Plants Go to War

A Botanical History of World War II

JUDITH SUMNER

McFarland & Company, Inc., Publishers
Jefferson, North Carolina

ISBN (print) 978-1-4766-7612-8
ISBN (ebook) 978-1-4766-3540-8

LIBRARY OF CONGRESS AND BRITISH LIBRARY
CATALOGUING DATA ARE AVAILABLE

Front cover images World War II Victory Garden poster (U.S. War Food
Administration); *inset top to bottom* Tents were carefully constructed
and tested (U.S. National Archives); Tomato beds in the hydroponic farm
on Ascension Island (U.S. Army); U.S. troops learned to maneuver in dense
jungles on Bougainville and other Pacific islands (U.S. National Archives).

Printed in the United States of America

*McFarland & Company, Inc., Publishers
Box 611, Jefferson, North Carolina 28640
www.mcfarlandpub.com*

Plants Go to War

Table of Contents

Preface

As with many of my generation, I grew up listening to war stories, but in my case these involved chemistry rather than combat. My father enlisted as a bench chemist with the 43rd Chemical Laboratory Company at Schofield Barracks on Oahu, where he became known for developing a field kit used in identifying Japanese weapons captured during combat in the Pacific theater. However, his war stories focused on the everyday problems that vexed Army chemists, mostly involving plant products, including latex, quinine, fibers, chicle, chocolate, and even charcoal and early plastics. In short, at a time when synthetic organic chemistry was still a comparative start-up, plants provided most of the natural products and chemical derivatives essential to the war effort. In some cases, including quinine and latex, plants provided the natural models for products that were synthesized by the end of the war.

Richard Evans Schultes, the father of modern ethnobotany, often commented that historians stumble because they know little about plants. According to his world view, botanical knowledge is fundamental to understanding civilization and interpreting conflict. In fact, Schultes himself was involved in wartime botany. As part of his work for the Rubber Plant Investigations Office, he collected *Hevea* specimens and seeds for cultivation at experimental rubber plantations. The war could not have been won without rubber, but the same might be said about wheat, cotton, lumber, quinine, and penicillin, all with botanical origins. This book is my contribution to Schultes' desire for history viewed and interpreted through a botanical lens. My goal has been to write an encyclopedic synthesis of civilian and military plant uses and botanical connections as they relate to World War II, a project that far exceeded my original expectations.

Autarky was a universal wartime aim, with Allied and Axis countries struggling to supply food, drugs, clothing, fuel, and matériel. Plants provided the bulk of the wartime diet in the U.S. and abroad; civilians cultivated vitamin-rich carrots, cabbages, potatoes, and soybeans. By 1944, 44 percent of all food in the U.S. was grown in 20 million victory gardens. Agricultural crops provided rations that were shipped worldwide, augmented by fresh crops from military farms tilled on foreign soil. On the medical front, quinine was the first effective anti-malarial drug, while knowledge of local vegetation was essential in controlling scrub typhus in the Pacific. Penicillin-producing fungus grew on an industrial scale in a corn-based bacteriological medium, coincidentally a fungal strain isolated from a decaying melon. Once pharmaceutical drugs could no longer be obtained from German-occupied Europe, County Herb Committees foraged English hedgerows for medicinal plants.

Rubber was essential for gas masks, tires, and barrage balloons, while cotton, hemp, and nettle provided fibers for clothing, canvas, and cordage. Wood was used to build aircraft and barracks and to fuel vehicles, while conifers in the Hürtgen forest were intentionally weaponized using overhead German artillery shells. Paper balloons crafted from native Japanese mulberries were used to carry bombs across the Pacific and over the continental United States. Coal, the fossilized remains of ancient forests, was an essential wartime energy source, and coal-powered vehicles became common in Europe and Japan. Jungle warfare, military survival, and camouflage techniques required basic botanical knowledge that saved lives. Botanical gardens and herbaria served as wartime repositories of useful information, from timber characteristics to ethnobotanical lore useful in survival situations. Perhaps not surprisingly, the war years were also a time of worldwide botanical collecting, research, and discovery. Plants provided the raw materials for construction and survival, practical information often provided by herbaria and botanical gardens, sometimes recorded as anecdotal collectors' notes on individual herbarium sheets.

The wartime botanical story includes the German zeal for farming and native botany, reflected by the medicinal herb farms at concentration camps and *Lebensraum*, the acquisition of agricultural territory outside of German borders. Civilian survival often depended on the cultivation of *Schrebergarten* on the outskirts of German cities. On a symbolic level, Germans staged harvest festivals and planted Hitler oaks and lindens in rural villages and conifers in a swastika pattern visible only from the sky. Whether in the aftermath of firestorms or atomic blasts, vegetation returned, but native plants were often replaced with non-native ruderal taxa. In Hiroshima and Nagasaki, a few original trees survived the atomic bombs, regenerated, and live today as a symbol of rebirth after vast destruction.

Incidentally, names can deceive. Operation Market Garden, Operation *Sonnenblume* (sunflower), and certain ships had names that suggested plants. The flower class corvettes included the HMS *Azalea*, *Campanula*, *Hydrangea*, and *Orchis*. The *Marigold* was a U.S. Army hospital ship, while the *Aloe* class ships included the USS *Aloe*, *Boxwood*, *Catalpa*, *Eucalyptus*, and *Holly*, all tasked with positioning anti-submarine and anti-torpedo underwater netting. *Feuerlilie* (fire lily) was the code name of a German anti-aircraft missile, and mulberry harbors were portable, pre-fabricated enclosures developed by British military engineers. None of these events, vessels, or devices had any particular botanical connection.

Many have helped in identifying clues and finding information about botanical connections to World War II. Richard Howard kept meticulous correspondence files associated with his 1994 paper on the wartime role of botanists in the Pacific region, and these letters and other materials were immensely useful in uncovering information about cinchona, agar, forestry, medicinal plants, survival manuals, and several other related topics. His comprehensive review paper suggested many topics to explore in depth and thus enriched and expanded the scope of this book. Lisa DeCesare, former archival librarian at the Gray Herbarium, helped in locating Dr. Howard's papers at Harvard. Librarians at the Pusey Library, Harvard University Archives, Countway Library of the Harvard Medical School, and Schlesinger Library provided generous access to their collections. Judith Warnement at the Harvard Herbaria Botany Libraries helped to locate the camouflage manuals written by Arnold Arboretum staff, and Julie Pallant provided access to the complete files of the Harvard Camouflage Committee at the Harvard Forest.

Maureen Horn, former librarian at the Massachusetts Horticultural Society, provided access to their archives and seed catalogue collection. Suzanne Wheeler and other librarians at the Richards Memorial Library tracked down numerous rare and out-of-print memoirs and sources. Laura Hastings of the Centre for Economic Botany (Kew) sent useful information on the County Herb Committees. Holly Watson shared her archival research on the successful wartime farming efforts at Mount Holyoke College. The family of Professor Walter Pauk shared notes on the remarkable interviews in which he described the liberation of Dachau and his involvement with providing food to former prisoners. Kenneth Helphand provided guidance with finding images of the subsistence gardens at the Lodz ghetto. John Coster-Mullen offered useful suggestions for discovering information about trees that survived the atomic explosions in Hiroshima and Nagasaki.

I am particularly indebted to the many U.S. Army historians who authored the numerous volumes of the *U.S. Army in World War II Series*. Often known as the green books, these detailed histories of World War II pointed the way to many topics for further research.

Stephen Sumner, my husband, collected numerous anecdotes and historical footnotes with botanical connections. He was an enthusiastic sounding board as the project moved forward, and his vast knowledge of military history helped me to contextualize much of the information that I discovered and documented. Stephen provided ongoing support and interest during this lengthy project, for which I am thoroughly grateful. Most importantly, he believed that this book should be written and helped me to get the job done. Given the scope of the project, I am certain that there are omissions, which I regret, and errors, for which I am solely responsible.

1

Victory Gardens

For many Americans, the Great Depression was a time of nutritional desperation. Many families survived by growing vegetables in relief gardens, subsistence-level vegetable plots cultivated during the worst years of the economic crisis, from late 1929 through the mid–1930s and beyond. In fact, many of these gardens still existed in 1939, when Hitler invaded Poland and England and France declared war on Germany. Still cultivated or fallow, Depression-era relief gardens were the starting point for the World War II victory garden movement in the United States.

These were not the first American wartime gardens. Years earlier, Charles Lathrop Pack initiated a World War I garden campaign to enable the United States to ship food abroad in response to European shortages. In 1919, the National War Garden Commission published Pack's pamphlet on the role of vegetable gardens on the American home front: *Victory Gardens Feed the Hungry—The Needs of Peace Demand the Increased Production of Food in America's Victory Gardens.* As part of Pack's plan to alleviate widespread postwar famine in Europe, Americans had to grow some of their own produce on the home front. Posters encouraged Americans to "Sow the seeds of Victory!" and to consider "Every garden a munition plant." Known originally as war gardens, these plots were renamed victory gardens after the war. He argued effectively that the United States must continue to provide food to Europe as a strategy to circumvent anarchy.

As first lady, Eleanor Roosevelt promoted plain meals, practical domesticity, and simple living; indeed she viewed herself as a role model for American women. With war looming in Europe, she wanted a White House vegetable garden, but at first Secretary of Agriculture Claude Wickard rejected the notion of a national vegetable garden movement. He predicted the waste of fertilizers and pesticides if amateurs took up gardening and economic ruin to American farmers if householders successfully grew their own fruits and vegetables. Oddly, Wickard's men could not agree upon a victory garden site at the White House. Wickard staunchly opposed displacing ornamentals for vegetables, so the rose garden could not be tilled, and the tennis court site was pure red clay that demanded soil amendments, in other words—tons of manure.

Following Pearl Harbor, canned goods were rationed, as was the gasoline needed for transporting produce from farms to markets. Military needs were demanding; each U.S. soldier consumed a ton of food per year. Moreover, under the Lend-Lease policy enacted in March 1941, the U.S. supplied food to its allies. England, Russia, China, and other allies received shipments of American-grown food, including grains, canned fruits, and canned and dehydrated vegetables. Metals used in can manufacture posed yet another problem; tin was scarce because 90 percent of the U.S. supply historically came from Japanese-occupied Malaysia. By 1942, the War Production Board authorized can collection as part of patriotic salvage drives, but available food-safe metals were needed to produce cans to ship for military use.

Well-tended, productive vegetable gardens would help to offset the food demands of the Lend-Lease program and the military. Food for the home front was best grown close to where it would be consumed, with as much food as possible preserved in home kitchens—a reprise of the war gardens and kitchen economies of World War I. In short, Americans once again needed the small-scale farming skills that were promoted and honed by the United States Department of Agriculture during the World War I.

Wickard soon faced reality. In 1941, he convened a National Defense Garden Conference in Washington, D.C. Participants included garden clubs, seed suppliers, radio stations, publishers, and youth organizations, along with staff from the Works Project Administration, Office of Civil Defense, and the Department of Agriculture. Planning was grassroots in nature; local defense councils named victory garden chairmen from the ranks of local gardeners with leadership potential. However, there was reluctance to engage in urban gardening. Presumably city dwellers were not skilled gardeners, and city sites might not support vegetable growth. Some even speculated that the costs incurred with urban gardens might exceed the value of the crops harvested. Authors of the *Guide for Planning the Local Victory Garden Program*, the 1942 report on Wickard's meeting, noted, "The conference agreed that due to the desirability of conserving seed, fertilizer, and spray material as well as the avoidance of disappointing results, home vegetable gardens should be confined to farms, small- and medium-sized towns, and suburban areas … while city gardening has health, recreational, and morale values, city back yards are seldom successful in the production of vegetables as the soil is usually

A Guide for Victory Gardeners in New York and Neighboring States. **INDEX INSIDE FRONT COVER.**

Extension agents, local officials, and businesses published a vast number of pamphlets and bulletins for new gardeners. Many were aimed at women and youth, who did much of the wartime vegetable cultivation (New York State).

poor and other conditions unfavorable. Therefore, it is desirable to continue the landscape improvement of city yards and not to destroy lawns and ornamental plantings for the sake of a few vegetables."[1] In due course, however, they were proven wrong.

With a nation of amateur gardeners poised to cultivate their plots, extension agents provided essential, practical advice—on soil preparation, plant selection, crop cultivation and fertilization, and food preservation. Optimistic gardeners invested in pressure cookers to preserve their crops and set about the business of deliberately gardening for victory. During the 1942 growing season, the first year of the World War II victory garden campaign, approximately 15 million families tilled the soil to grow some or all of their own botanical foods. By 1943, the number had increased to 20 million, and about 40 percent of fresh fruits and vegetables came from these victory gardens.

By following the copious advice provided by legions of extension agents and other information sources, almost any soil patch with sunlight could be sufficiently improved to provide the mineral nutrients and drainage that plant growth requires. Victory gardens were installed in any arable soil (or soil that could be rendered arable) including lawns, backyards, flower gardens, public parks, school yards, vacant lots, and factory sites, including many urban sites. By 1943, the White House had also joined the victory garden movement, although Mrs. Roosevelt did not do the planting, weeding, and watering herself.

Crops and Cultivation

Suggestions for victory gardens arrived quickly through many channels, fueled by the duel realities of food and gasoline rationing. Both canned foods and gasoline were redirected from the home front to military troops, and victory gardens were the obvious national answer to both shipment and supply woes. Farmers would feed the fighting men, while victory gardeners would supply the home front. Government agencies, universities, botanical gardens, corporations, and scientific organizations developed educational publications and strategies, which included pamphlets, bulletins, booklets, films, classes, and clubs. Just months after the National Defense Garden Conference in late 1941, *Victory Gardens* (*USDA Miscellaneous Publication No. 483*) argued for country and suburban gardens, but discouraged city dwellers from attempting to cultivate plots. Concern centered on seeds, and the overleaf warned, "Unusual demands are being made on domestic supplies of vegetable seeds. Do not waste them."[2]

In fact, during the years prior to the outbreak of war in Europe, Americans had relied on seed stock imported from Europe. This may have been the source of the sentiment against urban victory gardens; if seedlings perished in compacted soil or shaded alleys, seed stock was wasted and not easily replaced. Gardeners were generally advised to cultivate reliable crops: beans, cabbage, carrots, parsnips, winter squash, tomatoes, and various leafy vegetables (lettuce, chard, kale, beet greens, and turnip greens). Beets and turnips were valued more for their leafy shoots than their edible tap roots, which reflected the concern for vitamins over food calories alone. Cooking diminished vitamins, causing some to advocate growing tomatoes and cabbage, which could both be consumed uncooked. The harvest lent itself to preservation; tomatoes and beans could be canned, while cabbage, carrots, and winter squash could be stored fresh for months.

This was not the time for crops such as celery and cauliflower that required labor-intensive blanching, the elimination of sunlight that in turn prevents chlorophyll synthesis.

Celery culture involved excavating a trench and mounding soil around the elongated leaf stalks to keep them pale green and mild-flavored. Following the same principle, cauliflower leaves were tied over the central "curd" (a mass of undeveloped flower buds) to keep it white. Both crops demanded too much of novice gardeners, who needed predictable outcomes with minimal special handling. Instead emphasis was on crops that were well understood, culturally adaptable, widely grown, highly productive, and vitamin rich; the *Victory Gardens* list satisfied all of these requirements. The pamphlet also emphasized the importance of a garden plan, successive plantings, and limited fertilization; chemical fertilizers remained in short supply for the duration of the war years.

International Harvester Company distributed *Have a Victory Garden* in time for the 1943 growing season, a pamphlet aimed at land owners who were familiar with basic garden practices. Author L.A. Hawkins suggested a one acre garden of "large fruit and small fruit and vegetables" and provided direct advice, "Get at the garden in time. Make a plan for it…. Get the seed. Make up your mind when you will plant the different things—then plant them." He argued that the garden "means a real home where the children will love to invite their friends because they have something to give them—strawberries, raspberries, cherries and apples." He wrote for a farm audience but still emphasized cultural information and crop-specific diseases and pests, from corn smut to cabbage worms. Poor or gumbo soil could be improved with the addition of manure (he suggested 20 to 30 tons per acre), and he trusted experienced gardeners to grow challenging vegetables such as asparagus, leeks, celery, and cauliflower.[3]

At times the experts disagreed. While the USDA *Victory Gardens* pamphlet encouraged restraint in selecting plants, Hawkins criticized experienced gardeners who did not grow a wide selection of foods in their large farm gardens: "It is very common not to find over 10 or 12 different kinds in the home gardens where there should be 25 or more. A garden in which 25 kinds of vegetables are growing offer a choice variety and the menu can be varied so much from day to day that we do not get tired of eating garden products…" His long cultivar list included warm weather crops such as eggplant, okra, and watermelon; he clearly anticipated southerners as a significant segment of his victory garden audience.

The Milwaukee Magazine, a railroad publication, made special note of *Have a Victory Garden* in its March 1943 issue. In light of the national goal of 18 million gardens, the Milwaukee Railroad offered free plots to its employees, a way to use vacant land to help the war effort and to allow workers the opportunity for "providing themselves with certain necessary foodstuffs that they might otherwise be able to obtain only in small quantities under rationing limitations." Superintendents issued employee permits for victory garden plots on railroad land that was safe and unoccupied.

Other publications chimed in with victory garden advice. *Science News-Letter* ran articles by Frank Thone, a plant ecologist who worked as a staff writer at the Science Service. In "Vegetables for Victory," published before the first growing season of the victory garden campaign, Thone reminded readers about the looming seed shortage, "We formerly imported most of our vegetable seeds from Europe, and we have not yet fully established American seed-growing industries. There is not an actual shortage, but there can be if everyone buys too much and plants too thickly, as home gardeners as apt to do." Addressing novice gardeners, he suggested careful measurement of the garden plot to prevent seed waste, while conducting efficient crop succession to ensure fresh crops for several months. Thone advocated rotted manure over chemical fertilizers and suggested that gardeners compost dead leaves, manure, weeds, clippings, and vegetable parings from the kitchen in "a back corner of your lot." He recommended inoculating the pile with garden soil, which "introduces a complex swarm of fungi, bacteria and small earth-animals that reduce the raw vegetable tissues to the good black humus that makes soil fertile."[4]

Thone was clearly a biological gardener, with an abiding appreciation of soil microbiology and nutrient recycling; in fact, he described commercial fertilizer only as a last resort for those without decayed manure or leaf-mold. He went on to explain in detail the correct spading strategy for soil, which involved completely inverting and overturning the soil—not merely stirring it in place. In contrast to *Have a Victory Garden*, which advocated using a cultivator to weed garden rows, Thone frankly described the reality of hoeing and weeding by hand, "And if you are not willing to do the weeding, better not start a garden at all: an unweeded garden is largely a waste of fertilizer, labor, and seed." He reminded gardeners, "Save all weeds and throw them on the compost heap; thus you will harvest good out of evil."

In "Victory Gardens," an article published before the second growing season of the victory garden campaign, Thone reflected on the value of tomatoes as a victory garden crop, "Allot a very generous share of your space to tomatoes. They are by far the most important soldiers in the whole Victory Vegetable army; agreeable to eat, easy to feed to children, easy to put up for winter, rich in vitamins and minerals."[5] In that vitamin-conscious era, Thone was correct; tomatoes provide 17 mg of vitamin C per 100 mg of tomato, more than carrots (6 mg/100 mg), cucumbers (2–8 mg/100 mg), or lettuce (5 mg/100 mg). Wartime conditions limited access to citrus fruits, so vitamin C was an ongoing nutritional concern. In contrast, oranges contain 44–79 mg of vitamin C/100 mg. Tomatoes fell short of that level as a high vitamin C vegetable, but on the other hand, they thrived in temperate gardens and were a versatile crop known to both immigrant and native-born Americans. Tomato plants (*Solanum lycopersicum*) are inherently sprawling, tropical weeds that tolerate a range of growing conditions, as long as they receive sunlight and water. Tomatoes could be eaten fresh or preserved for pantry storage and winter use; the low pH of tomatoes was sufficient to inhibit bacterial growth, making them suitable for water bath canning without the use of a pressure cooker.

Ironically, tomatoes became mainstream American vegetables only about a century before World War II. Based on flower structure, early botanists and herbalists recognized tomatoes as relatives of alkaloid-laden nightshade family (Solanaceae), which includes the toxic plants henbane, mandrake, and belladonna. Although tomatoes do not contain the strongly hallucinogenic tropane alkaloids synthesized by henbane and mandrake, the vines do produce toxic glycoalkaloids. In fact, many viewed tomatoes with suspicion and were reluctant to incorporate the fruit into daily meals. During the eighteenth and early nineteenth centuries, tomato vines were cultivated as botanical and culinary curiosities, and it was not until 1835 when Dr. John Cook Bennett described tomatoes as "the most healthy article in the Materia Alimentary" that Americans began to view tomatoes as palatable rather than dangerous. Bennett's essay was reprinted in home and farm journals, and he contended that tomato nutrition could be concentrated and sold in capsule form. In fact, tomato capsules were marketed for liver problems and bilious attacks, a dietary fad that soon waned, but public perception of the tomato changed for the better. Nevertheless a short-lived wartime experiment with tomato culture did raise concerns about toxic alkaloid levels. Soil nematodes often destroyed southern crops, so some growers grafted tomato shoots to the roots of thorn apple, a species known for producing the

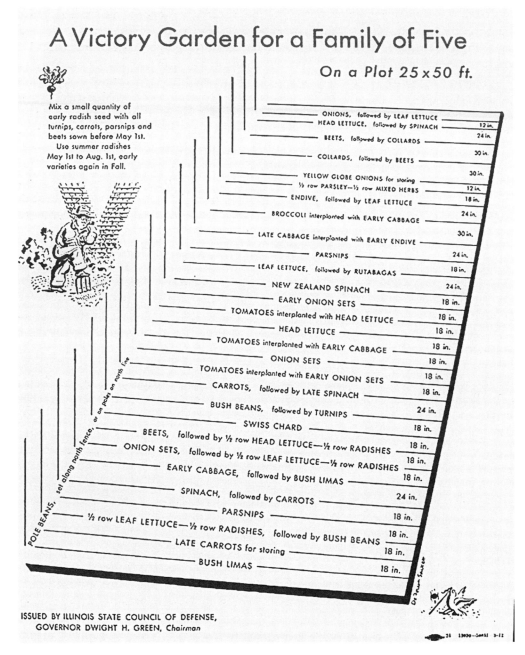

A Victory Garden for a Family of Five

On a Plot 25 x 50 ft.

Mix a small quantity of early radish seed with all turnips, carrots, parsnips and beets sown before May 1st. Use summer radishes May 1st to Aug. 1st, early varieties again in Fall.

Crop	
ONIONS, followed by LEAF LETTUCE	
HEAD LETTUCE, followed by SPINACH	12 in.
BEETS, followed by COLLARDS	24 in.
COLLARDS, followed by BEETS	30 in.
YELLOW GLOBE ONIONS for storing	30 in.
½ row PARSLEY—½ row MIXED HERBS	12 in.
ENDIVE, followed by LEAF LETTUCE	18 in.
BROCCOLI interplanted with EARLY CABBAGE	24 in.
LATE CABBAGE interplanted with EARLY ENDIVE	30 in.
PARSNIPS	24 in.
LEAF LETTUCE, followed by RUTABAGAS	18 in.
NEW ZEALAND SPINACH	24 in.
EARLY ONION SETS	18 in.
TOMATOES interplanted with HEAD LETTUCE	18 in.
HEAD LETTUCE	18 in.
TOMATOES interplanted with EARLY CABBAGE	18 in.
ONION SETS	18 in.
TOMATOES interplanted with EARLY ONION SETS	18 in.
CARROTS, followed by LATE SPINACH	18 in.
BUSH BEANS, followed by TURNIPS	24 in.
SWISS CHARD	18 in.
BEETS, followed by ½ row HEAD LETTUCE—½ row RADISHES	18 in.
ONION SETS, followed by ½ row LEAF LETTUCE—½ row RADISHES	18 in.
EARLY CABBAGE, followed by BUSH LIMAS	18 in.
SPINACH, followed by CARROTS	24 in.
PARSNIPS	18 in.
½ row LEAF LETTUCE—½ row RADISHES, followed by BUSH BEANS	18 in.
LATE CARROTS for storing	18 in.
BUSH LIMAS	18 in.

POLE BEANS, set along north fence, or on poles on north line

ISSUED BY ILLINOIS STATE COUNCIL OF DEFENSE,
GOVERNOR DWIGHT H. GREEN, Chairman

Garden plans often reflected a standard plot of 25 × 50 feet, although many productive victory gardens were significantly smaller. Inter-planting tall and short varieties and sowing successive crops prevented fallow land (Illinois State Council of Defense).

same tropane alkaloids as belladonna. Alkaloids produced by the roots apparently crossed the graft and entered tomato fruit, making them potentially quite toxic.[6]

By the mid–nineteenth century, many American gardens included tomatoes, and tomato canneries supplied Union troops. George Washington Carver recommended tomatoes as appropriate additions to the diets of poor southerners, who often suffered from vitamin deficiencies resulting from itinerant lives as migrant workers and over-reliance on dietary corn. In 1858, J.H. Walden recommended supporting the vines on slats or boards to allow more space in urban gardens. Walden's sound advice was reiterated by Thone in 1943, "…get more tomatoes from your space, by training the plants up to stakes and keeping them pruned strictly back to one stalk apiece. Immigrant farmers using this method set their tomatoes as close as only two feet apart." Thone preached a doctrine of common sense, encouraging gardeners to plan their plots to take advantage of maximum sunlight and minimum shading, with tall plants such as staked tomatoes and pole beans on the north and east, and low growing plants such as carrots and beets to the south and west. He also favored backyard gardens over allotments a distance from home, noting that "it is an advantage to do your gardening at home—saves time in getting to work, in a year when there isn't too much spare time at best; saves labor in getting the vegetables from earth to the kitchen, and lets the housewife step out at will to harvest a few carrots or enough lettuce for a salad…"[7]

In addition to tomatoes, essential crops included vitamin-rich vegetables such as carrots, various leafy greens (chard, collards, kale, lettuce, cabbage, mustards, and beet greens), and squash. Carotenes, vitamin A precursors, are abundant in green, yellow, and orange crops; these were essential to preventing night-blindness, a serious affliction especially in war time. Tomatoes are pigmented by carotenes, and gardeners had their choice of color: the covers of the W. Atlee Burpee seed catalogues for 1944 and 1945 illustrated tomato cultivars "Marglobe" (red) and "Jubilee" (yellow). However, carotenes are most abundant in green plant tissues where they function as an accessory pigment in photosynthesis, absorbing additional wavelengths and funneling this light energy to chlorophyll. This explains why a single cabbage varies in carotene content, from generous levels (up to 50 times higher) in the outer green leaves to minimal levels in the inner white leaves of the head. Cabbage also has high levels of vitamin C (35–115 mg/100 g), a nutritional advantage that was more valued and utilized in wartime England than in the U.S.

Beans cultivated for their pods also provided carotenes and other vitamins, while those grown for their seeds were an alternative protein source during a time of meat rationing; dried bean seeds are typically about 22 percent protein. Most victory garden beans were varieties of *Phaseolus vulgaris*, including string-beans, kidney, pinto, pea bean, navy, and haricot cultivars. Those with full scale farm gardens could follow the advice from International Harvester and grow such diverse crops as watermelon (not yet valued as a source of the anti-oxidant carotene lycopene) and parsnips, an under-utilized root crop with a high vitamin C content comparable to tomatoes. *Have a Victory Garden* suggested lesser known crops such as artichokes, salsify, kohlrabi, leeks, and cress, but these were grown infrequently in small backyard gardens. Most victory gardens could not even accommodate potatoes, cabbages, and corn, which required more space than the 1,500 square foot home victory garden recommended by the U.S. Department of Agriculture.

Garden Strategies

The goal of a successful victory gardener was a continuous food supply rather than a summer glut that exceeded need. This required strategizing, from selection of early and late varieties to successive plantings as crops were harvested. For instance, *Victory*

Gardens (*USDA Miscellaneous Publication No. 483*) suggested sowing radishes at ten day intervals to ensure a longer season. Crops such as radishes, beets, turnips, and mustard greens were replaced with beans (such as refugee snap beans, which could be consumed as edible pods or dried seeds) or collards. USDA publications also coached local leaders to encourage reseeding of fallow areas with late season varieties of endive, kale, cabbage, and Chinese cabbage cultivars.[8] Other late crops included broccoli, spinach, and potatoes; regardless of what was grown, the point was to start fall crops in mid-summer to ensure a reliable late harvest.

Hotbeds were another means for extending the growing season by providing earlier crops. These were small glasshouses that relied on microbial activity and sunlight as heat sources; the goal was to start young plants outdoors and to have them ready to transplant once garden temperatures were reliably warm and frost was unlikely. *Have a Victory Garden* noted that a hot bed could promote crop maturation by days or weeks; the manual provided detailed instructions on selecting a sunny site, excavating a pit, constructing a frame, and installing window sash that could be opened or closed, depending on air temperature. The hotbed was filled with a deep layer of manure, in which a mixed population of microbes degraded organic material through respiration and produced heat that promoted seedling growth.[9]

Manure required careful handling in order to maintain steady warmth, involving methodical turnover and tamping down. The goal was a temperature of about 65 degrees Fahrenheit, which could be adjusted in the daytime by opening the sash for ventilation or by insulating the hotbed at night with straw. Any higher or lower temperatures could prove disastrous for seedlings, causing them to succumb to soil fungi or die outright. Gardeners were advised to allow time for "hardening off" by completely opening or removing the sash so that the seedlings were fully exposed to seasonal weather conditions. This procedure conditions seedlings by increasing cellular sugar concentrations, depressing the freezing point of their tissues and making damage by cold conditions less likely.

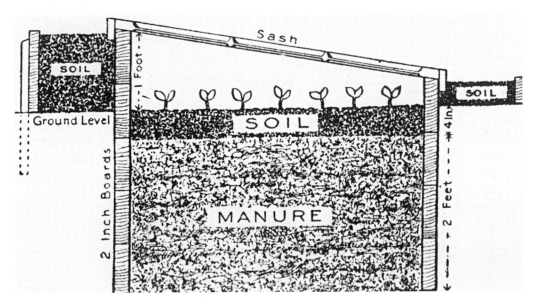

Hotbeds were ground-level glasshouses used to extend the growing season by relying on the microbes in manure to produce heat for seedling growth.

Successful hotbed crops included tomatoes, peppers, and eggplant, tropical species that require warm soil to germinate and grow. Vegetables aside, victory garden publications frequently suggested that gardeners should still cultivate flowers to promote home front morale in trying times. Familiar flowerbed species such as marigolds, petunias, morning glories, colcus, ageratum, and cosmos evolved in tropical regions, and their seedlings thrived alongside vegetable plants in the warmth of a well-tended hotbed.

Soils and Fertilizers

Novice gardeners encountered soils that ranged from the compacted clay of vacant lots (along with cinders, bricks, and other debris) to the rich loam of former flower gardens. Community allotments typically provided initial plowing and harrowing, but home gardeners were faced with the trial and error task of improving soil to promote successful plant growth. As Frank Thone noted in the *Science News-Letter*, there was no blanket advice to serve all sites, "Soils differ too much from region to region, even from one part of a township to another, for such shotgun advice to be valid…. A soil's natural fertility is generally indicated by its color. A black soil is usually a fertile soil; a gray soil usually less so … yet they may be capable of good production if well managed." He distinguished between mechanical and chemical improvements, recommending manure or composted humus as the best soil amendments for home victory gardens. Thone steered gardeners away from commercial fertilizers; used alone on dense clay soils, they provided nutrients but did not improve soil texture, and both are essential for successful vegetable culture.[10]

The *Journal of the New York Botanical Garden* devoted its March 1943 issue to a discussion of victory gardening, largely an analysis of the demonstration victory garden developed and cultivated onsite during the spring and summer of 1942. The local soil comprised about a foot of topsoil over "cold, stiff, gray clay" requiring "sympathetic management." The narrative described the autumn process of double-digging a few-inch layer

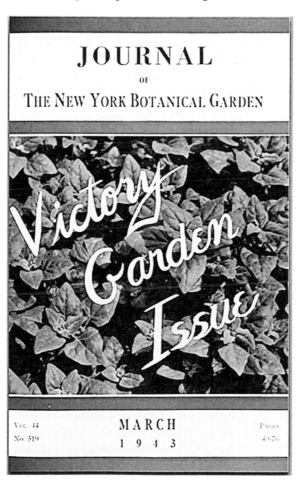

JOURNAL
OF
THE NEW YORK BOTANICAL GARDEN

Victory Garden Issue

Vol. 44
No. 519

MARCH
1 9 4 3

Pages
53-76

Botanical gardens supported the victory garden campaign by cultivating demonstration gardens and offering advice for novice gardeners. Horticulturalists at the New York Botanical Garden shared their experience in the March 1943 issue of their journal (New York Botanical Garden).

of manure into the garden to a depth of two feet. Winter snow and frost then acted to weather and smooth soil clumps, resulting in tilth, friable garden soil with satisfactory drainage and crumble. The strategy of breaking up clay involved the addition of calcium in the form of ground limestone, which helped to transform dense clay soils into small particles.[11]

Historically, natural materials such as guano and animal bones were used to provide plant nutrients, but the exact chemical requirements for plant growth were not precisely known. However, by the 1940s, plant physiologists had compiled the list of known elements needed by all green plants for normal metabolism. Micronutrients typically occur in trace amounts in soil and do not need to be provided; these elements include boron, chlorine, copper, iron, manganese, molybdenum, and zinc. Secondary macronutrients include calcium, magnesium, and sulfur, which some crops may require depending upon local soil conditions. Primary macronutrients include nitrogen (N), phosphorus (P), and potassium (K). These are almost universally required in garden and agricultural soils to promote maximum growth and production, and commercial fertilizers typically contain these elements in a specified N-P-K ratio, with the nitrogen in a usable form such as ammonia.

Phosphorus and potassium had geological origins. Phosphate deposits were mined in several states, and Canada exported potash (water soluble potassium salts) to U.S. fertilizer plants, in contrast to World War I when Germany still controlled most of the known potash supplies. Nitrogen posed a challenge, but in the early twentieth century, German chemist Fritz Haber developed a process that converted atmospheric nitrogen to ammonia, a significant chemical achievement in light of the wartime demand for both fertilizers and explosives. The Haber process required high temperatures and pressures, which explains the decision to build early nitrification plants near Tennessee Valley Authority hydroelectric dams. Although victory garden pamphlets often recommended the use of commercial fertilizers with known N-P-K ratios, home gardeners encountered shortages. However, by 1943, the War Department and Department of Agriculture authorized a standard victory garden fertilizer with an N-P-K ratio of 3-8-7. Due to ammonia demands for munitions, nitrogen levels were lower than in pre-war garden fertilizers, but the product was widely promoted as adequate for average garden use.

Home gardeners often made the mistake of growing the same crops in the same spot, which drained soil nutrients and encouraged species-specific pests. The horticulturalists who tended the New York Botanical Garden demonstration garden planned for crop rotation on a three-year cycle, with the exception of the beds devoted to edible perennials like rhubarb and herbs. Sections of the garden were assigned to three general categories: leafy vegetables, root crops, and warm weather crops such as tomatoes, peppers, and beans. These were shifted within the garden annually, and the gardeners applied specific nutrients as needed. The genus *Brassica* (which includes cabbage, broccoli, and kale) benefited from deep digging with manure and top dressing with limestone; root crops were covered with wood ash, a rich source of potash. Crop rotation was the only way to avoid some common diseases, such as the slime mold infection that causes clubroot in cabbages. The strategy avoided establishing populations of species-specific pathogens and diminished the effect of nutrient depletion over several growing seasons. By 1943, garden staff decided to include more tomatoes and a more crops for winter storage (beets, onions, carrots, rutabagas, parsnips, and salsify) and to eliminate corn, which produced too little to justify its allotted space.[12]

Fertilizer shortages spawned creative thinking about nutrient recycling. In coastal areas, gardeners used fish trimmings and algae, both rich in nitrogen and other mineral salts. Other options were also considered; for instance, the operators of municipal sewage works suggested the sludge produced from human waste might serve as an available, effective, cost-free victory garden fertilizer.[13] However, feces can transmit disease and intestinal parasites, so there was legitimate concern about spreading sewage sludge from unknown sources on home gardens. Sewage requires high heat for sterilization, and home cooks still would have been prudently advised to peel and boil any crops fertilized with sewage sludge and to avoid raw salad crops entirely.

Of particular concern was *Salmonella typhi* (the bacterium that causes typhoid fever), which could have remained viable in sewage sludge long enough to cause an infection. In an era before the widespread use of antibiotics, a typhoid epidemic on the home front would have been disastrous. It was suggested that sludge might be safely dug into garden soil in the fall, allowing the fecal bacteria time to die and decompose; however, concern about the spread of disease explains why sewage never achieved widespread use in the United States as a victory garden fertilizer. Nevertheless, some gardeners no doubt recycled "night soil" from their own families in gardens or compost piles. In fact, this was a traditional practice that was not at all remotely dangerous if all family members were free from infection.

Pests and Diseases

Home growers soon learned that victory gardens attracted herbivores. Garden pamphlets and bulletins suggested commonly used insecticides and poisons, an arsenal of toxic compounds that were effective but potentially hazardous to use. Arsenic was the active ingredient in products such as Paris green (copper (II) acetate triarsenite), a green crystalline powder used to eliminate both insects and rodents. Its name dates from its use to rid the Parisian sewer system of rats, and other wartime uses included aerial spraying to kill mosquito vectors of malaria in Italy, Corsica, and Sardinia.

An advertisement for the W.E. Barrett Company in the *Providence Journal* (May 4, 1945) reminded gardeners that "victory gardens will help stretch your point budget," referring to the food rationing system (see Chapter 4), and suggested Paris green as effective against potato beetles. Lead arsenate was less soluble and supposedly less toxic than Paris green; some advice-givers suggested combining the two as a broad-spectrum insecticide. Snarol, a powder described as an "arsenical bait" (probably lead arsenate) provided a toxic meal for cut-worms, snails, and slugs. *Have a Victory Garden* advised using a combination of Bordeaux mixture and lead arsenate to avoid the wilt diseases that kill the vines of cucumbers, musk melons, pumpkins, and squashes. First developed to combat fungal diseases in French vineyards, Bordeaux mixture is compounded from copper (II) sulfate ($CuSO_4$) and slaked lime ($Ca(OH)_2$). It was thought to prevent wilt disease (then believed to be a fungus), while lead arsenate killed the striped cucumber beetles that are its vector. In fact, the microbe that causes wilt in cucumbers and other curcurbits is *Erwinia tracheiphila*, a Gram-negative bacterium closely related to *E. coli* and *Salmonella*. With sustained use during the war years and later, arsenic and lead accumulated to potentially dangerous levels in gardens and orchards, resulting in the need for soil remediation in old garden and orchard sites.

Not all insecticides depended on heavy metals; some utilized toxic organic compounds. Nicotine, an insecticidal alkaloid, was the active ingredient in products such as Black Leaf 40, nicotine-pyrox spray, and nicotine sulfate, which were marketed for aphids and other insect pests such as harlequin bugs that ruined cabbage crops in southern victory gardens. Nicotine is now a known carcinogen, but as an organic compound, it was easily degraded by soil microbes. Endosulfan ($C_9H_6Cl_6O_3S$), sold under the trade name Thioban, was a highly toxic agricultural chemical used to eliminate insects and mites; it was also available to home gardeners to treat diseases of tomato crops. Endosulfan is now recognized as a neurotoxin that can persist in habitats for years, especially in low pH conditions in which bacterial activity is low. It was also used extensively on potatoes and cotton, two crops with high military demand. Of course, wartime gardeners and farmers did their best with the insecticides available; toxicity was not completely understood, and home front and military needs for food and fibers were a definite reality. In fact, gardeners were encouraged to pursue problems with military zeal. According to the *Victory Garden Leader's Handbook*, "Don't let the Victory Gardener be dismayed at the onslaught of greedy bugs, any more than at the fifth column of weeds. Local experienced gardeners or bulletins will tell you how to blast the miniature Japanazis in a hurry."[14]

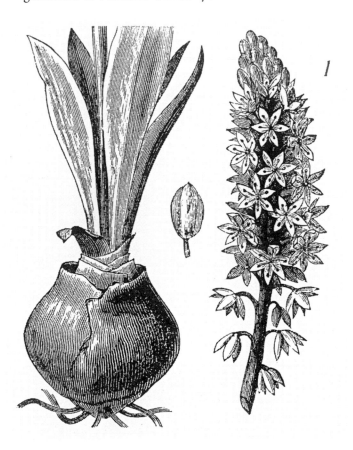

Mammals were deterred with chemical weapons. An article in *The American Biology Teacher* advocated creosote, lysol, and naphthalene to discourage moles; strychnine-laced oats as bait for field mice, ground squirrels, and pocket gophers; and cyanide-based fumigants to exterminate burrowing rats. Instructions advised gardeners to "Force the calcium cyanide dust into the burrows, then close all openings. The dust creates a gas that destroys rats. Avoid breathing the dust so far as possible. Use it only outdoors."[15] A less potentially hazardous rat poison originated with red squill (*Drimia maritima*), an onion relative that produces potent cardiac glycosides (see Chapter 7). Although the plant is bitter, rats readily consume it and die from the effects of the toxin scilliroside. Red squill has long been known as an effective rat poison, and by

Red squill was cultivated during the war years as an effective rat poison. Its potent cardiac glycosides include scilliroside, which was safer than the common practice of using cyanide against garden vermin.

the 1940s, it was grown as an experimental crop that could be used to make effective bait traps.

Seed Catalogues, Seed Saving and Cultivars

With each year of the victory garden campaign, gardeners were urged to conserve seeds, sow moderately, avoid seed hoarding, and buy only the seeds needed for a single growing season. As the war persisted, the victory garden campaign sought more gardeners, which meant higher seed demands. Even though American suppliers had ramped up production, reliable seed stock remained a concern for the duration of the war. *The Victory Garden Leader's Handbook* cautioned against squandering seeds, "Impress upon each gardener the importance of buying only the seeds called for in his garden plan.... Careless buying and use of seed is unpatriotic."[16] Manuals discouraged dense sowing and later thinning, and instructions made clear that gardeners should sow only sufficient seed for a crop and no more. Beets and Swiss chard posed a particular challenge in this regard because each "seed" actually comprised a few single-seeded fruits joined structurally at the base of the flower. When sown individually, these produced a cluster of seedlings that required thinning to produce successful crops, regardless of USDA caveats. Of course, the thinned greens were edible, and wartime recipes recommended their use in this era in which kitchen thrift equated with patriotism.

Seed catalogues featured vegetables, both fresh and preserved, accompanied by a patriotic message and cover design. In 1942, the Hall's Seed Company reminded customers to "Garden for Defense—Plant Hall's Premium Seeds" and "Ye Reap What Ye Sow." The vegetables illustrated were American dietary mainstays (tomatoes, peas, beans, beets, carrots, and corn), photographed enticingly in the foreground, with mason jars of canned vegetables arranged in military rows toward the rear of the cover design. By 1944, jewel-like jars of carrots, beets, and beans dominated the front of the cover, perhaps to remind growers to select crops for canning. Pansies, petunias, sweet peas, zinnias, and marigolds, were relegated to the back catalogue cover.

In 1942, Oscar H. Will & Company of Bismarck, North Dakota, offered Will's Defense Garden Collection for $1.25 postpaid, consisting of sixteen different seed packets and an instructional leaflet for a garden layout of 2000 square feet. By 1943, this offer was renamed Will's Victory Garden Collection, in alignment with the national victory garden campaign. The victory message was clear; the 1944 Will's cover design illustrated a large V filled with fresh produce, superimposed on a photograph of pantry shelves laden with colorful mason jars. Similarly, the W. Atlee Burpee Company's 1945 catalogue cover shows the red petioles of Swiss chard in a prominent V formation suggestive of victory, with carrots and beets positioned to resemble dropping bombs.

The diversity of cultivars was impressive. Gardens for Defense, the 1942 vegetable seed catalogue from the Holland American Seed Company of Grand Rapids, offered early, midseason, and late varieties for most crops. For instance, a gardener could keep the kitchen supplied with wax beans by planting successive rows of round-pod kidney, unrivaled, and sure-crop cultivars. There were 45 different bean cultivars offered for sale, including bush and pole varieties, stringless pods, dwarf and giant types, lima beans, and beans for eating fresh or dried. Cabbages also spanned the growing season; Copenhagen market was described as an extra-early variety that tolerated crowding, while late varieties such as Wisconsin-Hollander, were described as good for sauerkraut and winter storage. Sauerkraut forms when thinly sliced cabbage undergoes fermentation by *Lactobacillus* and *Leuconostoc*, bacteria that produce lactic acid, a natural preservative. It was rich in vitamin C and could be kept in jars and crocks almost indefinitely. *The American Women's Voluntary Services Cook Book* even suggested a use for fermented cabbage beyond the table: "Sauerkraut may be used as a rug cleaner. Expensive velvet rugs and tapestries in the National German Museum are cleaned with it."[17] Apparently the moist, shredded cabbage effectively removed dust and grime.

Hybrid cultivars were relatively unknown, so seed saving was a reliable way to prepare for the next season. A *Science News-Letter* article suggested that gardeners collect and dry seeds for their 1944 gardens; recommended crops for seed-saving include beans, tomatoes, potatoes, and melons. Of course, melon varieties are notorious for cross-pollinating and producing hybrid offspring, so gardeners might have been surprised with unexpected traits in their next crop. However, the article did caution against saving the seed from hybrid corn, a relatively new development that originated in the 1920s with four inbred corn varieties. These were crossed in pairs, producing plants that were more robust and productive than either parental variety, a phenomenon known as hybrid vigor or heterosis.[18]

By 1941, farmers in Indiana, Iowa, and Illinois were growing mostly hybrid corn (see Chapter 6). Frank Thone described the deeper roots, stronger stems, and higher yield of these early hybrids as "nothing less than an agricultural revolution."[19] However, this came at an expense; hybrid seed had to be purchased each season because saved seed did not reliably yield the same combinations of desirable traits that occurred in the hybrid parents. Victory gardens with enough square footage for corn may have grown a hybrid variety such as 'Bantam Evergreen,' described in the Gardens for Defense catalogue as larger and later-producing than one of its parents, the open-pollinated variety 'Golden Bantam,' a dwarf cultivar long prized for its small but delectable ears. Nevertheless, only two of the fifteen corn cultivars described in the Gardens for Defense catalogue appear to be hybrids; the others were open-pollinated varieties for which seed could be saved and used to produce a consistent crop. *Have a Victory Garden* made no mention of hybrid corn, which remained largely an agricultural crop for the duration of the war.

Seeds embedded in fleshy fruits posed their own problems. Home gardeners were advised that tomato pulp was best removed by scraping seeds into water, allowing the pulp to ferment, and drying the seeds on paper or cheesecloth for the next season; it is now known that fermentation enhances germination rates by removing the inhibitory compounds in the pulp that surrounds each seed. Jars with small lid ventilation holes provided protection from insects, mice, and moisture. Of course, some crops such as lettuce and radish only produced seed if they were not harvested and allowed to flower, so these seeds were typically purchased from commercial sources.

Have a Victory Garden urged gardeners to purchase seeds from reputable sources because good seed suppliers do on a large scale what the home gardener does when saving seed: Avoid seed collection from subpar plants. The process of roguing involved, "going over the fields and destroying all plants not up to standard or true to type," which sometimes meant the removal of a high percentage of the potential seed stock. During wartime, this may not have happened as systematically as in the past, either due to labor shortages or to the desire to maximize production during a time of high seed sales. Moreover, age and viability of purchased seed was unknown, so *Have a Victory Garden* suggested a simple germination test on wet blotter paper. Corn often will not germinate after a year, while other species remain viable for a few years if the seeds are stored in cool, dry conditions. In fact, gardeners were often better off saving the seeds of the open-pollinated plants that grew well in local victory gardens. The booklet strongly recommended that "as much seed as possible should be saved at home. Practice individual selection of plants and save seed for the next year. Individual plant selection means watching the plants that seem extra hardy, vigorous, resistant to disease and insects, and yet typical of the kind of vegetable. Such plants should be saved for seed production."[20]

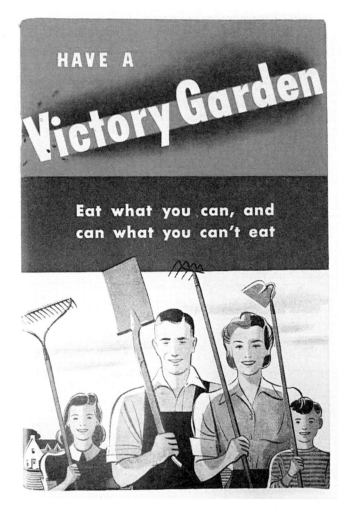

L.A. Hawkins wrote *Have a Victory Garden* for farmers and landowners with basic knowledge of cultivation and food preservation. In contrast with the restrained advice of extension agents, he recommended cultivating at least 25 various crops, including labor-intensive crops like celery and cauliflower (International Harvester Company).

Of course, open-pollination meant that half of the genes of the next generation came from the pollen of another plant, so despite careful selection of the seed-producing plant, the pollen-producing plant was an unknown member of the same species. Following pollination, each pollen grain produces a tube that delivers sperm to the egg inside the immature seed (ovule), and each mature seed contains an embryo that is the offspring of two parental plants, perhaps with some genetic differences. Genetically speaking, saved seed could share the same maternal line but have varying paternal lines. In other words, the crosses that occurred in open-pollinated cultivars could deliver some surprises during the next growing season, if saved seeds were planted.

Spreading the Word

Americans heard the victory garden message: Plant, preserve, and consume your own vitamin-rich vegetables. Government leaflets and university bulletins abounded, and with the start of the victory garden campaign in 1942, the popular press was also quick to respond. Grosset and Dunlap published *Food Gardens for Defense* by M.G. Kains, a former horticulturalist at the Department of Agriculture who specialized in small-scale farming. According to the dust jacket, "Based upon latest Department of Agriculture methods, this practical handbook shows you how to get the most in delicious foods of high nutrition value out of a small plot of ground. It covers virtually every problem the home gardener is likely to encounter." While not as widely read as much of the free literature, Kains' book helped to spread the word about the need to grow food on the home front.[21]

Popular magazines predicted garden success. At the start of the campaign, *Life* magazine reported in "Gardens for U.S. at War" that nearly six million amateur gardeners would be "digging and delving for vegetables and vitamins" in 1942. In addition to broadcasting the patriotic message of home front gardening, the article recapped much of the advice in pamphlets and bulletins. Cartoon sketches suggested strategies for dealing with insects and weeds, described in the text as "a fierce delight in annihilating enemy weeds and bugs." A detailed chart illustrated planting and harvesting times by zone for corn, tomatoes, squash, bush beans, peas, beets, carrots, Swiss chard, radishes, and lettuce. Nor was morale overlooked; the article mentioned the satisfaction of outdoor work and a well-tended, successful garden as "the things that bring satisfied peace to wartime worriers..."[22]

The following spring, *Life* magazine predicted 18 million victory gardens and described several in diverse locales: Copley Square in Boston; the zoo in Portland, Oregon; St. Patrick's Home in the Bronx; Golden Gate Park and city hall plaza in San Francisco; the Naval Air Station at Olathe, Kansas; Wellesley College; and the Cook County Jail in Chicago, where prison staff forbid the cultivation of corn, which might have allowed prisoners to hide from guards. The *Life* article noted, "Everybody was tucking seeds to bed in the moist spring soil—movie stars, soldiers, admirals, airline hostesses, nuns and prisoners." But novices needed sober reminding about the labor to come, "Many are unaware that although gardening victories are planned in April, the real heat of battle does not develop until July, when the gardener must struggle against incessant heat, bugs, the hot sun and laziness."[23]

As early as 1941, the New York City WPA had circulated a striking poster with the message "Grow it yourself—Plant a Farm Garden Now." War was again on the horizon, and agencies and organizations remembered the importance of vegetable gardening during World War I. Soon the Office of War Information, the National Garden Bureau, and the WPA War Service Project designed, printed, and disseminated posters bearing memorable mottos: "Plant a Victory Garden—Our Food Is Fighting—A Garden Will Make Your Rations Go Further" (1943), "War Gardens for Victory—Grow Vitamins at Your Kitchen Door" (1943), "Grow Your Own—Be Sure" (1945), and "Your Victory Garden Counts More Than Ever" (1945). Putting theory into practice, vegetables replaced the flower beds at Rockefeller Center, which featured red cabbage with a parsley border and Swiss chard with a carrot border.[24]

The Department of Agriculture released the film "Victory Garden" in 1942, which began with a message from Claude Wickard, Secretary of Agriculture, "A Victory Garden is like a share in an airplane factory. It helps win the War and pays dividends too." The narrator described an American family and a quarter-acre garden that they cultivated, all according to advice supplied by the county home demonstration agent and Department of Agriculture publications. A scale model illustrated their garden plans, and garden footage shared techniques for planting, thinning, and cultivating crops. The message was clear: Gardening requires work, but the results are well worth the effort.

The victory garden message appeared routinely in women's magazines—in articles, advice columns, and advertisements. *House & Garden*, *Better Homes and Gardens*, and *Good Housekeeping* shared information on planning, planting, and cultivation. *House and Garden* predicted 25.5 million families would plant victory gardens, exceeding the Department of Agriculture estimate of 18 million.[25] Many articles integrated vitamin awareness, crop selection, wartime recipes, cooking practices, and food preservation—all elements of the national concern for nutrition. By the second season of the victory garden campaign, magazines produced informative short movies, including "Gardens of Victory" (*Better Homes and Gardens*, 1943) and "Canning the Victory Garden Crop" (*Good Housekeeping*, 1943).

Advertisements pivoted on victory garden references. Vigoro fertilizer provided a free booklet "How to Make a Better Victory Garden," and Ferry's Seeds distributed a packet-sized garden plan with planting times and crop suggestions. A half-page advertisement for Wesson Oil in *Good Housekeeping* (June 1943) featured "Ode to a Victory Garden," three quatrains extolling the value of gardens, vitamins, and salads, supplemented with a recipe for an oil-based salad dressing that could be adjusted to taste with India relish or honey: "Give rationed meals variety, With salads when you sup, To keep them tasty as can be, Let Wesson dress them up!"

Victory gardens were also deployed to promote products as diverse as coffee, toothpaste, cheese, sanitary pads, and natural gas in advertisements that appeared in magazines such as *Good Housekeeping* and *Life* between 1943 and 1945. Despite a national emergency, the tone was often light-hearted, but interwoven with the patriotic message: Victory gardens provided for the home front so that food supplies could be redirected to the military, to our allies, and to occupied countries. After extolling the vitamin content and versatility of its product, a Velveeta advertisement (*Good Housekeeping*, March 1944) advised, "Right now the plans for your Victory Garden should be shaping up.... This year every family must produce as much of its own food as possible ... for our nation will need tremendous food supplies to make and hold a just, victorious peace. Plan now to plant a garden of the most nutritious vegetables."

Urban Victories

Victory gardens thrived in cities, from Brooklyn backyards to the Boston Fenway, despite early reservations from the Department of Agriculture. Due to the combined factors of inexperience and poor soil conditions, urban gardeners often needed more help than their suburban counterparts, but advice came rapidly from local authorities and horticultural organizations. Perhaps most importantly, urban victory garden campaigns transcended social class. In New York, gardeners cultivated plots at the vacant Charles Schwab mansion on Riverside Drive and on land surrounding the Rockefeller Institute of Medical Research (now Rockefeller University). Affluent matrons grew tomatoes on rooftops and in townhouse gardens; the City Garden Club of Manhattan organized tours to victory gardens owned (if not maintained) by Mrs. Andrew Carnegie and Mrs. George Whitney. The Brooklyn Botanical Garden provided plots in its Oriental Garden for families lacking land, while gardeners in Jackson Heights tilled four large lots between 84th and 87th avenues. Macy's offered expert advice for novice gardeners as part of their Vegetables for Victory merchandising campaign.

In Boston, the Victory Garden Committee identified unoccupied areas citywide with potentially arable land. By 1943, there were 49 sites in the program, mostly city parks, but also some former industrial and private land judged to be suitable for victory gardens. Boston park employees took applications from new gardeners, delineated plots, assigned sites, distributed pamphlets, and provided instruction. No area was sacred, no matter how iconic or historic; the Boston Common and lawns surrounding Copley Square and the Museum of Fine Arts were among the public lands that were excavated, tilled, and planted with vegetable crops.

The Massachusetts Horticultural Society functioned as the regional gardening hub for the duration of the war years. In addressing the annual meeting on May 7, 1945, society president John Ames noted, "The Society has been active in promoting many wartime activities and will continue to do its part along these lines. Horticultural Hall has been a center for the distribution of literature having to do with victory gardens and the preservation of food, and last summer a well-attended series of lectures on canning was given in the small hall by representatives of the State College."[26] This was probably the first time that many Bostonians had wielded a hoe or monitored the gauge on a pressure cooker.

Public lands were widely cultivated as victory gardens, with plots allocated to local residents. Horse-drawn plows were used to break up the sod on the Boston Common, which was then tilled and planted with vegetable crops (U.S. Army).

In addition to the Brahmins who supported the work of the Massachusetts Horticultural Society, some talent rose from the ranks. Henry Wendler began as supervisor of gardening for the Boston public schools, a position he had held since 1922, promoting children's garden schemes and classroom use of botanical specimens. He took a leave of absence from Jamaica Plain High School and in February 1943 became assistant director of victory gardens for the city of Boston. That spring, Wendler was everywhere in the city—delivering lectures, leading workshops, and sharing advice. As part of the Boston Victory Garden Committee lecture series, Wendler lectured on "The A, B, C's in the Art of Using Fertilizer, Seeds, and Muscle for Cultivation of the Soil." He offered public lectures for hundreds in attendance at Horticultural Hall on soil preparation, garden layout, seed varieties, fertilizers, and insecticides. Novices could also view the demonstration gardens cultivated on Boston Common, where five model plots provided produce for city hospitals and charities. Adjacent to the gardens, attendants staffed an information booth that did double-duty as a radio studio; three times weekly Mayor Tobin's Victory Garden Committee broadcast a garden advice program from the demonstration plots on Boston Common.

Wendler provided practical advice for local problems, for instance the need to "sweeten" acidic, calcium-deficient soils with lime, which could be accomplished by adding wood or coal ashes (both are sources of calcium ions). Either soil treatment improved the sickly beets languishing in Boston victory gardens. As an ambassador for victory gardening, Wendler also addressed groups such as the Women's Italian Club at the Statler Hotel on April 21, 1943. The program included the garden lecture, lunch, and a program of Italian and Spanish song and dance, and no doubt some women took Wendler's advice to heart. Bostonians (many of them women) grew 20,000 victory gardens, and they exhibited produce at the 1943 and 1944 Victory Harvest Shows at Horticultural Hall. War bonds were awarded to contestants with the best exhibits of vegetables artfully arranged on evergreen or autumn foliage. During these years, the *Chicago Sun* sponsored a similar harvest event at Soldier's Field, and New Yorkers displayed victory garden produce in the lobbies of RKO theaters.[27]

City sites often demanded tremendous preparation before planting could occur. Fenway Gardens (still cultivated and now a Boston Historical Landmark) started with a model garden planted by Professor Paul Dempsey to show best practices, including soil preparation, cultivation, and handling of seedlings, but before gardening could commence, the site required thousands of cubic yards of fill to raise the land above the height of the adjacent Muddy River. Soil (much of it excavated from the underground subway system) was moved to the site, but it tended toward poor quality with metal shards, bricks, rocks, and other debris to remove. Water was available for gardeners to carry to their plots. Despite these challenges, 260 plots were planted and harvested during the 1943 growing season, and the Fenway Garden Society organized at a 1944 Harvard Club meeting.[28]

Success in Boston was mirrored statewide. By 1944, nearly every Massachusetts city and town had a Home Garden Committee, and the Massachusetts Home Garden and Food Preservation Program offered seasonal suggestions for organizing and improving the victory garden movement. The theme for 1944 was "more pounds per garden," with close attention paid to soil improvement, fertilizer application, and cultivar selection. The number of factory and workplace gardens also increased each year; local committees provided supplies such as seeds and fertilizer and encouraged boys and girls to become involved with victory garden plans and activities. At Mount Holyoke College in Hadley, students resumed the active gardening campaign that they waged during World War I. Classroom instruction included lectures on agriculture and collaboration with the nearby Massachusetts State College (now the University of Massachusetts) on vegetable gardening. About ten acres were tilled, and the produce supplied the campus dining rooms. Students did the planning and the work, in 1944 harvesting 500 bushels of potatoes, 128 bushels of cabbages, 72 bushels of tomatoes, and 8,000 ears of corn, enough to feed the college community and local WAVES for three months.[29]

Children's Gardens

Victory gardens planted and cultivated by children were not a novel concept in the 1940s. During World War I, school children had grown vegetables as part of the United States School Garden Army, organized in 1917 by the federal Bureau of Education as a means to provide local produce. With World War II looming, national attention again turned to youth as a potential labor source to address food shortages and emergencies, and education journals took up the mission to integrate war gardens and education. In the spring of 1942, articles proposed that school staff identify sites and develop garden plans as part of the curriculum, with some educators recommending curricular shifts toward "life activities" such as work, hobbies, and play, with reduced emphasis on traditional reading and writing. The plan also included gardens that children would plant and cultivate at home, based on agricultural training at school.

Teachers of science, home economics, agriculture, and even art were drafted into the school garden movement, which included encouraging and supervising children's gardens at home. Earl Gabler of the school of education at New York University realized that science teachers might lack enthusiasm for an unexpected curriculum unit on agriculture, but maintained that help with a school garden program might be forthcoming if teachers could be persuaded "to deviate from the course of study in general science or biology."[30] Frequent advice aimed at educators encouraged wartime flexibility, and the message was clear: Teachers should be willing to integrate school gardens into the curriculum. The labor provided by high school students was a valuable resource, but this was a radical shift away from traditional textbook science to hands-on cultivation with unpredictable outcomes.

Nevertheless, some teachers willingly incorporated plant propagation in botanical studies. For instance, biology students at Ellsworth High School in Iowa started tomato, pepper, and cauliflower seeds in homemade wooden flats, but apparently they had trouble with damping off fungi or other microbes that killed seedlings at soil level. Reflecting standard practice at the time, their teacher recommended sterilizing seeds with an antifungal mercury compound (chlorophenol mercury, sold under the brand name Semesan) but discouraged the use of manure "as the presence of organic fertilizers often causes bacterial rot."[31] Many argued that all wartime biology courses should include just such a practical spring gardening unit that covered plant selection, planning gardens of various sizes, specific cultural information, and seed germination, including the effective use of cold frames. Food preservation was also part of the broader lesson, with discussion of canning and winter storage of appropriate crops.[32] Thus the task list for classroom teachers became daunting: planning garden lectures or symposia, building demonstration cold

School curricula shifted during the war years to include victory gardens. Children cultivated vegetables for their school lunches, including city plots such as this victory garden on 1st Avenue between 35th and 36th Streets in New York (Library of Congress).

frames, installing model gardens, organizing seed sales, managing seedling distribution, developing garden plans, arranging publicity, obtaining and organizing government and extension bulletins and pamphlets, and mimeographing instructional sheets and booklets.

Planning and cultivating victory gardens for younger children usually followed the advice disseminated by local victory garden committees. Amateurs needed help with identifying garden sites that were well-drained, with adequate soil and sunlight, which could be a particular problem with shaded school yards. One excellent layout design utilized beds that were 24 feet long by 4 feet wide; paths between the adjacent beds allowed children to work without trampling plants and compacting garden soil. Concern for young gardeners' safety centered on pesticide use and known chemical hazards; Earl Gabler suggested using rotenone and pyrethrum (see Chapter 6), rather than arsenic-based compounds to battle insects.[33] Both are plant-based compounds that at the time were considered relatively safe to use, but shipping difficulties with South American imports of *Lonchocarpus* (the most common source of rotenone) and Japanese imports of *Chrysanthemum* and *Tanacetum* (pyrethrum sources) caused wartime shortages.

A primary goal was supplying school lunchrooms with fresh vegetables. Children consumed the crops that they cultivated, which conserved the national food supply, eliminated canning and shipping, and encouraged the consumption of vitamin-rich botanical foods. The *Victory Garden Leader's Handbook* noted that "rural and city schools can have gardens planned and managed on a scale that will provide a large part of the fresh and processed vegetables for school lunches."[34] Attention was paid to frost-resistant crops that could be grown in the early spring while school was still in session, including peas, lettuce, onions, and Chinese cabbage, followed by beets, carrots, and potatoes, which tolerate cool nights and even light frost. Before the war, many children had not eaten such a diverse diet, and some may have had mixed feelings about increased vegetable consumption.

In *My Book to Help America* (1942), Munro Leaf reminded young citizens to eat "what we should when we should, without grumbling, or pouting, or crying about it," a reference to the higher vegetable content of wartime American meals.[35] Of course, children were probably interested in eating what they grew; *Victory Gardens: Handbook of the Victory Garden Committee* optimistically advised teachers and parents that "school gardening may also help develop a favorable attitude toward the eating of vegetables" and suggested soybeans (ironically, the Japanese variety known as *bansei*) as an ideal crop for children to cultivate.[36] The plants resist attack from the Mexican bean beetle, which devour the leaves of many legumes down to their vascular skeletons, thus toxic insecticides could be avoided. First grown for their oil and flour, soybeans eventually appeared in recipes for casseroles and other baked dishes, but their popularity as a fresh vegetable for wartime meals never took hold (see Chapter 4).

Summer crops such as tomatoes and beans that require warm soil were best reserved for summer cultivation at home. Of course, much of the responsibility for maintaining and supervising school and home gardens extended beyond the typical school year, so teachers' work with school and home victory gardens often extended into the summer months. At the start of the 1942 growing season, parents in Highland Park, Michigan signed enrollment cards promising their assistance, and students recorded their labor, expenses, production, canning, and net profit. School staff visited students' homes to assess and score their victory gardens numerically for cultivation, planning, insect and disease control, and overall effort. The most productive crops were tomatoes, carrots, string beans, beets, and Swiss chard, and successful young gardeners received certificates "in recognition of your patriotic efforts." Kodachrome slides documented these first gardens, which in turn were used to recruit more gardeners in 1943.[37]

During the spring of 1943, grammar school students at the Fitzgerald School in Detroit started their victory garden project with soil study and site selection, part of "scientific gardening instruction." Students in grades four through eight cultivated the plot and recorded their work in garden journals, each "with a decorative cover and pages to be filled in as the garden work progressed." Seedlings were started in the conservatory and then moved into the garden as the weather allowed, and gardening at school continued through late June. By the end of the school year, 1,200 additional seedlings were grown and transplanted to home gardens for summer cultivation.[38] In Chicago, over 14,000 children gardened in public parks; city workers removed sod, plowed, and laid out the initial plots, from which children used sticks and string to mark 5' × 12' beds. To prevent waste, Marshall Field and Company department stores provided packets, each with a diagram of the garden layout and the exact quantity of seeds to sow in 5' rows. Crops included lettuce, radishes, kohlrabi, bush beans, Swiss chard, carrots, beets, and for morale, zinnias and petunias. Children planted, thinned, transplanted, weeded, and cultivated under the watchful supervision of volunteer teachers. Despite the low 1943 spring temperatures, drenching rains, and resulting mud, the first year of the park gardens resulted in high yields that were harvested for home kitchens.[39] Similar children's gardens grew nationwide in schoolyards, backyards, reclaimed lots, and even rooftops, and the harvests comprised a legitimate contribution to the national war effort. Even with victory in Europe within sight, the Department of Agriculture appealed to teachers to continue cultivating crops. American farmers supplied the Lend-Lease Program, which by 1944 required 10 percent of the national agricultural harvest, largely due to food shortages in Russia. School gardens compensated for the nationwide wartime shortfall in vegetables.[40]

Harvest exhibits were a common theme across the children's victory garden movement. The Fitzgerald School in Detroit displayed the produce from students' 1943 home gardens, including foods canned with parental help. In August of the same year, Boston school children were invited to exhibit produce, flowers, and homemade tools and storage lockers at Horticultural Hall. There was particular interest in unusual crops; students from the John Cheverus School of East Boston exhibited chicory, salsify, peanuts, okra, and garlic. Boston youth packed the hall with 2,500 individual exhibits, and the Massachusetts Horticultural Society awarded certificates to children who maintained their plots in the best condition throughout the growing season. These included plots in school gardens, community gardens, or backyards—provided that a qualified teacher inspected at least twice during the growing season. According to an article in *The Boston Daily* on August 27, the judges worked in "clamlike silence," inspecting each vegetable considered for an award with "almost microscopic" acuity.[41]

Adults also learned from the school garden movement. Agriculture instructors at Jamaica Plain High School in Boston published a useful leaflet with information for tyro gardeners, plans for planting a 20' × 40' garden, cultural notes, supply list, and an offer for soil analysis provided at the school. Victory garden exhibits became increasingly widespread and ultimately included adult gardeners. With the motto "Grow Food to Win the War," the Boston Victory Garden Committee organized city-wide exhibits in September 1943 and 1944. These events filled Horticultural Hall with victory garden produce, with a junior division that included youth through age eighteen. The entry categories for vegetables included tomatoes, snap beans, beets, carrots, corn, and greens; requirements stipulated that contestants enter several identical specimens of one crop, artfully arranged on evergreen or autumn foliage.[42]

With parents absent, preoccupied, or busy with war work, gardening provided a worthwhile pastime, but in many communities, organizations like Boy Scouts and 4-H clubs vanished for lack of leadership. Youth had free time with minimal supervision and few organized activities. Juvenile delinquency became a growing problem; indeed, some sociologists and educators feared that a generation of young Americans would suffer irreparable harm. Juvenile delinquency became a popular topic in the press and media, and short films such as "Youth in Crisis" and "As the Twig is Bent" (both released in 1943) traced causes and possible cures for the youth crime wave; the latter assumed its title from the botanical imagery of Alexander Pope: "Just as the twig is bent, the tree's inclined." Social deterioration during wartime resulted in mischief by idle youth; an alarming article in *Life* magazine detailed youth crimes including vandalism, arson, robbery, car theft, bigamy, rape, and murder.[43] Boys a few years too young for the draft were derailing trains, and simultaneously derailing their own lives. Girls also garnered concern when they ran after soldiers and behaved provocatively in public places, rather than helping at home.

Victory gardens thus became a nationwide strategy for keeping adolescents busy and crime-free. According to *The Rotarian* magazine, gardening could prevent juvenile

Scouts, 4-H, and other youth groups fostered an interest in gardening activities; here Professor Harry Nelson shows a group of San Francisco Girl Scouts how to transplant seedlings with success (U.S. National Archives).

delinquency by providing a worthwhile activity, "Take a batch of boys—any boys with steam in their veins and time on their hands. Then take a couple of vacant lots. Stir the two together, add a few fat packets of seeds, and pop the two into the hot oven of Summer. This recipe will make a Victory Garden which will score two victories; one over the food problem; another over juvenile mischief.... Victory gardening yields more than food ... it can steer into safe channels those boiling energies of youth which, unguided, often burst out as mild or serious forms of juvenile delinquency. With Dad and Mother home less and less, that sort of steering becomes more and more necessary. Maybe a Victory Garden can provide it.... If the lads get good crops, fine!—but its infinitely more important that they themselves grow straight, in this time of laxer home supervision, and ready for good citizenship tomorrow."[44] Rotary Clubs recruited boys, girls, teachers, county agents, and 4-H leaders and helped them to start victory gardens; time was well-spent, excess energy expended, and the best gardeners received $25 war bonds.

Similar goals were set by other organizations. Nationally 4-H clubs began the "Feed a Fighter" campaign, endorsed by President Roosevelt. The goal was to produce enough food to feed a serviceman for twelve months, although the food would actually be consumed on the home front, thus redirecting food supplies to the military. Members were challenged to grow 110 bushels of tomatoes or can 500 quarts of vegetables, and one 4-H member in North Carolina raised enough food to supply 34 soldiers. The program was met with enthusiasm; in North Carolina alone, 91,000 4-H members participated and earned the honor of naming two naval ships, the USS *Tyrell*, named for a county in North Carolina, and the USS *Cassius Hudson*, which honored the man who instituted agricultural demonstration work in North Carolina.[45]

Boys' Life, the Boy Scout magazine, promoted victory gardening during the first year of the campaign. Editor James West encouraged all Scouts to grow a garden during the summer of 1942, reminding readers that "the success of our war efforts depends upon producing and conserving food.... Gardens are the source of more than one-half the essential foods."[46] The following spring the magazine featured an illustrated column "Repairing Garden Implements," which showed boys how to repair broken handles and tangs and also how to construct a wooden garden rake from maple, ash, or hickory, followed by an article a year later that encouraged Scouts to earn merit badges in gardening by growing tomatoes, lettuce, radishes, carrots, beets, and beans.[47]

With the end of the war in sight, many victory gardeners abandoned their plots, but Scouts were encouraged to stick with gardening for the duration. Just a few months before the end of the war, the magazine featured "Weed 'Em and Reap," a fable-like story about a bully who intimidates a Scout; as the story unfolds, we learn that garden work helped young men to become quite strong.[48] Additional support came in the form of awards; the National Victory Garden Institute, founded by New York businessmen at the beginning of the war, distributed medals for the General MacArthur Award to thousands of Boy Scouts and 4-H members with productive gardens.

Despite the serious specter of a food shortage, there was room for levity in promoting and encouraging victory gardens. Walt Disney Studios contributed cartoon images to various print materials, including posters for the Green Thumb contest that featured the motto "3-V's—Vegetables, Vitamins, Vitality," a Donald Duck victory garden comic book, and various other signs and record books for recording garden activities. Disney did not produce a cartoon film about victory gardens, but "Barney Bear's Victory Garden" (MGM, 1942) and Popeye's "Ration fer the Duration" (Paramount Studios, 1943) both centered on the victory garden theme from a strictly comic viewpoint, both with some sly humor that likely appealed to both children and adults.

The Harvest

World War II victory gardens fulfilled myriad goals, from fostering good nutrition and morale on the home front to redirecting agricultural crops to the armed forces and Lend-Lease program. Food shortages were circumvented, and strategic metals were conserved by decreasing the need for commercially canned foods. By 1943, Americans cultivated 20 million victory gardens, which produced an estimated eight million tons of produce, 40 percent of the fresh produce consumed in American homes. Based on an average garden size of 500 square feet, U.S. victory gardeners cultivated 700 million acres, an area about the size of Rhode Island. Gardens produced vegetables in places as diverse as public parks, wealthy estates, schoolyards, prisons, and convents. Home-canned produce lined pantry shelves, as suggested by the increase in pressure cooker sales from 66,000 in 1942 to 315,000 in 1943.

Ironically, as the war progressed, many victory gardens did not meet the dimensions suggested in the first wave of Department of Agriculture publications. A small plot of 100 square feet met the needs of many families for fresh vegetables, and this was a size suitable for backyards in densely populated areas. Despite the early reservations of Secretary of Agriculture Claude Wickard, city gardeners followed advice, improved the soil, and worked cooperatively to produce successful harvests. School children gardened as well, assuming adult responsibility for food production and developing lifelong horticultural skills. Food was indeed a weapon, and mobilizing a nation of vegetable growers helped to win the war.

Once victory was in sight, interest in victory gardening waned. In 1945, Americans cultivated 17 million plots, down from the 1943 peak of 21 million vegetable gardens. Nevertheless local organizers continued to promote the message—that victory gardening was a patriotic, thrifty, fun, healthy means to a reliable supply of fresh produce. "The Facts about 1945 Victory Gardens," a typewritten bulletin for leaders, urged gardeners to "Grow your own and play safe. If you have your own fruits and vegetables, you won't have to worry about crop failures in other parts of the country, bottlenecks in transportation or distribution, or anything else that might keep you from getting what you want when you want it."[49]

There was widespread concern that Americans might start to let down when the end of the war was in sight; in fact, many Americans were planning post-war landscapes that excluded vegetable plots. Once the victory garden campaigns ended in 1946, Americans abandoned the goals of the victory garden campaign; they were ready to move on and become active consumers. In the words of David McCullough, by the end of 1945 President Truman "failed to comprehend how a people who had shown such dedication and will through the war could overnight become so rampantly selfish and disinterested in the common good."[50]

In the post-war years, a shift occurred toward food security for Cold War preparedness. A few years after the war, *Kiplinger's Personal Finance* reported that "victory gardens went out with V-J Day, but now the Department of Agriculture is urging people to get busy and establish a brand new type of backyard garden to be known as a 'Freedom Garden.' The spade, hoe, trowel, mulch and bug powder are to be just the same, however, as in the old Victory Garden."[51] By 1952, after the Berlin Blockade and Airlift of 1948–49 and at the height of the Korean War, victory gardens were renamed again. Readers of the *Science News-Letter* were urged to "Plant a 'liberty' garden. You will at the same time be helping America's defense effort. And you will be assuring for yourself and your family, as well as your friends also perhaps, a steady and ample supply of vitamin-packed vegetables and other foods."[52] The advice resembled wartime victory garden bulletins, now backed with the message of atomic-era self-sufficiency. The connection between peace time national defense and vegetable gardening in an apocalypse was not stated bluntly, but with nuclear war a possibility, food security for survivors was a new national concern.

2

Dig for Victory

By the 1930s, about two-thirds of the food consumed in England was cultivated or raised abroad, amounting to 20 million imported tons annually. Port cities received foods from Argentina, various European countries, and current or former British colonies, including the United States, Canada, Australia, New Zealand, India, and Burma. These imports provided two-thirds of the essential dietary calories and half of the proteins that the British consumed, a potentially dangerous situation with war looming in Europe. Among the botanical foods that were routinely imported to England were the grains used for baking bread and the fruits that prevented vitamin-deficiency diseases; in fact, by the 1930s, 70 percent of the grains and 80 percent of the fruits consumed in England were harvested abroad and imported through shipping lanes. This suggested an obvious strategy to Axis countries: England could be forced into compliance if food shipments to the island were blocked.

With the invasion of Poland, England declared war on Germany in September 1939, over two years before U.S involvement as an ally. Food became an immediate weapon of war. Soon German U-boats patrolled the seas around England, rendering shipping lanes hazardous, leading to food shortages, and affecting the national diet. Fresh fruit and vegetables from Europe dwindled with shipping hazards and German occupation. Wheat from Australia and New Zealand was cut off or redirected to the American military, in compensation for Lend-Lease shipments sent from America to England. Many botanical products, including tea, spices, tapioca, sugar, and vegetable oils, disappeared from the marketplace as the war spread in Asia. Palm oil shortages affected not only diet by also the manufacture of soap, which became an increasingly scarce commodity. The 1941 Lend-Lease Act provided some relief, but the real solution to wartime food security lay in food production on English soil.

Garden Plans

Following the First World War, kitchen gardens and war gardens waned, replaced by perennial borders and verdant lawns. The cool English climate and high soil calcium content fostered excellent turf, but homeowners were advised at the onset of the new war with Germany to replace ornamental plantings with vegetable gardens. Of course, many gardeners anticipated that the war would be over in a year. They transplanted perennials into crowded beds and anticipated replanting ornamental gardens, not realizing that home vegetable gardens would remedy food shortages for the better part of a decade.

In the fall of 1939, facing problems with critical imports, the national Grow More Food campaign distributed a leaflet titled "Food from the Garden." Experienced gardeners immediately noticed several errors, such as the advice to plant the sprawling squash plants (known as marrows) just a few inches apart. The publication was assembled in haste and distributed when it was too late in the season to sow winter crops; campaign advice assured gardeners that crops such as cabbages could survive cold, but the winter of 1939–40 was the harshest in years. Snow and freezing temperatures reduced savoy cabbages, Brussels sprouts, and other typically winter-hardy crops to mush, discouraging for the novices who sowed these crops for the first time in the fall of 1939.

When food imports from Belgium and Holland ceased, the Ministry of Agriculture redoubled its efforts to encourage self-sufficiency in food production. Those who lacked land were encouraged to cultivate allotments, traditionally a piece of land equivalent to ¹⁄₁₆th of an acre (302.5 square yards) leased from a local council or landowner. The concept dated back to the 19th century when small plots for vegetable cultivation were made available to landless workers. Food shortages during World War I were remedied through the cultivation of 1.5 million allotment gardens, so once again public parks, properties and cricket fields were divided into garden plots. Gardening was encouraged across social lines: in April 1940, Princesses Elizabeth and Margaret Rose were photographed with a wheelbarrow and implements in a garden at Windsor Great Park, suggesting that the royal family had also taken up the cause.

The motto "Dig for Victory" appeared on a multitude of posters and free leaflets that covered topics including winter crops, digging, composting, food preservation, potato blight, and roof gardening. Morale was also part of the picture. Ministry officials recalled the salutary effects of gardening during World War I, which served to "to steady the nation's nerves," and they anticipated a similar outcome.[1] In fact, gardening leaflets became so commonplace that officials used them to hide in plain sight useful information in the event of a German invasion. One such pamphlet was titled "Country Man's Diary—1939" and advertised "Highworth's Fertilisers—Do their stuff unseen until you see results!," but inside it contained information on explosives, booby traps, and the training of guerrilla units. The fictional product was named for the Wiltshire town near where troops trained.

In the late summer of 1940, the Ministry published a four-page leaflet titled "Grow for Winter As Well As Summer," in which errors in the original Grow More Food leaflet were corrected, and information was distilled into four pages. Bearing the Dig for Victory logo of a boot on a spade, the revised leaflet employed telegraphic language to convey the goal: "Vegetables for you and your family every week of the year. Never a week without food from your garden or allotment…. Vegetables all the year round if you DIG WELL AND CROP WISELY." The publication provided basic information on layout, sowing times, and crop rotation, with emphasis on cold tolerant, often winter hardy crops including "savoys, sprouts, kale, sprouting broccoli, onions, leeks, carrots, parsnips, and beet." With correct crop choices for the typically mild English climate, victory gardens could provide British families with fresh vegetables even during the cold months.

Initial plans called for gardens of approximately 90 by 30 yards, with vegetables that fell into a few basic categories. Root crops included carrots, parsnips, beets, and swedes (also known as rutabagas, the result of an ancient hybridization between turnips and

kale or cabbage), which in many areas of the country could be harvested well into the winter. Legumes included broad beans, runner beans, and peas, dietary essentials because the protein in their seeds could replace the nutrient value of rationed meats. Green crops such as cabbage, broccoli, kale, and Brussels sprouts were vitamin-rich crops that could often overwinter in the garden, and these occupied five full rows in the Ministry garden plan. Savoys are wrinkle-leaved cabbage cultivars, which are planted in July and harvested during the fall and winter, even into March. While cabbages have a single massive terminal bud, each axillary bud in Brussels sprouts forms a small, cabbage-like head with similar potential as a vitamin-rich crop for potential winter harvest. Along with broccoli and kale, all of these crops are cultivars of *Brassica oleracea*, a single species bred into distinct cultivars since ancient times. Kale is closest to the wild type, and Brussels sprouts may be the most recent variety, developed in Belgium during the eighteenth century. Cabbages were probably first bred in Germany during the twelfth century, an ironic beginning in light of the impor-

The Ministry of Agriculture replaced the Grow More Food campaign with the Dig for Victory campaign during the summer and fall of 1940; wartime posters and instructional leaflets featured the compelling image of a boot, shovel, and soil (Ministry of Agriculture, United Kingdom).

tance of cabbages in providing a staple crop for the British home front.

Leeks, shallots, and onions (all bulbs produced by the genus *Allium*) were grown more for flavor than vitamin or nutrient content. Onions were still viewed with some suspicion as foreign vegetables with a persistent aftertaste, but as the war continued, they became an increasingly valued crop to enhance bland vegetable dishes. Lettuce and spinach could be sown after other crops were harvested, but emphasis on salad vegetables was minimal, despite vitamin concerns. Tomatoes were absent from early English victory garden plans, in contrast to American gardens in which they were commonly grown and valued for salads, cooking, and canning.

Some frustrated gardeners took liberties with the tidy rows diagrammed in Ministry publications. Following the advice of wartime manuals on the topic of garden layout, vegetables had potential that was both nutritional and ornamental. As described in *101 Things to Do in War Time 1940*, "…even with the growing of the more prosaic but valuable vegetable, it is still possible to obtain decorative effects and to include some favourite flowers, which may be left in clumps here and there amidst green vegetables."[2] The object was to emphasize foliage and to plant a decorative landscape using the attributes of vegetable plants (and occasional flowers), as done when gardening with ornamental species. Carrots provided a lacy border, while alternating clumps of rhubarb and beets created an interesting pattern of color and textures. Climbing legumes made a pleasant background for the border, and various brassicas could be tucked between hills of potatoes and clumps of leeks.

Allotment Gardening

Not all families owned land, but all needed to eat. A potential gardener without a garden site was encouraged to cultivate an allotment, one of the available plots carved from public properties and under-utilized private land, sometimes as part of a compulsory agreement with the land owner. In fact, allotment gardening was nothing new. During World War I, nearly two million allotments provided food, but numbers and interest waned in the following two decades.

However, allotments provided an immediate self-help option for urban dwellers, and in October 1939, the Ministry of Agriculture announced its intention to make 500,000 plots available. The national goal was one allotment for every five households, with the implied assumption that gardening would involve sharing labor and produce. Most importantly, this was not dilettante horticulture, and gardeners were expected to stay the course. Allotment societies administered the scheme, inspected sites for maintenance, and assessed plots for productivity. Newspapers and garden magazines published allotment news, including cultivation tips, records set, and extraordinary achievements, such as stories of extraordinary gardeners who singlehandedly cultivated several plots to supply needy families and neighbors.

All available land was scrutinized for its food-growing potential, including public and royal parks, city squares, school playing fields, recreation grounds, pastures, zoos, old cemeteries, and historic sites. Even the moat surrounding the Tower of London was subdivided into allotments

The Dig for Victory campaign encouraged civilians to cultivate allotments wherever land could be found, including landscaped gardens; this local poster used humor to pressure residents into replacing lawns with vegetables (Ministry of Agriculture, United Kingdom).

with particularly rich soil. Of course, tilling potentially arable land required the destruction of vast lawns; advice leaflets suggested that rectangles of turf should be cut, peeled away from the earth, stacked neatly, and allowed to decompose—either into potting soil or into a raised bed for cultivating marrows, various types of squashes that favor warm earth.

The "Dig for Victory" message supplanted the Grow More Food campaign during the summer and fall of 1940. The phrase first appeared in Ministry of Agriculture leaflets published late in 1939 and may have originated as a headline in the *Evening Standard*. A series of topical "Dig for Victory" leaflets provided basic information on digging techniques, winter crops, composting waste, potato blight, seed saving, fruit trees, roof gardening, and various means of food preservation. Posters featured a foot on a spade, with variations that included "Dig for victory now," "Dig for Victory on Allotments and Private Gardens," "Your own vegetables all the year round…. If you dig for victory now," "Dig for Survival," and "Dig for Dear Life." Posters encouraged experienced gardeners to "Help the new victory diggers with their problems…. Play your part in the Dig for Victory campaign."

The Dig for Victory campaign appealed directly to women to provide for their families. Farm crops supplied the military, so at a time when most meals were vegetable-based, it was up to women and children to grow food for home tables (Ministry of Agriculture, United Kingdom).

Carrying On

As the war wore on and interest in gardening waned, mottoes reflected the need to continue; "Dig on for victory" was followed in 1945 by "Dig for victory still." The final "Allotment and Garden Guide" predicted that "you'll know only too well that the end of the war has not meant the solution to all of our problems."[3] In reality, ongoing austerity required continued self-sufficiency in the post-war era, and allotments provided essential food for years after the war had ended.

In 1942, the Ministry of Information released "Dig for Victory," a short movie that galvanized key arguments for gardening—avoiding queues, providing for family needs, working outdoors, and helping to win the war. Food crops were compared to weapons, like the large barrage balloon tethered above the filmed allotments, but the narration did not mention the German intention to starve England into surrender. Other Ministry of Information short films focused on digging and cultivation of allotments, sowing, and planting, and some Pathé films were based on the content of Dig for Victory leaflets. All were destined for distribution to theaters, where they were projected before the feature film to home front audiences of women, children, and elderly theater-goers.

The BBC Home Service was also critical in promoting the message of food self-sufficiency. Cecil Henry Middleton had broadcast "In the Garden" since 1931, studied as a student gardener at the Royal Botanic Gardens (Kew), and worked with the Surrey Council as a horticulture instructor. Middleton addressed his radio audience with a conversational tone, in contrast to the Latin-laced, impersonal broadcasts of the Royal Horticultural Society. Radio advice departed from pre-war lawn, rockery, and border cultivation to practical food production. For the duration, Middleton traveled, published, and broadcast garden advice; he advocated the manual removal of pests, careful storage of crops that could be saved for winter consumption, and above all—patience. He guided a generation of novice allotment gardeners in producing food for the British home front.

Bombing led to more gardening. Explosions caused drastic changes to the landscape, but newly cleared sites provided more garden space. "Dig for Victory" included footage of a garden cultivated in the rubble of a bombed school yard, and British Pathé newsreels in 1942 featured well-tended crater gardens near Westminster, which according to the narrator converted "ruins into radishes and litter into leeks" and in Bayswater, where the "the bomb started the digging and the enterprising owner finished it." The message to the enemy was one of triumph over disaster and defiance in the face of adversity; a bomb served the function of a trowel in overturning earth and preparing a site for planting. The rooftop garden of Selfridge's department store was damaged by an incendiary bomb and subsequently replanted with vegetables, supplying the restaurant of the store.

Bombing cleared land for additional gardens. In 1942 British Pathé newsreels featured well-tended crater gardens near Westminster, which converted "ruins into radishes and litter into leeks" and in Bayswater, where the "the bomb started the digging and the enterprising owner finished it" (Pathé).

In London, east end residents formed the Bethnal Green Bombed Sites Producers' Association that worked with boys' groups to convert bombed sites into productive gardens. No easy task, preparation involved removal of rubble and sieving of soil to remove glass shards and shrapnel; however, by 1942 thirty Bethnal Green bomb sites supported allotments. An article in *Life* magazine provided photographs of vegetable gardens cultivated in the cellars and foundations of buildings demolished in the East End and Kensington areas of London.[4] However, the most publicized bomb site gardens were those cultivated within the sloping sides of an unleveled bomb crater. There were probably relatively few crater gardens, but the defiant act of growing food in the bombed landscape appealed to wartime sensibilities. Productive gardens sprouted in unexpected sites, including narrow alleys, rooftops, train yards, and window boxes. Unfortunately, not everyone wanted to work in order to harvest, and some pilfering did occur; it seemed that onions were particularly vulnerable, perhaps because a single bulb could flavor an otherwise uninspired dish. As the war progressed, theft of vegetables was equated with looting from bomb sites and rewarded with harsh punishment. In the eyes of wartime law, vegetable were weapons, used to nourish workers on the home front and to liberate agricultural crops to fuel the military.

As the age of conscription for men increased, many women assumed sole responsibility for gardening. A Ministry of Agriculture poster appealed directly to women, "Women! Farmers can't grow all your vegetables…. You must grow your own." By 1943, it was estimated that 10,000 women grew vegetables in England and Wales. Victory gardening had become another category of women's war work, an expected part of wartime culture. An advertisement for Yardley cosmetics illustrated a young woman with a garden fork, wheelbarrow, and cabbages, with the message, "Put your best face forward." Of course, a garden image for this company was entirely appropriate; beginning in 1873, lavender (*Lavandula angustifolia*) was incorporated into scents and soaps, and it may have served women well in wartime. Years before the war, herbalist Maud Grieve recommended lavender oil to prevent mosquito bites and to treat depression and fatigue.[5]

British colonies also adopted the Dig for Victory campaign. Early in 1942, Prime Minister John Curtin promoted the campaign to encourage home agriculture in Australia. Morale was a concern, in light of the feared Japanese invasion of Australia, and digging for victory was a way to channel worry into a productive pastime. Many Australians were already self-sufficient gardeners, efforts supported by the popular press that frequently published insightful advice. The *Cairns Post* provided instructions for composting and suggested laying out beds with north-south orientation to allow for morning sun, and narrow beds allowed for convenient cultivation, without the need to trample soil to reach weeds.[6] Australian gardeners routinely practiced both composting and contour plowing, strategies essential for enriching and preserving good garden soil. Some Australian gardeners became *de facto* farmers, selling excess produce and donating funds to help the war effort and social service organizations such as the Salvation Army and YWCA, which in 1942 organized the National YWCA Garden Army Scheme. In 1943 the Melbourne Garden Army of over 1000 women tended several community gardens, each with a required minimum size of one-half acre. Housewives, office workers, and Girl Guides all lent a hand, and sale of garden produce supported the Red Cross and Australian Comforts Fund.[7]

The Canadian government also actively encouraged victory gardens, following initial concern that amateur gardeners might waste valuable seed stock and fertilizer supplies.

The Canadian Ministry of Agriculture distributed pamphlets and by 1943, officials argued persuasively that homegrown vegetables lessened the cost of providing for military needs, allowing funds to be used for guns and other equipment. During the 1943 growing season, Canadians planted and cultivated over 200,000 victory gardens, which on the average each yielded over 500 pounds of produce for civilian tables.

Cultivars and Propagation

As imports decreased, more food was needed to supply both the military and the home front. British farmers sowed wheat and barley to replace foreign grain, and they planted fodder for livestock. As a result, farms produced fewer potatoes, a dietary staple that was nutritious, storable, and easy to prepare. To compensate, the first Dig for Victory leaflet suggested that home gardeners grow six rows of potatoes in a standard 90 by 30 yard allotment; thus tuber plantings increased as wheat imports dwindled.

Potatoes are specialized underground stems of *Solanum tuberosum*, tubers that are adapted for food storage. Each bears several buds (the "eyes") with the potential to grow into aerial stems, and these are used in asexual propagation, rather than seeds. Cultivation begins with burying seed potatoes (pieces of tubers) in several inches of soil; these sprout green shoots that photosynthesize and store starches in a new crop of tubers, cloned replicas of the parent plant. As a propagation strategy, cloning is efficient and effective in producing a reliable crop, but also means that diseases can be propagated along with each generation of tubers.

Gardeners learned that potatoes were a good first crop for newly dug land. Seed potatoes did not require the finely tilled soil of plants propagated by small seeds, and potato fields were easily established in rough soil. However, with increased demand for seed potatoes, some unscrupulous suppliers sold pathogen-infected stock that could endanger crops in an entire region. Victory gardeners were advised against planting potatoes of unknown provenance, but many of the older potato cultivars were better-flavored than disease-resistant strains. The best seed potato stock was certified into classes depending on its origins and susceptibility to wart disease, caused by a parasitic fungus (*Synchytrium endobioticum*), and breeders continued to develop productive cultivars that were resistant to this disease and also to potato blight (*Phytophthora infestans*), the fungus that caused potato famines in the 1840s. The appropriately named 'Home Guard' was a prized Scottish cultivar bred in 1943 and propagated widely; it was resistant to wart disease (but not potato blight) and produced a large, early crop.

Despite the advice and propaganda, the garden remained the testing ground in which gardeners learned what grew and what did not, depending on local climate and soils. Regional food preferences were another consideration; certain fruits and vegetables were essential for local tastes and recipes, while other were merely tolerated. For instance, celery was considered a difficult crop for new gardeners, requiring careful fertilization, trenching, and banking of soil around the stalks to produce the blanched vegetable sold by greengrocers. Once buried by mounded soil in the excavated trenches, celery stalks (elongated petioles that support leaves) do not produce chloroplasts and so remain pale and mild flavored. Nevertheless, gardeners in northern counties invested time in cultivating celery because it was a mainstay of the late afternoon meal known as tea.

Tomatoes were initially ignored, but suburban gardeners with pre-war glasshouses learned to start the plants indoors and move them into the garden once the danger of frost was past and warm temperatures approximated Central America. Ripening was a problem without intense sun, but the Dig for Victory leaflet "Tomato Growing Is Not Difficult" noted that green fruits could be ripened in the dark indoors or preserved in chutney recipes. Nevertheless, tomatoes remained a curiosity for many; the vines cultivated in the 1943 demonstration allotment plots at the Royal Botanic Gardens (Kew) attracted more attention than the giant *Victoria* water lilies. The golden variety 'Sunrise' set fruit reliably even late in the season, and despite a cool, cloudy summer, nineteen plants produced 75 pounds of fruit.

Ministry of Food policy officially discouraged certain crops, even national favorites like cucumbers and strawberries. Cucumbers are low in nutrients compared to other vegetables, and their cultivation in glasshouses became a finable offense. Strawberries were also considered a luxury fruit that should not occupy valuable glasshouse space, and gardeners were encouraged to till and replant old strawberry beds with potatoes. Fruit trees presented another ambivalent situation because many neglected orchards were unproductive, and Ministry authorities suggested strongly that they be replaced with vegetable plots. Nevertheless, domestic fruits were desperately needed to replace the vitamins in imported citrus and bananas. Although allotment gardeners were not advised to plant fruit trees, those with established orchards were encouraged to maintain productivity. The Dig for Victory leaflet "Better Fruit: Disease Control in Private Gardens" promoted a rigorous regime of spraying apple, pear, and plum trees. Berry-producing shrubs such as blackberries, raspberries, currants, and gooseberries also needed careful pruning and attention to produce crops worthy of preservation.

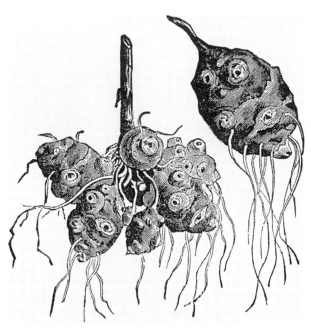

Regardless of their unattractive appearance and the myth that they cause leprosy, Jerusalem artichokes were a good first crop for newly dug land. The rhizomes proliferated in soil that was heavy and cold, and the plants tolerated partial shade.

At the same time, leaflets from the Ministry of Food and magazines such as *Garden Work* and *Gardeners' Chronicle* promoted unfamiliar vegetables that might provide a change from the dietary routine of cabbage, carrots, and potatoes. Many had shunned Jerusalem artichokes (*Helianthus tuberosus*), the underground rhizomes of a New World sunflower relative, because of their reputation for causing flatulence. Some may even have recalled the old legend that artichokes cause leprosy (now known as Hansen's disease, caused by the bacterium *Mycobacterium leprae*) because the bumpy rhizomes suggested the misshapen digits of lepers. Nonetheless, as an alternative to traditional root crops, the rhizomes provided some variety for those willing to cultivate and consume them. Like potatoes, Jerusalem artichokes were a good first crop for soil that had just been spaded; the rhizomes proliferated in soil that was heavy and cold, and the plants tolerated partial shade. The crop was convenient to harvest because the rhizomes could be lifted from the ground as they were needed. Jerusalem artichokes were not to be confused with native English globe artichokes (*Cynara scolymus*), grown for the edible bracts that were considered a frivolous vegetable in wartime.

Jerusalem artichokes were among the crops featured by the Royal Horticultural Society in their Dig for Victory touring exhibits, which consisted of mounted photographs and cultural information transported in large wooden crates. The display served as an alternative to flower shows when these became impossible to organize, and the instructional boards provided cultivation advice for potatoes, beans, peas, carrots, celery, tomatoes, Brussels sprouts, cabbage, onions, and parsnips. Displayed at public sites such as libraries and town halls, these exhibits spanned 55 feet of wall space; photographs duplicated those in *The Vegetable Garden Displayed*, first published in 1941 (and still in print).[8] The selfsame photographs eventually helped Germans to cultivate vegetables after the war, when translations of the book were sent abroad to assist with rebuilding.

Spinach may not have been a favorite, but it grew quickly, provided high vitamin content, and intercropped well with other vegetables as row space became available. Late in the growing season, summer spinach varieties were replaced by Good King Henry (*Blitum bonus-henricus*), a perennial crop that was originally classified along with spinach in the genus *Chenopodium*. Good King Henry was cultivated in medieval and Elizabethan gardens as a sallet green, and by World War II was best known as a European weed; as a victory garden plant, its leaves provided carotene, vitamin C, and 6 percent protein, twice the level of spinach.

As part of the Lend-Lease program, the U.S. sent seeds to England in time for sowing in the spring of 1942, and members of 4-H clubs mailed seed packets to British youth. Shipments included vegetables cultivated in American victory gardens. The maize variety known as sweet corn was an American favorite, although U.S. gardeners were discouraged from cultivating it unless they had a sizable plot. No recipes or suggestions for serving sweet corn appeared in English wartime cookbooks or leaflets, so it is doubtful that many grew a corn crop for human consumption. In Europe the grain was long regarded as fodder, so some may have added maize to silage but not to soup. Of course, in England the word *corn* referred to any grain or cereal crop. The Corn Production Act of 1917 protected the growers of wheat and oats with guaranteed prices, and its repeal in 1921 in response to lower wheat prices abroad resulted in over reliance on imported wheat at the beginning of World War II.

As the war progressed, supply and demand resulted in onion scarcity. In the 1930s, imports from Bermuda, Brittany, Spain, and the Channel Islands accounted for 90 percent of onions consumed in England, but these disappeared as U-boats patrolled the sea. With meat rationing in place, demand increased because onions flavored main dishes prepared from minimal meat and plenty of root vegetables. The few available onions were given as gifts, awarded as prizes, or set aside to flavor special occasion meals. "Onions, Leeks, Shallots, Garlic," Dig for Victory Leaflet Number 2, explained *Allium* cultivation, long considered difficult for novices. The major problem was soil; onions did not thrive in newly spaded plots and grew better in land that had been tilled for many years. In fact, many of the favored cultivars were selected and bred in the ancient kitchen gardens of large country houses. A further complication was the shortage of onion sets, the small offset bulbs produced asexually by a single parent plant. Home gardeners grew onions from seed, a lengthy process that required transplanting and fertilizing seedlings with wood ash and dried blood.

Most onion cultivars suitable for cooler climates were long-day types that required at minimum 14 hours of daylight to form bulbs. The cultivation of sizable bulbs was theoretically possible, but daylight was a limiting factor, depending on when the seeds were planted. However, varieties imported from southern regions required less light (typically 12 or 13 hours) and so formed bulbs reliably over a longer growth season. Climate was another issue; despite encouraging advice from the Ministry of Food, the 1941 onion crop largely rotted, and drying onion bulbs for storage was an ongoing struggle (see Chapter 6). The Women's Institutes organized an onion growing scheme in various areas (Oxfordshire was particularly prolific) and harvested thirteen tons in 1942, but onion shortages persisted for the duration of the war. Some rural families resorted to foraging hedgerows for native chives, wild *Allium* species that served as onion substitutes.

Onion shortages in Germany spawned a rumor that the Nazi government had seized the crop for poison gas research, speculation that was probably based on the eye irritation caused by slicing the raw bulbs. When bulb tissue is damaged, enzymes break down sulfur-containing compounds to release the volatile compound propanethiol S-oxide that reacts with water to form sulfuric acid, which irritates eyes. There may also have been practical interest in the antibiotic properties of *Allium*, based on research conducted at the Moscow Laboratory of Experimental Biology in the early 1930s. Researchers found that raw onions emit compounds that stop the growth of bacteria such as *Staphylococcus aureus* in severe wounds and amputations, a medical application of particular interest in wartime (see Chapter 7). No doubt the German government also directed much of the onion crop, along with other storable vegetables, to the military kitchens that supplied meals for German troops.

Ground Work

The Dig for Victory campaign advised intensive planting, which soon depleted soil nutrients and diminished soil structure. The traditional soil additive was animal dung, which supplied both minerals and humus, but increased levels of agriculture and gardening resulted in heightened demand for this essential commodity. Moreover, with the start of the war, many farm animals were slaughtered to eliminate them from the food chain. Land was needed for vegetable cultivation rather than meat production, so fewer manure-producing farm animals existed during the war years. Available dung was sent preferentially to farms, and thus gardeners turned to any available source of mineral nutrients or organic matter that could add minerals and improve texture.

Many traditional gardeners distrusted artificial fertilizers, and in place of manure, they dug a variety of other waste directly into their garden soil, where the processes of weathering and decomposition released nutrients and yielded humus. Home gardens and allotments were enriched with dressings of dug-in coal soot; wood ashes; mortar from bomb sites; household sweepings; lawn clippings; straw bedding from stables; tea leaves; leaf mold; scraps of thread, wool, and other fibers; and dried and pulverized animal bones.

As a soil amendment, wood ash posed a conundrum. On the one hand, as the charred remains of plant tissue, ash provided necessary minerals for plant growth. When wood burns, sulfur and nitrogen disperse as gases, but potassium, magnesium, and essential trace elements persist in the particulate remains. However, lye (potassium hydroxide) forms as water percolates through wood ashes, and this had the potential to change soil pH to excessively alkaline levels. As a result of naturally occurring calcium carbonate levels, soil pH in many areas of England was already in the alkaline range. Excessive alkalinity caused by the addition of wood ash potentially interfered with the uptake of phosphorus, iron, and manganese, resulting in nutrient deficiencies and subpar plant growth. The problem of soil alkalinity explains the suggestion made by some botanists and horticulturalists that wood ashes be used to construct paths rather than to enrich soils.

Composting was the logical strategy to minimize mineral loss by recycling plant waste back into garden soil, but the process was unknown to many. Dig for Victory Leaflet Number 7, "Manure from Garden Rubbish (How to Make a Compost Heap)," provided basic instructions and set the stage for *Manures for the War-Time Garden* by S.B. Whitehead, a longer treatise on converting all manner of garden and household refuse into nutrient-rich soil amendments. The term *manure* was used in a broad sense to imply the dung-like attributes of compost, which includes both humus (partially decomposed plant tissues that improve the texture of compacted soils) and mineral nutrients that plants require for maximum productivity.[9]

Whitehead suggested additional refuse to include in compost piles, including dust from vacuum cleaners, bracken ferns, feathers, animal fur, blood, fish trimmings, sewage sludge, and even night soil from chamber pots. Colonial experience also advanced composting; botanist Sir Albert Howard observed Indian farmers who composted any available organic waste (from old clothes to discarded roof thatch), using ancient techniques that yielded humus and recycled nutrients. The goal was to have wartime gardens in England become as self-sufficient as their Indian counterparts, possible only if gardeners worked deliberately to improve depleted soils through composting. In 1944, the message was featured in the short animated film "Compost Heaps for Feeding," produced by Pathé News and the Ministry of Information and featuring information from the Ministry of Agriculture. The cartoon illustrated anthropomorphic microbes converting and packaging soil nutrients and described compost piles using a wartime metaphor as "a sort of canteen for the plants, simple and cheap."

Unlike compost, commercial fertilizers did not provide humus, but they promised high yields nevertheless. Products included National Growmore fertilizer, introduced in 1943 and rationed carefully. The name was an adaptation of the Grow More Food program that pre-dated the Dig for Victory campaign, and the advertising posters reminded gardeners "Do Not Black-Out Your Garden." Growmore fertilizer provided a 7-7-7 mixture of nitrogen, phosphate, and potassium-containing mineral salts and contained proportionately more nitrogen than the standard American victory garden fertilizer that had an N-P-K ratio of 3-8-7. Newly spaded soils with high clay levels also required lime as a source of calcium ions, which attracted clay particles into larger particles, allowing water to drain and air to penetrate the soil. Farmers also needed lime, and shortages occurred although calcareous rocks occur in many areas of England.

One composting strategy combined inorganic fertilizers and organic matter. The Adco method was developed in England in the early 1920s, and the process relied on a proprietary product that was added to piles of compostable waste, as described in *101 Things to Do in War Time 1940*, "All waste vegetable refuse, weeds, pea and bean haulms, waste leaves of all kinds, cabbage stalks, etc. should be piled together and treated with Adco, according to the directions supplied. In the course of time, the chemical action of Adco causes the waste to decay and provide a very valuable manure and dressing for the ground … as a rule, nothing should be burnt if it can decay in the compost heap."[10] Chemically speaking, the Adco process and product relied on superphosphate (monocalcium phosphate), which promotes the growth of soil bacteria such as *Bacillus*. In turn, the bacteria produce cellulase, the enzyme that breaks down the cellulose in plant tissue, without which plant materials cannot become compost. Adco probably accelerated the natural process of bacterial growth and activity, which produced compost more rapidly.

The Adco method also appealed to former colonists who were digging for victory. The *Cairns Post* advised Queensland victory gardeners that "weeds, grass, lawn clippings, even kitchen vegetable scraps, must be religiously saved and stacked for rotting down, later to be returned to the soil to build up texture, moisture capacity and plant food." Instructions were clear: A six inch layer of vegetation was sprinkled with superphosphate and other inorganic fertilizers, and this was repeated several times to build the compost pile. Ideally, the pile was turned and rebuilt after two months, with the outer intact materials buried in the center for bacterial decomposition.[11]

Extending the Season

In many areas of England, the mild climate allowed vegetable gardening nearly year-round, but cool temperatures could still limit crops grown in the early spring and late fall. As in the U.S., hot beds and cold frames were encouraged as a means for establishing and growing crops at the extremes of the growing season. Moreover, many suburban homes had pre-war glasshouses that had been used for growing chrysanthemums and other ornamental plants, and these were soon co-opted for vegetable seedlings. The downside was that glasshouses required camouflage because the panes reflected from the sky (see Chapter 11). Nevertheless more glasshouses for victory gardeners would have been ideal, but shortages of glass, timber, brick, and fuel made new construction nearly impossible, but a miniature alternative was close at hand.

Cloches functioned as knee-high greenhouses positioned directly on garden soil, where they concentrated warmth that sped seedlings to maturity. They were assembled from glass panes held together with a system of clips, wires, and hinges, either free-standing or organized into tunnel-like "barns." Chase Continuous Cloches (manufactured by Chase Protected Cultivation Ltd.) offered products that were ready to assemble and available in various sizes and configurations, including tent, barn, and taller T-style types for growing and ripening tomatoes. Most gardeners opted for simple tent-style cloches, two glass panes leaning together to make a protective, transparent seedling shelter. The set-ups could be moved around the garden to protect successive plantings of early crops such as peas and lettuce. To promote interest, the Chase company published *Cloches Versus Hitler—A Guide to Intensive Vegetable Cultivation*, which provided cultural information for gardening with these small-scale glasshouses. Author Charles Wyse-Gardner (a likely pseudonym) advised starting seedlings inside the warm climate of a cloche; he promised two or three crops annually if instructions were followed. In 1944, with the end of the war in Europe in sight, the manual was republished as *Cloches Versus Hunger*, and translations were sent to Germany to help with post-war rebuilding and food shortages.

Cloches often needed repair or replacement, and an early plastic known as Windolite provided an alternative to glass panes. Reinforced with netting and advertised as a British substitute for glass, Windolite was translucent, flexible, and inexpensive. Wartime handbooks provided instructions for cutting Windolite into strips with shears and tacking the plastic onto batten, long strips of squared-off wood; the ideal length was three feet, coincidentally the width of the plastic rolls. Windolite cloches resembled Quonset huts in shape and protected seedlings in many wartime gardens.

The process for Windolite manufacture was proprietary, but its composition was based on products with botanical origins. As an early celluloid-based plastic, Windolite was synthesized from cellulose with added $-NO_2$ groups (the highly explosive compound known as nitrocellulose), combined with camphor. Cellulose is a complex carbohydrate composed of linked glucose molecules; plant cell walls consist of

Camphor, a cinnamon relative, had numerous uses, including medicine and manufacturing; combined with cellulose, it was used to make the first Windowlite plastic used in making garden cloches.

cellulose fibrils which support and encase each living cell, and wood and cotton fibers were the major cellulose sources. Camphor was originally distilled from the wood of a tropical tree related to cinnamon (*Cinnamomum camphora*). Prior to World War II, Japan exported large quantities of Asian camphor wood for medicinal uses in the U.S. and Europe; however, by the 1940s most camphor used in manufacturing was made from pinene, derived from turpentine tapped from various conifers.

Sheltering in the Garden

With the declaration of war against Germany, the Royal Air Force anticipated 600,000 deaths and over a million other casualties during the first two months of air raids. Fortunately, these estimates were high, but they resulted in preparedness for bomb attacks, beginning with simple shelters that could be installed by homeowners. The idea of a sectional steel shelter originated in 1938 with Sir John Anderson, Lord Privy Seal, who was responsible for developing survival plans for anticipated air-raid attacks. Known as Anderson shelters, these structures became a common feature of the landscape, with over two million installed in suburban gardens.

Anderson shelters were fashioned from corrugated steel covered with garden soil and perhaps sandbags. Installation began by excavating to a depth of four feet deep and then assembling the fourteen metal sheets that composed the shelter. The original design provided sufficient space to protect four adults and two children without the need to crawl or crouch, a small room roughly six feet high, 4.5 feet wide, and 6.5 feet long; later versions were larger and could shelter twelve people. Ideally, the shelter was covered by fifteen inches of dense soil, which needed to be compacted in place with the back of a shovel. The 1941 Ministry for Home Security "A.R.P. at Home: Hints for Housewives" leaflet reminded householders that the soil layer was the real protection inside Anderson shelter, suggesting, "Do go and look at your shelter and see whether the earth is really thick enough—if it is not, remedy matters now—you may be thankful one day." An article in *Scientific American* underscored the message with cutaway diagrams of deep bomb penetration into earth layers; Anderson shelters protected against "concussion and flying debris," but not against direct bomb hits.[12] In contrast, Morrison shelters were intended for indoor use; they resembled tables with steel mesh sides, which some gardeners later removed to use as trellises.

Bombing raids mandated nights spent in the shelter, so folding cots, warm bedding, small tables, chamber pots, and other comforts were commonplace. Candles were recommended rather than oil lamps, which could spill flammable fuel. The 1941 "A.R.P. at Home: Hints for Housewives" leaflet described a small stove assembled with two clay flowerpots encasing a candle; it provided some heat to a chilly shelter, and a kettle could be balanced on top for making tea. Unlike an oil stove that could jeopardize normal respiration in a confined space, a single candle consumed negligible levels of carbon dioxide.

Some shelters flooded in the rain and required bailing and a sump for drainage, so coconut matting (made from the inner coir fibers of the coconut drupe) or wooden flooring helped shelterers to avoid mud or standing water. Some owners covered shelter walls with felt, plasterboard, linoleum, paper, varnish, or paint (sometimes with sawdust added) to discourage dripping condensation. Rainfall caused leaks, mitigated by digging drainage channels around the shelter, sealing the steel sections with tarred or oiled cloth, caulking joints with tarred or oiled rope or high clay soil, or inserting a layer of linoleum under the soil floor. Linoleum was a botanical product, compounded from solidified linseed oil, pulverized wood and cork, and pine rosin, supported by a fabric backing made from sisal, jute, or hemp fibers. The oil content rendered the material both waterproof and flammable, but presumably linoleum in Anderson shelters was buried in soil and not exposed to sparks or fire. However, after the Japanese bombing of Pearl Harbor, there was enough concern about the flammability of linoleum that it was removed from the decks of most U.S. naval warships.

The dark, damp, cool shelter environment suggested mushroom culture to some gardeners; the British Mushroom Industry, located in the Covent Garden Market, provided spawn and manure-free compost to those wanting to experiment with growing mushrooms in Anderson shelters, cellars, or spare rooms. *101 Things to Do in War Time 1940* provided detailed instructions for tiered wooden boxes layered with compost and straw and planted with spawn (seeds of rye or another grain that have been inoculated with mushroom spores).[13] It took about two months for the first crop to mature, and mushroom production continued for a few more months. Buckets of rhubarb were also cultivated inside Anderson shelters; well-fertilized plants sent up tender, pale shoots in the dark interior.

There was concern that bare soil signaled a likely machine gun target, so many hastened to camouflage a new Anderson shelter with fast-growing plants. The mounded shape of an Anderson shelter suggested a rockery that could be landscaped with alpine species, and strawberry beds were another option. Many considered the fruit frivolous in wartime, but strawberries had the advantage of asexual reproduction; each crown produces stolons, horizontal stems that root and produce a clone of the parent plant, colonizing bare soil quickly. Rambling roses were yet another option, but most gardeners used their shelters to cultivate vegetable marrows, various cultivars of *Curcurbita pepo* (the same species that includes pumpkins and winter squash). Marrow vines thrived in the warmth and camouflaged shelters effectively; the mature marrows provided an excellent food source that could be alternately baked, boiled, or stuffed.

Before the war, British geneticist J.B.S. Haldane and others had favored centralized, deeply excavated shelters, on the theory that these would be safer than makeshift sheltering at home. However, official strategy advocated decentralized sheltering whenever possible, fearing an enormous impact on national morale if hundreds died during a direct hit on a communal shelter. Nevertheless, Haldane argued against simple home shelters; he had seen firsthand bombing during the Spanish Civil War and believed that preparedness for war with Germany was insufficient.[14] Despite initial concern that some would refuse to leave deep underground protection, communal shelters were eventually constructed in cities, and London underground train stations were also co-opted as nighttime shelters. Home and communal shelters coexisted for different populations, but Anderson shelters required garden space and effective installation. They provided protection from bomb blasts and shock, and these simple garden structures saved countless lives during the war. In many cases, sheltered families survived even when their houses were destroyed. Anderson shelters were repurposed after the war as garden sheds, and some were even relocated to post-war allotment gardens.

Although simple, Anderson shelters were a step up from an earlier alternative. In 1938, the Air Raid Precautions Department of the Home Office published the "Pamphlet on Garden Trenches," which detailed the steps in building a slit trench for immediate protection from a bomb attack. These were deep rectangular excavations several feet away from buildings; parks, playing fields, and church yards were ideal sites. Some slit trench shelters were reinforced with joists and protected by planks, corrugated metal, or masonry, while others were merely open pits in which to shelter from splintering glass or building collapse. As with Anderson shelters, slit trenches were prone to flooding, and soil walls could collapse, but despite their hazards, they provided basic protection. They were also excavated in fields and lawns in Hawaii, Australia, and perhaps other regions in which aerial bombing attacks were anticipated.

Women's Institutes, Children and Wartime Gardening

With men conscripted and away from home, British women and children cultivated many of the home front vegetable gardens and allotments. Women's Institutes, regional organizations devoted to rural living, met early in the war to instruct members on basic skills, cultivation, and soil types and amendments. These were not decorous meetings with tea and a talk; members brought their own gum boots and spades for experiential instruction. With the goal of putting more produce into the local food pipeline, members distributed seeds, cleared derelict and waste sites of brambles and debris, and planted cabbages, Brussels sprouts, peas, artichokes, and root crops, including potatoes, carrots, swedes (rutabagas), and parsnips. Some allotments were devoted to a single staple crop, such as potatoes, that could be shared, sold, or donated to local hospitals.

Agricultural fertilizers were chronically in short supply, and so WI gardeners diligently utilized any organic material with potential for soil enrichment. They collected straw, manure, poultry droppings, garden waste, vegetable peels and trimmings, leaf mold, and night soil from household privies. Lime from derelict tennis courts provided soil calcium. WI members resurrected a government campaign to salvage household bones, part of a large salvage agenda that included paper, rags, and rubber. Bones were dried and ground as a calcium-rich garden fertilizer; there was canine competition, but WI members outwitted dogs by anchoring collection bins firmly to trees. Bone collection was smelly, unpleasant work, but nothing was wasted nor neglected in the WI drive to produce food.

Abandoned gardens and fallow land became productive through the combined efforts of Women's Institutes and youth who were recruited as helpers, including evacuees and local schoolchildren. British children also joined the gardening effort as school yards and playing fields were tilled into vegetable allotments. School gardeners assumed horticultural teaching roles as science lessons evolved into practical lessons on vegetable cultivation. Competitions determined the most productive plots, and some schools acquired additional village land for vegetable gardening. Model allotments on school grounds encouraged the parents of students to tend their own wartime gardens.

Produce supplied school kitchens, and some was sold to raise school funds or shared locally with school families, faculty, and villagers. School lunches became more common during the 1940s, including the so-called Oslo meal, which required no cooking and no meat: it comprised a plate of vitamin-laden salad vegetables and slices of whole meal bread, served with cheese and milk. Originating in Norway as a vitamin-rich school meal, this menu used the carrots and other vegetables cultivated at school. Ministry of Food advisor Marguerite Patten referred to it as the health meal and suggested the menu for home tables as well.[15] Studies suggested that children thrived on the Oslo meal, and it appeared in pamphlets on rationing and menu planning, as a way to use allotment crops, save fuel, and provide a convenient, mostly vegetarian meal of non-rationed foods.

Schrebergarten

As in England and America, wartime vegetable gardens provided produce to urban German families, but there were distinct contrasts with the victory garden movement in Allied countries. Many allotments in Germany were known as *Schrebergarten*, named for the nineteenth century naturopathic physician Dr. Daniel Gottlieb Moritz Schreber who operated an orthopedic clinic in Leipzig. Schreber was a proponent of natural harmony, including fresh air and vigorous exercise; his ideas on childrearing included the notion that children should spend plenty of time outdoors in playgrounds supervised by a staff of teachers and military personnel. During the late 1800s, Schreber's followers in Leipzig established parks with children's gardens, but parents soon took over the cultivation tasks, growing vegetables and constructing simple structures on these allotments.

By the end of World War I, Schrebergarten were recognized as valuable assets worthy of protection, and the Small Garden and Small-Rent Land Law of 1919 solidified the rights and fees for leasing allotments. At a time of growing industrialization, *Shrebergarten* provided urban dwellers with fresh vegetables and modest outdoor space, and by the 1930s the movement had extended to other German cities, Switzerland, and Austria. Regarded by many as an emblem of the bourgeois, conservative middle class, the Schrebergarten movement served as a medium for the "blood and soil" militaristic patriotism that brewed in pre-war Germany.

Another garden movement originated in Berlin, beginning with land planned for development on the periphery of the city. Various agrarian groups and societies acquired land parcels that attracted working class families to spend time in these comparatively rural sites. During the 1870s, some urban-dwellers built colonies of summer houses (*Laubenkolonien*) on plots on the outskirts of Berlin; occupancy might have been temporary, so improvements were limited to simple structures and fenced gardens. These

Postwar gardens were cultivated on the land surrounding the bombed remains of the Reichstag building in Berlin. British engineers plowed the land and turned it over to local residents for vegetable plots (British Armed Forces, No. 5 Army Film and Photographic Unit, Wikimedia Commons).

allotments produced sufficient vegetables to augment working class diets; leasing fees were high, but time in nature compensated for grueling hours spent in factory jobs.[16]

As productive vegetable gardens away from city centers, *Schrebergarten* saved lives during both world wars when chronic shortages, high prices, and a thriving black market posed significant problems to food security. As food supplies dwindled during World War II, gardening became subsistence agriculture, and a well-tended allotment on the edge of town provided both food and shelter. *Shrebergarten* produced adequate vegetables for families who found little or nothing in the marketplace, but fertilizer shortages affected crop yield from these intensively cultivated sites. Imported nitrates were scarce due to Allied attacks on German vessels, and the few shipments that did arrive were directed to munitions plants rather than fertilizer production. Thus desperate gardeners resorted to bartering for soil nutrients; an article in *Collier's* mentioned a German newspaper advertisement offering to trade a service of valuable china for compost.[17]

During the Allied bombing of German cities, some families relocated to their gardens, and the sites also sheltered and fed persecuted Jews who hid in *Schrebergarten* for months or even years. Post-war housing shortages meant that Schrebergarten continued as emergency housing for German families with no other options than to live in a simple structure erected on a garden site. Gardening continued as an essential postwar activity, even for families without an allotment on the edge of the city. Photographs and *Deutsche Wochenschau* newsreels showed vegetable plots cultivated by *Hitler Jugend* near the bombed remains of the Reichstag building in Berlin (*Reichstagsgebaude*), which had been used for Nazi meetings and functions. It was a target during the Battle of Berlin in 1945; the structure was rebuilt in the 1990s following German reunification and is now the Bundestag.

3

Vitamins and Food Preservation

The Great Depression began with the stock market crash on October 29, 1929, coincidentally just months after the first Nobel Prizes were awarded for vitamin discovery and isolation. For many, the Depression was a period of sustained deprivation; jobs, money, and food were in short supply nationwide, and dietary deficiencies frequently accompanied relief-era stringencies. Although strategies for assessing malnutrition were imperfect, President Roosevelt declared in his second inaugural address on March 4, 1937, that one third of Americans were nutritionally needy; poorly-understood diseases such as scurvy, pellagra, and beri-beri affected people who were chronically hungry and nutritionally naive.

In light of events in Europe, there was concern for the impact of a sickly population in building national defense; military might and home front productivity required diets with adequate calories, proteins, and vitamins.[1] Despite a lack of ready cash during the Depression, Americans with relief gardens and root cellars survived nutritionally. Even subsistence meals of whole wheat bread, sweet potatoes, and green cabbage prevented scurvy, pellagra, and beri-beri, although most home cooks could not explain why. Ironically, it was during this time of deprivation that scientific knowledge of vitamins unfolded. Between 1928 and 1943, fourteen Nobel prizes recognized discoveries in vitamin physiology, isolation, structure, and synthesis—including vitamins A, C, and the B complex. Only vitamin B12 lacked a botanical source, but eventually it was added to enrich soy products.

Vitamin Knowledge

Vitamins are essential to metabolism, often functioning as cofactors that enable enzyme activity. Cells cannot synthesize these essential nutrients, so vitamins come from diet, most frequently from botanical foods. For instance, vitamin C functions as a cofactor in several reactions, including collagen synthesis; lack of this vitamin results in scurvy, with symptoms that include bleeding gums, skin sores, and overall malaise. Various fruits and vegetables are the primary sources of vitamin C, including citrus, cabbage, green peppers, and tomatoes. Pellagra, another deficiency disease, results from lack of one of the B vitamins (B3, also known as niacin), a molecule supplied by whole grains, leafy vegetables, carrots, and legumes. Initial symptoms of pellagra include dermatitis, but dementia and death can occur in severe cases. Beri-beri results from the lack of another

B vitamin (B1, also known as thiamine), present in whole grains, legumes, leafy vegetables, and potatoes. Thiamine functions in the basic metabolism of carbohydrates, and the symptoms of its deficiency include the psychological effects of confusion, lethargy, and depression. Perhaps the most ironic aspect of thiamine deficiency is its link with upward mobility, fueled by increasing social preference for food made from white, refined flour rather than whole grains.

During the Depression years, food access and preferences resulted in deficiency diseases, the result of itinerant lives and meals dependent on starch and pork fat. The most common dietary starch was refined flour, in which the bran (outer layers of the grain) and germ (embryo) had been removed. Diets were often low in niacin, riboflavin, thiamine, and folic acid, B complex vitamins supplied by various fruits and vegetables. However, pure white flour was perceived as more refined and socially upscale than whole grain flour, which milled brown bits of germ and bran along with the white endosperm. With pre-war concern about the effect of nutritional deficiencies on conscription, President Roosevelt convened the National Nutrition Conference for Defense in May 1941. The public outcome was the Recommended Daily Allowance (RDA) system for essential nutrients, including vitamins A, C, D, and the B complex. In short, the RDA were soon a key element in the plan to improve national defense; nutritional concerns centered on American military and civilian needs, as well as refugees and others who might need emergency rations. Many Americans simply did not eat enough vitamin-rich botanical foods, the combined effects of regional tastes, nutritional ignorance, and poverty. The RDA system galvanized nutritional knowledge into a cogent defense message: a nutritionally deprived nation could not produce tanks, fight abroad, or maintain home front morale.

The Vitamin War

A complex array of U.S. government departments and other offices assumed national nutrition as one of their responsibilities: the Department of Agriculture, the Office of Defense Health and Welfare Services, the Sanitary Corps of the War Department, the War Food Administration (and its Nutrition Division), the Office of War Information, the Food and Nutrition Board and Committee on Food Habits (both arms of the National Research Council), and more than two dozen other agencies. Anthropologist Margaret Mead chaired the Committee on Food Habits, which aimed to understand the effect of social patterns on food preferences. She viewed the war as an opportunity for permanent social change and applied her objectified research style honed in Bali and Samoa to analyze Americans. Nor did she hesitate to correlate social status with food preferences, noting the desire of recent immigrants for white bread.[2] Of course, the real object was encouraging more fruit and vegetable consumption on a national scale, but small successes were the sole result; local women's groups received gardening advice, canning instruction, and new recipes to try. To sway public opinion nationwide would have required vast numbers of leaders and instructors, even using the small group social networking strategies that Mead favored.

Mead decried the option of providing cafeteria-style, vitamin-rich meals for needy families because as a social scientist, she placed kinship ties above nutrition. In short, she maintained that this type of dining would have undermined family structure, precisely the complaint from interred Japanese Americans whose children elected to eat American-style foods with their peers rather than traditional meals with their elders. Wartime rationing limited civilian access to sugar and meat, to the extent that meals depended on vegetables for both calories and nutrients. Nutritionists in the U.S. and England categorized foods by function, with one group focused specifically on vitamin content: Group I [warmth and energy-producing foods] included sugars, starches, and high-fat meats like bacon. Group II [body-building foods] supplied animal protein, although many might have argued that legumes belonged in this category because of their potential to replace meat in the diet. Group III [protective foods] included vitamin-rich fruits and vegetables, as well as products such as margarine that could be enriched with added vitamin content. The idea was that vitamins protected people from physical and mental diseases and potential wartime rigors. Hence vitamin-rich botanical foods were deemed protective in function.

In 1940 the *British Medical Journal* published a series of articles titled "The Nation's Larder in Wartime," based on talks before the Royal Institution on vitamin access across socioeconomic levels. Calories were not the problem because the poor had access to potatoes, a starchy staple crop. Rather the issue was with vitamin-rich, protective foods. Graphs of fruit and vegetable consumption (excluding potatoes) versus income revealed a positive correlation with socioeconomic levels; the poor survived on sugar, starch, and fat and suffered vitamin deficiencies. Even vitamin D posed a problem in areas such as the London eastside. Its synthesis requires sunlight, but sufficient rays did not penetrate shaded alleys and narrow streets, resulting in cases of childhood rickets.

Sir John Orr, a Scottish physician who won the 1949 Nobel Peace prize for work in nutrition, argued that all vitamin requirements could be provided by a plant-based diet of vegetables and oatmeal, with the addition of some milk or cheese. Supplemented by a few rationed ounces of meats and fats, this was the botanical diet that nourished British families during the war years when consumption increased for many impoverished families. Imported fruits and vegetables were scarce, but cabbage supplied vitamin C, and carrots yielded vitamin A. The precursor to vitamin A is beta-carotene, a pigment that occurs in orange and yellow fruits and vegetables and leafy crops such as spinach and chard.

Other locally-grown crops that supplied vitamin C included currants, tomatoes, radishes, watercress and related mustard greens,

The British government encouraged the cultivation of black currants as a wartime source of vitamin C. Syrup prepared from the fruit was distributed free of charge to children and pregnant women, and the Ministry of Food relied on black currants to prevent cases of scurvy among civilians.

swedes (also known as rutabagas, the result of an ancient hybridization between turnips and kale or cabbage), and turnips. Currants were one of the most esteemed protective foods; in particular, some cultivars of black currants (*Ribes nigrum*) yield up to 200 mg of vitamin C /100 grams of fruit, in contrast to approximately 54 mg of vitamin C/100 grams in oranges and lemons. The British government encouraged currant cultivation during the war years, and most of the crop was preserved as syrup (marketed under the name Ribena) which was distributed free to children and pregnant women. The Ministry of Food was concerned that children might not eat vegetables and counted on currant syrup to prevent cases of wartime scurvy among civilians. Black currant syrup was so successful that the Vegetable Drugs Committee pursued a similar strategy with rosehips collected from the hedgerows that separated adjacent fields. Each rosehip is a hypanthium, a cup-like structure containing the small, seed-like fruit (achenes) produced by each rose flower. Because of their tough anatomy and hairy interior, rosehips were difficult to crush into juice, but the resulting syrup was worth the effort; it had high levels of both vitamins A and C, with a palatable taste that resembled plums or guava (see Chapter 7).

In the United States, currants had also been valued for medicinal wines and preserves. However, it was discovered that *Ribes* serves as an alternate host for white pine blister rust (*Cronartium ribicola*), a parasitic fungus on nursery stock imported to the United States in 1900. The fungus has a complex life cycle that requires both currant bushes and white pine trees. Beginning in 1918, state and federal legislation forbid the planting of any currants in the U.S., and during the 1930s, the Civilian Conservation Corps removed many currant shrubs. Consequently, there was no equivalent use of black currant syrup in the U.S. during the war years, and laws remain in several states including Maine and Massachusetts against cultivating non-resistant currants and gooseberries (*Ribes grossularia*) because of the potential danger to white pine, a wood with essential uses for lumber and other wood products.

The stress associated with war led to great interest in vitamin B1 or thiamine, which became known as the "morale vitamin," perhaps because of the psychological effects known as Wernicke's encephalopathy associated with beri-beri. According to the results of a 1941 study at the Mayo Clinic, vitamin B1 deficiency led to weakness, inattention, quarrelsomeness, loss of dexterity, sensitivity to pain, and a variety of physical complaints, including anemia and low blood pressure.[3] Physicians concluded that the amount of the vitamin needed was a function of activity level and that diets of white flour and polished (white) rice contained insufficient B1 levels. The movement to enrich flour began with Dr. Russell Wilder, a nutritional chemist at the Mayo Institute and first chairman of the Food and Nutrition Board of the National Research Council. Working with colleagues, he established nutritional standards for white flour. By early 1942, federal law mandated that bread be enriched with thiamine, riboflavin, niacin, iron, calcium and vitamin D, all seen as essential in a wartime diet.

Vitamins and patriotism were linked inextricably during the war years. Vitamin consumption and conservation were patriotic pursuits, including growing vitamin-rich vegetables and preserving vitamins through correct cooking practices. Military and civilian focus was on carrots as a food capable of improving night vision, but for those who disliked carrots, an inexpensive product advertised as "vitaminized margarine" supplied fat-soluble vitamins such as A and D. Other products also provided vitamins that ordinarily occurred in fruits and vegetables. Baker's Chocolate manufactured an eight ounce bar that was fortified with vitamins A, B1, and D, and the Vitamins for Britain Committee worked with the Life Savers Corporation to produce "Vitamin Sweets" designed to provide a daily dose of vitamins A, B1, B2, C, and D. The British-American Ambulance Corps distributed the candies to children who did not have access to fresh produce, but questions arose about the stability of the vitamins and the reliability of the product to improve nutrition.

Other vitaminized products included various capsules, milk, prepared foods, cosmetics, tobacco, and patent medicines. The latter included Lydia Pinkham's Vegetable Compound, a proprietary mixture dating to 1875, which contained black cohosh (*Cimicifuga racemosa*), a medicinal plant with known estrogenic properties. The Vegetable Compound was still marketed during the twentieth century and became the topic of ribald drinking lyrics sung by service men during both world wars: coincidentally, the inventor was memorialized by the eponymous B-17 bomber *Lydia Pinkham*, flown by Lt. Robert Dea Peterson, who was later imprisoned at *Stalag Luft 1* in Barth, Germany. Vitamin doughnuts each promised "pep and vigor" along with 25 units of vitamin B1. They nevertheless proved unpopular with consumers, perhaps because the War Food Administration insisted upon the wording "enriched flour" doughnuts, rather than the claim that the doughnuts themselves were enriched. In fact, there was no extra vitamin content beyond the levels in whole grain; enriched flour merely replaced the vitamins lost in milling with the removal of the bran and germ.

Seed catalogues and victory garden manuals emphasized the importance of cultivating crops for their vitamin content. "Victory Gardens—A Practical Manual for Planting a Vegetable Garden" (1942), a local bulletin distributed by the Boston Victory Garden Committee, featured the headline "Vegetables, Vitamins, Victory" and a chart of vegetables and their vitamin content; Swiss chard had the highest vitamin A content (24,000 units/100 grams), green peppers had the highest vitamin C content (3,600 units/100 grams), and various legumes were promising sources of B complex vitamins. The USDA publication "Victory Gardens" (1942) began with the claim, "We need minerals and vitamins" and attributed the number of rejections for military service under the Selective Service Act to widespread dietary deficiencies. It went on to caution that "nutrition experts advise that people get their vitamins from food rather than from indiscriminate use of synthetic preparations."[4] An early poster from the National Garden Bureau showed a young woman carrying a basket of crops, proclaiming, "War gardens for victory—Grow vitamins at your kitchen door." The message was clear: Victory gardens will provide food for the table and vitamins for home front health and morale.

Dr. Russell Wilder, the nutritional chemist who pioneered enriched flour, even speculated about vitamin deprivation as a weapon of war. Before American involvement in World War II, Wilder argued that Hitler intended to deprive conquered countries of thiamine; he noted "depression, exhaustion, and feelings of inferiority" as possible outcomes of thiamine deficiency, which he postulated as a German strategy to control occupied countries.[5] Whether in fact there was a specific German plan of vitamin deprivation is difficult to say, but it was certainly feasible. Thiamine deprivation could have been easily accomplished by withholding whole grain bread (or its equivalent in enriched flour) and legumes from the diet. In planning the military diet, the Wehrmacht certainly benefited from German knowledge of vitamin chemistry and sources from botanical foods, and Hitler also relied on vitamins for his own health. Dr. Theodor Morell dosed Hitler with various vitamin cocktails and injections, suggesting keen awareness of vitamin benefits and deficiencies.

Keeping and Canning Food

Victory gardens challenged home cooks to store fruits and vegetables for year round use. Food preservation involved several means: root cellar storage, canning, drying, pickling, and freezing, depending upon the crop and the available resources. The goal was to avoid waste, which required strategic cultivation and preservation. Growth conditions, family preferences, regional tastes, and vitamin content all factored into selecting crops for long term storage and use. The simplest method involved keeping root crops, apples, celery, and cabbages in unheated cellars or pits under conditions that inhibited over-ripening and sprouting. Depending on the crop, *Have a Victory Garden* recommended traditional root cellars, bank shelters (constructed outdoors and insulated with mounded soil), or shallow pits protected with built-up layers of straw and soil.[6] The goal was to maintain consistent cool temperatures, so that apples, potatoes, and other storable crops were metabolically inactive and protected from the damaging effects of hard frost on plant tissue. The degree of protection needed depended on latitude; warmer climates required less insulation to forestall heavy frost damage.

Root cellar crops like carrots and parsnips were often buried in moist sand to prevent shriveling, while cabbages survived well in protected outdoor pits. In all storage, good drainage and ventilation were essential. Crops soaking in rainwater invariably rot, and living plant tissue needs oxygen and releases carbon dioxide; stored garden produce literally needed to breathe, so crops needed careful arrangement on shelves or in boxes. A single decomposing fruit or vegetable releases ethylene, a natural plant hormone that signals ripening, thus occasional inspection of cool-stored crops was essential to prevent one or two rotting items from spoiling the contents of the entire root cellar. In contrast, a few crops such as pumpkins and winter squash benefited from warm storage, so attics and furnace rooms were also used for storage.

The relatively milder English climate made outdoor storage possible for many crops. Cabbages and leeks overwintered in the garden, while the technique known as clamping was used to store potatoes, onions, swedes, and other root crops in a protected outdoor pile. Clamp construction began with a well-drained site covered with a straw bed about five feet in diameter and eight inches deep. Foliage and stems were removed to curb decomposition. Then the vegetables were arranged into layers, with the largest at the bottom, to make a stable mound about three feet high. The pile was insulated with another six inch layer of straw, which was then covered with several inches of tamped-down soil. The top was left open to form a straw-lined chimney, which allowed metabolic heat to escape and thus forestalled decomposition. Vegetables were removed by burrowing into the side, selecting what was needed, and then sealing up the layers. Of course, clamps formed obvious mounds that were subject to both human and animal pilfering, so they were best constructed in private sites. They also took time to construct, and there were simpler options. The lack of central heating allowed for successful indoor storage, more so than in warm American homes; the Dig for Victory Leaflet No. 3 "Storing Vegetables for Winter Use" advised the layering of fresh vegetables in unheated bedrooms and attics, where they kept fresh for months.

As during World War I when the National War Garden Commission encouraged Americans to "Can Vegetables and Fruit and the Kaiser Too," cooks and gardeners were again advised to can surplus produce for winter use. Canning had a military origin that dated from the early 1800s, when Nicholas Appert perfected the hermetical seal as part

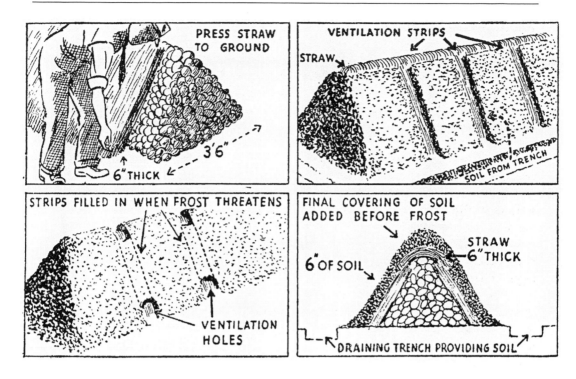

The mild English climate made outdoor storage possible for many crops. A technique known as clamping was used to store potatoes, onions, swedes, and other root crops in an insulated pile of straw and soil. The vegetables were removed by digging into the side, selecting what was needed, and then sealing up the layers (Ministry of Agriculture, United Kingdom).

of a competition to provide food supplies for Napoleon's troops. Canning technique combines heat and pressure to kill the spores of the soil microbe *Clostridium botulinum*, which produces a highly potent nerve toxin that interferes with the release of acetylcholine. *Clostridium* thrives in anaerobic conditions, and even a microscopic soil particle can bear hundreds of its heat-resistant spores. Non-acidic vegetables such as corn, carrots, pumpkin, and beans were at particular risk for botulism, and tainted food was potentially deadly depending on the extent of bacterial growth.

The average survival rate among those who inadvertently ingested the botulinum toxin was 50 percent, so extreme caution was in order. Not surprisingly, botulinum toxicity suggested its possible use as a biological weapon, and by the 1930s Japanese researchers from Unit 731 (a laboratory division that conducted research on chemical and biological agents) had killed prisoners in Manchuria with experimental doses. There was also concern that Germany planned to use the weaponized toxin against an Allied attack. More than a million doses of the available vaccine were on hand to provide some protection against a possible aerosol botulinum attack on D-Day.[7]

Safe canning of most crops required a pressure cooker, but even before the war, not all families had this equipment. Some home cooks instead relied exclusively on the hot water bath method, in which canning jars were covered with water and boiled in a large kettle. This strategy was safe for acidic foods like tomatoes and pickles because *Clostridium* will not growth at low pHs, but it was a risky practice for most vegetables. Nevertheless, the 1934 *Ball Blue Book* described a hot water bath alternative to pressure cooker

A variety of publications offered information on food preservation. Canning and drying were new to many Americans, but they were essential skills in preserving summer crops for winter meals. Pressure cookers were shared, and canning jars reused in an effort to preserve foods and avoid the waste of victory garden crops (U.S. Department of Agriculture).

canning, the so-called intermittent method that was popular in southern states. Boiling alone did not kill bacterial spores, but the intermittent method involved boiling in a hot water bath three times, separated by stretches of several hours. The timing allowed spores to germinate between each boiling, and the activated spores were quickly killed by high heat. The 1943 *Home Canners Textbook* reminded home cooks that they must follow instructions carefully to avoid waste; the manual addressed a "citizen army of growers and canners" who in wartime practiced "the 'old fashioned' American virtues" necessitated by a national emergency.[8]

Periodicals provided practical advice for canning techniques and safety, but their directions did not always agree. The *Journal of Home Economics* warned of the dangers of oven canning, a method advocated by the *Ball Blue Book* (1943), *Kerr Home Canning Book* (1943), and *Canning at Home: Cornell Bulletin for Homemakers 583* (March 1943).[9] Oven canning was supposedly safe for acidic fruits, but Cornell home economists chronicled cases of spoilage and accidents.[10] This was not work for amateurs, but many inexperienced homemakers canned during the war years, and instructions were not always closely heeded. Not only were trays of hot glass jars dangerous to handle, but pressure inside tightly sealed jars mounted with increasing temperature; instructions made it clear that jars placed in the oven should be only partially sealed to allow room for expansion. Some mistakes were inevitable, but an explosion involving glass shards was potentially life threatening. Regardless of the technique used, home cooks were advised to boil home canned foods for fifteen minutes to denature any bacterial toxins that might be present. Of course, excessive heat and water affected vitamin content to the extent that any sort of canning method posed a nutritional compromise; calories were preserved, but vitamin content was definitely diminished.

Metal was in high demand for military tanks and airplanes, and as a result, pressure cookers were in short supply. Cooks with pre-war pressure cookers and kettles were encouraged to share their equipment; cookbooks and extension bulletins encouraged community canning bees to promote both home front morale and food preservation. *Good Housekeeping* recommended the sharing of pressure cookers, noting that they were out of production in 1942.[11] By 1943, the magazine advertised "Canning the Victory Crop," a film produced by the Good Housekeeping Institute for viewing by women's clubs and victory garden groups. In rural areas, the Food Distribution Administration, a Division of the Department of Agriculture, organized community canneries with commercial equipment; use of the cannery required a donation of 5 to 10 percent of the canned food to school lunch programs. These canneries saved crops that otherwise would have gone to waste, such as thousands of gallons of cherries that were preserved at a Utah facility in 1943 for use in schools and welfare programs.[12] Eventually some wartime pressure cookers became available, but these were often cheaply made, with malfunctioning gauges and ill-fitting lids and gaskets. Some cooks even used laboratory autoclaves to sterilize jars of food.

Canning jars from past years were reused, including those with glass lids sealed with a rubber ring and bale wire. The rubber used for both jar rings and pressure cooker gaskets was a strategic material that began as natural latex produced by various plant species (see Chapter 10). During the war years, scrap drives included rubber, and canning jar rings were among the household items collected for recycling. A vast number of military supplies required rubber, from gas masks to rafts and flotation devices, but home canning of foods was equally important to the war effort by freeing up commercially canned food for military use. However, subpar rubber rings affected home canned foods. Wartime products such as Bull Dog Jar Rubbers, manufactured by the Boston Woven Hose and Rubber Company, probably contained some synthetic rubber in addition to natural latex, explaining the odd flavor of some home-canned food. Boiling new rings with potato parings helped to remove the rubbery taste, which could infiltrate canned foods.[13]

The goal of home canning was three-fold: limiting metal use, reducing food transport from farm to cannery and table; and freeing up food for military use. Despite the challenges and potential hazards, canning was a home front activity for the duration of the war. As cans of fruits and vegetables became increasingly scarce in markets, home canning increased; even commercial producers encouraged home canning to alleviate shortages due to military demand. In April 1943, Del Monte launched a poster campaign to encourage women to cultivate victory gardens and to can the surplus crops. Government posters also marketed the message. "We'll have lots to eat this winter, won't we, Mother?" asked a child on a 1943 Office of War Administration poster, which advised "Grow your own. Can your own." Canning was clearly a practical manifestation of home front patriotism. "Of course I can! I am as patriotic as can be—And ration points won't worry me!" proclaimed a 1944 War Food Administration poster that illustrated a homemaker holding three jars filled with homegrown produce.

Pride in a pantry lined with gleaming jars (or perhaps a preference for commercial products) may have caused some women to hoard. *Good Housekeeping* advised that "the tender green peas, the rich red tomatoes, gold corn, yellow wax beans, and all the other vegetables and fruits you took such pride in canning last year can help to add color, flavor, and health to your meals."[14] To encourage the use of jars in the larder, the magazine suggested recipes including green beans in chive sauce and canned pears with black cherry sauce. Of course, despite shortages and rationing of certain foods, Americans still had plenty of food available in grocery stores and were never in danger of starvation, whether or not they cultivated gardens or canned produce at home.

The situation in England was comparatively desperate, and there was concern about potential malnutrition on the home front as German U-boat attacked ships carrying food imports from Europe and North America. Victory gardens and allotments were essential to year-round food security, but home canners struggled with minimal equipment and few supplies. Pressure cookers were rare in England, even before the war. Sugar was closely rationed in amounts insufficient for home canning, and thus wartime manuals suggested preserving fruit, whole or pureed, in water by a method known as cottage bottling. Before the war, sugar was traditionally used to preserve canned fruits not processed in a pressure cooker, but in wartime England many cooks relied on heat alone to preserve fruit and vegetables. For instance, *101 Things to Do in War Time* recommended packing quartered apples and pears into clean bottles, filling with water, and boiling thoroughly.[15] Unlike the intermittent method of canning used in the U.S., the British instructions did not suggest a second or third boiling, perhaps to save fuel. Other options included using golden syrup or honey as part of the bottling liquid, but the latter potentially introduced another hazard; honey could contaminate bottles with *Clostridium*, the result of contact between bees and soil in nature. The Ministry of Food Leaflet No. 24 "Preservation of Tomatoes" described an oven sterilizing technique in which whole tomatoes were baked in canning jars for at least ninety minutes, then covered with brine and sealed.

Concern for spoilage and botulism toxicity reignited interest in Campden powder, a chemical sterilization technique developed in the 1920s at the Fruit and Vegetable Preserving Research Station in Chipping Campden, Gloucestershire. The powdered compound consisted of potassium or sodium metabisulfite, first available as an aqueous solution and later in tablet form. The Ministry of Food organized distribution of the formula to local chemists and pharmacists across England, and Boots became one of the major purveyors. One tablet in a cup of water yielded a sulfite solution of about 900 parts per million, which effectively killed food borne bacteria. The method was promoted as cold sterilization, a means to preserve food without the use of valuable fuel; however, bisulfate can be toxic if measured incorrectly, and the use of Campden tablets in canning ceased after the war. Home canners were advised to boil canned fruits for fifteen minutes, a step that denatured botulinum toxin and removed bisulfate ions, but also decreased the vitamin content. Current MSDS list respiratory irritation, asthma, nervous system complaints, and possible organ damage as among the potential hazards associated with these compounds.

Another chemical strategy used sulfurous fumes, produced by burning crystalline sulfur (known as sulfur flowers) to yield sulfur dioxide. The site of combustion was an iron spoon placed inside a canning jar; the upended jar contained the fumes, which killed any bacteria. Then boiled fruit was ladled into the jar, which was covered with parchment paper and made air tight through the application of a thin layer of glue. Parchment paper is itself a botanical product, made by treated wood pulp with sulfuric acid, which causes cross-links to form among the cellulose molecules. The end result is a heat resistant, dense paper with various culinary applications. Bottled under ideal conditions, the fruit was sterile, sealed, and suitable for long-term storage at room temperature.

Jam provided quick energy, appealing taste, and some vitamins, and it was a staple food in the working class diet. Sugar preserves by dehydrating microbial cells, by attracting water molecules by osmosis and decreasing water concentration to a level that cannot support microbial growth. Local British flora included several species suitable for jams and jellies, mostly members of the rose family (Rosaceae): plums, apples, crab apples, strawberries, quince, black currants, and brambles. Brambles are species of *Rubus* (*R. fruticosa* and related species), which hybridize freely and produce blackberries and raspberries. The hypanthia (hips) produced by mature rose and hawthorn flowers were also collected for fruit preserves (rosehips were valued as a source of vitamin C; see Chapter 7). Fruit jams and jellies compounded with sufficient sugar (the usual standard was 60 percent) were definitely safe from spoilage, but rationing forced home cooks to experiment with alternatives to table sugar (sucrose). One option was golden syrup, a pale solution that like molasses is a byproduct of sugar refining. Both golden syrup and honey contain the simple sugars (monosaccharides) glucose and fructose, in contrast to sucrose, which is a disaccharide of linked glucose and fructose molecules. Pound for pound, simple sugars should attract roughly the same amount of water as sucrose; however, glucose encourages bacterial growth, so only highly concentrated glucose solutions were truly antimicrobial.

Rationing did not allow for the 60 percent sugar content in traditional jam recipes made at home. Saccharin supplied sweetness to jam mixtures, but it provided neither quick carbohydrate energy nor protection against microbes; the sweet-tasting powder is benzoic sulfimide, a coal tar derivative developed at Johns Hopkins University in 1878 and at first manufactured only in Germany. Coal tar is the viscous liquid that remains after coal is gasified into coal gas or carbonized into coke, and coal originated from the fossilized remains of flooded forests and swamps, which formed combustible sedimentary rock. Thus saccharin has a botanical origin although it provides no dietary calories. In 1901, Monsanto Chemical Works (later Monsanto Company) began as a major producer of saccharin. The safety of saccharin was debated, but sugar rationing during both world wars resulted in spikes in its use as a substitute for rationed cane sugar. Some cooks used saccharin to replace up to three-fourths of the sugar in a batch of jam.

Like sucrose, salt provides osmotic protection against microbes, and by adding a couple of teaspoons of sodium chloride, the amount of sugar could be decreased by half. However, the gelling of jam requires both sugar and pectin, a carbohydrate component of cell walls and the area between adjacent cells. In the boiling process, pectin from fruits dissolves into solution; the addition of sugar attracts water and allows pectin molecules to form an insoluble matrix of fibers, the backbone of the gel. Lacking sufficient rationed sugar, cooks often added gelatin (derived from collagen, a structural protein in animal connective tissues and bones) to obtain the desired semi-solid texture normally imparted by the interaction between pectin and sugar.

Tapioca, typically used in Victorian era puddings, was another ingredient used to thicken wartime jams. Derived from the roots of cassava or manioc (*Manihot esculenta*), the starch becomes translucent when it is boiled in water. Coincidentally, at the same time that cooks used tapioca to thicken jams, British women and children imprisoned in Southeast Asia relied on tapioca as a dietary staple. Manihot cuttings rooted easily in poor soils and could be harvested frequently; the crop was a reliable source of carbohydrates and vitamin C, with the *caveat* that the bitter roots required peeling, shredding, boiling, and washing to remove the cyanide-yielding glycosides linamarin and lotaustralin that release prussic acid (HCN). For many, cassava starch provided a bland alternative to starvation during years as prisoners of the Japanese.

The Hedgerow Harvest

The Women's Institutes movement began in Canada during World War I and subsequently organized across England to teach traditional farm skills and link rural populations. During World War II, Women's Institutes implemented a national jam-making scheme that preserved surplus cultivated and wild fruit. With the declaration of war against Germany in the early fall of 1939, ripening crops were ignored. Foreseeing unprecedented waste, the national WI headquarters appealed to the Ministry of Food for sugar supplies. Local WI chapters organized jam-making efforts using volunteer labor; borrowed kettles, bottles, and jars; and 430 tons of government sugar; their efforts initiated the Co-operative Fruit Preservation Scheme, which lasted for the duration of the war and saved tons of fruit from decomposition. The goal was vast: to harvest and preserve fruit collected from private gardens, allotments, hedgerows, forests, fields, and abandoned sites. Because home refrigerators were still relatively rare, preserved fruit was a significant contribution to the English diet. Moreover, jam-making was good for home front morale and sent a message of defiance to Germany. Commercial jam companies continued their work, but the WI contributed tons of jam to the national supply chain; members donated labor but relied on government-supplied sugar reserves.

Preservation centers served as regional sites for washing, processing, boiling, canning, and sealing. These were established in large houses, school and farm kitchens, public buildings, and other spaces with sufficient room for women, stoves, equipment, and fruit. Conditions were often cramped, and plumbing varied, but Lord Woolton, Minister of Food, visited frequently to view the work and offer encouragement. Glass bottles were filled and sealed with parchment, but some WI members also learned the process of professional canning with apparatus such as the Dixie Hand Sealers donated by the U.S. and Canada. Canning technique required precise attention to detail; for instance, exactly twenty cranks of the handle crimped and secured the metal lid on each filled tin, no more and no fewer. Mobile canning vans from the U.S. were equipped with zinc sinks and copper boilers;

The Hedgerow Harvest campaign urged British civilians to forage for wild fruits in gardens, hedges, forests, and fields. Local Women's Institutes provided the labor needed to preserve millions of pounds of fruit into jam for the civilian food supply (Ministry of Food, United Kingdom).

mounted on Ford V8 chassis, these could be moved through the countryside to areas with bumper crops in need of rapid processing.

Fairness was paramount when dealing with rationed goods, thus despite hours of volunteer work, Women's Institute members could not purchase more than their fair share of preserved fruits. Detailed records tracked the sugar used in making jam, which in turn was sold by local shops and WI market stalls or donated to organizations that provided meals. There were some hard feelings about allocating sugar to the WI for jam during a time of strict sugar rationing, but the Ministry of Food backed the fruit preservation scheme as fair and beneficial for the nation. Jam production continued despite bombing, including intense raids during the Battle of Britain in the summer and fall of 1940. This was a season with a particularly fine fruit harvest; WI members made jam by day and sheltered from bombs at night. By the end of the season, there were 2,650 WI preservation centers across the country, making not only jam but also jellies, juices, chutneys, bottled whole fruits, and fruit cheeses. The latter were made from thick fruit puree into homogenous preserves with a consistency that could be sliced with a knife.

As might be expected, the Co-

"GROWMORE" BULLETIN No. 3 OF THE MINISTRY OF AGRICULTURE AND FISHERIES PUBLISHED BY HIS MAJESTY'S STATIONERY OFFICE PRICE 4d. NET

Bulletins and periodicals described the process of jam-making from cultivated crops and foraged fruit. Government recipes mandated 60 percent sugar, but home canners sometimes resorted to the use of saccharin when rationed sugar was in short supply (Ministry of Agriculture, United Kingdom).

operative Fruit Preservation Scheme spawned a bureaucracy that sought consistent products with no possibility of spoilage. Local inspectors judged sample jars, and they required strict adherence to the high-sugar jam recipes that osmotically inhibited any possible bacterial growth; the goal was the production of preserves that were well-sealed and remained sterile under a variety of conditions. Inspectors noted contaminants, such as dead wasps, and sometimes required that fruit be re-boiled. Marguerite Patten, a Ministry of Food home economist, encountered WI stalwarts who had been making jams and jellies for generations without the mandated 60 percent sugar. In her memoirs, she described jam-making instruction; there was often disagreement with an undercurrent of grumbling about which recipes to use at regional fruit preservation centers—tried and true local methods or the high-sugar mixtures mandated by the Ministry of Food.

Women's Institutes preserved 12 million pounds of fruit between 1940 and 1945, providing nutritious foods from crops that otherwise would have gone to waste. The tongue-in-cheek motto "jam and Jerusalem" summarized the WI wartime contribution, the latter referring to the bracing hymn sung at WI meetings, a musical setting of a poem by William Blake that extolled aspects of the English landscape:

> And did those feet in ancient time
> Walk upon England's mountains green:
> And was the holy Lamb of God,
> On England's pleasant pastures seen!
>
> And did the Countenance Divine,
> Shine forth upon our clouded hills?
> And was Jerusalem builded here,
> Among these dark Satanic Mills?
>
> Bring me my Bow of burning gold;
> Bring me my Arrows of desire:
> Bring me my Spear: O clouds unfold!
> Bring me my Chariot of fire!
>
> I will not cease from Mental Fight,
> Nor shall my Sword sleep in my hand:
> Till we have built Jerusalem,
> In England's green & pleasant Land.

Dehydration and Freezing

Other food preservation techniques were revived during the war years. Living plant cells are 90–95 percent water (most of it stored in the vacuole, which can occupy 90 percent of cell volume), and dehydration eliminates the water. Salting involved dehydration by osmosis, in which water moves from high concentration inside the cell to lower concentration outside of the cell. Fresh green beans were often packed in crocks or jars between layers of salt for long term preservation. Onions, celery, peas, spinach, carrots, parsnips, and fruit were dehydrated by oven-drying on shallow trays. Household manuals suggested lining wooden or wire drying trays with hessian, coarse cloth woven from jute, hemp, or sisal fibers, and maintaining a low oven temperature of 160 degrees Fahrenheit.[16] In England, apple slices were tossed in a jar containing sulfur dioxide from a sulfur candle or crystals (which killed microbes and inhibited activity of tyrosinase, the enzyme that causes fruit discoloration), dried in a low oven, and then safely stored in tins. Many such strategies consumed considerable time, such as preparing tomato paste, spreading it to dry, and then cutting it into cubes for keeping. Salt and heat both removed water, rendering the tissue metabolically inert for indefinite storage away from vermin or moisture.

Commercial food companies also resorted to dehydrated alternatives during the war years, both to save metal and to decrease shipping weights. Baked beans were available in dehydrated form as a replacement for canned beans, but cooks also had the traditional option of using dry beans. It was important to food companies to keep their product in the public eye, even if supplies were not available; the Burnham and Morrill Company generously offered their recipe for B&M baked beans to anyone who requested it.

The Lend-Lease Act depended largely on shipments of dehydrated foods to alleviate shortages in Europe. *Science News-Letter* extolled the role of dried, compressed foods in feeding desperate Allies; dehydrated vegetables were packaged as dense blocks, which required soaking for twenty minutes, followed by boiling.[17] For instance, a double serving of the borscht developed for Russian troops was the size of a match box. Potatoes revealed particularly dramatic effects, losing 88 percent of their weight and 90 percent of their volume when dehydrated and compressed for Lend-Lease shipments. Vitamins were also essential; by late 1942, a million gallons of dehydrated orange juice had been shipped to England, a ready source of vitamin C during the years of scarce imported citrus fruit.

The Army Quartermaster Corps suggested the most likely foods for preparation and export to Allies, and tile presses and similar devices were retrofitted to produce the food blocks. The prepared blocks were packaged in cellophane, manufactured in the U.S. by the Dupont Corporation as an alternative to metal cans. Cellophane is itself a botanical product, made from cellulose-containing cell walls harvested from wood, hemp, or cotton fibers. The cellulose is treated with alkali, carbon disulfide, sulfuric acid, and extrusion to produce a solution of viscose, from which cellophane film is made; simply put, cellophane is a glucose polymer derived from plant cell walls, closely related chemically to rayon that was used extensively during the war as a lightweight cloth for printed escape maps.

Production of dehydrated food peaked by the end of the war, with the processing during 1944–45 of 196 million pounds of beets, cabbage, carrots, potatoes, rutabagas, sweet potatoes, and potatoes.[18] *American Cookery* reported on samples of dehydrated fruits and vegetables prepared by Department of Agriculture scientists; turnips, sweet potatoes, onions, cabbage, carrots, string beans, orange juice, and cranberry sauce were reconstituted instantaneously in water, with the prediction that virtually all postwar foods would be sold as dehydrated packets, ready to soak or boil into table-ready meals. However, although dehydrated produce saved space and weight on transport ships, postwar consumers were not anxious to continue with wartime ways. Despite speculation that dehydrated packets would supplant fresh fruits and vegetables, the prediction that "The day is coming when a woman can buy a boiled dinner, and carry it home in her purse.... Then a well-stocked pantry will be reduced to some small boxes" proved incorrect.[19]

Freezing foods was another option that circumvented the use of the strategic metals used in canning. Working in Labrador as a naturalist, Clarence Birdseye experimented with the quick freezing of various foods, including cabbage, and by 1925, he had founded two companies devoted to the mass production of frozen foods, including peas, spinach, raspberries, loganberries, and cherries. As a preservation strategy, freezing halts the metabolism of both plant tissue and microbes that cause decomposition; however, ice crystals puncture cell membranes and cell walls, resulting in defrosted vegetables that are soggy and limp. Quick freezing produced smaller ice crystals that were less likely to damage cells, and this was Birdseye's achievement: rapid freezing at temperatures of -50 degrees Fahrenheit, which preserved cell structure.

Frozen foods became increasingly popular and common on the home front, and Birdseye pursued the best varieties for this means of preservation; he investigated as many as 105 pea varieties before finding the ideal cultivar for freezing.[20] To prevent desiccation over time, frozen foods were securely packaged in a variety of waterproof materials made from plant cell walls, including cardboard, waxed paper, parchment, and cellophane.

4

Botanical Diet and Cookery

The onset of war demanded full attention to food—its production, quality, distribution, availability, and preparation. In short, the military required top drawer nutrition in order to fight, and civilians needed groceries. Simultaneously, the U.S. supplied food to England, the Soviet Union, and other allies through the Lend-Lease program enacted on March 11, 1941. As a further complication, ships carrying food imports such as sugar and coffee were needed to transport soldiers and matériel. Thus in the spring of 1942, several months after the Japanese attack on Pearl Harbor, the U.S. Office of Price Administration (OPA) instituted food rationing.

Americans received their ration stamps through distribution sites at local schools. Each stamp featured an illustration, including stylized images of wheat and fruit, a reminder to civilians that controlled access to critical foods equated with military strength. Meats, butter, fats, and oils required red stamps, while blue stamps controlled certain botanical products such as canned fruits and vegetables, juices, soups, and catsup. Of course, availability dictated *de facto* rationing. Foods that were not available for purchase, while technically unrationed, were limited for home front use. Seemingly inexplicable food shortages occurred periodically during the war years, affecting essential foods like flour, beans, and vegetable shortening; such shortfalls resulted from subpar planning, increased military needs, and shipping or supply problems.

Sugar

During World War II, the first and last rationed food in the U.S. was sugar, sucrose crystals processed from sugar cane (*Saccharum officinarum*) or sugar beets (*Beta vulgaris* var. *esculenta*). The experience of World War I portended that forward thinking civilians might again hoard sugar. However, military diets required sources of quick energy; rationing bulletins reminded consumers that a typical soldier consumed twice as much sugar as a civilian, so sugar rationing was essential to the war effort. Food aside, there was also a chemical demand for military sugar; sucrose was fermented into the alcohol needed to produce smokeless powder, the nitrocellulose-based propellant used in guns.

Wartime concern for sugar cane supplies was legitimate. Japanese occupation limited American access to Philippine sugar, and imports from Hawaii were curtailed when cargo ships converted to military needs. These islands supplied about one-third of U.S. sugar imports. Both regions were ideal for sugar cane cultivation because the perennial, tropical grass thrived in hot, low-lying fields. As a species with C4 photosynthesis, the leaves of sugar avoid dehydration by closing their stomata during the day. At night when the stomata open, carbon dioxide is absorbed, held temporarily by a four carbon compound, and eventually used in photosynthesis to yield six-carbon sugars. These simple sugars (monosaccharides) are converted to the disaccharide sucrose in cane juice, which is pressed, heated, and filtered to yield refined sugar crystals. Sugar beets (see Chapter 6) were a temperate alternative that could be cultivated in the mainland U.S. and yielded sucrose identical to sugar cane.

Combat and emergency military food rations (K and D rations) included high-calorie chocolate, candies, and sugar packets, all made possible by home front rationing. However, sugar was also essential for cooking and baking, preserving canned fruits, fermenting alcohol, and pickling or preparing certain condiments. Sugar availability dictated the rationing of canned fruits in syrup, as well as commercial jams and jellies, but fruit could be preserved in home kitchens. Cooks could secure a higher sugar ration for home canning, provided they completed the necessary paperwork and self-reported figures from the previous season documenting the amount of sugar used and the number of jars canned. Rationing policy allowed a pound of sugar for each five quarts of bottled fruit, as well as five pounds per family member for use in jams, jellies, sweet pickles, relishes, and catsup.

Rationing was promoted as a fair way for all civilians to share goods that were in high demand, including such botanical items as sugar, coffee, and canned fruits (U.S. Office of Price Administration).

There were alternatives to sugar cane and sugar beets. Molasses, a by-product of sugar cane processing, was valued for its high iron content, some of which may have originated from the metal vats used in boiling down the cane syrup. Its sugar content included both simple sugars (glucose and fructose) and sucrose, and its dark color was best disguised in spice cakes such as Betty Crocker's wartime version of Haddon Hall gingerbread. Sugar beet processing also yielded molasses, but byproducts such as the nitrogenous compound glycine betaine and various mineral salts made it unpalatable for humans, but edible for fattening livestock. Other sugar alternatives included starch from corn (*Zea mays*), hydrolyzed with acid to produce glucose, a simple sugar that was used in several ways: to ferment alcohol and vinegar, to make jam and jelly, and to make corn syrup that could replace sugar or cane syrup in standard recipes. Wartime editions of standard cookbooks often provided the corn syrup equivalents for sugar. An industrial use involved the use of corn sugar in coating steel molds, which improved the finished surface of various molded steel parts. Using similar chemistry, potato starch yielded simple sugars that were used in European kitchens.

Honey was another wartime option. It is the modified, concentrated floral nectar that pollinating bees collect as a food source for their larvae. Honeybees ingest and regurgitate the nectar until it comprises mostly simple sugars (glucose and fructose), in contrast to the sucrose (a disaccharide) in sugar. Evaporation helps to reduce the sugar content, rendering honey antimicrobial; water molecules are attracted to sugar, decreasing water concentration by osmosis to levels that cannot support microbial growth and also interfere with enzymatic activity. Honey was a resource that could be stored indefinitely, and honey recipes proliferated in wartime publications. Food companies encouraged home baking even when standard supplies were scarce or rationed. For instance, 1942 and 1943 advertisements for Arm and Hammer baking soda provided recipes for sugarless chocolate cake and coconut cookies, both sweetened with honey. Maple syrup, the boiled and concentrated sap of sugar maples (*Acer saccharum*) was another temperate sugar source that supplemented imported sugar. An article in *Life* detailed the production of maple syrup as a substitute for cane sugar.[1] In March 1942, Vermont school children received an extra week of vacation to help with collecting maple sap that would be boiled into syrup.

The weekly sugar ration in the U.S. was one half pound per person, roughly half of pre-war consumption, and nutritionists rejoiced in the health benefits of decreased sugar intake. Tooth decay was a major concern because of its high incidence in military inductees. Medically speaking, the relationship between sugar intake and the frequency of dental caries was just becoming clear, but many suspected that it had something to do with acid-producing oral bacteria that thrived in sugar-laced saliva. An article in *Time* reported that rationing might mitigate "the rampant decay of American teeth,"[2] while *Science News-Letter* predicted that Americans would add more grains, vegetables, and milk to their diets, although sweets were important for morale.[3] Candy and confections required rationed sugar for their manufacture, and supplies of other ingredients such as chocolate and tropical nuts were often limited. Sugar rationing in the U.S. continued until 1947, when sugar supplies

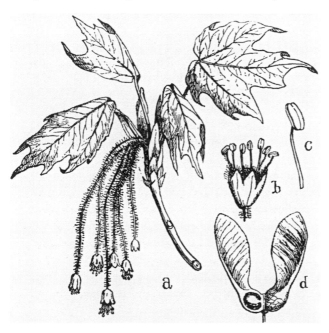

Maple syrup, the boiled and concentrated sap of sugar maples, was a wartime substitute for sugar cane. In 1942, Vermont school children received an extra week of vacation to help with collecting maple sap to boil down into syrup.

again reached pre-war levels. Chocolate was largely redirected to the military (see Chapter 5), although soldiers complained that military chocolate bars did not equal pre-war products.

A 1942 convention of American candy manufacturers revealed makeshift wartime recipes for civilians. Soybeans and peanuts substituted for imported nuts, and corn syrup, dried fruit, and even sweet potatoes replaced some of the sugar.[4] Candy mixtures were extended and stretched with botanical ingredients including peanut butter, cereal, meal, cornstarch, and stale bread. Candy diversity also suffered, with many pre-war varieties not manufactured for the duration of the war. Some sweets originated with wartime ingenuity, including M&Ms and the candy rolls known as Smarties. Beginning in 1949, the latter were manufactured from colored and flavored glucose; the small disks were shaped using machinery that produced compressed gun powder pellets during the war.

Coffee

Coffee was another imported commodity in high demand by the military. Ground from the roasted seeds of *Coffea arabica*, coffee was the most commercially important beverage plant and a key source of caffeine. Many civilians also considered coffee an essential part of their diet, particularly those engaged in war work and nighttime duties. Concerned about hoarding when coffee rationing began in late 1942, the Office of Price Administration asked consumers to disclose the quantity in their cupboards by self-reporting the "pounds of coffee owned on November 28, 1942, minus 1 pound for each person included in this Declaration whose age is stated on War Ration Book One as 14 years or older."[5] Grocers tried to convince shoppers that coffee packaged in paper bags (a wartime strategy to conserve metal) lost its freshness in a few weeks, so hoarding was an unwise economy. Coffee was an exclusively tropical crop that thrived in Brazilian soils at elevations of 4,500 feet, a point not understood by some novice victory gardeners who sought to purchase and plant coffee seeds.[6]

Like sugar, the weekly coffee ration provided for about half of pre-war consumption, about a pound per person every five weeks, sufficient for a cup each day. Shortages were the result of combined factors that subverted supplies; there were fewer ships with space for food imports, German U-boats

Chicory taproots were traditionally used to extend supplies of coffee beans, an imported crop in high demand by the military. Wartime ground coffee available to civilians worldwide typically contained roasted chicory.

attacked ships sailing from Brazil, and U.S. troops needed coffee to function. Some supplies arrived from Central America and Mexico by train, but demand remained high just to supply the U.S. military, which requisitioned ten times more coffee after the onset of war in 1941. President Roosevelt asked Americans to re-brew their coffee grounds; housewives used smaller amounts and kept their percolators on the stove longer in an effort to extract every possible ounce of the water-soluble brew.

Various concoctions of molasses, chicory, chick peas, soybeans, barley, and other grains were used to stretch the available coffee beans, or at least to make a potable dark liquid. Coffee additives were nothing new; chicory (*Cichorium intybus*) was a common nineteenth century adulterant to mixtures marketed as coffee. Preparation involved roasting and grinding the taproots of the perennial European herb, which was widely naturalized and cultivated in North America. By some accounts, nearly all of the wartime coffee sold in the U.S. and Europe contained substantial amounts of chicory, and many Europeans preferred the chicory mixtures to pure coffee. The bitter taste of chicory stems from sesquiterpene lactones such as lactucin rather than caffeine, and thus its stimulant properties do not equate with pure coffee.

Although German military interest in caffeine and other performance-enhancing chemicals peaked during the war years, a 1941 handbook for Hitler youth described caffeine as a known toxin.[7] Nazi medical policy discouraged caffeine consumption because of suspected carcinogenic or nervous effects, and varieties of *Ersatzkaffee* were brewed from roasted oats and other grains. This was not dissimilar from an American product that was also brewed for health reasons. As a disciple of the food faddist J.H. Kellogg who founded the Battle Creek sanitarium, C.W. Post advocated molasses and roasted, ground wheat as a coffee substitute. His mixture was first marketed in 1911 under the brand name Postum and enjoyed popularity as a wartime substitute for rationed coffee.

Margarine

Margarine originated as a military invention, initiated as a challenge from Louis-Napoléon Bonaparte for a cheap butter substitute for the French navy and working classes. In 1869, the French chemist Hippolyte Mege-Mouries compounded the earliest margarine from an emulsion of beef fat in skim milk, but later versions relied on botanical chemistry. Developed in Germany in 1906, the hydrogenation process allowed for the use of unsaturated vegetable oils by converting them to solid fats suitable for a butter substitute. In the chemical process, unsaturated (double) bonds between carbon atoms are broken, and hydrogen is added to produce a saturated, solid, white, botanical fat. Seeds often contain oils that serve as food storage for the embryo, and thus oil could be pressed from seed crops such as cotton, peanut, and soybeans for hydrogenation into wartime margarine. Margarine was rationed during the war because it contained vegetable oils, but it was more widely available than butter.

Palms provided another source of raw materials for margarine manufacture. Oils from the fruits and seeds of the South American oil palm (*Elaeis oleifera*) and oil from the seeds of coconuts (*Cocos nucifera*) provided saturated fats, unique because most vegetable oils are unsaturated. Various palm oils contain high concentrations of palmitic acid, the 16-carbon fatty acid that was also used during World War II in manufacturing the incendiary mixture known as napalm. During 1942–43, a group of Harvard organic chemists led by Louis Fieser combined gasoline with the aluminum salts (essentially a soap) of napthenic and palmitic acids; the term *napalm* was based on the first two syllables of the fatty acids. The result was a thickened, adhesive liquid that burned slowly and at a high temperature, and it was used in flame throwers and incendiary bombs (see Chapter 10). Incidentally, napthenic acid also has a photosynthetic origin, at least in part; it occurs in petroleum, which originated with vast organic deposits of ancient algae and other plankton.

Butter color stems from the yellow carotenoid plant pigments consumed by grazing cows. These molecules absorb and funnel light energy into photosysnthesis, and they are also the precursor to vitamin A synthesis in human diets. Wartime recipes often suggested margarine as a butter replacement, and enriched "vitaminized" margarine provided vitamins A and D (see Chapter 3). In an effort to make their product resemble butter, margarine manufacturers used a yellow pigment derived from the fleshy arils that surround the seeds of annatto (*Bixa orellana*), a tropical American shrub. Nevertheless dairy farmers opposed butter substitutes and lobbied against any attempts to tint margarine a butterlike yellow. To avoid the high taxes on pre-tinted margarine, some manufacturers included a packet of coloring that had to be kneaded or creamed into the mixture with a wooden spoon.

Margarine from soybean and other seed oils was also a common wartime commodity in Europe, even in Germany where Hitler opposed its use. He likely viewed margarine as undermining German dairy farmers and pro-agriculture Nazi policy. Moreover, as someone with vegetarian leanings, Hitler perhaps associated vegetable-based margarine with earlier formulations made from beef tallow or hydrogenated whale oil. Color posed yet another concern; German chemists synthesized azo food dyes from coal tar, the chemical remains of coal (fossilized plant matter from Carboniferous forests) converted to coke or gas. The azo dye known as butter yellow (methyl yellow or dimethylaminoazobenzene) tinted margarine a deep yellow color. However, Nazi influence oversaw health and diet, and by the late 1930s German researchers confirmed Japanese studies suggesting that butter yellow caused liver cancer. Reich officials worked to ban coal tar dyes as a preventive measure to preserve German "racial hygiene," but concern persisted that German housewives would view white margarine as an inferior wartime product.[8] Nazi policy discouraged food imports, which included annatto. Indeed another wartime food additive with coal tar origin was saccharin, first synthesized by German chemist Constantin Fahlberg working at Johns Hopkins University. Saccharin substituted for rationed sugar during both world wars, but by 1939, German policy also discouraged its use because of suspected carcinogenesis.

Rationing, Meals and Botanical Foods

The ration system depended on the perception of fairness and the practice of frugality. Policies were aimed at keeping home front morale high, despite shortages due to military needs and the Lend-Lease program that supported Allies. The cost (in terms of ration points) and varieties of rationed commodities shifted depending on supply and demand, but the idea was equal access for all. Posters extolling thrift and kitchen strategies targeted American housewives, pitting the home cook against the enemy. Food needed fair rules, thus hoarding was widely publicized as unpatriotic, suggestive of panic-buying or black market trading. Nevertheless there was a legitimate temptation to secure and stash supplies that later might disappear, particularly in the case of staple foods. Flour was a possible concern; to prevent hoarding, the Pillsbury Company assured customers that "American housewives will be able to buy peacetime high-quality flour for the duration," so stashing multiple sacks was unnecessary.[9] There was widespread speculation that a thriving black market could undermine fair access to goods, with better-off families able to purchase items at inflated under-the-counter prices.

Consumers, primarily housewives, were asked to pledge that they would not pay more than the government-mandated price nor purchase desired goods on the black market. Government posters reminded consumers "Rationing Means a Fair Share for All of Us" (OPA, 1942) and "Rationing Safeguards Your Fair Share" (OPA, 1943), while extolling them to "Keep the Home Front Pledge—Pay no more than Ceiling Prices…. Pay your Points in full" (OPA, 1944). Many botanical foods were prone to hoarding, including canned and dried fruits, sugar, cooking oils, spices, and imported items that might be scarce due to rationing and demand, but which could remain inert for months or even years on pantry shelves. Of course, some unfairness seemed inevitable in any rationing system, the combined effect of rural economies, preferential treatment, and racial segregation. Farmers may have favored family members and friends, and black people forced to queue at the end of long lines sometimes received less than their fair share of rationed foods.[10] Rationing resulted in heightened vegetable consumption because desired cuts of meat were often in short supply; it seemed that no one had meat of the desired varieties in pre-war quantities. Animal protein was limited based on availability and quality, which had the effect of shifting American diet in a vegetable direction.

With the start of war, canned fruits and vegetables were in high demand by American troops in the U.S. and abroad, and by early 1943, these foods were also controlled by rationing. During a nationwide radio address, Claude Wickard, director of the War Food Administration, explained that fruits and vegetables were not in short supply. In fact, supplies were high, but military and Lend-Lease obligations consumed half of all available canned, dried, and frozen fruits and vegetables. The monthly ration amounted to a few cans per civilian, shifting nutritional demands from canned fruits and vegetables to available fresh produce. By 1943, in addition to coffee and sugar, rationed botanical foods included dried fruits, dried beans, canned and frozen fruits and vegetables (including soups), and vegetable oils, which included oil-based margarines.

The point system introduced in 1943 allowed some choice in rationed foods based on supply and demand and affected largely botanical foods: canned vegetables, fruits, and juices; frozen vegetables and fruit; dried fruits; and canned soups. Lower point values were assigned to foods in greater supply; for instance, canned spinach typically required fewer points than green beans, although both were green vegetables. The point system operated in addition to the stamp system, so a single purchase involved a complex exchange of cash, stamps, and points. Consumers found the system confusing and cumbersome; an article in *The High School Journal* suggested that schools could help by instructing students and their parents on the best strategies for food purchases.[11] By this point in the war, the commercially preserved fruits and vegetables in a family's larder depended on preference, either a few choice items or large quantities of foods that were in less demand.

Some nutritionists viewed nationwide rationing as an opportunity for influence or even control of civilian diets. Staff writers at the *Journal of Home Economics* approved of the new point system and suggested that trained home economists be posted in all grocery stores to explain food purchasing strategies.[12] Later in 1943, an official in the U.S. Food Distribution Administration proposed a system in which workers would receive part of their salary as coupons exchangeable for specific foods by category. Dr. Mark Graubard, a biochemist, was frustrated by the food choices he observed and wanted to mandate healthy eating, "The nation has a vested interest in the health of its citizens, a right to insist that they shall not clutter up clinics and hospitals and lose valuable production time through preventable ill health."[13] The scheme was clearly designed to promote botanical foods, but to some it suggested paternalism and even socialism. Graubard based his proposed system on the Basic Seven nutritional classification developed by the U.S. Department of Agriculture (precursor of the four food groups and food pyramid) and publicized widely as part of *The National Wartime Nutrition Guide*[14]:

1. Green and yellow vegetables
2. Oranges, grapefruit, and tomatoes (or raw salad greens or cabbage)
3. Potatoes and other vegetables and fruits
4. Milk and milk products
5. Meat, poultry, fish, or eggs (or legumes or nuts)
6. Bread, flour, and cereals
7. Butter and fortified margarine

Six of the seven categories of coupons potentially required the consumer to purchase botanical foods: yellow and green vegetables; oranges, tomatoes, grapefruit, and raw cabbage; salad greens, potatoes, other vegetables, and fruits; peas, beans, or nuts; bread, flour, and cereals; and fortified margarine made from vegetable oil. Thus a family that disliked yellow and green vegetables would lose some of the breadwinner's salary if coupons went unused, which may explain why the system did not gain widespread support. Some foods were simply unfamiliar; for instance, most civilians were more likely to eat oranges rather than grapefruit. Although grapefruit contain less vitamin C than oranges, a campaign was mounted to advertise the crop as the "commando fruit" rich in vitamin C. By 1944, *Life* magazine published advertisements for the Florida Citrus Commission with the message, "Ask a Jap what it feels like to be up against men who are fortified with Victory Vitamin C."[15]

Some Americans opposed rationing altogether, preferring open competition to government allocation systems for limited goods. Rose Wilder Lane, daughter of Laura Ingalls Wilder, was a founding member of the Libertarian movement, for which she coined the name. She espoused the agrarian self-sufficiency described in the *Little House on the Prairie* series of books and during the war years modeled this herself by farming, gardening, and canning at her home in Danbury, Connecticut.

Cooking for Victory

The Depression brought issues of nutrition and food security for one third of all Americans, who survived the lean financial years on diets high in fat and low in vitamins and protein. Fat, starch, and sugar provided cheap calories, but the lack of fruits and vegetables caused vitamin deficiencies. Itinerant lives often rendered gardening impossible, but vegetable plots prevented many cases of malnutrition. Within the social instability of the Depression era, nutrition evolved into a legitimate national concern. In *It's Up to the Women*, published at the beginning of Franklin Roosevelt's first presidential term, Eleanor Roosevelt troubleshot family issues from household budgets to adequate nutrition. She advocated for the meal plan developed by Cornell University home economists, subsistence-level menus designed to keep a family of six barely nourished, noting that "many of the meals we have used ourselves at the White House. They have been worked out under the direction of experts on home economics, and will serve as a sample for balanced, inexpensive home rations."[16]

The Cornell menus pivoted on plants: grains (including oatmeal, cornmeal, and farina, a whole-grain cereal made from wheat), dried beans, potatoes, carrots, cabbage, and canned tomatoes. Most meals were meatless and plainly seasoned, and menus omitted appetizers or baked desserts. The purpose was to forestall malnutrition using cheap, easily-stored, botanical ingredients, and the meals were reminiscent of the cereal mush and vegetable soups and stews prepared years earlier in the New England Kitchens. The practical goal of this nineteenth century scheme was to convince cash-poor families to eat cheap, nutritious food, mostly vegetables and grains. However, failure ensued because immigrants preferred their own recipes over the straightforward dishes devised by social reformers. Ellen Richards, founder of New England Kitchens, continued to teach the strategies for nutritional survival on a minimal income, which involved cooking and eating plenty of vegetables and cereals as part of a scientific approach to domestic practice. Forty years later, Cornell home economists channeled the same strategic practice of a plain botanical diet into the Depression era fare served at the White House.

In solidarity with cash-strapped families, Eleanor Roosevelt described simple living at the White House, declaring to a reporter, "I am doing away with all the kickshaws—no hothouse grapes—nothing out of season."[17] Her culinary goal centered on economical meals as models for destitute Americans, which earned dinners at the Roosevelt White House a dreary reputation. She wanted to mirror simple living, but the president, a known *bon vivant*, detested culinary austerity. In fact, some Roosevelt biographers have speculated that Eleanor exhibited passive-aggressive behavior in running the White House kitchen as retribution for her husband's infidelity. Either way, Depression-era meals for the First Family featured botanical foods, including vegetable stew, creamed spaghetti with carrots, baked bean soup, scalloped tomatoes, spinach and cabbage salad, carrot relish, rice pudding, stewed prunes, and oatmeal cereal. Moreover, during an era when many favored white flour, the Cornell recipes stipulated bread made from whole grains and scotch wafers mixed up from rolled oats, milk, and a bit of fat.

Depression meals reflected the high cost of meat and produce, and thus wartime rationing and ceiling prices improved food quality and accessibility for many cash-strapped families. A 1942 voluntary "Share the Meat" campaign prepared Americans for rationing, but many were already accustomed to frequent meatless meals. In short, meat fueled the military. Soldiers received and consumed the best cuts, while civilians mixed animal protein with unrationed botanical foods; vegetables, grains, and legumes could all stretch a pound of meat to feed many. In preparing beef stew, *The American Women's Voluntary Services Cook Book* advised readers to, "Use a variety of vegetables. Potatoes, green beans, carrots, celery, turnips, rutabaga, cauliflower, cabbage, onions, lima or navy beans, and peas are good in a stew."[18] A cereal advertisement recommended that you

"S-T-R-E-T-C-H your meat with Cream of Wheat." *Meat Point Pointers—Wartime Meat Recipe Book* recommended that meatballs and patties be variously mixed with bread crumbs, cracker crumbs, oats, rice, barley, corn, cornmeal, chopped macaroni, and onions to stretch a pound of meat to serve six or eight.[19] *Victory Meat Extenders* suggested dishes that depended on vegetables or grains to stretch the meat ration to serve several: meat pies, creamed meat, stews, timbales, patties, croquettes, loaves, and various types of dumplings and bread-based stuffing.[20] Meat dishes and casseroles were often imaginative, involving unexpected combinations such as beef and pumpkin pudding or spaghetti sauce prepared with tomatoes and liver.

Of course, there were also coincidental health benefits to rationing, which many realized by the end of the war. Wartime meals featured available vegetables and minimal meat. It took hours to scrub, scrape, and trim raw vegetables and then to assemble, simmer, or bake the stews, soups, and casseroles described by rationing bulletins and cookbooks. At a time when many women were functioning as single parents and busy with war work, long cooking times must have posed a challenge. Some considered one-pot meals to be a regression to immigrant meals and poverty status; middle-class taste ran to plates with separate meats and vegetables. Rationing meant that the meat portion might have been quite modest, while combining meat with vegetables ensured portions of sufficient size, with adequate nutrients and calories. War meant sacrifice on the home front, and the theme was clearly a patriotic message to *make do* by using botanical foods to substitute for the meat that nourished the military.

Any recipe labeled "victory" was particularly plant-based and thrifty. A recipe for victory meatballs used appreciably more oats than beef, and victory vegetable soup called for onion, tomatoes, parsley, cabbage, carrots, green beans, potatoes, and celery, as well as barley or rice.[21] *American Cookery* magazine featured a victory pie with unsweetened apple slices in a thin crust,[22] while Alice Winn-Smith's version used honey or corn syrup in place of sugar.[23] Depending on crops and demand, grocery stores featured victory specials, foods that could be purchased in large quantities and prepared into patriotic meals without allegations of hoarding.

Social change progressed with changes in diet. Susan B. Anthony, great niece of the nineteenth century women's rights advocate, confronted the issue of women's time in *Out of the Kitchen—Into the War*, "Lurking behind the nutrition posters, the committees and conferences, is the hoary notion that in the solemn business of winning a war women's chief contribution should come through more hours of shopping and more conversation about food, meat cuts, vegetables and vitamins.... Women's time is expendable—that was the only conclusion you [could] come to."[24] Her thinking was aligned with Eleanor Roosevelt (her distant cousin) and nineteenth century social reformers who envisioned communal feeding programs that would assume much of the burden of kitchen work; she disagreed with Margaret Mead, who was concerned about the effect of communal meals on family structure (see Chapter 3). Anthony believed that a postwar economy would require that women remain in the workforce after the war, and she promoted public cafeterias and school lunch programs to provide food for all. In fact, communal eating at work, schools, nurseries, canteens, and low cost restaurants was an important wartime reality that drastically retrenched in the decade following the war.

Corporations adapted their wartime advertising to feature meals made from available ingredients. Advice on menu-planning came in the barrage of pamphlets, bulletins, product leaflets, and newspaper articles on managing the wartime kitchen. For instance, cabbages are large, temperate vegetables that provided vitamin C, and the vegetable was an ideal extender for dishes containing rationed ingredients. *Bright Spots for Wartime Meals—66 Ration-Wise Recipes* recommended a congealed egg salad stretched in volume with plenty of shredded cabbage.[25] Banana shortages were common, and in 1942 the Fruit Dispatch Company of New York recommended a recipe that used a single banana to flavor a family-sized cabbage salad. In cities such as Chicago and San Francisco, voluntary or appointed block brigade captains visited homes to share information on nutrition, menu planning, rationing, gardening, canning, as well as to caution against black market purchases. Radio spots featured home economists and extension staff who lectured on ration points, cookery, and nutrition.

Wartime waste of any sort was unpatriotic—including food, fuel, and vitamins. Peeling vegetables was discouraged to save edible tissue, and nutritionists recommended short cooking times using minimal water to preserve water-soluble vitamins such as vitamin B1 (thiamine) and vitamin C.[26] Conservation and consumption of vitamins were essential to the war effort, but home economists disagreed about vegetable cookery; some held that small-cut vegetables cooked quickly and saved fuel, while others argued that larger pieces with less surface area lost fewer vitamins. However, there was consensus on the value of cooking water that contained any water soluble vitamins and minerals. Home economists and nutritionists agreed that any water in which vegetables were cooked should be served or saved to use as a vegetable stock in soups, sauces, or gravies.[27]

To compensate for the preponderance of plain meals, authorities shared pointers on maintaining mealtime morale. A medical doctor quoted in *Good Housekeeping* magazine suggested sprinkling herbs on stews and preparing new salads, presumably with victory garden crops, all in an effort to "see that mealtimes are the bright spots in the day."[28] Housewives were encouraged to take time to make appealing meals from the available supplies, devising clever dishes from minimal meat and seasonal vegetables. Of course, many choice vegetables were unavailable from farmers, who were advised to cultivate crops that required the least work for the largest harvest and to avoid fruits and vegetables that required special cultivation, careful handling, and refrigeration. Cauliflower, lettuce, asparagus, artichokes, celery, and cucumbers were scarce, while cabbages and root crops filled the bins in local markets. Another *Good Housekeeping* article asked "Do They Eat Around the Vegetables?" and urged home cooks to "make up for the lack of variety by cooking available vegetables expertly, by concocting new ways to serve them, by combining two vegetables."[29]

Many youth were unfamiliar with vegetables beyond the most common pre-war cultivars. A wartime poll asked college students, "In order that we may add variety—will you be willing to try anything once? There are many vegetables richer in beauty and energy values than the … pea and green bean. Are you willing to learn to like a few of them?"[30] Perhaps for the first time, students were encouraged to eat unfamiliar vegetables as part of a college meal plan, and for many, this was their first taste of root crops such as turnips and parsnips. National defense was the motivation; botanical vitamins and nutrients were essential to the health and stamina of young men queued for military service.

Norman Rockwell's painting "Freedom from Want" (1943), third in the series known as the Four Freedoms, illustrated the culinary desires of mainstream Americans, with meat (in this case, turkey) as the mainstay. Vegetables, fruit, and cranberry sauce completed the meal. Rockwell based his illustrations on the 1941 State of the Union address in which Roosevelt explained why the United States entered the war. Rockwell himself noted the resentment voiced by Europeans, who endured surely greater hardships than Americans, against the abundant, idealized meal illustrated in his painting. Select cuts of meat, roasted and then carved at the table, were part of the upward mobility that had reduced botanical foods to side dishes. In fact, many Americans also yearned for untrammeled food access during the war years; one pot meals of meat and vegetables resembled immigrant diets.

Rationing, victory gardens, and food preservation reversed the meat-eating trend, at least for the war years. Meatless meals used animal proteins such as milk, eggs, cheese, or fish, but the usual expectation demanded some meat or meat flavoring at virtually every meal. Animal proteins (various combinations of meat, fish, eggs, and dairy foods) provided sufficient protein and fats, while vegetables provided mass, carbohydrates, some protein, and most of the vitamins. T. Swann Harding, a strategist who wrote extensively on agriculture, viewed a rationed diet as "just good enough to prevent the physical and mental deterioration that might result in defeat."[31] His message was bleak but truthful: High-quality meat protein provided troops with the strength and morale for military engagement, while on the home front, a largely vegetable diet maintained baseline civilian health. Of course, there was not yet concern about high levels of dietary salt and saturated fat, thus a vegetable-based diet was comparatively more conducive to long term health.

Legumes Replace Meat

Legumes, seeds of the large legume family (Fabaceae), became essential wartime protein substitutes for meat and eggs. Legume roots host symbiotic *Rhizobium* bacteria, microbes that convert atmospheric nitrogen to forms that the plants use to synthesize amino acids, the building blocks of proteins. In turn, legume seeds convert starchy storage tissue (endosperm) into protein; the cotyledons (embryonic leaves) of legumes store protein content that varies from 20 percent in lima beans to 37 percent in soybeans.

Civilian meals called for beans to replace rationed meat. *American Cookery* suggested all-vegetable luncheons of green peppers stuffed with fresh lima beans accompanied by green beans and cabbage.[32] Other legume options included baked bean loaf, peanut and carrot loaf, kidney bean salad, lima bean scallop, savory lentils, lentil soup, cream of bean soup, and pinto rarebit. A General Mills pamphlet included a recipe for peanut butter loaf, a quick bread with peanut butter substituted for shortening.[33] Sample menus from the *Health-for-Victory Meal Planning Guide* featured legumes in various dishes, including sandwich fillings of peanuts or beans mixed with chopped pickles, relishes, carrots, and other vegetables.[34] Sandwiches were of particular interest because it was essential that war workers carry nutritious food to their jobs; "Eat Well to Work Well" cautioned homemakers and boarding house cooks that "the lunch you send may determine the success of our war, the future health of your family, and whether your worker will have a job when the war is ended. Know food values in making lunches.... Eating good food helps to lead to the highest quality of work, and that leads to victory."[35] Nutrition, much of it legume-based and home grown, equated with the patriotic will to win the war.

Baked beans, a familiar pre-war dish, were typically made with one of the many cultivars of *Phaseolus vulgaris*, the species that includes haricot, kidney, pea-bean, and black bean varieties. However, with appeal to young men and a protein content of 22 percent, canned baked beans were needed for military messing, thus home front supplies were erratic. A *Good Housekeeping* advertisement (September 1943) described B&M beans as "Hearty as meat and potatoes.... Again on sale," but home cooks could also write to the company in Maine for a recipe to use if canned beans ran low. In 1943, Brer Rabbit molasses provided a bean recipe that combined dried navy beans with unrationed molasses and used stovetop simmering rather than baking to save fuel.

Because of their high protein and oil content, soybeans (*Glycine max*, also known as soya) earned particular attention. The species originated in southeastern Asia, and by the 1940s there were 1000 varieties, including the cultivar 'Rokusun' that was recommended for home gardens in the southern U.S. A single bushel of soybean seeds yielded 48 pounds of flour and 11 pounds of oil, which explained the wartime effort to convince consumers to eat a crop that many considered fodder. Bulletins and pamphlets recommended that home gardeners cultivate soybeans; one-sixth of an acre supplied a large rural family with enough soybeans for routine inclusion in their meals. Black populations were a particular concern because many still subsisted on low protein Depression-era southern diets. Thus some suggested that soybeans be grown in particular to augment diets of low-income Americans and also for overseas shipment to Allies, claiming optimistically that the cooked beans "have a rich flavor that is pleasing to most people."[36]

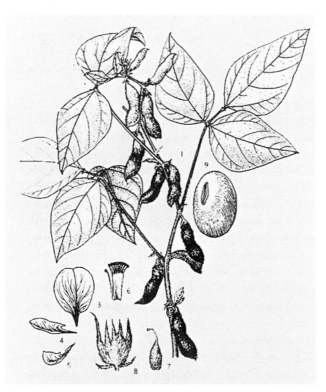

Soybeans were considered the nutritional equivalent of meat, and they appeared often in wartime recipes, from baked goods to casseroles. Their unique chemistry also made the beans suitable for making the maritime product known as Aer-o-foam, used to fight fires at sea.

Families were encouraged to add soybeans to wartime meals. As a cheap protein source that contained all of the essential amino acids, soybeans remedied some dietary deficiencies—if people could be persuaded to eat them. Soybeans have a characteristic flavor due to the enzymes that digest soybean oil molecules into small, aromatic fragments, and a slight bitterness results from the isoflavones known as phytoestrogens. The combined effect is a "beany," slightly rancid flavor. Quick cooking of soybeans denatured the enzymes and prevented oil breakdown, and this was the key to preparing palatable dishes without the off-taste caused by aromatic molecules. However, cooks soon learned that dried soybeans required overnight soaking and longer cooking times than other legumes; recipes in the *Journal of Home Economics* suggested boiling pre-soaked soybeans in an open kettle for four or five hours. Then they were ready for baked dishes or to extend meat.[37]

Despite problems with taste and texture, the *War Emergency Bulletin* suggested soybeans as "meat substitutes ... as a vegetable, as a toasted nut, or ground into grits or flour."[38] *American Cookery* praised soybeans as a luncheon dish, such as a loaf made from bacon, tomato juice, celery, green pepper, and boiled soybeans.[39] Soybeans that had been soaked, fried, and salted were recommended as a nutritious food for school children. However, due to their low starch content, soybeans never yielded the creamy texture of other cooked beans. They also tended to boil over into a foamy mess, the result of protein interaction with saponins, seed coat compounds that can account for 5 percent of soybean mass. Saponins have a soapy nature, with separate polar and non-polar regions that are soluble in water and fats, and they stabilize the bubbles that form from soybean proteins in water. This aspect of soybean chemistry proved useful in developing the maritime product known as Aer-o-foam, a fire retardant credited with saving Navy personnel during fires at sea (see Chapter 6). Known among World War II sailors as "bean soup," the patented soybean-based foam quelled marine fires by floating on top of burning fuel. Based on soy proteins originally isolated by the chemist Percy Julian, Aer-o-foam exploited the same chemical properties that vexed home front cooks: the ability of soybean proteins to form a thick, stable bubble layer.

Military messing demanded enormous quantities of enriched wheat flour, and so Americans were urged to substitute soy flour for wheat flour in bread recipes and to use soy flour in thickening soups and stews. Soy flour was a key ingredient in the soybean bread, biscuit, and cookie recipes advocated by the *Health-for-Victory Meal Planning Guide*.[40] Yeast bread made entirely with soy flour lacked volume and texture because the protein gluten is absent from soy flour. As dough rises, gluten allows the mixture to form bubbles that capture the carbon dioxide produced by yeast; soy flour alone will not rise as expected because of the absence of gluten. However, the enzymes that degrade soybean oils into aromatic fragments also act serendipitously to extend the length of gluten molecules, making bread dough made with some soy flour relatively more elastic. Thus wartime recipes for yeast breads suggested substituting soy flour for up to half of the wheat flour.

Concerned about civilian food needs, the New York State Food Commission relied on Cornell University nutritionists to develop innovative soybean uses, resulting in a successful bread-baking mixture known as the Cornell formula. Sarah Gibson Blanding co-led the commission; she was a London-trained economist who served as dean of the College of Home Economics. Raised on a Kentucky farm, Blanding had practical knowledge of agriculture and pushed for soybean uses beyond traditional boiling and baking. One early strategy involved germinating soybeans into sprouts; the commission recommended converting canneries into factories to utilize Chinese bean sprouting techniques on a vast scale. Wartime soybean sprouts pre-dated the popularity of Asian cookery, but they were nutritious and cooked quickly. According to the *Report of the State Food Commission*, soybean sprouts were the equivalent of a fresh vegetable; they cooked more quickly than dried beans, contained more vitamin C, and were popular on the home front.[41] On the other hand, soy-based sausage disappeared quickly from the marketplace; the product relied on flour milled from soybeans, cotton seeds, and peanuts, compounded with onions and spices to make a mock, meatless "soysage." It had the dim appeal of most wartime food substitutes.

Bread Strategies

The most influential work of the New York State Food Commission involved bread and depended on the work of Clive McKay, a Cornell nutritionist with a lifelong interest in the connection between diet and longevity. Experimenting with the diet of laboratory rats, McCay developed a high protein mixture of enriched white flour, soy flour, wheat germ (the milled embryos of wheat grains), and powdered milk. The prototype was field-tested in New York mental hospitals, where patients thrived on the formula, even those who were willing to eat only bread.[42] Loaves of the Cornell bread were described as having a rich golden crumb; this resulted from the soy flour and was the primary reason for their appeal, during a time that average Americans disdained dark, whole grain bread. During the war, school lunch programs, hospitals, commercial bakeries, and home bakers relied on the Cornell formula, which provided not only protein, but also iron, calcium, vitamin E, and B vitamins. A 1943 luncheon menu at the New York governor's mansion included muffins and corn sticks made with the Cornell mixture, as well as a soybean soufflé, soy sprout salad, and sautéed soybeans; the goal of the event was to introduce soy-based foods for home front meals. Toward the end of the war, Pillsbury Flour Mills marketed Golden Bake Mix, an unrationed convenience product that combined soy and wheat flour; it contained 20 percent soy flour, 20 percent protein, and promised a nut-like flavor when mixed into muffins, pancakes, and waffles.

Cornell bread provided a rich wartime source of vitamins and proteins, a timely option when protein deficiency due to rationed meat was a potential problem. Well into the 1950s, articles and recipes extolling the Cornell formula appeared in magazine articles and popular cookbooks such as the *Joy of Cooking*. Following her service with the New York State Food Commission, Blanding left Cornell to become president of Vassar College, one of the Seven Sisters colleges that educated capable young women. In the post-war era of overcrowded colleges, Blanding welcomed 170 male veterans of World War II who used the GI bill to attend Vassar classes.

Making Do

Cooks had to be nimble, able to reconfigure dishes based on available foods, and many meals depended on cookery rules learned during World War I. Alice Winn-Smith noted in the preface of *Thrifty Cooking for Wartime*, "In reality, they are not new rules, but rather the best and thriftiest of the old ones…. Many of them were used during the First World War by thousands of American women…. American housewives of today are united in one great Army, for one noble purpose—VICTORY. Just as necessary as shouldering a rifle, is the shouldering of our responsibilities in the home."[43] In the home front kitchen, housewives solved the meal dilemma by strategically planning for the palatable preparation of available foods. Imagination was essential; Winn-Smith modeled culinary patriotism in the recipes that she proposed: a meatless loaf made with beans (boiled and sieved), peanut butter, onion, and bread crumbs; soups made from turnips and green pepper or asparagus and green beans; and victory garden vegetables variously baked, stuffed, breaded, steamed, scalloped, or glazed She also advocated using edible trimmings, for instance her recipe for a salad of beet tops and grated orange rind, the epitome of thrifty cookery.

Newspapers and magazines shared recipes tailored to seasonal harvests, supply, and demand. For instance, the 1943 bumper crop of sweet potatoes required diverse recipes for their preparation. *Good Housekeeping* suggested sweet potato stew, sweet potato hash, and sweet potatoes flavored with orange juice and grated rind.[44] However, oranges were often scarce because of military demand. A full page Sunkist advertisement acknowledged that oranges might be infrequent; it reminded consumers that vitamin C was also in cabbages and tomatoes and to use victory garden crops, such as beets and potatoes, as sources of "protective" vitamin-rich foods.

Cooking became an experimental enterprise. Traditional recipes were often set aside for lack of ingredients, or substitutions were devised for scarce, rationed, or point-assigned foods. Temperate herbs replaced imported spices, and paperboard boxes (a wood pulp product) replaced familiar spice tins. Black pepper, ground from the fruits of a tropical vine (*Piper nigrum*), was essential to American palates, and commercial substitutes were concocted from mixtures of cereals, hot red peppers (*Capsicum* spp.), and pepper hulls and oils. Inventive cooks may have used fresh leaves of water pepper (*Persicaria hydropiper*, a buckwheat relative that is widely naturalized) or seeds of nasturtium flowers (*Tropaeolum majus*) for their peppery flavors. Herbal cookery was still relatively rare, but wartime recipes recommended herbs to flavor bland ingredients; in a *New Yorker* cartoon, a hostess informed her luncheon guests that "If everything has a funny taste, don't worry. It's just herbs."

Once pre-war spice tins were empty, Old World species such as cinnamon, cloves, and nutmeg were difficult to obtain; military campaigns, Japanese occupation, and German submarine activity interfered with harvesting and shipping. Cinnamon (*Cinnamomum zeylanicum*) originated in Ceylon (now Sri Lanka) and much of the crop was cultivated in Burma (now Myanmar), Malaya, and the West Indies, regions drastically affected by the war. Cassia (*Cinnamomum cassia*) is a closely related species from Burma that sometimes substituted for true cinnamon; it was cultivated in China and probably rarely shipped during the war years.

Cloves (*Syzygium aromaticum*) originated in the Moluccas, but were commonly cultivated in Indonesia and the West Indies. Oil of clove, pressed from the dried flower buds, had uses in dentistry and cytological slide preparation, so it is likely that medical demand took precedent over kitchen needs. Nutmeg (*Myristica fragrans*) also originated from the Moluccas and was cultivated in the East and West Indies. German submarines actively pursued ships leaving the British West Indies, affecting nutmeg (as well as mace, made from the outer covering, or aril, of the nutmeg seed), cloves, and other exports from these islands. But despite shortages, wartime recipes continued to call for Old World spices. For instance, pumpkin pie recipes took note of sugar shortages and substituted corn syrup and maple syrup for part of the sugar, but still specified cinnamon and nutmeg for traditional flavoring.[45]

Fortunately, cooks had an alternative that was widely cultivated in the New World tropics; allspice (*Pimenta dioecia*) seemed to combine the presence of cinnamon, cloves, and nutmeg. Spice flavors result from the presence of essential oils, which impart specific flavors when present in various combinations. Cinnamon, clove, and nutmeg all contain eugenol, in addition to other terpenes and terpenoids such as linalool, camphene, and geraniol, as well as safrole and cinnamaldehyde. Allspice combines eugenol with a complex array of terpenoids that yield an ideal flavor as a baking ingredient. Native to Central America and the West Indies, allspice trees naturalized widely in the American tropics,

Allspice from the New World tropics was a wartime substitute for cinnamon, nutmeg, and cloves, which it resembled in flavor; it became widely used when shipments of other tropical spices dwindled due to wartime conditions.

and Jamaican imports supplied American kitchens during the war.

Vanilla flavoring was another tropical commodity that was sometimes in short supply. Vanilla orchids (*Vanilla planifolia*) were widely cultivated in Mexico, Madagascar, the Seychelles, and other islands, but wartime shipments were unreliable. Ready-made vanilla extract was made by soaking the orchid capsules in alcohol to extract the vanillin, but there were synthetic alternatives because vanilla was in short supply even before the war. Eugenol derived from clove oil was a chemical starting point for the laboratory synthesis of vanillin; however, by the 1930s, artificial vanillin was synthesized from the waste liquid collected from the acid sulfite treatment used to produce wood pulp. Thus some of the vanilla flavoring in wartime kitchens likely originated as lignin, the hardening substance in the cell walls of xylem or wood cells. The *Betty Crocker Cook Book of All-Purpose Baking*, a wartime booklet, suggested substituting orange and lemon, alone or combined, to flavor cakes.[46] *Thrifty Cooking for Wartime* recommended pounding and grinding the seeds of *Prunus* (plums, peaches, and apricots) to yield a substitute for almond flavoring, perhaps a task that could be done by children.[47] Perhaps the author was unaware of amygdalin, the cyanide-yielding glycoside in *Prunus* seeds. Prussic acid (hydrogen cyanide) is released when the seeds are damaged in any way, although if only small amounts are consumed, cyanide concentrations do not cause severe toxicity.

Because chocolate was an essential part of military rations, with specialized bar formulations for field and tropical settings, baking chocolate was often scarce (see Chapter 5). Wartime recipes often specified cocoa powder as a substitute for chocolate, with a small amount of added fat to make up for the missing cocoa butter. One popular recipe (known as wacky cake or crazy cake because of its unlikely ingredients) relied on cocoa powder and vegetable oil, rather than eggs, butter, or baking chocolate; leavening of the batter depended on a reaction between vinegar and baking soda that yielded carbon dioxide.

The war in the Pacific affected imports from southeast Asia, including the tuberous roots of manioc or cassava (*Manihot esculenta*), the source of tapioca starch used to thicken puddings and some other dishes, including wartime jams that lacked sufficient sugar to gel (see Chapter 3). When boiled, the starch granules form soft translucent spheres held together by gelatinous starch, which in turn provide the texture of tapioca pudding. Although native to South America, cassava was introduced to tropical areas worldwide where it served as an emergency high-energy food during famines. Many refugees survived by eating cassava during the Japanese occupation of Malaysia, but careful preparation was essential to remove the cyanide-yielding glycosides that yield prussic acid (HCN) when they are digested (see Chapter 11).

The Minute Tapioca Company of General Foods relied almost exclusively on crops grown in Java, so an alternative was needed during the war in the Pacific. In 1942, Nebraska farmers began to grow the waxy varieties of sorghum (*Sorghum bicolor*) from China, with seeds that yielded a starch similar to tapioca, which also had potential as an adhesive in manufacturing plywood for wartime use. Food was the first priority, however, and starch from waxy sorghum made satisfactory wartime desserts. However, General Foods changed the name of their product to Minute Dessert because it no longer contained true tapioca. The *USDA Yearbook of Agriculture* noted that waxy sorghum was a highly adaptable new crop that could be made into puddings that were "pleasant to eat ... especially good for people unable to swallow solid food after a tonsillectomy," with future uses in textile sizing, paper production, and industrial adhesives.[48] Coincidentally, the leaves and germinating seeds of some sorghum varieties like cassava also yielded cyanide, but apparently this was not a problem with the waxy types used as a wartime food starch.

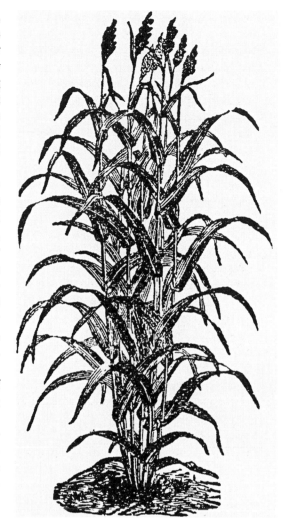

Waxy sorghum from China was cultivated for use in puddings, once Japanese occupation blocked exports of tapioca from Java. Sorghum starch was also investigated for use as an adhesive in plywood manufacture, textile sizing, and paper production.

Wild plants provided additional vegetable options, and magazine articles encouraged wartime cooks to forage outdoors for edible plants. Fiddleheads, the springtime crosiers (curled fronds) of wild ferns were described as an asparagus substitute that could be "cleaned to remove the brown fuzz which covers them ... washed and treated as other greens for canning." The carcinogenic potential of ferns such as bracken (*Pteridium aquilinum*) was not yet known, nor was the toxicity of pokeweed (*Phytolacca americana*), which was recommended as a "palatable green." We now recognize its toxic saponins and alkaloids and the potential of pokeweed to cause stomach upset, convulsions, and even blood anomalies. Perhaps a better plant for foraged meals was miners' lettuce (*Claytonia perfoliata*), a small wildflower with high vitamin C content. California gold miners prized the species as a scurvy preventative, and it was recommended for wartime foraging. Patricia Allen noted that miners "ate it raw, they ate it boiled with jerky, and there were no more deaths from scurvy" and highly recommended a cooked wartime vegetable dish of garden peas and miners' lettuce.[49]

Thrifty Cooking for Wartime suggested gathering berries, apples, figs, and nuts, noting that "the United States is so richly blessed with fruits and berries that the occasional pie made from these materials will be a treat easily afforded."[50] Foraging also yielded substitutes for unavailable foods. Imported Mediterranean capers (*Capparis spinosa*) were scarce during the war, but some cooks revived the folk practice of using the flower buds of marsh marigold or cowslip (*Caltha palustris*) as a caper substitute, noting that "smart farmers might profit from the cultivation of the cowslip, for the pickled buds are a very effective substitute for French capers."[51] This was unlikely, since growing marsh marigolds would have required flooded agricultural fields. Moreover there were possible problems with toxicity. The slightly sharp taste of true capers results from mustard oils, which are lacking in marsh marigolds; however, herbalists have long noted the irritating quality of all parts of the plant, attributable to protoanemonin which causes skin and mucous membranes to itch and blister. Perhaps boiling and pickling to make a caper-like relish helped to eliminate some of the protoanemonin, a toxin found throughout the buttercup family (Ranunculaceae). High levels can cause symptoms ranging from nausea to paralysis, so marsh marigold consumption was definitely ill-advised.

Feeding England

By the 1930s, England depended largely on imported food, the result of soil diminished by centuries of farming and the desire to support the Canadian wheat harvest. English ports received shipments from Europe, as well as the U.S., Canada, Argentina, Australia, India, and Burma; in fact, over half of the protein and two-thirds of the calories in the English diet came from offshore farms. Food imports included most of the flour (almost 90 percent), cooking oils (over 90 percent), sugar (over 70 percent), and meat (about 50 percent) consumed in English homes. Thus when German U-boats (an abbreviation of *Untersee-Boot*, or submarine) sank England-bound ships with edible cargo, the situation threatened widespread hunger. In short, Hitler planned to activate English surrender by means of strategic starvation.

Even when the U.S. was not yet in the war, American food imports to England involved peril. Despite their escort vessels, cargo ships were particularly vulnerable in the mid–Atlantic, where U-boats traveled in packs and torpedoed convoys. Between February and April 1941, U-boat attacks destroyed 1.6 million tons of food, in addition to the loss of lives and ships. In the spring of 1941, shortages of dairy foods and cured meats occurred after the German invasions of Denmark Norway, Holland, Belgium, and Luxemburg, followed by the surrender of France in June. Luftwaffe bombing of milling and processing plants caused even further shortages.

The newly formed Ministry of Food established price controls in September 1939, the month that Germany invaded Poland and England declared war on Germany. Controlled items included several of the botanical items that housewives sought for their larders: sugar, flour, potatoes, and dried fruit. Food rationing began in January 1940 with limits on sugar, bacon, and butter; eventually the scheme extended to include meat, cheese, milk, eggs, fruit preserves, and sweets. With war looming, housewives had already been advised to lay in a supply of emergency food, including tins of beans and other vegetables, cocoa, flour, cereal, dried fruit, jam or marmalade, tea, coffee, and sugar. Pamphlets such as the "A.R.P. [Air Raid Precautions] Home Storage of Food Supplies" described the management of a home larder, which was not considered hoarding as long as the stored food did not exceed a ten day supply.[52] Food writer M.F.K. Fisher recommended that home cooks acquire for their households an "iron ration" (an ironic reference to World War I emergency combat rations) comprising tea, whole wheat biscuits, sugar cubes, and tomato juice; these botanical foods could tide a family over during blackouts and bombing raids.[53] Given the shortages of desired foods, Londoners were dismayed on September 7, 1940, when food warehouses on the docks burned during an air raid. Melted sugar cascaded down the streets, but waste was reduced the next day when East End housewives collected chunks of cooled sugar to use in their kitchens.

The Ministry of Food worked diligently to deliver its messages about diet, cookery, vitamins, and food conservation through all available media, including programs, classes, posters, bulletins, leaflets, radio, and films. Their wartime influence was enormous; for instance, between March 1942 and November 1946 over 200 brief Ministry "Food Flash" films were produced and shown in theaters. Each one reached an estimated audience of 20 million and used dry humor to provide updates on rationing and food preparation. Early morning "Kitchen Front" BBC radio programming shared pertinent recipes for available foods, broadcast just before housewives joined the queues at local shops. Charles Hill, known as the Radio Doctor, chimed in with information on nutrition and health. The fictional charwomen known as Gert and Daisy provided humorous commentary on wartime cookery and recipes, eventually collected in *Gert and Daisy's Wartime Cookery Book* (1940).

Information helped to ease the transition to a home front diet based largely on vegetables, bolstered by small quantities of rationed foods. The Ministry of Food categorized foods according to metabolic function: Body-building foods were high in protein, warming foods were high in carbohydrates, and protective foods were vitamin-rich. Rationing sought to provide fair access to all of the metabolic food groups, particularly body-building foods, including meat, eggs, and cheese. Typical recipes stretched a half pound of meat to feed a family, revealing and resolving dietary inequities that correlated with class structure. Protein consumption decreased for many middle class English, while it actually increased for many working class families despite wartime stringencies.

Rationing dictated that plants grown on English soil were the key to wartime diet and nutrition. Vegetables (including potatoes), fresh fruit, and bread filled the gaps left by rationed foods, but some needed instruction in preparing vegetable meals. The Royal Horticultural Society published "Simple Vegetable Cookery" (1940) to supplement the first Grow More Bulletin "Food from the Garden" from the Ministry of Agriculture (see Chapter 2). Food writers also embraced the challenge, and wartime cookbooks flooded the market. Ambrose Heath, who wrote for *The Times* and *The Manchester Guardian*, published 29 cookbooks between 1939–1945, including *Cooking in Wartime* (1939), *Good Food without Meat* (1940), *Making the Most of It* (1942), *Simple Salads and Salad Dressings* (1943), and *Vegetables for Victory* (1944). He also contributed to the BBC Kitchen Front broadcasts with advice on vegetable cookery. Thus the overall effect was an involuntary national shift toward vegetarianism, with careful attention paid to preparation because vitamin conservation often involved cooking vegetables quickly in minimal water. The

Ministry of Food short film "Two Cooks and a Cabbage" compared quick and slow cooking times for two halves of the same cabbage, demonstrating that quick steaming yielded the most vitamin-rich, appealing cooked vegetable. *101 Things to Do in Wartime* recommended steaming and pressure-cooking to conserve fuel and prevent the loss of water-soluble vitamins such as B and C. A three-tier steamer could accommodate an entire meal, although new metal cookware was scarce during the war years.[54]

Rationing reflected the tension between civilian wants and military demands, and as the national beverage, tea brewed from the leaves of *Thea sinensis* posed a particular conundrum. Fearing shortages and possible hoarding, Ministry officials seized control of all supplies a few days after war was declared on Germany, closed the London tea market, and established ceiling prices for wholesale and retail sales. The situation clearly reflected national preferences; unlike the U.S., coffee was never rationed in England during the war. An early proposal suggested replacing individual brands with a national wartime tea blend, but immediate public outcry resulted in these plans being dropped. Many remembered with contempt the fixed-price blend known as National Control Tea sold during World War I. The war in the Pacific posed additional complications for the tea market, but colonial growers in India and Ceylon (now Sri Lanka) continued to export to England, supplying about 95 percent of needed supplies in 1940. The rest of wartime tea that year came from British East Africa, while the Ministry of Food monitored the worldwide tea market.

Predicting brisk sales, Horniman's Tea issued its "Special Wartime Catalogue of Free Gifts" in 1940. Once Germany invaded the Low Countries in May 1940, tea from the Dutch East Indies became available at low prices to the English market. Axis countries knew of this British need; Italian propaganda portrayed the English as weakened by excessive amounts of afternoon tea. As early as 1937, a fascist Italian exhibition ridiculed the tea custom as bourgeois.[55] Tea supplies varied for the duration of the war, and housewives endeavored to brew the maximum volume from the weekly ration of two ounces of tea per adult, which would have yielded about twenty cups, perhaps a few more if the leaves were boiled for a second brewing. Shortages encouraged interest in tea herbs, including medicinal species in use since ancient times, and some followed the suggestion of Marguerite Patten to collect and dry blackberry leaves which she described as "Delicious and very like India tea."[56] Known as brambles, the leaves of blackberries and raspberries (*Rubus* spp.) do contain tannins and flavonoids similar to those in *Thea sinensis*. Other traditional tea herbs included peppermint, chamomile, and hyssop.

Commercial additives promised to extract more from the tea ration, but these did not deliver. One product that claimed one hundred more cups from a pound of tea leaves turned out to be nothing more than 90 percent sodium bicarbonate.[57] It may have persuaded some that more tea flavor was actually extracted because the alkalinity of sodium bicarbonate altered the color reflected by the tea tannins known as thearubigins. These polyphenolic compounds produce dark-colored negative ions when tea brewed in water with a high pH and a paler shade of brown when acidity (such as lemon juice) is added.

Although tea alone provides few nutrients, there were nutritional implications of the tea shortage. Tea consumed with milk and sugar supplied both vitamins and calories and was an essential part of the light supper (a meal known as tea) served in many English homes. However, artificial milk (often nothing more than flour suspended in water) often substituted for canned milk, and reduced sugar rations meant limited amounts for tea. Saccharin was a wartime sugar substitute derived from coal tar (see Chapter 9), used for both tea and cookery. There was not the same suspicion of carcinogenesis as in Germany, and some tried to stretch their sugar ration by adding crushed saccharin tablets. In contrast, the compo tea favored by British military was prepared with plenty of real sugar and genuine canned milk, both home front luxuries until well after the war. Tea shortages persisted for several years after the war, and rationing finally ended in October 1952.[58]

Honey could supply the tea table, and households with gardens were encouraged to try their hand with bee-keeping. *101 Things to Do in Wartime* noted that "bee-keeping is a profitable occupation and in war-time it is especially useful owing to the considerable food value of honey, and its value in replacing sugar for many purposes."[59] The Ministry of Agriculture offered advice pamphlets on building and maintaining hives. Moreover, bees were also reliable pollinators of garden crops, but the space for gardens and hives exceeded the means of many urban working poor who had tea as their evening meal.

A concurrent point system controlled access to other high demand items, including Lend-Lease goods such

Tea was a critical commodity in wartime England. With shortages possible, there was an early proposal to replacing individual brands with a national wartime tea blend, resulting in immediate public outcry. Colonial growers in India, Ceylon (now Sri Lanka), and British East Africa supplied their wartime tea crops to England.

as canned vegetables (beans, peas, and tomatoes), canned and dried fruit, and dried peas, as well as biscuits and breakfast cereal. The point system discouraged food hoarding by those who could afford to buy in bulk, helping to preserve good morale and a sense of fairness. In fact, some aspects of rationing policy pivoted on morale; for instance, pickles, relishes, and various sauces were never rationed because they were considered essential to appealing meals that encouraged home front optimism. Biscuit types decreased from 350 to twenty varieties, but some kinds were always available because many considered biscuits and tea an essential part of their evening meal. Beer and ale also fed morale, although the barley used in brewing could have fed millions of chickens, enough to supply several more eggs to the weekly family ration. Breweries remained open, with *de facto* daily rations of no more than a cup or a pint of diluted ale, depending on supplies.

Chocolate was in chronically short supply, with queues forming at shops that received small shipments. As in the U.S., most chocolate was supplied to British troops as part of their rations. Shortages were felt acutely by a nation that enjoyed sweets; according to Frances Blackwood, an American newspaperwoman who spent six weeks in

England during 1942, chocolate was the one food that the English missed most. Candy bars were coveted gifts, and some families "would cache bits of cooking chocolate and allow themselves a tiny nibble each night after dinner."[60] As a substitute, cookbooks suggested mixing up a chocolate spread from cocoa powder and cooked potato. These few luxuries aside, most meals depended on locally grown crops that demanded clever cookery and flavoring to prevent a sense of repetition.

Food shortages and queues were commonplace, so availability resulted in *de facto* rationing, as was often the case with imported fruits and vegetables. Oranges, lemons, and bananas vanished from ports, as did other tropical and warm weather crops such as almonds, coconuts, tapioca, and spices. The few available oranges were reserved as a valued source of vitamin C for children and expectant mothers; peels were saved for marmalade and for flavoring bland dishes such as potatoes. Adults resorted to orange juice substitutes that were nothing more than citric acid dissolved in water. Greengrocers continued to display bunches of artificial bananas; by the end of the war, dry banana powder appeared on the shelves, but it was not popular. Former and current colonies shipped food to England, but fresh fruit was impractical to send by ship because of its weight and volume. For instance, apples from Nova Scotia were dehydrated or converted to vitamin-enriched juice before being sent to England.

American Lend-Lease shipments included canned and dehydrated foods packaged for efficient shipping (see Chapter 3). Fear of a German invasion in 1940 caused further concern, but Lord Woolton, Minister of Food, assured the civilian population that there was sufficient stored food to provide for weeks of basic rations. Government supplies were often stored in suburban locales, although food was often most needed in city neighborhoods where centralized feeding stations provided meals after bombing raids. Damaged foodstuffs were salvaged for use, but it was not uncommon to find bits of glass and metal in stored reserves. Eighty percent of bombed food stores were salvaged and used; badly damaged flour made its way into dog biscuits, and tainted grains were fed to farm animals.

Shortages were exacerbated in December 1941 with the entry of Japan into the war and subsequent Japanese occupation of Pacific locales. Asian tea and rice imports dwindled, and similar shortages occurred with sugar and tropical oils, including the Malaysian palm oil used to manufacture soap. Minister of Food Lord Woolton requested that Nigeria, then a British colony, ship peanuts to England; 400,000 tons provided both cooking oil and peanut butter for sandwiches, which were typical "shelter snacks" during evening bombing raids. Oil palms (*Elaies guineenensis*) yield oil from both the seeds and inner fruit wall (mesocarp); the Allies used the latter, a rich source of palmitic oil, in manufacturing margarine, soap, and bombs. Soybean and other vegetable oils substituted in margarine production, but palmitic oil (in the form of an aluminum salt) was used as a gelling agent for petroleum in the development of napalm, which fueled both flamethrowers and incendiary bombs. Salts of naphthenic acid (derived from the refining of crude oil, with chemistry traceable to ancient marine phytoplankton) were combined with the salts of palmitic acid, the origin of the term *napalm*. As the war progressed, even the Japanese suffered palm oil shortages. According to U.S bomb disposal personnel, their Japanese counterparts were able to disassemble unexploded bombs and save the napalm oil mixture for soap manufacture.[61]

Early in the war, an appointed Scientific Food Committee calculated the minimum food needed for civilian survival and presented it as a "basal diet," consisting of vegetables (potatoes provided most of the 2000 daily calories), oatmeal, and bread, augmented by a weekly half pint of milk and single ounce of fat. The SFC plan was to use the basal diet as the basis for food rationing, but Churchill opposed the scheme as depressingly stringent, which perhaps reflected his own relationship with food. With access to vegetables and meat raised or hunted at Chartwell, his family estate, he was able to eat comparatively well during the war years. Georgina Landemare volunteered to cook for Churchill and his wife during the war, and in 1958 she published her wartime recipes as *Recipes from No. 10*, recently republished as *Churchill's Kitchen*.[62] As a skilled cook, she had kitchens at 10 Downing Street and at the Cabinet War Rooms, an underground London bunker. Churchill's food preferences ran to the best, and Landemere did her utmost to provide dishes that made good use of common foods prepared in a superior way. Her soups used potatoes, cabbage, carrots, onions, beans, and swedes (also known as rutabagas, the result of probable ancient hybridization between turnips and kale or cabbage); main courses involved meat, often rabbit and mutton from Chartwell, dressed with sauces and vegetables.

Bread flour remained a concern because wheat imports occupied most of the cargo area on ships coming to England. German U-boats menaced ships carrying wheat from Australia and New Zealand, resulting in shortages of wheat flour. In particular, bread availability posed a major shift for working-class British for whom the standard evening meal was "bread and scrape," white bread spread with margarine or drippings, accompanied by hot tea with sugar and canned milk. Sugar, tea, canned milk, margarine, and meat (the source of drippings) were all stringently rationed. Fats were in such short supply that some cookbooks suggested using refined mineral oil (known as liquid paraffin) in baking and frying. The oil is a mixture of alkanes derived from petroleum distillates, considered edible, but it interfered with the uptake of fat soluble vitamins such as A and D and may have been carcinogenic. Petroleum results from deposits of phytoplankton and other organisms under deep sedimentary deposits.

The Ministry of Food discouraged any form of food waste such as feeding bread crusts and crumbs to domesticated pigs, and wartime leaflets featured wheat-conserving recipes that used stale bread to stretch meat rations, make puddings, and convert into fairy toast (thin toasted bread) or dried cubes ("wheatmealies") to eat with a bit of milk and sugar. Meanwhile bread boxes nationwide were scrubbed and aired to prevent spoilage caused by bread mold. Another dietary option was to eat more homegrown English potatoes as a source of carbohydrates, energy, and vitamins; nutritionally speaking, both bread and potatoes provide carbohydrates and vitamins. In the Food Flash film "Now Wait a Minute," the Ministry of Food delivered a succinct message: Save ships by eating potatoes instead of bread.

Another conservation strategy involved baking with whole grain flour, although most English consumers much preferred white bread with a homogeneous texture. The Ministry of Food encouraged millers to process more of the entire grain, rather than removing the wheat germ (embryo) and outer bran layer, a process that yielded darker, more textured flour. The extraction rate quantified the amount of the grain converted to flour; white flour had an extraction rate of 70 percent, although by 1941, the recommended level increased slightly to 75 percent. By 1942, the Ministry of Food launched a campaign to convert all flour and bread to whole meal status, which increased overall yield of both flour and vitamins compared to an equal quantity of grain milled into white flour. Calorie content was not affected because bran is largely undigestible cellulose, but increased mass (approximately 12–15 percent of the original grain weight) was added to on hand flour supplies by the milling of the outer grain layers.

The product was known as national flour, with a mandated extraction rate of 85 percent for much of the war, and it was milled from imported and British wheat. It was baked into loaves of wartime national bread and was the flour available for general home use. Vitamin content increased in proportion to extraction rate; for instance, levels of thiamine were approximately nine times higher in national flour than in pre-war white flour. Thiamine (also known as vitamin B1) was of particular interest in wartime as a metabolic compound associated with morale and mental health (see Chapter 3). Rumors circulated that Hitler planned to subdue enemy and occupied countries through blockade-induced thiamine deficiencies, so from a defense perspective, national flour should have been welcomed. Some medical doctors even predicted an increase in fertility as a result of the high levels of vitamin E in the whole grain flour; they postulated that the consumption of vitamin-E deficient white bread since the 1870s had caused a decrease in the national birthrate.

Public displeasure with national bread was patent. As M.F.K. Fisher noted in her wartime food memoir, *How to Cook a Wolf*, typical British households considered white bread a sign of refinement. Most disliked the slightly darker color and coarser texture that resulted from milled bits of germ and bran, and the loaves were described as gray and mushy.[63] Bread was not sold until the day after baking, so that slices were thinner and more uniform, but housewives still complained that national bread sliced poorly and dried quickly. Many considered jam, much of it produced by the Women's Institutes (see Chapter 3), essential in making national bread palatable. Nonetheless, in contrast to pre-war white loaves, national bread was more nutritious and did not require the addition of synthetic thiamine.

By 1942 government policy required the addition of 10 percent of other English grains (barley, oats, and rye) or potato starch into national bread in an effort to "dilute" wheat supplies and avoid bread rationing, However, the Ministry of Food aimed for loaves that were uniform in quality and so expected all of the national flour to have consistent proportions of grains. Government subsidized oats were cheap and plentiful, but the grains required special machinery to remove the outer husk layers, yielding only a 40 percent extraction rate. Moreover, oats were needed to feed horses in some areas of the country. Barley was needed for brewing, and potatoes yielded a crude flour substitute. The effect of wheat dilution on the national loaf was demoralizing, but helped to keep bread freely available for the duration of the war, although a postwar grain shortage resulted in bread rationing between 1946 and 1948.[64]

In home kitchens, cooks were encouraged to experiment with alternatives to wheat flour. Cakes mixed up with national flour were too dense, but housewives soon learned that they could lighten the batter by adding imported corn flour, which was in sufficiently high demand that it was controlled by the point system. As an advisor for the Ministry of Food, Marguerite Patten devised ways to incorporate oats into familiar recipes for bread, buns, cakes, scones, and biscuits.[65] Oven-toasted oats substituted for imported nuts, and soups and stews were thickened with oatmeal, including a meatless wartime soup made from oatmeal, milk, onions, and carrots. Imported American soy flour was available, and cooks were advised to mix it with water to make an egg substitute for baking. They could also cook with soyaghetti, a version of spaghetti made from American soy flour, and purchased sausages contained a high percentage of soy flour. However, the favorite use for soy flour was nonessential; mixed with margarine and almond essence, milled soybeans could be molded into cake decorations that somewhat resembled marzipan.

A relentless campaign promoted cooking and eating vegetable crops grown in victory gardens and farms. The Ministry of Food organized a Food Advice Department that offered cookery instruction in markets, canteens, factories, hospitals, schools, and shops. Ministry posters, pamphlets, bulletins, and films delivered the sustained message that English-grown vegetables promised a healthy wartime diet. Potatoes and carrots stretched meat rations with essential vitamins and carbohydrates, providing the nutritional scaffolding for many meals. Both were categorized as energy (high carbohydrate) and protective (high vitamin) foods. Potatoes stored copious starch, and the freshly dug rhizomes also provided much needed vitamin C. As biennials, carotene-rich carrots stored sugars in their robust taproots, which fueled the second season of growth, flowering, and seed production.

Ministry of Food leaflets and bulletins used cartoon characters to remind civilians (children especially) to eat their vegetables, but with little meat in the weekly ration, there was minimal choice aside from homegrown produce. Peeling was discouraged to save calories and vitamins, and Potato Pete was often drawn with the caption, "Good taste demands I keep my jacket on."[66] The character promoted potatoes as a key ingredient for thrifty main dishes and alternative to bread baked from imported wheat, and they appeared at virtually every meal—boiled, baked, fried, stuffed, or mixed into pastry or pies. The "Song of Potato Pete" reminded consumers that versatile potatoes could replace imported wheat; it was recorded as a popular song:

> Potatoes new, potatoes old
> Potato (in a salad) cold
> Potatoes baked or mashed or fried
> Potatoes whole, potatoes pied
> Enjoy them all, including chips
> Remembering spuds don't come in ships!

Dr. Carrot and a cartoon family drawn by Disney artist Hank Porter (Carroty George, Pop Carrot, and Clara Carrot) encouraged civilians to eat plenty of carrots. Posters reminded civilians of night-blindness and bombing raid blackouts, a potentially fatal combination, and extolled carrot benefits to eyesight: "Carrots keep you healthy and help you to see in the blackout" and "Night sight can mean life or death." Better vision became an incentive for carrot consumption on both the home front and battlefront. Carrots contain carotenes, the starting point for vitamin A synthesis, which contributes to the production of rhodopsin that is essential for normal color and low-light vision. In reality, carrots cannot improve vision beyond normal limits, as wartime propaganda implied. Even though vitamin A claims were grossly overstated, the message was clear: Carrots thrived in the English climate and put food on the table; they could win the war, if they were eaten in sufficient amounts.

The Ministry of Food encouraged carrot cookery in every possible way, including soups, stews, curries, casseroles, pancakes, and salads, often combined with potatoes and other vegetables. Marguerite Patten suggested carrot-cap salad (boiled potatoes topped with shredded carrots and dressed with vinegar and oil), potato basket (a potato crust filled with cooked carrots), and carrot sandwiches (grated or cooked carrots combined with celery, cabbage, chutney, curry, etc.)[67] Lord Woolton pie, named for the Minister of

Food, featured root crops (carrots, parsnips, turnips, potatoes, and swedes) covered with an oatmeal crust. Its successful preparation pivoted on liberal seasoning or flavorful gravy, and onion was essential in the otherwise bland filling. Variations of the recipe appeared widely, including a version flavored with bacon rind, bay leaf, and nutmeg which was featured in *Life* magazine as typical of the British wartime diet.[68]

Carrolade (also known as carolene), regarded as a substitute for orange juice, was made from the juice of sugared, grated carrots and swedes pressed through muslin. Mock apricot flan used potato or oatmeal pastry filled with cooked carrots mixed with a few spoons of plum jam and flavored with almond essence; Marguerite Patten noted that "The carrots really do taste a little like apricots," no doubt due to the addition of almond for flavor.[69] Almonds, plums, and apricots are all species of the genus *Prunus* that produce cyanogenic glycosides and similar essential oils. Carrots were preserved in low-sugar jam and marmalade mixtures, where they helped to stretch scarce citrus supplies. The Easter 1941 Pathé newsreel showed children with large toffee-dipped carrots on sticks, a wartime substitute for ice cream, conveying a subtle message that carrot consumption was enjoyable. Even carrot leaves were recommended for soups and salads, although mature plants may have had some slight alkaloid toxicity.

Most of the nutrition in carrot taproots was in the storage cells of the cortex, the darkly pigmented layer surrounding the core of water-conducting xylem cells. Victory

In England, carrots were an essential wartime crop used in main dishes, salads, sandwiches, baked goods, marmalades, and carrolade (also known as carolene), a substitute for orange juice. The Easter 1941 Pathé newsreel showed children with large toffee-dipped carrots on sticks, conveying a subtle message that carrot consumption was enjoyable (Pathé).

garden crops were grown to maximum size, and thus after months of growth, a cambium layer formed around the original xylem core of herbaceous carrot roots. Cell divisions in the cambium increased root diameter by developing secondary xylem, also known as wood; in short, carrots became hard and tough when they were grown for an entire season. However, they could be combined in infinite ways with cabbage and potatoes, two other highly productive crops that could be harvested at will. For instance, in a wartime version of the Irish dish known as champ, cooked carrots and cabbage were mounded on mashed potatoes and seasoned with salt, pepper, and a bit of margarine.

Countless other British recipes relied on the vegetable trio of carrots, cabbages, and potatoes, essential to food security during the war, but none of the species was indigenous to England. Carrots (a cultivated variety of *Daucus carota*, known commonly as Queen Anne's lace) originated in Asia, and the Moors introduced them to Europe. Romans introduced cabbages (*Brassica oleracea*) from the Mediterranean region; each plant is a massive terminal bud that unfurls and flowers during the second season of biennial growth. Wartime recipes also included Brussels sprouts, a cultivar of the same species, characterized by a robust stalk with axillary buds resembling miniature cabbages. Potatoes originated in the Andes where they were discovered by 16th century Spanish explorers, and sailors adopted them as fare that prevented scurvy. Within a hundred years, they spread into England and Ireland where they were favored as a source of cheap calories for feeding the poor. M.F.K. Fisher observed that "potatoes are one of the last things to disappear, in times of war, which is probably why they should not be forgotten in times of peace."[70]

Many vegetable-based recipes from the Ministry of Food and other sources were time-consuming and complicated to prepare. Women had war jobs that filled daytime hours, stood in queues for rationed foods, often were the sole caretakers for children and elderly parents, and sheltered at night during blackouts and bombing raids. Complex cookery instructions were one more wartime responsibility, at a time when food (mostly vegetables) was limited in scope and supply. Mature crops often required long simmering to become palatable, despite advice from the Ministry of Food to preserve vitamins by quick cooking in minimal water. Fuel shortages posed another problem, but hay box cookery provided a thrifty option for those who could improvise with household materials. In anticipation of wartime fuel shortages, herbalist, gardener, and prolific author Eleanor Sinclair Rohde published *Hay Box Cookery*, and her methods were shared and published widely.[71] Instructions called for lining a wooden box (such as a

9

Originally introduced to England by the Romans, cabbages were an essential ingredient in the vegetable-based recipes provided by the Ministry of Food; combined with carrots and potatoes, they were the mainstay of many meals. A Ministry of Food short film "Two Cooks and a Cabbage" demonstrated that quick steaming yielded the most vitamin-rich cooked vegetable.

lead-foil lined tea chest) with several sheets of newspaper, followed by several inches of hay packed tightly on the bottom and sides. A covered soup pot nested in the middle, covered by a cloth pillow stuffed with more hay. It was essential to bring the pot to a boil on the stove and then to place it immediately in the hay box so that heat was retained and cooking continued for hours. Several inches of hay insulation kept the covered pot quite hot, but success required that the box be kept closed for several hours. As with other means of fireless cookery, the technique required planning ahead. Porridge put in the haybox at night would be ready for breakfast, and soups and stews could simmer all day.

Hay box cookery was botanical in both form and function: vegetable-based meals simmered in hay-insulated wooden boxes. The method suited soups, stews, porridge, root crops, and dried peas and beans that required long cooking times. Lacking hay, cooks used newspaper, blankets, and carpeting to achieve the same effect. The Ministry of Food provided instructions for making a portable hay box from a gas-mask carrier (or alternately a large biscuit tin), which served as an insulated lunchbox for hot dishes. In the pamphlet "Your Anderson Shelter This Winter" (1940), the Ministry of Home Security recommended insulating a glass bottle for hot drinks while sheltering at night.[72]

Wartime conditions created challenges for obtaining, preparing, and serving food, and ingenuity and compromise were essential. Crops cultivated alongside railway tracks supplied the staff canteens of the London Passenger Transport Board, and food stores were used regardless of bombing and surrounding destruction. It was not uncommon to find potatoes or cabbages with embedded shards of glass or metal. Bombing caused chaos in areas where homes were destroyed, leaving survivors with neither shelter nor food. First aid manuals recommended hot tea with sugar as an antidote to shock among bombing survivors, but food was also needed—sometimes for weeks after a raid. Mobile canteens, built to order by Ford for the British War Relief Society, ventured into bombed neighborhoods to serve soup, baked beans, and sandwiches prepared from available supplies. Each mobile canteen had two 25-gallon vacuum-jacketed containers that retained heat, much like huge hayboxes, with volume to feed 250 people. Convoys of canteens and lorries loaded with food supplies and Soyer stoves remained in bombed neighborhoods until families secured shelter. Victorian chef Alexis Soyer pioneered the use of these portable stoves during the Crimean War, and during the Blitz they were managed by the Women's Volunteer Service and The Queen's Messengers. Each lightweight unit consisted of a drum and furnace that could be fueled by botanical fuels such as coal, peat, and wood (see Chapter 9), as well as gas and animal dung. Soyer stoves were suitable for baking bread and other foods on site.

By 1943, over two thousand British Restaurants were serving 600,000 meals daily, often in schools converted for feeding and housing residents displaced by bombing. Vegetables provided most of the nutrition because in keeping with their wartime policy, Ministry of Food communal feeding centers prepared meals with just single servings of animal protein—meat, eggs, milk, *or* cheese. According to Frances Blackwood, an American newspaperwoman who spent six weeks in England during 1942, British Restaurant meals were as good as those served in private restaurants, suggesting that rationing and stringencies affected all social levels, regardless of income or status.[73] However, food preferences did reveal class differences and pre-war deprivations. For instance, a survey of children from the Limehouse school in East London revealed their desire for chipped (fried) potatoes, pickled beets, and fried onions, and a nearly universal dislike of cooked root crops such as carrots, turnips, and parsnips. Many of these children preferred canned pineapple, peaches, and blackberries over fresh fruit, which many of them had never seen.[74] One healthy option for school children was the Oslo or health meal (see Chapter 2). Consisting of unlimited servings of salad and whole grain bread, accompanied by milk and cheese, in terms of nutrients it far surpassed the suppers of "bread and scrape" (white bread and margarine or drippings) that caused many vitamin deficiencies.

Not all urban children remained with their families. Beginning in 1939, the Committee on Evacuation organized a scheme to transport children, pregnant women, and infirm or elderly people to reception areas away from bombing raids. Most evacuees were children, and many left Dickensian poverty in cities such as London, Liverpool, and Glasgow for their first experience with rural village life. Often these children were scrubbed, deloused, and re-clothed before acclimating to country settings. Host families were encouraged to billet as many children as they could accommodate, with the support of the Women's Voluntary Service, local Women's Institutes, and local evacuation officers. In *A.R.P.—Air Raid Precautions*, British geneticist J.B.S. Haldane speculated that evacuation of schools was the most efficient option. Children followed their teachers' instructions, and there were enough country estates and farms within one hundred miles of London to billet most London children of school age. In fact, entire schools did evacuate to the countryside during the war years.[75]

Food for billeted youth posed a challenge, and advice abounded. Home cooks were encouraged to feed their evacuees a diet of mostly potatoes, bread, legumes, root crops, and steamed vegetables, including economical pies with plenty of vegetables and minimal meat or fish.[76] Bisto, a pre-war product that promised flavorful gravy, advertised its use specifically for stretching meat supplies: "Your evacuees! To make the most and get the best out of every scrap of meat, use Bisto."

Over time, evacuated children became accustomed to rural life and country food, and some helped with farm work such as apple picking, harvesting hops, and mowing fields. There were nevertheless dangers that came with hoards of city children transplanted to the country, sometimes with minimal daytime supervision. Newspaper articles reminded host families to warn their evacuees about the dangers of eating wild fruit— especially red and black berries—because several toxic species thrive in English gardens and hedgerows. For instance, common yew shrubs (*Taxus baccata*) produce the toxic alkaloid taxine. Its red arils (berry-like outgrowths from the base of each seed) are non-toxic, but hungry children could easily have ingested enough of the poisonous seeds to become nauseous and even convulse. Nightshades posed another hazard; the black berries of *Solanum nigrum* and the red berries of *S. dulcamara* both contain the toxic alkaloid solanine that causes vomiting and hallucinations. Even the red berries of holly (*Ilex aquifolium*) and the black berries of ivy (*Hedera helix*) contain a potent mix of secondary compounds that could sicken a child.

Something from Nothing

War demanded some unexpected strategies, and self-sufficiency, humor, and patriotism all played parts in encouraging compliance with Ministry of Food policies. Food conservation was an essential part of the Ministry of Food message; a familiar poster reminded consumers, "Better Potluck with Churchill today than humble pie under Hitler tomorrow—Don't waste food!" Cooks were encouraged to avoid peeling vegetables to conserve vitamins and to use all edible trimmings in cookery, such as a simple soup made of peapods, boiled until tender and sieved into a puree.[77] With the exception of solanine-rich potato leaves, the green tops of root crops such as radishes, beets, turnips, and carrots were used in making soups and salads. There was some legitimate concern about consuming carrot leaves, which some gardeners knew as phototoxic; an allergic rash can develop if the wet carrot tops are collected and handled in bright sunlight. The reaction results from skin contact with falcarinol, a naturally-occurring antifungal compound, but eating reasonable amounts of carrot foliage was quite safe.

Cooking water contained soluble vitamins, and it was saved for cooking or drinking. M.F.K. Fisher suggested collecting vegetable water in an old gin bottle and mixing it with lemon or tomato juice. Even parsley stems could be steeped in hot water and added to the mixture, which she described as a "veritable treasure jug for vitamins and minerals that otherwise would have gone down the drain."[78] Writing in a somewhat subversive tone, probably in reaction to the barrage of advice from the Ministry of Food, she advocated balancing vitamins over the day—rather than insisting that each meal contain each known vitamin. She suggested simple no-meat menus such as green salads or hot cereal with syrup and fruit and preached a message of upbeat wartime gastronomy, despite strict rationing.

Foraging for edible wild plants was another option. The Ministry of Food published "Hedgerow Harvest" (1943) to encourage the collection of wild nuts and fruits to supplement home front food supplies.[79] These hedges that border agricultural fields were planted hundreds of years ago; they have grown into biodiverse, semi-wild habitats in which shrubs and small trees reseed to form a dense thicket of brambles (*Rubus* spp.) and other woody species. Hedgerow fruit suitable for home jam-making (see Chapter 3) included rowans (*Sorbus aucuparia*), elderberries (*Sambucus niger*), sloes (*Prunus spinosa*), and hawthorns (*Crataegus* spp.) Collectors were cautioned to treat the hedgerow plants with care, "None of this harvest should be wasted, but be exceedingly careful how you gather it in … don't injure the bushes or trees." However, care had to be taken to avoid the red berries of black bryony (*Dioscorea communis*), a tropical yam relative that colonizes the dense hedges and contains highly toxic saponins. In rural areas, children collected wild fruits that grew along roads and in fields and hedgerows, including elderberries, whortleberries, and mulberries. Nothing edible went to waste; along with acorns and beechnuts, windfall fruit too damaged for the jam pot provided food for pigs, which were often fattened and shared among families as a means to supplement the meat ration.

Anticipating food shortages, women's magazines urged their readers to forage. Native nuts included chestnuts, walnuts, cobnuts, and filberts; even beechnuts replaced almonds in some wartime recipes. Chestnut trees (*Castanea sativa*) were a Roman introduction that quickly naturalized in hedgerows; along with walnuts (*Juglans regia*) they were saved for holiday use by packing them in crocks layered with sand. Cobnuts are the fruit of common hazel (*Corylus avellana*), a close relative of filberts (*C. maxima*), and both were prolific in hedgerow habitats. The nuts were husked and layered in salt. Elderberry and hawthorn flowers could be fermented into wine, and oxalic acid in sorrel (*Rumex acetosa*) imparted a lemon-like flavor; a quarter pound of the leaves flavored an entire pot of broth-based soup. In *They Can't Ration These*, Vicomte de Mauduit argued that wild foods could feed many during wartime stringencies, if the English just knew what to collect.[80] Dandelion and nasturtium flowers and leaves made vitamin-rich salads, and mushrooms were another wild option, presuming that the collector could recognize the nontoxic species. He recommended soup made from nettles (*Urtica dioecia*), also used for their medicinal properties and bast fibers (see Chapters 7 and 8). Cooking disarmed the notorious stinging trichomes (hairs), and protein accounted for up to 25 percent of the dried weight. Another option was samphire, an inclusive common name for succulent, salt tolerant species such as *Crithmum maritimum*, *Inula crithmifolia*, and *Salicornia europaea*, which could be cooked like potherbs, sliced into salads, or pickled. Their succulent habit evolved from selective pressure to conserve water under salty growth conditions, in which osmosis causes plant tissues to dehydrate. Even before the war years, fish mongers in coastal towns included these edible species in decorative window displays.

Mauduit even recommended dried grass stalks as a vegetable for human consumption, referring to claims made by American chemists that twelve pounds of hay

Foraging for edible wild plants was promoted by the Ministry of Food, but care had to be taken to avoid the red berries of black bryony, a tropical yam relative that colonizes hedgerows and contains highly toxic saponins.

contained as many vitamins as 340 pounds of fruits and vegetables. Of course, these calculations ignored the absence of cellulose-digesting enzymes or cellulolytic bacteria in human stomachs, meaning that much of the grass tissue would have remained intact even after passing through the alimentary canal. Nevertheless, edible grasses could help to prevent scurvy and other deficiency diseases, and they were routinely eaten by prisoners of war as a vitamin source (see Chapter 11). In the preface, David Lloyd George described *They Can't Ration These* as "a valuable contribution towards our national defence," but Mauduit was later imprisoned in England for treasonous talk, ending up in Dachau where he died at the end of the war. German bombing raids caused the proliferation of an edible species that colonized burned sites. Rosebay willow herb, also known as fireweed (*Chamaenerion angustifolium*, syn. *Epilobium angustifolium*, see Chapter 11), blanketed bombed sites; young shoots could be eaten like asparagus, and mature leaves were used as a green vegetable. Even after the war, books such as *British Herbs and Vegetables* (1947) continued to mention "neglected wild species" such as samphire and rosebay willow herb as potential foods during a time of ongoing shortages and rationing.[81]

An ongoing challenge to the home cook was how closely she could approximate pre-war dishes using unrationed foods, and there were many opportunities to experiment. Cookbooks and magazines suggested simulating meat and egg dishes with botanical substitutions; potatoes could bulk up an eggless mayonnaise, and mock sausages were shaped from seasoned lentils and potatoes. Once shortages occurred because many fishermen entered the Navy, mock fish dishes were made from rice flavored with anchovy essence. Despite wartime conditions, the Ministry of Food urged festive holiday observances. Traditional fare was considered essential for morale, but pre-war Christmas meals were nearly impossible during a time of rationing and shortages. In her *Book of Household Management*, Isabella Beeton described roast fowl with sage and onion stuffing; the Romans introduced sage from the Mediterranean region to England, and the flavorful terpenes of sage were essential to simulating the taste of genuine roasted fowl in the English fashion. Thus wartime versions of mock goose and mock duck were molded from mashed lentils, potatoes, and apples, seasoned liberally with sage and onion; correct seasoning was essential to culinary memory, and herbs such as sage were easily grown in gardens and allotments. Cooks used apples, carrots, potatoes and oatmeal to replace imported fruits and nuts in traditional Christmas puddings, and Cecil Middleton (see Chapter 2) recommended that gardeners excavate rhubarb roots and force them in greenhouses as a substitute for fruit. Christmas cookery leaflets from the Ministry of Food suggested colorful beetroot and carrot salads and savory vegetable pastries, and magazines featured cakes mixed up from national flour and iced to resemble the Anderson shelters in many suburban gardens. Traditional simnel cakes, essential to Lenten observances of Mothering Sunday, were sweetened with marmalade (probably made from carrots) and decorated with mock marzipan made from soy flour, margarine, and almond essence.

England survived despite the food stringencies of the war years, but rationing of various foods continued for nearly a decade. Meat rationing ended in 1954, following a decade of austerity that included the rationing of bread and potatoes after extensive postwar crop failures and spoilage. Chicago attorney, author, and experimental farmer Ezra Parmalee Prentice considered the long term effects of austerity on health and development.[82] He feared that the English were consuming a deficient diet that resembled pre-nineteenth century meals of "bread and relishes," referring to the salted eels and fish that flavored a largely bread diet. Beef and fats were scarce, and the value of botanical vitamins was not understood; in short, he observed that malnutrition was a scourge of early England but improved during the nineteenth century. Prentice drew parallels with postwar England, noting that "rationing in England is severe, and the effects of undernourishment may be expected soon to show in the offspring of undernourished parents."[83] His concern centered on the effect of nutrition on intelligence because he speculated that deficient diet might affect intelligence and industry, comparing the situation to the stunted ponies that graze on depauperate pastures in the Shetland Islands.

The farming interests of Prentice and his wife, Alta Rockefeller Prentice, centered on using agricultural genetics to prevent worldwide famine. At Mount Hope Farm in Williamstown, Massachusetts, they bred cattle and chickens and grew grains, vegetables, and fruit—scientific agriculture that portended the Green Revolution. Nevertheless Prentice overlooked the vitamin-rich botanical foods that bolstered English meals, or perhaps he believed that meat was essential to nutrition. During the war years, the English diet shifted toward fruits and vegetables; meat became a condiment rather than a staple, and plants comprised the backbone of most meals. Gardening and farming continued out of necessity, so there were still plenty of cabbages, carrots, and legumes, and communal meals shared nutritious food fairly among the urban poor. On balance, although the English were lean after the war, they were healthy and devoid of deficiency diseases.

The German Home Front

Official German policy extolled the value of a vegetable diet as the key to good health, and healthy civilians were essential to the Reich. Propaganda posters reminded all *"Dein Korper gehört dem Führer"* [Your body belongs to the Führer], and youth publications such as *Gesund durch richtige Ernährung* [Health through Proper Nutrition] promoted soybeans as a meat substitute. Moreover, according to the popular press, Hitler was a vegetarian. A *Homes and Gardens* magazine article noted, "A life-long vegetarian at table, Hitler's kitchen plots are both varied and heavy in produce. Even in his meatless diet, Hitler is something of a gourmet..."[84] Vegetables for his meals came from the farm that was part of the complex at Obersalzberg, a Bavarian settlement that Nazi officials took over during the 1930s and the location of Hitler's *Berghof* residence. Martin Bormann, one-time private secretary to Hitler, had established the farm as a model for the expansion of German farms in eastern Europe, but montane conditions and short growing season made its long success unlikely. The stony soil could not yield enough feed for the farm animals, but fruits and vegetables grew under glass; these were also shipped to the kitchen at the Führer headquarters in Prussia.[85]

Perhaps Hitler's diet was propagandized to encourage vegetable consumption. In rambling *Tischgespräche* (table talks) during 1941 and 1942, Hitler extolled a raw vegetable diet as promoting longevity and children's health, preventing cancer, and curing vitamin deficiencies such as beri-beri. However, an article in *The New York Times Magazine* noted that occasionally he "relishes a slice of ham ... and delicacies such as caviar."[86] By all accounts, he also had a rapacious taste for sweets, which apparently he theorized were good for the nerves. One cook recalled that Hitler favored in particular a dessert known by those around him as Führer cake, a single layer flavored with apples, raisins, and nuts.[87]

Hitler enjoyed asparagus in particular, but not without ridicule. A perennial crop, asparagus stalks were easy to harvest as young shoots, which became tough with maturity but were never truly woody. Asparagus (a monocot with scattered vascular bundles embedded in soft tissue) never differentiates a vascular cambium, the cell layer that divides to make wood, so unlike many mature crops asparagus remains relatively succulent. Standard etiquette called for eating the stalks with a knife and fork, but Hitler followed the Bavarian tradition of sucking whole, cooked asparagus into his mouth, one at a time. In Heidelberg, a group of privileged university students mocked his manners.[88] The *Chicago Daily Tribune* reported that six of the offenders were punished at a concentration camp, and henceforth the term "asparagus-eater" referred to an opponent of the Nazi regime.[89]

A couple of other timely asparagus references are worth noting. A popular song in the early 1930s used asparagus as a phallic symbol, which Hitler may have recalled. In *"Veronika, der Lenz is Da"* [Veronika, Spring Has Arrived] the Comedian Harmonists sang of asparagus in spring, *"Veronika, der Spargel wächst, ach Du Veronika, die Welt ist grün, drum laß uns in die Wälder ziehn"* [Veronika, the asparagus is growing, Oh my Veronika, the world is green, So let's go wandering into the forests]. The sextet enjoyed spectacular success in pre-war Germany, but disbanded in 1934 when the Nazi regime censored songs and halted performances because of the singers' mixed Jewish and gentile backgrounds. By 1944, asparagus again appeared in the news, but this time as a military strategy against aerial invasion. *Rommelspargel* (Rommel's asparagus) were actually small trees, felled and erected as a vertical defense system in Normandy fields. Field Marshal Erwin Rommel ordered troops to install over one million of these logs and interlace them with barbed wire, planning that during an invasion the system would damage gliders and interfere with paratroopers (see Chapter 9).

Reich policy discouraged high meat consumption as a matter of food-chain efficiency. Ninety percent of the carbohydrate energy in grain is lost when it is fed to cattle, thus milling the grain for bread is vastly more efficient when many need to eat. Concern for public health was certainly another factor, likely stemming from Hitler's personal fear of cancer and his tendency toward hypochondria. Robert Proctor has convincingly linked the Nazi plan to fight cancer to Reich pro-vegetable food policy, presaging modern medicine.[90] In particular, stomach malignancies were on the rise during the decades preceding the war, perhaps due to the consumption of preserved meats, toxic food dyes, contaminants, adulterants, and aflatoxins (carcinogenic fungal toxins) in stored grains. Reich policy advocated a fresh botanical diet free from artificial colors such as coal tar dyes, with high fiber content, whole grain breads, and few fats. Herbal teas were encouraged over coffee (see Chapter 7), and alcohol was widely discouraged. Official policy disdained English cookery; radio propaganda from Berlin declared, "Thousands have died of the errors of English cooking. It has thrown humanity back by centuries in the field of morals."[91]

The German shift toward a botanical diet began with the distribution of ration cards in 1939. Limited meat rations (500–700 grams/person weekly) meant increased consumption of native-grown vegetables, and a one-pot (*Eintopf*), meat-flavored vegetable stew became the wartime norm. German-grown rye, rather than imported wheat, was baked into wartime bread. Using the money saved by serving one-pot meals on Sundays, well-off families were encouraged to donate to a winter relief fund for the poor (*Winterhilfswerk*). Rationing affected luxuries such as coffee, sugar, and jam, but eventually even staple starches like flour, bread, and potatoes were controlled. Limits on plant and animal fats (vegetable oils, margarine, butter, and lard) translated into bomb production because the triclyceride hydrolysis yielded glycerin, which combined with nitric acid produced the explosive nitroglycerin. During the 1860s and 1870s, Alfred Nobel experimented with combinations of nitroglycerin with diatomaceous earth (sedimentary deposits of the single-celled algae known as diatoms) and nitrocellulose to produce explosives, including dynamite and rocket propellants. In short, civilian limits on fried foods and pastry meant more German matériel to fight the Allies.

A battalion of government agencies and organizations controlled food rationing and wartime nutrition on the German home front, with overlapping influence and control. In addition to the *Reichsnährstand* (Reich Food Corporation) which oversaw food production and distribution, administrative offices included the *Reichsministerium für Ernährung und Landwirtschaft* (Ministry of Food and Agriculture), *Reichsgesundheitsamt* (Ministry of Health), *Reichsarbeitgemeinschaft für Volksernährung* (Reich Working Group for Public Nutrition), *Hauptamt für Volksgesundheit bei der Reichsleitung der NSDAP*

(Center for Public Health of the Reich Administration of the NSDAP), *Sachverständigenbeirat für Volksgesundheit* (Expert Commission on Public Health), and the *Reichausschuss für Volkswirtschaftliche Aufklarung* (Reich Committee for National Economic Education). Nazi party officials dictated food and agricultural policy, managed supplies, provided recipes and nutritional advice, and fought waste. They also imposed rationing and nutritional policy in Austria, following the March 1938 *Anschluss* in which the neighboring country was accessioned to Germany. As supplies ran low, food policy relied on the 1941–44 *Hungerplan* that prioritized food access for Germany over occupied countries. The plan mandated that Germans would never go hungry, with starvation planned and anticipated in occupied countries. Food (mostly grain) was exported from occupied regions of the Soviet Union to Germany for civilian and military use (see Chapter 11). Indeed Hitler's planned accession of the Ukraine stemmed from food deprivation during World War I and the desire to establish food security for Germany.

Nevertheless as the war progressed, rationing reflected shortages, and there were violent outbreaks at markets in German cities. According to the *Reichsgesundheitsführer* [Reich health leader] Dr. Leonardo Conti, daily calories dropped to 1,358 for a normal consumer (*Normalverbraucher*), which was insufficient for health and work. By 1945, the weekly bread ration dropped to about 2.5 pounds, from five pounds in 1939. Plant fats such as vegetable oils and margarine also dwindled, and meat was limited to less than a half pound weekly.[92] Thus German wartime cookery involved vegetables that were easily to cultivate and store in vast quantities: potatoes, cabbages, carrots, swedes, and dried legumes (pulses) comprised the nutritional backbone of the diet.

Older Germans recalled with anxiety the miserable *Kohlrübenwinter* [turnip winter] of 1916–17, in which daily meals depended almost entirely on *Brassica napus*, the turnip variety known also as rutabaga or swedes. The root crop was probably an ancient hybrid between two familiar vegetables, *B. campestris* (turnips) and *B. oleracea* (cabbage and kale), but many thought of the

Wartime cookery in Germany involved vegetables that were easily to cultivate and store in vast quantities, including the turnip variety known as swedes or rutabagas. The *Völkischer Beobachter*, the Nazi party newspaper, recommended using swedes in soups, stews, sauces, patties, vegetable dishes, salads, and even as a mueslitype cereal; there were also contests for the best swede recipes.

root crop as fodder. Swedes lacked the carbohydrate content and calories of potatoes, but they provided vitamins A and C and were filling and easy to store. German and Austrian civilians read articles in the *Völkischer Beobachter*, the Nazi party newspaper, that recommended swedes in soups, stews, sauces, patties, vegetable dishes, salads, and even as a muesli-type cereal; there were contests for the best swede recipes. Germanic tastes ran to meat and potatoes, and a defiant Viennese pundit authored a "swede creed" that mimicked the format and cadence of the Lutheran Apostles' Creed. It circulated underground, and Nazi leaders would have taken a dim view of the humor:

> I believe in the swede,
> The comprehensive diet of the German people.
> And in swede jam,
> Its worthy kin and companion,
> Conceived in the municipal sales stall,
> Born at the behest of the *Kreisnahrungssamt*,
> Which has caused all of my dreams of potatoes to die and be buried,
> Having suffered at the hands of extortionate farmers,
> Having been squashed and gone moldy as table fruit,
> From whence it will return as spread for Germany's heroic sons,
> I believe in war,
> The general society of blood suckers,
> The community of scroungers,
> The raising of taxes,
> The reduction of meat rations,
> And the eternal duration of bread ration cards.[93]

Many wartime meals were known as *hotchpotch*, a broad vernacular term for thickened vegetable soups and stews. Lower classes knew hotchpotch well; versions of it were closely related to the economy soup developed about 1800 by Sir Benjamin Thompson, an American physicist who emigrated to England and later Bavaria, where he served in German government. Thompson (later named Count Rumford) was charged with compounding a cheap, nutritious food for workhouses and military prisons. His plan known as the *Rumfordsche Suppe* nourished the poor with a barley-thickened mixture of potatoes, vegetables, pulse, and bread crumbs, traditionally served with a large piece of rye bread. The recipe crossed class lines, becoming the basis for many military meals prepared for the military and for the soup kitchens that Count Rumford started in German cities. Barley (*Hordeum vulgare*) was an essential ingredient; as cultivated grain dating back to the Fertile Crescent, it grew well under a wide variety of conditions and was long known in Europe as a peasant food. Most importantly, the amylopectins (branched starch molecules) in barley grains absorb copious water, converting thin soups into passable stews. Thus barley played a key role in massive feeding campaigns, both before and during the war. In the event of severe food shortages, there were Reich plans for centralized food preparation using coal-fired cauldrons to prepare hotchpotch from government caches.

Incidentally, the Swiss botanist Augustin Pyramus DeCandolle also recognized the plant-based nutrition of the *Rumfordsche Suppe* and organized a scheme to serve it to the poor in the years following the French Revolution. It is possible that cultural memory of this austerity vegetable meal persisted in France during World War II, when vegetable gardens saved many families and high-calorie soup would have been welcome. Through cooperation of the Vichy government, France sent about one-fifth of its food to Germany, at a time when agriculture also suffered due to lack of fertilizers, fuel, and labor.

Hitler extolled native fruits such as apples over imported oranges and bananas, a message of Germanic genetic superiority as it applied to the plant kingdom (see Chapter 12). Of course, promotion of native fruit was also a move toward autarky and away from dependence on shipping lanes. Civilians were encouraged to eat their fill of native fruit in season and to preserve the rest; the *Nationalsozialistische Frauenschaft* (National Socialist Women's League) organized classes in making fruit jams, pickling, and storing crops in hay-lined root cellars. Finding food was women's work, and meals were often concocted from minimal supplies because a shortage of workers meant that some crops were not harvested or perhaps even planted. Lacking gardens of their own, some urban women ventured into rural areas to trade valuables for potatoes and flour, a practice known as *Hamsterfahrten* (hamster trips) that became particularly widespread toward the end of the war. *Hamster* is derived from the German verb *hamstern* [to hoard], based on animal instinct to collect and hide food. In the wartime barter economy, farmers' wives acquired china, linens, ornaments, and furnishings in return for food, but not without criticism. One Reich poster illustrated an anthropomorphized female hamster carrying full bags, with the warning *"Hamsterin, schäme dich"* [Hamster, shame on you].

Hoarding and black market trading undermined Nazi policy and could result in prison or execution, but civilians needed food regardless of Reich ideals. For many, illicit means were the only way to acquire the botanical calories and vitamins needed to forestall malnutrition. Official advice from the *Reichausschuss für Volkswirtschaftliche Aufklarung* (Reich Committee for National Economic Education) suggested that stock or thin soup could be converted to a main dish by thickening it with flour paste. Typical recipes stretched a pound of meat with six pounds of root vegetables, flavored with an onion or two, but chronic shortages led to the rumor that the government had seized all available onions for poison gas research (see Chapter 2).

For most Germans, survival pivoted on potatoes. In the *Last Train from Berlin*, Howard K. Smith chronicled the effect of potato shortages caused by the cool, wet summer of 1941.[94] Sodden fields resulted in a small crop because potatoes need oxygen, which diffuses slowly through water-logged soil. Early frost compounded the problem. Unlike temperate root crops such as carrots and turnips, potatoes (native to South America) cannot tolerate freezing temperatures, and tubers died and rotted before they could be harvested. As a result of shortages, potatoes were rationed, and queues formed for the meager available supplies. It was estimated that peeling wasted 15 percent of the edible tissue, so housewives were advised to cook potatoes with their skins intact to conserve both vitamins and food. City-dwellers kept the occasional milk cow and traded kindling for potato peels to use as fodder. Some even repurposed peels as a soap substitute; the glycoalkaloids in potatoes are saponins, naturally occurring soaps that can produce a meager lather. The cellars of bombed homes were plundered for stored potatoes, which were used even if they were penetrated by glass shards. After harvesting, dried potato plants were burned as fuel or processed as a source of cellulose for explosives.

By the end of the war, all vegetables were scarce, and the most fortunate families were those with plots of arable land or area to forage. Some experimented with extending bread flour with starch ground from horse chestnuts, peas, potatoes, or acorns. The latter needed soaking to remove varying levels of toxic, bitter tannins; their use was perhaps ironic in light of the symbolism of oaks and acorns on Nazi medals and standards (see

Chapter 9). Sawdust was another option with no nutritional value (humans lack enzymes to digest cellulose), but it increased volume and was no doubt incorporated into many *ersatz* foods. Foraging was officially encouraged, including the ingredients for sorrel, rosehip, and elderberry soups; dandelion and daisy salads; and chickweed stew thickened with oatmeal and potatoes.[95] Other edible plants were species typically used as fodder, including serradella (*Ornithopus compressus*, a legume that colonizes dry ground), clover, and alfalfa. Seed cakes (pressed waste that remained after the processing of rape and flax seeds for oil) doubled as food for both humans and livestock. Desperate bakers mixed pulverized lichens into bread dough, which was nearly the equivalent of eating mushrooms. Lichens are a symbiosis of algae and fungi, with most of the mass consisting of the chitin-rich fungal cell walls. Housewives devised substitutes and experimented with *ersatz* products such as rice patties flavored to resemble meat or fish.

Tea was brewed from bramble leaves (*Rubus* spp.) and pansy flowers (*Viola tricolor*), and coffee substitutes were compounded from mixtures of roasted rye grains, rice, almonds, and spices. The German conglomerate I.G. Farben made synthetic "beans" that were ground into *ersatz* coffee enhanced with chemical aroma and added caffeine, but their actual content is unknown.[96] Perhaps this was the coffee provided as part of the meager diet for slave workers who provided labor for I.G. Farben at the Auschwitz concentration camp. Hamburg residents likely rejoiced when RAF planes dropped small sacks of genuine coffee as a commentary on German economic policy; warehouses were full of genuine coffee beans for foreign trade, but only *ersatz* grain mixtures were available in the shops of Hamburg, a major shipping center. Spice shortages due to curtailed imports posed additional problems for German cooks trying to simulate pre-war meals. Organic chemists synthesized substitutes for cinnamon, nutmeg, pimento, and cardamom, but sales were limited to small packages due to possible carcinogenicity. *Kunsthonig*, artificial honey, was nothing more than a concentrated solution of beet sugar in water.

Although Nazi medicine linked alcohol consumption to cancer, it is not surprising that Germans consumed high levels of alcohol during the years of Nazi control. Wartime ale was brewed with less barley, which meant decreased fermentation and lower alcohol content, which may have increased consumption. To keep pace with demand, chemists resorted to an industrial process that used wood to yield potable ethanol (not to be confused with methanol or wood alcohol, which is highly toxic). Cellulose from wood cell walls was treated with sulfuric acid to yield sugars, which could then be fermented by yeast—yielding about fifty gallons of alcohol for each ton of wood or sawdust, thus avoiding the need to grow and ferment fruit or grains. In the U.S., similar chemistry was used to produce butadiene for the production of synthetic rubber (see Chapter 10). There was even an attempt to collect the potable alcohol that evaporates during the baking of bread; yeast ferment the starch in bread dough because oxygen does not penetrate the dense mixture, yielding alcohol as a waste product. Heinrich Himmler, *Reichsführer* of the SS, instructed subordinates to investigate a device that could capture ethanol fumes from bakery chimneys. He estimated that the bakery at Dachau would yield 100–120 liters daily, but the plan proved unfeasible.[97]

Wood was also used for cultivating edible yeast (*Torula utilis*, not to be confused with the *Saccharomyces* that ferment wine), a process developed during World War I as a source of fodder for military horses. However, the exigencies of World War II led to the use of *Torula* (known as beefsteak yeast) as a protein supplement for humans. These yeast thrived on the liquid fraction of beech wood pulp, the five carbon (pentose) sugars essential for *Torula* culture but useless for alcohol production. A ton of beech pulp supported the growth of 200–240 pounds of yeast; thus widespread German stands of European beech (*Fagus sylvatica*) potentially contributed 38,000 tons of edible yeast to the wartime food supply, which may have helped to alleviate protein shortages.[98] The yeast *Candida tropicalis* (then classified as *C. arborea*) was also cultivated on beech waste, yielding twice the protein and four times the calories of lean meat.[99] However, there were possible problems with this potential food. *Candida tropicalis* is now recognized as a potential pathogen that can infect patients with cancer or low immunity, but whether this affected Germans who consumed the fungus is unknown.

Yeast provides another example of convergent evolution of British and German wartime food strategies. During World War I, brewers' yeast (cultured on sugar or molasses) was used to make Marmite, a savory spread issued as part of military rations. Support for Marmite stemmed from the discovery that yeast provided high levels of B vitamins and thus helped to prevent beri-beri. During the Second World War, German POWs received Marmite as a supplement to prison rations. After the Marmite shortages of World War I, Australian entrepreneurs developed Vegemite as a substitute. World War II posters advertised "Vegemite: Keeping fighting men fighting fit." In the Pacific Theater, some Japanese soldiers may have been poisoned by botulism when Australians intentionally punctured and abandoned cans of Vegemite; anaerobic *Clostridium* bacteria are soil-borne, and the optimum temperature for growth is 95°F. The cells would have multiplied quickly in tropical temperatures, and there is no known antidote to the botulinim nerve toxin.

Across Europe

Food shortages in other European countries also reflected ingenuity in the face of wartime exigencies, and foraging was widespread. In Norway, wild nettles and dandelions provided vitamins in soups and vegetable dishes, and government posters encouraged Oslo residents to pick berries to supplement their meals. Sugar rationing made jam-making difficult, but berries were bottled for winter use, sometimes with melted candle wax in place of paraffin.

Yeast shortages meant a return to the old method of fermenting a culture in a medium of boiled potatoes, sugar, and salt. As in England and Germany, Norwegians used yeast as a nutritious spread, thickened with boiled crisp bread and flavored with spices. Vegetables replaced much of the meat in main dishes, and potatoes replaced flour in cake baking. Potato flour was also essential in Switzerland, which was surrounded by Germany. Rationing controlled access to all starchy staple crops, including rice, oats, wheat, barley, and legumes, and the bread ration amounted to about a half pound daily. Bakers were required to store their bread for a day (later two) after baking; loaves were easier to slice thinly, but bread stretched with potato starch became moldy after a few days.

Before the war, the Netherlands imported grains for bread, but a 1930s plan for self-sufficiency resulted in enough stored grain to feed the civilian population for seven months. Traditionally, home grown rye was fodder, but as in Germany, it was more efficient to bake these grains into bread rather than feed them to animals. With the start of war, most livestock were eliminated, and meat consumption plummeted. Arable land increased as former pastures were ploughed under, and land devoted to fodder was planted with food crops. Much of the farming was done by expert former flower growers, and vegetables were abundant and unrationed until the desperate winter of 1944 (see Chapter 11). Overall the botanical diet had a salutary effect on vitamin deficiencies; scurvy, night-blindness, and beri-beri were rare during the war years.[100]

Rye was planted because its yields exceeded wheat in the Netherlands climate. Potatoes were the most common vegetable, and along with rye comprised the backbone of the daily diet. Wartime bread was under government control, baked from rye and other grains and supplemented with starch from potatoes and legumes. German occupiers seized control of coffee, cocoa, and fat reserves, which they forcibly exported for use in Germany. Fortunately rapeseed (*Brassica rapa*) thrived in the Netherlands and yielded oil for margarine and cooking. The species originated as a Eurasian field mustard that colonizes roadsides; selection has resulted in several cultivars, including turnips and Asian cabbage varieties, as well as varieties with oil-rich seeds.

France had both tight rationing and a flourishing black market. By 1941 most nutrients came from the daily ration of a half loaf of bread and a few potato slices, perhaps with a bit of meat or cheese. Although the standard baguette varied from pre-war quality, bread quantity was essential; posters encouraged civilians to *Economisez la pain* (save bread) by cutting loaves thinly and saving crusts for soup. Bakers used whatever flour was available, including rice and maize. Vegetables provided the rest of the diet, but farmers and markets in occupied areas were forced to sell produce to the Nazi military officials in return for nearly worthless German marks. Simple luxuries also disappeared, except for purchases on the black market; chocolate vanished, saccharin replaced sugar, and chicory and barley mixtures substituted for coffee.

Imports from French colonies in North Africa halted with the Allied invasion in 1942, and previously scorned vegetables like turnips became more acceptable. Although the practice was illegal, there were excursions into the countryside to barter with farmers for food. Production decreased by nearly half because farmers lacked seeds, fuel, and machinery, and many abandoned their land as German troops advanced. Nutritionists were concerned about epidemics of influenza, diphtheria, and tuberculosis due to malnutrition, and incidence of these diseases increased as access to calories and vitamins dropped. In early 1941, the endless queues spawned food riots, to which Nazi officials responded with a forty day halt in potato distribution.[101]

Mussolini anticipated a short war and avoided bread rationing in Italy until late 1941, but price controls dictated what could realistically be purchased. There were shortages of olive oil, sugar, potatoes, and flour, which was extended and adulterated with starches, sawdust, and marble dust; wartime bread and pasta were poor quality. Nearly one third of Italian beef cattle were shipped to Germany in return for raw materials, so civilians were encouraged to eat four meatless meals weekly. However, fruit and vegetable shortages ensued, further complicated by exports of Italian fruit, vegetables, and wheat to Germany in return for coal. Like Hitler, Mussolini had vegetarian leanings, in his case the result of gastric bleeding. He boasted of his frugal ways, but inflationary prices made purchasing food difficult for many on the Italian home front. The Allied blockade halted imports from other areas, and Italy produced insufficient wheat to feed the home front, despite improvements in agriculture before the war. By 1943, occupying German troops caused even greater food shortages and hardships.

The Japanese Home Front

Like England, Japan relied heavily on pre-war food imports, including rice and soybeans, two essential staples. To manage home front needs during the war, including food distribution, the Home Ministry organized a hierarchy of community councils and neighborhood associations to distribute rations and organize local gardens. Rationing was implemented in 1940, following the inevitable decrease in farm production that accompanied conscription, with a daily civilian rice ration of about twelve ounces. Other staple, starchy crops included sweet potatoes, white potatoes, wheat, and naked barley, a cultivar with easily removable hulls (*Hordeum vulgarum* var. *nudum*). Vegetable and fruits augmented the diet, including cabbage, peas, beans, carrots, eggplant, carrots, onions, leeks, turnips, pumpkin, cucumbers, tomatoes, apples, plums, peaches, pears, tangerines, and persimmons. Western influence was clear; most of the produce were varieties of the same species consumed in Europe and the United States, but inevitable shortages resulted from the need to cultivate calorie-rich staple crops. Eventually the daily ration of cultivated vegetables was limited to a few ounces, which affected urban dwellers more drastically than those in rural areas. Many traveled for hours into the countryside to purchase produce directly from farmers; this circumvented rationing, but government officials turned a blind eye to desperate mothers scavenging food to feed their families.

Rice provided the caloric backbone of the Japanese diet. It was easily cultivated in a densely populated country; paddies were maintained on small plots of land, terraced mountainsides, and reclaimed land, but wartime supplies were insufficient for both civilian and military needs. In an effort to stretch the supply, rice was extended with dried noodles, wheat, barley, and potatoes or cooked as unhulled (brown) grains, which could cause gastric bleeding and illness. The wartime meal known as *nukapan* consisted of fried wheat flour and rice bran; it was generally despised but kept starvation at bay. By 1945, only half of the ration was actually rice, and most were eating rice gruel, a thin mixture of grains in water. Nothing was wasted; rice straw was woven into traditional tatami mats used to cover windows and prevent bomb injuries from splintering glass. Production of rope from rice straw was one of the jobs performed by Allied prisoners of war in Japan; rice straw mats and ropes became valuable wartime commodities and were among the most likely items to be pilfered.

Soybeans were a cheap source of protein, but about half of the beans consumed were imported from China and Korea, leading to severe shortages when Allied warships and submarines interdicted shipments into Japan. Soy foods included soybean paste (*miso*), which came in sweet and salty varieties, as well as soy sauce (*shoyu*), bean curd (*tofu*), steamed soybeans (*natto*), soybean sprouts (*moyashi*), and soybean oil. The preparation of *miso* and *shoyu* relied on fermentation by the fungus *Aspergillus oryzae*, lactic acid bacteria, and yeast. These salty fermented foods had a long shelf life and were considered essential to Japanese cookery and nutrition. However, at least some strains of *Aspergillus* produce aflatoxins, carcinogens that may have contributed to the above average incidence of stomach cancer in Japan. In contrast, Nazi medical policy berated fermented, salty foods as possible causes of stomach cancer.

Two large taproots were part of the Japanese diet, both crops that were easy to grow and harvest. Burdock (*Arctium lappa*), known as *gobo*, is a weedy Eurasian species that was often an ingredient in *miso* soup. *Daikon* is a cultivated radish (*Raphanus sativus*) with elongated white taproots, which were pickled, simmered, or mixed into condiments.

Radishes originated in Asia, and as with other members of the mustard family (Brassicaceae), their sharp flavor results from an enzymatic reaction between sinigrin, a glucosinolate, and the enzyme myrosinase. The end product is isothiocyanate, flavorful in small amounts, but a severe irritant at higher levels. A botanical connection involves its role as the chemical model for synthetic mustard gas, which was first used by German soldiers against the Allies at Ypres in 1917. Known as yellow cross (the marking on the shells) or yperite, the volatile oil lacked color, odor, or taste, but after several hours, victims developed burns and blisters; some were permanently blinded. There was concern that mustard oil might again be used as a poison gas during World War II, thus rubber gas masks with charcoal filters (see Chapters 9 and 10) were standard wartime equipment for many soldiers and civilians. Fritz Haber, a pacifist German chemist, worked out the synthesis of mustard oils used in gas attacks; however, his work also led to the synthesis of alkylating agents, broad spectrum cancer drugs developed in the 1940s. Haber also developed the chemical process of nitrogen fixation, resulting in synthetic ammonia that could be used to make both agricultural fertilizers and nitric acid for explosives (see Chapter 6).

Foraging for wild edible plants was officially encouraged. City residents scoured vacant lots for leaves (dandelions, chrysanthemums, chickweed, knotweed, thistles, and other familiar weedy species that seemed edible), grasses, and seeds. Chryanthemums (*Chrysanthemum indicum*) had long been regarded as a symbol of longevity, and the stylized sixteen-petal flower of the imperial seal was engraved on Japanese rifles. Perhaps ironically, the plants became an emergency wartime food for civilians. For those who could travel into the countryside, mountain vegetables (a collective term for any wild edible plants) staved off starvation; foraged foods included mushrooms, bark, chestnuts, mulberries, bamboo shoots, and wild onions. Acorns were collected and ground into flour. Ferns such as the widespread bracken (*Pteridium aquilinum*) were collected and eaten, but not without some risk; this species contains the carcinogenic compound ptaquiloside, which causes gastric cancers in areas where it is frequently eaten as a vegetable. Bog rhubarb (*Petastites japonicus*) was another foraged plant with potential carcinogenic effects. Known from both Europe and Japan, this composite (family Asteraceae) contains pyrollizidine alkaloids that exhibit tumor activity and liver toxicity; its astringent shoots required soaking in wood ash or baking soda to improve palatability before they could be consumed.

Mugwort (*Artemisia princeps*) was widely collected because it was common and edible. As with several other foraged species (including knotweed, bamboo, and bracken), mugwort has weedy growth and rapidly colonizes wide areas with robust rhizomes. The leaves were a wartime vegetable, but traditional uses included the medicinal practice of moxibustion, in which the dried leaf hairs (trichomes) were ignited briefly on the skin of afflicted body parts. Mugwort also had potential anti-malarial effects, with secondary compounds (artemesinin and related terpenes) known to kill the parasitic *Plasmodium* species that cause the disease. Malaria occurred in Japan and perhaps became more widespread with wider rice cultivation (the mosquito vectors of malaria require water for their larvae) and the possible introduction by military returning from Pacific islands.

Communal kitchens allowed women to work in rural farms, but by the end of the war, daily rations were reduced to about 1,500 calories, the result of a poor rice harvest and the loss of Japanese ships that carried imports. *Time* magazine reported desperate conditions at the end of the war; even cabbage was rationed to a single leaf every few days, and civilians cultivated vegetables in window boxes and air raid trenches.[102] Diseases such a tuberculosis and rickets were widespread among malnourished civilians, and there was frequent theft of fruits and vegetables. Japan surrendered in August 1945; had the war continued into the winter of 1945–1946, starvation would have been widespread.

Food shortages also affected the 120,000 Japanese-Americans who spent the war years in inland internment camps. Communal mess halls provided meager meals of rice, boiled potatoes, and bread, along with canned vegetables and fruit, processed meat, and offal. Many of the internees were farmers who soon planted camp gardens to augment sub-par food supplies; simultaneously the internment of thousands of expert Japanese-American farmers affected food supplies nationwide. Cultivated crops included traditional vegetables like *gobo* and *daikon*, and nearby camps traded produce for greater variety. Strawberries, corn, Chinese cabbage, beets, romaine, lettuce, spinach, and watermelon helped to round out the government diet.

At Manzanar, where food was particularly scarce, workers making camouflage nets were rewarded with watermelons for their productivity. However, food shortages remained a central issue, and protests and strikes occurred frequently. Eight hundred workers at Santa Anita ceased net making to protest miserable meals of mostly bread and sauerkraut.[103] Facilities for preparing *tofu* and *shoyu* were built, but many yearned for certain foods, such as the marine kelps known as *kombu* (*Saccharina japonica* and related species) used for soup stocks, pickling, and tea. Japanese algae were unavailable during the war, but hundreds of tons of bladder kelp (*Nereocystis luetkeana*) were harvested from the California coast and shipped to internment camps.[104]

5

Feeding the Military

During the Depression era of the late 1930s, vitamin deficiencies undermined the health of many Americans, a significant concern with war on the horizon. Military might demanded nutritious food, as defined by the relatively new field of vitamin science. In the past, armies survived on meager rations (such as Civil War hardtack and salted meat), reinforced with bartered and appropriated foods. In contrast, military messing during the Second World War involved strategy; planned meals provided vitamin-laced nutrition following menus developed for specific conditions and climates.

Military Meals

Military meals reflected the guidelines developed by the National Academy of Sciences and the National Research Council, which meant a diet with plenty of vitamin-rich fruits and vegetables. There was initial concern that young men might shun vegetables in favor of a diet of meat, bread, and sweets. However, Depression era stringencies may have worked in favor of balanced meals; hungry young men ate botanical foods because in many cases their families survived the Depression by eating homegrown crops. The Quartermaster Corps made certain that military meals included plenty of vegetables. Moreover a "clean plate" was expected prior to second helpings of meat, a strategy to improve nutrition by requiring vegetable consumption to satisfy hunger.[1] As a concession to flavor, the Quartermaster Corps developed a kitchen pack of spices and condiments that cooks could use to improve bland dishes that relied heavily on preserved vegetables. Sailors and combat soldiers often spent weeks away from fresh foods, relying instead on a diet of canned and dehydrated foods and field rations. Providing fresh vegetables to soldiers worldwide posed several complex challenges. As part of the Food Service Program instituted during the summer of 1943, the Office of the Quartermaster General encouraged victory gardens on military posts, and there were anecdotal reports of soldiers who planted gardens with seeds sent from home. There were also military farms and hydroponic sites, both discussed in greater detail in Chapter 6.

Conscription officers encountered cases of malnutrition and deficiency diseases among recruits, and nutritious food was the certain way to build able-bodied soldiers. Investigators experimented with possible military uses of vitamin-rich diets, such as the all-carrot diet developed at Northwestern University Medical School. Rats raised on a steady diet of fresh carrots had higher tolerance for the low oxygen levels at 30,000 feet altitude, which suggested a possible diet for high-altitude airmen.[2] However, typical military meals provided both the high calorie content essential to physical activity and the comfort of familiar foods cooked in standard "American" style. Daily calorie consumption was 4,300, sufficient to fuel the health, stamina, and energy of young fighting men. Despite the physical rigors of basic training, an average enlistee gained twelve pounds during his first months as a soldier. No wonder when asked about the military view of wartime needs, Donald Nelson, Chairman of the War Production Board, summed it up bluntly, "Astronomical quantities of everything and to hell with civilian needs." A 1943 poster from the Office of War Information proclaimed, "Do with less—so they'll have enough. Rationing gives you your fair share."[3]

Civilian sacrifice made for excellent military messing, and meat was a case in point. American civilians each ate a couple of pounds weekly (still incredibly generous by European wartime standards) and made the rest of their meals from homegrown and unrationed botanical foods. In contrast, *per capita* military meat consumption was about a pound daily, reinforced by all manner of vegetables, fruit, bread, and desserts, washed down by gallons of milk. Parents of young sailors were assured of balanced meals, prepared in immaculate battleship galleys with the dual goals of "health and contentment."[4] Supplying Navy vessels involved strategic planning, with fresh, dehydrated, and frozen foods delivered by provisions stores ships. Of course, battle conditions delayed arrivals, and there was often heavy reliance on canned vegetables and fruits.

Vegetables and fruits were essential as vitamin sources, and American troops consumed more than ever before. At times canned crops were scarce in markets because army need was high, which resulted in rationing of cans of high demand foods. Peas were an army favorite; Green Giant advertisements reminded housewives, "Peas have gone to war.... After meeting war demands, we are of course doing our best to supply our friends at home. If your grocer is out of Green Giant Brand Peas, don't despair. He may have a new supply next week, or next month. Because of necessary government wartime control, the supply is 'parceled out' and shipments are permitted only at certain times."[5]

Potatoes were served for both vitamins and energy, and each soldier consumed about 23 pounds each month. The minimum standard ten-day army menu specified potatoes at least once and often three times daily.[6] Potato crops were cultivated worldwide, with the exception of lowland tropical areas, so they were readily available to nourish troops. Although home front cooks were instructed to conserve vitamins by leaving vegetables unpeeled, soldiers preferred potatoes without skins, although peeling potatoes for hundreds was onerous. In 1942, *American Cookery* described a mechanical improvement in army kitchens, "K.P. has been revolutionized! This automatic peeler takes the skins off an entire bag of potatoes in only ten minutes"[7] The device utilized centrifugal force to remove the outer periderm ("skin") from each tuber. Anatomically-speaking, this outer layer originates from a cork cambium, similar to the growth of bark on woody plants.

The centrifugal potato peeler probably did not remove the slightly indented axillary buds ("eyes") that were used in asexual potato propagation. When planted, a single bud produced a clone of the parent plant, explaining the simplicity of potato cultivation. Cloning over many generations resulted in genetically homozygous crops that were susceptible to the fungus *Phytophora infestans*. The Irish potato famine resulted in mass immigration to England and America during the 1840s, and the fungus at times reappeared; an outbreak during the cold winter of 1944–45 limited the potatoes available to feed American troops in Europe. At the same time, scientists at the Maine Agricultural

Experimental Station in Orono were researching potato blight as a possible biological weapon, a notion suggested by high levels of potato consumption in Germany.[8]

Strategic Planning

In 1943, the Office of War Information released the short film "Food for Fighters," which explained the need for scientific food strategies. The Army Quartermaster Corps Subsistence Laboratory experimented with caloric needs, calorie content of various foods, and climatic effects on diet. Shipping caused concern for weight and volume, and so food dehydration demanded study; in particular, fruits and vegetables lent themselves to drying and powdering for later reconstitution with water. *Army Food and Messing: The Complete Manual of Mess Management* included an entire chapter on cooking with dehydrated ingredients, which alleviated the dual problems of spoiled fresh food and rusted cans, which occurred quickly in the tropics.[9]

Field experience soon demonstrated that dehydrated fruits and vegetables were compact, easily transported, and conveniently stored. Edible fruit and vegetable tissue is largely composed of parenchyma cells; each has a large, water-filled central vacuole, so dehydration simply reflects the high water content of plant cells. Before drying (which on average removed 90 percent of the original weight), fruits and vegetables were scrubbed, peeled, seeded, and cored. As long as dehydrated plant tissue was protected from moisture and pests, it was safe and ready to use indefinitely. A pound of dehydrated cabbage soaked for a few hours yielded sixteen pounds of cabbage ready for coleslaw; dried potatoes rehydrated into over four pounds of peeled potatoes, ready for frying, soup, stew, or salad. Using only dehydrated supplies, soup and apple pie for one hundred men required just a few pounds of various vegetables and four pounds of apples. In fact, this technology seemed so perfect that many nutritionists and food writers predicted that postwar homemakers would prefer packets of dehydrated ingredients over fresh market produce.

Nutritious food was worthless if not eaten, so the challenge was to convert dietary insights into meals that reminded troops of home. Menus reflected regard for foods that appealed to young, male appetites. *American Cookery* featured an article on Mary Barber, who served as special food consultant to the Secretary of War as an adjunct at the Army Quartermaster Corps Subsistence Laboratory. Recruited for wartime service from the Kellogg Company, she had submitted a set of menus to the Quartermaster, based on those that she had developed for a fraternity house. Barber insisted on vegetable variety, and the minimum standard ten-day menu included fruit for breakfast and two or three vegetables at all other meals, plus salad at the main meal midday; she noted, "The brass hats have determined that this Army is going to have every vitamin in the alphabet, served as appetizingly as possible."[10] Vegetable diversity no doubt surprised new enlistees, who may not ever have eaten parsnips, turnips, eggplant, or asparagus, but army recipes intentionally enticed young male palates. Turnips were flavored with bacon, and parsnips were braised in beef stock and dressed with sugar and cinnamon; eggplant was fried, and asparagus was served on toast, blanketed with a cream sauce.

Army messing included regional foods, particularly vegetable dishes that catered to the relatively high number of recruits from southern states. Collard greens were boiled with bacon, and canned corn was used in fritters. Prepared, canned hominy also appeared on the minimum standard ten-day army menu. Known as lye hominy, it was made by soaking dried field corn kernels in a lye solution (a process known as nixtamalization). The effect was to weaken the grain wall by degrading the hemicellulose molecules that cross-link with cellulose, allowing the starchy endosperm to soften and expand, but there were also nutritional benefits. The alkaline lye solution simultaneously destroyed carcinogenic mycotoxins that accumulated in stored grains infected with fungi and increased the available levels of niacin and lysine, an amino acid. Army nutritionists probably realized that southerners who ate more hominy than corn had a lower incidence of pellagra, a condition caused by niacin deficiency. Hominy was thus a welcome addition to the basic army diet, either as a vegetable or ground into hominy grits, eaten as a cereal. Army breakfasts also included weekly dishes of prunes, ordered by Mary Barber for their high riboflavin content. Fruit-based desserts provided both vitamins and calories; apple, blueberry, pumpkin, coconut, raisin, and cranberry pies appeared on the ten-day menu.

Concern also centered on the nutritional value of rice, which was served regularly in garrison kitchens. The husked grains lost 95 percent of their vitamin content; however, a method known as the Huzenlaub process, developed by Erich Huzenlaub and Frances Heron Bacon, used vacuum drying and steaming to preserve 80 percent of the nutrients and pest-proof the grains. Known as converted rice, the product sold well to U.S. and British forces. The product had a long shelf-life without spoiling or insect infestation, so it was suitable for storage and shipping to field kitchens. Converted rice was sold exclusively to the armed forces for the duration of the war and only marketed to the public after 1945. Despite the improved vitamin content of converted rice, army regulations stipulated that Filipino troops be provided with brown (unpolished) rice. There was concern that the rice-based Filipino diet might lack essential nutrients needed by combat troops, including the thiamine provided by whole-grain foods.

Citrus crops supplied the military, which explains the shortage of oranges for civilians, and there were some unexpected uses. The 442nd Infantry Regiment (a highly decorated all-volunteer group that included native Hawaiians and interned Japanese-Americans) celebrated Lei Day on May 1, 1944, by stringing orange skins into leis, details recorded by the chaplain.[11] They perhaps realized that citrus was related to *Pelea anisata*, also a member of the citrus family (Rutaceae), an indigenous Hawaiian species with fragrant capsules that were often strung into traditional leis. Named by Asa Gray in honor of Pele, the volcano goddess, *Pelea* leaves have oil-producing glandular cells that resemble those in citrus rinds and release an orange scent when crushed. In fact, Hawaiians named the first introduced orange trees *alani*, the local name for *Pelea*.

Daily Bread

Thiamine was recognized as affecting morale and stamina (see Chapter 3), and there was concern that servicemen consume sufficient levels to be effective soldiers. The vitamin became a major military concern, especially because recruits received as much as 40 percent of their daily calories from bread that accompanied their meals. Whole grain flour was one of the best dietary sources of thiamine, but only 2 percent of American households purchased whole grain bread. No doubt most enlistees preferred white bread, but standard military menus did not specify bread varieties, and whole grains were encouraged for their vitamin content. As a compromise, *Army Food and Messing*

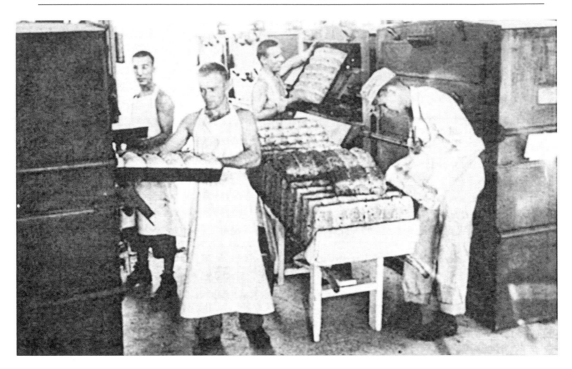

Bread provided thiamine and calories in the military diet, and by early 1942, federal law mandated that all bread be enriched with thiamine, riboflavin, niacin, iron, calcium and vitamin D. Bread-baking on a military scale posed other problems involving cleanliness, microbes, and spoilage, but for many young soldiers, bread was the favorite part of the meal (U.S. Army).

recommended bread made from half whole wheat and half "issue" (white) flour, which following army guidelines had to be labeled "imitation whole wheat bread." It supplied more thiamine than standard white loaves, but by early 1942, federal law mandated that all bread be enriched with thiamine, riboflavin, niacin, iron, calcium and vitamin D.[12]

Bread-baking on a military scale posed other problems involving cleanliness, microbes, and spoilage. Bread attracted animal pests; store rooms had to be well-ventilated and secure against rodents, and shipments needed close inspection for signs of insect life. Grain beetles could be sifted out before baking, but avoiding infestation was far preferable. Under tropical conditions, flour tended to develop mold; air-borne spores could taint hundreds of loaves, especially if they were not allowed to cool and dry slightly after baking. Some strains of the bacterium *Bacillus subtilis* (sometimes classified as *Bacillus mesentericus*) thrive on the starch in dough, causing the baked bread to spoil and separate into long, sticky strands. Known as rope, it was spread by heat-resistant endospores that survive in oven temperatures. Under warm conditions, bacterial endospores quickly contaminated flour stores and kitchen equipment; like various bread molds, rope became a particular problem for military kitchens in the tropics. Rope-infected bread released a strong odor that resembled cantaloupe melons and was completely inedible. One known preventative involved adding vinegar to bread dough; acidic pH halts growth of rope bacteria, which thrive at pH 5.5–8.5. Rope bacteria were ubiquitous in wartime conditions, described in the Army technical manual *Methods for Laboratory Technicians* as "found in soil, water, dust, laboratory contaminations," and even in traumatic wounds.[13] Mycoban, calcium proprionate marketed by Dupont, promised to control rope fungi and became popular with military cooks. The spores also vexed German military bakers, who used similar products, Halogen and Ropal, in baking rope-free loaves.

Field bakeries provided bread for combat troops, which was much preferred over the crackers and biscuits packaged in operational rations. Baking occurred under field conditions, which required even greater attention to cleanliness, animal pests, and possible contamination. Field kitchens often relied on portable ranges adapted to burning wood (as an alternative to gasoline), which could be gathered locally. In the New Hebrides, Army bakers devised makeshift mixers from scrap lumber and converted oil drums into ovens that could bake eight loaves at a time; bakers in Papua New Guinea dug wells to provide fresh water and ground hard biscuits into crumbs to recycle flour.[14] Noting the success of the British army with field baking, some U.S. battalions requested and received field bakeries from England. Each mobile unit included a generator, mixer, and three ovens that far surpassed U.S. Army ovens in productivity and convenience. Company B, 95th Quartermaster Bakery Battalion was selected for special training with British army bakers; within a week of their arrival in North Africa, they produced 21,000 pounds of bread daily.[15] There was widespread agreement that the addition of decent bread made operational field rations more appealing.

Breast yeast posed another microbial challenge in producing large quantities of bread under field conditions. Shipping blocks of live compressed yeast was impossible under tropical conditions because active yeast cells (*Saccharomyces cerevisiae*) die at temperatures exceeding 104° F; in short, fresh yeast often spoiled before food shipments arrived. Innovative army cooks stationed on Kiriwina Island near Papua New Guinea leavened bread with fermented coconut milk, which presumably resembled a sourdough starter prepared with wild, airborne yeast.[16] However, the more practical solution came from Fleischmann laboratories, where trial and error experimentation resulted in granular dried yeast for military use. The method involved culturing yeast at low nitrogen levels, extruding the cultures in long strands, and air-drying for several hours. The process reduced water content to 8 percent and increased chances of long term cell survival. Inactive yeast cells were more tolerant of temperature extremes than compressed yeast and could be quickly rehydrated in warm water; thus foil-packaged dry yeast became the standard leavening agent for bread in both field and garrison kitchens.

Not all bread was eaten. According to anecdotal reports, sailors in the U.S. Navy used loaves with the ends removed to filter torpedo fuel into potable alcohol. The fuel was compounded from ethanol mixed with methanol (highly toxic wood alcohol, so-called because it was originally distilled from wood) and a pink dye. Bread absorbed some of the methanol and dye, but there were still cases of blindness caused by drinking torpedo fuel with wood alcohol. To discourage sailors from imbibing, oil pressed from the seeds of a known purgative (purging croton, *Croton tiglium*) was added to the fuel mixture. It caused severe cramps and diarrhea, although some soon learned that distillation could separate the oil from alcohol.

Field Cookery

Away from garrison kitchens, preparation of thousands of meals posed a constant challenge, particularly when troops were marching to a new locale. In addition to portable field kitchens, fireless cookers were an option for field cookery. These resembled large versions of hay boxes (see Chapter 4) scaled up for military use; layers of dried grasses, paper, and fibers conserved heat in the inner tinned food receptacle. Food was heated over a fire and then transferred to the insulated cooker, which could be easily transported while cooking continued with the reserved heat.[17] Most vegetables took two or three hours when prepared in a fireless cooker; mature plant tissue required long cooking times.

The Quartermaster Corps managed food shipments to the European and Pacific theaters. The typical 3,000 miles voyage from New York to Liverpool took about two months, in contrast to the four or five month trip from San Francisco to Australia, where most Quartermaster supply shipments landed in the southwest Pacific. Vast quantities of food and other supplies deteriorated and spoiled *en route*. Burlap and cotton sacks of flour, sugar, and rice were particularly vulnerable to quick degradation, but even canned foods, generally considered nonperishable, were liable to climate conditions. Salt water, heat, humidity, and microbes worked synergistically to rust cans and lids, disintegrate labels, decay wooden boxes, and degrade cardboard. High temperatures accelerated deterioration, with breakdown occurring twice as fast at 90° F compared to 70° F. Glass food jars broke when shipping cartons disintegrated due to moisture and microbes; bacteria, fungi, insects, rats and other pests quickly invaded anything edible, leading to waste and shortages.[18]

Most Pacific islands lacked receiving ports or storage warehouses, so shipments were offloaded onto exposed beaches. Simple paulin oases were sometimes assembled from tarpaulins and bamboo poles, but buildings were essential to remedy the waste and inefficiency of open air storage. The trunks of coconut palms worked well as dunnage for stacking and organizing supplies, and storage shacks were constructed with roofs thatched from palms, including the fibrous leaves of nipa (*Nypa fruticans*), a ubiquitous Pacific species colonizing tidal areas. Nipa was used locally in hut construction, which provided a model for food storage structures. Spoiled food was nevertheless a common sight, and as

Pacific islands often lacked ports and storage, so storage shacks were constructed with roofs thatched from palms, including the fibrous leaves of nipa, a ubiquitous Pacific species colonizing tidal areas. Nipa was used locally in hut construction, which provided a model for food storage structures.

much as 40 percent of the food shipped for military use was ruined before it could be consumed. Anecdotal reports from New Caledonia in late 1943 described a hundred thousand rusty food cans with decomposing contents.[19] However, by the end of 1942, Quartermaster staff developed V-boxes, shipping containers reinforced with sisal fibers, which were somewhat better than wood for food transport. Sacks with waterproof walls replaced the cloth sacks used for various staples; these were also manufactured from botanical materials (see Chapter 8), including asphalt-laminated paper and cotton.[20]

Food storage in temperate climates required ingenuity as well. Supplies stored aloft in suspended wooden boxes were protected from animal pests on the ground, and vegetable bins made of wood slats allowed air circulation and prevented build-up of ethylene (a natural plant hormone that signals ripening), thus preventing over-ripening and spoilage. An underground cooling box could be built using the hay box design, with the space between two wooden boxes insulated with sawdust, straw, hay, or grass. Wooden boxes provided protection from many animal pests, and a wooden box wrapped in water-soaked burlap constituted a make-shift refrigerator.[21]

Field Rations

In wartime parlance, the term *ration* applied to a military meal. A-rations were kitchen-prepared meals prepared with fresh or frozen ingredients, while B-rations were prepared from canned foods. However, all meals could not be practically prepared in garrison or field kitchens, especially under combat conditions. To serve the need for food during combat, in 1938 the Army Quartermaster Corps Subsistence Laboratory developed the Type C field ration as a nutritious, high energy meal that could be shipped in small wooden crates and consumed in the field. Maj. W.R. McReynolds, first director (1936–38) of the laboratory, described the C-ration as having, "all the vitamins, fuel and regulating food, and is far better in edibility and palatability than any meal that can be cooked in a peacetime Army mess, let alone a rolling kitchen in gas and shell attack."[22] Combat troops were issued three C-rations daily. Although these canned meals were developed for limited use (no more than a few consecutive days at a time), as a result of problems with shipping and spoilage, some soldiers consumed C-rations alone for several weeks.

Each type C ration contained a canned prepared meal (such as stew, hash, ham with beans, or chicken and rice) known as the M-unit. Vegetables in the M-unit included onions, potatoes, carrots, and lima beans, cooked with meat into a soft, bland, ready-to-eat mixture. This main dish was accompanied by a B-unit can, which contained several botanical ingredients, including hard tack (a cracker-like bread), candy, and powdered coffee. There was also an artificial lemonade powder made from citric acid, but its sour flavor was despised, and some soldiers used it to scour ovens and wash floors. The entire ration provided 3,000 calories, calculated by the National Research Council as adequate to support moderate physical activity. Ironically, the C-ration main dishes closely resembled many home front meals of meat simmered with root vegetables, although with a higher meat content.

Type C rations were widely regarded as bland and monotonous. They existed for sustenance alone, and some men developed digestive problems after a steady three-day C-ration diet. The M-unit was more palatable when heated, so troops requested and welcomed shipments of canned denatured alcohol, which was toxic and potentially hazardous. As an alternative solid fuel, inventor Norman Stark devised bars of paraffin and sawdust that burned long enough to heat canned rations; these were labeled "Fuel Tablet—Ration Heating" and shipped with rations into combat areas. The field rations also included a paper packet containing several other botanical products: a wooden spoon, chewing gum, sugar tablets, tobacco, and toilet paper.

Chewing gum was originally made by flavoring the latex-containing sap from various tropical trees, including jelutong (*Dyera* spp.) and sapodilla trees (*Manilkara zapota*), but this posed a challenge as the war continued. Jelutong was native to Malaysia, and sapodilla trees originated on the Yucatan peninsula, although by the 1940s there were cultivated plantations in British Honduras, Guatemala, and southeastern Mexico. Harvesting involved climbing the trees and slicing into the bark with a machete, which released the flow of raw sap known as chicle. A single tree could yield sixty quarts, but they could be tapped only once every few years. Chicle processing involved boiling, washing, neutralization with alkali, and drying; the final product was a water-insoluble powder that could be filtered, sterilized, flavored, and molded into chewing gum.

Chicle demand ran high during the war, primarily for chewing gum to supply C-rations, but it was also used in making adhesive surgical tape. Latex (known as *sorva* or *leche caspi*) from the Amazonian tree *Couma macrocarpa* was also used as a chicle source during the war years; Amazonian Indians had long used it to make waterproof canoes, and the latex was sweet and palatable even before processing. Eventually, however, efforts were redirected to synthesizing a chemical base for chewing gum production, which would solve the problems of harvesting, shipping, and shortages. Manufacturers adopted butadiene-based synthetic rubber, originally developed during the 1920s at I.G. Farben by the German chemist Walter Bock. Supplies of natural rubber diminished following

the 1942 Japanese occupation of rubber-producing areas in southeast Asia, but the butadiene-based rubber replacement was already being manufactured in the U.S. However, even synthetic rubber had a botanical origin. Butadiene was made from ethanol, made by fermenting the sugars in cellulose from the plant cell walls that compose wood (see Chapter 9).

During the course of the war, chewing gum symbolized American military forces and their local presence. Hundreds of pounds were included in the more than sixteen million tons of supplies used in the Normandy invasion, and American troops distributed chewing gum to Japanese children in the early days of post-war occupation.[23]

Chicle for chewing gum included in C rations came from the sap of tropical trees including sapodilla. Harvesting required climbing the trees and slicing into the bark with a machete; processing involved boiling, washing, neutralization with alkali, and drying. The final product was a water-insoluble powder that could be used to make chewing gum and the adhesive on bandages.

Military Chocolate

Research on a military chocolate bar began before World War I with combinations of cocoa (processed from the seeds of cacao, *Theobroma cacao*), egg albumin, and casein (a milk protein), a mixture that proved nauseating. With the help of Milton Hershey and his chocolate company, Colonel Paul Logan, head of the Quartermaster Subsistence School, revived the project in the 1930s. Their original formula specified 1:1 proportions of sugar to unsweetened chocolate (a considerably lower sugar to chocolate ratio than other chocolate confections), which explains the comparative bitterness of earlier formulations. The bar was further fortified with powdered skim milk and cacao fat and flavored with vanilla. The addition of one part oat flour to fifteen parts of the melted chocolate transformed the mixture into a stiff paste, which had to be kneaded and pressed into molds by hand.

The D-ration consisted of three four-ounce chocolate bars, which supplied 1,800 calories, and it was considered an adequate short-term emergency substitute for daily meals. D-rations were field tested at army bases in the Philippines, Hawaii, Panama, and Texas; as intended, the bars resisted melting until the temperature reached 120° Fahrenheit, so they were suitable for tropical climates. Known as the Logan bar, the final product was released for general use in 1939.

The foil-wrapped D-ration bars were packed in cardboard boxes, sealed against possible gas contamination, and shipped in wooden crates into combat areas. By late 1942, Hershey produced ten million D-rations annually, which explains the need to ration chocolate on the home front. Despite rationing, civilians discovered that chocolate candy bars were scarce; advertisements helpfully suggested slicing a bar into small pieces. Cake recipes used powdered cocoa, and ground nuts were used to extend chocolate into spreadable pastes. Nestle's advertisements reminded consumers that "U.S. troops fight on chocolate diet," "Chocolate is a fighting food," and "Chocolate and cocoa fight with our forces around the world." Their campaign sought to keep the Nestle brand name familiar despite chocolate shortages and rationing.

There were universal complaints about the bitter flavor and hard texture of the Logan bar; some even used pen knives to shave slivers from the bars. Colonel Logan had intentionally specified that the D-ration should definitely lack the flavor of typical confectionary (he suggested that it should taste just a little better than a boiled potato), out of concern that appealing bars would not be saved as emergency combat rations. Of course, American troops stationed abroad shared many K-ration bars with others, especially hungry European children who found the chocolate quite acceptable.

Palatability of the bars was later improved when they became part of other packaged operational rations, such as the K-rations designed for paratroopers. Thiamine was eventually added to D-ration chocolate as a line of defense against beri-beri, a nutritional disease common in tropical countries with a rice-based diet; the reputation of thiamine as the "morale vitamin" (see Chapter 3) probably also suggested its addition to combat rations. D-rations were also part of ration boxes issued to U.S. Air Force flight crews. Packaged in boxes labeled "Air Crew Lunch," these packages contained D-ration chocolate, hard candy, chewing gum, and fruit bars for quick energy while in flight. They were designed to be opened while wearing flight gloves. However, perhaps the most clever wartime use of chocolate was invented by Charles Fraser-Smith, who worked for the Ministry of Supply in developing devices and equipment for British intelligence officers in German-occupied Europe. He provided British intelligence officers with garlic-impregnated chocolate bars, so that they had the scent of the French civilians whom they impersonated. Reportedly there were also German plans to booby-trap a chocolate bar as part of a planned assassination attempt on Winston Churchill. British MI5 intelligence officers learned of their intention to encase a thin steel explosive in actual chocolate, but the plot was never implemented.

Operational Rations

Rations for extreme climates demanded special attention. The Army Quartermaster Corps Subsistence Laboratory developed and packaged daily rations for four men, designed specifically for troops in cold, high altitude regions or tropical jungles. Mountain rations comprised foods that provided energy and digested slowly. Provisions included biscuits, cereal, fruit bars, dehydrated potatoes, and pre-cooked rice, so that meals could be assembled easily at high elevations. Jungle rations required foods that could tolerate high temperatures and perhaps avoid the need for making a fire, and supplies included peanuts, raisins, and pre-cooked cereal. However, both mountain and jungle rations were obsolete by 1943, replaced by individual K-rations that could be easily carried and used under challenging conditions.

K-rations excluded some of the botanical foods in mountain and jungle rations and replaced them with animal proteins. The goal was concentrated nutrition compacted into the smallest possible volume, specifically for short term use by mobile units such as airborne troops and tank corps, regardless of climate. Each unit fit precisely into the pocket of a paratrooper's uniform and included a D-ration chocolate bar as a source of quick energy; however, much of the sustenance came from meat, eggs, and cheese. K-rations did include fruit bars and cereal bars (engineered following the principle of pemmican, which Native Americans compounded from venison, fat, and fruit), along with high protein biscuits baked from one part soy flour and seven parts wheat flour. These were highlighted in the Office of War Information short film "Food for Fighters," perhaps to let civilians know that the military was also eating soy, at least in its operational rations. Despite the nutritional benefits and ease of growing a large soybean crop, garrison kitchens avoided soy flour. Perhaps Quartermasters and Army cooks were unfamiliar with its use and benefits; although grocers sold wartime soy-based spaghetti, soy pasta was considered unsuitable for military tastes.[24] Medical advice, however, described soy as an "unexcelled substitute for meat" that was used frequently in the German military diet, suggesting that the U.S. Quartermasters should follow suit.[25]

Climate was an ongoing concern as the war in the Pacific developed. In 1943, the Quartermaster released a modified version of military chocolate known as the tropical bar. The new field ration retained the familiar hard texture but was sweeter than the Logan bar, which it replaced by 1945. Tropical bars held their shape even after an hour at 120° F, a temperature at which a standard chocolate bar would have completely melted. Most importantly, tropical bars provided basic nutrients, even for troops weakened by dysentery. Butter also softened and liquefied in tropical temperatures; however, buttered bread provided essential calories in military meals, so the army aimed to supply two ounces of butter daily whenever supplies and refrigeration allowed. Working with the Kraft Cheese Company, researchers at the Quartermaster Corps Subsistence Laboratory

Specially formulated bars of tropical chocolate held their shape even after an hour at 120° F, a temperature at which standard chocolate would have melted. As a field ration, the bars provided basic nutrients, important for troops weakened by dysentery (U.S. Army).

determined that adding hydrogenated cottonseed oil (with a melting point of about 122° F) raised the melting point of butter from 90–95° to 110° F. The final product was a hard, waxy, much reviled butter substitute known as Carter's spread, named for its inventor, Lt. Robert F. Carter. In 1942, cans of Carter's spread shipped to troops in Africa, but "... not without eliciting considerable adverse criticism. One observer remarked that no single item had been the butt of more jibes than Carter's spread. It was described by one soldier as having a 'greasy tang.'"[26] By 1943, the product was replaced with a mixture of butter and cheese.

Troops in desert or mountainous regions were often relatively isolated, so rations could be easily packaged into a single box to supply several men. The 5-in-1 (and later 10-in-1) ration packs provided basic B-ration foods for small groups bivouacked remotely. These included botanical foods such as potatoes, cabbage, bean soup, and tomato juice that were typical of garrison meals, but packaged in a dehydrated or concentrated state for long distance shipping. Meals prepared from 5-in-1 ingredients were generally well received, but Quartermasters concluded that they lacked sufficient calories and vitamins for sustenance long term. According to one report of soldiers fed with 5-in-1 packs, "Vitamin deficiencies were manifested in skin lesions, lassitude, and neuritis."[27] Of course, 5-in-1 rations were often consumed in extreme locales, including desert heat that undermined appetites and mountainous cold that required more calories to maintain bodily heat.

Perhaps the best received operational rations were those developed for Thanksgiving, Christmas, and New Year holidays of 1943–44. Special meals with fresh fruits and vegetables were considered essential for morale. For example, the Fifth Army in Italy received special perishable food shipments from the 67th Quartermaster Refrigeration Company, including olives, celery, apples, and walnuts, produce that provided relief from ordinary rations. Of course, refrigeration was not always necessary. Depending upon location, the army also obtained an abundance of local produce through contracts arranged by the Quartermaster Corps; following the fall of Sicily, an inadvertently large Quartermaster order for citrus fruit resulted in enough lemons for each soldier to have nearly a full bushel.[28]

Caffeine

Stamina and alertness function synergistically, which explains the importance of various sources of caffeine in wartime. As a plant alkaloid, caffeine has long been consumed to combat drowsiness. Some claim that it is the oldest and most common psychoactive drug, a stimulant that affects the central and autonomic nervous systems by blocking the receptors for adenosine, which causes drowsiness. Both Allied and Axis soldiers swallowed caffeine tablets for alertness under combat conditions, but they also consumed coffee, tea, and Coca-Cola as caffeine sources.

Caffeine evolved in nature as a deterrent against insects and other herbivores. More than sixty plant species synthesize the alkaloid, including coffee (*Coffea arabica*), tea (*Thea sinensis*), kola (*Cola acuminata* and *C. nitida*), and chocolate (*Theobroma cacao*), which contains low levels. Chicory and various grains used in making *ersatz* blends and coffee substitutes contain no caffeine and so were useful only as a hot infusion flavored with sugar for energy. U.S. Army cooks prepared coffee in large quantities, but they were cautioned against preparing coffee too early or reusing grounds; coffee beans were stored in airtight containers to retain flavor and potency. In contrast, tea was essential for British and Canadian soldiers. Each of their Composite Ration Packs contained blocks of dehydrated tea, milk, and sugar, so only hot water was needed to prepare the staple beverage known as compo tea. Sugar provided calories and energy, but the milk proteins denatured when heated and formed the much-despised scum that characterized compo tea.

Coca leaves were used to flavor the original proprietary formulation of Coca-Cola, which was sold during the 1936 Berlin Olympics. Bottles were distributed at German workers' events and Hitler Youth rallies, and advertisements appeared in magazines and youth publications. In 1942 the Coca-Cola Company produced "The Free American Way," a short film that contrasted life in Allied and Axis countries.

Coca-Cola originated in the nineteenth century as a quasi-medicinal tonic that promised vitality and strong nerves. Originally flavored with coca leaves (*Erythroxylon coca*) and kola nuts (*Cola acuminata* and *C. nitida*), the original formulation remains a proprietary secret. Coca is the source of the psychoactive alkaloid cocaine, which was eliminated from the formula in 1903. Kola provided high levels of caffeine (2 percent of dry seed weight in *C. nitida*). With vanillin flavoring and additional caffeine (botanical compounds supplied by the Monsanto Company), Coca-Cola became known as a coffee alternative, and wartime advertisements promoted it as a military beverage: "At ease ... for refreshment," "Coca-cola goes along," and "Here's to our G.I Joes."

However, the presence of Coca-Cola in Europe pre-dated the war. By

1929, the Coca-Cola Company sold the beverage across Germany and during the 1936 Berlin Olympics. Bottles were distributed at German workers' events and Hitler Youth rallies, and advertisements appeared in magazines and youth publications. Despite political differences between the U.S and Germany, the commercial message of Coca-Cola reflected the idealized values espoused by the National Socialist Party. By the time that the Nazi regime invaded Austria and annexed the Sudetenland, Germans had consumed Coca-Cola for a decade; however, in 1942 the Coca-Cola Company produced "The Free American Way," a short film that contrasted life in Allied and Axis countries. Apparently the Coca-Cola Company decided to co-exist with Nazi eugenic and anti–Semitic practices. Concerned with competition, the German-owned Afri-cola soft drink company tried to sway public opinion by alleging that Coca-Cola had Jewish origins. In fact, the Hebrew letters on bottle caps merely certified that the drink was kosher.

Hitler held caffeine in contempt (at least for civilian consumption) and insisted that bottles be labeled with warning labels. To counterbalance negative impressions of their product, the Coca-Cola Company displayed the swastika prominently at corporate meetings.[29] German physicians suspected that caffeine might harm youth, but Nazi doctors experimented with the potential of caffeine to enhance mental acuity or physical prowess.[30] Wartime advertisements urged German workers to take a coke break ("Mach doch mal Pause"), but cola syrup became scarce when the corporate headquarters in Atlanta stopped exporting their secret version of the flavoring to Nazi Germany. In 1940, Max Keith, director of the German subsidiary Coca-Cola GmbH, devised a fruit-flavored alternative sold under the name Fanta, an abbreviation of the German cognate *Fantasie*. It was manufactured from beet sugar and waste products that included pomace (the remains of apples pressed for juice) and whey (the liquid that remains after milk proteins are curdled and strained in cheese-making). Fanta gained popularity both as a wartime beverage and as a sweetener during a time of sugar rationing.

Coca-Cola was a familiar American product, and bottling plants opened across Europe as Allied forces liberated occupied areas. By the end of the war, General Eisenhower wanted to serve Coca-Cola to a Russian war hero but wondered if Stalin would resent the symbol of American imperialism. To compromise, a local bottling plant devised a clear version of Coca-Cola, bottled and sealed with white caps bearing red stars.

Supplying the Axis

Germany military doctors believed in the power of vegetables to cure mental and physical illnesses, seen in the high botanical content of meals for those serving the Third Reich. Perhaps the vegetable bias resulted also from recent vitamin science and Hitler's own quasi-vegetarian diet, or perhaps it was merely the result of meat shortages that occurred when farmers entered the military. Writing for *Time* magazine before the U.S. entered the war, Viennese physician Dr. Max Gerson noted the vegetable content of German military rations, which he attributed to "the newer knowledge of the science of nutrition." He also noted the use of soybeans, rye bread, and yeast extract in bolstering military nutrition; clearly he believed that Americans could learn lessons from German dietetics.[31] A captured German military cookbook included the recipe for soup made from soy flour and beer and recommended adding soy flour to vegetables, gravy, meat dishes, and dumplings; there was clearly the sense that the U.S. military had much to learn about the benefits of soybeans in military diets.[32]

Field kitchens followed German troops into battle; known as *Gulaschkanone* (after the goulash that they stewed and their cannon-like profile), the vehicle housed a double-walled kettle that encased an internal glycerin layer. These were engineered to prevent direct heat from burning or scorching the thickened broth of *Eintopf* meals, the one-pot soups and stews that were the backbone of the German military diet. *Gulaschkanone* were relocated as battle lines shifted, and the glycerin provided sufficient insulation that cooking continued even after fires were extinguished. *Kochkiste* (hayboxes) were also used to simmer meals while on the march; rye straw was easily gathered from fields, although sand was another available insulator.

Eintopf preparation depended on a generous vegetable larder, a nutritional shift from the First World War when German soldiers survived on a steady diet of sausage and potatoes. The meat to vegetable ratio in a typical *Eintopf* was 1:4 or 1:5, with meat left in visible chunks to promote morale. The dishes used kale, kohlrabi, cabbage, spinach, turnips, and other vegetables. German food technology focused on dehydration, thus *Gulaschkanone* were stocked with packets of dried cabbage, carrots, celery, potatoes, tomatoes, applesauce, jam, and *Bratling* powder, a mixture of vegetable and meat protein that was used for thickening *Eintopf* dishes. Dried peas and lentils supplied additional protein and made a good base for soups, but as imported peas became scarce, military cooks were instructed to use rye to thicken *Eintopf* dishes. Rye gluten is particularly sticky, and addition of the flour transformed broth to a dense soup. Probably as a last resort, military cookbooks provided instructions for thickening *Eintopf* dishes with agar, the algal product used to solidify bacteriological media. Its laboratory use was first identified by Walther Hesse in the laboratory of the German microbiologist Robert Koch. Prior to World War II, Japan was the primary producer of powdered agar, a phycocolloid isolated from the cell walls of red algae; there were agar shortages in the U.S., but it is possible that the German military received supplies from Japan.

The *Deutschen Gartenbaues* (German horticultural society) of Berlin functioned under Reich command once Hitler came into power, and their role was essential in providing successful vegetable crops. *Die Gartenbauwirdschaft*, their weekly newspaper, provided detailed information for growing, harvesting, packaging, and transporting botanical products needed by the German military, demand heightened by new knowledge of vitamins and their role in metabolism and mental health. There was concern about vitamin deficiencies and their effect on strength, stamina, and military outcomes. As the war progressed, vegetable content of military meals increased, more likely due to shortages of meat than to dietary ideals.

Potatoes provided about 60 percent of daily calories and theoretically enough vitamin C to prevent scurvy. Recruits consumed over two pounds daily, but peeling and boiling resulted in vitamin loss, as did prolonged winter storage. Both German and U.S. researchers realized, however, that there is natural variation among potato varieties in terms of both vitamin C levels and retention.[33] German plant breeders attempted to produce potatoes with higher, stable levels of vitamin C; the unstated goal was to transform ordinary potatoes into the dietary equivalent of imported citrus fruit. Nevertheless vitamin C shortages vexed the German military for the duration of the war, and there were efforts to bolster vitamin consumption with packets of yeast extract and vitamin-infused candy supplied in field rations. American medical journals reported that 20 percent of young men in the *Luftwaffe* suffered from "vitamin C hypovitaminosis," resulting in dental diseases and tooth loss, as well as cardiac palpitations known as soldier's heart. Synthetic vitamin C (ascorbic acid) was produced in the 1930s, but apparently was not widely used in Germany. Nor did the German military follow the Russian practice of steeping pine needle tea as a scurvy preventative, a practice credited with saving lives during the siege of Leningrad.[34] In the U.S., speculation mounted that there were too few healthy young men to enter the German army, although in both the U.S. and Germany, physical standards for soldiers decreased as the war progressed.[35]

Military bread included whole-grain rye loaves of *Kommisbrot*, which were flavored with molasses and leavened with a sour dough yeast culture. These were heavy, nutritious loaves that provided the daily requirement of vitamin B1 (thiamine), considered essential for normal mental function and morale. Some *Kommisbrot* was canned for consumption on U-boats, and a long-lasting version of dark bread (known as *Dauerbrot B* or *Wittler Dauerbrot*) was wrapped in glassine (a glossy paper that is impervious to moisture and oils) and sealed in foil. Protected from microbes and drying, it remained palatable for months or longer. Another long term preservation method involved encasing loaves in plastic, a unique German process that involved dipping the loaves in a mixture of polyvinyl acetate, talc, and chalk. The process was sufficiently unique that it was featured in the contemporary press as a significant German wartime advance.[36]

Kommisbrot was served with *ersatz* butter (actually margarine) made from coal, the compressed remains of fossilized Carboniferous plants. Using coal from the Ruhr Valley, the German soap chemist Arthur Imhausen developed a method for extracting paraffin from coke (the remains of coal heated at high temperatures). In turn, the paraffin yielded fatty acids that were easily converted to both soap and artificial butter; once dyed yellow and enriched with vitamin A, it was used to supply the military. U.S. newspapers described the *ersatz* product as another example of German ingenuity.[37]

Dry breads included *Zwieback* (also known as *Feldzwieback*) and crispbread (*Knäckebrot* or *Knäcke*). Long baking eliminated water from the dough and no additional fat was added (aside from the approximately 2 percent fat in rye and wheat flour), so dry breads were suited for long-term storage. They were an essential component of the emergency field provisions known as iron rations. *Zwieback* more closely resembled typical bread mixed up from wheat, rye, or potato flour. The small loaves were flavored with caraway seeds, baked until hard, and packed in reusable cloth bags for distribution. These bags (*Zwiebackbeutel*) were crafted from cotton, linen, or rayon (a wartime alternative to silk that was woven from cellulose fibers obtained from wood pulp). *Hartkeks* (also known as *Keks*) were sweet, dry biscuits or cookies that were also packed in *Zwiebackbeutel* for soldiers on the march or in combat. Soldiers were encouraged to eat pieces of dry breads over the course of the day, to supplement their *Kommisbrot* ration with the extra vitamins and calories needed to maintain high activity. The labels on pocket-sized cardboard boxes promised soldiers, *"Knäckebrot stahit deine Körper und macht dich widerstandsfähig gegen Krankenheit!"* [Crispbread armors your body and makes you resistant to disease!]

When flour supplies were limited, sawdust was used to stretch supplies of rye flour by adding it to bread dough, up to 1 part sawdust to 2 parts flour. Military bakers were instructed on preparing sawdust from pine and birch trees; only the inner bark was used, which is phloem (food conducting tissue), so the sawdust was not actually wood but rather fresh tissue that contained high sugar levels. Once dried and pulverized, it did provide some nutrients. Sawdust from wood provides no nutrients because humans cannot digest cellulose. Soy flour was also used to enrich military bread, but it was used to incorporate protein rather than to increase carbohydrate content. A soy flour product known as *Edelsoja* was mixed into main dishes, soups, vegetables, and grains to bolster protein content when animal proteins were in short supply.

Combat conditions and difficult terrain limited the transport of *Gulaschkanone*, so some soldiers relied on field rations (known as iron rations) for extended periods. The full iron ration included *Zwieback* or other dry bread, dehydrated vegetables, and *ersatz* coffee; this was usually a decoction of roasted grains (such as barley) and molasses, sometimes extended with chicory and dried figs. *Gulaschkanone* were equipped with mounted coffee mills (*Kaffeemuhle*); perhaps they were used to grind roasted grain or acorns when coffee was scarce. Another standard item was *Erbswurst* (pea sausage), a mixture of pea flour and bacon, which was easily rehydrated into a thickened soup. As a military ration, it dated from the Franco-Prussian War when the war ministry considered feeding troops solely on a diet of pea soup and bread. The original *Erbswurst* formula was invented for the Prussian government by Johann Heinrich Grüneberg in 1867, and later it was sold to the Knorr food company, which packaged pea soup for the German army during World War II. German soldiers fought for days on iron rations, but anecdotal reports suggest that they much preferred American rations, which they sometimes captured and consumed. American peanut butter, chocolate bars, and chewing gum surpassed German iron rations in their flavor and appeal.

Rations for aviators and tank and mountain troops required lightweight, long-lasting foods that could be easily stored in a pocket. Based on the concentrated nutrition of Native American pemmican, *Pemmikan-Landjaeger* were pressed bars with concentrated proteins, fats, and vitamins. Botanical ingredients included soybean flour, dried fruit, cranberries, tomato pulp, and green pepper, in addition to yeast and meat. They resembled the K ration bars carried by U.S. paratroopers. Glucose crystallized from grapes (*Traubenzucker*) was a source of quick energy, and paratroopers carried a supply of another grape chemical, tartaric acid, which precipitates as crystals inside wine barrels. The powdered crystals of tartaric acid could be dissolved in stagnant water to make potable water; a weak tartaric acid solution also had medicinal properties as a diuretic, laxative, antiseptic, and skin coolant.

Rations sometimes also included chocolate, a military mixture of cocoa combined with coffee and cola. The intent was to incorporate caffeine to enhance performance, and the standard *Scho-Ka-Kola* bars issued to soldiers contained about two percent caffeine. The German policy regarding caffeine was clearly ambivalent. Hitler shunned caffeine personally, and youth were warned about the caffeine content of Coca-Cola; however, the Reich considered caffeine a potential chemical for enhancing the performance and stamina of young soldiers. German soldiers were also supplied with the stimulant methamphetamine (marketed as Pervitin tablets, which became widely known as *Panzerschokolade* (tank chocolate) because of its use by soldiers engaged in intense combat). The drug was first synthesized in 1893 by the Japanese chemist Nagai Nagayoshi using ephedrine, an alkaloid that he isolated from *Ephedra*, a genus of gymnosperms that are often xerophytes. Pervitin was also known as Herman-Göring-Pills (*Hermann-Göring-Pillen*, named for the Nazi military leader) and as Stuka-Tablets (*Stuka-Tabletten*, named for the dive bomber aircraft *Sturzkampfflugzeug*). Pervitin may have promoted morale and aggression, as well as counteracting fatigue, and it was also used by Allied forces. The chemistry of methamphetamine has no connection to the chemistry of chocolate.

Some rations were developed as gifts from the Führer for wounded or ill soldiers, rather than as provisions for fighting troops. Known as *Führergeschenk*, these were boxed assortments of desirable foods including sugar, marmalade, honey, and flour. The marmalade was likely made from substitutes for imported citrus, and the sugar was no doubt from beets rather than sugar cane. Bees produce honey from flower nectar, but the honey in the Führer gifts was possibly an *ersatz* product (*Kunsthonig*) made from sugar syrup and coloring. Across Europe, many beehives were lost during the war years, and so beet sugar was used to make a thickened syrup that was also included in soldiers' rations. The *Führer-paket* was an assortment of foods for soldiers on leave and included basic supplies such as dried legumes, cereals, starch, sugar, and flour. The likely intended purpose was to provide basic nutrition for a soldier on leave, as well as to alleviate shortages in his family's larder. The gift rations were labeled "*Ein kleiner Dank des Führers an seine Soldaten*" [A small thanks to his soldiers from the Führer] and "*Ein Gruss des Führers an seine Verwundeten*" [Greetings from the Führer to his wounded].

The efficiency of the *Gulaschkanone* did not compensate for the difficult conditions encountered by German soldiers who found themselves with inadequate food while in combat. Anecdotal records from the Battle of the Bulge suggest that some German soldiers survived on captured American rations, D-ration chocolate bars in particular. Plundering of abandoned homesteads yielded stored foods such as fruit preserves, apples, and potatoes. Forests provided edible plants, including fruit such wild apples and bilberries (*Vaccinium myrtillus* and related species) and Iceland moss (*Cetraria islandica*, a lichen), which required several hours of boiling to become palatable. Some hungry German soldiers also dug the starchy rhizomes of rushes and stripped pine cones for their edible seeds.

In contrast to the centralized meal preparation in other armies, Japanese soldiers survived largely on individually-cooked rations of rice and vegetables, supplemented by a small amount of meat. The Imperial Japanese Government issued mostly botanical foods, with most of the calories and nutrition provided by polished rice mixed with barley. Soldiers preferred polished (white) rice over brown rice, and grains with the outer layers removed could be stored longer, but vitamin deficiency was a concern. Thus barley was added to increase thiamine levels; it has about four times as much thiamine as polished rice and could forestall beri-beri, the deficiency disease that was rampant in Asia during the nineteenth century. Symptoms included nerve damage, muscle weakness, and shortness of breath, which would have been disastrous in combat.

Japanese rations as intended also included sweet potato, cabbage, bean sprouts, and radishes, oranges, lychee fruit, pickled vegetables, pickled plums, soy sauce, and miso (both prepared from fermented soybeans; see Chapter 4). The diet as planned was adequate, but food shortages and shipping problems meant that many troops were often desperately short of provisions. Rice arrived by ship, but often troops went for two or three weeks without this staple ration. Emergency rations were planned, including hardtack biscuits, uncooked rice, hard candy, and vitamin pills, but these were often lacking or tightly controlled. For instance, in Burma (now Myanmar) emergency rations could only be consumed with permission from a commanding officer.

Military meals of rice, thin miso soup (see Chapter 4), and a bit or meat or fish were inadequate to support men in combat. To survive, Japanese soldiers on Pacific islands foraged for fruit, coconuts, palm shoots (including the soft inner fibers of coconut palms), and potatoes, which could be fermented to produce an alcoholic mash. Taro (*Colocasia esculenta*) was another staple crop easily planted with asexual rhizome cuttings and cultivated in jungle habitats. On Numfor (Noemfoor) Island in Indonesia, American soldiers discovered a hilltop Japanese garden with hundreds of acres of papaya, cassava, and taro.[38] Of course, both cassava and taro required cooking for safe consumption. The tuberous roots of cassava contain hydrocyanic acid (HCN), which is removed by repeated washing and boiling, and taro rhizomes contain needle-like crystals of calcium oxalate that degrade with baking or boiling. They contain less vitamin C than fresh potatoes (13 mg/100 grams, compared to 21 mg/100g in potatoes), but still helped occupying Japanese troops to avoid scurvy while surviving on a subsistence rice diet.

On inhabited islands, invading and occupying Japanese forces appropriated local crops. In the Philippines, the Japanese army requisitioned local vegetable, fruit, and grains, and the military-controlled government was urged to cooperate with the cultivation of rice, soybeans, and cassava, as well as vegetable gardens. However, the officially mandated double planting of rice failed, despite the introduction of *milagrossa* and *horai* rice cultivars from Japan. Local governors were required to allocate unfarmed lands for agriculture and to distribute seeds, tubers, and seedlings for planting; failure to comply endangered local people because Japanese military needs prevailed in the

Soldiers on Pacific islands were sometimes forced to forage for foods such as taro cultivated in local gardens and farms. Safe preparation of the rhizomes required baking or boiling to breakdown needle-like crystals of calcium oxalate.

event of shortages.[39] A similar situation occurred in Papua New Guinea, where the plundering of yams, cassava, maize, sugar cane, pumpkins, melons, taro, and other staple crops cultivated by indigenous people led to widespread starvation. Japanese soldiers continued to hold out on islands such as Papua New Guinea and Morotai well into the 1950s (one emerged as late as 1974 from the jungles on Lubang), where presumably they survived for years by jungle foraging and perhaps small scale gardening.

6

Agriculture at War

Food fueled the war, both at home and abroad. In early 1940, American farmers had vast quantities of stored foods, Depression-era crops that cash-strapped consumers had been unable to buy. Many Depression-era farms had functioned at a subsistence level, with crops of corn and beans traded for goods and services in a bartering economy. Mechanical equipment and fertilizers were scarce, and crop yields reflected natural soil fertility and climate. Pending warfare meant major agricultural change. Even before the bombing of Pearl Harbor, Secretary of Agriculture Claude Wickard urged in September 1941, "…The largest production in the history of American agriculture to meet the expanding food needs of this country and the nations resisting the Axis."[1] With the start of war in Europe, boon years began for American farms. The need to feed troops and to supply Lend-Lease partners provided an immediate market for all of the food that American farms could produce; even the baled cotton stored in warehouses was soon commissioned for military uniforms. Spurred on by food for defense propaganda, American farmers increased their harvests and adapted to wartime demands.

Mobilizing Farms

During 1941–1945, climate and rainfall were generally ideal, and there were no major infestations of insects or plant pathogens. Hybrid seed was highly productive, and the addition of fertilizer and limestone improved soil nutrients for maximum yields. Thus there were only manmade challenges in increasing agricultural production while waging war abroad; farmers vied with the military for both men and metal. In short, farms needed to produce the maximum yields with the fewest workers and minimal impact on the production of matériel. Mechanization decreased the need for men, but tractors and other machinery required the steel also needed to manufacture airplanes, tanks, guns, helmets, and ammunition. Farm equipment was rationed and in short supply, and thus farmers became experts at repairs and recycling of machinery, including the combines and gins required for certain crops. Wartime USDA posters advised "Contour Farming Saves Soil, Water, Fertilizer" and "Victory Patterns in the Air, on the Land—Contour Farming Means Bigger Wars Crops," assuming that tractors were available and that they had tires and fuel.

The Department of Agriculture promoted the slogan "Food will win the war and write the peace," and posters proclaimed food as a weapon, but American agriculture lacked coordination and clout. Unlike Germany and England, where the Reich Food Corporation and the Ministry of Agriculture dictated crops and targeted productivity, the Department of Agriculture exercised comparatively less control; the War Food Administration, Bureau of Agricultural Economics, and Forestry Service all had a hand in American wartime agriculture. Turf battles ensued, and various officials recommended rather than ordered, which explains why U.S. farmers grew too much cotton and sweet potatoes, too many or too few peanuts, and other disparities between supply and demand. Extension service home economists developed recipes to use surplus crops, and Americans were expected to adjust their appetites accordingly. A peanut glut in 1943 resulted in extension service recipes for peanut butter in sauces and casseroles, and *Women's Day* and *Good Housekeeping* helped by publishing recipes to promote sweet potatoes.

Storage provided another set of challenges. There were incidents of widespread food spoilage, such as the tons of early potatoes that rotted in train cars during the spring of 1943. Huge crops required vast areas for cold storage; even caves were used to preserve produce before it could be used or processed. In Atchison, Kansas, a former limestone mine provided sixty acres of subterranean food storage during the war years, where the War Food Administration arranged to store tons of fresh vegetables, fruits, and other perishables at a constant temperature of 32° Fahrenheit.

Agriculture moved toward botanical diversity, as previously imported crops were grown on native soil. Essential war crops included peanuts, potatoes, sweet potatoes, sugar beets, carrots, tomatoes, cabbage, spinach, kale, onions, corn, and legumes (soybeans, peas, and beans), as well as hemp and cotton for fibers and guayule as an alternate source of rubber (see Chapter 10).[2] Nevertheless, the Steagall Amendment of 1941 promised price supports for a limited number of crops that in terms of vitamins and calories could provide a nutritious, mostly vegetable diet (dried peas, soybeans and other beans, peanuts, potatoes, and sweet potatoes), as well as the cotton needed for uniforms. There was particular concern for previously imported crops, including flax and hemp (see Chapter 8), as well as castor beans.

There were also looming shortages of seed stock, which became additional essential crops. Many farm and garden seeds had been imported from Holland and were subject to control by Nazi occupiers. To provide sufficient supplies for farms and victory gardens, fields were cultivated and harvested specifically for seed. For instance, irrigated areas of Arizona and Idaho were sown successively with oats, increasing the initial investment of 25 pounds to 40,000 pounds of seed stock within a year.[3] Limited seed supply meant that seedling survival was essential; inventors tinkered with various seed coatings that provided fertilizer, insecticide, fungicide, and in the case of legume seeds, the *Rhizobium* inoculant that ensured their growth.[4] At least one method was patented, and seed coating strategies are still in use as a means to establish healthy seedlings.

In the years leading up to the war, Japanese-Americans cultivated thousands of acres as truck farms in California. With the bombing of Pearl Harbor, suspicion of immigrants led to the internment of thousands of these highly skilled farmers; as a result, 200,000 acres of farmland were sold or confiscated from their original owners. Dust Bowl survivors and European immigrants tended the farms that for years had produced 40 percent of the fruits and vegetables cultivated in California—including such essential crops as tomatoes, green peppers, and celery. These comparatively inexperienced farmers did not achieve the productivity of Japanese farmers, the agricultural outcome of inexperience and fewer workers in the fields.

Civilians pitched in where they could. Some participated in harvesting crops, and others saw opportunities for cultivating new crops. For instance, J.A. Jamison, a Florida school superintendent, decided to grow rice in the Everglades. He began with a small pond on wasteland, which in its first season yielded fifty or sixty bushels. His plan was to use the rice as chicken feed, a cheap alternative to the corn that farmers bought as chicken feed, and he encouraged impoverished chicken farmers to plant rice in any available pool of water.[5] In fact, rice cultivation continues in the Everglades, mostly as a means of improving drainage and tilth (the suitability of the soil for sowing seed) in sugar cane fields that can be flooded seasonally.

Military Farms

Providing fresh vegetables to troops worldwide posed complex challenges, and necessity resulted in military farms cultivated abroad. No doubt few enlisted men thought that they would farm while fighting, but as part of the Food Service Program put in place during the summer of 1943, the Office of the Quartermaster General encouraged vegetable cultivation in the Pacific theater. Some servicemen farmed with seeds and tools sent from home; using their collective gardening knowledge along with available supplies, they planted and harvested crops at tropical latitudes. Small gardens helped to boost morale and supplement food for companies and squadrons. On a larger scale, South Pacific islands provided the best arable soil for full-size farms planted and cultivated by the U.S. troops. The largest agricultural tract was on Guadalcanal, where produce from 1,800 acres supported soldiers in the Solomon Islands.

Other farm sites included Espiritu Santo, Efate, New Caledonia, Bougainville, Papua New Guinea, New Georgia, and tropical Australia. The first year (1943) involved experimentation to see what would grow; as expected, successful crops included corn, tomatoes, okra, and watermelons, species that thrive in heat. Delays in obtaining seeds, fertilizer, insecticides, and tools hampered Army farmers grappling with tropical conditions, but any fresh foods were better than none. Tropical insects posed a considerable challenge, and some island soils were depleted of minerals after years of intensive sugar cane farming.[6] Nevertheless, good farming sites were discovered, and plantings occurred on a regular schedule to yield ongoing harvests. Soldiers with farming experience were detached to work on Army farms, but not all sites were maintained by U.S. military personnel. Indian, Chinese, and Melanesian farmers cultivated cabbage, carrots, celery, cucumbers, radishes, and squash in the fertile volcanic and alluvial soils of the Fiji Islands, which proved ideal for growing many of the temperate vegetables familiar to Allied troops.[7] In Australia, the Army Farms Unit cultivated papaws, mangoes, and custard apples along the Adelaide River for troops and military hospitals; they also operated a coffee plantation in Papua New Guinea and shared seed supplies with villagers.[8] Military gardens attracted the attention of local people, no doubt because some of the crops were unfamiliar. Packets of American garden seeds were among the items (along with cloth, knives, canned meat, and tin-plate bowls) bartered in exchange for labor during the construction of airfields in Papua New Guinea.[9]

The Army Air Force instituted hydroponics as an efficient option for growing crops on remote coral atolls that lacked arable soil for traditional agriculture. The first hydroponic farm was built on Ascension Island, a military refueling stop, to provide fresh

War Theatre #7 (Ascension Island)
FIELDS & INSTALLATIONS

Orig. 4x5 neg rec'd 26 March 1946 from Composite Force 8012, AFO #877, c/o P.M., Miami,
(over) Florida.

Construction Of The Hydroponics Garden
On Ascension Island. 7 February 1945

73729 A.C.

INDEXED

War Theatre #7 (Ascension Island)
FIELDS & INSTALLATIONS

Orig. 4x5 neg rec'd 26 March 1946 from Composite Force 8012, AFO #877, c/o P.M., Miami,
(over) Florida.

Tomato Beds In The Hydroponics Garden
On Ascension Island. 7 February 1945

73733 A.C.

INDEXED

produce that otherwise had to be flown into the site. Vegetable plants rooted easily in a growth medium made of inert volcanic gravel; they were watered with a solution of mineral salts that provided nitrogen, phosphorous, potassium, and other essential plant nutrients. Developing botanical knowledge about necessary plant micronutrients was essential to success in combining and mixing the mineral salts, including those needed in trace amounts such as boron, iron, and manganese. The typical method involved building beds at successive levels so that the nutrient solution flowed by gravity from one to the next and was then pumped to the top. Additional hydroponic farms were constructed on British Guiana, Iwo Jima, Okinawa, and Wake Island, all areas where the tropical climate worked in favor of productivity. On Wake Island, a single hydroponic bed of 120 square feet yielded 20 heads of lettuce, 30 pounds of tomatoes, and 40 pounds of corn weekly.[10] Other environments also supported wartime hydroponics. The British Air Ministry established hydroponic farms in the deserts of Iraq and on the Persian Gulf island of Bahrein, the site of oil fields. At the end of the war, American troops in Japan soon realized that the custom of fertilizing crops with night soil could cause dysentery, the result of enteric bacteria and intestinal protozoa that colonized the soil. A 55-acre hydroponic farm solved the gastrointestinal problem and supplied occupying troops with fresh vegetables for the next fifteen years.

Hybridization and Hybrid Vigor

In 1900, the rediscovery of Mendel's experiments with garden peas established the option of making controlled crosses within a species, yielding hybrid offspring with known and desired genetic traits. Mendel's meticulous work demonstrated that inheritance is controlled by discrete particles (genes) that pass to offspring following the laws of probability. In breeding agricultural crops, hybrid seeds result from crossing two inbred parental strains with different characteristics, such as disease resistance, drought tolerance, or high yield. When grown to maturity, hybrid offspring may outperform either parental strain; this phenomenon known as hybrid vigor or heterosis was first described in 1908 by American corn geneticist George Harrison Shull, who conducted early experiments in hybridizing corn. Another early hybridizer was Henry Wallace, who produced "Hi-bred" corn that increased yields from four to ten bushels per acre; he was among the first to realize that appearance, vigor, and yield were not connected. After a boyhood spent with George Washington Carver as a mentor, Wallace went on to become secretary of agriculture (1933–40) and vice president (1941–45), bringing his knowledge of farming and plant breeding to the executive branch during wartime.

Most small-scale U.S. farmers were content with their pre-war yields, growing food for their families and cash crops that generated modest income. However, war functioned

Opposite, top: **The first Army Air Force hydroponic farm was built on Ascension Island, a military refueling stop, to provide fresh produce that otherwise had to be flown into the site. Vegetable plants rooted easily in a growth medium made of inert volcanic gravel, and they were watered with a solution of mineral salts that provided plant nutrients.** *Bottom:* **Tomato beds in the hydroponic farm on Ascension Island were arranged at successive levels so that the nutrient solution flowed by gravity downhill and was then pumped to the top. Additional hydroponic farms were constructed on British Guiana, Iwo Jima, Okinawa, and Wake Island, all areas where the tropical climate worked in favor of productivity (both photographs, U.S. Army).**

as a catalyst for change as farmers were reminded unrelentingly that food was a weapon. The scientific approach to farming, spread by county extension agents in the 1930s (but often viewed with suspicion by experienced farmers) came into its day. Genetic advances were part of the shift to modern farming; corn fields planted with hybrid seed increased bushel yield per acre by more than two-fold, and so its wartime appeal was obvious. However, many farmers preferred the large, even-rowed corn from open-pollinated varieties to less symmetrical ears produced by hybrid seeds.[11] Of course, there were early assumptions that hybrid seed and chemical fertilizers would worked synergistically to push harvests higher, but hybrid corn did not necessarily grow better with the addition of chemical fertilizers. Some varieties grew tall, spindly stems that snapped under the weight of the ears, a problem known as lodging.[12] However, despite initial challenges, hybridization improved several wartime crops including tomatoes, onions, squash, cucumbers, sugar beets, and corn.

Luther Burbank was another early plant hybridizer known for producing numerous varieties of ornamental plants and stone fruit. In 1872, he developed the 'Russet Burbank' potato variety, which he selected from South American stock that had some resistance to late blight. By the 1940s, this variety was grown widely and used to prepare dehydrated potatoes for military messing; by the end of the war, the J.R. Simplot Company had shipped 33 million pounds of dried potatoes to the armed forces. Although his ideas on evolutionary science were vague (he thought that magnetism and vibrational forces were important influences), Burbank was a recognized expert on genetic selection who later applied the principles of plant breeding to human populations. In his 1909 treatise, *The Training of the Human Plant*, he compared human reproduction to horticultural crosses; in Chapter 6, "Marriage of the Physically Unfit," Burbank discussed eugenics, later known as the philosophical underpinning of Nazi racial and ethnic discrimination, "It would, if possible, be best absolutely to prohibit in every State in the Union the marriage of the physically, mentally, and morally unfit. If we take a plant that we recognize as poisonous and cross it with another which is not poisonous and thus make the wholesome plant evil … this is criminal enough. But suppose we blend together two poisonous plants and make a third even more virulent, a vegetable degenerate…. What then shall we say of two people of absolutely defined physical impairment who are allowed to marry and bear children?"[13] Of course, Burbank had no means to predict the Nazi ideal of "racial hygiene" and the suffering that it ultimately caused, and similar comingling of human genetics and agriculture occurred in England. A popular eugenics poster from the 1930s used the planting of seeds as a metaphor for selective human reproduction, with the message "Only healthy seed must be sown! Check the seeds of hereditary disease and unfitness by eugenics."

In short, plant hybridization provided a strategy for combining ideal traits into a single variety and for increasing per-acre yields using genetically-controlled traits, but the seeds required annual production and purchase. Those who saved seeds from hybrid plants soon realized that their offspring did not necessarily replicate parental traits, and the results were often disappointing. In the case of wind-pollinated crops such as corn, planting alternate rows of two varieties resulted in hybrid seed as air-borne pollen landed on the stigmas (the tip of the corn silks) and fertilized the ovules. Thus, in order to avoid the chance of self-pollination, farmers had to remove the cluster of male flowers from the seed-producing plant, a process known as detasseling. This made hybridization labor-intensive, but crop productivity soared once most farms cultivated hybrid varieties which were remarkably uniform and easily harvested.[14] By 1933, Marcus Morton Rhoades identified a trait that controlled male sterility, which could be bred into genetic lines, making detasseling unnecessary. Apparently the technique was not widely used in producing hybrid corn during the war years, and one of the most labor intensive tasks of the Women's Land Army was tassel removal.

Increased yields meant more corn to feed to livestock, process into starch and oil, and ferment into ethanol. Some of the corn ethanol was converted to butadiene for the synthesis of rubber.[15] However, pigs and cows competed for corn-based animal feed, and there were widespread problems with moving corn from Midwestern farms to cattle and pig farmers. An article in *Time* magazine complained bitterly about disorganized supply, demand, and transport; as milk producers, cows seemed more important, but many favored pork for meat, and both species needed corn in their feed. Governors of several states cautioned residents to eat little meat and to anticipate milk rationing because livestock farms were not getting the corn shipments necessary to

Hybrid corn yields meant more corn to feed to livestock, process into starch and oil, and ferment into ethanol for fuel and industry. Some of the corn ethanol was converted to butadiene for rubber synthesis, and starch from corn was used to make a substitute for TNT (U.S. Department of Agriculture).

supply both military and civilian needs. Midwestern farmers took advantage of the confusion by selling their crops at high prices to itinerant buyers, who shipped the hybrid corn directly to hog farms.[16] There was little wartime waste; cornstalks and the stems of other robust grasses such as sugar cane were used to make fiberboard and plastics.[17]

Some corn was also used to make explosives. Nitric acid reacts with cornstarch to produce nitrostarch, a viable substitute for TNT in the event of a shortage. Nitrostarch was highly sensitive to impact, and the half pound blocks were easily ignited with a spark; the 502nd Parachute Infantry Regiment used it in Europe, including Operation Market Garden. The Japanese army also used nitrostarch as the primary ingredient in a cluster of seven small bombs launched by a 70-mm barrage mortar. Each was held aloft by a rice paper parachute and designed for mid-air detonation.[18] Corn had been cultivated in Japan since the early 1900s, so the starch was readily available. Alternately, the Japanese may have manufactured nitrostarch from tapioca (the original ingredient used in nitrostarch), derived from the roots of cassava (*Manihot esculenta*), a tropical root crop.

Sugar Beets, Soybeans and Oil Crops

Other hybridized wartime crops included sugar beets and soybeans. Sugar beets (*Beta vulgaris* var.*esculenta*), a biennial cultivar with pale, elongated taproots, provided an alternative that yielded sucrose chemically identical to cane sugar. Beet sugar could be used for foods and for fermentation into alcohol, both for beverages and industrial processes that included the manufacture of explosives. Originating from wild beets (*B. vulgaris* var. *maritima*) that colonized European coastlines, sugar beets were known since ancient times. Natural variations in size and sugar content provided the genetic diversity for selecting and breeding several varieties. The pale roots known as mangel-wurzels or mangolds were commonly cultivated for fodder or silage, but they have also served as a survival food for humans. Other varieties were bred for edible sucrose; Napoleon encouraged their cultivation as part of an embargo against British sugar imports, and by the late nineteenth century successful crops were widely cultivated in both the U.S. and Europe. New England abolitionists supported sugar beet culture to circumvent slave labor in cane fields. Thus sugar beet crops were nothing new, but war caused a resurgence of interest in both the U.S. and Europe.

During World War II, cultivars were grown widely as an alternative to Hawaiian and Philippine sugar imports. Agricultural posters encouraged farmers: "Plant More Sugar Beets—Sugar is energy—Let's give 'em plenty." Successful beet farms in Oregon, Montana, Idaho, Utah, and North Dakota depended on the expertise of Japanese-American farmers recruited to work in the fields. These farmers, interned at the onset of the war, had grown sugar beets as a cash crop on family farms in California. With the onset of war, they were relocated to internment camps away from coastlines, but their expertise was essential to growing beet crops, which by 1942 supplied 40 percent of the annual U.S. sugar supply.

Sugar beet crops adapted to various soils and were suited to machine cultivation. Hybridization experiments yielded new varieties that exhibited hybrid vigor, including disease resistance, cold tolerance, and resistance to bolting. Cylindrical rings of cambium cells produced horizontal growth that yielded robust taproots, where the plants stored sugar during the growing season. Sugar concentrations peaked in the fall, and harvesting occurred before freezing temperatures hardened the ground. In terms of root anatomy, there was little woody growth despite the differentiation of cambium layers, so the taproots were easily crushed or sliced. Sugar extraction was easier than with the tough stems of sugar cane, but sugar beet processing did not yield palatable molasses. The thick syrup left over from sugar crystallization contained raffinose (a sugar that humans cannot digest) and the nitrogenous compound betaine, but the waste liquid was used during the war years to fatten cattle and to ferment into industrial alcohol.

German chemistry resulted in an ignominious use of sugar beets beyond sucrose and alcohol production. When conducted at temperatures higher than 1,000 degrees Centigrade, beet root processing releases hydrocyanic (prussic) acid. This method was known as the *Schlempe* process, named for the firm that owned rights to the chemical process (*Schlempe* is also the term for the nitrogen-rich waste that remains after sucrose is removed from sugar beets). The company was part of the Degussa corporation, which used the cyanide in manufacturing the product known as Zyklon B. Originally developed as a pesticide, this mixture of hydrocyanic acid and porous adsorbents was first used widely (including in the U.S.) for delousing clothes and sanitizing agricultural buildings.

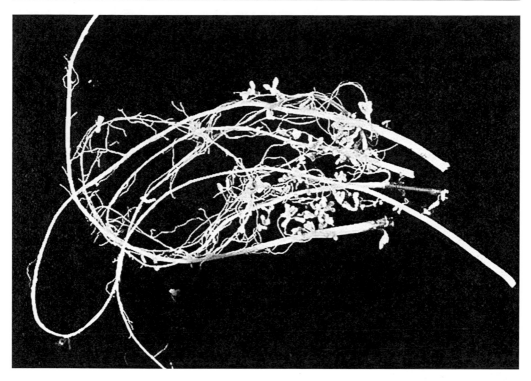

Soybeans improve soil nitrogen levels by hosting symbiotic nitrogen-fixing bacteria in nodules that grow on their roots, so farmers soon learned that soybean growth was not limited by the application of nitrogenous fertilizer. The U.S. Department of Agriculture had acquired nearly three thousand varieties from Asian breeders and promoted soybean planting widely during the war years (U.S. Department of Agriculture).

The adsorbent portion consisted of diatomaceous earth, sedimentary layers that accumulate from the siliceous cell walls of the single-celled algae known as diatoms. Vast deposits were mined in Germany, in areas such as the northern region of Lüneburg Heath.

During the war, Zyklon B was used to fumigate German barracks, hospitals, and ships. The pellets were later used in the gas chambers at Auschwitz-Birkenau and other Nazi death camps to exterminate millions of prisoners from German-occupied Europe. SS (*Schutzstaffel*) officers were responsible for handling canisters of the highly toxic mixture of beet-derived cyanide and algal cell walls, each bearing the warning label *Giftgas* (poison gas). Death resulted from the effect of cyanide on blocking cellular respiration, which over several minutes resulted in suffocation.

Like other legumes, soybeans improve soil nitrogen levels by hosting symbiotic nitrogen-fixing bacteria in their roots (see Chapter 4). *Rhizobium* bacteria convert atmospheric nitrogen to ammonia, so farmers soon learned that soybean growth was not limited by the application of nitrogenous fertilizer. The U.S. Department of Agriculture had acquired nearly three thousand varieties from Asian breeders and promoted soybean planting widely. Hybridization helped to eliminate agricultural problems like lodging (collapse of mature plants due to weakened stems) and shattering (breakage of the mature pods), and supposedly some of the new varieties had improved flavor. Presumably they lacked the enzymes that digested soybean oil into smaller fragments, or perhaps had lower phytoestrogen levels which improved the "beany" taste that some found objectionable (see Chapter 4). Chemists tinkered with ways to improve the taste of soy-based foods, and several methods were patented.

The plants tolerated acidic soils and low rainfall, but they could not survive frost. However, the only real problem was caused by soybean roots that grew more than six feet deep; they tapped deep groundwater, disrupted the aggregate structure of soil, and caused erosion. Farmers nevertheless saw the advantage of soybeans in enriching soil nitrogen levels and so used them in regular crop rotation. Not all soybean crops were grown to harvest beans; some farmers plowed mature plants directly into the soil or fermented them into silage. During the 1930s, most soybeans were used to feed livestock, but soon they became a staple wartime protein substitute in home front meals (see Chapter 4). Demand was high for soybean meal and flour, and the oil was used in making margarine. Soy flour was an essential ingredient in high protein K-ration biscuits that were baked from one part soy flour and seven parts wheat flour (see Chapter 5). Lend-Lease imports to England and the Soviet Union included soybean-enriched sausages, soups, and cereals. In response to demand, by 1942 the soybean harvest was 188 million bushels, harvested from fourteen million acres cultivated in thirty states.

Aside from food, the various uses for soybean proteins and oils included soaps and cleaning compounds, insecticides, industrial and lubricating oils, paints, varnishes, printing ink, linoleum, oil cloth, oiled (waterproof) clothing, candles, rubber substitutes, textile fibers, plastics, paper coating, and sizing.

Aside from food, the various uses for soybean proteins and oils were diverse: soaps and cleaning compounds, insecticides, industrial and lubricating oils, paints, varnishes, printing ink, linoleum, oil cloth, oiled (waterproof) clothing, candles, rubber substitutes, textile fibers, plastics, paper coatings, and sizings. Soybean varieties such as 'Roanoke' were selected specifically for their high oil content and grown widely in southern states. In 1941, Henry Ford revealed the prototype of a car manufactured entirely from soy-based plastic; the project ended as wartime demands increased, but the complex chemistry of soybean proteins and oils soon found numerous wartime uses. For instance, plywood lamination (see Chapter 9) required waterproof glue, which could be made by combining ground soybeans with a phenolic resin.[19] Rubber shortages were a critical wartime problem, and a soy-based polymer known as Norepol was developed as a substitute for imported latex (see Chapter 10).

Soy-based foaming solutions included the "bean soup" foam invented by Percy Julian, known as Aer-o-foam (see Chapter 4) and eventually marketed for firefighting by National Foam System, Inc. in Philadelphia. Their patent application (U.S. Patent 2,413,667) noted that the firefighting foam surpassed earlier mixtures that used licorice and oak bark to stabilize the bubbles. The success of Aer-o-foam pivoted on soybean chemistry; burning ships were literally surrounded by floating soy byproducts that quelled the danger of fire and fuel. Combined with water, the bean proteins provided a rigid framework for bubble formation, which allowed the carbon dioxide bubble layer to float atop burning fuel and smother contact with air. The U.S. Navy stockpiled and carried Aer-o-foam to spray on oil and gas fires, which can be particularly hazardous at sea. An article in *Time* magazine described the soy-water mixture as "a thick, snowy blanket of carbon dioxide bubbles.... In one Pacific sea fight 118 warship fires were reportedly snuffed out by foam."[20] Early orders for Aer-o-foam surprised the manufacturer, Fisher Longstreth Boyd, a lifelong Quaker, who did not think of the product as matériel. Nevertheless in early 1942 his Philadelphia firm managed to fulfill the U.S. Navy order for 200,000 gallons, which protected thousands of sailors from fire at sea.

In addition to soybean oil, various other botanical oils were essential during wartime, as lubricants, waterproofing chemicals, paints, varnishes, and chemical starting points for industrial processes. Acreage planted in oilseed crops such as flax and peanuts increased more than 40 percent during the war, and farmers were offered five dollar per acre incentives in return for each acre seeded with an oil crop.[21] Linseed oil is pressed from the seeds of flax (*Linum usitatissum*), a temperate Eurasian species that is also used for linen fibers (see Chapter 8). The seeds yield a drying oil used in compounding paints, varnishes, linoleum, and printing ink, products that were all in high demand during the war years. The seed coats and remaining endosperm tissue were pressed and used as fodder; in Germany, seed cakes made from flax waste doubled as an emergency food for humans.

Oil pressed from the seeds of peanuts (*Arachis hypogaea*) was used as a margarine ingredient, lubricant, and as a starting point for soap synthesis. Like peanuts, soybeans (*Glycine max*) are legumes that improve soil nitrogen content through their symbiotic relationship with nitrogen-fixing bacteria. Castor beans (not true legumes but rather the seeds of *Ricinus communis*, a member of the family Euphorbiaceae) were also grown for their oil (long known as a laxative and purgative), which had valuable wartime uses in waterproofing fabric, lubricating airplane engines, and making paints, inks, soaps, airplane coverings, and plastics.[22]

Castor bean imports came from China, but farmers in California, Arizona, Texas, and Oklahoma raised successful crops, encouraged by wartime incentives for crops with strategic uses. Interest in castor beans extended beyond their industrial uses;

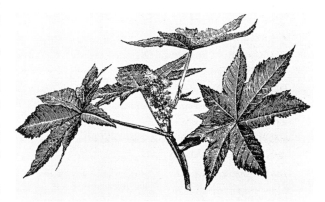

Castor beans were grown for their oil, which had valuable wartime uses in waterproofing fabric, lubricating airplane engines, and making paints, inks, soaps, airplane coverings, and plastics. The seeds contain the protein ricin, a powerful nerve toxin considered for weaponization as aerosols and small cluster bombs.

the seeds synthesize the protein ricin, a powerful nerve toxin considered for weaponization in several ways. During World War I, ricin-coated bullets and shrapnel were used for animal experiments, but ricin tended to denature from heat exposure, rendering it inactive. During World War II, ricin-containing aerosols and small cluster bombs were tested in at the Dugway Proving Ground in Utah. Although the U.S. could have produced a thousand tons of ricin annually from processing castor oil, ricin was never used as a weapon. The reason may have centered on ethics, or perhaps ricin was rejected because it takes days rather than minutes to kill. Seed cakes left over from pressing the oil each contained about a gram of ricin, so they were used as fertilizer rather than fodder.

Plant Nutrients and Soil Fertility

Successful farming depended on soil management, which was of particular concern after the Dust Bowl years of the 1930s. The U.S. Soil Conservation Service promoted crop rotation as a sound strategy to sustain soil fertility, improve yields, maintain soil structure, and eliminate pests and pathogens that might persist from season to season. It was not a new concept, especially with crops with high nutrient demands such as cotton; years earlier George Washington Carver had suggested alternating crops of cotton with legumes, which helped to restore soil nutrients. Erosion control, also essential to soil conservation, involved the construction of waterways, ponds, and terraces across agricultural land.

Added to agricultural fields, limestone (calcium-based minerals) neutralized acidity and increased numbers of soil bacteria, a process known as liming. Low pH was often caused by an excess of aluminum in the soil, resulting in hydrolysis in which –OH ions from water cling to aluminum ions (Al^{+3}) and H+ ions (acidity) are released into the soil. The U.S. government subsidized the process of crushing limestone (usually calcium carbonate) to make the product known as marl, and farmers soon realized that working it into the soil increased crop yields by a measurable percent. Calcium intervenes chemically by replacing the H+ ions on the surface of soil particles; H+ ions combine with carbonate ions ($-CO_3$) to release carbon dioxide and water, and soil pH increases. In fact, both soil quality and plant growth benefited from the addition of limestone. Calcium is essential for cell wall growth and cellular signaling, and trace amounts of magnesium provided the Mg^{++} ions need for chlorophyll synthesis. In short, applied chemistry helped to prevent the horrific soil conditions of the 1930s Dust Bowl, an environmental disaster that destroyed thousands of acres of Great Plains farmland.

Mineral fertilizers were another significant factor in improved crop yields. Based on years of research at land grant universities, wartime agriculturalists knew that plants needed several chemical elements for growth. In addition to carbon, hydrogen, and oxygen (from water and air), plants used nitrogen, phosphorus, potassium, calcium, sulfur, and magnesium, along with trace amounts of boron, chlorine, manganese, iron, zinc, copper, molybdenum, and nickel. Standard fertilizers bolstered the levels of the most essential elements (nitrogen, phosphorus, and potassium), while powdered limestone or even bones provided calcium. Inorganic fertilizers known as N-P-K mixtures combined nitrogen, phosphorus, and potassium-containing compounds, including ammonium nitrate and some of the same compounds used in explosives. Soil generally provided sufficient trace amounts of the other elements, including magnesium, the core ion in chlorophyll molecules.

By the early 1940s, U.S. agriculture demanded millions of tons of N-P-K fertilizers to support intensive agriculture and wartime crops. Corn, wheat, soybeans, and cotton crops removed nutrients from the soil, but crop rotation became impossible in fields devoted exclusively to these high-demand crops. Fertilizer chemicals were mined as minerals and often imported in huge quantities. Sodium nitrate (known as Chile saltpeter, different from the usual potassium-based saltpeter) was obtained and shipped from mines in South America. For years, potassium came from potash-rich regions of Germany (potash refers to the potassium salts that can be used by plants), but by World War I, U.S. farmers relied on Nebraska deposits; Canada later supplied much of the potassium for wartime fertilizers. Phosphate deposits were more common, and eventually both potassium and phosphate compounds were produced by chemical processes.

With the exception of legumes, crop plants could not use atmospheric nitrogen (N_2), and so a chemical process that converted nitrogen gas into ammonia was a major advance that alleviated some of the dependence on sodium nitrate deposits. German chemist Fritz Haber perfected the process of nitrogen fixation, yielding synthetic ammonia that could be used to make both fertilizers and explosives, for which he won the 1918 Nobel Prize in Chemistry. After World War I, he was credited with preventing widespread starvation in Europe by discovering a way to improve soil nitrogen with ammonia rather than relying on nitrate deposits. The German BASF Corporation bought rights to the reaction, and by 1931 was producing industrial levels of ammonia using a scaled-up technique known as the Haber-Bosch process; ironically, Haber died two years later, on route to Palestine while fleeing the Nazi regime. The U.S. adapted the Haber process to produce the ammonia needed for vast amounts of wartime fertilizers. The federal government built ten chemical plants to convert atmospheric nitrogen into ammonia, reduction reactions that required high pressure and temperature. The source of the hydrogen was methane from natural gas, a breakdown product of plant cellulose and other organic matter.

Fertilizers were used prudently during the war years, but the only agricultural crops that did not need nitrogen-enriched soil were legumes, which have symbiotic nitrogen-fixing *Rhizobium* bacteria that colonize nodules in their roots (see Chapter 4). Victory gardeners were supplied with standard low-nitrogen victory garden fertilizer with an N-P-K ratio of 3–8–7. Due to the needs of munitions manufacture, nitrogen levels were lower than in pre-war garden fertilizers, but the product was widely promoted as suitable for cultivating small crops (see Chapter 1). Fertilizer application on any land other than agricultural fields was forbidden; golf courses and lawns survived without added nutrients during the war years. Farmers were instructed to avoid fertilizing spring-sown grain (snow provided some minerals) as well as watermelon and cucumber crops, which were considered low in food value. An exception was made for cucumbers planted for processing into pickles for military messing. Nutrients were scrutinized from all angles; for instance, the leftover meal from processing oilseed crops, previously used for fertilizing fields, was repurposed as wartime animal feed.[23]

Farmers took advantage of legumes such as alfalfa as productive cover crops, a technique that controlled soil erosion and enriched its fertility. Along with contour plowing and crop rotation, this was a tried-and-true method that helped to save Dust Bowl farmlands of the southern plains during the 1930s. By 1942, a perennial hybrid variety of alfalfa held promise for improving soil fertility and erosion problems, as well as for feeding livestock. It resulted from careful crosses among four varieties, resulting in a shrubby perennial that could be propagated by cuttings rather than crossed to produce seed.[24] Apparently this variety did not appeal to farmers, who found broadcasting seed easier than planting rooted slips over vast acreage. Alfalfa was also interplanted and harvested together with sorghum (*Sorghum vulgare*) a tropical grass used traditionally for making syrup. They were fermented into silage and provided a good balance of soy protein and sorghum calories. The soy and sorghum mixture did not require the addition of molasses (a waste product from processing both cane and beet sugar), which was often used to promote fermentation in silage, but was in short supply during the war years because it could be fermented into industrial alcohol.[25]

Soil cultivation involved tools and labor, and some wartime innovations deserve mention, including the efforts of an Alabama farmer in adapting military flame throwers for weeding agricultural fields. Built with two burners, the gasoline-fueled device hooked on to a tractor for dragging through the field, where it "spread a sheet of fire close to the surface of the soil on opposite sides of the row." Aside from the occasional burned leaf, tall crops such as sugar cane, cotton, and corn supposedly suffered no damage while weeds wilted and died from the blast of heat. Weed roots remained buried "as binders for the soil" that discouraged erosion.[26] Agricultural flame throwers were never mass produced, but following USDA endorsement, farmers were encouraged to make and use the devices in their fields. They were certainly more efficient than hand-hoeing, but how many such devices were actually made and used is unknown. Another petroleum-based option was the use of organic solvents that killed weeds. They could be sprayed around parsnips, carrots, and celery (the recommended amount was eighty gallons per acre) without damaging the seedlings. Standard Oil manufactured the compounds and sold them under the name Sovasol; they were used in dry-cleaning and paint manufacture but were highly toxic. It also unknown how many farmers adopted their use for cultivating fields, a process that would have resulted in contaminated soil.[27]

Pests and Pesticides

There were no major insect attacks on agricultural crops during World War II, but pesticides were considered essential to productivity, and shortages loomed. In 1942, the director of the Bureau of Entomology and Plant Quarantine noted, "The war has greatly curtailed the supply of materials that enter into the manufacture of many of our most potent insecticides, fungicides and grain fumigants, and a large part of the work ... has been concerned with finding substitutes."[28]

The use of lead arsenate and calcium arsenate increased by half during the war, but botanical insecticides were still the most widely used. The most important was pyrethrum, the secondary compounds (known as pyrethrins) produced by the flowers of *Chrysanthemum* species native to the Balkans (*C. cinerariifolium*) and the Caucasus region (*C. coccineum* and *C. marshallii*). At the time, pyrethrum was valued as being nontoxic to humans and animals, residue-free, and non-flammable. We now know that it is potentially toxic, with possible neurologic and endocrine effects that depend on exposure; moreover, pyrethrin compounds may also cycle in ecosystems where they kill invertebrates and perhaps fish and reptiles. However, in wartime pyrethrum killed not only field and garden insect pests, but also lice, fleas, and the mosquito vectors of malaria and yellow fever. Pyrethrum bombs (actually aerosols) helped to eliminate the danger of malaria for troops fighting in the South Pacific. Japan was a leading grower and exporter of pyrethrum flowers. When war cut off supplies, growers in California, South America, Africa, and Australia began planting and cultivating *Chrysanthemum*. Harvesting, drying, and packaging required time and care, thus the development of an efficient harvesting machine was a significant innovation. Developed by USDA engineers, the apparatus allowed two farm workers to harvest four acres of flowers in a day.[29]

Rotenone, a toxin synthesized by the roots of various tropical legumes, was another botanical insecticide with extensive agricultural uses. It was first known from roots of the Malaysian genus *Derris*, woody vines long used to stun fish and poison arrows. Known locally as *tuba*, the cultivated species included the *D. elliptica* and *D. trifoliata*. By 1940, U.S. farmers were using 6.5 million pounds annually, but imports diminished with the start of war with Japan. The fall of Singapore eliminated imported roots by half, but eventually *Derris* plantations were cultivated in Guatemala and Ecuador. The South American genus *Lonchocarpus*, also a fish toxin, provided an alternate rotenone supply during the war years. The dried roots of *Lonchocarpus* contain a higher percentage of rotenone than *Derris* roots, and pulverized with clay they made an effective insecticidal powder. The roots required two or more years to mature, so farmers in Brazil and Peru inter-planted the vines with traditional food crops including bananas and plantains; they then worked diligently to excavate and bundle the mature taproots. Traditional farms were small sites carved from rain forest habitats, where *Lonchocarpus* vines thrived.[30]

As with pyrethrum, more is now known about rotenone toxicity; the compound kills red blood cells and may cause neurological damage that resembles Parkinson's disease. Nevertheless millions of pounds of South American roots protected U.S. farm crops and victory gardens during the war years. Concern about pyrethrum and rotenone shortages spurred the development of synthetic pesticides, and DDT eventually replaced much of the pyrethrum once used to kill lice, particularly the species that carried typhus in the South Pacific theater.

Biological Warfare and the Wartime Food Supply

There were no major insect infestations that threatened strategic crops during the war years, but there were attempts at weaponizing insect pests. Colorado potato beetles were first discovered in the Rocky Mountains, where they consume the leaves of native nightshade (*Solanum rostratum*). Apparently they tolerate toxic solanine alkaloids, which are also synthesized by potatoes (*S. tuberosum*), tomatoes (*S. lycopersicum*), and eggplants (*S. melongena*). Potato beetles soon invaded U.S. agricultural fields and moved east toward Ohio and New England. Despite bans on potatoes imported from the U.S., potato beetles established themselves in several European countries when they were probably imported inadvertently with supplies and equipment during World War I.

As early as 1937 the geneticist J.B.S. Haldane suggested that potato beetles might be dropped by airplanes onto agricultural fields in England, and Germany and other countries shared the same fear. As the main ingredient (and most of the calories) in *Eintopf* meals (see Chapter 4), potatoes were the backbone of the German diet. During the war years, Germans consumed three times more potatoes than Americans, and significant crop loss would have meant widespread famine. The invasion of France revealed that their scientists were investigating potato beetles as biological weapons, research that ended with German occupation. Nevertheless, a major beetle infestation was potentially catastrophic; hundreds of German inspectors remained on the lookout for potato beetle attacks, toiling in more than 200 million acres of potato fields.[31]

Despite Hitler's early opposition to biological warfare, by 1943 German scientists in the working group known as *Blitzableiter* had a diversified research program of biological warfare to use on the Allies. Investigations centered on aggressive weeds that might be dispersed into agricultural fields; on plant diseases such as potato blight and wheat rust; and on aphids, moths, flies, beetles, and other pests of strategic crops (including wheat, corn, potatoes, rapeseed, and even pine trees), but Colorado potato beetles remained the insect of choice. Estimates suggested that German scientists would need to breed and stockpile a minimum of twenty million potato beetles to stage an effective attack on English potato fields. Rearing the insects from larval through adult stages would have involved greenhouses filled with potato plants. In October 1943, entomologists experimented with releasing 40,000 live beetles from airplanes flying over German farms.[32] Of course, there was the risk of infecting German crops so subsequent experiments were conducted with artificial wooden beetles. Some English claimed that beetle "bombs" (cardboard boxes filled with several dozen insects) were dropped over British fields; there were also reports that young evacuees helped with catching and killing the beetles, although there is no concrete evidence that German potato beetle attacks ever did occur.[33]

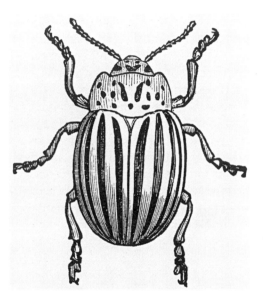

Colorado potato beetles were first discovered in the Rocky Mountains, but they established themselves in several European countries, probably imported inadvertently with supplies and equipment during World War I. Germans feared beetle attacks from Allied countries; meanwhile their scientists experimented with breeding thousands of beetles to attack English potato fields. There was no concrete evidence that such attacks ever did occur.

As part of the work done by the infamous Unit 731, Japan pursued research on nematodes that damage roots and plant pathogens such as smut and rust. There was particular emphasis on pests and pathogens that could affect crops in the Pacific Northwest, as well as potent herbicides that could be sprayed over agricultural fields in the U.S. and Soviet Union. Realizing the need for possible retaliation during World War II, the U.S. initiated a program of anti-crop biological warfare that extended into the Cold War years, including chemical herbicides and defoliants. Much of the work is now declassified and included research into diseases that affect wheat, rice, soybeans, sugar beets, and cotton. Herbicide research stemmed from knowledge of plant growth hormones; it was known that high amounts of natural hormones such as indole acetic acid (a naturally occurring auxin) killed plants, so wartime efforts centered on finding chemically stable synthetic versions that could kill potato and rice crops. Although such compounds were never used to destroy Axis crops, one outcome was the discovery of 2,4-D (2,4-dichlorophenoxyacetic acid), a synthetic auxin that is toxic to broad-leaved plants. By 1945, 2,4-D was marketed to U.S. farmers to use as a selective herbicide against agricultural weeds. Decades later the compound was used as a component of the military defoliant known as Agent Orange.

Harvesting Labor

The war took workers away from American farms. Many men volunteered for military service, some were drafted, and others left for work in defense industries. By late 1942, *Time* magazine predicted catastrophe. There were six million U.S. farms, and food production surpassed World War I by 40 percent; however, labor dwindled as a projected three million farmers left U.S. farms.[34] In the *San Francisco News* on March 9, 1942, John Brucato described a possible solution, "Farm groups today are asking people in the cities to give earnest consideration to plans for the entire family combining their annual outings with a bit of work in the fields or orchards. Proponents of the 'Victory Vacation' point out such vacations not only would be patriotic but would also be a matter of good health, through exercise and fresh air…."[35] In a Farm Mobilization Day speech delivered on January 12, 1943, President Roosevelt encouraged Americans to redouble the effort to grow food. Despite shortages of machinery and fertilizers, manpower remained the most critical need; eight thousand soldiers were sent to Maine, New York, and North Dakota for temporary farm duty rather than combat. Conscientious objectors, interned Japanese Americans, and migrant workers also planted, cultivated, and harvested crops. The responsibility for farming (not just victory gardens) was shared by all on the home front; emergency labor also came from women, children, teenage members of the Victory Farm Volunteers, and retirees.[36]

Secretary of Agriculture Claude Wickard, a former Indiana farmer, may have doubted the ability of women to assume responsibility for family farms. No doubt there were questions about women's stamina and strength. Many small farms were already struggling with growing new crops such as peanuts and soybeans, and thousands of family farms were abandoned or sold during the early years of the war. Nevertheless, women were the single greatest force in keeping U.S. farms on track with productivity; in short, most wartime agriculture was accomplished by three million American women, half with farm experience and half as "green" volunteers placed by the USDA for hands-on training.

The Women's National Farm and Garden Association began in 1914 as an organization of American women with botanical interests. The group took its direction from the British Women's Farm and Garden Union, established in 1899 as a training program for young women who wanted to make a living as horticulturalists and farmers. The American founder, Louisa King, was a flower gardener, prolific garden writer, and garden editor of *McCall's* magazine. Practicality allowed for quick adaptation to wartime needs; during World War I, the WNFGA took a serious interest in food security, training the Women's Land Army Units known as farmerettes. By 1940, they again mobilized the Women's Land Army in preparation for another war. They had the backing of Eleanor Roosevelt through her work with the Office of Defense. There was the group sense that there was nothing more essential to nation defense than adequate food supplies.

Following the attack on Pearl Harbor, there was widespread support for training home front Americans, mostly women and children, to farm. Despite the resistance of Secretary Wickard, plans moved forward with reorganizing the Women's Land Army, and USDA administrators realized that inexperienced women would need to be part of the workforce. In January 1943, a committee representing twenty organizations met in New York to plan basic strategy, followed by a conference in Washington, D.C., on emergency farm labor to map out precise plans for an updated WLA. With prodding from President Roosevelt, Wickard instructed agricultural colleges and extension services to recruit, organize, and train women for farm work. A *New York Times* article by M.C. Wilson, head of training at the USDA, explained the plan to the public; men in combat and women on farms would win the war together.[37]

A press release on April 10, 1943, described the updated Women's Land Army as a division of the new United States Crop Corps, an agency entrusted with the efficient harvesting of crops. Funding came from the Emergency Farm Labor Program, and Florence Hall was appointed director; she was a USDA extension home economist who noted that women would bring skills to farming that included "dexterity, speed, accuracy, patience, interest, curiosity, rivalry and patriotism."[38] Extension service home economists designed a uniform of practical blue denim overalls with a matching jacket, but it was not widely adopted because denim became scarce as textile manufacturers began weaving fabric for military tents.

Physically fit women could opt for the Women's Land Army at age eighteen, and thousands did join. Recruitment aimed at town and city residents, and booths at Macy's, Gimbel's, and other department stores offered brochures and encouragement. Volunteers could live at home and travel by day to their assigned farms; depending on the region, they planted crops, hoed rows, pulled beets, shocked wheat, harvested fruit, and gathered nuts for wages at the local rate. Much of the work was back-breaking labor such as thinning rows of seedlings, picking cotton, and detasseling hybrid corn.

State colleges offered courses in growing vegetables and greenhouse management, and women's magazines encouraged their readers to plan vacation time so that they could help with local harvests. The campaign was effective; over a quarter of all farm workers during World War II were women who learned enough about hands-on agriculture to get the job done. Posters encouraged young women to "Pitch in and Help" and "Harvest War Crops" by joining the Women's Land Army, but the U.S. Crop Corps also advertised widely for volunteers of any age. Posters urged Americans to heed the "Call to Farms" and to "Work on a Farm This Summer," "Help Harvest," and "Be a Victory Farm Volunteer." For the duration of the war, families were encouraged to spend their vacation time helping with harvesting, and school calendars adapted to local harvests so that students could join the Victory Farm Volunteers.

Men remained in short supply for farm work, so it is not unreasonable that attention turned to the more than 400,000 enemy captives who were interned for the duration of the war in U.S. prisoner of war camps. The prisoners were German, Japanese, and Italian soldiers; they were housed in 155 base POW camps (plus more than 500 branch camps), which were located nationwide. The Geneva Convention mandated that rations and housing equal U.S. military standards. Either pine barracks or canvas tents were used, depending on the site, and the quantity and quality of American food surpassed typical Axis rations. German POWs favored white bread and real coffee, after years of whole-grain rye loaves of *Kommisbrot* and *ersatz* coffee. Some enterprising men fermented fruit, potato peelings, and rationed sugar into a crude wine for evening parties, until guards seized the contraband drink. Many of the first captives were from the *Afrika Korps*, the elite German expeditionary force led by Field Marshall Edwin Rommel. They surrendered in May 1943, and more than 150,000 German soldiers were transported to POW camps.

Many spent the war working on U.S. farms, either voluntarily or through required labor. Their work was paid, but most of the wages that POWs earned went toward their own support and toward improvements at the POW camps. Officers were not expected to work in the fields, and many spent the rest of the war cultivating their own flower and vegetable gardens in the U.S.

Governors of agricultural states vied for prison camps, which were organized in haste on vacant land and former Depression-era CCC camps. Desperate farmers sought POW labor, regardless of their Nazi beliefs, and so branch camps were established closer to the farms where many of the prisoners worked in the fields—cutting sugar cane, harvesting fruit, picking cotton, and other essential tasks. POWs planted rice in Louisiana, harvested root crops in Nebraska, cut asparagus in Illinois, and harvested peaches, citrus fruit, and pecans in Texas.[39] The first wave of *Afrika Korps* prisoners adhered to Nazi ideals and believed in German victory, so they were first viewed with suspicion, followed by cautious optimism as their work became valued. They often experienced more civil and considerate treatment than black farmhands.[40]

Nevertheless cotton was a challenging crop for German prisoners to cultivate and harvest. Most had never seen anything like it; the economic variety of cotton was selected during ancient times from the wild American species known as upland cotton (*Gossypium hirsutum*), one of several fiber-producing species in the genus (see Chapter 8). The shrubby plants produce spiny capsules that each contain a boll, a cluster of seeds covered with long white fibers, trichomes (plant hairs) which in this case are mostly cellulose. Cotton fibers are soft and absorbent, and its wartime uses ranged from uniforms and bandages to paper and explosives. Each year 25 million U.S. acres of cotton needed harvesting, work that was arduous and often painful; cotton picking involved yanking the intact boll from each sharp-tipped capsule, while dragging a heavy collecting sack along the rows. German soldiers were remarkably fit and strong, but soon learned that this was exhausting field work. Few Germans could compete in the field with experienced cotton pickers, and some frustrated or rebellious POWs stuffed their long shoulder sacks with stalks, soil, or stones to meet the weight quota. Planters complained that some of the cotton was so contaminated with debris that it could not be ginned. Despite these acts of "petty sabotage," German POWs were often treated with considerable respect in the Jim Crow South. Planters did not enforce quota expectations with POWs; in contrast, black field hands were expected to harvest two hundred pounds or more daily, perhaps because they were supposed to be accustomed to the harsh conditions of cotton fields. Thus German involvement in King Cotton spawned some wartime racial tensions.[41]

As might be expected, some POWs excavated escape tunnels under agricultural fields, but many, if not most, were content with spending the remainder of the war farming rather than fighting. Farm families and prisoners sometimes ate meals together, and after the war some families sponsored former POWs who wanted to immigrate to the U.S. When films of Nazi atrocities reached the U.S. at the end of the war, outraged *Afrika Korps* POWs burned their desert khaki cotton uniforms in protest.

Farming in England

At the onset of World War II, England depended on imports for two-thirds of its food, but German U-boats soon pursued ships carrying supplies to England. Hitler planned to bring about an English surrender through drastic food shortages and ultimately starvation. The only alternative was to reinvent English agriculture by reducing the amount of meat consumed and cultivating sufficient botanical foods for human consumption. In short, land yielded more food and more calories when planted with crops than when used as pastures. Data compiled by John Richardson Marrack revealed the agricultural reality: One acre of farmland could produce 3.7 million calories of potatoes or 1.8 million calories of wheat, but merely 160,000 calories of beef.[42] Simply stated, wartime agriculture required that grass be ploughed under and former pastures planted with food for humans; the goal was to harvest sufficient calories and vitamins to prevent starvation on a national scale.

However, soils often lacked plant nutrients, the result of intensive farming for grain and vegetables since ancient times. Despite its calcareous reputation, some English soil was even deficient in limestone, and other nutrients such as nitrogen, phosphate, and potassium were minimal. As harvests dwindled, abandoned agricultural fields reverted into pastureland populated by indigenous grasses and acid-loving bracken fern (*Pteridium aquilinum*), which was nearly impossible to eradicate, making the land suitable only for grazing animals. Even this was not ideal; bracken is toxic to some livestock, although animals usually avoid eating its leathery fronds. However, when the loss of French potash imports caused widespread shortages, some farmers returned to the traditional use of bracken as a potassium-rich mulch for potato crops. These old fields were low input-low output, semi-natural habitats, quite different from arable land that is deliberately tilled and enriched for crop production.

By 1939, there were 17 million acres of pastures in England that were once agricultural fields, in comparison to 12 million acres that were still being actively farmed. Hedgerows, the living fences that separated adjacent fields, overgrew in height and width, casting shade and encroaching on land that once grew crops. In comparison to the early nineteenth century, arable land diminished by one-third; however, cheap produce was available from European farms and market gardens. Thus by the 1930s most of the 350,000 farms in England depended on animal husbandry rather than crop production.[43]

With war on the horizon, abandoned fields were needed for strategic crops such as wheat and potatoes, managed by a government-mandated plow-up program that aimed to convert old pastures back into useful farmland. Many farmers were still using horses, but the scale of the plow-up demanded mechanization to achieve its goals. Ford manufactured wartime tractors in England, but massive gyrotillers were more suitable for overturning derelict fields, heathlands, bogs, and marshes; they cut through overgrown brambles and shrubby heath and routed out roots with ease. The goal was to prepare two million acres for spring planting in 1940, and gyrotillers moved from farm to farm converting abandoned acreage back to agricultural land. For daily use, many farmers preferred the Trusty Tractor, which resembled a large rototiller; it could plow tracts of various sizes and harrow soil into a fine tilth ready for seed.

Heathlands posed a unique situation as widespread ecosystems that resulted from the clearing of oak forests for fuel, becoming shrubby habitats with nutrient-poor, acidic soil. Such areas may have exhibited the effects of allelopathy; some plant species release toxins (allelochemicals) into the soil as an adaptation to establish territory. Although it was probably not recognized at the time, the common heath species *Calluna vulgaris* and some related species release toxins that can drastically inhibit seed germination. Converting heathlands to arable land was challenging because of the shallow soil and hard moorpan layer that impeded root growth, but allelopathy may also have impeded seed germination and the growth of some crops.

Time was of the essence in reinventing English agriculture. The Ministry of Agriculture pushed farms to plow by day and night; an article in *Life* noted that despite the blackout "...new regulations were adopted permitting illuminated ploughing by night.... Masked headlamps light the furrow line as an English farmer helps to meet his government's demand for more potatoes, wheat, beets, and turnips."[44] This may have been wartime publicity, but agriculture did in fact operate under strict government guidelines, with expectations of maximum possible harvests of strategic high calorie crops—particularly wheat and potatoes, but also carrots and tomatoes for their vitamin content. Horticulturalists and flower growers plowed up rose bushes, perennials, and flowering bulbs that had taken generations to produce; they were replaced by wartime crops.

War Agricultural Executive Committees (known as the War Ags) were based on a similar management system established during World War I. In September 1939, a note in the journal *Nature* described their emergency mission: "The Minister of Agriculture has appointed a War Agricultural Executive Committee, for each county in England and Wales and has made an Order ... authorizing these committees to exercise on his behalf certain powers conferred on him by the Defense Regulations for the purpose of increasing home food production in time of war ... they will be given as free a hand as possible to proceed as a matter of urgency with all possible steps to increase the production of foodstuffs in their areas. Their immediate task is to see that additional land is brought under the plough with all speed. The aim is to obtain for next year's harvest an increase of about 1½ million acres in the tillage area in England and Wales.... The committees have already been holding informal meetings and have made good progress with their preparatory work."[45]

The reinvented War Ags oversaw county farms as the local arm of the Ministry of Agriculture. Each committee surveyed land, prescribed crops for cultivation, determined the best land for specific crops, and assessed harvests. As part of a national survey described in the *County Circular No. 227* (May 1940), private farms were graded A, B, or C depending on their productivity and potential; factors such as soil fertility, drainage, and vermin infestations were assessed to determine needed improvements. War Ag orders could be compulsory, and most significantly, they had official power to take over farms that failed to meet targeted expectations. As noted in a confidential Cabinet document, "...in the light of each farm's circumstances, the Committee shall have power to serve orders requiring the work to be done, or ... to take possession of the land. The Committees will also assist in allocating to farmers their shares of the available supplies of labour, feeding-stuffs, and fertilizers.... Steps are being taken to augment supplies of ploughs and certain other kinds of farming tackle."[46] Experienced farmers at times found War Ag advice to be uninformed and meddlesome, but the scheme did manage to increase farmland by 14 percent (1.7 million acres) before the second growing season of the war.

Soil posed several challenges to War Ag wisdom. Fertility had waned after centuries of farming, and the most common type of soil was characterized by heavy clay and few pores. Known as gleysol, it had a tendency to retain water rather than drain. Rain and snow caused water-logged fields, but plant roots need oxygen, which diffuses more slowly through water than through air. Thus successful crops demanded drainage, a problem that many farmers needed to solve prior to sowing seed. Water flow was modified by digging ditches, laying clay pipes, or plowing at a depth of about sixteen inches with a mole plow, also known as a subsoiler. The bullet-shaped plow broke apart subsoil hardpan clay, creating drainage channels in the process. By providing oxygen for root respiration, wartime drainage work was an essential part of land reclamation, and more than four million acres were proactively drained by 1944.[47]

Plowing at first seemed to improve soil fertility, probably by stimulating the activity of soil microbes. Some lowland areas also benefited from wartime weather; harsh winter frosts, followed by low spring rainfall, worked synergistically to release and retain the ions of key nutrients. Nevertheless, soil nutrients tended to decline with each successive year of plowing and cultivating. The solution was to plow and plant more land, even small tracts alongside roads, landing strips, and factories. Unlike the U.S. where yield per acre increased dramatically, wartime food production in England increased only because more land was tilled, not because yield increased.[48] The War Ags supported ley farming (their term for crop rotation) in which fields were sown with legumes that improved nitrogen levels, and fallow fields were avoided. A typical rotation involved sowing clover (a legume, also known as a ley crop) following root vegetables and barley crops and prior to sowing wheat. The clover provided forage while simultaneously enriching the soil with nitrogen.[49]

Fertilizers of all types remained in short supply, despite stockpiling that began as early as 1936. Some artificial fertilizers were imported and could be used successfully on potatoes, sugar beets, carrots, onions, and flax, but farmers were suspicious of inorganic mineral-based mixtures and preferred the familiar method of manure-spreading. Fertilizers worked synergistically with environmental conditions to result in unanticipated problems. For instance, the 1941 onion crop suffered from imbalanced soil nutrients (low potash and high nitrogen, perhaps from artificial fertilizers), wet weather, and cool temperatures. Day length was also a factor in bulb development for some onion cultivars, and the dreary August weather did not help. Much of the crop resembled leeks rather than typical onions, a developmental anomaly known as bull-neck; they were edible but needed to be used immediately rather than dried for long term storage. The result was a national shortage at a time onions were particularly sought after for flavoring main dishes of mostly vegetables. Home cooks had to reserve onions at the green grocer.

Crop rotation decreased the number of wireworms (the larvae of click beetles) that tunnel through potatoes and carrots, but infestations of various other root and tuber-eating pests continued. Some farmers sowed mustard seeds and then plowed the plants into the soil; presumably the mustard oils (chemically related to mustard gases) killed soil herbivores. Soil sterilization was also widely practiced. War Ags provided the necessary equipment, which involved using a portable steam boiler. Soil was covered with a tarpaulin, a pipe was inserted underground, and the soil blasted with steam to temperatures of 212° F—sufficient to kill any herbivorous insect, grub, or worm. Of course, some beneficial microbes and invertebrates like earthworms and centipedes were also destroyed. However, steam sterilization did eliminate damage to potatoes, an essential crop that replaced much of the wheat in civilian wartime diets.

Potato blight, caused by the fungus *Phytophthora infestans*, was an ongoing problem, especially during wet, warm growing seasons. Some home gardeners used powdered mothballs (naphthalene, now recognized as carcinogenic) as a fungicide for potatoes grown in allotments, but farmers were more likely to spray their potato fields with Bordeaux mixture, a solution of copper sulfate and slaked lime (calcium hydroxide). Potato blight also affected tomatoes (potatoes and tomatoes are related members of the family Solanaceae), which War Ags encouraged many farmers to cultivate as a valuable source of both vitamins A and C.

The shift toward a wartime botanical diet meant that livestock numbers dwindled just as the need for their dung was highest. In planning for a mostly botanical human diet, the Ministry of Agriculture had not considered the importance of animals in fertilizing agricultural fields. Grain crops in particular benefited from sheep dung, and harvests in some areas decreased because there were fewer sheep to provide manure. Alternatives were explored, including sewage and sludge, and some farmers tried to recycle nutrients back into the soil by adding ammonia and lime to rotting straw following grain harvests. Straw was also bundled and coiled into the traditional skeps that housed bee hives, but its most important wartime use was as fodder for milk cows, either dry or in silage.

The English enjoyed sugar, which was among the first foods rationed in January 1940 (see Chapter 4). Cane sugar imports were drastically curtailed, but the Sugar Beet Act of 1925 assured that an identical product could be made from native-grown sugar beets. Concern for sugar shortages stemmed from World War I; by the start of World War II, there were over 300,000 acres planted in sugar beets, which grew to a healthy size (each often the size of a child's head) in the English climate. As in the U.S., sugar beets became an important crop that provided 95 percent of the wartime sugar consumed in English homes. There was harvesting equipment invented that sliced away the leafy crowns and lifted the heavy taproots, but for small scale farmers the work of pulling the taproots by hand and removing excess soil was notoriously back-breaking. Nevertheless the effort was worthwhile because single acres each supported 25,000 plants and yielded tons of table sugar at the eighteen processing plants that converted beet taproots into sucrose. Originally sugar beet leaves were plowed back into the soil to decay, but a wartime innovation involved using them in making silage.

Imported cattle feed was in short supply, so the "Make silage, Make sure" campaign provided instruction on silo construction and silage management. Pamphlets described silo construction using brown paper and pitch (pine resin) to line a wire enclosure built around wooden posts. Farmers could use other materials such as corrugated metal, as long as the interior was airtight. Sugar beet tops, straw, wild grasses, nettles, and other weeds were all suitable for shoveling and compressing into the silo. Silage depended on fermentation to release nutrients from plant tissue, a process that required anaerobic conditions. The ensiled matter compacted over several days into a fermented, nutritious botanical mash; lactic acid bacteria and other microbes converted carbohydrates to simple organic acids and proteins to smaller peptide molecules. The decrease in volume led some farmers to reject silage as wasteful, when in fact ensiled plant matter provided more accessible nutrients than fresh straw and leaves. Many farmers initially doubted the process and preferred to store chopped hay for winter feeding, which required warm sun and dry weather; however, more adopted silage-making as they were faced with the challenge of feeding milk cows. War Ags added silage officers to their ranks, tasked with explaining its nutrient value, use as winter fodder, and preparation; most importantly, silage made good use of energy-rich plant matter that humans could not consume.[50]

The Land Army, Schools and Harvests

During the war years, labor was in drastically short supply across England. Posters asked volunteers to "Lend a Hand on the Land," and in June 1939, the Ministry of Agriculture reinvented the Women's Land Army of World War I. Lady Denman, the national chair of the Women's Institutes (see Chapter 3) served as honorary director. Young women volunteered in impressive numbers (30,000 during the first few months), but beginning in December 1941, some entered as part of the National Service Act (No. 2) which required the conscription of young unmarried women or childless widows, ages twenty to thirty.

Many young women left offices to join the Women's Land Army. One in three land girls came from an urban area, and many of the early volunteers may have sought refuge from anticipated bombing, although it should be noted that in some areas Land Army girls worked close to military action, with only ditches for protection. Young women replaced men who joined the military. Most were assigned to farms, but some were employed in large private gardens that cultivated vegetables for nearby villages or schools, while others worked directly for War Ags and moved from farm to farm for seasonal work and tasks. In the *Land Girl Manual*, Wilfred Edward Shewell-Cooper addressed the basics of gardening; he was an organic gardener who also advised the army on growing fresh vegetables and advocated cultivating the small plots around radar stations and anti-

The Women's Land Army replaced men who joined the British military. Most members were assigned to farms, where their work included all aspects of agriculture: sowing seeds, spreading manure, trimming hedgerows, hoeing carrots, picking peas, digging potatoes, harvesting beets, cutting hay, threshing, and roof-thatching (Library of Congress).

aircraft guns, but much of the practical training occurred in the field. Land Army work included all aspects of agriculture: sowing seeds, spreading manure, trimming hedgerows, hoeing carrots, picking peas, digging potatoes, cutting hay, threshing, and even roof-thatching.[51]

The work was strenuous, and conditions were often miserably cold and wet, but *The Land Girl* magazine provided tips for making do, amusing short stories, recipes, and encouraging words. The first page of the April 1943 edition noted that there was still much to be done, "Everyone is overtired and overworked and the Land Army in particular has won a nice comfortable bed of laurels on which it is very tempting to rest. But there can't be any rest for us until we are producing those forty-seven million meals a day which our ships now have to bring, instead of sending men and munitions to the Second Front."[52] Despite some farmers' skepticism, most Land Army girls were up to the work, and by 1940 the organization had 80,000 members. Commissioned by the Ministry of Agriculture, Vita Sackville-West chronicled WLA history in *The Women's Land Army*; the book included firsthand accounts of farm experiences, photographs of girls at work, and lyrics and music to "Back to the Land," the official anthem[53]:

Back to the land, we must all lend a hand,
To the farms and the fields we must go.
There's a job to be done,
Though we can't fire a gun
We can still do our bit with the hoe.
When your muscles are strong
You will still get along,
And you'll think that a country life's grand.
We're all needed now,
We must speed up the plough,
So come with us back to the land.

Back to the land, with its clay and its sand,
Its granite and gravel and grit,
You grow barley and wheat
And potatoes to eat
To make sure that the nation stays fit.
Remember the rest
Are all doing their best,
To achieve the results they have planned.
We'll tell you once more
You can help win the war
If you come with us—back to the land.

In addition to on the job training, girls attended month-long educational programs at agricultural programs such as the Northamptonshire Farm Institute. Studley College provided more formal agricultural training for young women who planned to join the Land Army. The school had a history dating back to 1903, when Daisy (Frances Evelyn) Greville, the Countess of Warwick, decided to endow an agricultural college. She purchased Studley Castle as part of her progressive plan to provide practical training to young women who needed work. A socialite with socialist leanings, Daisy Warwick had an interest in natural history. Her extended family included both Captain Fitzroy of the HMS *Beagle* and Charles Francis Greville, for whom the botanical genus *Grevillea* is named; she installed gardens and even a small zoo at her home.

By 1926, the Ministry of Agriculture had recognized Studley Horticultural and Agricultural College for Women as a training program, and young women pursued two and three-year courses in horticulture, market gardening, beekeeping, colonial life, and other aspects of agriculture considered suitable for young women. Daisy Warwick died in 1938 and so did not live long enough to see young women in the reorganized Land Army; she had opposed World War I, so her reaction is difficult to predict. Nevertheless Studley became synonymous with women's farm work during the Second World War. Magazine advertisements for Land Army uniforms described "ladies agricultural outfits" including khaki coats, breeches, and overalls as identical to those worn at Studley College. Despite her contribution to training young women for wartime service cultivating crops, Daisy Warwick is perhaps now best remembered for her colorful personal life and her 1905 John Singer Sargent portrait "The Countess of Warwick and Her Son," painted in an idealized natural setting, presumably in Warwickshire. Politics aside, she would have been pleased with the Studley College students who earned top honors in the rigorous Royal Horticultural Society exams administered in the spring of 1942.

The Waterperry School of Horticulture for Women was another established training ground for young women who planned to farm during the war years. Founded by Beatrix Havergal and Avice Sanders to train daughters from upper class families, the college was based at an Oxfordshire estate, fully equipped with a 50-bedroom mansion house, fertile agricultural fields, flower gardens, and greenhouses. With the start of war, the Waterperry School plowed up most of its land for food crops. Socially diverse Land Army girls joined forces with enrolled students for theoretical and practical training; together they cultivated bumper crops of potatoes, cabbages, tomatoes, and even onions, which farmers often had trouble growing. The local War Ag donated a Fordson tractor and plow to the successful operation. Potatoes were harvested in 2,500 willow baskets woven by members of local Women's Institutes, who also helped with repairing the Wellington rubber boots that were part of the Land Army uniform.

Children also labored in fields across England. For years prior to the war, school vacations were arranged to overlap with harvest seasons, and school officials tolerated absenteeism during times that local farmers were particularly busy. With wartime labor shortages a reality, farmers soon discovered that even quite young children excelled at digging potatoes, picking berries, and harvesting peas, while older youth did the heavier work of hoeing, cutting hay, and making silage. With over 6.5 million acres of former grassland under cultivation and almost 100,000 fewer skilled men, children's labor became essential to successful planting, cultivation, and harvesting. School holidays were scheduled to accommodate harvest weeks, so that children over age twelve could work in the fields; younger children also participated, albeit unofficially. Some schools adopted local farms as routine work sites.

From the start of the war, schools were inundated with information on gardening and small-scale farming. Children studied Ministry of Agriculture Dig for Victory leaflets and listened to BBC radio broadcasts such as "The Practice and Science of Gardening," which began in 1940. Students were instructed on crops to grow at home, so the idea of organizing school-wide work camps to assist farmers was not completely unexpected. By 1941, there were 335 agricultural work camps for school-age children, organized by both private and public schools. Logistics were a challenge, from suitable footwear to adequate meals; children often camped in the fields, so the farm stay often began with stuffing straw into mattress covers made of ticking. The Ministry of Food published a leaflet "Catering Arrangements for Schoolboy Harvesting Camps" (1941), which relied heavily on canned beans, rice, dried fruit, and New Zealand honey for basic meals. Local farmers' wives often sent cakes, tarts, and buckets of tea into the fields.[54]

The Ministry of Agriculture established the Schoolboy Harvest Camps Advisory Committee to provide advice on arrangements and safety provisions, but there was legitimate concern that children's labor might be exploited and their education might be compromised. After considerable haggling, a 1942 government order specified that children could not work more than seven hours daily, and they could not miss more than twenty school days annually. All work was strictly voluntary, and recreation time was scheduled during the work day; children were paid for their farm work, unlike a similar scheme in Germany in which children were expected to work as a voluntary honor.

During the spring 1944 planting season, German planes dropped bombs that detonated if handled. There was concern that children might be injured or killed by these explosives, but close supervision managed to avoid any disasters. Plans were made for children (and in some cases entire schools) evacuated from cities to train at selected farms, so that they could continue schooling and learn farm work, all under the watchful eye of local War Ags. For country children, the experience may not have been too different from helping on family farms, but for children evacuated from urban areas, rural farm environs must have been quite eye-opening. Despite early doubts from many farmers, most children were hard workers who enjoyed the experience, and many acquired lifelong skills.[55]

Beginning with the 1941 harvest season, prisoners of war provided additional labor on English farms, with wages specified by the Geneva Convention. Farmers sought POWs for some of the heaviest work, such as digging beets and excavating ditches; by the 1943 harvest, over 40,000 Italian prisoners were agricultural workers in England. In contrast, German POWs were viewed with distrust and thought of as being fanatical, but the need for farm labor outstripped any hypothetical danger of having prisoners at work in British fields. At first Germans worked in closely guarded gangs, but supervision loosened once farmers observed their work ethic and agricultural knowledge.

Ultimately agricultural land bore the scars and effects of warfare. Airfields were constructed on the same sort of land that lent itself to productive farming—flat and dry. During the course of the war, 450 new airfields consumed thousands of acres of potentially arable land, along with improvements to existing fields. The Ministry of Agriculture had two weeks to raise objections and suggest alternative sites, but ultimately the Air Ministry decided which farms became airfields. Bracken fern was a problem in some pasturelands; once the rhizomes had a foothold, the only way to eliminate the invasive fern from airstrips (to allow visibility from the sky) was by repeated mowing, which depleted the stored food in the rhizomes. In many areas, farming and airplanes co-existed as farmers plowed and planted strips of land alongside and between adjacent runways. Other uses of potential agricultural land included POW and military camps, ordnance factories, barrage balloon and artillery sites, and ammunition dumps.

As a further complication, there was concern than German planes might land on farms, release troops, and fly off to pick up more men and supplies. Anticipating an invasion, posts made of wood or concrete were placed in fields as part of a plan to block the landing and takeoff of enemy aircraft. The posts interfered with cultivating and plowing, but it was the unanticipated poor traction of airplane tires on plowed soil that finally halted their installation.[56] Other anti-invasion measures involved the excavation of deep ditches across prime farmland. Over time the rural landscape became pocked with bomb craters and shell holes and punctuated by 28,000 concrete guard posts (known as pill-boxes) and other fortified defense structures. By 1944, almost ten million acres in England were given over to military uses, including wooded tracts and lanes used for military training because the landscape resembled Normandy.

Despite the hardships endured, Henry Williamson noted in retrospect the overall salutary effects of the Second World War on agriculture, "It has taken a war to put British farming on its feet, and to bring back to us generally that work is the true basis of life in the world. A nation that neglects its land, and its peasants—which are its rootstock—will perish.... The war has brought us back to the fundamentals of life; and when it is over, on the basis of our new hard economy, we shall build a fine civilization in this country, and its Empire, on the simple virtues of life."[57]

German Agriculture, Hereditary Farms and Plant Breeding

Allied countries observed changes in German agriculture in preparation for war. Local agricultural committees advised farmers on planting rapeseed and other oil-producing seeds, root crops, soybeans, vegetables, and forage crops, as well as flax and hemp. Government stockpiles grew, and there were plans for equitable food distribution. However, Nazi agriculture exceeded the need for food, fodder, and fiber production. Farming was embedded in Third Reich ideology, in which agrarian ideals led to *Lebensraum*, a quest for "living space."

Richard Walther Darré, the *Reichsminister für Ernährung und Landwirtschaft* (minister of food and agriculture) extolled the notion of *Blut und Boden* (blood and soil) as the ideological link between Aryan farming families and the land. Inherent was the hereditary right of able Aryans to cultivate German food plants in German soil (or colonial farmlands), tied to the widespread promotion of rural and agrarian virtues. Both Darré and Rudolf Hess, deputy to Adolf Hitler, followed the principles of biodynamic farming espoused by Rudolf Steiner, whose teachings pivoted on the notion of self-sufficient organic agriculture. On a scientific level, biodynamic farms functioned as "organisms" that recycled animal manure into the soil that produced fodder. However, spiritualism also influenced biodynamic practices. Seed sowing and crop harvesting were aligned with cycles of the solar system, notions interwoven with the mysticism of Aryan origins. Yet despite their appeal to ideologues, Steiner's notions were never implemented on a large scale; food production was too critical for experimental ventures, and not all Nazi leaders were equally invested in this amalgam of organic and mystical farming.[58]

Lebensraum translated into land appropriation to establish new colonies, where Aryan families could farm and reproduce to serve the Reich. German Farmers were actively recruited into Nazi party membership because their families would be needed to emigrate and till new soil abroad. Thus Darré was also named both *Reichsbauernführer* (leader of farmers) and head of the *Reichsnährstand* (Reich Food Corporation), the government agency that controlled all aspects of agriculture and food production, including cultivation, pricing, and distribution. The *Reichsnährstand* defined agriculture broadly to include far-reaching control over grazing lands, forestry, soil cultivation, gardening, viniculture, and bee-keeping. The corporation comprised a hierarchy of bureaus and unions that supervised such areas as specific crops (potatoes, sugar beets, grain, etc.), soil, forestry, legal matters, farm education, machinery, and breweries. Farmers were recruited to join the *Reichsbauernrat* (Reich Farmers' Council), which advised the local *Bauernführer* (farmers' leader). A *Bauernführer* network across rural Germany extolled Nazi agricultural philosophy and enforced Darré's agricultural policies.[59]

Hereditary farming was established before the war with memorable thanksgiving festivals (*Reichernstedankefest*) that celebrated the harvest seasons between 1933 and 1937. As part of a regular rotation of party events, these events were under tight Nazi management. Festival grounds were installed on a hilltop outside of Hamelm in Lower Saxony, with architectural features designed by Albert Speer. As staged propaganda, harvest celebrations were organized to forge a bond between Hitler and German farmers, with an altar-like monument, processions, national anthems, military displays, and staged battles. Most important was the *Reichserbhofgesetz* (land heritage law) first announced at the 1933 festival. It guaranteed that certain German land (*Erbhof*) passed from father to son (or following the patriline, if there were no sons), establishing the hereditary farms that linked *Blut und Boden*. The idea of peasant farmers (*Bauern*) leaving land to male heirs was extolled as part of agrarian ideology, connecting racial purity to a hereditary right to cultivate family land. The policy encompassed one third of the three million farms in Germany.

Labor on Nazi-era hereditary farms was performed by members of the *Hitler-Jugend* (Hitler Youth), the *Bund Deutscher Mädel* (League of German Girls), and the *Reichsarbeitsdienst* (Reich Labor Service), which conscripted young men and women during the war years. German youth were required to farm due to the need for settlers in new eastern territories (Bundesarchiv Bild 183-E10868, Wikimedia Commons).

Despite the practical need for food production, there was a romantic aspect to the *Reichsnährstand* bureau that oversaw hereditary farming, elevating the peasant farmer and his love for the fatherland, family, fields, and harvests.[60] In reality, however, hereditary farmers sowed government-mandated crops and sold them at government-controlled prices. Despite *Reichsnährstand* regulations, Hitler held that farmers had a right to sell their surplus produce once their government obligations were settled. In one of his rambling *Tischgespräche* (table talks) in 1942, he defended the right of peasant farmers to sell perishable fruits and vegetables, by-passing middlemen, ignoring food distribution protocol, and profiting from their own labor.[61]

In fact much of the labor on hereditary farms was performed by members of the *Hitler Jugend* (Hitler Youth), the *Bund Deutscher Mädel* (League of German Girls), and the *Reichsarbeitsdienst* (Reich Labor Service), which conscripted young men and women during the war years. Farming was not optional for German youth because of the need for settlers to farm in the new eastern territories. *Hitler Jugend* each experienced an obligatory year of agricultural work (*Landjahr*), which could be extended into a four year training course (*Landdienst*) at model farms (*Landsdienstlehrhof*) and certification as a "new farmer" (*Neubauernschein*). However, as the war progressed, few young men could be spared for farming in the Reich. Estimates are that women did half of the wartime farm work, despite the Nazi plan for more pregnancies.[62]

Agricultural research in the Third Reich focused on practical matters with an eye toward future colonies abroad, including Darré's plan to reclaim and settle former German colonies in Africa. Botanists examined soil micronutrients and their effect on plant growth, plant diseases, and drought resistance. Tolerance for dry and saline soils was part of a larger interest in agriculture under various conditions, particularly environmental conditions in Africa. During the 1930s, plant physiologist Heinrich Walter of the botanical institute in Stuttgart focused on colonial agriculture, making several research trips to Africa. At the botanical institute in Munich, Walter Mevius studied the effect of drought on nitrogen fixation, which provided insight into the planned cultivation of soybeans and other legumes in dry habitats; Karl Höfler, a plant physiologist at the University of Vienna, observed the effect of drying on individual plant cells of plant species adapted to living in full sunlight. Other investigations examined the various effects of drought on grains, illuminating the role of transpiration (loss of water vapor) in developing drought resistance. Mevius established a working group in agricultural botany to handle funding requests in the *Forschungsdienst* (Research Service), one of the complex network of agencies overseeing crop research during the Third Reich.[63]

As with other Nazi science, some agricultural research verged on pseudoscience. Friedrich Boas compiled *Dynamische Botanik*, a text that sought to create a new discipline focusing on dynamic plants and their significance for farmers, but his work was scientifically inscrutable. On a more practical level, he studied blueberries as a potential food source, part of a working group studying edible forest plants. The native German blueberry is the low-growing shrub *Vaccinium myrtillus*, but after some early breeding experiments, it was largely replaced by *V. corymbosum*, a highbush North American species that produces larger fruit that are easier to harvest. This contradicted the Nazi notion that German plants were inherently superior to non-native species, but sometimes usefulness trumped principle, which was also the case with the soybeans (native to Asia) that provided both oil and protein. By the early 1930s, Germans were importing more of these legumes by rail and sea than any other country. Concerned with German dependence on imports, I.G. Farben (the chemical, dye, and drug conglomerate) supplied eastern European farmers with soybean seeds and nitrogen-fixing *Rhizobium* bacteria needed to inoculate the soil. As a result, farmers in Romania, Yugoslavia, and Hungary provided Germany with soybeans that replaced Chinese imports.

If soybeans could nourish the military, Nazi leaders were willing to appropriate a non-native plant species; soybeans were renamed *Nazi-bohne* (Nazi beans) and promoted as a healthy meat alternative. However, the species was a non-native crop cultivated on foreign soil, sometimes by the Slavic people whom Hitler held in contempt, all utterly inconsistent with Nazi philosophy. Soybeans thrived in eastern colonies, and they were the focus of early genetic crosses using seed stock from I.G. Farben; the ultimate goal was to develop cultivars that thrived in Germany, but the species defied consistent adaptation to the local climate. Regardless of their non-native origin, tons of these legumes were milled into *Edelsoja*, the soy flour that increased the protein content of military rations. Perhaps to encourage soy use in the American home front, a *Science News-Letter* article reminded readers that German soldiers were consuming plenty of soy flour; a captured military manual recommended adding it to vegetables and using it as an egg and milk substitute in cooking.[64]

Plant breeding followed the political agenda of Darré and the Nazi party. In 1937, the Kaiser Wilhelm Institute laid out these goals in a small booklet titled *Die politischen Aufgaben der deutschen Pflanzenzüchtung* (The Political Objectives of German Plant Breeding), which pointed to the need for food (particularly proteins and oil) and fibers from plants adapted to German climate and soil conditions. The breeding of new cultivars would move Germany toward autarky by reducing dependence on food, fodder, and fiber imports; it also supported the *Lebensraum* expansion of German farming and the *Drang nach Osten* (drive eastward) into Slavic countries.[65] Thus the goal of Nazi-governed plant breeding was patent: eugenically approved people would cultivate genetically improved plants. The *Generalplan Ost* (General Plan for the East) envisioned German-style villages landscaped with herbaceous and woody species native to Germany. Plant geneticist Konrad Meyer directed the plan, which ultimately displaced and killed millions of local people.

Grains were a strategic crop, long regarded as the backbone of agriculture. Stylized heads of grain appeared in the symbol of the *Reichsarbeitsdienst* (Reich Labor Service), which during the Nazi regime required compulsory service (often agricultural work) from young men and women. Among plant breeders there was considerable interest in wild type grains, the original genetic stock from which agricultural varieties were selected and bred. This stemmed from both propaganda and practicality; Nazi officials insisted that bread grains historically originated in Germany, and wild plants provided the genetic raw material for potentially more productive cultivars. However, not all German scientists supported a German origin for bread grains. Based on her research, geneticist Elisabeth Schiemann's contended that the center of wheat and rye evolution was the Near East, as she explained in her book *Entstehung der Kulturplanzen* (Origin of Cultivated Plants, 1932). She also disagreed with the Russian geneticist Nikolai Vavilov, who held that the greatest genetic diversity occurred in the area where a species originally evolved. Nevertheless, Schiemann's work was valued. During the war years, despite taking a stand against the pseudo-Darwinian doctrine used to justify eugenic practices, she supervised the department of crop history at the *Kaiser-Wilhelm-Institut für Kulturpflanzenforschung* (Kaiser-Wilhelm Institute of Crop Plant Research).[66]

In 1938–39, the *Schutzstaffel* (SS) organized a scientific expedition to Tibet that focused in part on obtaining grain specimens for genetic experimentation. Interest in Tibet followed the Nazi belief that Tibetans were racially "pure," a quality that they may have ascribed to Tibetan plants as well; Aryans supposedly arose in central Asia, so exploring this region had mystical, pseudo-historical, and scientific implications. Under the umbrella of the SS foundation known as *Ahnenerbe* (ancestral inheritance), Heinrich Himmler recruited the explorer Ernst Schäfer to head the expedition, which ultimately collected the seeds of hundreds of varieties of oats, barley, and wheat. The seed stock was eventually housed at the SS Institute for Plant Genetics at Lannach, Austria, under the control of botanist Heinz Brücher.

Brücher also plundered collections from Russian field stations, including the diverse wild seed stock of essential grains collected by Vavilov. There was particular interest in finding wild, cold-tolerant grains because as part of the *Lebensraum* plan he planned to develop productive cultivars adapted to the eastern European climate. At Rajsko, a Polish village that became an Auschwitz sub-camp, Germans learned small-scale farming, with crops adapted to eastern territories and minimal mechanization. In addition to the model farms, the Rajsko botanical and farming units included market gardens that supplied vegetable crops and hothouse flowers to the German SS and military, all part of Himmler's plan for Auschwitz to be a seat of plant breeding and agricultural research. Meanwhile, by 1943 the Kaiser Wilhelm Institute for Biology planned to install its own seed bank, as part of the new Kaiser Wilhelm Institute for Cultivated Plant Research. Functionally it clearly overlapped with the SS Institute at Lannach; both were located in Austria, planned to breed agricultural strains for eastern territories, and focused on Russian seed stock as a source of genetic diversity.

Kaiser Wilhelm botanists settled into quarters at the Vienna *Vivarium*, part of the Prater public parkland, a building outfitted with naturalistic aquaria, terraria, and climate-controlled growth chambers. The latter were essential for physiology and breeding experiments under specific conditions such as light and temperature extremes. German botanists had noted Trofim Lysenko's earlier research in cold-treating grains of winter wheat for spring planting (a process known as vernalization), and they were also curious about using controlled light (photoperiods) to breed wild potatoes from South America. The *Vivarium* enabled these sorts of experiments for a short time; Kaiser Wilhelm botanists soon relocated to the Tuttenhof Manor near Vienna before the *Vivarium* was destroyed in bombing raids at the end of the war. Himmler in particular supported this work on plant growth and climate, a field in which he shared a simplistic interest. In a 1944 letter to an SS officer, he noted that the elongated roots of the autumn crocus or meadow saffron (*Colchicum autumnale*) could predict a severe winter, information that Hitler supposedly shared with him.[67]

Plant breeding is a painstaking process that requires repeated cycles of cross-pollination and selection, so it is not surprising that interest arose at the Kaiser-Wilhelm Institute in using radiation to develop new cultivars. High frequency radiation is mutagenic, and German botanists regarded it as a source of instant genetic variation. X-rayed seeds (including Tibetan grains, apparently obtained from the SS Institute at Lannach) might exhibit resistance to cold temperatures, drought, pests, and plant diseases; however, mutations occur randomly, and most random genetic changes are deleterious. Finding a desirable variation was unlikely but succeeded in at least one case. Genetic crossing had failed to produce a strain of barley that was resistant to mildew fungi, but the irradiation of 20,000 Tibetan grains instantly yielded a mildew resistant variety.[68]

Spontaneous mutations in nature were also of interest. Geneticist Hans Stubbe investigated soil nutrients and reported results linking plant mutations to high levels of sulfur, nitrogen, and phosphorus. He also noted a higher incidence of mutations in older seed stock and posited that environmental conditions might be the cause.[69] Stubbe's botanical studies dovetailed with his reputation as an ardent eugenicist concerned broadly with the notion of genetic health. Nevertheless, in 1938 he was among the scientists sent to a work camp for indoctrination, perhaps because of his prior Marxist leanings.[70]

A genetic anomaly known as polyploidy (organisms with one or more extra chromosome sets) also received attention. Based on the observation in nature that polyploid plants are often more robust than their normal diploid counterparts (with two sets of chromosomes), German botanists hypothesized that mutated strains of agricultural plants might produce larger harvests. Fritz von Wettstein, director of the Kaiser Wilhelm Institute for Biology, was particularly interested in trying to increase the amount of sugar produced in Germany by developing polyploid sugar beets. By 1937, U.S. scientists were inducing polyploidy in crop plants including hybrid cotton varieties by halting cell division following chromosome division, which resulted in extra sets of chromosomes. The technique involved colchicine, an alkaloid that occurs naturally in the corms of the autumn crocus (*Colchicum autumnale*) and which had long been used to treat gout. Using colchicine, German researchers attempted to create polyploidy varieties of useful plants, but successful results with practical applications would have taken years to develop. In 1941, Joseph Straub authored *Wege zur Polyploidie: Eine Anleitung zur Herstellung von Pflanzen mit Riesenwuchs* (Paths to Polyploidy: A Guide to Producing Vegetables with Giant Growth), a manual on the potential of polyploidy in developing new cultivars. However, outcomes with developing polyploid crops were mixed, with some experiments resulting in sterile offspring or plants with abnormally large cells.[71]

Allied countries used available intelligence, much of it related to German agriculture, to predict war outcomes. A graph of strategic materials in the *Illustrated London News* compared the production of strategic materials by Allied and Axis countries, including fertilizers (phosphates and potash), sugar, wheat, and cotton.[72] Germany produced abundant potash but less wheat than the U.S. or England, and it became obvious that the Germans would need additional grain to supply their workers and military. Nazi policy dictated that farmers cultivate more rye to replace wheat imports, which resulted in a change in the grain proportions used in wartime bread (see Chapter 4). Even though rye thrived in the climate and acidic soils of Germany, during the war years grains were not used to fatten livestock because they were needed for human survival.[73] Early and late cover crops yielded potential silage, but there was insufficient labor to build additional silos.

As in England, the German military requisitioned land for roads, aerodromes, and fortifications at a time when more acreage was needed for agriculture; during the period of rearmament in the 1930s, over two million agricultural acres were converted to military use. Thus attempts were made to make the most of any available land. Only the most productive crops were cultivated, liberally fertilized with nitrogen and potash, which improved yields to a point. In 1909 the German chemist Fritz Haber had perfected a process that converted atmospheric nitrogen to ammonia (see Chapter 1). Germany had extensive natural potash deposits; in fact at the end of the war one of the deep potash mines was supposedly used to hide the research library of the German Chemical Society. Labor shortages meant less soil preparation, but increased levels of potash and nitrogen compensated somewhat to keep some yields fairly level despite minimal tilling and harrowing. Neither plant nutrient was in short supply at the start of the war, but nitrogen supplies dwindled with demands from munitions manufacturers for synthetic nitrogen compounds.

Limestone and phosphate were limiting factors, and alternate sources were sought for these plant nutrients. Human bones from the concentration camp at Oswiecim in Poland were collected and sold to the firm of Schterhm, which processed them into superphosphate.[74] Also known as monocalcium phosphate, superphosphate provided both calcium (the primary element in limestone) and phosphorus essential for plant growth. However, phosphate shortages affected crops that need high levels of this micronutrient, including potatoes and sugar beets. Beets were a reliable wartime sugar source, and potatoes produced not only food but fuel; fermented tubers yielded alcohol, which was used to fuel streetlights, cars, stoves, and even German aircraft. Rye thrived on the acid soils in most of Germany, but many grain fields were replanted with root vegetables, a wartime strategy to obtain more calories/cultivated acre. However, by the end of the war, potato and sugar beet yields declined dramatically as a result of diminished soil phosphate. The condition known as *Rübenmüdigkeit* (beet fatigue) became common, and there was confusion about to improve yields; farmers believed erroneously that manure caused growth of the non-sugar producing beetroot tissue, when in fact the addition of soil nutrients would have increased sugar levels.[75]

By 1945 other factors affected food shortages in Germany, including poor seed quality, unfavorable weather, and shortages of labor and machinery. There was often minimal thinning and hoeing after seeds were sowed, so crop plants competed with each other and with weeds. By the end of the war, chemical fertilizers were in short supply, and even manure was scarce. Limited rye and barley cultivation meant that there was less fodder for pigs and chickens, and fewer farm animals translated into shortages of manure for fertilizing fields.[76] By mid–1944 the German rocketry program demanded ethanol for liquid fuels; at a time when food was scarce, the single launch of a V2 rocket required fermentation and distillation of an estimated 30 metric tons of potatoes. Over three thousand of these *Vergeltungswaffen* (vengeance weapons) were fired at targets in England, Belgium, France, and the Netherlands, requiring over 6.6 million pounds of potatoes to produce sufficient liquid fuel.

Not all German agriculture was under Aryan control, and a remarkable training program arose from the anti–Semitic policies of the Third Reich. The 1935 Nuremberg Laws prevented Jewish youth from enrolling in universities, but the *Reichsvertretung der Juden in Deutschland* (National Representative Agency for Jews in Germany) established farm schools for Jewish youth. Beginning in the spring of 1936, students trained at the Gross Breesen Agricultural Training Camp in Silesia. Planned with the goal of emigration to Brazil, the curriculum included both farming and coffee tree cultivation; practical instruction was supplemented by evening lectures, cultural programs, and Portuguese language study. The Brazil plan fell through after the training camp was forced to close in 1941, but many Gross Breesen alumni escaped from Nazi Germany and pursued farming and other livelihoods in the U.S. and other countries worldwide. For instance, the Van Eeden Settlement in North Carolina provided ten acres of land to Jewish immigrants who wanted to farm, but some lacked agricultural experience and turned to other lines of work.

Farming in Japan

Japan relied more heavily on a botanical diet than other industrialized countries. Agriculture reflected the mountainous Japanese landscape; farmers planted on tracts of level land wherever they could, but less than 20 percent of the land was arable. All farmland was cultivated intensively, and an advantage to having several small fields was that a variety of crops could be cultivated depending on variations in soil and terrain. Small farms typically comprised fifteen to twenty defined plots; peasants grew rice in flooded paddies, while upland sites (often terraces carved from hillsides) were densely planted with fruits and vegetables. Soils ranged from sandy loam to gravel, with varying levels of nutrients and pH, and sometimes contained volcanic ash.

Farming methods were carefully honed with centuries of experimentation and experience. In the pre-war years, Japanese harvests were among the highest per unit land worldwide, but much of this productivity pivoted on manual labor rather than fertile land. Following fall rice harvests, the drained paddies were quickly replanted in vegetables, wheat, barley, and the grain known as naked barley (see Chapter 4). Many fields were too small for standard machinery, so families eked out a living on a few acres with manual cultivation and harvesting, followed by efficient replanting to avoid fallow land. Fertilizers were essential for productivity and included both inorganic fertilizers and night soil.

There were very few tractors in Japan, and most farm horses had been requisitioned for military use, so the remaining draft animals served several farms. Wartime production shortages also meant that families shared equipment, including the motorized pumps needed to irrigate paddies. Nearly three million young Japanese men left farms and entered the military, so women, children, and the elderly all worked to increase the harvest by manual labor and to reclaim any arable land for planting. Public parks, schoolyards, and baseball fields were tilled and planted with vegetables and grain, and youth labored to deforest hillsides for farming. Entire schools relocated to rural areas to help with farm work, with lessons taught during evening hours. Evacuated children were often hungry due to food shortages, but those who helped local farmers with weeding and harvesting were paid in rice and sweet potatoes.

In the 1930s, there was increased dependence on rice imported from Korea and Formosa, setting the stage for shortages when shipping lanes were blocked during the war years. Rice (*Oryza sativa*) had been cultivated since ancient times, but it is unique in having varieties selected for wet and dry conditions. Most of the rice crop grown in Japan consisted of semi-aquatic varieties cultivated in paddies, although some non-aquatic strains were sown in upland fields. Traditional paddy fields were banked by hand-built dikes designed to accumulate rainfall or contain irrigation. High rainfall during the early summer benefited the growing season, while drier conditions during August and September favored rice grain maturation and harvesting. Draft animals had the extra benefit of producing manure, another source of micronutrients for intensively cultivated paddies and fields.

Most calories came from rice, wheat, and others grains, supplemented by white and sweet potatoes cultivated in upland fields. Upland areas were planted in diverse fruits and vegetables, including cabbages, onions, eggplant, burdock, apples, pears, persimmons, and tangerines, but elongated white *daikon* radishes covered nearly half of arable upland agricultural fields (see Chapter 4). Soybeans provided essential protein and had been cultivated for centuries for use in *miso, shoyu, tofu, natto, moyashi*, oil production, and various synthetic chemical processes (see Chapter 4); in the pre-war years, over a million tons were grown and used annually. Typically the plants were grown in single rows along the dikes that surrounded rice paddies, and farmers often kept the harvest for their own use. Ultimately soybeans posed a situation similar to rice, with increasing dependence on imports from China; between 1920 and 1938, Japanese soybean crops declined by nearly a third, while imports more than doubled, setting the stage for wartime shortages.[77]

Some crops were essential economically as exports. Japanese farmers cultivated pyrethrum daisies as a source of insecticides, and the loss of pyrethrum imports posed a challenge to U.S. farmers and gardeners during the war years. Mulberry culture fueled the silk industry; about half of all Japanese farming families were involved in sericulture, either by raising caterpillars for their silk-containing cocoons or by cultivating their food, the leaves of mulberry (*Morus* spp.). Following an economic downturn in the 1920s, some also worked in silk mills to supplement modest farm earnings. However, the Depression left most Americans and Europeans unable to afford silk clothing, so Japanese farm families suffered drastically from the loss of silk income. The pre-war economy was so desperate that many Japanese foraged for edible bark and roots to survive.

Parachute construction used silk for its strength and light weight, but wartime shortages of Japanese silk encouraged chemists at the Dupont Experimental Station to develop nylon for parachute construction. Nevertheless silk was in high demand, and stockpiles were among the first raw materials exported from occupied Japan to the U.S. aboard the *Marine Falcon* in March 1946.[78]

However, the war soon resulted in major shifts in Japanese agriculture, with planting redirected to staple crops, particularly rice. However, labor shortages impacted the work of transplanting rice seedlings from seedbeds into paddies, and the harvest of 1941 was disastrous due to this and other factors. In 1941, a Temporary Agricultural Land Management Ordinance mandated efficient land use, specific staple crops (primarily rice, wheat, barley, and soybeans), and the elimination of nonessential crops such as tea and flowers. Melons were also discouraged due to their low caloric yield and sprawling growth habit. Local officials encouraged cooperation by suggesting the theft of watermelons from the fields of farmers who did not comply.[79] Local agricultural stations established standard cultivation practices for each prefecture and village. Prescribed methods included planting times, fertilizer application, crop selection, and the distance between rows. Productivity trumped palatability, so government subsidies for seed stock favored high-yielding varieties. For instance, productive strains of *Norin* and *Okinawa* sweet potatoes replaced the more flavorful *Oiran* and *Genji* cultivars. Prefectures established specific production goals for strategic crops, including staples (grains, potatoes, and soybeans) and fibers (hemp, ramie, and jute, see Chapter 8). Seeds were distributed to encourage sunflower cultivation because the pressed seeds yielded an edible oil.

Farmers who ignored standard practices and missed targets could lose control of their land, in a system that functionally resembled the War Agricultural Executive Committees in England. Government efforts were aimed at projects that would earn immediate results, and land was converted into wartime rice paddies using irrigation strategies and make-do methods. Clay pipes were in short supply, so hollowed bamboo stalks and wooden logs were used as temporary means to funnel water into flooded fields. Rice seedlings were started in hotbeds warmed by decomposing leaves and rice straw, a technique promoted and subsidized widely during the war years to encourage earlier planting and to increase yields. However, beginning with the failed rice harvest in 1941, wartime harvests of this essential crop routinely fell short of target goals, the result of shortages of labor, machinery and fertilizers; in short, national rice harvest goals became a formality unrelated to agricultural reality. With dwindling food supplies, sweet potatoes became the vegetable of choice during the last two years of the war. The starchy tubers yielded 30 percent more calories per acre than rice, provided vitamins A and C, and grew on reclaimed land that was unsuitable for other crops.[80]

By the spring and summer of 1945, the last few months of the war, city-dwelling Japanese civilians were encouraged to live as urban farmers among the bombed ruins. The *Photographic Weekly Report*, the official weekly news magazine, described clearing rubble and planting staple crops on city blocks leveled by Allied bombing raids. The March 28 issue included this advice: "Leave no place untilled, Leave no spot unsown, For this land of the emperor, Is the mother of victory's provisions."[81] The June 11 issue provided official instructions for excavating dugout homes in leveled streets (similar to the bomb shelters excavated in home gardens), with the recommendation of planting bare soil with squash plants for camouflage, similar to the practice in England of planting Anderson shelters with a cover crop of marrows.[82] Foraged weeds and wild plants supplemented cultivated crops; civilians were encouraged to eat anything edible, including roots, leaves, grasses, nuts, and seeds (see Chapter 4). By the end of the war, Japanese agriculture and diet had become matters of resourcefulness and self-discipline rather than nutrients and calories.

7

Medicinal Botany

At the start of World War II, about half of all pharmaceutical drugs included botanical derivatives in their formulations. Drug shortages were anticipated because many medicinal plants were imported, some from Europe and others from the tropics, and concern increased with global hostilities. Trade in botanical drugs occurred in European cities, including Hamburg and Rotterdam, which drastically affected worldwide access to pharmaceuticals.

Essential Drugs

Critical drug plants in limited supply included belladonna (*Atropa belladonna*), henbane (*Hyocyamus niger*), quinine (*Cinchona* spp.), red squill (*Urginia maritima*, now recognized as *Drimia maritima*), and lavender-cotton (*Santolina chamaecyparissus*). European growers supplied belladonna, henbane, and red squill; quinine was obtained from feverbark trees cultivated in the Dutch East Indies, and santonin was derived from lavender-cotton plants imported from Asia.

These plants had diverse medicinal uses. Belladonna and henbane were sources of potent tropane alkaloids such as atropine and scopalomine, which had narcotic and sedative properties, and they appeared in formulations ranging from laxatives to painkillers. Atropine from belladonna was a known antidote to organophosphate nerve agents such as sarin and tabun. Germany produced these chemical weapons in large quantities but never used them against Allied troops, but stockpiles of atropine-loaded syrettes resulted in a wartime belladonna shortage. Originally imported from Europe, belladonna was cultivated in New Jersey, Pennsylvania, Tennessee, Virginia, Ohio, and Wisconsin. Huge dryers desiccated two tons of leaves daily.[1]

Quinine was used to prevent and treat malaria, but the compound was also used in cases of shingles, whooping cough, psoriasis, and sepsis. Lavender-cotton was a vermifuge against intestinal parasites. Red squill, a bulb-producing species in the lily family (Liliaceae), is native to the Mediterranean region, and its cardiac glycosides were used to regulate heartbeat. The plant was also widely used as a wartime rat poison; known doses of scillaren glycosides can be cardiotonic, but uncontrolled levels added to rat bait were lethal. In addition to destroying stored food, rats were potential vectors of disease. Biological warfare was a legitimate concern; the Japanese experimented in the infamous Unit 731 with the aerial spraying of the plague bacterium (*Yersinia pestis*) that is spread by rat-borne fleas.

166

In the Pacific theater, wild rats were reservoirs for the microbe that causes scrub typhus, and red squill rat poison was standard military issue for many years.[2] Thus rat poison reserves were considered essential to national security and military health, but imports of red squill were blocked by German submarines. Rather than seeking alternatives, the USDA Agricultural Research Service cloned European bulbs for successful cultivation on experimental farms in California. The individual bulbs weighed up to a kilogram and were macerated into chips or powder for drying and long term use. There were also attempts to select cultivated strains with high glycoside concentrations that could thrive in the California climate.[3]

All of these species were originally imported from areas potentially affected by war with Germany and Japan. Even before the attack on Pearl Harbor, practical concern resulted in the cultivation of medicinal plants in the U.S. In the spring of 1941, Harvard University botanists worked with faculty of the Massachusetts College of Pharmacy to plant a medicinal plant garden at the Arnold Arboretum. The two-acre experimental site was landscaped with woody medicinal species including witch hazel, sweet gum, sassafras, buckthorns, bayberry, and sugar maples, while herbaceous species were transplanted into beds. Much of the plant list resembled a colonial garden, including yarrow, bugleweed, tansy, angelica, sage, thyme, parsley, and rosemary, herbs with known medicinal properties. However, the goal was not to recreate a historic garden. Plant choice was clearly strategic, to identify easily cultivated species for use in treating ailments from congestive heart failure to wound care.[4]

Belladonna, henbane, red squill, and lavender- cotton (all temperate species) were planted in the Massachusetts College of Pharmacy garden, but the National Formulary (now merged with the United States Pharmacopeia) sought safe substitutes for wartime use. For instance, thorn apple (*Datura stramonium*) was cultivated for use in cathartics as a belladonna alternative.[5] Both species are members of the family Solanaceae (a family known for producing tropane alkaloids) that synthesize atropine and related compounds, but thorn apple naturalizes widely and grows aggressively, and it was collected from the wild for wartime use. Eventually wartime crops of belladonna were successfully cultivated in Wisconsin and Pennsylvania, and henbane was collected from naturalized populations in Montana.[6]

There were other wartime substitutions, including the temporary use of Indian species of valerian

Thorn apple was cultivated as a wartime substitute for belladonna and its medicinal alkaloids. Both species synthesize atropine and related compounds, but thorn apple naturalizes widely and grows aggressively.

(*Valeriana wallichii*) and rhubarb (*Rheum australe*) to replace European valerian (*V. offic-inalis*) and Chinese rhubarb (*R. palmatum*). However, not all plants of a single genus shared similar medicinal properties. Shortages of aconite root (*Aconitum napellus*) from the central European Alps resulted in investigations of Asian aconites, but either the potent alkaloids (primarily aconitine) were lacking or undesirable side effects occurred.[7]

Other plants cultivated in the garden included tansy (*Tanacetum vulgare*) and pink-root (*Spigelia marilandica*), both effective vermifuges when administered in controlled doses. Lily of the valley (*Convallaria majalis*) and foxglove (*Digitalis* spp.) were grown for their cardiac glycosides. Autumn crocus (*Colchicum autumnale*) was used to treat both gout and typhus. Although European supplies were low, the bulbs multiplied easily in the New England climate, and the alkaloid colchicine was also used to develop polyploid strains of agricultural plants (see Chapter 6). Meadowsweet (*Filipendula ulmaria*) was a possible substitute for the European willows used in manufacturing aspirin. These species all produce salicin, isolated by German chemists and valued for its anti-inflammatory and analgesic properties. Ironically, Germany lost the aspirin trade-mark as part of the reparations negotiated in the Treaty of Versailles at the end of World War I.

Plants were also cultivated with military uses in mind, including species used his-torically for wound treatment. Yarrow (*Achillea millefolium*) was known since ancient times as a hemostat, and garlic and onions (*Allium* spp.) were used as antibiotic dressings. Various mints had antibiotic potential, including bugleweed (*Ajuga reptans*, a folk cure for gangrene) and species of *Mentha*, *Hyssopus*, *Monarda*, and *Lavandula*. Various mus-tards (*Brassica* spp.) were also potentially antibiotic. New World medicinal plants included several used by Native Americans and adopted as folk remedies; at least three of these were used historically to treat malaria, including fringe tree (*Chionanthus virginicus*), jack-in-the-pulpit (*Arisaema triphyllum*), and Oregon grape (*Mahonia aquifolium*).

Home Front Medicine

Civilian health was considered part of patriotic duty, and proprietary medicines advertised their products in light of wartime preparedness. Over-the-counter remedies included Vaporub and Va-tro-nol from the Vick Chemical Company of North Carolina. Vaporub was intended for external use and was compounded with botanical terpenes and terpenoids, including camphor, menthol, and thymol, and oils of nutmeg, eucalyptus, and cedar leaves. Va-tro-nol was a similar aromatic combination, with the addition of the alkaloid ephedrine from *Ephedra*, and advertisements for the "Vicks plan" suggested that it be used as a throat medication to treat colds. Menthol, thymol, and camphor are all derived from various mints, and the latter is also isolated commercially from a cin-namon relative, the camphor laurel (*Cinnamomum camphora*). All have antimicrobial and antiviral properties, so the advertising claims may have had a medical basis.

Home front medicine included first aid. With the threat of bombing in England, families were advised to have on hand a kit of basic items that included several botanical products. Basic medicines included ammoniated tincture of quinine, used as a home remedy for colds and fevers. Now obsolete, it appeared in the British Pharmaceutical Codex until 1963 and was a medical carryover from tropical colonies, where quinine from feverbark (*Cinchona* spp.) was used to treat malaria. Tincture of myrrh (prepared from the resin of the tree *Commiphora myrrha*) was another common remedy that was valued for its antiseptic properties and used as a home cure for periodontal diseases.

Poultices were common home remedies for congestion, pain, or minor infections, typically prepared by wrapping macerated or powdered plant matter in oiled silk (made by impregnating silk cloth with a drying oil, usually linseed oil from the seeds of flax or linen, *Linum usitassimum*). The lightweight, waterproof cloth could wrap and contain poultices, for instance those made from linseed meal (ground flaxseed) or a moistened mixture of powdered mustard and flour. Materials for bandages included surgical lint, made by scraping fibers from linen and used for dressing wounds; an antiseptic dressing was made by steeping the lint fibers in a saturated boric acid solution. Cotton bandages were part of a standard first aid kit, essential for stopping blood flow, binding fractures, for making slings, and for holding wound dressings in place. Wartime shortages meant that these were often made from household cloth such as flannel, and first aid charts illustrated the correct use of triangular and roller bandages during air raids.

Battlefront Medicine

Military medical chests included several botanical drugs. Routine complaints such as headaches and toothaches were treated with aspirin from willows and eugenol from cloves, and aloin (from *Aloe*) and *Cascara sagrada* were standard cathartics. More powerful drugs included digitalis, quinine, and opium, which had ancient roots as a military analgesic. Military drug supplies included both opium powder and the purified opium alkaloids morphine and codeine, drugs that have alleviated more suffering than any other botanical medicine.[8] As in earlier wars, morphine was the most important military drug during World War II, alleviating pain and allowing healing to occur when agony interfered with rest.

Wild opium poppies (*Papaver somniferum*) originated in Eurasia and migrated with humans across Europe, the archeological evidence for their use dating back to the Neolithic and Bronze Ages. Early selection probably favored the most chemically active poppies, so the weedy plants that colonized agricultural fields may have been potent populations in terms of their analgesic and psychoactive properties. Opium poppies synthesize 26 alkaloids, including morphine, codeine, laudanine, papaverine, and thebaine, with the potential of addiction. In the early nineteenth century, the German pharmacist Friedrich Wilhelm Sertürner isolated morphine, the first known plant alkaloid, and experimented on animals and humans to determine safe and effective doses. He named his *principium somniferum* for Morpheus, the Greek god of sleep.

During the Civil War, dependency on opium or purified morphine became known as the soldiers' disease, but the danger of addiction or overdose did not outweigh the benefits of a reliable analgesic for injured troops. By World War II, soldiers received injections of morphine while still on the battlefield. Frontline medics administered the drug subcutaneously using syrettes, packaged "hypodermic units" strategically developed and patented in 1939 by the E.R. Squibb and Sons drug company (U.S. Patent No. 2,219,301) both as a way to save lives and to sell morphine to the U.S. military. Each syrette had a hypodermic needle attached to a collapsible tube containing a pre-measured morphine dose; they were also used to administer atropine, the known antidote to organophosphate nerve agents such as sarin and tabun.

The capsules of opium poppies produce morphine, in high demand for military use. The drug was administered in combat using syrettes, pre-measured hypodermic units developed by E.R. Squibb and Sons drug company as a way to market the powerful analgesic to the U.S. military during World War II.

The standard form of the drug used was morphine tartrate, an easily soluble salt prepared by combining a morphine solution with tartaric acid, an organic acid typically isolated from grapes. As with any form of morphine, overdosing was possible, especially in cold temperatures when blood circulated more slowly and the drug was slower to act. A standard procedure involved affixing the empty syrette to a soldier's clothing, to avoid additional doses that could result in death.[9] Along with wound dressings and sulfanilamide drugs, morphine syrettes were considered critical to battle. There were anecdotal reports that supply problems resulted in shortages, which forced the rationing of available morphine to the wounded men who were expected to survive.

Opium in another form was used to control dysentery, which could be bacterial or amoebic in origin. Paregoric was a tincture compounded from opium and three other botanical ingredients: camphor, oil of anise, and benzoic acid. It had anti-diarrheal properties that were needed by troops stationed in the Pacific and Mediterranean regions where dysentery was potentially deadly. Ethnobotany provided other clues; based on Maori practices, New Zealand troops treated dysentery using dried leaves and decoctions of koromiko (*Hebe stricta* and *H. salicifolia*). The active ingredient is now known to be a phenolic glycoside with apparent anti-protozoal activity.

Reliable opium supplies were critical to the war effort. The poppies thrive in warm temperate habitats, particularly in rich soil that has been recently plowed. China, India, and Turkey provided opium for wartime purification, but there was legitimate concern that shipping blockades could cause shortages at a time when pharmaceutical morphine demands were high. There was also a market for edible poppy seeds, so California farmers began cultivating culinary varieties. Due to the interest in poppy cultivation, Congress passed the Opium Poppy Control Act of 1942, which sought to control the illegal narcotic trade by requiring licenses to grow the crop. The seeds could be harvested from the edible varieties, but any collection of the opium-containing latex from their capsules was clearly on the wrong side of the law. Of course, many were quick to point out that many cultivars developed for their seeds contain minimal quantities of the narcotic latex. Crops were also cultivated for wartime pharmaceutical use, despite the legal ambiguities surrounding the growing of opium poppies in the U.S. In 1942, California authorities granted permits for sowing two thousand acres with opium-producing cultivars, but without the knowledge of the Federal Bureau of Narcotics. Opium poppies were often in plain view on open roads, and federal officers feared that the marketplace would be flooded with illegal narcotics. However, many of the poppy fields failed, the result of farmers' inexperience and variations in climate and soil that resulted in low morphine production.

As a result of the Allied blockade, Germans cultivated opium poppies wherever they would grow, including city lots. The plants were used both for their medicinal alkaloids and for the cooking oil that could be pressed from their seeds. Opium shortages in Germany resulted in alternative methods of morphine extraction using the dried capsules, leaves, and stems (collectively known as poppy straw), usually considered waste products of opium and poppy seed production. Traditional harvesting involved collecting the liquid latex from cuts made in the immature capsules, a labor-intensive process that ignored residual alkaloids in other plant parts. The chemical method perfected in the 1920s involved using sulfuric acid to break the bonds between meconic acid and the poppy alkaloids, followed by several extraction and precipitation steps. The process yielded alkaloids even from cultivars grown for edible seeds and not opium, supplying the German military with morphine. English chemists devised a similar method known as the Gregory process, in which entire poppy plants were cooked in acidic solutions and the alkaloids extracted using acid-base reactions. In fact, most pharmaceutical morphine is now extracted from poppy straw rather than latex.

In Germany, the Merck pharmaceutical company developed a botanical drug mixture known as SEE (an acronym for scopalomine, ephedrine, and eukodol) or Scophedal. SEE was used for surgical anesthesia during the 1930s and then adapted for frontline casualties during World War II. Scopalomine may have mitigated frightening memories, but as with other tropane alkaloids, hallucinations were a possible side effect. Scopalomine-producing species include henbane (*Hyocyamus niger*), aconite (*Aconitum* spp.), belladonna (*Atropa belladonna*), and nightshades (*Solanum* spp.), all with various ancient associations to witchcraft practices. Ephedrine originated as an alkaloid isolated from the Chinese shrub *Ephedra sinica* and related species used in traditional medicine, but the wartime drug was probably synthetic rather than imported. It functioned in maintaining blood pressure levels in severely injured soldiers. Eukodol (also known as oxycodone) was a semi-synthetic drug made from the opium alkaloid thebaine; it replaced heroin, a highly addictive form of morphine with two additional acetyl groups, produced by Bayer Laboratories.

Scopalomine also functioned as an effective truth serum, limiting inhibitions while encouraging conversation and leaving no residual memory of interrogation. During World War II, the Office of Strategic Services (OSS, the precursor to the CIA) investigated the use of low doses of scopalomine for interrogating U-boat crews and high-ranking POWs. The secretive studies were conducted using U.S. Army personnel under the guise of research for a shell-shock treatment, and Josef Mengele conducted similar research in Germany. As with other potent phytochemicals, dose was critical because high scopalomine levels brought about delirium, severe hallucinations, and tachycardia.

In Germany during the years prior to World War II, there was considerable concern regarding the decreased birthrate, so it is interesting to note that obstetrical medicine turned to tropane alkaloids to ease the rigors of childbirth. Midwives had traditionally managed labor pains with mandrake (*Mandragora officinarum*), a source of tropane alkaloids since ancient times. Based on research begun in 1903, Dr. Karl Gauss and Dr. Bernardt Kronig developed *Dämmerschlaf*, a drug mixture known as twilight sleep, in which they administered a mixture of scopalomine and opiates (usually morphine) during labor. The goal was a synergistic combination of anesthesia and amnesia, and apparently some found the mixture of botanical drugs to be effective. Women came from abroad to have their children at the Freiburg clinic operated by Gauss and Kronig.

Medical journals touted the benefits of twilight sleep, and the method became known in the U.S. Maternal pain was alleviated or at least forgotten, and infants were spared the toxicity of ether and chloroform. The popular press, such as *McClure's* magazine, published laudatory articles on painless childbirth, and women clamored for twilight sleep at lying-in hospitals across America. At the Jewish Maternity Hospital in New York, a three month trial of twilight sleep with 120 women was deemed a complete success, and the National Twilight Sleep Association organized in 1915 to disseminate pamphlets and leaflets and organize lectures and campaigns.

Twilight sleep was simultaneously encouraged in Germany. The German population had plummeted, and there was concern for populating the German military. During the Nazi regime, mothers received rewards and awards for bearing children for the Reich. The practice of *Dämmerschlaf* encouraged women to bear children, but was eventually abandoned due to the negative side effects of the plant alkaloids, including hallucinations so strong that some laboring mothers required restraint. Ironically, both SEE and *Dämmerschlaf* relied on opiates and scopalomine for their effects. An increased birthrate ensured growth of the German military, and twilight sleep and SEE eased the pain for both laboring mothers and their soldier sons.

Ephedrine was also used to synthesize a potent stimulant that was widely used during the war. Chemically speaking, ephedrine is a substituted amphetamine (meaning that it is based on the amphetamine ring structure), and it served as the molecular starting point for methamphetamine, which was first synthesized in Japan in 1888 (see Chapter 5). By 1938, Temmler-Werke in Germany was producing large quantities of the drug, most likely starting with synthetic ephedrine rather than the natural product. As documented at the Nuremberg trials, concentration camp prisoners were used as test subjects; experiments showed that methamphetamine users could forego sleep and still perform at high levels. Known as Pervitin (methamphetamine hydrochloride), methamphetamines were widely used in the German military, where the pills were known as *Panzerschokolade* (tank chocolate) and *Stuka-tabletten* (Stuka tablets). Tank crews and airplane pilots relied on the pills during periods of stress and minimal sleep, but the drug was potentially addictive; Adolf Hitler received methamphetamine injections during the last three years of his life. Production levels of eight to nine million tablets per year suggest that Pervitin use was widespread even among German civilians during the war years.[10] In Japan there was widespread methamphetamine use among both military and factory workers who used the drug to enhance productivity. U.S. pilots also relied on methamphetamines to eliminate fatigue and improve focus during long bombing raids.

Wounded soldiers sometimes required infusions of blood plasma, and alternatives were needed for times when supplies were low. In terms of their chemistry, plasma substitutes required large molecules that attracted water (i.e., hydrophilic compounds) and formed a colloidal solution which retained fluid volume in blood. Various options were explored, including pectin which had long been used to stabilize foods; the complex polysaccharides are derived from plant cell walls and can differ in their component sugars and branching patterns. Most of the research relied on pectin derived from citrus skins, the standard specified by the *U.S. National Formulary*, although apple pomace (the skins and other tissue remaining after pressing for juice) was another source of commercial pectin. The ability to attract and retain water is universal, explaining the medical use of pectin as a demulcent and to control diarrhea. Plant pectins also seemed to have potential as plasma substitutes, for instance in managing cases of plasma loss associated with severe burns. However, investigations at the Henry Ford Hospital and the University of Illinois yielded mixed results. A conference on pectin use in 1943 highlighted 500 clinical cases with no ill effects such as blood clotting or coagulation. Toxicity was debated, and there was concern about the effect of pectin injections on soldiers suffering from shock. Ultimately the military use of pectin as a plasma substitute was rejected.[11]

Other botanical substances were investigated as plasma substitutes, including cotton fibers oxidized with nitrogen tetroxide into a powder which dissolved in bicarbonate solutions. This yielded soluble cellulose that attracted and held water. Researchers at Columbia University experimented with various cotton solutions; however, there were concerns about possible effects on kidney function and blood clotting, and the option was dropped.[12] Although never officially approved for military use, coconuts (*Cocos nucifera*) provided the best emergency alternative to blood plasma, particularly in the Pacific theater where coconut palms were part of the landscape.[13] The trees are nearly ubiquitous because the fruit float and remain impermeable to sea water for weeks, allowing for long distance dispersal among atolls and beaches.

Each coconut houses a large seed (the familiar coconut of commerce) containing copious endosperm, the white tissue that provides nutrition for the germinating embryo. Immature coconuts still retain some of the endosperm as a liquid, sometimes known as coconut water. This naturally sterile solution of minerals, amino acids, and simple sugars (glucose and fructose) can be transfused on an emergency basis if blood or plasma supplies are low. Under desperate conditions, British troops in Ceylon (now Sri Lanka) and Japanese troops in Sumatra both used intravenous drips of coconut water. Recent analysis reveals that coconut water contains electrolyte levels closer to cellular levels rather than extracellular plasma; the solution is relatively hypotonic (lower in solutes) and acidic compared to plasma, which means that is not ideal for transfusion. However, coconut water served to prevent some cases of shock among casualties during make-do wartime conditions.[14]

Malaria and Quinine

Malaria is a parasitic disease caused by the protozoan *Plasmodium*, with symptoms that include intermittent fevers, chills, debility, anemia, jaundice, seizures, coma, and possible death. The vectors are female *Anopheles* mosquitoes which transmit the bloodborne disease by their bites; because the insects breed in areas with standing water, malaria has long been associated with swampy habitats. Once in the blood stream, *Plasmodium* protozoa enter red blood cells and reproduce. Fevers and chills occur when the infected blood cells rupture and release more *Plasmodium* into the blood. Among the species that parasitize humans, *P. falciparum* is the most severe; *P. vivax*, *P. ovale*, and *P. malariae* cause chronic infections with relatively milder symptoms.

The reliable preventative and treatment was quinine, a drug derived from feverbark trees (*Cinchona* spp.) indigenous to the Peruvian Andes. It is concentrated in the bark and is one of at least 24 alkaloids produced by the species. Local people had used *Cinchona* species for malaria since ancient times, and during the 16th century they shared the cure with Jesuit priests. By the 18th century, imported feverbark allowed European countries to colonize the tropics without fear of malarial fevers. By the 1930s, Dutch growers had established *Cinchona* plantations in Java that supplied nearly all of the quinine used

6

Feverbark was essential in preventing and curing malaria, but the worldwide supplies cultivated in Java were ultimately controlled by Axis countries. The U.S. National Formulary Committee encouraged local pharmacists and drug wholesalers to return unused quinine and totaquinine (a mixture of feverbark alkaloids) for military use.

worldwide; operations included the Bandoengsche Kinenfabriek, the largest quinine processing plant in the world. Following the occupation of Holland in May 1940, the Nazi government assumed control of the Dutch Kina Bureau, which oversaw all aspects of quinine distillation and processing; stored supplies of quinine were shipped to Berlin for German military use. Subsequently, the Japanese invaded Java in March 1942 and seized control of the Dutch-operated *Cinchona* plantations, where high-yielding varieties supplied most of the global quinine demand.

The disease was not limited to the tropics. During the Depression years, malaria was still prevalent in swampy regions of several southern states. Beginning in 1942, the Office of Malaria Control in War Areas (which eventually became the Centers for Disease Control and Prevention) monitored and managed the malaria problem near military bases, which were often located in lowland areas with *Anopheles* populations. Eradication of mosquitoes meant the elimination of their breeding sites. Although the Tennessee Valley Authority drained wetlands, there were still known malarial regions in Louisiana and Arkansas, and so some troops stationed in the South needed quinine. There was even greater need anticipated following the Pearl Harbor attack, with war predicted in northern Africa, tropical Asia, and the Pacific region. There was also the possibility that troops could encounter malaria in Europe. Beginning in October 1943, the German army flooded lowland areas in Italy including Agro Pontino and Agro Montano, regions with indigenous *Anopheles* mosquitoes that spread malaria. This was arguably biological warfare, but the flooding was ineffective because Allied troops were administered anti-malarial drugs. In addition, German mine blasts left thousands of craters where mosquitoes bred; malaria reinvaded areas of Italy where it had been long eradicated, increasing cases of the disease among local people.[15]

Quinine was a critical drug, and in 1941 the U.S. had no source of feverbark trees; government stockpiles had to last until new *Cinchona* plantations could be established or an alternative drug identified. At the time, quinine was a component of several proprietary drugs and health tonics, and it was an essential ingredient in treatments for several ailments, ranging from anemia and amoebic dysentery to typhoid, typhus, and varicose veins. A 1942 conservation order from the War Production Board restricted limited quinine use to an anti-malarial drug and local anesthetic (quinine and urea hydrochloride). With the conservation order in place, most pharmacists and suppliers had no need for quinine supplies; the National Formulary Committee encouraged pharmacists and wholesalers to return unused quinine and totaquinine (a mixture of *Cinchona* alkaloids) for military use.

There was a synthetic alternative to quinine. The drug known as atabrine had anti-protozoan activity, but the pills caused nausea, diarrhea, and yellowed skin. It was rumored that atabrine caused impotence and sterility, falsehoods spread by Japanese propaganda. First synthesized in the 1930s by the chemical and dye conglomerate I.G. Farben, the compound was based on the chemistry of dyes derived from coal tar, the chemical remains of coal (fossilized plant matter from Carboniferous forests) converted to coke or gas. Atabrine (variously known as atebrin, mepacrine, or quinacrine) eliminated German dependence on Holland for quinine. Eventually several U.S. pharmaceutical companies also synthesized atabrine using intermediate compounds from various dye and chemical firms. Millions of atabrine pills were shipped annually to military bases in the Pacific; troops exposed to malaria received doses of quinine or atabrine, but many had to be frightened or cajoled into taking the drugs. Posters, signs, and films warned of the dangers of malaria, and commanding officers were told to require that the pills be swallowed.

There were five times more cases of malarial infections than combat injury in the Pacific. Military doctors soon discovered that daily doses of anti-malarial drugs were essential to preventing the disease, rather than treatment in response to exposure. The first epidemic occurred in the spring of 1942 among U.S. troops stationed on Efate in the New Hebrides, followed by significant outbreaks on Guadalcanal, Espiritu Santo, and other islands with *Anopheles* populations. The effect of malaria on military strength cannot be overstated; at one point, General MacArthur complained that two-thirds of his troops either had malaria or were recuperating from the disease, which made fighting impossible.[16] Ultimately there were over a half million cases of malaria among Americans stationed in the Pacific and southeastern Asia. Some experienced recurrences, which were treated with plasmoquine, like atabrine synthesized from coal tar dyes and reliable in curing chronic infections of *P. vivax*. News of serious malaria infections certainly concerned civilians; an article in *Good Housekeeping* reassured wives and mothers that atabrine and quinine were effective in preventing or curing the disease and that swamps and "protective vegetation" were removed from areas where military were bivouacked.[17]

Some regions such as the Fiji islands and New Caledonia lacked endemic *Anopheles* mosquitoes, so malaria was absent. However, in areas with mosquito populations, the incidence of malaria was linked to landscape and vegetation. Most of the malarial islands in the Pacific region were volcanic in origin, mountainous, and densely forested, with annual rainfall exceeding one hundred inches. Nocturnal mosquitoes became diurnal in deeply shaded jungle habitats. Streams and rivers flowed toward the coastline, and water was retained by alluvial silt and clay soils. Natural standing water was nearly impossible to eliminate, and pools of any size allowed mosquito reproduction; supply dumps and bivouac sites increased man-made microhabitats with standing water. Military vehicles compacted soils and reduced drainage, while tire ruts, shell and bomb craters, and foxholes also created ephemeral ponds in which *Anopheles* reproduced. War Department manuals advocated ditching, drainage, and the discarding of empty cans, oil drums, barrels, and coconut shells where mosquito larvae might live.[18]

In tropical America, malarial mosquitoes bred in bromeliads (family Bromeliaceae), epiphytic plants with sheathing leaf bases that catch and retain rainwater (known botanically as phytotelma, bodies of water held by terrestrial plants). On Trinidad, bromeliads (particularly the genera *Gravisia* and *Guzmania*) colonized immortelle trees (*Erythrina poeppigiana*), which were planted widely to shade cacao plantations. The trees were dangerous to climb, but high pressure spraying with copper sulfate killed the epiphytes and *Anopheles* larvae. To protect troops from malaria, the removal of epiphytic bromeliads became part of wartime preventative medicine.[19] Even the outer husks of coconuts sometimes retained sufficient water for mosquitoes to breed, but removing coconut palms from tropical islands would have been impossible.

Malaria control teams focused on distributing insecticides along with netting and burlap (made from sisal or jute fibers, see Chapter 8), which served as cloth screens inside tents. Some troops used hammocks that could be covered with netting, but these required trees for suspension and provided minimal protection in combat areas.[20] Pyrethrum bombs combined freon with pyrethrins (produced by the flowers of *Chrysanthemum* species, see Chapter 6) and sesame oil (pressed from the seeds of *Sesamum indicum*). Kept under pressure in steel containers, the bombs released a fine aerosol mist that killed *Anopheles* mosquitoes upon contact.[21] Dichlorodiphenyltrichloroethane (DDT) also killed mosquito larvae and allowed troops to fight with reduced danger of malaria. The compound was organic but non-botanical in origin, although plants do absorb DDT from habitats where it has been sprayed. There was awareness of possible dangers to plant life and pollinating insects from the mass production and widespread use of DDT; however, the difficult choice was in favor of using the insecticide.[22] Waging a successful war in the Pacific would have been impossible without the use of DDT to eliminate the vectors of malaria.

Human contact was another possible problem because those already infected with *Plasmodium* could transmit the disease to troops through blood transferred by mosquito bites. Drug supplies were shared with local people, but there was also the possibility of malaria infections from Japanese troops bivouacked in the same area. The Japanese military had meager supplies of quinine and atabrine, relying often on larvicidal sprays and citronella oil, a botanical pesticide that was steam-distilled from lemongrass (*Cymbopogon nardus* and *C. winterianus*) and used to repel mosquitoes. Malaria became widespread in the Japanese military, and most prisoners arrived with chronic infections.

In 1942 the Board of Economic Warfare assumed responsibility for the wartime quinine shortage. Working with civilian botanists, they developed a plan to obtain *Cinchona* bark from South America, collect seed stock, and establish Central and South American plantations that would supply the Allies. Wild *Cinchona* populations occur in the Andes range, from Bolivia north to the countries of Venezuela, Colombia, and Costa Rica, at altitudes ranging from sea level to 11,000 feet. Bolivia had agreed to ship bark to the Dutch Kina Bureau, but Columbia, Peru, and Ecuador signed agreements to supply both *Cinchona* bark and purified quinine to the U.S. The Columbia *Cinchona* Mission secured buying privileges for high yielding bark, and in return promised assistance with establishing local plantations.

William Steere from the University of Michigan and F. Raymond Fosberg from the USDA worked collaboratively to organize teams of botanists and foresters to scour the region for high-yielding trees (a minimum of 2–3 percent quinine in the dry weight of the plant tissue). In an effort to prepare future botanists and foresters for work in *Cinchona* plantations, Fosberg wrote the *Columbian Cinchona Manual* which detailed the techniques of cultivation and harvesting.[23] The goal was to obtain bark for immediate quinine purification and to collect seeds of high-yielding trees for future propagation. Teams identified several previously unknown populations, but their field work was complicated by the tendency of *Cinchona* species to hybridize, resulting in highly variable quinine concentrations. Rather than collecting and testing every possible specimen, botanists detected high quinine levels using the simple Grahe test, in which shredded bark releases reddish fumes when it is heated in a dry test tube. Trees with quinine content were then marked for later seed collection, and voucher specimens were sent to the National Herbarium at the Smithsonian Institution. The related genera *Ladenbergia* and *Remijia* were also collected for possible breeding and hybridization. Some species in these genera yield quinine and the related alkaloids cinchonine, cinchonidine, and quinodine, which had potential anti-malarial activity.

Over two years, *Cinchona* missions visited Colombia, Ecuador, Peru, and Venezuela. High elevations and high rainfall made physical work a challenge, and botanists on these missions endured altitude sickness, amoebic dysentery, and malaria. Fungi destroyed clothing, supplies, and field notes. Harvesting was arduous, and there were few local people who had the necessary skill to strip bark efficiently without killing trees. The traditional method involved mossing, a technique in which strips of bark were peeled away from the trunk and the wounds were covered with moss, which provided antibiotic protection during healing. Using seed stock collected on the missions, plantations were established in Costa Rica, Guatemala, Colombia, and Ecuador, which depended on research in the areas of vegetative propagation, plant diseases, and grafting techniques.

Cinchona field work was halted in 1944 when chemists, rather than botanists, seemed to control the future of malaria drugs. At Johns Hopkins University, the Office for the Survey of Malaria Drugs organized and disseminated chemical and pharmacological data for thousands of clinical trials. In an effort to find drugs superior to atabrine, 14,000 various compounds were tested for anti-malarial properties; this involved painstaking chemical synthesis and experimental trials which led to drugs such as chloroquine.[24] The laboratory synthesis of quinine was another option, a way to produce the drug without growing trees, harvesting bark, and purifying the alkaloid. Supported by Edwin Land of the Polaroid Corporation, a team of organic chemists used organic precursors to synthesize quinine, known previously only as a natural plant compound. Their work was hailed as a chemical solution to the wartime quinine shortage. According to the *New York Times*, "The war has brought forth many a wonder of research but none more wonderful than the success of Drs. Robert B. Woodward and William E. Doering in synthesizing quinine. Behind this outstanding achievement stands nearly a century of vain effort—vain partly because organic chemistry had not developed the concepts and techniques required. Yet the failures contributed much to ultimate success by indicating the path to be pursued."[25]

Although described at the time as the total synthesis of quinine, the Woodward-Doering method did not yield the pharmaceutical product in time for wartime demand. However, it did reveal the importance of synthetic organic chemistry in replicating molecules originally evolved by plants. Ironically, Sir William Henry Perkin's earlier attempt at quinine synthesis resulted in the discovery of the first synthetic dye, a mauve color.

His serendipitous discovery in 1856 established the chemical basis for the aniline dyes used for dress blue uniforms and the discovery of atabrine, the first wartime quinine substitute.

Scrub Typhus

Poorly understood at the beginning of the war, scrub typhus is caused by the bacterium *Orientia tsutsugamushi*, originally classified in the genus *Rickettsia*. The species is an obligate intracellular parasite, meaning that it must live inside host cells with which they share some basic metabolic functions. Symptoms include fever, gastrointestinal upset, muscular pain, hallucinations, and rashes. Latter stages of the potentially deadly disease involve encephalitis, spleen enlargement, and tissue swelling in the heart and lungs.

The disease is spread by biting mites, often known as chiggers, resulting in the dark scabs (eschars) that characterize the disease. The mites inhabit a region now known as the tsutsugamushi triangle, extending from northern Japan and eastern Russia south to northern Australia and west to Afghanistan and Pakistan. Typical scrub typhus regions are defined by habitats populated by rats and other small rodents, which are hosts for the mites and bacteria; larval mites acquire the bacteria by biting the rats. Scrub typhus is spread to humans by mites, while rodents serve as a reservoir of the disease.

The plant habitats associated with the disease included tropical grasslands and scrub forests characterized by stunted woody plants. For instance, troops in Papua New Guinea encountered kunai grass (*Imperata cylindrica*), which grows six to ten feet tall and provides shelter and food for thousands of rats. Blades of the grass were sharp, and maneuvering through kunai fields was a physical challenge. Even worse, time spent penetrating kunai fields resulted in scrub typhus infections, the result of bites from mites associated with rats. In Ceylon (now Sri Lanka), Indonesia, and the Philippines, habitats colonized by elephant grass (*Pennisetum purpureum*), also harbored the tick vectors of scrub typhus.

Botanists working with the U.S. Typhus Commission examined the flora of scrub typhus regions in Burma (now Myanmar) to investigate possible links between vegetation and mites, which seemed to be attracted to certain plants such as the legume *Cassia kleinii*. Although three thousand herbarium specimens from scrub typhus regions were shipped to the Smithsonian for analysis, the field work was inconclusive in determining the plants that attract mites. Grassy and wooded areas were all possible mite habitats, depending upon local agricultural practices. It was common in scrub typhus areas for fields to be cultivated for a few seasons and then abandoned when soil fertility diminished. Fallow land was quickly taken over by grasses, and rats colonized abandoned gardens and villages; thus mite infestations and scrub typhus multiplied with the spread of agriculture.[26]

In Burma during 1944, the U.S. 5307th Composite Unit (known as Merrill's Marauders) suffered from the synergistic effects of scrub typhus, malaria, dysentery, and poor nutrition that resulted in hospitalization and deaths. Men were tagged with medical diagnoses, in some cases "A.O.E." (accumulation of everything) and evacuated on stretchers made from bamboo poles rigged with clothing. Troops also encountered scrub typhus in Japan after the war, where the disease became known as Japanese river fever or tsutsugamishi disease. The War Department *Military Sanitation Manual* noted that the

Scrub typhus is spread by biting mites in habitats populated by rats and other small rodents, including grasslands and scrub forests characterized by stunted woody plants. Typical vegetation included kunai grass and elephant grass, which harbored the vectors of the bacterial disease; abandoned farms and villages were invaded by rats carrying the disease (U.S. Army).

disease was associated with flood plains along rivers "especially during hemp harvesting season," in which field activity must have disturbed local rat populations.[27]

Control measures included eradicating rats and burning fields of kunai grass near bivouac areas. The *Jungle Warfare* field manual advised against sleeping on the ground and noted that vegetation should be cleared and burned near bivouac sites.[28] British troops headed to Burma viewed "Six Little Jungle Boys" (War Office, Directorate of Army Kinematography, 1945), a cartoon-format training film that illustrated kunai grass and contact with mites and mosquitoes as a warning against scrub typhus and malaria. Combat troops were issued tight-fitting, one-piece jungle suits made of cotton herringbone twill printed in a camouflage pattern. The suits were designed to protect against mite and mosquito bites, but they were impossibly hot and heavy for the tropics, and the lack of a drop-seat was impractical in an area with widespread dysentery. A redesigned two-piece, light cotton suit was better accepted and prevented some cases of scrub typhus.[29]

Clothing was sprayed with citronella oil, a botanical pesticide that was steam-distilled from lemongrass (*Cymbopogon nardus* and *C. winterianus*), widespread species in the Old World tropics. Citronella oil is a mixture of terpenes including geraniol and citronellol and was known as McKesson's oil of citronella. The oil was bottled under pressure to make the aerosol bombs for use inside tents and buildings, and it was also used as a wartime substitute for chaulmoogra oil in treating leprosy. With shortages of citronella from Java, oil of pennyroyal (*Mentha pulegium*) was a temperate substitute for true citronella oil and also a well known abortifacient; German troops relied on pennyroyal cultivated in Spain as an insect repellant.

Botanical Antibiotics

Many plants produce secondary compounds with antibiotic properties, and some botanical materials have the ability to suppress bacterial growth. Wounds needed sterile dressings, which in some cases made use of sphagnum moss (*Sphagnum* spp.). The genus colonizes wetlands across North American and Europe, and during World War I, the harvested wild moss provided antimicrobial, highly absorbent wound dressings. During World War II, volunteers again harvested sphagnum moss from bogs, fens, and moors. *Sphagnum* is acidic and naturally antimicrobial, so no sterilization was needed; processing simply involved drying and cutting the moss into layers for wound dressings. The desiccated moss absorbed at least twenty times its weight in fluids (the result of hollow cells interspersed with living tissue) and kept injured tissue clean and dry. *Sphagnum* dressings were particularly valued before antibiotic drugs were widely available, when an infected wound could mean the loss of a limb. Research in Russia supported similar use of *Sphagnum* there; their wound treatments also included resin (balsam) collected from fir trees (probably *Abies nordmanniana*), now known to have antibiotic properties against *Staphylococcus* strains and several other bacteria.[30]

In 1858 Louis Pasteur described the antibacterial properties of garlic (*Allium sativum*), and the genus had a long history in folk medicine as a treatment for tuberculosis and colds. The genus also includes onions (*A. cepa*) which have a similar chemistry. The sulfur-containing compounds alliin and allicin act against several bacteria and fungi; when garlic tissue is damaged, a series of chemical reactions converts alliin into allicin, which is antibiotic to both *Salmonella* and *Staphylococcus*. During World War I, the practice of using garlic in field dressings for wounds was common across Europe, and the Russian Red Army continued the practice during World War II. The Russian technique used only the vapors released by ground onions in a closed container over the wound; tissue healed quickly, and bacterial infections subsided as a result of the vapor treatment.[31] By this point, the antibiotic properties of *Allium* species were documented in the laboratory using steam-distilled oil of garlic and assay methods developed in penicillin research.[32] At the time, however, medical interest in botanical antibiotics waned with the discovery and widespread availability of sulfa drugs and penicillin.

Oil from leaves of the tea tree (*Melaleuca alternifolia*) was another wartime antibiotic with broad spectrum activity against bacteria, fungi, viruses, and protozoans. Captain James Cook had observed that aboriginal Australians used the boiled leaves for skin eruptions, and he carried specimens back to England for study. It was not until the 1920s that studies at the Sydney Technological Museum revealed the strong antimicrobial properties of tea oil; however, the medicinal potential of tea tree oil was eclipsed by penicillin investigations during the same decade. Nevertheless tea tree oil was included in the first aid kits supplied to Australian troops who fought in the Pacific theater. It was widely used to treat minor wounds, insect bites, and infections, including the infected ulcers that were known generally as jungle rot. These lesions were very likely polymicrobial, colonized by various bacteria including *Mycobacterium ulcerans* and species of *Staphylococcus* and *Streptococcus*, which suggests the broad antibiotic activity of the oil. Field hospital staff saturated bandages with tea tree oil to minimize wound infections. Harvesters of tea tree leaves were sometimes exempt from conscription because the oil was essential to military medicine.[33]

Burns required special treatment. During World War I, tannic acid was used for burns caused by mustard gas, and research during the 1920s confirmed its effectiveness in healing and preventing infection. Tannic acid became a standard treatment adopted by the Bureau of Medicine and Surgery of the U.S. Navy.[34] Tannins are naturally occurring phytochemicals that discourage herbivores by interfering with digestion, and they are also known to be antibiotic against *Staphylococcus* bacteria that may infect burned tissue. Applied as tannic acid jelly, the treatment sealed the burn wound, prevented fluid loss, and forestalled infections. The idea originated with the traditional Chinese practice of using strong tea to treat burns, but tannic acid used in Western medicine was extracted from oaks (*Quercus* spp.) and sumacs (*Rhus* spp.), including galls caused by wasps.

In England, home front advice manuals suggested stocking the first aid cabinet with tannic acid jelly, at a time when civilians anticipated bombing and carried gas masks in the event of a chemical attack. However, treatment with tannic acid proved dangerous for certain combat wounds. During World War II, military doctors discovered that treating severely burned faces or hands with tannic acid caused crippling of the fingers and immobility of the eyelids, resulting in long term mutilation. Among British doctors, preferred treatments for severe burns included Peruvian balsam, a resin derived from the bark of a South American leguminous tree (*Myroxylon balsamum* var. *pereirae*), which contains several bioactive terpenes with traditional uses in healing.[35]

In contrast to the usual protocol, victims of the infamous 1942 Cocoanut Grove fire treated at the Massachusetts General Hospital did not have applications of tannic acid to keep their burns free of infection. Patients were administered penicillin, and their wounds were covered with cotton gauze and petroleum jelly, a new method that maintained sterility and promoted healing. Petroleum jelly was derived chemically from petroleum, a fossil fuel produced by microscopic algae and other plankton. Presumably as a result of the treatment used on Cocoanut Grove burn victims, the U.S. Army revised its use of tannic acid for burns in favor of simple gauze coverings.[36]

Penicillin

The antibiotic drug penicillin resulted from its serendipitous rediscovery in 1928 at Saint Mary's Hospital (London) by Alexander Fleming who noticed the ability of a mold (later identified as *Penicillium notatum*) to stop growth in *Staphylococcus* cultures. He soon ascertained that the mold could kill other bacteria, including *Streptococcus* species and *Corynebacterium diptheriae*, the causative agent of diphtheria. In nature, penicillin most likely evolved as a toxin that killed microbes competing for the same food source, and it can be adapted to cure microbial infections in medicine. However, once the therapeutic potential of penicillin was apparent, culturing sufficient *Penicillium* to produce a pharmaceutical drug was a challenge.

Although *Penicillium* is a fungus (classified in the Kingdom Fungi rather than Kingdom Plantae), there are botanical links to its pharmaceutical origins and production. Microbiologists at Oxford University tried a variety of culture methods for growing large quantities of *Penicillium*, essential for purifying and testing penicillin for its antibiotic potential. Young women known as "penicillin girls" were employed to inoculate the cultures and operate a fermentation apparatus, but wartime conditions compromised large scale production.

By 1941, there was heightened demand for a reliable antibiotic in England, where the war with Germany was in its third year. Microbiologists Howard Florey and Norman Heatley traveled to the USDA Northern Region Research Laboratory in Peoria, Illinois, where attention turned to culturing large quantities of *Penicillium*.[37] Corn steep liquor proved to be an ideal growth medium, a by-product of milling corn grains that had been soaked and softened in water. The liquid that drained from the milled grains contained nutrients from corn endosperm layers and embryos, a rich solution of vitamins, amino acids, and carbohydrates.

Corn steep liquor fueled the rapid growth of *Penicillium* to ten times previous yields. Perhaps this was not surprising because cornmeal was already well known in the U.S. as a standard growth medium for various fungi; its preparation was described in the War Department manual for microbiologists.[38] Microbiologists cultured various *Penicillium* strains isolated from decaying fruits and vegetables and soil samples from several locations. The fungus cultured successfully in Peoria was collected from a decaying melon at a local market, and this single wild type strain yielded all of the penicillin used during the war years. The melon mold was later identified as *P. notatum* (now also known as *P. chrysogenum*), commonly found in nature on moist soil and decaying fruits.[39]

The catastrophic fire at the Cocoanut Grove nightclub in Boston occurred on the evening of November 28, 1942, when a spark may have caused the ignition of artificial palm trees, rattan, bamboo, and other tropical-style decorations. Nearly five hundred people died, including many men and women in the military, and survivors with severe burns were treated at Boston hospitals. Still in the early stages of developing penicillin, the Merck drug company shipped 32 liters of *Penicillium* culture medium to Boston; the liquid contained penicillin from the cultured fungi and was administered to burn patients at risk for *Staphylococcus* infections in burns and skin grafts. Dosing was experimental, but many of the patients avoided infections and survived their severe burns. This success of penicillin as an antibiotic spurred its further development as a pharmaceutical drug.

The War Production Board assumed responsibility for developing penicillin as a pharmaceutical drug, which meant scaling up production and solving problems with extraction. Trials demonstrated that penicillin could cure infections caused by combat wounds or field surgery, so its wartime use was essential to saving lives and returning men to combat. In particular, penicillin treated gas gangrene, a necrotic infection usually caused by the anaerobic soil bacterium *Clostridium perfringens*. Perhaps ironically, many military recruits from southern states had grown up eating bread leavened by *C. perfringens*. So-called salt-risen bread recipes relied on a starter of wild microbes that could produce gas in anaerobic bread dough; baking removed any trace of living bacteria, which were also known to cause food poisoning.

Such opportunistic infections as those caused by *C. perfringens* had long been a hazard of combat wounds and field surgery, and penicillin provided the first reliable cure. However, there was a degree of natural resistance to penicillin that presaged modern problems with antibiotic resistant strains. In cases of chronic wound infections, three-fourths of the bacteria were *Staphylococcus* species; 19.9 percent did not succumb to penicillin treatment, and 9.4 per cent acquired resistance during the course of treatment.[40]

Movie theater newsreels highlighted penicillin as a miraculous drug and featured images of fermentation and purification. Soon there was civilian demand for penicillin,

Medical trials demonstrated that penicillin could cure infections caused by combat wounds so its availability was essential to saving lives. Newsreels described the drug as a wartime miracle; its use in curing venereal diseases was less well publicized (Movietone News, 1944).

but supplies for home front use were rationed on a case by case basis. Posters reminded civilians that "thanks to penicillin…. He will come home!" and "Penicillin saves soldiers' lives." By 1944, several drug companies were involved in penicillin production, with the goal of having high reserves of the drug in place before the D-Day invasion of Europe. Some captured Allied penicillin may have been used topically to treat Hitler's wounds following an assassination attempt by a bomb blast on July 20, 1944. An oak table absorbed much of the impact of the detonation, but Hitler was left with multiple abrasions and bleeding and was treated with ephedrine.[41]

Penicillin also cured syphilis and gonorrhea, bacterial infections caused by *Treponema pallidum* and *Neisseria gonorrhoeae* respectively. Sexually transmitted diseases were equally as likely to prevent a soldier from fighting as a combat wound, and opportunities to contract such infections were rife. Posters warned soldiers that "she may be a bag of trouble" and "She may look clean, but pick-ups, good time girls, prostitutes spread syphilis and gonorrhea." One particularly lurid poster featured a skull wearing a purple orchid fascinator, with the advice that "the 'easy' girlfriend spreads syphilis and gonorrhea which unless properly treated may result in blindness, insanity, paralysis, premature death."

Troops were advised against sexual contact generally, but the War Department was also realistic. The wartime V-kit provided a self-administered ointment containing a sulfa drug and calomel (mercurous chloride, the traditional albeit dangerous cure for venereal diseases), but the advent of penicillin provided a more reliable option. Soldiers soon learned that penicillin cured gonorrhea in a day and syphilis in a week, which inadvertently may have encouraged more sexual contact. Nevertheless, by the last year of the war venereal diseases posed less of a threat to military and civilian populations. Penicillin was provided to civilians known to spread venereal diseases, including desperate women in ravaged European cities who traded favors for food, as well as the comfort women in occupied Japan.

Penicillin killed several pathogenic bacteria efficiently and soon replaced sulfa drugs, which were first developed in the 1930s by Bayer chemists working at the I.G. Farben chemical conglomerate. Beginning with a red dye that showed antibiotic potential in laboratory mice, their investigations led to Prontosil, the first drug that provided a possible treatment for several different types of infections. Sulfa drugs slow bacterial growth by inhibiting the enzymatic pathway that produces folic acid, so they were bacteriostatic rather than bacteriocidal. In contrast, penicillin killed bacteria by interfering with cell wall synthesis, which causes the cells to rupture.

The dyes used in sulfa drug synthesis were derived from coal tar, the viscous liquid that remains after coal is gasified into coal gas or carbonized into coke. Coal originated from the fossilized remains of flooded forests and swamps, which formed combustible sedimentary rock. Sulfa drugs were standard issue in military first aid kits, such as the Carlisle kits used in the U.S. Army. The packets of sulfanilamide powder were dusted on field dressings and open wounds to prevent sepsis and used to prevent gangrene and amputations associated with immersion foot, a condition associated with prolonged exposure to cold water.[42] The drugs were also used for intestinal infections, but side effects included confusion; some doctors contended that pilots should not receive sulfa treatments.

However, sulfa drug use continued in cases of Hansen's disease, also known as leprosy. Beginning in 1940, sulfa drugs became part of the standard treatment, along with the traditional treatment that used chaulmoogra oil pressed from the seeds of *Hydno-carpus* and *Taraktogenos* species, trees native to Malaysia and Asia. The oil contains hydnocarpic and chaulmoogric acids, both antibiotic against the bacterium *Mycobacterium leprae*, which causes the disease. During the war, 69 cases of Hansen's disease occurred among military personnel, who were honorably discharged and admitted to the National Leprosarium in Carville, Louisiana.[43]

Not all investigations of antimicrobial compounds resulted in pharmaceutical antibiotics. Chlorophyll, the green photosynthetic pigments of algae and plants, had long been known to inhibit bacteria growth, and by the early 1940s, articles in the popular press extolled chlorophyll as an antibiotic and possible wonder drug. Physicians at Temple University Hospital used chlorophyll solutions and ointments to treat gum disease, peritonitis, abscesses, skin ulcers, and other infections; they claimed improvement or complete cures in over a thousand patients, with no tissue damage or side effects.[44] They used chlorophyll from nettles (*Urtica* spp.), while another team at Stanford University used laboratory-grown *Chlorella* (a unicellular green alga), which promised an unlimited supply of chlorophyll.

The potential of chlorophyll for treating combat wounds was of great interest because the extracts killed Gram-positive bacteria, including *Staphylococcus* and some of the microbes that can cause gas gangrene. However, the instability of chlorophyll undermined its medicinal use. In plant cells, chlorophyll occurs inside chloroplasts, where the molecules are embedded in the internal thylakoid membrane system. The long hydrocarbon "tail" of each molecule extends into the membranes, while the rest of the molecule consists of a porpyrin ring, a magnesium ion surrounded by a nitrogen, carbon, and hydrogen (similar to the heme groups in hemoglobin, which have iron in place of magnesium). Extracted chlorophyll molecules are fragile and susceptible to slight changes in pH; the acidity or alkalinity of wounds can vary slightly depending on the bacterial infections, which might affect antibiotic activity. Later studies revealed that the antibiotic effect of chlorophyll can be short-lived. Some *Staphylococcus* cultures resumed growth after a brief period of stasis, and investigators concluded that the cells developed resistance to chlorophyll when used as an antibiotic.[45] Because of its potential to mimic the color of vegetation from the sky, chlorophyll was also investigated as a camouflage paint, but molecular instability was once again a problem in making a usable product (see Chapter 11).

Agar

With the bombing of Pearl Harbor, agar became a critical war material. Japanese industry was the major producer of processed and powdered agar worldwide, and supplies from Japan halted. The uses of agar were diverse, as a laxative, thickening agent in jellied foods, pill coating, compound for making dental impressions and molding prostheses, and sizing agent in the finishing of cloth and paper. Most importantly, however, agar was an essential ingredient of bacteriological media, and the laboratory culture of microbes was essential to wartime food safety and medical practice.

At the beginning of the war, the U.S. War Production Board assumed control of all available agar supplies. There was enough agar on hand (about 200,000 pounds) to last for a year, if its use were limited to laboratories.[46] Suspended and heated in water, purified agar forms a semisolid gel that is ideal for laboratory culture media. There are very few bacteria that can digest agar, which tolerates sterilization and thickens media for use in Petri dishes and test tubes. Other ingredients, from cornmeal to yeast extract, provide the essential nutrients that support bacterial growth. Military demand for agar was expectedly high; the *Technical Manual for Laboratory Technicians* described the preparation of seventeen agar-containing media, for use in culturing microbes from water, food, milk, blood, urine, tissue, wounds, and any other material suspected of microbial growth.[47]

Chemically speaking, agar is based on the complex polysaccharide agarose extracted from the cell walls of red algae (Phylum Rhodophyta). In nature, agar has an adaptive role in forestalling desiccation because it absorbs several times its weight in water, which prevents algae in tidal zones from drying out in the sun. Although the polysaccharide is present in many red algae, a few species provided the commercial product; these were harvested, processed, and exported by Japan, from which the U.S. had received 600,000 pounds annually.[48] Most of Japanese agar was extracted from red algae indigenous to the eastern coast of Asia, primarily *Gelidinium corneum* and its relatives.

Wartime concern for agar shortages in the U.S. resulted in quick progress in agar collection and processing. The War Production Board commissioned surveys along the Gulf of Mexico coastline and from Cape Henry to Key West to locate populations of red algae for harvesting; a processing plant was established at Beaufort, North Carolina that produced agar for the duration of the war.[49] Along the Atlantic coast, *Graciliaria confervoides* is a fast-growing red alga with free-floating, filamentous masses that were easily collected and dried in the sun. *Gelidinium cartilagineum* and a few related species thrive along the southern California coastline, and shortly after the attack on Pearl Harbor, divers were harvesting large quantities of the wild algae as a substitute for Japanese agar.

Axis countries had access to Japanese agar, but other countries also had drastic shortages for hospital and laboratory use. Russia, China, Australia, and New Zealand established wartime agar industries using red algae indigenous to their coasts. School children and civilians (including local Maori people in New Zealand) assisted with collecting algae along coastlines. There were investigations into cell wall polysaccharides from other species such as *Hypnea musciformis* as possible agar substitutes, but these typically yielded compounds without the gel strength of Japanese agar.[50] Irish moss (*Chondrus crispus*) yielded the polysaccharide carrageenin, also used in thickening foods; during the war, it was used to make "Carragar," an inferior substitute for true agar.

County Herb Committees

In England, reliance on pharmaceutical drugs imported from Europe led to shortages and a pending medical crisis. German occupation of Europe and U-boats in shipping lanes interfered with drug shipments to England, and by the early 1940s, there were critical shortages of essential drugs in hospitals and homes. The winter 1941 meeting of the Royal Pharmaceutical Society recognized the depleted national supplies of drugs such as belladonna and colchicum but noted that substitute British remedies were available for use.[51] The National War Formulary listed the drugs that were available and recommended alternatives and equivalents for compounding essential pharmaceuticals; the few available familiar pharmaceutical drugs were reserved for military use.

Botanists at the Royal Botanic Gardens at Kew joined with the Ministry of Health in 1941 to organize the Vegetable Drugs Committee, a plan to collect medicinal plants from the countryside. Fortunately many of the species used by European drug companies were also indigenous to Great Britain, so it became a matter of finding, collecting, drying, and transporting native plants to drug companies for processing and use. Hedgerows, the dense living fences planted to mark boundaries, were particularly diverse habitats for both herbaceous and woody medicinal species. The Committee provided specific instructions for identification, collection, and preparation for shipping, including careful drying and bundling of the botanical collections.

Women's Institutes, Scottish Women's Rural Institutes, Girl Guides, Boy Scouts, pensioners, school children, and evacuees participated in herb collection and drying. Country life was a radical change for children evacuated from bombed cities, and local Women's Institutes were often involved with settling the children with local families and overcoming obstacles in the inevitable clash of rural and urban cultures. Nevertheless children settled in, often for years, and participated in daily rural routines such as farm activities and herb collecting. WI members shared insights in a report "Town Children through Country Eyes: A Survey on Evacuation," which detailed the condition of children whom they cared for in their homes.[52] Vitamin deficiencies, parasites, and basic hygiene raised significant health concerns that resulted in postwar family allowances.

Accuracy was essential in herb collection. Botanists at Kew produced a set of forty printed cards to aid with identification, and collectors received instruction in the form of publications and lectures. In an effort to improve the plants that they would receive, the wholesale drug supply firm Brome and Schimmer published *Herb Gathering*, authored by two experienced herb farmers. The text covered about seventy indigenous medicinal plants in nontechnical language, with emphasis on accurate identification and careful handling to avoid bruised plants, which could affect the active principles.[53]

Among the most important herbs was foxglove (*Digitalis purpurea*), a source of cardiac glycosides used to regulate heartbeat in cases of congestive heart failure. Their importance for many cannot be overlooked, and they may have saved the life of Winston Churchill in 1943. While traveling to Tunis to plan the D-Day landings with General Eisenhower, Churchill developed pneumonia, accompanied by a high fever and spells of atrial fibrillation. He was treated with a new sulfa drug (penicillin was not yet available) and digitalis to stimulate and regulate heart beat, a drug combination that resulted in his recovery. Incidentally, a few months later in March of 1943 President Roosevelt was also treated with digitalis when his physician, Dr. Howard Bruenn, prescribed "digitalization" to stimulate Roosevelt's heartbeat. Predating modern diuretics and beta-blockers, the drug was often part of the standard treatment plan for advanced heart disease and hypertension, the conditions that led to Roosevelt's death from a cerebral hemorrhage two years later.[54]

The Ministry of Supply issued monthly herb newsletters that provided updates on the progress of collection in different areas; the first *Herb Collectors Bulletin* (1942) noted that in Derbyshire "the Clifton and Mayfield Boy Scouts dried seventy-six pounds of foxglove at their headquarters. They hope to do much more this year and the county committee is looking around for drying depots."[55] The medicinal compounds in foxglove degraded if the plants were not handled with care and dried quickly, and this was true for other species as well. In most cases, sun drying was insufficient, and some form of heat was needed to evaporate water and completely dehydrate the plant tissue. Kew botanists advised that collectors spread the plants on drying racks (made from lace curtains tacked to wooden frames) and then dry the plants in a coke-heated shed at 90–100 degrees Fahrenheit.

Environmental conditions and the genetics of local populations sometimes affected concentrations of secondary compounds, at times to an advantage. Cardiac glycoside levels in foxgloves were the highest in July, the ideal collection time; moreover, plants grown in Wales often had particularly high glycoside levels, so Welsh collectors were encouraged to collect and dry foxglove leaves.[56] Foxgloves are biennials that flower during the second growing season, but to untrained eyes, comfrey, primrose, and other species can resemble the vegetative rosette of coarse leaves produced during the first year. To prevent misidentification, some botanists recommended that collectors limit their collections to plants in flower. Foxglove seeds were also collected as a source of the cardiac glycoside digitalin; the *Herb Collectors' Bulletin No. 3* recommended stripping the mature capsules into a pillow case and then sorting them out to release the seeds.[57] Collectors were encouraged to leave some capsules on the plants to encourage reseeding of natural populations.

Other native medicinal plants in high demand included belladonna (*Atropa belladonna*, the source of belladonna, sedative tropane alkaloids), autumn crocus (*Colchicum autumnale*, a treatment for gout), and valerian (*Valeriana officinalis*). Collectors also gathered and dried traditional herbs including wild thyme (*Thymus polytrichus*, an antiseptic), burdock (*Arctium* spp., a diuretic), colt's-foot (*Tussilago farfara*, a demulcent useful in treating colds), black horehound (*Ballota nigra*, a treatment for spasms and worm infections), male fern (*Dryopteris felix-mas*, a vermifuge), elder (*Sambucus nigra*, used to treat influenza), and juniper berries (*Juniperus communis*, a diuretic and carminative). Some medicinal plants are highly toxic even in small quantities and required careful handling and identification. They share in common the matter of dose; controlled amounts can be therapeutic, while higher levels may be lethal. Children were not allowed to collect belladonna, and eventually this species and several others (aconite, henbane, foxglove, and thorn apple, *Datura stramonium*) were cultivated in plots at Kew and some private gardens. Cultivation eased the burden of identifying and collecting plants that were both rare and poisonous.

As in other countries, plants were collected for wound dressings or laboratory media rather than drug production. The County Herb Committees oversaw the collection of peat moss (*Sphagnum* spp.) from bogs and wet moors to use as an absorbent sterile wound dressing. Its naturally acidic pH inhibited bacterial growth and helped to prevent infection. Collectors in northern areas were encouraged to harvest tufts of "long-stemmed" species for drying in the air; the moss was then packed into sacks and shipped to hospital supply depots. Algae specialists scoured the coastline seeking substitutes for the *Gelidinium* species used in agar production. County Herb Committees in coastal areas collected Irish moss (*Chondrus crispus*); as in the U.S. it proved inferior to true agar but could be used to emulsify cod liver oil and as a gelatin in tinned meat. However, discoveries of indigenous red algae populations of *Gelidinium* and *Ahnfeldtia* yielded some agar suitable for wartime laboratory use.

Vitamins were another wartime necessity, with particular concern for children's health. As shipments of citrus fruits became rare, research at Kew centered on rosehips as a rich source of vitamin C. Botanically speaking, each rosehip is the cup-shaped hypanthium that remains behind after a rose (*Rosa* spp.) drops it petals following pollination. Rosehips are often red-pigmented, and they contain the small, seed-like fruit (achenes) which are dispersed by birds. Primary school children gathered rosehips by the pound, amassing hundreds of tons annually. Rosehips resisted crushing, but they could be finely milled and then boiled. The final product was a thick syrup high in vitamins A and C, with a palatable taste that resembled plums or guava; it was administered primarily to infants and children as a scurvy preventative. Eventually Kew botanists determined that rosehips from the Lake District and northern counties contained appreciably more vitamin C than those from the south, and so collection sites were adjusted accordingly. Incidentally, a similar wartime program evolved in Russia, where rose varieties with high vitamin C content were identified and cultivated.[58]

Children also collected the seeds of horse chestnut (*Aesculus hippocastanum*). Long known as conkers, these were a rich source of aesculin and other glucosides (glycosides based on the simple sugar glucose). Aesculin was a familiar treatment for varicose veins, but it also had bacteriological uses in identifying possible pathogenic bacteria in milk, including *Streptococcus*. Glucose isolated from the seeds was used to make Lucozade, a sickroom beverage that provided some simple sustenance and fluid.

Beginning in September 1940, England experienced nighttime bombing raids, when the only option was to seek shelter and hope against a direct hit. Physicians predicted that millions would suffer psychological trauma from aerial bombing and possible poison gas attacks; a 1938 report submitted to the Ministry of Health anticipated panic, hysteria, and nervous breakdowns as collateral effects of war on the home front. Thus it is not surprising that the Vegetable Drugs Committee noted valerian (*Valeriana officinalis*) as one of the most essential medicinal species for its sedative properties. Newspaper columnists such as Mary Rose, who penned "Making the best of a 'Sheltered' Life" in the Manchester *Daily Sketch*, recommended personal items to improve spirits and counter fear while spending time in bomb shelters. In cities, there were communal shelters such as the underground tube stations that were deep below street level. Many flocked to these sites at night to catch a few hours of sleep, while others used indoor Morrison shelters or Anderson shelters excavated in gardens.

Women carried the major responsibility for war work, child care, cookery, rationing, and household tasks. Small wartime luxuries included face creams and powders, cologne, smelling salts, and nerve tablets, proprietary mixtures that often contained valerian. The use of valerian in wartime was nothing new; in *A Modern Herbal*, Maud Grieve described valerian as a "powerful nervine, stimulant, carminative, and anti-spasmodic." She noted the use of valerian during World War I: "The drug allays pain and promotes sleep. It is of especial use and benefit to those suffering from nervous overstrain.... During the recent War, when air-raids were a serious strain on the nerves of civilian men and women, valerian ... proved wonderfully efficacious, preventing or minimizing serious results."[59] Valerian was also used to treat soldiers who suffered psychological effects after fighting on the front lines; it was administered as a tincture to shell-shocked infantrymen during both world wars.

Ancient Greeks and Romans understood the medicinal properties of valerian, using it to calm stomachs and improve digestion. Dioscorides recommended the herb for heart palpitations, Galen mentioned it for insomnia, and Arabs deployed it to control aggression. In fact, the generic name *Valerian* is likely derived from the Latin verb *valere*, which commands us to be strong, while the specific epithet *officinalis* refers to the medicinal properties of the species. Valerian appeared in editions of *the U.S. Pharmacopoeia* between 1820 and 1930, becoming a popular remedy for "vapors," cramps, anxiety, headaches,

5

In England, the Vegetable Drug Committee noted valerian for its sedative properties, and wild plants were collected from the countryside and dried for wartime use. Valerian was administered to shell-shocked infantrymen during both world wars, and nerve tablets were proprietary mixtures that often contained the herb.

high blood pressure, nervous complaints, and even disruly behavior in children.

However, despite its long history of use, the mode of action of valerian is poorly understood and involves a complex chemistry. The active principles are concentrated in the aromatic rhizomes, robust underground stems that often colonize old garden sites. Valerian compounds include various valepotriates, sesquiterpenes, and several aromatic oils, and its efficacy may results from synergy among its chemical components. Women's magazines also recommended that nervous moods could be treated by eating plenty of lettuce. Wild lettuce (*Lactuca virosa*) had traditional herbal use as a mild sedative, but whether garden varieties offered the same anodyne effects is unknown. Lime tea was another option; brewed from the leaves of *Tilia europaea* and not a citrus fruit, it had traditional uses as a mild narcotic in cases of hysteria and palpitations.

There were commercial products that claimed to sooth wartime nerves with botanical extracts in alcohol. Advertisements for Wincarnis promoted the product as a tonic wine that contained "therapeutic herbs and spices," including gentian, mugwort, angelica, fennel, coriander, peppermint, cardamom, and cassia. Described as helpful for sleepless nights during bombing raids, Wincarnis claimed to provide B vitamins, which received particular attention for possible connections to psychological effects of confusion, lethargy, and depression (see Chapter 3). However, its soporific qualities likely stemmed from a relatively high 17 percent alcohol concentration rather than from its herbal content.

Due to palm oil shortages, soap was rationed to a few ounces weekly for personal washing and laundry, with potential health effects. Some gathered soapwort (*Saponaria officinalis*) as a substitute because its leaves could be worked into a lather, the result of glycosides known as saponins. The herb was long used in the fullers' industry to clean wool, and it grew widely, often at the sites of former Roman baths; however, soapwort was never on the County Herb Committee lists of collected plants. Soapwort also had ancient uses for treating skin complaints and venereal diseases, but was not part of the modern pharmacopeia although during soap shortages it was useful for washing. An advertisement for Ino brand toilet soap noted the use of starch and beetroot juice as substitutes for scarce powder and rouge, and reminded customers to buy the three ounce cake (the weekly ration) to "guard the health and beauty of your skin."

British colonies cultivated and shipped medicinal plants to England to supplement the harvest of certain species. Foxglove was cultivated in India, where it grew abundantly, and New Zealand supplied foxglove, deadly nightshade, thorn apple, and henbane; these were critical drugs, which justified long distance shipping. The Department of Scientific and Industrial Research (DSIR) had started a medicinal plants industry in New Zealand before the war, beginning with a five-acre experimental farm to determine the European species that could grow in the New Zealand climate and soil. By 1942, 26 acres of medicinal species were cultivated at Hastings. DSIR engineers designed a processing plant that used a trolley system to move trays of plants through heated tunnels; the dehydrated plants were then baled and tested for chemical content. In particular, thorn apple was used to treat asthma and bronchitis, and it was shipped to the Middle East, where some troops suffered from inhaling sand into their lungs.[60] Boy Scouts and Girl Guides in New Zealand assisted with collecting ergot (*Claviceps purpurea*), a parasitic fungus of rye and wheat. The toxic fungus yielded ergotamine, a potent vasoconstrictor used to control bleeding. It was also collected in the U.S., where Eli Lily obtained the crude drug from wheat grown in Minnesota.

German Herbalism

The Nazi regime revered nature, with harvest festivals, youth camps, and philosophical yearning for the Germanic outdoors. Aligned with these practices and ideals was the official preference for Germanic crop plants, which extended to native herbs, herbalism, and homeopathic medicine. Some of this policy may have been strictly economic; it was cheaper and easier to rely on native food plants and herbs rather than imported groceries and drugs. Thus Nazi medicine idealized and nationalized the practice of herbalism, which aimed to replace pharmaceutical drugs with German-grown plants.

Despite the known medicinal properties of many plant species, the policy seemed regressive, especially in light of the success of German chemists in developing effective pharmaceuticals and in replicating natural compounds through organic synthesis. Of course, German chemists had also advanced the study of coal tar derivatives, from aniline dyes to sulfa drugs, some with known carcinogenicity. Herbal medicine commingled with eugenics as part of a larger plan to improve German health, including reduction in the incidence of cancer. Medical doctors were under Nazi party control, beginning with the Reich Physicians Ordinance of 1936 and the "re-education" of practicing doctors through mandatory courses on racial hygiene and inheritance theories.[61] Gerhard Wagner, leader of the Reich Physicians Chamber, was a proponent of the *Neue Deutsche Heilkunde* (new art of German healing); he worked with Nazi leaders to encourage alternative therapies, including holistic and naturopathic treatments that used German-grown herbs. Wagner established a hospital in Dresden in 1934 which emphasized the teaching of alternative medicine and followed this up with courses on the tenets of the *Neue Deutsche Heilkunde* interlaced with racial purity.[62]

The aim of racial purity influenced medical practice, in short the notion of treating Aryan people with medicinal plants cultivated in German soil. According to Nazi propaganda, Jewish physicians represented the medical establishment that profited from synthetic drugs, and there was also suspicion of side effects. Geneticist Hans Stubbe posited that pharmaceutical drugs might cause mutations and damage to "genetic health," and in fact certain sulfa drugs may have been carcinogenic. Some Nazi leaders even advocated closing medical research facilities, despite the remarkable history of German progress in medicine and biology. Gerhard Domagk, the pathologist who developed sulfa drugs, received the Nobel Prize in 1939. However, the Nazi hierarchy did not allow him to accept the award, although some did realize that biomedical research was still essential to maintaining both military and civilian health.[63] In fact, Domagk's research led to the sulfa drugs widely used in the post-war tuberculosis epidemic in Europe.

German apothecaries first viewed the New German Medicine with optimism, seeing their elevation to the status of physicians as they compounded the drugs that replaced the products of big pharmaceutical firms. Even local druggists were soon part of the scramble for native-grown medicinal plants that would assure independence from imports. Pharmaceutical firms supplied the military demand for analgesics, sulfa drugs, and other essential medicines and so continued to exist, despite the idealized Third Reich vision of medicinal herbs dispensed by local apothecaries.[64]

Under the Nazi regime, there was considerable support for the study of medicinal plants as an integral part of the *Neue Deutsche Heilkunde*. By the late 1930s, universities offered courses in medical botany and field trips to view local flora, and a national working group formed to oversee the study of medicinal botany and the supply of herbal plants. Economy was certainly part of the story; the use of native plants to prevent and cure disease fostered German self-sufficiency, seen as an improvement over dependency on drug imports. Wild and cultivated plants were used to brew quasi-medicinal herbal teas that could serve as coffee substitutes. Propaganda photographs showed children busy with "*Teekrautersammlung, ein Kriegeinsetz der Jugend im Dienste der Volksgesundheit*" (collecting plants to brew for tea as youth wartime service for the people's health). As part of the Reich agenda and to conserve coffee supplies for military use, children were told to encourage their parents to drink these healthful teas.[65]

The use of German herbs was also part of the curriculum at the hundreds of Reich schools for brides and housewives, which provided detailed instruction on home management for women who married during the Nazi regime.[66] Ingredients included traditional tea herbs such as the flowers of German chamomile (*Matricaria chamomilla*) and raspberry and blackberry leaves (*Rubus* spp.) Chamomile in particular may have medicinal properties that were beneficial under wartime conditions, including possible antibiotic activity against *Staphylococcus aureus* and *Mycobacterium tuberculosis*, the bacterium that causes tuberculosis. Soap shortages encouraged experimentation with ivy and pine needles to remove dirt from clothing. Ivy (*Hedera helix*) contains saponins with soap-like properties, and pines (*Pinus* spp.) produce an essential oil that dissolves fats.

Beginning in 1935, civilians were encouraged to collect medicinal plants in areas including Westphalia, Wurttemberg, Hanover, Baden, Vienna, the Sudetenland, Moravia, and Bohemia. The Reich committee on medicinal plants directed the packaging of dried tea herbs into packets, and some were used as ingredients in ciders and preserves.[67] As in England, rosehips were collected as a source of vitamin C; official Reich policy discouraged imported fruit, so native sources of vitamin C replaced citrus in the diet. Fruits of the common sea buckthorn (*Hippophae rhamnoides*, also known as sandthorn or sanddorn berry) were made into a juice rich in vitamin C, with a few teaspoons administered to children daily. However, foraging alone was not a sustainable solution to the official policy of herbal medicine across Germany.

During the 1930s, the SS (*Schutzstaffel*) began a program of intensive herb cultivation at the Dachau concentration camp on land formerly blanketed by a coniferous forest. Based on organic practices such as composting and vermiculture, the *Plantage* (plantation) was one of several economic programs under the wing of the SS, which included over twenty agricultural sites. Led by Heinrich Himmler, *Reichsführer* of the SS, the *Plantage* herb gardens at Dachau depended on free slave labor to cultivate medicinal plants and decorative flower beds. The old forest land at Dachau required drainage in order to support crops; prisoners working without machinery converted wetlands into arable soil by excavating trenches, cutting peat to fill ponds, and spreading soil.

Forty acres were planted with species of traditional herbs and indigenous plants with known medicinal properties, and the overall plantation site included greenhouses, research facilities, herb drying and processing facilities, and a library. In addition to medicinal plants, culinary herbs were planted as replacements for imported spices; these included a substitute for black pepper that may have been the ground seeds of nasturtium (*Tropaeolum majus*), which contain sharp-flavored mustard oils. Plants grown at the Dachau plantation supplied most of the cooking herbs for the Germany military. In addition, a smaller herb plantation was developed at the women's prison at the Ravensbrück concentration camp, and no doubt more such projects were planned.

Himmler started an institute of medicinal plant research at Dachau, stemming from a personal interest in herbs, commingled with notions of a superior Nordic race, ancient traditions, and mysticism. Local schools assisted with collecting medicinal plants from the wild, and university botanists received grants for research and breeding experiments on medicinal plants.[68] Research at the Dachau plantation included careful translation of ancient herbals captured from religious orders, part of the wider effort to identify potentially medicinal European plants. Prisoners with artistic ability worked alongside scientists as botanical illustrators.[69] To mark Christmas 1942, Himmler donated a herbarium collection of dried specimens to the plantation library, documenting his personal regard for traditional herbalism. At the same time, prisoners were used as test subjects for the efficacy of medicinal plants; Himmler had them treated with herbal homeopathic remedies for conditions and infections caused by experimentation.[70]

Crops at the Dachau plantation included basil (*Ocimum basilicum*), thyme (*Thymus vulgaris*), balm (*Melissa officinalis*), rosemary (*Rosmarinus officinalis*), peppermint (*Mentha* x *piperita*), marjoram (*Origanum vulgare*), and sage (*Salvia officinalis*), members of the mint family (Lamiaceae) probably known since Neolithic times. Herbal literature documents literally dozens of uses for these species, from digestion and melancholia to gangrene and epilepsy. Terpenes in the essential oils confer some degree of antibiotic activity to each of the species, and all were suitable as tea herbs. Ironically, while various mints may grow and naturalize in Germany, they are actually native to other regions; basil probably originated in southeastern Asia, while the other genera evolved in the Mediterranean area.

Other herbs cultivated at the Dachau plantation were aromatic composites (family Asteraceae) including tarragon (*Artemisia dracunculus*), chamomile (*Matricaria chamomilla*), and marigolds (*Tagetes* spp.). Tarragon originated from Russia, and marigolds were a South American introduction. So-called German chamomile grew across Europe and northern Asia, and its evolutionary origin is unclear, while caraway (*Carum*

The Dachau plantation included glasshouses and hotbeds for use in cultivating and propagating traditional medicinal herbs, including non-native mints and composites; Reich policy overlooked or rewrote evolutionary history in claiming these plants as true "German" herbs. Prisoners provided labor and were used as test subjects for experiments in herbal medicine (Archiv der KZ-Gedenkstätte Dachau, DaA F 0513/21720).

carvi) and mullein (*Verbascum thapsus*) also had widespread Old World ranges. In short, although they were dispensed by apothecaries and used widely in Germany, the herbs cultivated at Dachau lacked Germanic origins; Reich policy clearly overlooked or rewrote evolutionary history in claiming these plants as true "German" herbs.

Prisoners at Dachau harvested herbs and used the drying room to install an illegal radio through which broadcasts from the Allies could be heard. The work of harvesting herb fields was back-breaking. The small flowers of chamomile and mullein were difficult to pick quickly, and prisoners who failed to meet the collection quota dreaded being called "into the open" for discipline. Both were apparently considered critical herbs; mullein flowers soaked in oil were used to treat ear infections, suggesting possible antibiotic activity, and chamomile had also long been used against infections, including tuberculosis.[71] Gladiolus (*Gladiolus* spp.) and perhaps other species were cultivated as a source of vitamin C. The need for vitamin C may explain unsubstantiated reports that gladiolus leaves were pulverized and used as an ingredient in *Pemmikan-Landjaeger* carried by German military (see Chapter 5).

Aside from herbs, crops included root vegetables and tomatoes, presumably cultivated for meals consumed by SS officers, although plantation workers smuggled food to malnourished prisoners elsewhere at Dachau. The SS herb plantation at Dachau functioned as a business supported by slave labor; local civilians could purchase garden seeds and other goods from an administrative office, and the enterprise supported Aryan health. Other cash crops included garlic, which had known antibiotic properties, and mallow (*Malva sylvestris*), a traditional demulcent used for treating coughs and sore throats. The latter was included in the Nazi tabloid newspaper *Der Stürmer* to illustrate the propaganda statement, "*Die Apotheke hilft dir durch ihre Heilkräuter*" [apothecaries help you with their healing plants]. Medicinal plants represented both the past and the future of German medicine. Himmler planned botanical expeditions to South America, where there were rumors of plants with miraculous curative properties to include in the *Neue Deutsche Heilkunde*; however, travel plans were postponed until after the war.[72]

Dr. Theodor Morell, physician to Adolf Hitler, did not necessarily adhere to herbal medicine, although several of the drugs that he administered did have botanical origins. Hitler received daily injections of the analgesic dihydroxycodeine (under the Merck trade name Eucodol), a semi-synthetic drug derived from thebaine, one of the alkaloids found in opium poppies. Hitler apparently suffered from convulsions or Parkinson's disease for which Morell prescribed Eupaverin (an opium poppy derivative sold by Merck as an anticonvulsant and muscle relaxant) and tropane alkaloids from deadly nightshade and other species of Solanaceae. A naturopathic mixture known as Euflat contained the opium alkaloid papaverine compounded with angelica root, aloe, and caffeine. Other botanical compounds in Hitler's pharmacopeia including quinine, strychnine, and cardiac glycosides isolated from curare plants in the genus *Strophanthus*, in addition to methamphetamines synthesized from ephedrine.[73] In short, Hitler was either quite ill with diverse symptoms, or Morell over-prescribed the available medications, both in scope and frequency.

In addition to pharmaceutical drugs, Hitler used several proprietary medicines with botanical ingredients, including *Franzbranntwein*, a liniment that contained oil from pine needles; A. Bohmert's *Waldmeisterei*, a mixture containing sweet woodruff, *Galium odoratum*; *Pinofluol Medizinische Fichtennadel Krauter Bader*, bath tablets containing spruce needles and herbs that promised to promote healthy nerves and relieve rheumatic pain; and an inhaler containing *Eucalyptus* oil.[74]

8

Fibers

Fibers are specialized plant cells that evolved as adaptations for survival in nature. Depending on the species, some fibers strengthen shoots, while others help to disperse seeds. Either way, their elongated structures consist primarily of cellulose cell walls, so fibers lend themselves to spinning and weaving. Many species have fibers as part of their anatomy, and since ancient times several such plants have been selected and bred for economic use. Pre-war U.S. government fiber stockpiles included burlap, cotton, flax, jute, kapok, Manila fiber, sisal, and silk, which all had critical uses in providing shelter, clothing, and the basic tools of war. Jute and sisal fibers were used in weaving burlap and mosquito netting, both essential in malaria control. Burlap was also used as camouflage cloth and for printing the cloth maps used in escape and evasion, but the difficulty and expense of importing jute from India became a wartime problem. In 1941 the Quartermaster General ordered that cotton replace jute wherever possible, and the huge stores of U.S grown cotton became the logical alternative to imported fibers. In fact, this was the typical trend for botanical products generally: the replacement of imported commodities with native grown crops, even if the substitutions were subpar.

Some fiber uses were quite innovative. The Quartermaster Corps used sisal combined with kraft paper to invent durable V-containers for shipping intact rations into the Pacific theater, preventing extensive loss and waste. Crude dolls crafted from burlap served as dummy paratroopers that were used to confuse spotters; in the U.S. these decoys were known as Oscars, while in England they were Ruperts, based on the name of the parachute company. Coir matting, a tough carpet made from the fibrous middle layer of whole coconuts (which are actually stone fruits or drupes), was used along with Sommerfeld tracking, wire mesh first developed by an expatriate German engineer living in England. Mesh was laid atop coir to stabilize roads built across the Normandy beaches and to construct runways for temporary airfields. British engineers also outfitted some Churchill AVRE tanks with large spools of coir matting that could be unrolled on muddy surfaces ahead of the advancing vehicle. Coir fibers were several inches long and remained strong even when saturated with water, which was a major benefit.

Known as loofah sponges, the fibrous vascular skeletons produced by the fruits of *Luffa cylindrica* (a cucumber and squash relative in the family Cucurbitaceae) were widely used as oil and water filters in shipboard engines. The fruits were a Japanese import, but following the attack on Pearl Harbor, the War Production Board encouraged successful loofah cultivation in Central America. Agriculture adjusted to wartime demand for other plant fibers as well: farmers cultivated hemp and milkweed as substitutes for imported jute and kapok that became impossible to obtain. Uniforms, tents, nets, cordage, maps, sandbags, bandages, boxes, tarpaulins, and the nitrocellulose (gun cotton) used in explosives all originated from botanical shoot and seed fibers.

Cotton

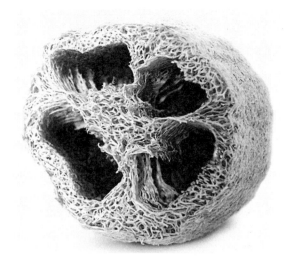

Cotton fibers originate as surface hairs that grow as single elongated cells from the epidermis of cotton seeds. One seed can produce 10,000–20,000 hairs, which most likely evolved as an adaptation for seed dispersal. Various species of *Gossypium* were domesticated in the Old and New Worlds, but the species known as West Indian cotton (*G. hirsutum*) was cultivated in pre–Columbian times and provided most of the cotton of commerce, including virtually all of the cotton supplied to the military during World War II. By the 1940s, cotton was the most important non-food crop worldwide, producing a high fiber yield for the effort invested in cultivation, harvesting, and processing. The fibers are strong and absorbent, making them ideal for uniforms, surgical dressings, and other military uses.

Wild cotton is usually a tropical perennial, but cultivars were selected both for long fiber length and for mutations causing annual growth, which yielded crops with uniform size and ripening times. Each plant produces capsules (bolls) with four or five valves that split to reveal the fiber-covered seeds. Hand-picking of cotton was labor intensive, followed by the ginning process that separated the seeds from the fibers. Eli Whitney and other

Top: The fibrous vascular skeletons of cultivated loofah fruit were used as oil and water filters in shipboard engines. The plants were widely naturalized in the tropics, where the non-fibrous immature fruits were an emergency survival food (Jerry Crimson Mann, Wikimedia Commons). *Bottom:* Cotton was the single most critical U.S. wartime crop, in high demand for food (cottonseed oil and animal feed), shelter (tentage, tarpaulins, and blankets), and clothing (uniforms). The fibers were also used to make absorbent cotton, bandages, mattresses, parachute ropes, and cordage.

inventors developed numerous cotton gin designs, which improved efficiency, increased U.S. cotton imports over sevenfold by 1800, and processed the cotton for Civil War uniforms.

During World War II, cotton became the single most critical U.S. crop, with 25 million acres in production and Axis prisoners of war performing some of the agricultural work (see Chapter 6). In 1941 there were sizable government supplies of the fiber, to the extent that some argued for replacing cotton fields with food crops; however, the needs for cotton were vast. From a military perspective, the fiber was cheap to cultivate in huge quantities, and it provided food (cottonseed oil and animal feed), shelter (tentage, tarpaulins, and blankets), and clothing (uniforms). X-ray technology helped with recognizing the ideal angles between cellulose fibrils and the long axis of the cotton fiber for maximum strength. The long fibers known as staples were spun and woven into textiles, while the shorter fibers (linters) were used for absorbent cotton, mattresses, and parachute ropes and other cordage. Cotton varieties with shorter staples yielded weaker fibers and were thus grouped with cucumbers, celery, and watermelon (foods that at the time were considered minimally nutritious) as nonessential crops for which fertilizer use was restricted.[1]

U.S. Army Carlisle model first aid packets included field dressings of absorbent cotton. Beginning in 1943, these were dyed green because medics and surgical units realized that white bandages were highly visible even in the dense forests of some Pacific islands; jungle camouflage colors were essential to avoiding attacks from Japanese snipers.[2] Other cotton uses included the manufacturing of plastics, varnish, paper, photographic film, collapsible boats, and as a source of cellulose for semi-synthetic fabrics such as rayon. The waste left over from processing cotton seed oil was used to make animal feed, fertilizers, and dyestuffs. Explosives including smokeless powder, gun cotton, and cordite were manufactured using cellulose from cotton fibers or alternative sources, which included peanut shells, cornstalks, and wood pulp. Cellulose filters were investigated but not adopted for use in civilian gas masks. By the end of the war, solid fuel for rockets consisted of half nitrocellulose made from cotton and half nitroglycerin, which was purified from salvaged cooking fat.[3]

Celluloid, an early plastic used for photographic and movie film (including wartime footage), was based on similar chemistry. Cotton fibers react with sulfuric and nitric acids to produce nitrocellulose, which was combined with camphor to produce a moldable plastic used to manufacture film, buttons, and trinkets. Camphor is an essential oil that is steam distilled from the Asian tree known as the camphor laurel (*Cinnamomum camphora*). It was stocked by Army medical field units where it was used for its stimulant and antimicrobial properties in treating trench foot (caused by prolonged exposure to wet conditions) and associated fungal diseases. Commercial crops came from Formosa, controlled by Japan during the war; however, with export limited, much of camphor used during the 1940s was semi-synthetic, derived from pine essential oils.

Anticipating the need for high quality cotton varieties, plant geneticists at the Bureau of Plant Industry used colchicine (see Chapter 6) to develop fertile hybrids that combined the traits of long fibers with annual growth and early maturity. There were also efforts to develop cultivars with pigmented fibers that would not require dyes. Experimental fields in Mississippi yielded bolls of green and brown cotton that would have been useful for manufacturing various textiles; Soviet geneticists even claimed to have developed red and blue cotton varieties.[4] However, pigmented strains produced shorter fibers that interfered with their use in cloth production.

Military uniforms required vast quantities of cotton. The fibers expand in water, so closely woven cotton fabric was water resistant and used to make outer clothing impervious to both wind and rain. Plane crews wore suits enhanced with electric heating coils; arctic combat uniforms relied on winder-breaker shells, jackets and trousers made of tightly woven sateen, which reduced the use of fur and wool. Long-staple Egyptian cotton was used for the herringbone weave known as Byrd cloth, which had a cooling effect when wet. Also known as herringbone twill, this rip-resistant cotton cloth was suitable as an outer layer under cold conditions and as a single layer for desert, tropical, and jungle uniforms. The latter had tape-fastened cuffs to protect against mosquitoes, ticks, chiggers, and leeches, and two-piece versions prevailed over the original one-piece design. However, herringbone twill became uncomfortably heavy in rain, and so by the end of the war tropical combat uniforms were sewn from lighter weight cotton poplin. British military stationed in the Far East and Middle East wore shirts made from green-dyed aertex, a loosely woven cotton cloth that traps air between its warp and weft. The Women's Land Army (see Chapter 6) also used aertex in their uniforms.

Oilskins were waterproof clothing made by using linseed oil (pressed from flaxseed, *Linum usitassimum*) to impregnate cotton or another botanical fiber such as hemp or linen woven into cloth for sails. In the form of jackets and trousers, oilskins (also known as tin cloth) were used by sailors and others who worked in wet conditions, including the Women's Land Army and U.S. troops in Arctic areas. Waterproof tents, hammocks, and duffel bags were constructed from cotton duck; the fabric was woven more tightly than canvas, dyed olive drab, and impregnated with chlorinated rubber that resisted fire and water. To conserve crude latex supplies, later versions of the standard cotton duck were waxed rather than rubberized. Tents ranged from two-man pup tents to squad shelters for several men.[5]

The wartime invention known as duck tape (waterproof cloth tape) came from an Illinois munitions worker and mother of two Navy sailors. Vesta Stoudt had heard about the difficulty of opening cartridge boxes while under fire (the paper tabs often tore and required a knife to break the waxed seal) and suggested that munitions boxes instead be sealed with waterproof adhesive cloth tape. She wrote to President Roosevelt in 1943, who forwarded her letter to the War Production Board, who in turn commissioned Johnson and Johnson to produce water resistant tape for munitions boxes using cotton duck fabric. The company already produced cotton surgical tape with adhesive rubber backing, a nineteenth century invention, and duck tape was a similar product.

High wartime demand for cotton impacted civilian life. The U.S. avoided clothes rationing (with the exception of leather shoes), but designs reflected wartime stringencies. In 1942 government guidelines aimed to decrease fabric use in women's garments by 15 percent to conserve fibers, and men's clothing was also cut along more spare lines. Wartime garments became shorter and narrower, with small seams and hems, thin sleeves, no cuffs, few pockets, and minimal ornamentation.

In England, clothes rationing began in January 1941 with the goal of conserving fiber supplies and redirecting labor toward outfitting the military. The Board of Trade spawned a complex bureaucracy that developed austerity guidelines for fabric use. Pockets, cuffs, seam and sleeve width, decorative embroidery, and pleats were all limited to conserve fabric and labor. Restrictions mandated short pants for boys under age thirteen. Following the Board of Trade guidelines, by early 1941 coupons were required for most clothing purchases. Although cotton was in short supply, expectant mothers received extra coupons to outfit babies, and one piece boiler suits (coveralls) were not rationed, presumably because they were needed by factory workers. By February 1942, the Utility Apparel Order controlled the weight and weaving pattern of fabrics, set price controls, and mandated designs that conserved fabric. Generic utility clothing replaced familiar British brands, and the elimination of metal zippers and rubberized elastic conserved critical materials. With bombing a reality, newspapers and women's magazines suggested coping strategies for comfort and safety. Shops advertised one piece jumpsuits for both adults and children to wear in shelters; these became known as siren suits and could be zipped up over pajamas, particularly useful when children had to be awakened and dressed quickly. The practical design was popularized by Winston Churchill who wore his own pin-striped siren suit to meet with heads of state.

Air raids required blackout conditions. U.S. civilians in urban areas were encouraged to make at least one room light tight and safe in the event of bombing or gas attack, and this required cotton. The *Cornell Bulletin for Homemakers: War Emergency Bulletin* provided detailed instructions for making draperies, shades, and baffles and suggested pasting light cotton cloth on windows to stop glass from splintering.[6] American cities experienced no aerial bombing, but the situation in England was dire, with frequent German raids across urban and industrial regions. Thus cotton blackout fabric was not rationed, although a few layers were sometimes needed to eliminate light to the satisfaction of local ARP (Air Raid Precautions) wardens. Although not officially condoned, some saved clothing coupons by sewing garments from blackout cloth.

Due to military demand, Axis countries experienced severe fiber and clothing shortages as the war progressed. German civilians encountered empty stores, and worn garments were nearly impossible to replace. Nazi policy encouraged donation of used clothing to the winter relief fund for the poor (*Winterhilfswerk*), while chemists developed experimental fibers from soybeans, potatoes, and cornhusks to stretch supplies of cotton. Technological advances included culturing *Aspergillus parasiticus* in bran (the outer husk layer removed from grain during milling) and then using the fungus as a source of enzymes to remove wool from sheepskins completely and without damage to the fibers.[7] In Japan, the standard civilian dress for men was a khaki cotton military-style suit, and many women wore simplified narrow kimonos or *monpe*, cotton jackets and loose pants that were convenient for quick dressing during air raids. However, cotton shortages resulted in rationing and frequent theft of cotton garments. Rayon was a possible alternative, but its manufacture required wood pulp as a source of cellulose, and the wood had to be imported. A synthetic fiber known as *sufu* combined paper mulberry bark (*Broussonetia papyrifera*, originally *Morus papyrifera*; see Chapter 9) and wood pulp, and it was combined with cotton to make a notoriously weak cloth. *Sufu* was a poor substitute for rayon, but by 1944 it was the only fiber available for civilian use. The clothing disintegrated after a few washings, so Japanese women were encouraged to invent ways to preserve *sufu* fibers. U.S. textile manufacturers used a similar strategy to spin the fibrous bark of giant redwoods (*Sequioadendron giganteum*) with sheep wool to make blankets, clothing, and felt hats.[8]

At the end of the war, the U.S. had over eleven million bales of stockpiled cotton. Despite wartime demands, some of the stock dated from the 1930s, and the Department of Agriculture sought ways to use the excess fiber. Prior to the war, Germany had imported almost a million bales of U.S. cotton annually, but even before the war, Hitler had promoted synthetic over botanical fibers in a move toward self-sufficiency. Both Germany and Japan had empty textile mills and civilians who needed clothes. Cotton exports to these countries helped to reinstate a peacetime economy, and it was in the best interest of U.S. farmers to promote the use of botanical fibers while providing a humanitarian service during the period of occupation.[9]

Bast Fibers

Cordage was critical for military needs, but export problems and Japanese occupation in the Pacific region halted the export of fibers traditionally used in its manufacture. Jute (*Corchorus capsularis* and *C. olitorius*) is a coarse fiber imported from India; it was used in making twine and burlap for sandbags, which the Quartermaster Corps replaced with cotton in 1941. Manila fiber is derived from mature leaves of *Musa textilis* (also known as *abacá* or Manila hemp, but unrelated to true hemp) originally imported from the Philippines. The species is in the same genus as bananas, and banana skins were also investigated as a possible fiber source. However, Manila fiber remained the premier crop for naval cordage.

Battleships each required 34,000 feet of rope of various dimensions, and thus with the Japanese occupation of the Philippines, the Quartermaster Corps substituted sisal (*Agave sisalana*) from Mexico for tent cordage and other less critical needs. The United Fruit Company and other growers cultivated wartime plantations of Manila fiber in Panama, Costa Rica, Honduras, and Guatemala. The perennial plants colonized fields asexually by growing stolons and required no replanting; Manila fiber crops supplied sufficient wartime cordage to make 3,000 miles of six-inch rope, mostly for the U.S. Navy.[10] Incidentally, some rope made from Manila fibers was recycled into the heavy paper stock used to make Manila folders (originally invented to hold files during the Civil War) and also used for military paperwork during World War II.

Hemp (*Cannabis sativa*) offered an alternative fiber crop that would avoid the problem of importing critical wartime materials. It originated as a temperate weedy species in western Asia, and varieties spread with human migration across Eurasia and worldwide. By World War II, hemp already had a successful history in North America. It was grown in the U.S.

9

Manila hemp is derived from mature leaves of *Musa textilis*, a banana relative originally imported from the Philippines. Wartime plantations wartime in Panama, Costa Rica, Honduras, and Guatemala supplied sufficient cordage to make 3,000 miles of rope, mostly for the U.S. Navy.

during colonial times when ships used hemp cordage and canvas sails; the word *canvas* is derived from the Greek word *cannabis*, meaning "made of hemp." Nineteenth century mills produced the hemp-containing duck cloth used on westward-bound covered wagons.

Hemp is an annual species with separate staminate and pistillate plants, and typical crops mature in three or four months. The wild species is variable, and since ancient times cultivars were selected for fibers, edible seeds, and oil, as well as medicinal or psychoactive properties. Fiber-producing varieties have minimal concentrations of the tetrahydrocannabinol compounds which impart psychoactive properties to marijuana, but prohibition supporters viewed *Cannabis sativa* broadly as an intoxicant and sought its outlaw. Subsequently the U.S. Marijuana Tax Act of 1937 aimed to curtail the use of marijuana as a drug and hemp for paper-making in favor of wood pulp; it also limited the use of varieties of *Cannabis sativa* for fibers and pharmaceutical drugs. There was particular concern about the effect of marijuana use on enlisted men. In fact, Army doctors maintained that its use undermined work ethic and responsibility and led to chronic intoxication and disciplinary problems.[11]

The bast fibers of hemp were an alternate resource for manufacturing cordage and canvas. Fiber-producing hemp has low levels of psychoactive tetrahydrocannabinol compounds, but prohibition supporters viewed marijuana cultivars as intoxicants and sought to outlaw cultivation of the entire species. Legal cultivation required registration under both the federal Marijuana Tax Act and state law.

Hemp is known botanically as a bast fiber in which long, flexible cells develop in the phloem (food conducting tissue) as a stem adaptation for tensile strength. Individual fiber cells can be about two inches long, and bundles of the flexible cells can be several feet in length. As an economic fiber, hemp fibers are four times stronger than cotton, but they require the labor-intensive process of removing the fibers from stem tissue, a process known as retting.

The U.S. Department of Agriculture established a hemp division to oversee wartime cultivation. Growers had to be registered under both the Marijuana Tax Act and state law, and forty hemp mills were built in Indiana, Minnesota, Iowa, and other states with hemp crops. The Department of Agriculture provided detailed advice for growers. Seeds were broadcast or sown in rows just four inches apart, resulting in dense growth. Competition for light produced tall, flexible plants with long fibers, rather than shrubby plants with woody growth. A government film "Hemp

The 1942 government film "Hemp for Victory" explained uses of the fibers and assured farmers that hemp cultivation would not deplete soil, although successful crops required high nitrogen content. Soil that grew good corn also supported productive hemp plants (U.S. Department of Agriculture).

for Victory" (USDA, 1942) assured farmers that hemp would not ruin soil, but it was also true that successful crops required moist, drained soil with high nitrogen content. Soil that grew good corn also supported productive hemp plants. Depending on water conditions, hemp roots extended deep into the ground, with a possible depth of over six feet.

Seed stock was an ongoing concern, and so hemp seed for national distribution was grown in Kentucky, where the fertile calcium-rich bluegrass soils produced remarkable yields. In 1941, the acreage devoted to hemp increased three-fold in Kentucky and Wisconsin, so in anticipation of future shortages, seed was set aside for planting in 1943.[12] Seeds dispersed from cultivated fields to roadsides and disturbed sites, and hemp naturalized easily into wild populations of *Cannabis sativa*, commonly known as ditchweed. Self-seeding hemp populations now occur in areas where it was cultivated as a wartime crop, including Indiana, Minnesota, Oklahoma, Missouri, and Nebraska.

With many U.S. farmers in the military, German prisoners of war and relocated Japanese-Americans labored in hemp fields. The harvest involved cutting the stalks and arranging them in shocks for drying. Farmers learned that stacked hemp tended to rot quickly, and extreme decomposition ruined some early crops.[13] Once dried, the stalks were retted, a managed process in which microbial activity destroys soft tissue around the fiber bundles and separates the useful fibers from the woody core of the stem. Warm, rainy weather hastened the process, which could take a month or two. Retting was labor intensive, but done correctly it resulted in soft fibers that were ready in October or November for processing in hemp mills.

During 1943 and 1944, U.S. farmers produced sixty million pounds of hemp fiber, with wartime uses that included rope, twine, fire hoses, parachute cords and webbing, oakum, heavy duty thread, and canvas. Oakum was a mixture of hemp fibers and pine tar (a gum made by heating pine wood at high temperatures with low oxygen), and it was used to pack cast iron plumbing and to caulk the decking of metal ships (see Chapter 10). Heavy duty thread for military footwear was an ongoing need, and unlike cotton, hemp resisted fungal rot. Canvas was woven with various combinations of hemp, cotton, and flax, depending on availability. Military uses for canvas were diverse and included the waterproofed canvas flotation skirts used on amphibious tanks, such as those involved in the D-Day invasion. The Ford Motor Company used canvas for the canopies of mobile canteen units that served food after bombing raids (see Chapter 4). However, despite the versatility of its fibers, the hemp project was discontinued once imports of jute and Manila fiber became available at the end of the war.[14]

Flax (*Linum usitassimum*) is probably the oldest fiber used in making textiles. Military demand for these bast fibers was high during World War II; they could be incorporated into canvas (see above) and spun into linen thread that was two or three times stronger than cotton. The thread resisted fungal rot, so it was in demand for stitching military footwear for tropical use. Flax was used in cordage, fire hoses, camouflage netting, parachute harnesses, and as the cloth in air plane wings.

Flax plants are annual herbs native to Europe and Asia, but the species has traveled worldwide with human migration, and no truly wild populations still exist. Like hemp, flax stems produce bast fibers, and the pressed seeds yield linseed oil; cultivars have been selected for high seed yield or long fibers. Puritans grew flax in New England to use in both cloth and paper, but by the twentieth century cultivation dwindled. By the 1940s, Oregon was the only state with flax farms and processing mills, built during the Depression by the Works Progress Administration.[15]

German occupation of France and Holland interfered with European exports, so sources of flax not controlled by Axis countries became critically important for military uses. The U.S. government encouraged flax farming in Peru and added more mills in Oregon; the 12,000 acres of flax grown in Oregon replaced about 40 percent of the imported fibers.[16] In England, similar concerns caused the Ministry of Supply to require flax cultivation in areas where the plants had not been grown for centuries, if ever. British farmers were resistant to growing an unfamiliar crop and lacked the necessary equipment for harvesting; however, local War Ags (see Chapter 6) had harvest quotas to meet, and they determined which land could best support flax crops. Flax fields in England quadrupled during the war years to 16,000 acres. Per government orders, flax was one of the few crops on which artificial fertilizers could be used (the others were staple foods including potatoes, carrots, and sugar beets), which reflects the wartime importance of this fiber crop. Flax matured in about three months; farmers then harvested the plants by hand, threshed them for seeds, and dried the stalks in shocks. The traditional retting process involved microbial activity to loosen and release the bast fibers from stem tissue. Australian and New Zealand farmers also cultivated flax crops to supply the Allies, as well as New Zealand flax (*Phormium tenax*), an unrelated plant that produces leaf fibers used in making sails and rope. As in England, the production of usable fibers required trial and error and often involved advice from botanists familiar with plant anatomy and local agriculture.[17]

Flaxseed was saved for replanting and for making oil and seed cakes, an agricultural feed prepared from the seeds after they are pressed to release linseed oil, which was used in waterproofing fabrics and making linoleum. The latter was a product manufactured from several botanical raw ingredients, including linseed oil, burlap, canvas, cork, wood, and pine rosin. Battleship linoleum was made for heavy use on decks, but it was flammable and removed from warships (but not U.S. submarines) following the attack on Pearl Harbor. A similar product made from cork and natural rubber was used on British ships, but it did not include linseed oil.

In England, flax became part of a wartime plan to infect German cattle with anthrax, in the event that Germany launched a similar biological attack on England. Known as Operation Vegetarian, the plan involved mixing anthrax spores into seed cakes and dropping them in cattle fields. Cattle consuming the cakes would have died and perhaps also would have infected German civilians with anthrax. Five million cakes were made in the event that they were needed, but these were incinerated after the war.[18]

Germany aimed for fiber independence. The military had long been dependent on flax for manufacturing linen, and as part of the agricultural and genetic agenda of the Third Reich, farmers sowed native flax seed on national soil. The *Lebensraum* plan of settling German farmers in eastern regions required flax varieties suited to cultivation in eastern Europe, but botanists at the Kaiser Wilhelm Institute (see Chapter 6) soon realized that successful plant breeding required time. Cross-pollination and selection depended on seasons and seed production; even with greenhouses that allowed two life cycles per year, plant breeding yielded slow results. Plans included an experimental flax farm of 150 hectares in Moravia, but the war ended before the fields were sown.

Some argued that developing new cultivars for eastern Europe was unnecessary because suitable strains already existed in the Soviet Union or occupied countries. Thus German researchers made botanical forays into Austria, Czechoslovakia, and Bulgaria to obtain fiber cultivars, and by 1940 the Reich Food Corporation ordered Kaiser Wilhelm botanists to abandon their breeding experiments and instead to use the seed stock of eastern flax varieties plundered from Soviet institutions. Other German research centered on fiber technology and adapting fibers to various uses; a process known as coagulation spinning shortened and "cottonized" flax fibers, so flax could replace cotton imports that halted during the war. Other fiber sources were investigated for possible use, including the leaves of nettle, yucca, and corn. The 1934 *Spinnstoffgesetzte* (fabric law) specified Nazi breeding policy for fiber plants, as well as fiber technology, conservation, materials testing, spinning, weaving, and even laundry techniques to extend the useful life of textiles. The dyeing of flax into military colors and blood removal from textiles were also areas of research interest.[19]

Nettles (*Urtica dioecia*) are robust perennial weeds with bast fibers that resemble flax, and both species were used in ancient times. The plants are covered with stinging hairs, needle-sharp trichomes that deliver a subcutaneous dose of histamines, but these are removed during retting. During World War I, the British Empire controlled 90 percent of cotton worldwide, so some German soldiers wore uniforms woven from nettle fibers. German civilians collected the wild plants, and farmers cultivated crops of field-grown nettles, which they learned would grow in the full sun if provided with nitrogen-rich, moist soil.[20]

Nettles produce high concentrations of chlorophyll, long used for coloring textiles, food, and soap; it was also investigated as a possible antibiotic (see Chapter 7). Extracted chlorophyll is typically unstable in light, but perhaps the relatively alkaline pH of nettle

Nettles have high levels of chlorophyll and produce bast fibers that resemble flax. German farmers cultivated nettles for fiber processing, and County Herb Committees collected wild nettles across England to dye uniforms and camouflage cloth. Kew botanists investigated nettle fabric to reinforce airplane construction, a scheme that ultimately proved impractical.

cells helped to stabilize the pigment molecules, which were also considered for possible use as a camouflaging paint. In England, the County Herb Committees (see Chapter 7) collected abundant local nettles to use as a natural dye for uniforms and camouflage cloth and perhaps in the manufacture of paper and rope. The first collectors' bulletin issued in 1942 by the Ministry of Supply noted that in Derbyshire "The Hathersage Women's Institutes dried fifty pounds of materials chiefly nettles in the attic of a house…" Local schools joined in the effort, and a village dance party in Northamptonshire required two pounds of nettles in lieu of a ticket.[21]

Botanists at the Royal Botanic Gardens (Kew) investigated nettles for wartime uses, including airplane construction using plastic panels and gears reinforced with fabric made from nettle fibers. Testing reveals that experimental parts were almost as strong as steel, but problems with collecting and processing rendered the plan of using nettles in aircraft impossible. Nettle farming was considered, but seemed impossible under wartime conditions. Plants had to be grown from rhizomes, and they needed fertile soil to produce long fibers. German factories had processing equipment that separated bast fibers stem from tissue, but in England, retting was the only option.

Milkweed

For years the standard filling used in life vests was kapok, the buoyant and waterproof fibrous seed hairs collected from the woody capsules of *Ceiba pentandra*. Kapok was used for the floating litters to evacuate injured soldiers and for the booms used to float the wooden decking of pontoon assault bridges. Other uses included cold weather gear; the British army used kapok to line full length canvas Tropal coats for use in sub-freezing temperatures. Originally native to South America, kapok trees were cultivated in Java, the Philippines, and Ceylon (now Sri Lanka), but with Japanese occupation of these areas, supplies of this strategic material soon dwindled. Newly established kapok plantations in Ecuador and Brazil took time to mature, so wartime substitutes were needed for life saving equipment and other uses.

Milkweed (*Asclepias* spp.) offered a likely option. The genus includes about 140 species native to the Americas, herbaceous perennials that could be collected from the wild or cultivated. The common milkweed (*A. syriaca*) was the most widespread in the U.S. and became the focus of wartime efforts. Each flower produces a pair of follicles that release numerous seeds, each bearing a tuft of fine hairs that evolved as an adaptation for wind dispersal. Known as milkweed floss, the fiber harvested from the seeds had buoyancy and insulating qualities similar to kapok. In 1941 The U.S. Navy tested lifesaving equipment made with milkweed floss and learned that slightly over a pound could support a sailor in water for over forty hours, leading to a national effort to farm, collect, and process milkweed floss for military use.

Farmers considered milkweed a noxious weed, but during the war years, they sowed fields with its seeds and harvested tons of the follicles. Plant breeders experimented with improving seed germination and floss quality, but there was also interest in milkweed fibers for use in cordage and in its latex as a substitute for imported rubber. Dr. Boris Berkman, a physician, patented a milkweed gin which separated the follicles and seeds from the useful fibers; he also envisioned diverse future uses for the processed floss, including flotation devices, food, fibers, building materials, explosives, insulation, and surgical dressings.[22] Researchers at the U.S. Department of Agriculture investigated erosion control using milkweed plants to bind the soil, an application suggested by its perennial growth and broad network of lateral roots. There was also

Floss from milkweed seeds replaced imported kapok in wartime lifesaving equipment, leading to a national effort to farm, collect, and process the plants for military use. Despite its reputation as a noxious weed, milkweed was also investigated as an alternative latex source, as a fiber for cordage production, and as a cover crop to control soil erosion.

interest in the edible unsaturated oil from milkweed seeds (said at the time to be similar to soybean oil, but now used externally for pain relief), as well as the waste leftover from pressing seeds as a possible animal feed.[23]

Michigan was rich in wild milkweed populations, particularly the area around Petoskey along the Lake Michigan shoreline, so the Milkweed Floss Corporation of America built processing facilities there. By 1942, this defense contractor had a huge drying oven and seven gins working full time. School children and Scouts helped with the wild milkweed harvest in rural areas; teachers organized and oversaw their students' efforts, and schools provided mesh onion bags for collecting the wild follicles. One life vest for the Navy required two bags of follicles, so "Two bags save one life" became the milkweed motto. The Milkweed Floss Division of the War Hemp Industries poster appealed to young collectors, "School children of America! Help save your father's, brothers,' and neighbors' lives by collecting milkweed pods."

Timing was important; hand-picking had to be done when the seeds were mature, but the follicles had not yet opened. September was the peak of the Michigan harvest, and community groups such as the Rotary and local businesses often joined the effort. Many donated the meager earnings per bag (typically twenty cents per pound) to the Red Cross. During the war years, wild milkweed was collected in 25 states and also in Canada, with collection depots across New England and the Midwest. Enough milkweed floss was produced or collected to fill millions of life vests and to insulate aviators' suits, sleeping bags, coats, vests, helmets, shoes, refrigerators, and gas tanks.[24] *Popular Science* also reported optimistically on the use of cattail fibers (*Typha* spp.) for life vests and insulation.[25] These fibers remained buoyant even after being submerged in water for a hundred hours, but availability was a potential problem. Cattail cultivation would have required planting and harvesting in marshlands, and thus milkweed offered an easier alternative to kapok.

Silk

Although it is not a plant fiber, silk production relies on a steady supply of mulberry leaves (*Morus alba*), the food of the silkworm moth. Silk fibers are made from fibroin, a structural protein that the caterpillars produce in their silk glands; in four days, a silk gland produces a billion fibroin molecules, a process fueled by the food energy provided by mulberry leaves. Each silkworm cocoon is a single silk filament that can be painstakingly unwound if the cocoon is soaked in warm water.

Silk is strong, lightweight, and a good insulator, making it useful for several military needs. Prior to World War II, Japan produced over half of silk worldwide; thus the fiber was a strategic material that became nearly unobtainable following the attack on Pearl Harbor. The War Production Board and the Quartermaster Corps conserved available supplies, and by the summer of 1941, the U.S. Army Air Corps had established priority in securing silk cloth for parachutes.

Other military uses for silk included officers' ties, garment linings, hat cords, thread, banners, medals, and the white shirtwaists worn by Army nurses. The Quartermaster Corps replaced silk ties with ties made of black worsted wool and later with olive drab mohair, but used cotton to replace silk in most military clothing. Cotton was mercerized to improve its strength and luster, which made it resemble silk more closely; the mercerization process used sodium hydroxide to alter cellulose bonding in cotton fibers, which coincidentally made them less prone to fungal attack. Another silk substitute was rayon, a fabric woven from fibers spun from cellulose obtained from wood. Despite early concerns that morale might be affected by medals and banners made from artificial silk, rayon was used in U.S. military regalia.[26]

Silk parachutes were wind resistant, lightweight, and compact. They were used by both pilots and paratroopers during World War II, and Germans bombers also used small parachutes to drop landmines. They were manufactured from closely woven, fine cloth which was highly valued on the home front during a time of fiber shortages; the only downsides were the tendency of silk to stretch or weaken when wet, and it was prone to insect attack. Some soldiers sent parachute silk to their families to sew clothing (particularly wedding dresses) and underwear. In Europe, parachutes on the ground signaled a possible German invasion, so civilians were ordered to turn them over to local authorities; however, many D-Day parachutes and others were repurposed into civilian clothing. Civilians donated unneeded silk for recycling into parachute cloth and other needs, but when silk stores were depleted, nylon (a synthetic polymer) replaced silk in Allied parachutes. It proved to be strong, elastic, insect resistant, fungal resistant, and cheap. The nylon used in textiles was often made from phenols derived from coal, the high-carbon sedimentary rocks made from Carboniferous period vegetation (see Chapter 9).

Silk was excluded from wartime civilian clothing, but with possible gas attacks in England, there were hooded protective suits of oiled silk, sewn from cloth impregnated with linseed oil. Mustard gas (see Chapter 4) was a known blistering agent that could damage skin. Harvey Nichols, a fashionable department store, advertised women's gas suits in green, amethyst, and rose hues, promising that they would resist toxic gas during the time that it took to traverse two hundred yards. Oiled silk was also used as a waterproof covering for surgical and wound dressings.

U.S. and British troops used escape and evasion maps printed on silk (later rayon) cloth. The detailed European maps were designed to help prisoners of war to escape captivity or to help troops avoid capture behind enemy lines. Unlike paper, silk maps were durable, did not rustle, and could be easily hidden inside clothing or tucked into a shoe. Maps were usually printed on both sides for efficiency, and pectin from plant cell walls (see Chapter 3) was used to stabilize dyes so that they would not blur in water.

Delivering the maps to prisoners required an ingenious strategy. Following the Geneva Convention, prisoners could receive relief packages containing small comforts and diversions, so board games were used to smuggle items into Axis prison camps. John Waddington, Ltd., the manufacturer of Monopoly in England, packed special game boxes for shipment to prisons; they worked under the auspices of the Licensed Victuallers Prison Relief Fund, a fake charity with a credible name. Certain Monopoly games were escape kits that included genuine German, French, and Italian currency; game boards with printed silk maps sandwiched between the cardboard layers; and metal files and compasses. Soldiers were told to look for the Monopoly games if they were imprisoned. Boards containing silk maps were marked with a red dot in the Free Parking square, and hundreds if not thousands of Allied prisoners used the maps and tools to stage successful escapes. After the war, many cloth maps were repurposed into scarves or clothing.

Manage, Make Do, Mend and Survive

Wartime shortages and rationing provided for the military at civilian expense. Clothing, bedding, and other household goods were impossible to replace with goods of prewar quality, thus fibers often had to last for the duration of the war. Wartime advice promoted repair and repurposing whenever feasible. Butterick printed patterns for patchwork skirts that could be stitched from cloth salvaged from worn dresses, and women's magazines featured countless ways to reuse scraps in creative ways. Garden string could be crocheted to make simple hats, and parachute cords could be used for trims and woven belts. Wartime scrap drives collected botanical fibers for recycling; old clothes, rags, threadbare blankets, and worn upholstery were sorted and reprocessed for uniforms, bandages, and other essential items.

In England, where clothes rationing began in early 1941, the cotton available for civilian clothing decreased by 75 percent. Fiber waste was on par with food waste; both required imports at a time when shipping was perilous at best. Rayon, a semi-synthetic fiber made from cellulose, did not wear as well as natural fibers, so sewing skills were in high demand to maintain pre-war garments. The Make Do and Mend campaign encouraged the care and repurposing of any available clothing or fabric. The phrase probably originated with the Royal Navy "make and mend" time for uniform maintenance. The campaign mascot was Mrs. Sew-and-Sew, a doll-like character who appeared in illustrated leaflets, advertisements, and magazines.

The Ministry of Supply produced "How to Make-Do-and-Mend," a short film (1943), which included footage of a sewing machine attachment for darning. However, most mending was done by hand, and neat darns were considered a badge of honor. Darning in particular was taught as a wartime skill, done with a simple running stitch to simulate the warp and weft of woven cloth. A Board of Trade leaflet "How to Darn Holes and Tears" offered instructions on technique, "It is better to darn as soon as garments begin to wear thin. Imitate, as well as possible, the texture of the fabric being darned."[27] Land Army members (see Chapter 6) darned uniforms with the thread unraveled from cotton and jute sacks, which were recycled when empty. The various Make Do and Mend leaflets advised on ways to patch worn spots, sew simple infant clothing and bedding, and make cloth shoes with braided rope soles. Children's clothing was made by cutting down adult garments; curtains were repurposed into dresses, which were later reinvented as baby clothes, cushions, or tea cozies. When thread became scarce, sewers unraveled the fibers in knitted garments and crocheted lace. Despite shortages in England, there was compassion for the desperate plight of civilians in occupied countries. Rural Women's Institutes (see Chapter 2) contributed sewing supplies including needles and cotton thread to send to France, where they would be needed after the war.

The Women's Voluntary Service (WVS, see Chapter 4) promoted the Make Do and Mend message and offered demonstrations. Volunteers also worked with the program that evacuated city children to the countryside, away from the dangers of bombing. Householders were responsible for providing for the children's needs, but the WVS helped by opening low cost clothing stores to provide evacuees with suitable garments for the country. Stuffed toys were crafted from rags and remnants, and extra mattresses were made from heavy canvas, linen, or cotton ticking filled with straw, the chaff remaining after the threshing of grains. Grasses such as wheat and rye provided a cheap, sturdy stuffing material, but insects were a possible problem when using natural materials; the Make Do and Mend leaflet "Getting Ready for Baby" recommended baking grain chaff for an hour, presumably a sterilization step.[28]

Conditions in Axis countries were equally difficult. In Italy, scrap drives recycled fibers into military uniforms, but civilian clothing was nearly impossible to purchase except at exorbitant black market prices. In Germany, soldiers were faced with shortages of cold weather clothing, and some lined their coats and uniforms with straw, rags, and paper. The Hitler *Jugend* (see Chapter 6) collected rags and worn clothing to recycle in war industries, but fiber shortages at the end of the war resulted in paper rather than cloth bandages. Lacking winter footwear for the Russian winter, some German soldiers on the eastern front wore *Strohschuhe*, straw overshoes made by women prisoners at the

Ravensbrück concentration camp and by women and elderly residents of the Lodz ghetto in Poland. These were constructed in the traditional manner used in making bee skeps, with a bundle of dried stems (probably rye) laced together with twine and then coiled into the desired shape. The grass stems contain silica deposits, a botanical adaptation that strengthens tissues mechanically and may discourage herbivore attack. Pine resin was used as a sealant against water and snow. The overshoes provided some insulation against frostbite, especially for those on sentry duty, but were cumbersome for walking in snow through Russian forests with notoriously dense and tangled undergrowth.

There were German efforts that resembled the Make Do and Mend campaign. Women were encouraged to participate in *Aus Alt mach Neu* (make new from old) and *Aus Zwei mach Eins* (make one from two). Needle and thread shortages complicated sewing efforts, and so housewives darned and mended with dyed string. Women's magazines avoided discussion of wartime hardships and rationing, but they did publish articles on remaking clothes and reinforcing garments for warmth. Promoting the Third Reich notion of a prosperous *Volk* culture, clothing patterns featured illustrations of traditional dirndl styles with stylized floral decoration, evocative of traditional peasant garb. However, neglected fiber crops and fewer imports resulted in clothing shortages; shop windows displayed merchandise, but shelves were typically empty. As in Italy, German civilians found it nearly impossible to replace their worn winter clothing, and even shoelaces were in short supply.

Wartime shortages of botanical fibers encouraged experimentation. Depleted silk supplies forced the use of rayon and others alternatives. Rayon production in Italy used cellulose from imported conifer wood. As a replacement, manufacturers turned to a giant Mediterranean grass (*Arundo donax*, known locally as *canna gentile*). The plants were easily propagated from rhizome cuttings and could grow over thirty feet tall. In reality, silk shortages in Germany dated from 1806, when Napoleon ordered destruction of German mulberry trees in order to establish French dominance in European silk markets. The Nazi party planned to reestablish the German silk industry by replanting mulberries, but demand for parachute cloth exceeded possible production levels. The chemical conglomerate I.G. Farben developed Perlon, a synthetic fiber used for parachutes, and as the war progressed, synthetic and semi-synthetic fibers were also woven into military uniforms, but there were problems with dye chemistry; German soldiers became known for having greenish skin, the result of the textile dyes that bled from their synthetic uniforms.

Fungi and Fibers

Fungi are an ongoing problem in tropical climates, conditions in which textiles and cordage seem to rot overnight. The Kingdom Fungi includes microbes that use the enzyme cellulase to digest the cellulose in plant tissue, a process that is essential to soil formation and composting. However, the same organisms can attack the cellulose in cloth and rope, a problem that was not anticipated until it was encountered in the Pacific theater where fungi caused billions of dollars of waste. Estimates are that half of the matériel shipped to the Pacific was destroyed by tropical fungi.

Because fungi thrive in warm, moist climates, botanical fibers were ideal habitats for cellulose-digesting microbes, including many previously unknown species. Within hours of arrival on Pacific islands, bales of clothing and canvas equipment were colonized by the small fungi known commonly as mildews. Cellulase enzymes caused the cloth to weaken, and green dyes turned yellow, rendering items useless for use in combat requiring camouflage. Canvas-topped jungle boots fell apart within weeks when fungal activity weakened both the canvas and the cotton stitching on shoes and boots. Soles separated from the uppers, which led to the substitution of linen thread that was more fungal resistant.

Tents, hammocks, tarpaulins, and webbing were all prone to failure once fungi began to dissolve the cellulose, and then the textiles disintegrated quickly. Under tropical conditions, mildew could ruin a tent in a few days; airborne-fungal spores landed on damp tent walls, and the lower parts were in constant contact with soil teeming with local fungi.[29] Government and university laboratories worked on identifying the organisms, including samples from many damaged items from the South Pacific. Eventually more than 4,500 cultures of fungi associated with deterioration were grown and identified. In 1944, one particularly aggressive strain of the fungus *Trichoderma reesei* was isolated from military textiles in the Solomon Islands, and it is now used in biofuel technology. The fungus produces high levels of the enzyme cellulase, used industrially convert to cellulose from plant matter into glucose for ethnanol fermentation.

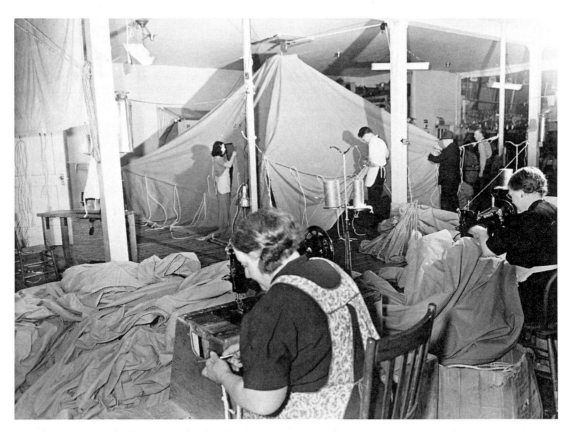

Tents were carefully constructed and tested, but textiles were prone to failure once fungi began to dissolve the cellulose; airborne-fungal spores landed on damp tent walls, and the lower parts were in constant contact with soil teeming with local fungi. Estimates are that half of the matériel shipped to the Pacific was destroyed by tropical fungi (U.S. National Archives).

Fungicides, waterproofing, and improved storage helped to control fungal growth. The problem was studied experimentally, with research on various commercial fungicides and their effect on textile engineering. However, various surface treatments against water, fire, and fungi added 50 percent to the weight of tentage, a problem for both transport and life of the fabric.[30] Cotton and jute sandbags were impregnated with copper compounds that inhibited soil bacteria. Some experimental fungicides were mercury-based and highly toxic, while others such as salicylanilide (based on the botanical compound salicylic acid, a phenolic acid used in aspirin synthesis and originally derived from willows, *Salix* spp.) were relatively safe to use on clothing.[31]

Various laboratories and committees worked on the problem, including the Tropical Deterioration Committee, a subsidiary of the federal Office of Scientific Research and Development, along with research mycologists in university labs. At the University of Pennsylvania, investigators attempted to study tropical fungi *in vitro* using a full size growth chamber that simulated daily changes in temperature and humidity. This "tropical room" included leaf litter inoculated with tropical fungi and populations of mites and insects known to carry fungal spores.

By early 1944, more realistic trials on fungal deterioration were conducted in the dense rain forests of Barro Colorado Island in the Panama Canal Zone; 1400 military items were tested under true tropical conditions, where microbes could be collected from nature and shipped to the tropical fungus collection at Harvard University.[32] Elso Barghoorn, a mycologist involved in the research on Barro Colorado, summed up the benefits of field research on fungal activity, "The green gloom of the forest, the dripping trees, and the saturated air make this an excellent location for the work we are doing ... one cannot study this problem by talking to people in well kept offices ... you have to live with the problem in the jungle where you don't have to look to find it."[33]

By the end of the war, rot-resistant cloth was made using cotton fibers treated with acetic anhydride to produce cellulose acetate, related chemically to the dope used to coat the fabric wings and fuselage of the Mosquito and similar aircraft (see Chapter 9). Cloth woven from a combination of cotton and acetylated cellulose fibers remained intact even after burial for several months in soil with high microbial populations; it had potential for food storage, sandbags, and tents for use in tropical or wet environments.[34] However, according to U.S. Army historians, the problem of fungal deterioration of botanical fibers was never really solved: "In any event no known methods offered complete protection against fungi. At the close of the war it was still reported that 'even under the best storage conditions' all types of canvas quickly deteriorated."[35]

Fiber Currency

Perhaps the most diabolical use of fibers involved several wartime schemes for printing and circulating counterfeit currency using paper made of botanical fibers rather than wood pulp. In one case, the U.S. replicated and printed Philippine pesos and released the bills as part of an effort to devalue the currency of the Japanese occupation. The plan required finding paper made of the correct botanical fibers; occupation pesos were probably printed in Japan on paper made from tough kudzu vines (*Pueria lobata*) and durable bark fibers of the Asian shrub known in Japan as *mitsumata* (*Edgeworthia chrysantha*).

In Germany, finance officials developed Operation Bernhard (named for the Nazi

officer who directed it) as a plan to undermine the British economy by releasing counterfeit bank notes. The scheme involved meticulous attention to design, paper, and printing. Concentration camp prisoners were recruited as excellent engravers, using ink
replicated by boiling grapevines in linseed oil to produce paper currency totaling 32 million pounds, which exceeded the funds in the vaults of the Bank of England at the time.
However, procuring the correct paper posed a complex problem. British currency was
printed on paper made of bast fibers from linen and ramie (*Boehmeria nivea*, a member
of the Urticaceae, nettle family). Germans used linen grown in Germany and ramie
imported from Hungary, but they resulted in a paper that was somewhat distinguishable
from legitimate English currency. Nevertheless the engraved images and ink appeared
entirely authentic to the unpracticed eye, and even Swiss banks accepted the Nazi counterfeits. The original plan had been to air drop currency for civilians to find, but ultimately
the fake bills were used and circulated by German spies working abroad.[36]

9

Forestry, Timber and Wood

War demanded wood for myriad uses, from gunstocks and ammunition boxes to ships, docks, pontoon bridges, railroad ties, airplanes, barracks, and hangars. In addition to lumber, wartime industries used wood pulp for manufacturing paper and cellulose from wood cell walls to make explosives, cellophane (see Chapter 3), gas mask filters, photographic film, and semi-synthetic textiles such as rayon. Wood cellulose yielded sugars for fermenting into the alcohol needed for synthetic rubber production. The U.S. Forest Service short film "Wood for War" (1942) summarized the wood products needed by the military; in short, over a thousand items used by the U.S. Army and Navy during World War II were made all or in part from wood or its by-products, the equivalent of 63 billion feet of board lumber (ten times the demand of World War I), half of it used for building boxes and crates used in shipping goods and matériel worldwide.

In the theaters of war, local timber had to be selected with care, which required knowledge of regional tree species. Wood could degrade or fail depending on its structure and resistance to natural conditions; for instance, when boring beetles ate through the telephone poles connecting Lae to Finschafen, the Signal Corps in New Guinea (now Papua New Guinea) instead turned to bamboo poles and living trees to hold telephone wires. As a result of local needs, knowledge of wood and wood products became a wartime focus, and botanists at the Arnold Arboretum of Harvard University compiled a preliminary list of trees native to the western Pacific region that would be suitable for construction. Identification of local timber required more than scientific names, so the U.S. Navy sent an artist to the herbarium in Boston to develop a set of lifelike tree illustrations based on dried plant specimens.

After the destruction of virgin forests for airplane construction during World War I, foresters and politicians became aware of the need to manage and conserve wood. However, even with the vast resources of the U.S. national forests (10 percent of timber came from national forests during the war), tree cutting exceeded wood production by about 50 percent during the war years. Wartime needs effectively deforested much of the U.S. because more timber was cut than could grow; seedlings need a few years of maturation to begin growth of the vascular cambium that produces wood (secondary xylem). There was plenty of acreage not needed for food production, so by the end of the war, American farmers were encouraged to plant tree seedlings and establish woodlots on private land. Wood became a cash crop to be planted and cultivated following the methods of scientific arboriculture, and forestry was recast as a branch of farming for those who usually grew food and fodder. By the 1940s, research had revealed that careful management of farmed woodlots could yield stronger timber with higher specific gravity than those produced by crowded seedlings competing for light in natural forests.[1]

The postwar wood shortage was not due to a lack of land but rather to the need for seedlings, growth time, management, and fire prevention.[2] Concern for destructive forest fires, including the threat of incendiary balloon bombs released by the Japanese (see below), resulted in the Smokey the Bear mascot, which was introduced by the U.S. Forest Service in 1944. A national campaign featured the slogan, "Smokey Says—Care Will Prevent 9 out of 10 Forest Fires," subsequently replaced in 1947 by "Remember.... Only YOU Can Prevent Forest Fires." The plan was to extinguish forest fires of any size or scope, a practice that came into question after the war years. Fire is a natural element of forest ecosystems, and ground fires routinely eliminate small brush. In short, allowing dead wood and leaves to accumulate can result in major fires that can destroy an entire forest, and more recent forestry practice often allows for controlled burns, ground fires that eliminate brush and the danger of destructive conflagrations.

Forests and Timber

During World War II, forestry was a practical science reinforced with conservation measures learned during the Dust Bowl era. Modern practices were the means of providing billions of board feet of timber during the war years. Conservation lessons were learned during World War I, when the demand for wood for airplane manufacture during 1917–18 resulted in panicked clear-cutting, which included virgin timber. By 1942, one third of the U.S. (630 million acres) was forested, most of it under commercial control with selective cutting and replanting as developing practices. Research on the triple threat of microbial diseases, insect damage, and forest fires was also on the uptick in time for wartime preparedness.[3] President Roosevelt had an avid personal interest in forestry and replanted his Hyde Park, New York property with tree seedlings. Practical issues of timber production were surely at the heart of his wider concern for American forests. Recalling a honeymoon visit to the managed woodlands of the Black Forest, Roosevelt observed in a 1931 speech, "For centuries European countries have been renewing and caring for their forests so as to get maximum benefit from them. We treat our timber resources as if they were a mine, from which the ore can be taken once and once only. The United States is using timber today four times as fast as it is being grown."[4]

President Roosevelt advocated reforesting abandoned farmland and managing forests as a national source of timber. In 1933, the same year that Hitler became the German chancellor, Roosevelt established the Civilian Conservation Corps, and over the next decade, three million young CCC workers planted three billion trees in national forests. Unlike the *Hitler Jugend*, the CCC did not officially prepare young men for military service; however, one in every six draftees had served in the CCC and the experience of outdoor teamwork proved useful. In 1942, *The Alaskan* attributed conservation work for taking "baffled, furtive, tough inner-city youngsters in and transforming them into bronzed, clear-eyed, well-muscled soldiers-in-waiting."[5]

As CCC workers entered the military, Boy Scouts took over forestry work and planted two million trees between 1942 and 1945. Former CCC camps in the Great Smoky Mountains housed conscientious objectors who did conservation work during the war years, and prisoners of war held in 700 U.S. camps provided an additional workforce for forest work. Japanese and German POWs saved U.S. timber by fighting wildfires in North Dakota, Texas, and Idaho. At Fort Devens in Ayer, Massachusetts, German POWs planted trees and practiced forestry in the oak and birch forests of the former World War I Camp Devens. Many were skilled carvers and spent their spare time crafting items from wood scraps. Some Fort Devens prisoners were relocated to Camp Stark in New Hampshire, a former CCC camp where they cut pulpwood for the Brown Paper Company, in Berlin, NH. They also forged local friendships and even crafted wooden toys for local children. As part of an interesting historical continuum, George Washington first planted and cultivated the land of Fort Hunt CCC camp in Virginia. As part of Roosevelt's reforestation plan, the CCC planted the old farmland with oak seedlings; following the war, German prisoners must have felt at home in the oak forests when the site was used for interrogation of former Nazis, including the rocket scientist Wernher von Braun.[6]

Wood Production

Trees begin life as herbaceous seedlings, and arboreal growth requires time. For the first several months, their stems consist of soft tissue with embedded vascular bundles, each with an inner layer of water conducting tissue (xylem) and an outer layer of food conducting tissue (phloem). Within a year or two, a layer of cambium cells grows horizontally from the center of each vascular bundle and merge to form a continuous internal cylinder of cambium cells. Wood (also known as secondary xylem) results from divisions of the cambium cells. In temperate trees, seasonal growth begins with wide diameter, thin-walled springwood cells, followed by narrower, thicker-walled summerwood; together these comprise an annual growth ring. Developing wood cells are reinforced with a secondary wall of cellulose and further hardened by lignin, a complex compound made from six-carbon aromatic alcohols.

Microscopic differences occur between conifer woods (softwoods) and the wood of flowering trees (hardwoods). Softwood consists of tracheids that function in both water conduction and support; in contrast, in addition to tracheids, hardwoods have tube-like vessel elements that form conducting vessels and thick-walled elongated fiber cells that are adapted for tensile strength. Softwoods lack fibers and are typically more brittle and prone to compression than hardwoods. High lignin content results in greater wood density, so conifer woods are also less dense as measured by specific gravity, which is the ratio of wood mass to the mass of an equal volume of water. The typical range of specific gravity in temperate species is 0.35–0.65. High specific gravity values indicate the presence of many thick-walled fibers that impart both tensile strength and density to hardwoods. For instance, black walnut (*Juglans nigra*, specific gravity = 0.55) was used during World War II for both gunstocks and airplane propellers; the high number of fibers made the wood both shock resistant and suitable for fine machining. In contrast, conifers such as white pine (*Pinus strobus*, specific gravity = 0.34) yielded lightweight lumber suitable for mass-produced ammunition boxes.

By World War II, recently planted forests provided useful scientific information about tree growth and timber production, which no longer had to be left to chance. It became standard practice to allow natural reproduction, so some mature trees were left standing to provide seed. Douglas fir (widely used in decking and plywood) required bright sunlight for seedling growth, so groups of mature trees were left after clear-cutting, a practice that limited shade to a confined area; fortunately the wind-dispersed seeds could repopulate widely. In addition, tree seedlings of essential species were nursery-cultivated for replanting at measured intervals. Observations revealed that crowding of hardwood saplings resulted in trees that grew vertically, expended less energy on lignin production, and yielded wood with decreased specific gravity. Selective thinning resulted in hardwood trees that grew faster and yielded stronger wood with higher specific gravity. In contrast, the specific gravity and strength of conifers (softwoods) increased as a result of crowding, which increased the proportion of thicker-walled summerwood cells.[7]

Managed woodlots yielded lumber with desired properties, but natural forests still provided valuable timber resources. In September 1938, a powerful New England hurricane uprooted thousands of trees, the equivalent of over 2.5 billion board feet of lumber, mostly pine. Private sawmills and the lumber market could not process and absorb the tremendous glut of wood, but wasted timber and possible forest fires were unthinkable. Organized through federal legislation and managed by the U.S. Forest Service, the Northeast Timber Salvage Administration purchased and preserved piles of hurricane-damaged timber for future use. The salvaged logs were stamped U.S. on the end, and deep lakes provided ideal submerged storage. Cold water temperatures combined with low oxygen

A 1938 hurricane uprooted thousands of trees across new England, the equivalent of over 2.5 billion board feet of lumber, mostly pine; the logs were stored in northern lakes where cold water temperatures, low oxygen, and high tannin levels protected against insects, decay, and fire. Eventually the timber was used to construct barracks and other military buildings (U.S. Forest Service).

and high tannin concentrations protected thousands of usable logs from insects, decay, and fire. Many ponds were dammed to provide additional aquatic storage.

The Civilian Conservation Corps (CCC) and Works Progress Administration (WPA) supplied labor, which included cutting the highly flammable, resinous pine branches that blanketed forest floors after the 1938 hurricane. Local women worked at the portable sawmills, which were set up near the water to cut lumber into enormous stockpiles for drying. In addition to pine, salvaged trees included maple, birch, beech, ash, oak, spruce, and hemlock. With war on the horizon and buildings needed, 425 million board feet of lumber were sold to the Eastern Pine Sales Corporation, a private company. Lumber from trees downed in the 1938 hurricane was eventually used in constructing World War II barracks such as those at Fort Devens in Massachusetts.[8] After the war, Fort Devens housed a branch campus of the state university for veterans studying on the G.I. bill. The makeshift campus utilized military buildings for classrooms and laboratories and provided basic college courses until 1949; the wooden barracks built from hurricane timber became college dormitories that housed twenty men per room.

Military Forestry

At the beginning of the war, most draft boards deferred forestry students from the draft, which changed as military needs evolved. Forestry schools trained foresters skilled in timber production and management, critical specialists who also had the necessary skills to understand aerial maps as part of the photo-interpretation units of the Army Air Force. Early in the war, the Corps of Engineers conducted forestry operations, but by 1942, specialist forestry companies prepared for work involving timber and construction. The 799th Engineer Forestry Company trained in the forests of the Pacific Northwest, moving on to wartime service in Alaska, France, Germany, and the Philippines. The 797th Engineer Forestry Company began at Camp Claiborne in Louisiana and moved on to India, where they cut wood for constructing the Ledo Road into Burma, much of it through uncharted jungle, including 507 miles of log road and 165 wooden bridges. They

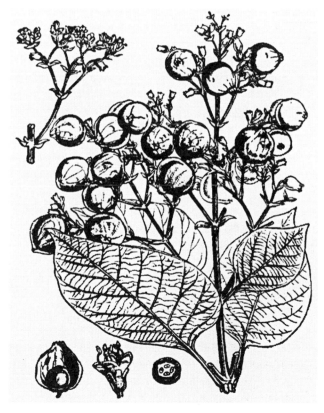

U.S. Army foresters working in India relied heavily on teak to construct the Ledo road into Burma, much of it through uncharted jungle; the project involved constructing 507 miles of log road and 165 wooden bridges.

learned about local woods in the field, relying on teak (*Tectona grandis*) and other hard-woods after discovering that ebony wood (*Diospyros* spp., specific gravity = 1.1) was so dense that it warped sawmill blades. Marines stationed in the South Pacific also conducted forestry work, including sites in the Solomon Islands where the 4th Base Depot of the Marine Corps felled and processed native woods for military use.

Pacific tree species were not necessarily well known to U.S. botanists, who hastened to lend a hand using herbarium collections. Collections of local trees were sent back to the U.S. for identification and assessment; specimens that arrived at the Arnold Arbore-tum of Harvard University included *Mastixiodendron stoddardii*, a new species native to the rain forests and volcanic soils of the Solomon Islands and named for its collector, Lt. C.H. Stoddard of the U.S. Navy.[9] In an effort to help with timber identification and uses, the Navy published reference books for use in theaters of war, including *Native Woods for Construction Purposes in the Western Pacific Region* by J.H. Kraemer (1944), which covered timber in the Solomon Islands, Papua New Guinea, and other archipelagoes. The text provided practical timber information: illustrations, guidelines for use, scientific names, and phonetic spellings of local names. Presumably much of this information was gleaned from herbarium specimens, perhaps based on collections at the Arnold Arbore-tum where lists of useful trees and illustrations for Kraemer's text were prepared. The work could be nomenclaturally complex; for instance, the sturdy leguminous tree *Albizzia acle* was known locally by thirteen local names, including *kita-kita*, *mabunga*, and *banuyo*. Specimen trees grew four feet in diameter with a dense termite-proof wood that was ideal for construction in contact with soil; however, if submerged in seawater, the timber was quickly honeycombed by marine worms.[10] *Native Woods for Construction Purposes in the South China Sea Region*, a companion volume on Asian woods, followed in 1945.[11]

Not all wood was cut for construction. At the end of the war, the U.S. Army in France (1944–46) was in desperate need of fuel, so the Quartermaster Corps established 28 camps to house 10,000 loggers who cut timber in shell-damaged beech and oak forests near Bayeaux in Normandy. Prisoners of war did much of the work and included skilled German foresters; logging was not selective, but a few dozen seed-producing trees were left standing in each acre. Operations continued into the nearly impenetrable under-growth of the Ardenne and Argonne forests, where there were still trenches and shell holes that dated from World War I. Old Army jeeps were converted into buzz saws that yielded 300,000 cords of fuel wood for military encampments and boards for chestpaling, the wood and wire mats used to traverse mud. Mature trees were used to make mine props for French coal mines, sufficient for mining three million tons of coal in the waning months of the war.[12]

Timber in England

Wartime wood demand sometimes included civilian needs. In England, the Blitz destroyed or damaged 450,000 homes, resulting in the need for emergency housing and furniture during and after the war. The first generation of emergency dwellings were short term huts assembled from asbestos panels installed on wooden frames, insulated with thin wood shavings known as wood wool. Prefabricated houses were designed to last for a decade; several models had wood framing and floors, and wood trim was stan-dard.

To furnish their homes, bombing survivors could obtain permits for purchasing utility furniture, a range of 22 chairs, tables, cupboards, and other basic items crafted from simple designs. As with utility clothing (see Chapter 8), utility furniture eliminated ornament but served the necessary function during a time of national emergency. The furniture was made from wood, typically oak or mahogany, presumably using pre-war imports. Plywood was not available, but to conserve wood some utility furniture was assembled from hardboard (compressed wood pulp) and then veneered with a thin wood layer. Manufacturers included F. Wrighton and Sons, Ltd., a company with flexibility in its wartime production lines. Their carpenters produced utility furniture for bombing survivors in England and wood fuselages and wings for the de Havilland Mosquito airplanes that bombed German cities.

England was originally forested, but over centuries woodlands were cut for fuel and did not regenerate. By World War II, England imported more wood than any other nation (85 percent), mostly from mainland Europe. Some wood for specialized uses came from the U.S., including walnut for rifle stocks and hickory and ash for tool handles, but with the U-boat blockade, native ash and beech replaced American timber. Various native woods were needed for building small boats, airplanes, and wooden landing tracks used for tanks and heavy vehicles during the D-Day landings on Normandy beaches. Small items were also in demand, including tent pegs made of beech, and a 1940 Pathé newsreel showed thousands of stacked pegs handcrafted in Buckinghamshire. However, many immature trees were felled for lumber during World War I, which decreased available timber during the 1940s. Thus with demand high and natural resources limited, woodland management became critical, and any standing timber on public or private land had wartime potential.

Wartime experiments focused on reforestation by transplanting nursery-grown tree seedlings into regions that were forested in ancient times, but the emphasis was clearly on immediate production. In 1939 the Forestry Commission established a Home Grown Timber Advisory Committee, tasked with designating mature woodlands for immediate cutting. Nearly half of all standing timber in England was felled to support military efforts during World War II, with the Forest of Dean and New Forest areas virtually cleared of native conifers suitable for lumber. Nearly 90 percent of the timber cut came from private lands such as the managed woodlands and landscape gardens surrounding country estates.

With most men in the military, the Women's Timber Corps was organized as a division of the Women's Land Army (see Chapter 6) tasked with forestry management. Based on forestry work done by women during World War I, the WTC recruited about six thousand young women who qualified based on their perceived resilience and enthusiasm. WTC members (known informally as Lumber Jills) worked in gangs that traveled widely to survey and measure trees, identify timber for selective cutting, and calculate cubic footage of wood yields. Wood in highest demand included beech, which was used in the manufacture of Mosquito aircraft, and conifer trunks (known as pit props) which were suitable for supporting the shafts of coal mines.[13]

Based on a 1940 survey, the Forestry Commission concluded that lighter work such as planting and brush trimming was possible for young women, a notion that was cast aside when mature trees needed cutting. In reality, WTC work was strenuous and potentially dangerous. Lacking power tools, the WTC used heavy axes and two-person hand saws to fell sizeable trees; women learned to notch trunks and then worked in teams to

The Women's Timber Corps was a division of the Women's Land Army tasked with forestry management. Known informally as Lumber Jills, members surveyed and measured trees, identified timber for selective cutting, calculated cubic footage of wood yields, and felled trees with axes and two-person hand saws (Ministry of Information, United Kingdom).

cross-cut the trunks, followed by branch removal and cutting into sections for transport. Board feet of lumber were estimated using a system developed by Edward Hoppus during the eighteenth century, a method of calculation that essentially squared off log measurements and used ready reckoner tables to estimate lumber yield. Young women with good mathematical skills were entrusted with these calculations, and the modest pay of WTC members was based on lumber yields.

As in the U.S., wood demand in England outpaced tree growth during the war years. The wood shortage forced foresters to consider trees that had not previously been used for lumber; the wartime edition of *A Handbook of Home-Grown Timbers* listed several new species, including apple, pear, and holly, as well as cedar of Lebanon, the picturesque trees in the cultivated landscape gardens of many great houses. The handbook provided information on durability, fire resistance, mechanical properties, and potential uses of wood that could be grown in England rather than imported.[14] Wood supplies were still so limited that restrictions were placed on the wood used for coffins (not to exceed 5/8" thickness), and low grade woods and even papier-mâché (a mixture of paper or wood pulp bound with glue or starch) became standard materials for coffin construction. Some local authorities even suggested that shrouds were sufficient for burial, a move opposed by undertakers who in some cases purchased timber and constructed coffins for military and civilian burials.

Combat

Combat can involve wood in several ways, from firearm and landmine manufacture to the landscape of the theater of war. Strength, density, and flexibility results from wood anatomy at a cellular level, and the correct combination of traits results in the selection of wood for particular uses. Ammunition boxes were made of pine, which was strong enough to hold the heavy contents but lightweight and disposable in the field. Standard trench shovels had oak handles that were easy to grasp while extricating heavy vehicles from the mud or digging trenches, foxholes, artillery emplacements, or graves. Oak wood is heavy and characterized by wide vascular rays, the ribbon-like radial files of cells which function in horizontal transport in tree trunks. Sometimes oak wood split along the vascular rays, but it was good enough for shovel handles.

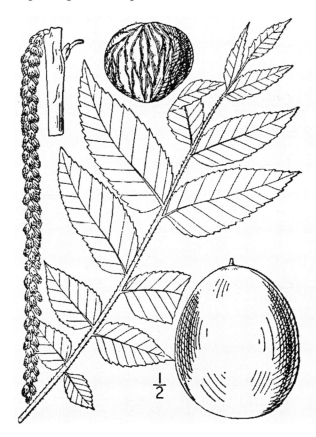

Black walnut (*Juglans nigra*) was traditionally the most structurally desirable wood for gunstock manufacture. Its density added balance to the mass of a standard rifle like the M1903 Springfield, and its cellular structure resisted shock and distortion during recoil. Walnut wood has a relatively high specific gravity of 0.55; the vascular cambium produces a high number of thick-walled fiber cells that contribute density and strength to the wood. Functional alternatives to black walnut included maple, birch, and beech (all with specific gravity = 0.62–0.64), which were used in various service weapons. Even

Black walnut was the optimum wood for gunstocks; its density added balance to the mass of a standard Army rifle, and its cellular structure resisted shock and distortion during recoil. Thick-walled fibers contribute characteristic mass and strength to the wood.

lighter weight elms were used, with specific gravity of about 0.45. However, the woods were light in color, so the gunstocks required staining to avoid detection. Various woods were also used to make realistic but lightweight dummy rifles for use in military training. Walnut was reserved for actual firearms, so these non-functional training rifles were made from cheaper timber, probably whatever was available. Wooden broomsticks (perhaps birch or maple) substituted for some of the real guns on the sixteen B-25B Mitchell bombers used in the Doolittle attacks on the Japanese islands. From a distance the painted dowels resembled the barrels of real guns; projecting from the tail cone of the bombers, they served as visual deterrents.

Oak is heavier (specific gravity = 0.63–0.68, depending on the species) than walnut but more prone to splitting. Nevertheless, German manufacturers such as Mauser resorted to oak during the years that they were manufacturing 50,000 rifles monthly and supplies of more desirable woods dwindled. Early Karabiner 98 rifles had walnut gunstocks, but by 1943 these were replaced with oak or laminated wood, made by gluing together thin sheets of walnut, beech, and elm. Laminated wood avoided the waste associated with machining solid gunstocks and so helped to conserve tight wartime wood supplies; it was also relatively stronger because the wood layers were oriented in different directions and so the final product resisted cracks or splits despite changes in temperature or humidity.

Some gun manufacturers eventually abandoned wood and wood veneers and turned to durofol, a composite material made from compressed wood impregnated with phenolic resins under high heat and pressure. However, oak and other available woods were used to make the unique *Stielhandgranate* (stalk hand grenades) used by the German army. These consisted of a steel or iron casing surrounding an explosive compound and mounted to a hollow wooden handle containing the detonator. Compared to American "pineapple style" grenades, the wooden handle made the "potato masher" design of the M24 *Stielhandgranate* easier to throw a distance of thirty feet or more.

Some German anti-personnel mines utilized wood to avoid discovery by metal detectors. The *Schützenmine* 42 (shoe-mine) was a six inch square wooden box that contained an explosive and a detonator, triggered by foot pressure on an internal pin that released the striker and caused detonation. The design was cheap to manufacture from available wood, which could dampen and decay when buried a few feet deep in soil or sand; nevertheless vast numbers of the *Schützenmine* 42 design were produced and deployed. During the Normandy invasion, dogs trained in detecting explosives helped to locate shoe-mines. Other undetectable non-metallic mines were made from plywood, cardboard, and wood waste; for instance, the *Topfmine* (pot mine) design had an outer casing manufactured from tar, sawdust, and cardboard, waterproofed and camouflaged with a coating of tar and sand. Some similar versions of *Topfmine* were molded from waste products left over from processing bituminous coal, which apparently resembled plastic.[15] Mines were often used to booby-trap abatis, anti-tank obstacles and field fortifications made from rows of entire trees felled in a way that the tree tops aimed at incoming tanks. These were particularly favored by the German and Soviet armies and were made from any available species.

Wood is highly flammable, and incendiary bombs that are dropped strategically on wooden buildings can cause the eruption of firestorms. Surrounding air is pulled into the fire, resulting in turbulence and updraft that draws in additional oxygen and can cause strong winds. Firebombing occurred during the Blitz with devastating effects. The

Allied attack on Hamburg, conducted during a spell of warm, dry weather in July 1943, resulted in a firestorm with intense winds that uprooted trees. Thus there was interest in understanding the physics of firestorms and the effect of incendiary bombs on Axis architecture. At the urging of President Roosevelt, model German and Japanese villages were constructed at the Dugway Proving Ground in Utah in 1943. Details included typical furnishings, authentic architecture, and accurate building materials, assembled with the guidance of refugee German-Jewish architects; much of it was constructed from wood. The plan was to assess damage after intentional bombing with incendiary devices, including gasoline-containing bombs recently developed by Standard Oil. Another village was constructed at Eglin Field in Florida, where Army Air Force B-17 bombers dropped bombs on Japanese-style wooden houses to determine the effects of fragmentation and incendiary devices.

The unstated goal was to understand the conditions necessary to start firestorms in German and Japanese cities. Fires were started, data collected, and the wooden structures were rebuilt for additional rounds of test bombing. In the case of the German buildings, heavy timber was simulated by wood (probably oak) imported from Russia. The heavy timber and wooden stairwells and attics contributed to the stack effect, which drew in air as the fire gained heat and resulted in uncontrollable flames. The replica Japanese houses were constructed from wood and paper, which burned quickly when ignited by incendiary bombs such as the M-69. These were filled with napalm, a combination of

Model German and Japanese villages were constructed at the Dugway Proving Ground in Utah, and they included typical furnishings, authentic architecture, and accurate building materials, much of it constructed from wood. The plan was to assess damage after intentional bombing with incendiary devices and to determine the conditions necessary to start timber-fueled firestorms in German and Japanese cities using incendiary bombs (U.S. Army).

gasoline, gelling agents (including latex, see Chapter 10), and the aluminum salts of naphthenic and palmitic acids (see Chapter 4). Trials were also conducted using bats to carry small incendiaries with timers (probably napalm), with the intention that the bats would start fires by roosting in buildings, a strategy never employed in a theater of war.

The compiled research from the model villages influenced the aerial bombing of Tokyo, Dresden, and other Axis cities that experienced wood-fueled firestorms. Wood anatomy and chemistry were factors to consider as well. Xylem cells (the water-conducting tracheids and vessel elements) are dead at maturity, and the hollow cells contain air that can fuel a fire; the less dense the wood, the more air is held in the xylem. During fires, the cellulose and lignin in wood cell walls undergo pyrolysis (thermochemical decomposition) at high temperatures, and thus denser woods like oaks and other hardwoods tend to burn more slowly than softwoods. Timber used in Japanese buildings included conifers (softwoods) such as native pine, cedar, and cypress species characterized by vertical resin canals in the xylem. In addition to lower wood density (specific gravity of conifer wood is typically less than 0.5), cells lining the canals produce highly flammable terpene-based resins, a chemical factor that contributed to the instantaneous fires caused by incendiary bombing in Japan.

Trees provided the raw material for corduroy roads used to navigate difficult terrain during combat. Trunks were placed horizontally and attached to side pieces (stringers)

Corduroy roads were used to navigate difficult terrain during combat. Tree trunks were placed horizontally and attached to side pieces (stringers) to provide stable footing across swamps and damaged roads. The technique was useful in stabilizing roads that became muddy, rutted, and eventually impassible due to damage from military traffic (U.S. War Department).

to provide stable footing across swamps and damaged roads. When military activity churned wet soil into impassable muck, the 111th Engineer Battalion laid corduroy roads for the Fifth Army in Italy during the winter of 1943–44. Engineers used trees felled from the banks of the Volturno River to stabilize roads that had become "streams of mud."[16] During the landing at the Anzio beachhead in Italy in January 1944, Army engineers lay corduroy logs to stabilize the rutted clay roads leading away from the beaches, augmented by woven straw matting that made a passable surface.[17]

Wood was used during the D-Day landings to support tanks and heavy vehicles on the Normandy beaches. Palings (boards used in fencing) were cut from sweet chestnut (*Castanea sativa*) and crafted into 1500 miles of tracks across the sand. Engineering tanks such as the British AVRE carried huge bundles of chestnut wood into battle, ready to launch the load into anti-tank ditches and artillery craters. The strategy of using masses of woody branches (also known as fascines) to traverse obstacles originated with the Roman army; the Romans also introduced sweet chestnut to England, but probably for their edible nuts and not as a timber tree. Sweet chestnut naturalized widely in southern England and was valued for its tannin-rich, weather-resistant wood that was used traditionally for fencing. Cultivation of sweet chestnut often depended on coppicing, a method in which woody growth recurs from living roots when trunks are cut close to the ground. Depending on the local climate, woodlands re-grew new trees every ten to thirty years, and this technique probably provided most of the wood used during the Normandy invasion for chestnut palings and fascines.

While not directly related to vegetation, the sand itself was another factor to consider. It was long known that the Normandy beaches varied in sand texture; some substrates were comparatively more stable and could support tanks and other matériel with less risk. These variations resulted from populations of diatoms, single-celled algae (Class Chrysophyceae) that produce mucilaginous strands, which make sand grains adhere to each other and to the diatom cells. Prior to the Normandy invasion, botanists at the British Museum analyzed samples from various

Tanks and vehicles involved in the D-Day landings in Normandy travelled across beaches on 1500 miles of tracks made from the wood of sweet chestnut. Engineering tanks such as the British AVRE carried huge bundles of chestnut wood into battle, ready to launch the load into anti-tank ditches and artillery craters, a technique of traversing obstacles that originated with the Roman army.

beaches to determine those with the richest diatom flora, where the sand was sufficiently stable to support tanks and guns, and this factored into selecting the landing sites.[18]

Mud was a problem during warfare on Pacific islands. In Papua New Guinea, local men assisted with road construction, which required continual work to keep them passable for Army jeeps; Papuans knew the local flora and could advise on selecting timber for particular uses in roads and bridges.[19] Corduroy foot trails were laid in areas where jeeps could not maneuver, but lessons were learned in the field. In the Buna region of Papua New Guinea, engineers soon discovered that corduroy roads sunk irretrievably into the mud if stringers were not installed first.[20] Often coconut palms (*Cocos nucifera*) were the only material available for building corduroy roads; the coconut fruit disperse by floating in seawater, so palms were nearly ubiquitous on Pacific islands. The mature plants are arboreal, but as monocotyledons they lack a vascular cambium and true woody growth. However, the stems are strengthened internally with flexible fibers and lignin-impregnated cell walls, which made them well suited for construction.

Japanese soldiers used coconut palms to assemble small pillbox forts and larger above-ground bunkers in areas with high water tables, such as the Buna area of Papua New Guinea. Coconut logs (some up to eighteen inches in diameter) formed the columns and beams, with a roof made of two or three layers of logs, covered with soil and camouflaged with transplanted vegetation.[21]

Bamboo provided another likely material for construction during combat. There are about 1400 species of these large grasses, and like coconuts, they can be tree-high monocots without true woody growth. Impregnated with both lignin and silica, bamboo stems are simultaneously lightweight, strong, and flexible. As in other grasses, bamboo growth occurs at the intercalary meristems, localized zones of dividing cells which are visible as external rings along the stems. The meristems divide quickly, resulting in rapid elongation of the outer stem tissues; internal cells do not divide at the same rate, so bamboo stems typically become hollow as they elongate and mature.

Army engineers used bamboo as a raw material to make items that were needed but not available. In the Pacific, bamboo poles framed simple shelters for storing supplies out of the rain; these were modeled on local huts thatched with palm leaves and were later replaced with warehouses made from locally milled lumber. Mats woven from bamboo, vines, and wire were layered with soil and rolled to make earthen barricades (revetments), and bamboo-framed baskets were used to deliver goods by parachute. Field hospitals used bamboo to devise shelters, platforms, beds, showers, latrines, orthopedic tables, and framing for surgical pavilions; split bamboo poles and balsawood were used to make litters.[22]

Army engineers produced thousands of grenades from hollow bamboo stems cut into sections and packed with dynamite and improvised shrapnel.[23] In the Philippines, U.S. troops encountered a similar sort of explosive made by the Japanese, so-called Bangalore torpedoes, tubular mines crafted from bamboo shoots.[24] During the Philippines campaign of 1941–42, hollow bamboo pieces were used as "envelopes" to airdrop General Morioka's orders to soldiers trapped at Silaiim that they should retreat from the beachhead by any means possible, even by swimming.[25] The Chinese prevented some damage to public buildings by constructing bamboo scaffolding designed to catch Japanese bombs before they landed and detonated. In northern Burma, the Chinese Army devised a bamboo bridge across the Shweli River, an engineering feat that U.S. engineers maintained for use by American infantry.[26]

Facing equipment shortages, Japanese troops assembled dummy airplanes from bamboo poles and wooden boards, which appeared realistic when seen from the skies. Many soldiers had only sharpened bamboo poles as weapons and retreated to bamboo thickets that served as natural forts (see Chapter 11). The Kachin rangers (from northern Burma) who fought with the Allies crafted *pungyi* sticks from bamboo poles that they sharpened, hardened in fire, and then pushed into the ground under dense foliage. Japanese soldiers frightened by Allied gunfire ran into the forest and impaled themselves on the *pungyi* points.[27] Meanwhile, as the end of the Pacific war approached, Japanese women practiced with bamboo spears and dummy wooden rifles to defend the Japanese home islands from an Allied invasion.

Hedgerows

The European landscape was dissected by hedgerows, densely planted with shrubs and trees that separated adjacent fields, defined land boundaries, and served as natural fences for grazing livestock. In Normandy, the landscape comprising fields and hedgerows was known

Bamboo was used for construction during combat. Impregnated with lignin and silica, the stems are lightweight, strong, and flexible, ideal for building shelters, earthen barricades (revetments), latrines, and the framing for outdoor surgical pavilions. Split bamboo poles were used to make litters.

as *bocage* (derived from the Anglo-Norman word *boscage* and *bosc*, the old French word for wood). Although manmade, the hedgerows developed a unique ecology and species diversity as plants and animals naturalized into the habitats. Throughout the *bocage* landscape of Normandy, woody plants rooted in the earthen berm surrounding each field, each with a rocky core of excavated stones. The largest berms were soil embankments about fifteen feet high and four feet wide, and vegetation added several more feet to the height of the hedgerow. Typical species in Normandy hedgerows included English oak (*Quercus pendunculata*), sweet chestnut (*Castanea sativa*), common hazel (*Corylus avellana*), hawthorn (*Crataegus monogyna*), sloe (*Prunus spinosa*), wild service tree (*Sorbus terminalis*), and holly (*Ilex aquifolium*). Although originally intended as boundaries, hedges provided both firewood and food. Edible fruits included some of the same wild foods that were foraged in England during the war years (see Chapter 4).

The *bocage* landscape dictated Allied and German strategies during the Battle of Normandy during the summer of 1944. With successive plowing, the hedges became higher than the fields they surrounded, and sunken lanes ran between adjacent hedgerows, probably the result of erosion from water flow and local traffic. Branches and foliage often overarched the sunken lanes, creating cave-like shaded sites for snipers and small anti-tank weapons. During the four years that they had occupied Normandy, German troops converted hedgerows into natural fortresses, keeping most of the dense woody vegetation untrimmed to obscure views of the landscape and lines of fire. The agricultural fields and orchards enclosed by hedgerows provided concealment and served as natural camouflage for German artillery and snipers. Openings were cut only to allow observation and gunfire, and field officers used wired field telephones to communicate.[28]

The *bocage* landscape of Normandy was defined by dense hedgerows surrounding agricultural fields; woody plants rooted in the earthen berm surrounding each field. German troops converted hedgerows into natural fortresses, keeping woody vegetation untrimmed to obscure lines of fire and to camouflage German artillery and snipers (U.S. Army).

It was difficult if not impossible to detect the precise source of enemy fire from within a hedgerow. Thus fields became fortifications protected by the earthen and rock berms and dense living hedges. Horizontal trenches and tunnels cut into the soil provided protection during artillery and mortar attacks; roots held the soil in place so several German soldiers could safely shelter and survive by excavating under a hedgerow. While English and Canadian troops knew of hedgerows from home, the *bocage* landscape was entirely foreign to most U.S. troops. The maze of green hedges was disorienting, so some tank crews assigned one member to serve as navigator. The *bocage* environment was so unique that Allied troops learned largely by trial and error the tactical strategies for fighting in the hedgerow-lined fields that had become German fortifications. The dissected landscape also interfered with the landing of the wooden gliders used to transport Allied soldiers and matériel.[29]

The *bocage* region of France was a mosaic of small fields, orchards, and hedgerows, which limited the use of tanks. From one aerial photograph, one representative section of Normandy revealed nearly four thousand hedgerow-enclosed fields in an area eight miles square.[30] Visibility was limited to a few hundred yards, and German mines were buried in the hedgerows. Local roads were bound by hedges, and lower regions of the landscape were often muddy, a situation that worsened with high rainfall during the spring and summer of 1944. Rain storms also limited the use of air power during the summer of 1944 hedgerow battles. Tank tactics required the ability to maneuver in difficult terrain with minimal visibility, while taking fire from German troops who bivouacked within the protected fields. Penetration and attack through the hedgerows was physically difficult and required new tank technologies for success.

The Allies repurposed numerous anti-tank obstacles in Normandy as a line of defense against German tanks. Known colloquially as Czech hedgehogs, these static three-dimensional structures were made from metal beams or timber, such as chestnut railroad ties, and tanks maneuvered around them. However, an ingenious solution to hedgerow assault repurposed metal from Czech hedgehogs into sets of five horizontal teeth that were welded onto tanks. Eventually the metal attachments were mass-produced to modify Sherman tanks battling in the *bocage* landscape, and those fitted with these welded metal "tusks" became known as rhino tanks. The attachments sliced through hedgerows and woody roots, making openings in the dense vegetation that were essential to moving tanks, troops, and artillery across the fields and orchards bordered by the complex hedge system. There were a variety of anti-hedge devices developed by Army ordnance units, including various prong and fork-like attachments for tanks, although dense hedgerows required dynamite to make an initial opening in the ancient woody growth.[31]

Forest combat was difficult and dangerous, particularly in the Hürtgen forest (*Hürtgenwald*), about fifty square miles of densely planted woodlands along the Roer River near the Belgian border. After penetrating the Siegfried line, U.S. troops reached the coniferous forest in the fall of 1944, where they discovered the wet valleys and steep hillsides of the of Hürtgen forest. In the months preceding the Battle of the Bulge, German forces defended the region vigorously by exploiting the forested environment to defeat the Allies' offensive.

The terrain was naturally rough and sodden, punctuated by swamps and gorges that became snow-covered as winter approached. Prior to the arrival of the Allies, German troops had constructed heavy log bunkers, buried mines (including *Schützenmine*,

In the Hürtgen forest, German troops timed artillery shells to detonate in the tree canopy, exploiting softwood anatomy to weaponize conifers into lethal shards. Tree bursts were a major factor in the Allied defeat and 33,000 casualties in the Hürtgen Forest in late 1944, considered by historians the longest battle ever fought by the U.S. military (U.S. National Archives).

shoe-mines in undetectable wooden boxes) in the forest floor, and felled trees to block the few winding roads. Tank use was limited in the forested landscape, so most U.S. forces fought in the open, but many were inexperienced with combat in a cold, rugged environment. From their log bunkers, German troops timed their artillery shells to detonate in the tree canopy, resulting in tree bursts that exploded conifer timber into sharp splinters. *Life* magazine described "close-ranked firs towering 75 to 100 feet … evil with whining bullets and bursting shells that leave broken trees and broken men in tangled fraternity…[mortars] bursting in the trees to shatter jagged fragments for yards around"[32] Thus the standard military practice of lying on the ground during an artillery attack was dangerous during a tree burst, when the best survival strategy involved standing flat against a tree trunk to avoid the penetrating shards.

The anatomy of conifer wood reveals why the trees became airborne daggers. At a cellular level, softwoods lack fibers, the elongated cells that lend strength and flexibility to hardwoods. Thus firs, pines, spruces, and other conifers have wood that is relatively brittle and that separates easily into shards upon impact. German forces exploited softwood anatomy to weaponize conifers; tree bursts were a major factor in the Allied defeat and 33,000 casualties in the Hürtgen Forest between September 19 and December 16,

1944, considered by historians the longest battle ever fought by the U.S. military. During the Battle of the Bulge that followed, Allied forces in the Ardennes region used conifers to their own advantage by strafing and dropping napalm on forests marked by German tank tracks in the surrounding snow. The conifers caught fire quickly due to their resin content, forcing German troops from their hiding places.

Construction, Boats, Airplanes and Plywood

Expeditionary forces during World War II needed vast amounts of wood in the field, more tonnage than any other commodity, for military housing and other buildings and for reconstructing damaged bridges and railways. Lumber was locally sourced by forestry companies that supplied troops with needed timber. Within a few days of arriving in Normandy after the D-Day landings, Canadian foresters set up saw mills, and within months they were joined by forestry companies from the U.S. and England. The Canadian and British forestry companies preferred felling the trees by hand with an axe and saw rather than with chain saws, but all Allied forestry companies had to adapt their techniques to various European tree species and sizes. The dense wood of ancient beech trees posed a particular challenge to the Canadians who had been felling pines in Scotland.

Shrapnel posed a significant problem. For instance, fighting in the Reichswald area of Germany resulted in so much embedded metal in forest trees that shards often broke the teeth of saw mill blades, and a similar situation occurred in northern Italy. Metal encased in dense wood was difficult to detect, and so timber from such areas was left for handling by firewood brigades, which were staffed by prisoners of war. Mines were another ongoing hazard for foresters felling local timber. In the Ardennes forest, German anti-personnel mines were difficult to detect in the dense undergrowth, and civilian helpers hesitated to enter forests that had not been cleared of mines. No wood was wasted; conifer branches were wired into bundles to use in filling bomb craters, and stumps and roots were excavated and split into firewood.[33]

Forestry companies in the Pacific theater encountered high biodiversity of tree species with an equally wide range of wood characteristics. Relatively little was known outside of the region with regard to uses of particular species, so the botany of specific tropical families became strategically essential. Choice of the incorrect wood for various uses, from telephone poles to marine pilings, could result in microbial decay, worm attacks, or timber that was impossibly dense or resinous for sawmills to handle. Botanists at the Arnold Arboretum of Harvard University pooled their knowledge and resources, and based on monographs and wood research, lists were prepared of native trees with potential uses in construction. The U.S. Navy dispatched an artist to prepare lifelike tree illustrations based on dried herbarium specimens of useful timber plants. Botanists also supplied the military with photographs of the scenery and vegetation of Papua New Guinea, the Solomon Islands, China, Japan, Formosa, and other areas where combat seemed likely.[34]

In July 1944, Australian botanists held a forest botany school in Papua New Guinea, which included lectures and field work on Pacific timber. Trial and error resulted in improved knowledge of useful local timber, including the trees to avoid because wood with a high incidence of druses (microscopic calcium oxalate crystals) dulled saw blades. Foliage of unknown trees was dried in plant presses heated over open fires or preserved in formalin for future identification. Local people contributed knowledge of wood uses and tree names in local languages and pidgin English. As a result of the compiled knowledge, Australian troops received voucher specimens, wood samples, and identification notes so that they could immediately identify useful timber in the field. One major need was the rebuilding of the pier for Liberty ships landing at Lae, an essential port for shipments of matériel. U.S. engineers built the original structure using wood from *Syncarpia glomulifera*, native to Queensland forests and supposedly resistant to marine invertebrates; however, the submerged timbers attracted marine worms and collapsed in a few months. The pier was rebuilt with resistant timber from local species in the family Dipterocarpaceae, rainforest trees known for producing buttressed roots and excellent hardwood.[35]

Plywood was particularly essential for wartime construction. Manufactured from thin wood veneers with their wood grain oriented at right angles, plywood had greater strength than a comparable thickness of lumber. It was used in military buildings, boats, and airplanes and soon became an essential war material with strict guidelines for its manufacture and use. The idea of laminated wood originated in the nineteenth century, but biological glues (such as those made from casein and albumin) were neither antimicrobial nor waterproof. Even a waxy sorghum variety (*Sorghum bicolor*) from China originally cultivated as a tapioca substitute was investigated as a possible plywood adhesive (see Chapter 4). Adhesives made from soybean by-products (see Chapter 6) were supposedly waterproof, but until phenolic resins were developed in the 1930s, plywood often deteriorated. Plywood made with these synthetic adhesives could be used outdoors or in water with no concern for weathering or separation of the veneers. The process of lamination required heat and pressure, and the resin was often stronger than the wood itself. The standard wood was Douglas fir (*Pseudostuga menziesii*), but hardwoods such as mahogany, birch, poplar, and basswood were used in making aviation plywood, which had to tolerate sheering forces and extreme temperatures. Metal and wood were often used side by side; for instance, German V-1 rockets had plywood wings affixed to a steel fuselage. Cardboard sirens made from wood pulp were affixed to the metal wings of Junkers Ju 87 (*Stuka*) airplanes and also to the bombs that they dropped on the Netherlands and France. The sirens instilled terror among civilian populations, and cardboard was a cheap substitute for metal.

Typical plywood had three or five layers, but boards made from seven to thirteen layers were stronger and more durable. Odd numbers of layers were the rule, so that the xylem cells (wood grain) in the upper and lower layers were oriented in the same direction. Experimentation revealed that plywood made from an uneven number of layers tended not to warp, and boards made from multiple thin layers could be bent in all directions without splitting, making them ideal for molding not only fuselages and hulls but also medical devices.

Working for the U.S. Navy, Charles and Ray Eames (later known for their eponymous modern chair designs) developed litters and splints for injured servicemen who required transport to field hospitals. Prototypes were fashioned using a homemade plywood-molding machine, work done in the evenings after Charles Eames finished his work as a set designer for MGM, working on films that included the wartime drama "Mrs. Miniver." The Eames' plywood litters and splints were durable, form-fitting, and safer than older methods; troops often improvised litters from blankets and bamboo poles, cots, or ladders, and the standard splints were made from basswood boards.[36] After the initial order for 5,000 splints in late 1942, the couple formed the Plyform Wood Company in California to produce thousands of plywood litters, splints, and airplane and glider components.

Other plywood uses included construction of hangars for the naval blimps that patrolled the U.S. coasts. The hangars were prefabricated from plywood, and even the arches were made from laminated wood. After the sections were assembled, the completed hangars were 1,000 feet long and sixteen stories high, requiring the wood needed for 250 typical houses. Thousands of wartime barracks and houses were also prefabricated from plywood and erected on the spot.[37] Although largely fabricated from metal, Quonset huts also made use of plywood in their design. These archetypal military buildings were an improvement on the prefabricated Nissen huts of World War I; they were open, general purpose buildings that could be used for used for virtually any military purpose, including barracks, offices, chapels, kitchens, latrines, and infirmaries.

THE ARMY & NAVY NEED 156,000,000 BOARD FEET A YEAR FOR HANGARS

Vast amounts of timber were needed to construct military structures, including plywood hangars for airplanes and blimps. Thousands of barracks and houses were also prefabricated from plywood and erected on the spot (U.S. War Department).

Named for Quonset Point (near the Davisville Naval Construction Battalion in Rhode Island), some huts were repurposed as college dormitories for returning veterans after the war.

During World War II independent contractors manufactured over 150,000 Quonset huts from sheets of galvanized steel curved into a semi-circular silhouette. The ends of the huts were made from plywood, and the completed structures were insulated with a lining of pressed wood. Steel construction was suited to temperate areas, but standard Quonset huts rusted in the tropics and retained cold in the Arctic. An all-wood version of the Quonset hut was designed with framework made of spruce or hemlock, sheathed with boards of waterproofed pressed wood, and outfitted with plywood floors. The prefabricated wooden huts took a few hours to erect, and they were lighter to ship, easier to insulate from the cold, and conserved tons of steel, a critical war material.

Aircraft design required aviation-grade plywood that could withstand the stresses of pressure changes, turbulence, sheering forces, and temperature extremes. Hardwood veneers (typically mahogany, birch, poplar, and basswood) were used to make the boards, which were tested following standards established by Germanischer Lloyd, an independent

Mosquito bombers were assembled by the de Havilland Aircraft Company Limited. The fuselage was made of imported wood, veneers of Ecuadorian balsawood alternating with Canadian birch. The unique plywood was molded over a concrete or mahogany form, utilizing the traditional *monocoque* method of a frameless shell; internal bulkheads made of spruce blocks and plywood provided additional strength (Royal Air Force).

technical agency in Hamburg, Germany. Batches of aviation plywood were screened for physical defects in wood grain, tensile and shearing strength, torsion, and strength following prolonged soaking or boiling.[38]

Known as the Wooden Wonder, Mosquito bombers were assembled by the de Havilland Aircraft Company Limited in fulfillment of a contract with the British Air Ministry. F. Wrighton and Sons, Ltd., a furniture manufacturer, manufactured both utility furniture for bombing victims and the wooden components of Mosquito bombers and other aircraft. The fuselage was made of imported wood, veneers of Ecuadorian balsawood alternating with Canadian birch. Native to tropical forests of South America, balsa trees (*Ochroma pyridale*) produce low density wood with numerous soft-walled parenchyma cells. It has a specific gravity = 0.12 (the lowest of commercial timbers) and so served as low-weight filler layers for the plywood comprising the fuselage. The unique plywood was molded over a concrete or mahogany form, utilizing the traditional *monocoque* method of a frameless shell; internal bulkheads made of spruce blocks and plywood provided additional strength. The wings were made from ribs of plywood and spruce, covered with madapolam (a densely woven cotton cloth) and lacquered with dope made of highly flammable nitrocellulose or other cellulose-based compounds (see Chapter 8), followed by camouflage paint. An advantage of wood construction was that the planes were barely detected by radar, but a downside of the design was the heavy dependence on glue that may have been affected by tropical climates. Wet conditions caused warping of wood, and ubiquitous tropical insects ate the glue between the plywood veneers. Far East monsoons and torrid heat were possible climatic factors in several crashes of these wooden bombers late in the war.

Late in the war, the German bomber known as the Heinkel He 162 *Volksjäger* was also made largely of wood, a cheap aircraft design that was quickly and easily assembled by semi-skilled and slave workers. Known informally as the *Salamander* (perhaps to hearten pilots by the mythological ability of salamanders to survive fire), its wooden sections including the frame, nose cone, and wings were manufactured by German furniture factories. Plywood problems caused crashes of the first Heinkel He 162 prototypes. Following the bombing of the Goldschmidt Tego Film factory that manufactured plywood adhesive, a highly acidic glue substitute caused wood to deteriorate and delaminate, but the Heinkel He 162 program continued until the end of the war with pilots trained in the Hitler Youth.

As the Allies moved closer to the Japanese home islands toward the end of the Pacific war, the Japanese military resorted to crashing explosive-laden airplanes into enemy ships. Their *kamikaze* airplanes were cheaply designed for one-way suicide missions by a single pilot. By the end of the war, the planes had simple wooden frames that were strong enough to carry bombs or torpedoes (sometimes just a full load of fuel), causing damage to the wooden decks of U.S. carriers. Some *kamikaze* pilots adopted cherry flowers (*yamazakura*) as their symbol; there have also been recent claims that some *kamikaze* attack flowers (*tokkobana*) were actually composites (species in the Asteraceae, in particular *Gaillardia* spp.) native to North and South America but naturalized in areas of Japan. The *Nakajima Ki-115* was a wood-framed airplane developed at the end of the war and known as *toka* (wisteria flower), but the planes were never used in combat. Some Japanese torpedoes also utilized wood; the Imperial Japanese Navy used type 91 aerial torpedoes equipped with *kyoban*, box-like wood covers designed to fall away upon impact with water. The design made the tailfins more aerodynamic after the torpedo was dropped from an airplane.

Engineless aircraft, such as the Waco gliders used in the Normandy invasion to carry troops and matériel, could carry loads that included jeeps and howitzers. These one-way aircraft were constructed from a tubular metal frame with a plywood floor and canvas covering; wood and cloth saved weight and were more expendable than metal. Gliders were towed by airplanes and then released, relying only on expert piloting and prevailing winds for flight. To prevent gliders from landing safely, German troops felled small trees and used the logs wired with explosives (known as Rommel's asparagus, see Chapter 4) as a defense system in Normandy fields. Field Marshal Erwin Rommel ordered troops to install over one million of these vertical logs to interfere with Allied gliders and paratroopers during an invasion. This strategy was effective in destroying at least one of the large wooden Hamilcar gliders that carried tanks and anti-aircraft guns for British airborne troops in the invasions of France, Belgium, and the Rhine region of Germany.

Gliders were effective when used, but production was hampered by wood shortages (spruce and birch) and the lack of sufficient airfield space for assembly and storage. In a plan to escape from captivity in Colditz Castle, British prisoners of war constructed a small glider from beech bed slats and scrounged wood, relying on texts in the prison library for engineering design and aeronautical physics. In place of canvas, cotton bedding sheathed the frame, made airtight with a dope mixture of millet grains (small-seeded edible grasses) simmered in water. The planned escape involved launching the glider from the chapel roof and navigating it across the River Mulde, but Allied troops liberated the prisoners before it was put in motion.[39]

Teak (*Tectona grandis*) was a critical material because its natural oils make even the unvarnished wood water resistant, and the wood resists cracking even under variable moisture conditions. The species is an arboreal member of the mint family (Lamiaceae) that can grow to 130 feet in height, and like other mints, teak trees synthesize terpenoids that resist microbial attack. Working in the monsoon conditions and rugged terrain of India and Burma (now Myanmar), the Army Signal Corps used local teak logs for telephone poles.[40] The trees thrived in the high rainfall conditions of Burma (Myanmar), and the Japanese acquired vast teak resources when they occupied the region. Teak had long been the wood of choice for decking on aircraft carriers, but much of the supply ended with Japanese takeover of the forests which provided probably half of all teak timber worldwide. In nearby Thailand, disputes arose between British companies and Japanese occupiers about ownership of teak logs harvested for local sawmills. Botanists at the U.S. Naval Research Laboratory, a wood testing facility at the naval yard in Philadelphia, investigated various wood types for resistance to decay, warping, cracking, and marine borers. Douglas fir (*Pseudotsuga menziesii*) was an available alternative source for decking in aircraft carriers, and it was also used in other boats and ships.

Known informally as the splinter fleet, small submarine chasers (110 feet long, in comparison to the larger steel subchasers) were built from planks of various conifers, often depending on availability. The hulls were typically constructed from long leaf yellow pine (*Pinus palustris*), with decking of white pine (*P. strobus*) and Douglas fir. Masts to hold radar equipment were made from Sitka spruce (*Picea sitchensis*).[41] In 1938, the U.S. Navy sponsored a challenge for various designs of patrol torpedo (PT) boats that were vetted in a "plywood derby." The goal was to develop highly mobile attack boats that could easily be manufactured at several plants using accessible materials, and the typical construction was hastened by pre-molding plywood into sections before assembly. The amphibious LCVP (landing craft vehicle personnel) boats manufactured by Higgins Industries were also largely plywood craft; their unique construction was visible in an "x-ray boat" (a complete boat on one side with a cut-away view on the reverse) that toured as part of the Salute to Wood program organized by the U.S. War Department. First launched on Lake Ponchartrain in Louisiana, the Higgins boats were known for their role in the D-Day landings and Normandy invasion. In contrast, British troops relied widely on collapsible boats built with a cedar slat floor, plywood bottom and stern, and canvas sides. Known as Goatley boats (the designer was Fred Goatley of Saunders-Roe Ltd.), they could be used variously as pontoons for bridges, as rafts, and as lightweight boats that could carry ten men. Early models were equipped with wooden paddles, while later Goatley boats were outfitted with motors.

Recently released CIA information reveals two small wooden submarine prototypes constructed specifically for the possible invasion of the Japanese home islands in the fall of 1945. Code-named "Gimik," the boats were designed to transport cooperating Korean prisoners-of-war to Japan, where they would infiltrate and collect intelligence prior to full scale invasion. The submarines each had a plywood hull that enclosed a watertight steel compartment for a three-man crew and were most likely made by John Trumpy and Sons in Camden, New Jersey. The firm built yachts and had a reputation for excellent workmanship in wooden boat construction. Teams practiced undetected landings with the wooden submarines along the southern California coastline. The plan was to transport the small boats on conventional submarines for release within one hundred miles of the Japanese coastline, an invasion rendered unnecessary by the Japanese surrender on August 15, 1945.[42]

In freezing conditions, wood and ice were used together in construction. During the winter of 1941–42, the German military constructed an ice and wood railway bridge across the Dnieper River near Kiev as a means to deliver supplies to the German Sixth Army by train. Local Ukrainians had successfully built ice bridges in the past, but a bridge large enough to support a train required structural reinforcement with wood. Working on top of the frozen river, Ukrainian laborers placed two layers of ice blocks, which were then flooded and frozen in place. On top of this embankment, two double rows of oak and pine logs functioned as reinforcing beams immobilized in ice; the railway tracks and ties were the final layer. The ice and wood structure was about five feet thick and could support an engine and train that weighed 120 tons. It remained in use by the German Sixth Army through the winter months of early 1942.[43]

With the loss of ships in the Atlantic, by 1942 Lord Louis Mountbatten and Winston Churchill became intrigued by the possibility of building unsinkable aircraft carriers from ice. As Chief of Combined Operations, Mountbatten had encouraged ideas for offensive operations, which resulted in the proposal to freeze carriers of solid ice that could serve as takeoff and landing points for airplanes protecting ships and for the refueling of cargo planes. The project was named Habbakuk (for an Old Testament prophet), and options were considered for construction of a prototype, including additives that might add tensile strength to ice made from water alone. An idea came from basic research on the behavior of wood cellulose in water, investigations conducted by Herman Mark, a former Kaiser Wilhelm Institute chemist and research director at I.G. Farben; he had fled the Nazi regime for the U.S. and worked as a polymer chemist during the war years. Mark's research included experiments with combinations of a slurry of wood

With the loss of ships in the Atlantic, by 1942 Lord Louis Mountbatten and Winston Churchill considered building unsinkable aircraft carriers from ice. Investigations led to the development of pykrete, a frozen slurry of wood or paper pulp and water. A model sixty feet in length was built on a lake in Alberta, Canada, but the project ended due to its high cost and the availability of other strategies to protect shipping lanes (National Research Council Canada).

pulp and water to produce reinforced forms of ice, investigations that led to the development of a composite building material made from wood or paper pulp (about 14 percent) combined with 86 percent water (by weight) and frozen into a solid. The mixture was known as pykrete, named for Geoffrey Pyke, a scientific advisor to Mountbatten.

Plans were made for a Habbakuk carrier 2,000' in length. To begin, a scaled down model sixty feet in length was built on a lake in Alberta, Canada, but it soon became apparent that the design required a large quantity of steel for internal reinforcement to prevent deformation of the pykrete mass. U.S. support for the planned carriers was lukewarm at best, and American steel would be needed for their construction. The Habbakuk project ended due to its cost, which would have run into millions of pounds, and the availability of other strategies to protect shipping lanes. More escort carriers were built to travel with convoys, and airplanes were equipped with larger fuel tanks, which allowed longer flights into the Atlantic.

Paper, Books and Balloons

Since the mid-nineteenth century, paper has been made from conifers using a process in which chemical and mechanical means convert wood into pulp, a slurry of wood cells in water. The macerated xylem is then rolled into thin sheets and dried. During World War II the military needed paper for over 2,800 items, from plasma containers to cartridge boxes. The primary source of pulpwood was spruce (*Picea* spp.), which has relatively high cellulose content and less resin than other conifers, and most wartime paper was made from spruce wood. However, pine, eastern hemlock, larch, and balsam fir were also used for paper production, particularly in northern New England where German prisoners of war labored to cut pulpwood for the mills of the Brown Paper Company in Berlin, New Hampshire.

Pulpwood for paper mills was long considered a renewable resource, but U.S. wartime demands outstripped available natural timber; more than 90 percent of timber forests grew on land controlled by private owners who could saw down their trees at will. Clear-cutting of forests was a traditional practice in some areas of the country, particularly the southern states where the building of new pulpwood mills stimulated overcutting of woodlots and natural forests. Scientists involved in managed forestry advocated selective cutting to keep growing stock in place and to provide seeds for germination and new seedlings, but their advice was often ignored. Even the ratio of surface area to volume recommended leaving small trees standing; it took twice as long to cut and peel saplings versus mature trees to obtain an equivalent amount of wood pulp, but nevertheless entire forests (mostly spruce) were leveled to print wartime newspapers.[44]

The U.S. War Production Board rationed paper and controlled details such as the size and margins of book pages. Paper drives organized by school children and Scouts were standard practice during the war years, often coupled with the collection of metals, rubber, and rags. Boy Scouts participated in the General Eisenhower Waste Paper Campaign of 1945, contributing 300,000 tons of paper for re-pulping; each boy who collected a thousand pounds of waste paper received a war service medal for his efforts. Civilians were urged to bundle (rather than burn) cardboard, waste paper, old magazines, and newspapers for recycling back into wood pulp, and similar shortages existed abroad. Campaign slogans were aimed at Axis enemies, including "Slap the Jap with Scrap" and

"Hit Hitler with Junk." Paper was conserved and reused, but disposable tissues were allowed; a 1942 advertisement encouraged civilians to, "Be patriotic and smother sneezes with Kleenex to help keep colds from spreading to war workers…. When half size will do, tear Kleenex in two." However, paper shortages curtailed production, so by 1944 advertisements reminded consumers that "paper, too, has a wartime job … and that's why there's not enough Kleenex Tissues to go around."

In England, wrapping paper for parcels had already dwindled and disappeared for the duration of the war; a 1940 Pathé newsreel showed a local butcher's sign that requested "Will Customers Please Bring Their Own Paper." The Ministry of Production assumed control of paper by 1942; newspapers and magazines were limited to 60 percent of their pre-war paper allocation, and then the old newspapers were saved for insulating beds in public shelters or collected for conversion back into wood pulp to make more paper. Newspapers such as *The Times* and *Daily Telegraph* were no more than eight pages long, with much of the content from the Ministry of Information. Salvaging paper was mandatory, and a common poster warned, "Any person burning or destroying waste paper is guilty of an offence against the national war effort." Envelopes were routinely reused, and stationers encouraged writing on both sides of the paper with small penmanship and narrow margins. Posters reminded civilians, "Tramcar tickets, paper bags, Old newspapers, label tags, Magazines and old school jotters, Cardboard packets, finished blotters—Save all the paper waste you can, And give it to the salvage man."[45] Only paper that might transmit communicable diseases was discarded as unsafe. Home and garden magazines recommended starting fires with dried plant matter such as fir cones, leaves, or bracken fronds rather than paper. Old rags were collected for making heavy duty paper such as charts for submarine navigation. Despite tight paper rationing, vast numbers of government pamphlets were published during the war years, with advice on all aspects of wartime life, including cookery, air raids, and the evacuation of children to the countryside.

Wherever possible, paper or cardboard (a thicker grade of paper sometimes also known as paperboard) replaced the metal needed for airplanes and tanks. Packaging of foods such as spices and shortening converted to paper and cardboard containers. In England, jars of preserved fruit were sealed with parchment paper and glue rather than metal lids (see Chapter 3). Cardboard (probably from made recycled paper) was used to make shell housings and waxed boxes for the Carlisle bandages used as field dressings for infantry. The U.S. Navy and Army Air Force used cardboard to make thousands of airplane models, including German and Japanese designs used in training troops to recognize silhouettes. Wartime wood shortages meant that even coffins included some cardboard in their construction. Nevertheless War Department policy was clear that crosses and stars of David must be constructed from wood as temporary grave markers in the event of isolated burials abroad; military manuals specified the style and dimensions of the wooden markers.[46]

A comparatively stronger type of paper was made using the Kraft process, in which most of the lignin was removed, with hydrogen bonds among cellulose molecules that strengthened the final product. As a substitute for wooden boxes, the Quartermaster Corps used Kraft paper combined with sisal fibers (see Chapter 8) to invent durable V-containers for shipping rations intact into the Pacific theater, preventing extensive loss and waste.[47] To conserve metal, aviation engineers in England even developed fuel tanks made of Kraft paper coated with glue; they were shaped around a cylindrical mold, outfitted with interior wooden baffles, and coated with cellulose-based dope. Sometime referred to as papier-mâché, the containers were designed as single-use drop tanks to be filled before flights and jettisoned prior to landing. The paper fuel tanks were sufficiently waterproof and resilient to alleviate the problem of carrying sufficient fuel on long flights, and when dropped they kept metal out of the hands of Axis countries.

In England, paper was essential to managing blackouts and surviving bombing raids. Incendiary bombs posed significant danger, so householders were advised to remove paper and other flammable items from attics. Conical lampshades were assembled from cardboard and used to direct light downward and away from windows and curtains, and windows were prevented from splintering by applying gummed strips of heavy paper. These could be applied in various decorative patterns, as suggested by household manuals and articles on coping in wartime; brown wrapping paper and flour paste could be used in an emergency.

Various commercial products promised protection from flying glass, but the use of transparent sheets of highly flammable cellulose nitrate was officially discouraged. Known as guncotton, it was used in making celluloid photographic films and explosives and was potentially dangerous during bombing conditions. As in Germany where bales of paper were used to surround unexploded bombs, the Ministry of Home Security noted that books provided protection from bomb splinters and thus suggested blocking windows with bookcases. The Japanese used tatami mats woven from rice straw (see Chapter 4) to bomb-proof windows; fearing gas attacks, they used cellophane (made from cellulose-containing plant cell walls, see Chapter 3) to seal rooms.[48]

Paper shortages affected book publishers, who instituted smaller book dimensions, page margins, and type face. Page count and print runs also decreased, and books were printed on lesser grades of paper. Similar shortages existed abroad and affected the availability of books. In England, the National Federation of Retail Newsagents, Booksellers, and Stationers advised customers: "Notice to the Reading Public—Shortage of Paper." Some books were available, and customers were advised to shop early in bookshops for wartime Christmas presents. In 1941, publishers noted a particular interest in books about the Soviet Union, one of the Allies, focusing on Russian history, the Communist party, and battles with Germany.

As training camps opened for new recruits, books for the military became a national concern. The American Library Association, United Service Organizations (USO), and Red Cross joined together to sponsor the Victory Book Campaign, which sought to collect and ship thousands of suitable titles to servicemen worldwide. They aimed for popular fiction (mysteries, westerns, adventure stories, and various best-sellers were most popular) and non-fiction books on technical topics including radio, architecture, aeronautics, and navigation. Guidelines stipulated that the books should not predate 1930 and should be of interest to young men. The goals were to boost military morale, to educate and improve, and to fill the empty hours away from home, as well as to keep men busy, away from local temptations, and involved instead in recreational reading. Posters asked donors to "Give more good books to our men in the armed services" and to bring donations to their local library. Congress also allocated funds to establish libraries at camps, posts, and other military installations.

The Council on Books in Wartime included authors, librarians, and publishers and promoted their motto that "books are weapons in the war of ideas." They worked with the Office of War Information to disseminate books about Axis countries, technical texts, and recreational reading, with the goals of encouraging peace, maintaining morale, and winning the war. However, their most significant project involved publishing the Armed Services Editions (1943–1947), books printed on magazine presses with reduced dimensions (about 4 × 6 inches), paper covers, and cheap paper.

Armed Services Edition books were designed to fit in uniform pockets. The small format also saved paper, a prudent strategy because 123 million copies of 1,322 titles were printed. Most titles were unabridged and included virtually all genres, from classics, poetry, and drama to current novels, science texts, and theology. The first sets of thirty titles were shipped overseas in wooden boxes, and the plan was to provide a new set each month for each 150 men on active duty. Books were also distributed to isolated units regardless of size and to hospitals, and individual books were handed out to troops traveling to Normandy for the D-Day invasion.[49] One of the most popular novels among the Armed Service Editions was *A Tree Grows in Brooklyn* by Betty Smith, a coming-of-age novel with a young female protagonist; the title refers to the tree of heaven (*Ailanthus altissima*), a fast-growing and resilient Chinese species that colonizes urban areas and serves in the novel as a metaphor for survival and overcoming adversity.

The Council on Books and Office of War Information collaborated again to disseminate books in European countries then occupied by the Axis. Titles were selected in the U.S. and translated into other languages; the plan was to dispel totalitarian thinking and to forge relationships with the U.S. using books that portrayed a positive view of American values, democracy, and the future of postwar Europe. Despite the tricky logistics of shipment, crates of books arrived in Normandy along with military supplies, and they were sent to local bookstores to sell. However, in occupied Japan and Germany civilians were too poor to buy books, and severe shortages of food and other essentials hampered the marketplace. Nevertheless in the U.S., 379,000 interned German prisoners of war were another ready audience for literature aimed at rehabilitation. Anti-totalitarian authors including Erich Marie Remarque and Thomas Mann were published in new editions, and German translations were prepared of Hemingway's *For Whom the Bell Tolls* and other works.

Paper served some remarkably unique military uses. German engineers designed electrical condensers made of paper coated with a thin zinc layer. They were cheap to manufacture, durable, and essential to both radio and radar technology.[50] Metal-coated paper could also be used to disrupt radar, an independent discovery in Germany, England, and the U.S. The material was known variously as chaff (U.S), window (England), and *Düppel* (Germany, named for the area in Berlin where it was invented) and consisted of black paper with a single layer of aluminum foil. Earlier plans had envisioned full-size sheets with propaganda leaflets printed on the reverse side, but dark paper cut into narrow strips was apparently more effective.

Bombers carried bales of the foil-clad strips and tossed them out en route to the target. The technical effect was a visual blizzard on enemy radar screens, which decreased the likelihood that incoming bombers would be detected and attacked. Chaff played a significant role in the attack on Hamburg in July 1943, the firebombing raids known as Operation Gomorrah. Until that point, Germany had not blocked Allied radar with *Düppel*, but they attempted to use it during the bombing of London in the fall of 1943. The retaliation did not work because the German bombers were detected by English night-fighter aircraft. With cycles of bombing and retaliation, chaff became common litter. In England, civilians collected the shiny strips and used them to make Christmas decorations, and no doubt chaff was recycled into munitions. After the holidays, salvage drives collected any sort of scrap paper from crackers or parcels for manufacturing cartridges, the outer coverings of bullets.

During the last winter of the war (between November 1944 and April 1945), Japan manufactured and released 9,300 balloons to carry incendiary bombs across the Pacific toward North America. The Japanese navy developed balloons of rubberized silk cloth, but paper quickly prevailed as an alternative to using silk and rubber, both critical materials in wartime. Strong winds at 30,000 feet (now known as the jet stream) carried the balloons across 6,200 miles of ocean in just three days, where they landed as far east as Michigan and Manitoba. The balloons were designed to set fires, particularly in the dense forests of the Pacific Northwest, but also on farms and in cities and suburbs.

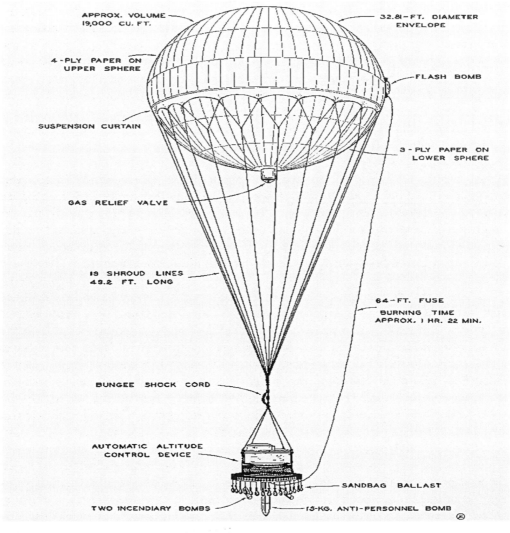

During the last winter of the war, Japan released 9,300 balloons carrying incendiary bombs across the Pacific toward North America, with the goal of causing forest fires and widespread panic. Japanese school girls assembled the balloons from botanical materials, including paper made from a native shrub and paste made from aroid rhizomes (U.S. Army Air Force).

The balloons were also designed to cause panic as potentially explosive weapons that dropped unpredictably from the sky. In a southern Oregon forest, a party of church picnickers discovered a balloon with an intact bomb that exploded, killing five children and the minister's wife. In an effort to avoid mass panic, federal officials asked the local coroner to state, "The cause of death, in my opinion, was from an explosion of undetermined cause," although cemetery markers stated clearly that the victims were killed by enemy action.[51] However, these were the only casualties that resulted from the balloon campaign, although there were several other explosions and small fires. Nevertheless Japanese wartime propaganda proclaimed widespread damage and death counts in the thousands, although most Americans were unaware of the bomb-laden balloons.

The U.S. Office of Censorship asked newspapers to avoid stories about the balloons so that the Japanese knew little about their effectiveness or whether balloons had in fact reached North America. However, after the deaths in Oregon, newspapers printed stories about the incendiary bombs to protect civilian safety. There were still an unknown number of unexploded bombs in unpopulated areas, and an educational program was mounted to remind people to avoid touching unidentified objects that they might discover in the woods. Forest rangers were warned of the dangers and ordered to report sightings or balloon remnants that they discovered.[52] There was fear that balloons might next be used to carry biological weapons to the U.S., based on Allied knowledge of the infamous Unit 731 of the Imperial Japanese Army, where covert research projects included the weaponization of the plague bacterium and smallpox virus for use in germ warfare.

The balloons were assembled entirely from botanical materials. *Washi*, a traditional paper made from the paper mulberry (*Broussonetia papyrifera*, originally *Morus papyrifera*), formed the balloon walls. Known in Japan as *kozo*, the shrubs and small trees are related to the mulberries known for their fruit (*M. alba* and related species), but this species is valued for its fibrous inner bark that can be pounded, combined with water, flattened, and dried into paper sheets. Botanically the fibers are similar to the bast fibers produced by hemp (*Cannabis sativa*, see Chapter 8), also a member of the mulberry family (Moraceae). A few sheets of the tough paper were pasted together to make thick wall layers that were assembled into an elongated sphere that held hydrogen gas. The complete balloons were 33 feet in diameter and could lift a load of 300 pounds at their flying altitude of 30,000 feet, enough to carry incendiary bombs aloft.[53] Using paper to carry bombs was not unknown; the U.S. also used parachutes made of heavy duty paper (probably made of wood pulp) to drop fragmentation bombs on Japanese airfields.

The paste was made from *konnyaku* (*Amorphophallus konjac*), a member of the aroid family (Araceae) that also includes taro (*Colocasia esculenta*). The potato-like rhizomes were dried and ground into a powder that when mixed with water yielded a viscous gel of complex polysaccharides. Traditionally, the rhizomes were pulverized for use in traditional dishes, but in wartime they were more valuable as a paste for balloon assembly. Workers were typically young girls who handled the materials deftly; entire schools converted overnight from academic lessons into balloon-assembly factories. They were tasked with applying the glue, which had the effect of sealing and strengthening the paper. The *konnyaku* gel was tinted blue so that it would be visible on the paper, which when wet required careful handling. Girls wore gloves and socks to prevent accidentally tearing the paper, and they were cautioned against wearing hairpins. To check for leaks, the balloons were inflated inside theaters and *sumo* wrestling halls. The finished product was intentionally devoid of identifying marks aside from single numbers and alphabet letters because Japan feared attack on the launch sites or manufacturers.[54]

The ruse worked well. When the first balloons were discovered, some suspected that they were being made in secret by German prisoners of war held in U.S. camps. However, Alfred Erling Porsild, a botanist at the Canadian National Herbarium, determined the Japanese provenance of the balloon bombs from pine needles and rice grains present in a sandbag used for ballast. A day after receiving the sample of unknown sand, Porsild flew to Boston to examine herbarium sheets of *Pinus* species at the Gray Herbarium of Harvard University. He quickly concluded that the specimens came from the main Japanese island of Honshu (which was correct) or less likely from South Korea, work that he could not discuss until after the war.[55]

Tenaka Tetsuko recorded in her memoir of wartime at the Yamaguchi Girls' High School that the schoolyard was converted to a drying site for the paper balloons. An ancient gingko tree was felled to eliminate shade, and in the event of rain, the operation moved into the gymnasium where a large hibachi burned charcoal and heated the air for drying the paste. Eventually the entire school relocated to the Kokura military arsenal, where the girls wore headbands labeled "student special attack force." A single balloon required six hundred sheets of paper, each the size of a traditional tatami mat; shifts worked day and night, with the nighttime workers receiving a bit of extra rice and a dose of tablets used by Japanese pilots to counteract drowsiness.[56] However, the girls were often starving and ate the edible *konnyaku* paste, which resembled foods like *poi* made from taro rhizomes. This may well explain why many of the balloons disintegrated in flight before reaching the U.S., which undermined the success of balloon bombs as weapons. Records reveal that many of the balloons were identified from paper fragments scattered across the landscape.[57]

Incidentally, once introduced to Fiji and other Pacific islands, paper mulberry was adapted for making traditional *tapa* cloth, which is similar to *washi*. In Tonga, then a British protectorate, local artists painted images of Spitfire aircraft on tapa to commemorate the work of the Tongan people in raising money for Britain to purchase four Spitfire fighters. In Japan, paper mulberry helped to extend cloth fibers when cotton and wool imports halted during the war. Fibers from mulberry tree bark were combined with wood pulp to make the synthetic fiber known as *sufu*, which was woven with cotton to make a notoriously weak fabric, and paper mulberry was probably also used in making some escape and evasion maps (see Chapter 8).

Another diabolical use of paper involved several wartime schemes for printing and circulating counterfeit currency. In one case, the U.S. replicated and printed Philippine pesos and released the bills as part of an effort to devalue the currency of the Japanese occupation. The plan required finding paper made of the correct botanical fibers; occupation pesos were probably printed in Japan on paper made from tough kudzu vines (*Pueria lobata*) and durable bark fibers of the Asian shrub known in Japan as *mitsumata* (*Edgeworthia chrysantha*). In Germany, finance officials developed Operation Bernhard (named for the Nazi officer who directed it) as a plan to undermine the British economy by releasing counterfeit bank notes. The scheme involved meticulous attention to design, paper, and printing. Concentration camp prisoners were recruited as excellent engravers, but paper posed a complex problem. British currency was printed on paper made of linen (see Chapter 8) and ramie (*Boehmeria nivea*, a member of the nettle family, Urticaceae).

Cork

Cork is the outer covering of a woody stem, the layered bark that functions in preventing water loss, which is produced by the cork cambium (phelloderm). Most woody plants produce cork tissue, but the commercial source is the bark of the cork oak (*Quercus suber*), the Mediterranean species first harvested three centuries ago for crafting wine stoppers. Cork cells are dead at maturity, but they are impregnated with suberin, a water-repelling wax-like biopolymer that prevents transpiration from woody tissues. Cork tissue resists injury and impact, and because the individual cells are watertight and air-filled, it is buoyant.

By World War II, there was high military demand for cork for the manufacture of gaskets, flotation devices, insulation, and linoleum. The Quartermasters used cork to insulate steel semitrailers that could haul frozen and fresh foods to divisions in the field; vitamins were important, and without cork insulation perishable vegetables would arrive in poor condition. Lightweight portable refrigeration units were developed for use on South Pacific islands, where the tropical climate made fresh foods impossible to maintain without reliable refrigeration. Powdered cork mixed with paint alleviated light reflection by adding texture to the surface of Army helmets, including the standard M1 model that was used by troops worldwide. The Swiss experimented with cork bicycle tires; they remained neutral during the war, but imports had to pass through Axis-controlled areas, resulting in severe shortages of rubber and other raw materials. With shortages of leather and rubber, cork was also used to make the lightweight inner sole of military shoes.[58] Cork responded well to compression, which explained its use as a lining material in Fat Man, the atomic bomb that was detonated over Nagasaki, Japan on August 9, 1945. A half-inch thick cork layer cushioned the explosive sphere of plutonium, which worked on the principle of implosion.[59]

Cork was not without problems. The small air pockets that give cork its insulating properties also provided surface area for microbes, and cork shipped into tropical regions was soon colonized by fungi. This was a particular problem with optical equipment in which the lenses were supported by cork pads; fungal filaments extended from the cork and damaged the polished glass surfaces.[60] Cork imports became unreliable as the war in Europe progressed; by 1942 the shipments from Spain and Portugal were limited, and imports had supplied more than half of the cork needed. Cultivated cork oak plantations in southern California were insufficient to meet wartime demand, so alternatives were considered.

One possible cork substitute was the spongy wood of the common Jamaican plant known as cow apple (*Annona palustris*), which had long been used to float seine nets and to seal bottles. However, sugar cane proved to be a better option. In the 1920s, the Celotex Corporation had experimented with the pulpy waste known as bagasse from sugar cane processing to engineer a material that resembled cork insulation. After the canes were pressed and the juice removed, the fibrous stems were dried and woven into half-inch thick boards that had the insulating properties of cork. They were also lightweight and relatively resistance to fungal decay. Early experiments with sugar cane evolved into the wartime product known as Cemesto, a composite of sugar cane stems, cement, and asbestos (now known as a carcinogen). It was widely used to construct office buildings and housing, including homes for Manhattan Project workers in Oak Ridge, Tennessee.[61]

Coal and Charcoal

During the Carboniferous period (360–299 million years ago), tropical climates blanketed much of the earth, and swampy conditions prevailed in lowland areas. A diverse flora colonized these wet forests; when these plants died, they often formed peat that eventually fossilized into coal, a combustible sedimentary rock. Many Carboniferous plants were giant forms of extant species including club mosses, horsetails, and various ferns, and their fossils hold the carbon dioxide and energy captured by photosynthesis millions of years ago.

Coal had numerous wartime uses, foremost as a fuel (including steel production) but also for its chemical derivatives. Coal soot and ashes provided soil nutrients to victory gardens when chemical fertilizers were in short supply (see Chapters 1 and 2). Synthetic organic chemistry depended on coal tar, the viscous liquid that remains after coal is gasified into coal gas or carbonized into coke, as the starting point for reactions yielding useful products. Coal tar was used in the synthesis of saccharin (see Chapters 3 and 4), anti-malarial and sulfa drugs (see Chapter 7), various dyes (see Chapters 4, 5, and 7), and even margarine (see Chapter 5). As the first pharmaceutical antibiotics, sulfa drugs were arguably the most valuable outcome of synthesis from coal by-products.[62] The synthetic nylon used in making parachutes (see Chapter 8) was made from phenols derived from bituminous coal and was described during the war years as another remarkable technical advance.[63]

Wartime demand for coal as a fuel for war industries was high, and mining continued apace. Demand for petroleum was also high, so the U.S. government encouraged homeowners to convert from heating with rationed fuel oil to coal, but by 1943 coal was also rationed. In light of their low wages, coal miners resented wartime price increases in food and clothing. Food rationing was another major issue in mining communities; heavy labor called for the nutrients supplied by meat, and miners could not function on a wartime diet of mostly vegetables. Miners' strikes eventually resulted in concessions that included extra rationed food to support heavy labor.

In England, men left the mines for military service, munitions plants, and construction work, resulting in the loss of 36,000 experienced miners. Eventually miners were exempted from conscription, but by 1943 the demand for coal meant that 10 percent of all young conscripts were randomly selected to work in coal mines rather than serve in the military. Known as the Bevin Boys (named for Ernest Bevin, the Minister of Labour and National Service), these 48,000 young men received six weeks of training; they then spent the war years underground doing work that was dangerous and arduous. Most had no experience with coal mines, and they came from all levels of society and education. Lacking uniforms, they were often maligned as conscientious objectors (some in fact were). Many of the Bevin Boys tried unsuccessfully to enlist in military service, but their work remained in the coal mines even after the war. Coal shortages persisted, so many of the Bevin Boys remained in service until the spring of 1948.

The Bevin Boys' safety depended on the strength and integrity of the wooden pit props that supported the mine roofs in deep coal tunnels. Most of these sturdy timbers were made from imported Canadian spruce, but as coal tunnels extended deeper, pit props were in high demand. There was no more than a seven month supply in early 1940, which demanded more timber production in England rather than relying on imports. Pit props could only be made from mature trees; a 1942 survey of woodlands listed full grown conifers, and the Women's Timber Corps felled and trimmed these trees to use in supporting the tunnels into deep coal deposits.[64]

In Germany, coal was in high demand for steel production. The smelting of iron ore required coke, which was made from bituminous coal heated at high temperatures under low oxygen conditions (destructive distillation). There were vast amounts of coal in central and western Europe, but there were problems with both labor and transport. About a third of German coal supplies came from occupied countries, where forced laborers worked slowly under deteriorating conditions, including reduced food rations and physical danger. Much of the coal used in Germany came from mineral-rich areas of Silesia (now Poland and the Czech Republic), but a lack of locomotives and freight cars meant that supplies were difficult to move across the region. Unused coal piled up, while factories needing steel slowed down or closed entirely.

During the war years, petroleum shortages resulted in fuel rationing, but in Europe this was not enough to provide a fair share of fuel for all of the vehicles that needed it. Coal provided one alternative. When coal combusts, 70 percent of its calorific value escapes as gas; however, if this coal gas is captured, it can be used to power a car. The gas included carbon monoxide, hydrogen gas, methane, and other small hydrocarbons that could be routed to a carburetor after filtering. Heather plants (*Calluna vulgaris* and *Erica* spp. in the Ericaceae, the heath family) have needlelike leaves with high surface area to volume ratio, and they were used as filters to adsorb particles from coal gas. Of course, the wartime use of coal gas was actually nothing new; during the nineteenth century, coal emissions were collected as "town gas" and transmitted through pipelines for cooking, heating, and illumination. The latter caused defoliation of city trees exposed to ethylene, a gas released by the burning of coal gas and also a naturally occurring plant hormone (see Chapters 3 and 5). For years botanists had noticed the effect of ethylene on trees, but whether gas-burning vehicles caused urban defoliation in wartime England remains unknown.[65]

In continental Europe and Japan, wood gasification served a similar function. In Germany alone, there were half a million vehicles outfitted with gasification (so-called Gazogene) units that burned wood and released a mixture of gases similar to coal gas. Germany lacks natural deposits of petroleum, and imported gasoline was available during the war years only to military and government officials or to local doctors; cars, trucks, and even some military tanks ran on wood gas rather than petroleum. As an alternative to wartime rationed fuel, the strategy of operating vehicles with wood gas became common across Europe.[66]

However, there was another alternative based on work done in the coal research branch of the Kaiser Wilhelm Institute. During the 1920s, German chemists had developed a means for producing a liquid fuel from solid coal, beginning with a gasification step that converted the solid coal to a mixture of hydrogen gas and carbon monoxide known as syngas. The Fischer-Tropsch process (a series of reactions named for the co-discoverers) then converted the gas into liquid hydrocarbons that could power vehicles. An alternate method for fuel production involved liquefying and hydrogenating coal (the Bergius process, named for its discoverer Friedrich Bergius), and both chemical strategies were used to convert coal into liquid fuel that resembled petroleum. The Bergius method converted coal for use in airplanes and cars, while the Fischer-Tropsch reactions yielded oils and diesel fuel. Production costs were higher than refining petroleum, but Nazi officials supported the project financially and provided forced labor to keep the fuel plants operating. Thus liquid fuel production provided a way to convert locally mined lignite deposits into 18 million tons of wartime fuel. Geologically speaking, lignite contained visible plants fossils and was barely considered coal; it was inferior to bituminous coal in terms of heat production, but was the only type of coal mined in many areas of Germany. Lignite is closely related to the gemstone known as jet, which decades earlier was carved for use in mourning jewelry.

Charcoal is made by burning coal, wood, or other lignified plant tissues slowly under low oxygen conditions, a process known as pyrolysis or destructive distillation. Charcoal can be burned as a fuel, but it had several other wartime uses including filtration. Gas mask technology burgeoned during World War I with the use of poison gases such as mustard gas in Europe. In 1917, the Bureau of Chemistry at the U.S. Department of Agriculture conducted testing of charcoal made from various types of woods, fruits, and seeds to determine the best samples to convert industrially to activated charcoal. Plant materials included coconut shells, nut shells, and peach pits, all examples of lignin-containing sclerenchyma tissue.

The treated charcoal had millions of minute pores, which resulted in remarkably high surface area that enhanced adsorption. During the last year of World War I (1918), the Red Cross, Boy Scouts, the U.S. Department of Agriculture, and the Food Administration mounted a campaign to collect tons of nuts shells and peach pits for charcoal gas mask filters. Civilians joined in the effort to amass peach, cherry, plum, apricot, prune, olive, and date seeds; these were actually pyrenes, the inner hardened fruit wall containing the seed of a drupe, also known as a stonefruit. Collectors also saved the shells of walnuts, butternuts, and hickory nuts, and all of these plant tissues were dried and sent to centralized collection centers.

During World War II, both the U.S. and England manufactured gas masks based on this technology. The U.S. Army Chemical Warfare Service adopted Whetlerite, activated charcoal made from wood and impregnated with copper; it filtered and adsorbed mustard gas and phosgene, but was relatively ineffective against cyanide compounds that the Japanese had stockpiled. Developments in England involved the addition of silver to activated charcoal, which helped to filter and adsorb cyanide. Chromium was another additive that enhanced the ability of charcoal to remove cyanide. Testing occurred under simulated tropical conditions, apparently out of concern for chemical agents in the Pacific theater.

Ironically, Pacific islands were populated with coconut palms, but during the war coconut shells were difficult to import for making activated charcoal. Thus research centered on developing effective forms of charcoal from wood and coal and also on developing filters that could remove toxic smoke particles. Mats made of cellulose and asbestos were one option, but scientists at the Massachusetts Institute of Technology and Arthur D. Little, Inc. found that the most effective filters for removing solid particles were made from esparto grass (*Stipa tenacissima*), a perennial species indigenous to northern Africa.[67] Its leaves were known for producing remarkably resistant, flexible fibers. In England, Rosalind Franklin worked diligently on identifying the most effective types of available charcoal to use in gas masks. She obtained coal samples from across the U.K., measured the density of the samples as a way to assess pore size, and experimented with ways to increase porosity. Based on her work, it was possible to predict the best coal for converting into charcoal for gas mask filters. She is better known, however, for the X-ray diffraction images of DNA molecules that provided data essential to the double helix model of DNA published by James Watson and Francis Crick in 1953.

Charcoal was also an essential ingredient in making gun powder, which despite the development of cordite (see Chapter 8) was still used in some World War II munitions. For instance, gun powder was the explosive used in the German antipersonnel "S" mine, which British soldiers named the "Bouncing Betty." When detonated with a small amount of the explosive, the mine released a dangerous volley of high speed steel ball bearings.[68] Willow (*Salix* spp.) and cottonwoods (*Populus* spp.) were long used in the U.S. for gun-powder manufacture. However, in England the charcoal of choice came from the wood of alder buckthorn (*Rhamnus frangula*, also known as *Frangula alnus*), which has a wide range across Europe, northern Africa, and western Asia. Prior to World War II, England imported the charcoal from Europe, but wartime shipping problems required the use of native timber from the New Forest area of southern England where botanists surveyed the countryside for alder buckthorn trees. In folk medicine the bark of alder buckthorn was known as a strong cathartic and easily collected from self-sown populations. The species was so common in England that it was rarely cultivated or grown as coppiced wood, a strategy in which shoots were cut and re-grown from rootstock. Lumber Jills from the Women's Timber Corps cut wild trees, peeled the bark, and bundled them for processing into charcoal for munitions.

Forestry, Forests and the Third Reich

Forestry during the Third Reich encompassed both economic interests and philosophical underpinnings. German folk character was rooted in forested landscapes, and forestry was under the broad jurisdiction of the Reich Food Corporation, which operated under the *Blut und Boden* (blood and soil) notion of a link between Aryan families and the land (see Chapter 6). Practically speaking, forests were a rich resource of wood for building and natural products developed as sources of cellulose and other useful chemicals. Nazi party officials took great interest in natural resources, and Heinrich Himmler even envisioned obtaining fuel from the roots of fir trees (see Chapter 10). In a typical duplication of control, Hermann Göring was appointed the Reichsminister of Forestry (1934–45), during the same period that he served as Reichsminister of Aviation and other party roles. Perhaps realizing the importance of forests to the wartime economy, he pushed for new conservation laws, including a change from clear-cutting to the *Dauerwald* (continuous forest) practice. Selective cutting kept forest ecosystems intact, but some historians have argued that its real significance was in providing an analogy between German forests and Aryan Germans. Much of the hiking, camping, folklore, and outdoor romanticism of the *Hitler Jugend* (Hitler Youth) and the *Bund Deutscher Mädel* (League of German Girls) arose from a practical *Weltanschauung* (world view) than envisioned Aryans in an idealized landscape of native Germanic vegetation.

Christmas trees (*Weihnachtsbäume*) remained a tradition during the Nazi regime, but they were officially dissociated from religion and instead became symbolic of a pagan celebration of the winter solstice. In 1942, the German newsreel series "Die Deutsche Wochenschau" (German Weekly Review; U.S. National Archives and Records Administration, films captured by Allied troops after the war) featured scenes from wartime celebrations in snowy, forested landscapes, a cheerful holiday message for civilian theater-goers in the midst of deprivations. Candles illuminated the evergreen branches, but swastika ornaments and toy tanks and bombers replaced stars and angels, and miniature gardens with figurines of woodland animals replaced mangers. Familiar decorations included the badges earned by donors to the *Winterhilfswerk* (winter aid program) to help civilians who lacked food and heat (see Chapter 4). Some German soldiers even managed to celebrate with a Christmas tree during the campaign for *Lebensraum*; one memoir from the eastern front noted, "We had a Christmas of sorts. We even had a Christmas tree. Not a big one but it was at least real and had been brought back from Germany by one of our returning convalescents. The aroma of those few German twigs in this desert was truly a breath of home. There were even a few candles to light.... We stood around the tree and sang the old familiar German carols.... We exist in a desert of snow and ice but within this desolation we had brought our German traditions, our songs and our spirit.... Like all married men I felt the loss of the family more keenly at such times, but it had been for their future that we were in Russia."[69]

However, the wartime demand for wood overruled *Dauerwald* ideals and Nazi propaganda. Woodcutting in German forests exceeded production despite official conservation policy. Wherever possible, wood replaced metal, which was needed for airplanes, tanks, and munitions. Metal lamp posts were replaced with wood, which eventually became difficult to obtain because of labor shortages. Desperate for heat during chronic coal shortages, civilians made illicit forays to cut firewood. In short, trees were still standing in the area that later became West Germany, but mature forests were depleted by as much as 27 percent in the area that became East Germany.[70] Military demands trumped ministry concerns for conservation; overcutting caused German forests to become drastically depauperate, taking decades to recover after the war. As part of the effort to reclaim timber after the war, German women were ordered to work as *Trümmerfrauen* (rubble women), organized into brigades to reclaim usable wood from bombed ruins. Their salvage efforts included removing oak timbers typical of German construction.

Adolf Hitler admired the straight growth of oak trees in comparison to the more gnarled and asymmetric growth of ancient beeches. Once he became chancellor of Germany in 1933, trees known as Hitler oaks (probably *Quercus robur*) and Hitler lindens (*Tilia* spp., probably *T. platyphyllos*, the large leaf linden, another straight-growing species) were planted in towns and villages throughout Germany. These trees figured in Berlin Olympics of 1936 when the German Olympic Committee presented saplings of *Q. robur* to medalists. The plan was to spread German oaks worldwide. Recipients included Jesse Owens who planted four of the saplings in the U.S.; one of these oaks survives at a high school in Ohio. Another oak with Nazi connections was a tree with legendary ties to the poet Goethe. During the construction of Buchenwald, prisoners tasked with clearing land were warned to avoid damaging the Goethe oak, which later burned during an Allied air raid in August 1944. Many of the Buchenwald prisoners saved chips of its charred wood.[71]

Stylized oak images based on *Quercus robur* were widely used during the Third Reich. The strength, resistance, and hard timber of oaks presumably symbolized military might; oak leaves equated with laurels (*Laurus nobilis*, the bay laurel of antiquity) in wreaths and garlands, and the staffs used to carry the flags of German army units were made from a single piece of seasoned oak timber. The personal flag (standard) used by Hitler included a garland of golden oak leaves, and newly married SS (*Schutzstaffel*) officers received a copy of *Mein Kampf* presented in an oak box carved with oak leaves and acorns. SS families had cast iron family trees with oak leaves, acorns, and slots for family photographs. Military combat medals, including the Knight's Cross of the Iron Cross, had oak leaves included in the design, and hats worn by German infantry bore cast metal pins of oak leaves and acorns. Willy Lange, a landscape architect in Berlin, advocated planting oak trees on the graves of fallen soldiers, converting cemeteries to memorial groves that resembled German nature gardens (see Chapter 12). Hitler's podium was often flanked by oak leaves, and the insignia of the *Blut und Boden* movement entitling Aryan families to land ownership (see Chapter 6) included oak leaves flanking a swastika. Coincidentally, it was an oak table that protected Hitler from a bomb blast during a 1944 assassination attempt (see Chapter 7).

Incidentally, the 87th Infantry Division of the U.S. Army also adopted the oak as a symbol. Their shoulder patch had a golden acorn on a green background, and their motto was, "Stalwart and Strong; and Sturdy as an Oak." They fought through the Battle of the Bulge, across Germany, and to the Czechoslovakian border, but were not among the Allied forces who organized the postwar denazification and rebuilding of Germany.

There were some uniquely Nazi forest connections. In 1994, a flight crew observed the outline of a swastika 200 feet wide in the Brandenberg forest reserve sixty miles north of Berlin; it consisted of one hundred deciduous larch trees (*Larix decidua*) planted in an otherwise evergreen conifer forest. For a few weeks each autumn, the larch needles revealed bright yellow carotenoid pigments before dropping. The origin of the forest swastika is unknown, but based on tree ring analysis, the configuration was planted in 1938. Whether its planting originated with a zealous forester or Nazi order is subject to speculation, but sufficient larch trees were subsequently removed that the image is no longer visible from the sky.

Another Nazi forest connection appeared in *Der Giftpilz* (*The Poison Mushroom*), an anti–Semitic children's book published in 1938.[72] The publisher was known for its anti–Semitic newspaper, but this picture book aimed to persuade a younger audience by using toxic fungi in German forests as a metaphor for Jewish people in Europe. In the illustrated pages, a young Aryan boy and his mother collect mushrooms in a picturesque Germanic forest, but some appear to be the bright red, toxic fly agaric (*Amanita muscaria*). Mother's warnings against picking poisonous mushrooms introduce a detailed discussion of anti–Semitic stereotypes; Jewish people are ridiculed and criticized, and children are warned away from any dealings with "poisonous people." There is, however, a botanical irony to the story. The fly agaric is one of the fungi that form mycorrhizal relationships with the roots of trees (including the European oaks that Hitler admired), a symbiosis necessary for nutrient cycling in forest ecosystems. Many trees cannot grow without the fungal filaments (hyphae) that colonize their roots and improve the absorption of water and dissolved minerals. In short, the poisonous mushrooms used to symbolize Judaism are essential to tree survival in German forests, surely not the message that *Der Giftpilz* intended.

The Homefront

Fuel rationing and shortages vexed home life during the war years. In England, conservation measures included making briquettes to burn from coal tar or coal dust, sometimes combined with dead leaves. Dried plant matter was collected as kindling, and wood replaced coal in coal stoves and furnaces. Timber was in short supply, but bomb sites and even driftwood provided wood for salvage and burning. Peat (layers of *Sphagnum* moss, see Chapter 7) was cut from bogs and wet moors and dried to use as fuel. As a means to conserve heat and fuel, rooms were closed off during the coldest months, and hot water heaters were packed with straw and enclosed in plywood boxes. With minimal coal available, former coal cellars were sometimes converted to bomb shelters, with the coal chute enlarged to provide an emergency exit.[73]

In Germany, the problem was not a shortage of coal but rather a shortage of trains to carry coal from mining areas to the cities. The particularly cold winter of 1939 resulted in frigid homes and shuttered factories, portending conditions for the duration of the war. German civilians endured winter cold and repeated the joke that Hitler ordered conversion from Celsius to the German Fahrenheit scale, so temperatures all (apparently) increased. As in England, they were told to collect and burn peat in place of coal or usable wood.

In Japan, civilians were limited to eight small sacks of coal or charcoal each winter, and the briquettes known as *rentan* were mostly sawdust and often disintegrated before they were burned. Some resorted to burning pine cones and magazines as fuel for cooking and heating. Public baths heated water with firewood collected by their patrons, and trees were felled from public parks and city streets to make coffins; chronic timber shortages meant that coffins were routinely rented and reused. With soap a rarity, Germans used wood ash; the lye that occurs naturally in the ashes reacted with fats to produce soap, so ashes were an effective cleaning agent for greasy dirt. The Japanese used lye and the leguminous fruit of honey locust (*Gleditsia japonica*), which are rich in the soapy glycosides known as saponins.

Wooden shoes were common during the war years as a way to save leather and rubber for military needs. In England wooden-soled shoes were known as woodies, and by 1943 there were versions with hinges for more flexibility. The Board of Trade issued directions for caring for wooden shoes; they required drying if wet, but never near a fire, and worn composition soles required replacement to avoid splintering of the wooden base. In Germany, clogs were made from the wood of beech and alder or from slats of laminated wood that resembled plywood. Much of the labor in crafting the wooden soles was done by prisoners in the Lodz and Warsaw ghettoes who crafted clogs in return for food and coal. In Italy, some shoe soles were made from thick layers of cork rather than wood. Uppers were made from miscellaneous botanical materials including cloth such as canvas and oilcloth (see Chapter 8), wood products such as cellophane and paper, and raffia (leaves of raffia palms, *Raphia taedigera*). In Japan, eventually all leather was reserved for military footwear, and civilians were limited to wooden clogs.

Civilian life often meant simple amusements. In England, unnecessary travel was discouraged, so magazines and handbooks suggested home projects using scrap wood for building garden frames, window boxes, chicken houses, and rabbit hutches.[74] Children were kept busy with homemade wooden puzzles, boat models, puppets, and pull toys, such as those described in "Improvised Toys for Nurseries and Refugee Camps."[75] For those without woodworking skill, editions of *The Mammoth Book of Working Models* (various editions published by Odhams Press) supplied ready-to-assemble heavy paper models of the SS *Queen Elizabeth*, a steam engine, and several other inventions. Airplane models made of wood doubled as an instructional tool for young plane spotters; it was known that model-building was required of German boys. Balsawood kits of bombers and other military aircraft were widely available both in the U.S. and England, and the wood was sufficiently strong that it was also recommended for making simple splints in the home practice of first aid.[76]

Christmas traditions continued in wartime England despite bombing raids. There were numerous suggestions for homemade decorations using botanical materials such as pinecones, holly, flour-based clay, *papier-mâché*, white-washed twigs, and window, the metallic paper used to interfere with radar (see above). Epsom salts were used to simulate ice crystals on natural greenery. Some commercial ornaments were available but made with cardboard hangers to conserve metal. *Christmas Under Fire* (Ministry of Information, 1941), a short documentary film aimed at an American audience, showed the British holiday celebration during the Blitz. Emphasizing the themes of defiance and resilience, the film featured images of Christmas trees in bomb shelters. In the U.S., Warner Brothers donated profits from showing the film to the Royal Air Force fund for constructing Spitfires, fighter planes equipped with wooden propellers and wing construction that utilized spruce wood.

History in Timber

Landscapes reflect history, and the growth of trees can mirror or even encapsulate wartime events. Military helmets, guns, shells, and grenades discarded in forests have become embedded in wood, which occurs when inanimate objects lean against bark for many years. Over many years, the seasonal growth of the vascular cambium occurs around the object, which over time becomes encapsulated in the secondary xylem (wood) as the sapling becomes a mature tree. Examples of trees with embedded military metal have been found in Russian forests and also in Europe. Some contain intact grenades or shells that were fired deep into the wood of a mature tree, where they remain undiscovered. Embedded munitions can explode if the wood is unknowingly burned, which presents a documented hazard if mature wood from battle-scarred areas is burned in fireplaces or stoves.

Tree rings may also record wartime events. The recent discovery of growth anomalies in Norwegian pines reveals the possible effect of a gas used to camouflage the German battleship *Tirpitz*. Dendrochronological studies show stunted or entirely stalled pine growth in 1945, the year that the ship traveled incognito in a chemical fog in the fjords of occupied Norway. Chlorosulfuric acid released into the air attracts water, which resulted in a cloud-like mist capable of hiding a battleship; the strategy worked, but not without unintended consequences. German forest ecologists have quantified the apparent effects of the airborne acid on tree ring formation, which in some trees lasted for years after the war. The complete absence of tree rings is a rare event, which in this case may well be an unanticipated side effect of camouflage by chlorosulfuric acid.[77]

Archeological traces of wood have helped to identify tunnels excavated by prisoners of war. During World War II, *Stalag Luft III*, an eastern German prison camp operated by the *Luftwaffe* in Lower Silesia (now part of western Poland), housed Allied troops who planned to escape captivity by means of excavation. Using shovels and ducts crafted from the tin cans that held Red Cross dried milk, prisoners dug and ventilated three tunnels (code-named Tom, Dick, and Harry), an intentionally redundant system in case guards discovered one of them. Excavations began in the interior of buildings and reached a depth of 30 feet to avoid German seismograph microphones that could detect digging sounds. Some of the excavated soil ended up in prisoners' gardens, but much of it was surreptitiously scattered on the grounds by prisoners who walked about with small bags of loose subsoil fastened inside their clothing.

A problem arose with the sandy subsoil at the camp site that caused tunnel walls to collapse. Internal support was needed, so prisoners unobtrusively collected wood to construct tunnel supports. Bed slats, furniture, and any other lumber that could be surreptitiously pried free from the barracks were dragged deep into the tunnels, where the boards were notched and built into wooden beams. Prison officials discovered one of the tunnels (Tom), and prisoners subsequently concentrated all of their efforts on excavating in Harry. Dick was used as a dumping site for soil. On March 26, 1944, 76 prisoners moved through the tunnel named Harry to the perimeter of the prison. Only three Allied soldiers escaped captivity; 73 men were recaptured, 50 of them were executed (a violation of the Geneva Convention) and 23 prisoners were returned to German camps. Soviet forces liberated the camp ten months later.

Sixty years after tunnel construction, the wooden beams had rotted, but they left distinctive signs of their presence in the sandy soil beneath *Stalag Luft III*. Lawrence Babits and a team from East Carolina University used ground-penetrating radar to locate disturbed areas of soil that indicated digging. They subsequently excavated the tunnel sites and discovered the remains of wooden construction, including areas of discolored soil that revealed the system of beams as well as the areas where boards were notched together.[78] An earlier escape plan at *Stalag Luft III* involved hiding the tunnel entry beneath a wooden vaulting horse. In 1943, prisoners evincing an interest in gymnastics constructed the wooden horse from the plywood boxes that contained Red Cross shipments. Placed at a site near the perimeter fence, the horse concealed the tunnel entry, digging tools, and excavation activity, while other prisoners practiced vaulting. A few prisoners did escape through this tunnel, but the horse disappeared at some point during the war years.

10

Oils, Resins and Rubber

Plants are virtual chemical factories, and despite the burgeoning of synthetic organic chemistry in the early 1900s, plants still provided botanical substances that were essential for military needs during World War II. Aside from medicinal compounds (see Chapter 7), plants synthesize various oils, waxes, resins, and latex, all with specific adaptive functions in botanical life cycles. Since antiquity, humans have adapted these compounds for essential needs and uses—from fuel and shipbuilding to munitions and machinery.

The botany of oils, resins, and latex pivots on understanding the adaptations associated with their production. Plant oils typically originate in seeds, which are adapted for dispersal and thus have limited space for food storage. Oils and other fats store three times more energy than starch, which in terms of mass and space, explains why fats have often evolved as efficient foods that support growth of germinating seeds. In contrast, resins and latex are secondary compounds (phytochemicals) that plants have evolved in response to environmental pressures. Natural selection has resulted in synthetic pathways that enhance survival, including evolution of resins and latex that seal wounds, deter herbivores, and prevent microbial growth.

Botanical Oils and Resins

Several crops cultivated by U.S. farmers produced seed oils that had diverse wartime uses. Linseed oil was used in paints, varnishes, linoleum, and printing ink (see Chapter 4). Soybean oil was compounded into soaps, insecticides, industrial and lubricating oils, paints, and varnishes (see Chapter 6). It also replaced limited supplies of linseed oil in making the linoleum used in military construction. Experiments with soybean oil resulted in waterproof adhesives for manufacturing plywood (see Chapter 9), and in making a latex substitute known as Norepol (see Chapter 6). Other essential wartime oils included castor oil which was used to waterproof fabric, lubricate airplane engines, and make paints, inks, soaps, airplane coverings, and plastics (see Chapter 6).

Aside from these familiar agricultural crops, some additional botanical oils had wartime roles. In Russia, vast sunflower fields produced seeds that were pressed for their edible and lubricating oil. German troops in Russia used it on their rifles, at low temperatures an apparent improvement over army-issue lubricating oil. The high oil content of sunflower seeds meant that they were a favored high-energy ration for Russian troops, but historians have noted that kilometers of sunflower fields actually depressed German soldiers, who had no prior knowledge of the vast size of the country.[1]

Botanical oils became wartime fuel substitutes as shortages of coal and petroleum forced Axis countries to consider botanical options as fuel for internal combustion engines. Once Allied forces occupied the Philippines and Okinawa, they blocked petroleum imports to Japan. In an effort to develop synthetic fuels, the Japanese agreed to collaborate with I.G. Farben, a plan that failed with the defeat of Germany. In the last months of the war, shortages of aviation fuel hindered Japanese planes from defending the home islands from Allied bombing; alternatives were sought from plants growing in Japan, with fuel research centered on plant oils and tissues that were potentially combustible: soybean oil, camphor oil, pine needles and roots, birch bark, and orange peels. Soybean oil was the only plant fuel pressed from seeds; most of the other oils were based on aromatic terpenes produced in vegetative parts of the plants. Investigations also included a potential fuel based on alcohol from fermented sweet potatoes, a plan reminiscent of Heinrich Himmler's failed plan to capture evaporating alcohol from bread baking in the Dachau bakeries (see Chapter 4), although it is unknown whether he intended the alcohol to be used as a fuel.[2]

Pine oil production became a successful wartime industry that utilized woody tree roots to distill a crude aviation fuel. Japanese civilians, including entire schools of children, collected tons of pine roots from the countryside. It was a labor intensive undertaking that required thousands of distillation devices to heat the roots to release the oils; the process required twelve hours, and pine oil yielded about only 4 percent in crude fuel. Nevertheless during the waning months of the war, Japanese civilians extracted thousands of gallons of fuel from native pines. Occupying U.S. troops reportedly used the fuel in their jeeps, but found that it quickly gummed up American engines.[3]

Based on optimistic reports from the Japanese Ministry of Agriculture, Himmler instigated an unsuccessful program to use German conifer roots for fuel. Nazi agriculturalists also pursued another ill-fated plan to develop fuels from geranium leaves, presumably the scented varieties of *Pelargonium* with high levels of terpene-based oils. Reportedly these were grown in large numbers in the agricultural fields at the Auschwitz concentration camp, but the plan did not yield a useful fuel.[4]

Since the era of wooden sailing ships, sailors had relied on pine trees as a source of caulking and waterproofing substances, known as pine sap, resin, or pitch. Chemically speaking, the sap is an oleoresin, a semi-solid of viscous terpenes dissolved in essential oil. It is sticky, waterproof, and weather resistant, making it an ideal substance to combine with fibers into oakum, a botanical product long used to caulk wooden ships and the decking of iron and steel ships. Its production involved heating resinous pine wood under low oxygen conditions, converting the sap to pine tar, which was then combined with the bast fibers from hemp to make oakum (see Chapter 8). The U.S. War Production Board assumed control supplies of Vinsol, a proprietary product made from the ground stumps of pine. Known for its thermoplastic properties, the resin is pliable when heated and solid at cooler temperatures; it was adapted for use in building military roads and runways and in making paperboard and early plastics that replaced strategic metals.

Turpentine has a related origin and similar chemistry; it can be made from pine sap using steam distillation or from wood (including stumps and roots) by using high heat under low oxygen conditions. From a military perspective, all of these pine products (resin, oakum, pine oil, turpentine, and turpentine-containing paints) fell under the broad category known as naval stores, critical substances for ship maintenance. Rosin was the solid fraction of pine sap that remained after heating and evaporation of more volatile terpenes; it was used during World War I to make military clothing that reportedly repelled gases for forty minutes, providing the basis for research that continued during World War II.

Natural forests of longleaf yellow pine (*Pinus palustris*) in the Gulf coast states for years had supplied most of the sap and wood needed for making naval stores. However, by the 1930s, the pine timber had been overharvested; virgin stands had vanished, and the forests were largely depleted. Naval stores were still critical materials, and oil from the seeds of Chinese tung trees (*Aleurites fordii*, also known as *Vernicia fordii*) offered an alternative to resin products from native pines. In China, the oil was used for making a caulk that resembled oakum and also for waterproofing paper, cloth, and wood. U.S. paint and turpentine manufacturers imported the oil for making their products, but during the 1930s hostilities between Japan and China affected supplies.

Responding to need, U.S. lumber companies established tung plantations where native pine forests had once flourished. Tung trees grew quickly under the same conditions that promoted pine growth: acidic soil, minimum annual rainfall of forty inches, and a week or two of freezing weather each season. Regional research labs were started in Georgia, Alabama, Florida, and Louisiana, and tung oil parades and festivals hailed the first crops. Over a half million tung trees were planted in the years prior to the war.[5] Because it hardens in air, tung oil had more diverse uses than pine products and was quickly adopted for military use. During World War II, the entire domestic production of tung oil supplied Army and Navy needs, including varnish, paint, inks, brake linings, lubricants, electrical insulation, naval stores, and linoleum manufacture. Liquid pressed from the shells of cashew nuts (*Anacardium occidentale*) had some similar uses. The oils hardened into to a lacquer-like layer used in electrical insulation and brake linings, eventually implicated in causing severe rashes among servicemen allergic to the tree, a member of the same family (Anacardiaceae) as poison ivy.[6]

The most insidious wartime use of resins involved fragmentation weapons. A note in the 1942 volume of *Gopher Peavey*, the University of Minnesota forestry school yearbook, described some of the little known uses of timber, "Forest products used in our war effort include … resin for shrapnel, and turpentine in flame throwers."[7] Shrapnel shells relied on pine resin to hold small metal pieces and protect them from deformation; the typical design involved a metal casing that contained steel balls in a resin matrix. After the shell was fired, a small amount of an explosive caused the resin to release the shrapnel from the nose of the shell into a cone-shaped discharge of steel balls at ground level.

In contrast, so-called sticky bombs had an external layer of resin that allowed them to stick to their targets, which were often tanks. In the original British specifications, an outer layer made of woven wood fibers encased a glass sphere attached to a wooden handle. The sphere contained an explosive (often nitroglycerin made from fats collected in home kitchens), and the outer layer was coated with resin; the idea was to throw the bomb (really a grenade) onto a tank, where it would adhere and detonate. Resin was essential to the success of the weapon, but in this case it did not have a pine origin. The British designs of the sticky bombs relied on a chemical improvement of birdlime, an adhesive spread on branches as a way to trap birds. In England, birdlime was commonly

compounded from holly bark (*Ilex aquifolium*), which was boiled for several hours, stripped, pounded, fermented into a mucilage, and mixed with oil to make the finished adhesive. The sticky bomb version of birdlime was developed by chemists at Kay Ltd., but its actual formula remains unknown. Adhesion was an ongoing problem in designing sticky bombs; they could not cling to tanks covered in mud or dust, and there was also the possibility that the resin coating could unintentionally adhere to a soldier's uniform. Later versions used magnets rather than resin, but these had to be placed by hand on the tracks or undercarriage of a tank.

Sticky bombs had an external resin layer that allowed them to stick to their targets, which were often tanks. Original British designs relied on birdlime compounded from holly bark, which was boiled for several hours, stripped, pounded, fermented into a mucilage, and mixed with oil to make the finished adhesive. However, the actual wartime formula remains unknown.

Latex, Rubber and Rationing

Latex is an emulsion of botanical compounds, primarily long-chain hydrocarbon compounds combined with various resins, alkaloids, and terpenes, depending on the plant species. As a natural product, it is known from about fifty species that produce latex in specialized laticifers, single cells or canals that form networks in various plant structures. In nature, latex probably repels hungry herbivores, but laticifers may also store compounds involved in botanical reactions or to sequester certain phytochemicals from cellular reactions.

Economically speaking, latex is the raw material for rubber production, an industry that started in the mid–1800s and expanded with the invention of cars and demand for tires. At the onset of World War II, rubber tree (*Hevea brasiliensis*) plantations in the Dutch East Indies produced 90 percent of the global latex supply. Like cinchona (see Chapter 7), rubber trees are native to South America, but they were cultivated in areas of southwestern Asia that fell under Japanese control during World War II. By the fall of Java in March 1942, Japanese interests controlled more than 90 percent of the global supply of latex. Synthetic rubber was not yet a practical option, and the U.S. had stockpiled only 660,000 tons of rubber, barely enough to supply civilian needs for a single year.

With thirty million automobiles on U.S. roads, tires were the major concern. Four days after the Pearl Harbor attack, the Office of Price Administration halted all tire sales to civilians, a temporary measure that was followed by rules for rubber use and allocation. Once local ration boards were established, they received a certain number of tires and

At the onset of World War II, rubber tree plantations in the Dutch East Indies produced 90 percent of the global latex supply. Like cinchona, the trees are native to South America, but they were cultivated in areas of southwestern Asia that fell under Japanese control during World War II. By early 1942, Japan controlled over 90 percent of the global supply of latex (C.J. Kleingrothe, Royal Institute of Southeast Asian and Caribbean Studies, Leiden University Library, Wikimedia Commons).

inner tubes and controlled their availability. Fuel rationing helped to prevent tire wear, and civilians were advised on tire care and inflation; damage, however minor, could not be overlooked. Seepage of water into minute cracks caused the interior cotton fabric to decay, and then the tires could not be retread, a standard wartime strategy for conserving rubber.[8]

Rubber could be reclaimed, so scrap drives included anything made entirely or partially of rubber: tires (including bicycle tires), bicycle pedals and handle grips, inner tubes, bath mats, hot water bottles, tennis shoes, boots, overshoes, gloves, rubber soles and heels, hoses, rain slickers, jar rings, bathing caps, tennis and golf balls and other sports equipment, tubing, gaskets, and rubberized flannel sheets. Recycling required time and energy, but the reclaimed rubber could be used for flooring, shoe heels, and for tread that could be applied to worn tires. On the home front, jar rings were needed to can victory garden vegetables; the Boston Hose and Rubber Company sold a wartime version known as Bull Dog Jar Rubbers, presumably made with minimal latex content. Elasticized underwear and rubberized footwear became difficult to obtain.

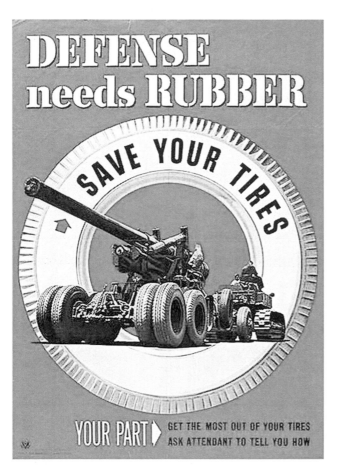

In 1941 civilians were advised to conserve car tires with advice on care and inflation; fuel rationing also helped to prevent tire wear during the war years. Local ration boards received a certain number of tires and inner tubes and controlled their availability (U.S. Office for Emergency Management).

In England, rubber use in clothing was limited to essential agricultural, industrial, and military needs, and rubber footwear for civilians was not allowed until 1947. Certain items requiring rubber were in high demand, including the standard Wellington rubber (gum) boots that were part of the Women's Land Army uniform; these were also needed by city children who were evacuated to the countryside. Eventually, the Board of Trade relented on the use of limited rubber for elastic corsets, which were a social convention considered essential to morale. However, shortages affected stretchable corset designs, and women were forced to revert to earlier lace-up styles with limited elastic rubber content.

Rubber Plants

Identifying alternative rubber sources posed a botanical challenge for several federal agencies involved with securing latex supplies, including the Rubber Plant Investigations Office of the U.S. Department of Agriculture. Several plant families produce latex, in particular the Euphorbiaceae (spurge family), Apocynaceae (dogbane family), Moraceae (mulberry family), and Asteraceae (sunflower family). However, only some species produce enough latex for rubber production on an industrial scale, and only certain species are suited to large scale growing. The latex (chicle) used in making chewing gum (see Chapter 5) came from various tropical trees including species in the Apocynaceae (*Dyera* spp. and *Couma macrocarpa*) and Sapotaceae (*Manilkara zapota*), and some chicle was also used as the adhesive on surgical tape.

The wartime pursuit of latex-producing plants assumed a shot-gun strategy. In retrospect, fast-growing herbaceous plants were the most likely emergency latex crops, compared to woody species that required years to mature. But most commercial latex came from the rubber trees native to Amazonian forests, which offered a starting point for botanical research. *Hevea* (the genus that includes *H. brasiliensis*, the most widely grown rubber tree species) is a genus in the Euphorbiaceae and perhaps offered alternative rubber sources. The other eight species of *Hevea* included wild populations in Cuba, Haiti, the Dominican Republic, Panama, Costa Rica, Venezuela, Colombia, and Brazil. Field botanists tapped wild trees early in the day to determine the ones with abundant latex flow that merited seed collection. There was considerable variation in latex production even within a single species of *Hevea*, a characteristic noted by ethnobotanist Richard Evans Schultes. He had been in Colombia collecting curare specimens as part of a National Research Council grant, but with the onset of war, he was exempted from military service and assigned to rubber research. As part of his work for the Rubber Plant Investigations Office, he collected 3500 *Hevea* specimens and three tons of rubber tree seeds for future cultivation. Based on the wartime field work of Schultes and others, experimental rubber plantations were established in Costa Rica and Haiti. However, the trees required seven to ten years to reach maturity, so new rubber tree plantations were not a solution to wartime demands.

Other genera in the family Euphorbiaceae merited investigation, including species of the tropical genera *Cnidoscolus*, *Micrandra*, *Manihot*, and *Sapium*. Several New World species were identified and tapped in the wild, but latex yields were minimal. However, there were other options, including plantations of the Panama rubber tree (*Castilla elastica*, family Moraceae) a pre–Colombian latex source that had been cultivated during World War I. Some of the surviving trees in Venezuela and Trinidad were tapped again for modest latex yields, using the old method of coagulating the latex with the highly alkaline juice pressed from moonflower vines (*Ipomoea alba*); alternatively laundry detergent (also alkaline) was used to precipitate the latex.[9] Native Brazilian populations of small trees and shrubs in the genus *Hancornia* (family Apocynaceae) yielded two thousand tons of usable latex, and the vines in the related genus *Cryptostegia* produced some latex as well.

One of the most promising latex-producing species was *Parthenium argentamum*, a Mexican desert shrub known as guayule which matures a couple of years after planting. A federal program known as the Emergency Rubber Project involved hundreds of botanists, chemists, geneticists, and agriculturalists who focused on guayule as a latex

One of the most promising latex-producing species was guayule, a Mexican shrub that matures a couple of years after planting. The federal Emergency Rubber Project involved hundreds of botanists, chemists, geneticists, and agriculturalists. Japanese-American scientists at the Manzanar internment camp cultivated guayule from cuttings and developed simplified methods for latex extraction from its shoots (Library of Congress).

source. They undertook the planting of guayule seedlings on thousands of acres in the Salinas Valley of California and began research on the genetics and seasonality of latex production. By 1942, local women and girls helped with weeding the beds and collecting seed, and Japanese-American scientists at the nearby Manzanar internment camp (see Chapter 4) cultivated guayule from cuttings and developed simplified methods for latex extraction from its shoots. A small amount of the latex added to reclaimed rubber improved its overall quality, which was the plan for using the guayule crop.[10]

However, botanists soon realized that climate affected latex content. Summer growth yielded no latex because its production required night temperatures below 50° Fahrenheit; only winter growth produced latex, which also required high levels of rainfall for a decent yield per acre.[11] Despite climatic variation, over 1,500 tons of guayule latex were collected during the course of the program, but as the end of the war approached federal efforts were abandoned. All of the seedlings were destroyed before the guayule latex program reached its full potential, ostensibly due to the demand for food crops.

Milkweed offered yet another latex option. The common milkweed (*Asclepias syriaca*) was already in use as a kapok substitute (see Chapter 8), and there were 140 species of the genus native to the Americas. The plants are herbaceous weeds that thrive along roadsides and in abandoned fields; as a possible latex source, milkweed barely needed cultivation, just collection from the wild. An article in *Popular Mechanics* described the nonflammable nature and comparative strength of milkweed latex (during tests it tolerated flame tests and a barrage of bullets) and projected a yield of 28 tons of latex per acre.[12] The harvesting method involved crushing the plants, followed by bacterial activity in which carbohydrates were converted to protein. Supposedly the high protein concentration accounted for resistance of milkweed latex to chemicals, including petroleum, so that it could be used to manufacture fuel tanks. However, early estimations of the latex yields from milkweed proved inaccurate; in reality, the shoots contain 1 or 2 percent latex and thus milkweed never achieved large scale success as a latex plant.

Several latex-producing composites (family Asteraceae) also merited attention because they were weeds adapted to temperate conditions. Species of *Hieracium* (hawkweeds), *Lactuca* (lettuce), *Tragopogon* (goatsbeard), and *Solidago* (goldenrod) were grown in experimental plots in Ottawa.[13] This was nothing new, but rather the wartime application of botanical information. Aware of rubber shortages during World War I, during the 1920s Thomas Edison had bred a high-yielding variety of *S. leavenworthii* from wild Florida goldenrod populations and used its latex to produce tires for his Ford car.

The Russian dandelion (*Taraxacum kok-saghx*, also in the family Asteraceae), was another promising source, but its taproots produced varying amounts of latex. According to data from Russian collective farms where they had grown the plant since the 1930s, the average latex content of dandelion taproots was 1 percent, which translated into a yield per acre of a paltry fifty pounds.[14] Nevertheless, dandelion research moved forward, and in 1942, 18,000 roots grown from Russian seed stock were harvested from experimental dandelion farms in Minnesota, Michigan, Wisconsin, and Montana. Using seed from the U.S. Department of Agriculture, Canadian botanists identified and crossbred dandelion strains with high latex production, and they also worked on cloning high-yielding strains; some of their fields produced taproots with 19 percent latex.

While research into botanical alternatives continued, the U.S. government tasked the Rubber Reserve Company and Rubber Development Corporation with shoring up

Taproots of Russian dandelion produce varying amounts of latex. Nevertheless, dandelion research moved forward, and in 1942, 18,000 roots grown from Russian seed stock were harvested from experimental farms in Minnesota, Michigan, Wisconsin, and Montana. Canadian botanists crossbred strains with high latex production and cloned high-yielding strains; some taproots produced 19 percent latex (W. Gorden Whaley and John S. Bowen, Ford Motor Co., Wikimedia Commons).

the long neglected rubber tree plantations in South America. Unable to supply latex at the low price of Pacific plantations, abandoned South American plantations now received much needed supplies: tapping equipment, machetes, kerosene, vegetable seeds, and outboard motors, along with a supply of atabrine to prevent malaria among the workers (see

Chapter 7). Old techniques were revived such as plastering tree trunks with a mixture of manure and soil, a practice that stimulated the growth of lateral branches from dormant epicormic buds below the bark. In return for aid, growers in Brazil, Peru, Bolivia, British Guiana, and other South American countries and colonies contracted to sell their latex to the U.S., thus supplying about a third of the latex needed for wartime rubber production.[15]

German Strategies

In 1939, the Nazi regime initiated a four year plan to reduce German dependence on imported rubber by using synthetic organic chemistry rather than botanical latex sources. Chemists at I.G. Farben pursued the development of synthetic (so-called buna) rubber, which required the addition of a small amount of natural latex to its formulation. Thus there was still a need for latex-producing plants, ideally species that could be grown in Germany. The SS (Schutzstaffel) had plundered seed stock from Russian field stations (see Chapter 6), including Russian dandelions that were planted and cultivated in agricultural fields at the Auschwitz concentration camp. The SS conducted breeding experiments with the goal of increasing latex production; thousands of dandelions were grown and their taproots tested for latex content, work done by captive Soviet scientists and 150 prisoners from the women's concentration camp at Ravensbrück. Results suggested that latex production was under genetic rather than environmental control, but following the liberation of Auschwitz in 1945, it was unclear whether the breeding program produced a high-latex cultivar.[16]

Meanwhile scientists at the Kaiser Wilhelm Institute of Plant Breeding conducted a parallel program on the genetics of latex-producing plants suited to the German climate. Working at the Rotes Luch estate near Muncheberg, an area where Russian dandelions thrived, geneticists used colchicine treatments to increase chromosome number (see Chapter 6). Their intent was to develop a robust polyploid strain; the treated roots were peeled using a centrifuge and tested for latex on site. Beginning in June 1943, Heinrich Himmler assumed oversight of rubber production in Germany and merged the Kaiser Wilhelm Institute program with the field station and laboratories at Auschwitz, with the obvious intent of organizing rubber production (both natural and synthetic) in one place. Hitler planned to grow the dandelions in German-occupied areas of Russia for export to German rubber manufacturers, but Russian farmers lacked interest in the crop. The dandelion fields were overgrown by weeds, resulting in the deportation of Russian farm families to forced labor camps.[17]

Ultimately several Nazi agencies and ministries (involving food, agriculture, farming, farmers, plant breeding, chemistry, and automotive production) had controlling interests in Russian dandelion research. Rubber production was of particular concern to the *Volkswagen* engineers who needed tires for their vehicles. Car ownership was part of *Kraft durch Freude* (strength through joy) program that offered leisure activities for the German middle class. Posters and medals associated with *Kraft durch Freude* bore images of alpine woodlands and Aryan outings in the Germanic landscape. However, the car factories were soon converted to manufacture *Kübelwagen*, lightweight military vehicles that were adapted from the *Volkswagen* design; they resembled U.S. jeeps and navigated bogs and mud with ease. All available rubber was diverted to the Nazi war effort, which included some novel uses. Designed almost exclusively for underwater travel, U-boats (particularly the diesel-electric models, the so-called Type XXI super-submarines) had a hull covered by rubber tiles that supposedly deflected sound waves; apparently this was an effective cloaking mechanism to avoid detection by Allied sonar. While on patrol, German U-boat crews plundered tires and inner tubes wherever they could be found, whether to use or to recycle (perhaps into rubber tiles) is unknown.[18]

German interests also included gutta percha, a latex harvested primarily from *Palaquium percha*, a Malayan tree species related to chicle sources in the family Sapotaceae. The trees grow slowly and must be felled in order to extract the latex, which forms in sacs in the leaves, cortex, phloem, and pith. Gutta percha is thermoplastic, meaning that it can be heated and

Gutta percha was harvested primarily from a Malayan tree species related to chicle sources in the family Sapotaceae. The latex is thermoplastic and resistant to salt water, making it ideal for insulating undersea telegraph cables. Gutta percha was also a standard item in military dentistry for filling cavities, and it was used in the surgical repair of severe facial trauma such as eye socket injuries.

molded, and then solidifies when cool. Its insulating properties and resistance to salt water made the unique latex the ideal material to insulate undersea telegraph cables. Plantations in Borneo, Sumatra, and Malaya were controlled by a few British companies, and presumably the Allies had sufficient supplies stored for wartime use, which included dentistry. Gutta percha was a standard item in military dentistry supplies for filling cavities, and it was used also in the surgical repair of severe facial trauma such as eye socket injuries. Apparently German supplies of Malayan gutta percha had dwindled, and botanists sought alternative sources; an issue of *Die Umschau* noted that a similar compound was isolated from a native German species of warty spindle tree (*Euonymus verrucosus*), which was sometimes cultivated in ornamental plantings.[19] In fact, the unrelated shrub is now known to contain 7–15 percent of a latex that closely resembles true gutta percha.

Military Rubber

There were vast military needs for rubber, from insulation and tarpaulins to tires and specialized clothing. Munitions workers wore rubber shoes with no metal parts that might cause a spark, and frogmen wore wool-lined rubber suits. Sherman tanks and B-17 bombers each required at least a half ton of rubber, and battleships needed about 75 tons. Various types of inflatable rubber boats were used in landings and assaults, and the

Decoys made from inflatable rubber tubes mimicked the dimensions and silhouettes of tanks and other equipment. These served as effective deception to confuse enemy intelligence about the number of tanks on a battlefield or the direction of invading forces; D-Day strategies included inflatable landing craft, trucks, and anti-aircraft guns, later described in the press as a "ghost army" designed to confuse Nazi troops (U.S. Army).

U.S. used decoys made from inflatable rubber tubes that mimicked the dimensions and silhouettes of actual tanks and other equipment, but were prone to puncture from shellfire. These served as effective deception (both on land and from the air) to confuse enemy intelligence about the number of tanks on a battlefield or the direction of invading forces. D-Day strategies included inflatable decoy landing craft, trucks, and anti-aircraft guns later described in the press as a "ghost army" designed to confuse Nazi troops.[20]

Rubber was essential to various types of military footwear, perhaps most importantly the boots designed for combat under wet, slippery jungle conditions. Following victories by Japan in Malaya, General MacArthur's staff examined the form and function of the equipment used by Japanese troops in jungle environments. Their items were lightweight and compact, allowing rapid, quiet movement. Troops wore *tabi* (or *jika-tabi*), shoes with canvas uppers and thin, split-toe rubber soles that allowed some awareness of soil surface and relief. The unique shoes enhanced the ability of Japanese soldiers to walk through rain-soaked mountainous landscapes, mud, and dense vegetation with relative ease. One of the Japanese owners of the Bridgestone Corporation, which also manufactured wartime tires, designed the original *tabi*.

Leather shoes deteriorated quickly in wet, hot climates, so new designs relied on the rubber and cloth model of *tabi*. U.S. jungle boots were designed with a corrugated rubber sole for traction in mud and on wet vegetated slopes, but by all accounts they were not as effective as *tabi* in navigating jungle terrain. The split-toe design was not adopted, but uppers were made from canvas or cotton duck that allowed ventilation. The jungle boots slipped on wet roots, logs, and slopes; the rubber soles were tiresome for walking; and there were complaints about fit and shrinkage of the cloth uppers. Men cut away the fabric that chafed their ankles, voiding some of the protection against leeches and insects. Nevertheless Army-issue jungle boots were supple and quiet for walking in vegetation, and engineers and others who worked in swampy areas favored shoes that drained water and dried quickly. The boots were shipped into the Pacific region by the thousands, although many troops preferred ordinary leather service shoes, sometimes modified with rubber soles and hobnails for improved traction during combat.[21]

Even with control of Asian and Pacific rubber plantation, the Japanese anticipated latex shortages, but their civilians were informed otherwise. Military needs included various armaments, anti-venom kits for snake bites, and parts for airplanes and tanks, and the Japanese press featured photographs of latex tapping and bales of dried rubber ready for industry. Optimistic articles in the Japanese press predicted that latex would be made into paints and petroleum and that rubber would replace metal, plaster, and wood.[22]

Health was an ongoing military concern. Troops were routinely exposed to venereal diseases such as syphilis and gonorrhea, despite graphic posters, official films, and other warnings about illicit sexual contact with prostitutes and local women (see Chapter 7). Despite sulfa drugs and penicillin, venereal diseases still cost time away from duty and medical supplies. In 1942, Army doctors stationed in northern Ireland were the first to practice prophylaxis against venereal diseases by distributing rubber condoms. Although the local Red Cross offered wholesome activities for soldiers, syphilis and gonorrhea infections still occurred; men were treated and not punished, but Army surgeons insisted on lectures on condom use. Officers, physicians, and chaplains all delivered the message, and condoms were distributed at the rate of six per man each month. Eventually military condoms were available at railway stations, local prophylactic stations, and even Red Cross clubs.[23]

By the end of the war, official condom policy was, "When properly used, venereal prophylaxis offers good protection against infection.... Condoms are provided free through medical supply channels and must be made easily available to the unit at all times."[24] Statistics revealed that manufacturing condoms was a valuable use of wartime latex supplies; according to the final logistics report of the U.S. Army, "The Army lost 1,280 man-days per thousand per annum in 1940 from venereal diseases; in 1945 it lost 244 man-days per thousand per annum."[25] In fact, many (perhaps most) of the hours saved were the result of condom use rather than antibiotics; syphilis still required a full week course of penicillin, and enlistees were accepted with active infections that required immediate treatment. Prophylaxis aside, troops found other inventive uses for condoms. For instance, unrolled onto the barrel, a condom protected a rifle from becoming clogged with mud or soil.

Gas Masks

There was widespread fear of chemical gas during World War II. Personal defense involved wearing a rubber gas mask that formed a gas-proof chamber and required breathing through a charcoal filter (see Chapter 9). The gas masks manufactured by many countries at the beginning of World War II were based on the technology developed during World War I and relied on rubber to make the molded face piece airtight. Germans had used mustard gas against the Allies at Ypres in 1917 (see Chapter 4) and thus during

World War II anticipated that the Allies would retaliate with poison gas bombs. Standard gas masks were issued to all German civilians, and children drilled for gas attacks by wearing masks during school assemblies. Mothers practiced placing infants and young children inside *Gaskettchen*, gas-proof chambers consisting of a wooden frame and rubberized fabric, hand-ventilated with bellows.

British civilians also anticipated poison gas attacks. Local Air Raid Precautions (ARP) workers carried wooden gas rattles, ratchet-based devices used to signal a possible gas attack with a characteristic clacking noise. ARP bulletins including "Personal Protection against Gas" (1937) and "Civil Defense Leaflet 2—Your Gas Mask" (1939) focused on the importance of carrying gas masks when away from home, keeping them nearby at night, and cleaning and maintaining masks weekly. Gas masks were packaged in standard boxes made of strawboard (cardboard made from straw pulp), but civilians were reminded that attractive carriers could be made by covering the boxes with varnish, paint, canvas, or glazed calico and adding shoulder straps.[26]

Poison gas bombs could drop at any time, so 24-hour vigilance was essential to survival. Evacuated children carried gas masks into the countryside, and mothers were reminded continually of the need for practice drills with young children to avoid panic in the event of a gas attack. As in Germany, infants were placed inside ventilated devices made of gas-proof cloth, and parents were instructed to have young children wear masks during playtime, to encourage familiarity with their potentially frightening appearance. Mickey Mouse–style gas masks made of red and blue rubber were designed to appeal to young children.

Nor was mustard gas the only possibility. It was known that the Germans also synthesized lewisite, an organic arsenic-containing compound that was both a blistering agent and lung irritant. Posters illustrated with a gas mask and flowers reminded civilians that lewisite smelled like geraniums, but the odor was only coincidentally similarity to the terpenoid-based floral scent. Following the German attack on Poland, the British government provided gas masks to Polish civilians. Gas masks were also made for dogs and horses, both domestic pets and military service animals, although thousands of household pets were euthanized at the beginning of the war due to anticipated food shortages. In England and other countries during World War II, gas masks were never needed against a poison gas attack, although ARP workers used them routinely to avoid the fumes and dust caused by incendiary bombs and bombing raids.

Gas mask design was an ongoing effort of the U.S. Chemical Warfare Service. The original M1 service model and its modifications were mass produced in three sizes that fit almost all head sizes. However, the masks were heavy and bulky, and soldiers often abandoned them or used the cases for other purposes. Some also discovered that the gas mask silhouette was an easy target for enemy snipers, but by 1943, a streamlined version known as an assault mask was available to troops stationed in Europe. These weighed half as much as the original gas masks and floated in water, important in the event of gas attacks during the D-Day invasion.[27] The new design was featured in *Popular Science* two months before the D-Day landings.[28] Climate led to additional problems. Gas masks made from reclaimed or synthetic rubber (see below) hardened during the cold European winter, making them impossible to fit. The only alternative was to use supplies of natural, newly made rubber to mold the face pieces, so the Chemical Warfare Service hired several French manufacturers to remake 400,000 gas masks. The heat and moisture of tropical Pacific climates also took their toll; gas masks deteriorated quickly from fungi that colonized rubber, cloth straps, and lenses.[29]

Following the attack on Pearl Harbor, there was widespread concern that poison gas attacks on the Hawaiian Islands would follow. The Chemical Warfare Service supplied nearly 500,000 new and used masks (some probably dating from World War I) that high school students and other civilians refurbished and repaired. Rubber padding was added to improve the fit of masks for school-age children and Asian physiognomy. Local first aid stations issued the masks to all Hawaiians over the age of seven years, but none were available for younger children and infants. In response to this need, Colonel George Unmacht (then in charge of civilian defense in the Territory of Hawaii, but later remembered for inventing a tank-mounted flame thrower) invented a gas-proof hood with attached bunny ears to appeal to young children. These were made in the territory from locally sourced materials including cloth treated with paraffin (insufficient rubber was available) and eyepieces of scrap celluloid (see Chapters 8 and 9).[30] The hoods were never needed, but thousands were distributed to civilian families and also to residents of the leper colony on Molokai. In the event of widespread need for civilian gas masks, the Chemical Warfare Service considered another version for U.S. children based on Mickey Mouse. In January 1942, Walt Disney met with Chemical Warfare Service staff to collaborate on the design, which unlike the ARP version included large rubber ears.[31] A supply of about one thousand were made but never used.

Military gas mask design was an ongoing effort of the U.S. Chemical Warfare Service. Gas masks made from reclaimed or synthetic rubber hardened during the cold European winter, making them impossible to fit and requiring retrofitting with new rubber parts. The heat and moisture of tropical Pacific climates also took their toll; gas masks deteriorated quickly from fungi that attacked rubber, cloth straps, and lenses (U.S. Army).

Barrage Balloons

Barrage balloons were stationary, strategically-placed blimps that were made from rubberized cotton fabric, filled with gas (hydrogen or helium), and tethered with cables. During World War II, the British military pioneered their use as anti-aircraft devices, positioning the balloons near docks, harbors, airfields, and other sites targeted by *Luftwaffe* bombers. Often described as kite balloons, the elongated shape allowed them to tolerate windy conditions more readily than a spherical design. Their function was simple: to complicate flight navigation because low-flying planes could be ensnared and damaged by the metal cables. Some balloons were also equipped with charges that in the event of a collision released a section of cable equipped with parachutes, designed to bring down a plane using weight and drag.

Barrage balloons protected against planes flying lower than 5,000 feet, forcing them to fly higher and into anti-aircraft fire. Later in the war, the balloons also provided some protection against German V-1 rockets. Although V-1 wings were equipped with wire-cutters to slice though metal cables, over two hundred of the rockets (which flew at about

Barrage balloons were stationary blimps made from rubberized cotton fabric. The British military pioneered their use as anti-aircraft balloons, positioning the balloons over London and other cities and near docks, harbors, airfields, and other sites targeted by *Luftwaffe* bombers. Low-flying planes could be ensnared and damaged by the metal balloon cables (Royal Air Force).

2,000 feet) were felled by barrage balloons. Members of the Women's Auxiliary Air Force learned how to inflate and maintain the 1,400 barrage balloons that by 1940 were tethered across England. A Ministry of Information film "Balloon Site 568" (1942) featured footage of young women working at balloon hangars and urged others to join up; training included wire-splicing, knot-tying, and techniques for maneuvering balloons which were typically tethered to trucks. Early in the war, refilling the balloons with gas was part of standard maintenance performed by the Women's Auxiliary Air Force; the natural latex used in making rubberized balloon cloth was slightly porous and allowed some gas to escape. By 1942, the U.S implemented barrage balloons to defend vulnerable strategic sites. Rubber manufacturers such as Shell Oil Company boasted in their advertisements of using less porous synthetic rubber to make barrage balloons gastight.

The U.S. began with a few barrage balloon companies, but by 1941 there were plans for 85 batteries that would each fly 35 balloons. Early equipment was imported from England, but 3,000 newly designed D-8 low altitude balloons were soon ordered from Goodyear. These closely resembled British designs which used less rubber and maneuvered more easily than a larger prototype designed by the U.S. for possible high-altitude flight. Camp Tyson in Tennessee was the site of rigorous training for balloon companies; these included the 320th Barrage Balloon Battalion, the African American company that traveled to Normandy and tethered barrage balloons over Omaha beach to stop German aircraft. At Utah beach, which lacked surrounding hillside, colored and numbered balloons directed Allied planes to landing areas.[32] Some ships in the English Channel also carried balloons to protect D-Day landing craft from strafing by low-flying German planes. Ultimately U.S. barrage balloons were used to defend the west coast, Hawaiian Islands, Panama Canal Zone, and Allied positions in Europe. The 36th Signal Heavy Construction Battalion tried to use a barrage balloon to drag telegraph cable across the Rhine River (the attempt failed), but instead used timber to suspend 1,600 feet of cable across the open water.[33]

Few American children ever saw them aloft, but in England about a third of all barrage balloons flew over the heavily populated London area. There was concern that the balloons might frighten children, many of whom were already traumatized by evacuation and bombing. Although the rubberized fabric and hydrogen gas were flammable and dangerous in shellfire, children were taught that the balloons were there to protect them. There were toy balloons and children's books that anthropomorphized barrage balloons into likable characters. *Bulgy, the Barrage Balloon* by Enid Marx (1941) and *The Story of Blossom, the Brave Balloon* by Phillip Zec (1941) familiarized children with the idea of large rubber balloons flying over local towns and villages. Apparently Enid Marx had to request clearance from the Ministry of Defense to include simplified illustrations of a barrage balloon, although the balloons were already a familiar sight on the British horizon.[34]

Occasionally barrage balloons broke free of their cables and caused damage, which resulted in the British idea of launching free-flying bomb attacks on Germany. Operation Outward released rubber naval weather balloons (about 8' in diameter) across the English Channel toward Germany. Each balloon carried either dangling wires (which caused short circuits when they touched power lines) or fire-setting devices including grenades and incendiary jelly. Some of the balloons carried incendiary devices particularly designed to cause forest fires; the design involved paraffin-coated canvas bags filled with wood shavings, equipped with fuses, and V-shaped to catch in the crotches of trees. Beginning in March 1942, over 99,000 balloons were released toward Germany from a coastal golf course in Felixstowe. The Women's Royal Naval Service assisted with balloon releases (1,000 per day at the height of the program), admittedly hazardous work because of the incendiary devices, but the balloons caused local disruption in Germany by setting forest fires and damaging electrical equipment.

Synthetic Rubber

Rubber shortages were finally solved by organic chemistry when the compounds known as elastomers captured chemists' attention worldwide.[35] While botanists were hunting for wartime sources of natural latex, chemists used botanical by-products to develop synthetic substitutes, including a rubber-like compound known as Norepol and made from soybeans (U.S. Patent 2,390,961, 1943). As early as the 1920s, German chemists had already made considerable progress with making synthetic rubber from two small organic compounds: butadiene and styrene. The process required the addition of sodium ions, so the German product known as buna rubber took its name from *bu*tadiene and *Na*. Butadiene had a botanical origin; it was made on a commercial scale from alcohol fermented from sugars derived from cellulose in wood cell walls. I.G. Farben operated their *Buna-Werke* (synthetic rubber plant) at the Auschwitz concentration camp using slave labor. In the U.S., fifty factories produced a similar combination of butadiene and styrene equal to twice the global pre-war production of natural rubber. By the end of the war, this synthetic product had largely replaced natural latex. Even military-issue chewing gum was made of butadiene-based rubber (see Chapter 5).

During World War II, incendiary bombs and flame throwers used napalm, made from gasoline combined with the aluminum salts of naphthenic and palmitic acids, both obtained from plant-based oils (see Chapters 4 and 9). Napalm required jelling agents to convert the liquid into a semisolid adhesive liquid that burned slowly and at a high temperature. Natural latex was the first jelling agent adopted, but shortages caused by the Japanese control of Asian rubber plantations resulted in the use of synthetic rubber with the gasoline and plant acids. The result was a sticky, flammable mixture that was first tested by Louis Fieser and other chemists at Harvard; further testing at the Dugway Proving Ground demonstrated the effectiveness of napalm in incendiary bombs.

11

Survival

Training for warfare in the Pacific began with practical lessons in the ecology of tropical Asia, Malaysia, and Pacific islands. With regard to island combat, the U.S. War Department field manual *Jungle Warfare* described "dense tropical growth including undergrowth, trees, vines, and giant ferns found at the elevations between the lower foothills or beaches and the high areas above the timberline."[1] In reality, troops encountered a range of tropical habitats, including beaches, mangrove swamps, bamboo forests, coconut groves, tall grass, agricultural plantations, rice paddies, and local farmland. Nevertheless Pacific combat often occurred in tropical forests and the surrounding dense jungles, requiring descent into valleys and ravines where Japanese troops encamped.

Preparation

The Imperial Japanese Army had prepared for jungle warfare since 1941. The training manual (translated as *Read This Alone—And the War Can Be Won*) written by Colonel Masanobu Tsuji included sections on terrain, climate, sugar cane fields, jungles, and bamboo groves, which defined the habitat in many tropical areas. The giant grass grew several inches in diameter and up to twenty feet high, with vast clones sprouting from horizontal surface rhizomes. Thus Japanese troops often used bamboo groves for defensive concealment and long term encampment, positions from which they attacked. Tropical forests were similarly useful in providing botanical defense; forts and bunkers made of logs from coconut palms were masked with transplanted jungle vegetation (see Chapter 9) and so virtually disappeared into the landscape. In short, Japanese troops exploited dense vegetation strategically, an approach that differed from the tendency of Allied troops to avoid or destroy tangled growth and thick underbrush.

With Japanese troops deeply embedded, Allied training emphasized suspicion above all else. However, exhausted troops sometimes hallucinated, and jungle conditions compounded battle fatigue and other psychiatric conditions. The scent of the jungle at night (probably methane from decaying vegetation) was sometimes mistaken for poison gas, and bioluminescent fungi on rotting logs were mistaken for Japanese signals.[2] In reality, the fungi decompose the lignin in wood cells, and bioluminescence may have adaptive value in attracting nocturnal animals that disperse fungal spores.

Warm temperatures and high rainfall fostered dense vegetation which harbored parasitic leeches, poisonous snakes, and the vectors of diseases including malaria and scrub typhus (see Chapter 7). Muddy gorges and precipitous valleys posed physical danger, especially if colonized by thorny plants or stinging nettles that could result in skin infections, and mountainous terrain meant that distance was often measured in time rather than miles. Few locales had accurate maps, and dense vegetation obscured trails in aerial photographs. Thus training manuals advised relying on local people to provide information about trails, which could change seasonally depending on rainfall, floods, fallen trees, and erosion. Nevertheless, training manuals for U.S. military personnel made the Pacific theater seem unrealistically innocuous, if not downright pleasant, suggesting that "...the soldier should attempt to practice his hobbies or cultivate new ones. If he is of the type who enjoys the outdoors, he will find plenty to do—hunting, fishing, and trapping. He might also make a hobby of the jungle itself by learning something about the birds, plants, insects..."[3]

Training occurred at camps in the Hawaiian Islands, Philippines, Australia, New Caledonia, and Saipan, sites where tactical marches involved dense vegetation and camouflaged positions, although some troops just trained where they landed. In the spring

of 1942, the 37th Infantry Division left Ohio and arrived in the Fiji Islands to provide reinforcement against a possible Japanese invasion; their training continued in Fijian rain forests and mangrove swamps, which provided field preparation for Guadalcanal and the Solomon Islands later in the war. In all of these areas, woody growth concealed enemies, so soldiers were trained in stealth and scouting under conditions with limited visibility, and they learned to navigate the narrow trails that Army engineers cut through dense underbrush and jungle vegetation. The Unit Jungle Training Center in the Kahana and Punaluu valleys on Oahu used obstacle courses, cross-country marches, and mountain climbing exercises to simulate fighting the Japanese in difficult terrain. Landing in forested areas, paratroopers were in danger of becoming trapped in the dense canopy and remaining undetected. In Papua New Guinea, a recent

U.S. troops learned to maneuver in dense jungles on Bougainville and other Pacific islands. Few locales had accurate maps, and dense vegetation obscured trails in aerial photographs. Training manuals advised relying on local people to provide information about trails, which could change seasonally depending on rainfall, floods, fallen trees, and erosion (U.S. National Archives).

Tropical vegetation covered Cape Totkina on Bougainville Island, where Marine Raiders posed in front of a Japanese bunker, excavated structures reinforced with coconut logs. Training encompassed basic survival and sanitation skills including strategies for avoiding the fungal diseases associated with trench foot; soldiers were advised to avoid bare feet and contact with mud (U.S. National Archives).

discovery along the Kokoda Track that crosses the Owen Stanley Mountains seemed to be the moss-covered remains of a World War II paratrooper.[4]

Training encompassed basic survival and sanitation skills including strategies for avoiding the fungal diseases associated with trench foot (see Chapter 7). Soldiers were advised to avoid bare feet and mud, but tropical fungi quickly decomposed leather shoes. Rubber-soled jungle boots had structural defects (see Chapter 10), and mud was often so deep that men needed help to extricate themselves. Supplying footwear for tropical habitats was an ongoing challenge for Army Quartermasters, although civilian shoes were rationed, which provided the raw material for military footwear. Magazine advertisements for Florsheim shoes featured a soldier beside palm fronds and reminded civilians that "fighting men are hard on shoes—you can't afford to be." As jungle conditions and fungal deterioration became better understood, botanical products including cotton, rubber, and canvas replaced wool and leather in clothing and other equipment. Nevertheless U.S. items were heavy and bulky compared to Japanese equipment, clothing, and footwear. Gunstocks swelled in the high humidity as wood cells absorbed water, sometimes causing metal parts of rifles to bind; linseed oil (see Chapters 6 and 10) was used to waterproof wood, but sometimes the only solution was to disassemble the weapon and shave away some of the wood.

Machetes were needed because weapons could become tangled in vegetation, and the grasses associated with scrub typhus (see Chapter 7) were several feet tall. Dense bamboo thickets were particularly difficult to navigate because of the surface rhizomes, but they provided useful building materials (see Chapter 9). In Burma, the U.S. 5307th Composite Unit (known as Merrill's Marauders, see Chapter 7) encountered bamboo forests so dense that they literally chopped and tunneled through the growth.[5] However, there were hazards associated with cutting bamboo, which could be dangerously sharp due to its high silica content. While traveling by Jeep in Burma Admiral Louis Mountbatten was temporarily blinded by a bamboo splinter that caused an internal eye hemorrhage.[6] In Borneo, crew members of a B-24 bomber were assisted by local Dayak tribesmen and were eventually rescued using a bamboo runway built over a rice paddy. In the Philippines and New Caledonia, native bamboo was used to construct field hospitals that sheltered injured soldiers. Local people in Papua New Guinea crafted litters from bamboo and balsa wood to use in carrying injured soldiers over jungle trails inaccessible to jeeps. Similar to Japanese forts and bunkers (see Chapter 9), dugouts reinforced with coconut logs housed portable army surgical hospitals and sheltered wounded men. At times, buildings were not an option; before the fall of the Philippines in 1942, the incidence of casualties outpaced the ability of U.S. Army engineers to construct hospitals. On the mountainous Bataan peninsula of Luzon, medical staff organized wards and operating rooms in the jungle, using sheets tied to trees for cover.[7]

Poisonous plants were another concern, and some species were potentially lethal. In jungle conditions, troops typically relied on prepackaged operational rations (see Chapter 5), but when rations were in short supply, young men might incorrectly assume that all fruit were edible. For instance, physic nut trees (*Jatropha curcas*) are native to Central America and Mexico but were widely naturalized on saline and waste soils across Indonesia and other Pacific islands. Occupying Japanese forces required that Indonesians cultivate the plants because the nutlike seeds yielded an oil useful for fuel and lubricating machinery, but they contain a toxic protein similar to ricin (see Chapter 6); survival manuals (see below) warned troops about ingesting them. Ackee (*Blighia sapida*), an African relative of the lychee nut, was another widely naturalized tropical tree that men were advised to avoid. With the exception of the edible ripe aril (seed covering), the fruit produce a deadly amino acid derivative known as hypoglycin A.

Deception and Camouflage

Military strategies included deception and camouflage, with models of natural vegetation and local landscapes that were crafted with botanical materials. In Germany, model villages made from papier-mâché served as decoys to deflect bombing attacks from populated areas. Wood was used to build decoys of landmark buildings and bridges in Hamburg, and wood and canvas replicas of refineries and arms factories tricked Allied flight crews into dropping their bombs. On a larger scale, the *Luftwaffe* assembled a crude full size model of Berlin across nine miles of countryside. Designed to be viewed from the sky, there were fake parks and dimly lit buildings with "roofs" of paper and cloth, arranged to resemble the urban landscape of Berlin during blackout conditions. Streets in the actual city were draped with brown and green burlap (see Chapter 8), which from an aerial view resembled the pointed tops of a coniferous forest. At some of the concentration camps, buildings had earthen roofs that blended into the forest to avoid Allied reconnaissance, and fences were camouflaged with branches cut from *Holzplatze*, the wood lots that supplied fuel. During the Blitz, there were controlled nighttime blazes that mimicked the appearance of British cities in flames; the fires were set using creosote, a highly flammable by-product of burning wood or coal. The Home Guard organized in response to fear of a German invasion. Members were usually above the age of conscription, but they trained to defend their towns and villages using guerrilla strategies. Uniforms included ghillie suits made from hessian, a coarse fabric woven from jute, sisal, or hemp and embellished for camouflage in the local landscape.

Similar deception occurred at certain sites in the U.S. The Lockheed airplane plant in Burbank, California was considered a likely bombing target, and so landscape painters and set designers from film studios aided in disguising the site as an apparent agricultural and suburban landscape when viewed from the air. Tarmac-covered parking lots and airfields were painted to resemble agricultural fields, while the main factory was hidden under wire mesh draped with painted canvas. Artificial trees and house frames covered with burlap completed a convincing natural scene. Muralists and landscape artists were suddenly in high demand for training camoufleurs to paint vegetation as it would appear from a distance, with the goal of protecting military sites by mimicking nature and concealing buildings. In Europe, it was impossible to camouflage an entire city, but the combination of light, color variation, tone, texture, and shadows could simulate natural vegetation. Urban roofs were covered with gray-green wood shavings that resembled grass from the air. Other botanical materials used in creating a textured landscape included wood chips, excelsior, burlap, and evergreen branches, all of which could be cemented in place and painted to match the local landscape.[8]

Green paint posed a particular conundrum because it absorbed infrared light, unlike

Before and after aerial photographs illustrate the camouflage of the Lockheed plants in Burbank, California to resemble an agricultural and suburban landscape. Parking lots and airfields were painted to resemble fields, and the main factory was hidden under wire mesh draped with painted canvas. Artificial trees and house frames covered with burlap created a natural scene (U.S. National Archives).

natural chlorophyll which reflected wavelengths greater than 700 nanometers. As a result, trees appeared light-colored when photographed with infrared film, while green-painted buildings, matériel, and artificial trees were seen as dark blotches in the landscape. In the U.S. Navy, there was interest in developing a chlorophyll-based paint to use in camouflage, but extracts of leaf pigments proved notoriously unstable in bright light. Botanists worked on developing a stable camouflage paint using pigments extracted from spinach leaves, and they developed a mixture that remained green even under high intensity light for 24 hours. However, the methodology for its production remains classified.[9]

There was concern that the U.S. mainland might be bombed by Axis countries, and the nursery industry reacted immediately, anticipating opportunities to sell trees, shrubs, vines, and ground covers to camouflage military sites. Trees for potential use in camouflage were classified by size and growth form (spreading, erect, deciduous, evergreen), and the American Association of Nurserymen provided information about availability of various species by region.[10] High school teachers wove lessons on camouflage into biology curricula; it was considered important that students learn to apply the principles of concealment and protective coloration in a practical way.[11] Floriculture specialists at Cornell University taught a course on camouflage techniques, and the Museum of Modern Art in New York developed circulating exhibits on camouflage for civilian defense. Museum staff also contributed to the design of easily-camouflaged, prefabricated houses based on steel grain bins designed by Buckminster Fuller.[12]

Botany became a practical science as botanists considered seasonality in the appearance of local vegetation and the effect of climate on transplanting woody plants used for concealment. Botanists at the Arnold Arboretum investigated quick-growing plants that could be cultivated for cover; a wartime issue of *Arnoldia* featured fast-growing vines for areas across the U.S. and noted "a great deal of interest in camouflaging various installations in this country, both public and private."[13] Recommendations included herbaceous and woody vines, both annuals and perennials with twining growth, rootlets, tendrils, and other adaptations for climbing growth. Species included familiar cultivated plants such as English ivy (*Hedera helix*) and Boston ivy (*Parthenocissus tricuspidata*), along with various honeysuckles (*Lonicera* spp.), clematis (*Clematis* spp.), and grapes (*Vitus* spp.), all of which could grow up and over buildings or cling to wire mesh.

The most infamous recommendation for a camouflaging vine was kudzu (*Pueraria thunbergiana*, also known as *P. Montana* or *P. lobata*), an east Asian legume (or perhaps a cluster of hybrids) described as "the fastest growing of all vines."[14] Kudzu vines were reliably hardy south of Philadelphia and could colonize marginal sites and nutrient-poor soils; symbiotic root bacteria fix atmospheric nitrogen (see Chapter 4), allowing the vines to grow in soil depleted of usable forms of nitrogen. In 1902, botanist David Fairchild of the Department of Agriculture warned of possible problems with uncontrollable growth, but kudzu was planted widely across southern states to control erosion. The Civilian Conservation Corps launched a breeding program in the 1940s, and by 1946 there were a half million acres of nursery-raised kudzu vines on road banks, along tracks, and on public lands.[15] Should the need arise for home front camouflage, Americans were ready to plant more kudzu, and U.S. troops introduced the vines to the Allied air and supply bases in the Fiji Islands. The plan was to grow the vine as living camouflage for Allied equipment, but under tropical Pacific conditions kudzu quickly became an invasive species with a growth rate that aggressively outpaced native Fijian flora.

Tactical camouflage was largely the responsibility of camouflage units in the Army

The most infamous wartime recommendation for a camouflaging vine was kudzu, now an aggressive invasive species. The Civilian Conservation Corps launched a breeding program in the 1940s, and by 1946 there were a half million acres of nursery-raised kudzu vines on road banks, along tracks, and on public lands throughout the southeast. Americans were prepared to plant more kudzu for home front camouflage, and U.S. troops introduced the vines to the Allied air and supply bases in the Fiji Islands to camouflage Allied equipment (United States Soil Conservation Service).

Corps of Engineers, but fundamental principles of concealment were essential to all in combat. Trained camoufleurs taught the basics of concealment and deception in the field, the art of learning to hide and blend equipment and installations seamlessly into the landscape. Nets were used to conceal large guns and other equipment, but had to be carefully merged with existing vegetation to achieve a natural look. Igloos of draped netting hid anti-aircraft guns, sited on sod and landscaped with cut shrubbery and small trees. Considering aerial perspectives, camoufleurs recommended draping garlands of burlap strips (see Chapter 8) for a gradual visual transition from concealed matériel into the natural vegetation. Small trees were wired together to conceal gun positions, and ammunition boxes were stored amidst leaf piles and underbrush or draped with netting to resemble hay bales. Natural materials such as leafy branches were cut and used, but these wilted and required frequent replacement; any signs of military habitation such as foot prints, debris, discarded vegetation, or clothing had to be hidden. Airplanes were draped with burlap, netting, or branches to conceal their shape and avoid reflections. Deception also involved decoy positions; brush piles resembling ammunition boxes, foot and tire tracks, and disturbed vegetation were intentionally staged to provoke enemy artillery.[16]

Camouflage nets were made of jute, hemp, or cotton (see Chapter 8). They were

Camouflage nets were made of botanical fibers, dyed natural colors, and garnished with cloth strips to resemble foliage. In the U.S., many nets were made by Japanese-Americans who had been relocated to inland camps. Residents of the Manzanar internment camp wove burlap strips into hemp nets by following a Greek key pattern that cast credible shadows from the sky; garnished with bits of burlap to resemble leaves, these nets were used to camouflage tanks and buildings (U.S. National Archives).

either knotted or woven, dyed natural colors, garnished with cloth strips to resemble foliage, and transported in canvas bags along with wooden poles and stakes. Netting was essential equipment that civilians could hand-produce; British fishermen and their wives knotted camouflage nets from hemp twine following specific patterns, and Women's Institutes (see Chapter 7) volunteered to garnish netting with pieces of green, brown, and black cloth, depending on its intended use. In the U.S., nets were made by Japanese-Americans who had been relocated to inland camps; residents of the Manzanar internment camp wove burlap strips into hemp nets by following a Greek key pattern that cast credible shadows from the sky. Garnished with bits of burlap to resemble leaves, these nets were used to camouflage tanks and buildings.

In the Hawaiian Islands, the Corps of Engineers recruited the dexterous makers of leis and fishing nets to craft large nets to conceal local installations. Netting was garnished with cloth that local artists dyed to match Hawaiian habitats. Mindful of possible detection from the sky, net makers took great care in dying garnished netting the precise color of local vegetation. Dummy airplanes made of wood and burlap were parked in fields to attract enemy fire, while real aircraft were cleverly concealed. The football field of the Punahou School was converted into a tree nursery for cultivating camouflage trees, using thousands of seedlings obtained from the Territorial Board of Agriculture and Forestry. Outside of Honolulu, a building for airplane maintenance was constructed with a concrete roof ten feet thick, topped with soil, and planted with pineapples for camouflage. Of course, early in the war there was also fear of Japanese attack in Alaska, where some Army posts were landscaped with trees and shrubs and military buildings were concealed with mud and driftwood.[17]

Woven cotton shrimp nets were too visible for use in camouflaging landscapes, but they were ideal as helmet netting to minimize surface shine while holding small twigs, branches, or pieces of burlap (often known as scrim) as camouflage. Helmet camouflage was described succinctly in the Army field manual *Camouflage of Individuals and Infantry Weapons*: "The main point is to break up the shape of the helmet with short natural material which will not readily catch in surroundings and which will not disclose the head when it is moved slightly.... No matter what kind of helmet camouflage you use, it is incomplete if the shadow underneath the helmet is not broken up by arranging the bits of foliage so that pieces of it hang over the rim of the helmet. Small irregular pieces of cloth, similarly arranged, will accomplish the same purpose."[18] Coarsely woven cloth such as burlap or osnaburg (a fabric woven from flax and jute and sometimes used by the Quartermasters for shipping goods) was sometimes substituted for helmet netting.

Natural materials were used to conceal in a variety of ways. Airdromes and landing strips needed green camouflage or the bare soil could be easily detected from the sky; the solution was to plant them with cover crops. Grasses could be mowed to resemble agricultural fields, and botanists at the Royal Botanic Gardens (Kew) researched the chamomile species traditionally used for lawns (*Chamaemelum nobile*, not to be confused with *Matricaria chamomilla*; see Chapter 7) as a suitable low-growing, spreading plant for landing strips. Some Spitfire pilots actually preferred landing on sowed airfields; they knew that when tires barely touched the tall grass, it was time to stall the engine for a perfect landing.[19] Tents were plastered with mud and local grasses, and deciduous or evergreen foliage mounted on wire frames was used to shield vehicles. Army camouflage manuals suggested using tarpaulins and branches to conceal piles of supplies and recommended that pyramidal piles be made to resemble small trees and shrubs from the sky.[20] Army camoufleurs investigated the use of fast-growing weedy plants as living camouflage for permanent installations; vines like kudzu could be trained up poles and over buildings to resemble trees and forests from the sky. Corps of Engineers camoufleurs noted the

Airdromes and landing strips needed green camouflage or the bare soil could be easily detected from the sky; the solution was to plant them with cover crops. Botanists at the Royal Botanic Gardens (Kew) researched the chamomile herb traditionally used for lawns as a suitable low-growing plant to camouflage landing strips.

difficulty posed by cut deciduous foliage that wilted and could not be easily replaced during combat, noting that "foliage that sheds leaves wilts in a day or less, depending on climate and type of vegetation."[21] Succulents and evergreens survived longer, but most areas of combat were characterized by deciduous local flora that wilted quickly when cut.

In response to problems with using plants in concealment, botanists at Harvard University formed a Camouflage Research Committee, with staff from the Arnold Arboretum, the Biological Laboratories, and the Harvard Forest (a forested tract in Petersham, Massachusetts) collaborating with the U.S. Army Engineer Board at Fort Belvoir in Virginia. Using North American, European, and Asian trees cultivated at the Arnold Arboretum and Harvard Forest, botanists and foresters explored myriad techniques for keeping foliage green, or at least appearing fresh and natural from an aerial view. At the Harvard Forest, meticulous trials were conducted on preventing transpiration, wilting, and browning in broadleaf and conifer species. Staff experimented with cutting techniques and timing, sunlight exposure, temperature, and strategies for providing water to cut plants. Much of their work centered on preventing the formation of polysaccharide plugs (tyloses) and internal bubbles (air locks) that blocked water conducting cells in cut stems. However, they also experimented with surface treatments including waxes, paraffin, and petroleum jelly to slow transpiration and plant hormones (auxins) to prevent leaf abscission and promote root development in cut shoots. Other investigations involved using copper sulfate and calcium carbonate to preserve natural leaf colors, based on earlier studies of chemical means for stabilizing chlorophyll.[22]

Data and outcomes were presented in a research paper in which the Camouflage Research Committee summarized the practical side of its work, "Foliage is the principal raw material of military camouflage, and the way it is handled may well affect the life of the soldier or even the outcome of the battle."[23] The final report was in the form of an instructional manual titled *Using Cut Foliage for Camouflage*; the text noted, "…with a little care and knowledge, the soldier can very easily erect natural camouflage that will last for several days. The purpose of this manual is to show how that can best be done."[24] The authors described techniques for camouflaging temporary sites using branches from trees that best resisted wilting; cut branches of apple, hawthorn, beech, linden, lilac, and some oaks lasted for several days if provided with sufficient water. Not all species were equally useful; willow, aspen, and walnut foliage wilted almost immediately, and some conifers like larch and hemlock lost their needles within a few days.

There was also the matter of seasonal variation. Spring foliage lost water rapidly because the cuticle (a waxy layer on leaf surfaces) was not yet fully formed, while fall foliage was tough and water-resistant, but sometimes dropped leaves because the abscission layers had formed in the petioles. Botanists observed that sun-exposed foliage cut from the top or sides of a tree remained green longer than shade foliage and that branches lasted longer if they were cut at night or during rain or fog rather than bright sun.[25] Results suggested that a cut branch six feet in length typically needed a quart of water daily, which could be provided in a bucket concealed using leaves and pine sap. Large branches stayed green longer than smaller ones and could be positioned on wire mesh or netting to achieve a natural look. Orientation was important due to color differences between upper and lower leaf surfaces and the growth pattern of branches in nature. The committee recommended arranging foliage with the upper surface in view to avoid excess transpiration from stomata concentrated on the lower epidermis, noting that haphazardly strewn vegetation caused an "unnatural appearance that may often be more conspicuous than no camouflage at all."[26] Even entire trees were sometimes felled and used, maneuvered into tarpaulin-lined water holes and secured in place by guy-wires.

Work done by the Camouflage Research Committee was not classified, and the perfected techniques were shared with visitors at the Friends of Harvard Forest field day on September 4, 1943. The Committee also advocated permanent natural plantings at Army installations. Virtually any of the thirty common European tree species could be transplanted as natural camouflage, and there were literally thousands of woody species for cultivating in the Pacific and Asian tropics. Troops were warned in particular against woody plants that caused dermatitis, including related resinous species in the genus *Rhus* (poison ivy, poison oak, and poison sumac); these are native to North America, and camoufleurs in training may have mistaken them as useful for hands-on camouflage.

Tropical areas posed particular challenges, prompting the Harvard Camouflage Committee to publish a second manual, *Using Cut Foliage for Camouflage. Supplement on Tropical Pacific Islands.* Dr. E.D. Merrill, chairman of the Camouflage Research Committee, developed a list of potential plants for concealment trials at the Plant Introduction Garden, operated by the U.S. Department of Agriculture in Coconut Grove, Florida. Tropical diversity posed a conundrum to the committee; there was an abundance of plant material to use for camouflage in the Pacific theater, but it was impossible for botanists to predict the indigenous flora that soldiers might encounter. Thus the Camouflage Committee decided to experiment with widely naturalized tropical species and encouraged Army camoufleurs to conduct trials with local plants by cutting three to five branches, keeping them in water and under sunlight, and recording the outcomes. Many islands had diverse flora but no single dominant species, so camoufleurs first had to determine which woody plants to employ.

Guidelines developed by the committee noted that many coastal plants such as mangroves, coconut palms, and she-oaks (*Casuarina* spp.) could be kept alive in saline or brackish water. The elongated, jointed branches of she-oaks were particularly useful in concealing outlines and shadows, and shade-grown branches seemed to last longer than those exposed to bright sun. Other common trees useful for camouflage included rubber trees (*Ficus elastica*), banyan trees (*Ficus benghalensis*), and Pacific species of *Hernandia* (related to Old World laurels) and *Barringtonia* (related to Brazil nuts), all with leathery leaves that resisted wilting. Palms and banana plants were tough-leaved and nearly ubiquitous on Pacific islands, but single large leaves placed on flat surfaces were easily detected from the sky; upright orientation and three-dimensional foliage were essential in achieving a natural appearance. The goal was to simulate the depth, shadows, and texture of tropical vegetation, which required attention to details and ongoing maintenance.[27]

There was also concern that camoufleurs might be injured or poisoned by tropical plant toxins. The sap of mango trees (*Mangifera indica*) caused rashes similar to poison ivy (both are in the cashew nut family, Anacardiaceae), and the stinging hairs of tree nettles (*Laportea* spp.) contained formic acid that caused severe blisters and pain. The rule of thumb for camoufleurs was to avoid trees with milky sap and when in doubt to consult the War Department publication TM10-420, *Emergency Food Plants and Poisonous Plants of the Islands of the Pacific.*[28]

The two manuals compiled by the Harvard Camouflage Committee were distributed widely to the Army Corps of Engineers camouflage companies and to military training centers, including the Infantry School at Fort Benning and Armored School at Fort Knox.

However, their research and conclusions had a mixed reception; some of the techniques described in the manuals were too laborious for combat settings, and some seasoned officers clearly thought that using vegetation in camouflage had become unnecessarily complex. Nevertheless, the techniques were adopted and taught at the Army Air Force jungle survival school in Florida and perhaps other sites.[29]

Of course, camouflage with foliage was sometimes the only option, even by sailors without specialized training as camoufleurs. One of the most innovative examples occurred onboard the HNLMS *Abraham Crijnssen*, a minesweeper in the Royal Netherlands Navy. Late in 1941 the ship survived battles in the Java Sea and was ordered to return to Australia. To avoid detection, the crew collected, cut, and arranged tropical trees and foliage on the decks and painted exposed areas to resemble coastal rocks, until the minesweeper credibly resembled a small tropical island. The ruse worked; anchored as a small "island" by day, the *Abraham Crijnssen* avoided detection by the Japanese military. The crew sailed at night, close to the coastline, and the *Abraham Crijnssen* was the last Allied ship and only minesweeper in its class to escape safely from Indonesian waters.[30]

Camouflaged clothing posed another challenge. Any glimpse of white or light colors was potentially lethal. Troops on Bataan and Guadalcanal learned quickly that white laundry was easily visible to Japanese snipers. Some used berries, tannins from tree bark, and coffee to dye white clothing, until supplies of olive drab underwear, socks, handkerchiefs, and towels reached tropical installations.[31] Medics and surgeons soon realized that cotton field dressings (see Chapters 7 and 8) had to be dyed green to avoid detection in jungle habitats. In field hospital settings, white bandages were so visible to Japanese snipers that some wounded men removed them rather than risking enemy fire.[32]

With an eye toward the war in the Pacific, in July 1942 General Douglas MacArthur ordered uniforms made of a pattern that would conceal troops fighting in dense tropical vegetation. Various patterns and color schemes were considered, including suggestions from the Corps of Engineers, but the final choice was developed by Norvell Gillespie, who was well known as a horticulturalist and garden editor at *Better Homes and Gardens*. Her camouflage design featured a mottled pattern of three shades of green and two shades of brown and resembled frog skin. The reverse side of the fabric revealed a spotted pattern of tan and brown, so uniforms could be turned inside out during a beach landing. Nor was this Gillespie's only contribution involving concealment; later in the war she shared information with the Arnold Arboretum about fast-growing vines suitable for living camouflage.[33] Meanwhile, combat experience in Papua New Guinea revealed the importance of jungle camouflage. Japanese snipers could often discern standard olive drab cloth among dense vegetation, so orders were sent to a Brisbane cleaning establishment to dye standard green uniforms with a mottled coloration. The dye that was used is unknown, but it made the cloth retain moisture and caused discomfort and skin ulcers; it may also have been absorbed through skin and excreted in urine.[34] Late in 1943, Marines were the first to use the new frogskin-patterned camouflage uniforms during combat in the mountains and forests of Bougainville Island, the largest of the Solomon Islands. Parachute cloth was printed with the same green pattern for use by paratroopers landing in densely vegetated areas.

Camouflage manuals advised combat troops to use common sense and materials at hand. Even the mottled frog skin pattern did not offer complete concealment in dark jungle habitats, and so uniforms and equipment were at times amended with paint, mud, charcoal, and/or grease for use in habitats with deep shade and dark foliage. Troops learned to cover foxholes, bunkers, and dugouts with woven reeds, branches, and grass and to mask sandbags with sod. Troops also learned how to move quietly and inconspicuously in low or dense vegetation, preferably in the shadows cast by trees, and to avoid isolated clumps of plants that often became targets.[35] These were all skills at which Japanese soldiers excelled, as well as the clever camouflage of mine fields with earth, burlap and sod.[36]

Military vehicles were often concealed in clumps of vegetation, camouflaged with branches and netting (which had to be propped up with tall branches to hide the shape of the vehicle) or by plastering the painted surfaces with natural materials. Burlap effectively obscured reflective windshields. Manuals suggested using fresh plant material to make a natural adhesive by boiling any sort of herbaceous tissue in water for hours until it became a thickened paste (presumably dissolved carbohydrates from cytoplasm and cell walls, including pectin), which could be used to attach leaves, grasses, and sand to the painted surface of trucks and other vehicles.[37]

Survival Manuals

In combat settings, there was the possibility of becoming separated from others or stranded without resources, and survival manuals provided essential information for living alone in nature, perhaps for weeks or even months. Generally speaking, these were pocket-size paperback books with practical information about food, water, and shelter in arctic, desert, and tropical climates. Details included nontechnical descriptions and illustrations of edible and poisonous plants; materials and instructions for constructing temporary shelters; and strategies for collecting potable water. Organizing such information was a challenge; prior to the war, there was no central repository of useful survival advice, although there were resources that included the worldwide field experiences of botanists, anthropologists, and ethologists.

The first survival manual published during World War II was a booklet authored by an Army officer for troops stationed in the tropics, a text that covered several fruit-producing species which were common and widely naturalized.[38] Survival in wild settings eventually attracted widespread wartime interest; according to E.D. Merrill (chairman of the Camouflage Research Committee and director of the Arnold Arboretum), there were 21 government agencies, museums, botanical gardens, and individuals eventually involved with compiling, writing, and publishing survival manuals for various climates and habitats. Sensing confusion at hand, in September 1942 the National Research Council convened a meeting to organize the effort of compiling accurate survival advice. Information was gleaned from diverse sources including technical reports, scholarly papers, regional floras, taxonomic revisions of various plant groups, and anecdotal information from travelers and explorers. Nevertheless, the multitude of manuals published during the war came from disparate sources and did include occasional inaccuracies or simplistic generalities. Manuals with incomplete or inconsistent botanical information included *Jungle and Desert Emergencies* and *Jungle Desert Arctic Emergencies*, both published (apparently in haste) by the Army Air Force in 1943.[39] The latter recommended drinking sap from lianas (woody vines) as a water substitute; however, several pages later in the text, there was a warning against plants with milky sap, which can be toxic or even lethal.[40]

One of the most widely disseminated survival manuals that dealt strictly with food resources was *Emergency Food Plants and Poisonous Plants of the Pacific*, also known as War Department Technical Manual 10-420, authored by E.D. Merrill and illustrated with detailed drawings copied in later survival guides.[41] The area covered by the manual included Polynesia, Micronesia, Melanesia, Malaysia, the Philippines, Indo-China, Thailand, Burma, and eastern India, encompassing vast botanical diversity, so Merrill limited the contents to 128 widespread plant species and groups with edible tubers, leaves, fruits, or seeds. Rare and highly endemic plants were omitted, and the instructions included directions for the safe preparation of botanical foods. As Merrill noted in a later article, "Naturally, widely scattered and very rare or local species should not be considered in any popular booklet on edible plants, hence a prime necessity ... is a wide field experience on the part of the compiler ... he must know what plants and plant parts may be eaten, either crude or processed—and some plant parts must be processed before they can be eaten in order to eliminate certain poisonous principles."[42]

Merrill's plant descriptions were accompanied by scientific names, illustrations of edible parts, and a spectrum of local names. Common edible species included bananas (*Musa sapientum*) and plantains (*M. troglodytarum*), various breadfruit species (*Artocarpus* spp.), and papayas (*Carica papaya*). Some less familiar edible species were virtually ubiquitous on islands that could support forests, including palms and tree ferns. The cut stems of rattan palms (*Calamus* spp.) released potable water, but Merrill recommended drinking the liquid endosperm (see Chapter 7) from coconuts (*Cocos nucifera*) as a water source. Young fruit were preferable because their liquid did not have the laxative effects of mature fruits with higher oil content. Solid coconut endosperm from mature coconuts was another reliable food source. In addition, many palms had edible buds, and some such as sago (*Metroxylon* spp.) had inner stem tissue with high starch content. Tropical ferns were present year round, and their carcinogenic potential was not yet recognized. He recommended the fiddleheads (crosiers or curled young leaves) of tree ferns (*Cyathea* spp.) and climbing ferns (*Stenochlaena palustris*) as emergency food; the semi-aquatic fern *Ceratopteris thalictroides* could be collected in swampy areas and eaten whole. About 1,500 fern species occur in the Pacific region, but as Merrill noted, many produced tough or bitter leaves so sampling was essential to determine palatability.

Aroids were also abundant, but they required careful preparation and cooking. Taro (*Colocasia esculenta*) was widely naturalized, but the starchy rhizomes were unpalatable raw. Merrill described them as not truly poisonous but rather as having "myriads of minute needlelike stinging crystals of calcium oxalate that are intensely irritating when brought in contact with tender skin."[43] He recommended that aroids be thoroughly boiled or roasted to break down the crystals and alleviate the intensely acrid flavor, but he considered some more dangerous than others. In the case of the Philippine corpse flower (*Amorphophallus campanulatus*), he noted, "The large tuber should never be eaten except after prolonged cooking ... consult informed natives before using this as food."[44]

The spurge family (Euphorbiaceae) included several toxic species that may have appeared edible at first glance. Merrill warned against castor beans (*Ricinus communis*, see Chapter 6) and the related physic nut trees (*Jatropha curcas*), both widely naturalized. The starchy roots of cassava (*Manihot esculenta*, the source of commercial tapioca) contain dangerous cyanogenic glycosides, which required cooking in several changes of water to remove safely. There was the possibility that it might be confused with tropical yams (*Dioscorea* spp.) or sweet potatoes (*Ipomoea batatas*), both entirely edible. Many

Pacific species had unknown toxicity, so Merrill advised caution and consultation with local people to determine safe methods of preparing unidentified wild plants.

There may also have been variations in toxin levels or susceptibility. Merrill listed Polynesian arrowroot (*Tacco leontopetaloides*, a relative of tropical yams) as a tuber that required cooking for edibility, but many local people supposedly ate them raw. He recommended observing the feeding behavior of local monkeys before eating unknown fruits, but palatability was sometimes the result of anatomy rather than chemistry. The cucumber relative known as loofah (*Luffa cylindrica*, see Chapter 8) was common, but the gourd-like fruits had to eaten while immature, before the tough vascular tissue matured. There were also many edible seeds, including pangi (*Pangium edule*, which needed careful preparation to remove cyanogenic glycosides), Indian almonds and related species (*Terminalia* spp.), and various legumes including hyacinth bean (*Dolichos lablab,* also known as *Lablab purpureus*)

The U.S. War Department manual *Jungle Warfare* provided this illustration to warn against highly toxic physic nuts; the trees were widely naturalized on saline and waste soils across Indonesia and other Pacific islands. Occupying Japanese forces required that Indonesians cultivate the plants because the seeds yielded an oil used for fuel and lubricating machinery, but they contain protein similar to ricin (*Jungle Warfare* FM 72-20, 1944 p. 109).

and pigeon pea (*Cajanus cajan*). Merrill included information on *Derris*, native Malaysian legumes that produce the insecticide rotenone (see Chapter 6). As an alternative to fishing with lines and hooks, the roots of *Derris* species could be crushed in water to stun fish, allowing them to be caught and safely eaten.

Not all U.S. Army field manuals were equally useful when it came to providing sound survival strategies. The War Department field manual *Jungle Warfare* included optimistic advice about finding food: "Whenever possible, one should try to get in touch with natives even though one may be able to talk with them only by means of signs. They can be most helpful in times when regular rations are not available…. Field trips, preferably under the guidance of informed friendly native inhabitants, are the best means of learning plant identification."[45] In terms of field botany, the most informative section of the manual was the appendix on toxic plants, which included a warning about the botanical source of strychnine.[46] Species in the genus *Strychnos* are woody vines that yield both the potent alkaloid strychnine and the curare toxins used on poison arrows.

Other manuals of tropical edible plants included *Friendly Fruits and Vegetables*, a text for Australian troops stationed in the Pacific.[47] It covered plants that might be cultivated in local gardens, starchy plants such as sago and breadfruit, fruits, nuts, and poisonous species. Shortages vexed Allied forces stationed in remote Pacific sites, and in response to the need for emergency rations in the Solomon Islands, Lucy Cranwell wrote *Food Is Where You Find It—A Guide to Emergency Foods of the Western Pacific*; the text included detailed information and illustrations of plants that provide sugars, starches, and oils; toxic species, including plants that could be used to stun fish; and botanical fibers and structural materials for building shelters.[48] The manual provided information that could have helped the 16th Brigade of the Australian Army in November 1942, when three days without rations forced men to eat grass and caused many to collapse on route to Popondetta in Papua New Guinea.[49]

The Bishop Museum in Honolulu was a repository of ethnobotanical knowledge amassed from field work in Polynesia, Melanesia, and Micronesia, information that could be converted to survival strategies for pilots or sailors marooned on tropical islands. *A Castaway's Baedecker to the South Seas* was aimed at airmen who might crash in the Pacific, and *South Sea Lore* covered practical uses for common tropical plants that could provide food, water, shelter, and clothing.[50,51] K.P. Emory, the author of both manuals, offered lectures and practical demonstrations for all branches of the services at the museum and at Army camps and field sites, and his mobile units reached 2,500 men. On Oahu he provided field instruction at the Unit Jungle Training Center and at a wild site in the Kahana Valley, and he set up additional lessons in the New Hebrides, adapting instruction to the local plant populations. He emphasized that not all islands were densely vegetated; some atolls posed a particular challenge because they could be extremely dry and devoid of dense vegetation. Emory advised eating purslane (*Portulaca oleracea*, a low-growing succulent weed) or the tender aerial roots of *Pandanus* palms as a source of fresh water, or collecting water that accumulated at the base of taro leaves.

The Bishop Museum offered an intensive survival course for officers, who learned practical botany to demonstrate for others. As Emory lectured, the officers prepared widely naturalized edible plants, including coconuts, breadfruit, bananas, papayas, sweet potatoes, taro, and yams. They learned to release liquid endosperm from coconuts by punching holes into the eyes, thin areas in the inner fruit wall (endocarp) where the root emerges from the germinating embryo. Coconut palms had other uses, including use of liquid endosperm as emergency blood plasma (see Chapter 7). Coconut palm fibers that grow around the young leaves were a cloth substitute, the fronds were used for thatching and weaving, the husk was used for lighting fires, and the flowers provided a sugary sap. Officers demonstrated how to weave sandals from various leaves (essential for avoiding foot injuries and infections caused by walking on coral), thatch a six-man shelter using palms, and devise mosquito netting from palm leaf fibers, traditional skills developed by Pacific islanders and meticulously documented by museum staff.[52] The U.S. Army provided men and a truck for collecting supplies of coconuts, palms, and other Hawaiian plants used in the demonstrations, and the Bishop Museum eventually accommodated an entire village built during the survival courses.

Botanists at the Field Museum in Chicago described edible plants of the New World tropics in *Edible and Poisonous Plants of the Caribbean Region*.[53] Aimed at soldiers stationed in Central and South America, the text included charts that identified edible fruits, seeds, leaves, and roots based on color, shape, size, surface, and location. Many edible plants such as mango, papaya, and avocado were probably familiar to some troops, but others such as various species of *Annona* (sweet sop, sour sop, and custard apple) needed safe identification. The section on poisonous plants included several species that also occurred on Pacific islands, including physic nut trees and others that have medicinal properties in controlled doses. The authors warned in particular against ingesting any plants with milky sap characteristic of the spurge family (Euphorbiaceae); in fact, of the seventeen poisonous plants described, six species are in this family and have milky sap. These included the manzanilla trees (*Hippomane mancinilla*) that colonized shorelines.[54] The fruits resembled small green apples, but contact with the milky sap, smoke from burning wood, or with the beach sand around the trees resulted in severe dermatitis, blisters, and temporary blindness. Victims of manzanilla poisoning were routinely evacuated from the region and dosed with morphine sulfate to relieve the associated pain.[55] Even some known edible species had potential dangers; the chestnut-like seeds of the Panama tree (*Sterculia apetala*) can be consumed, but the inner surface of the capsule is lined with trichomes (hairs) that cause severe skin irritation.[56]

Survival on Land and Sea shared tropical, arctic, and desert survival tactics gleaned from Smithsonian research and archives.[57] Desert survival included relatively few plant-based strategies; under dry conditions water was more important than food, so downed airmen were advised to carry supplies with them and to barter with local people for food. Signal fires were useful in helping searchers find a downed plane, but dry kindling and timber were often lacking in cold climates. Advice for arctic survival included making signal fires from driftwood, shredded birch bark, and heathers such as *Cassiope tetragona*. Salmonberry (*Rubus spectabilis*), crowberry (*Empetrum nigrum*), bilberry (*Vaccinium* spp.), and mountain cranberry (*Vaccinium vitis-idaea*) were recommended for their edible fruits. Other edible plants above the tree line included the leaves of mountain sorrel (*Oxyria digyna*) and dwarf willow (*Salix herbacea*) and the roots of wooly lousewort (*Pedicularis lanata*).[58] Below the tree line, edible buds could be collected from spruce and tamarack trees, along with inner bark from willows, alder, hemlock, and birch trees. Lichens were described as "low, moss-like plants" (in fact they are symbiotic associations of algae and fungi), which required soaking, drying, and pulverizing into powder that could be cooked into a bland but edible gruel. Ironically, lichenologists considered them only as a last resort, perhaps because research on lichen digestion and food value was inconclusive. As a realistic postwar review article noted, "Under such starvation conditions any type of food or plant may be used in an attempt to allay hunger. But under a preplanned program designed to educate personnel with a minimum of out-of-door experience …a greater emphasis of the more common vascular plants… in these regions would have been more applicable towards the preservation of life. Lichens are not easily recognized, and their preparation with fire presumes the accessibility of fuel which may not always be available."[59]

Nevertheless *Edible Plants of the Arctic Region* emphasized lichens as a reliable food source in arctic habitats, organisms that lost airmen and sailors should not be afraid to consume.[60] Edible species included Iceland moss (*Cetraria islandica*), reindeer moss (*Cladonia rangifera*), and rock tripe (*Umbillicaria* spp.), which were all widespread and commonly used by local people. The author, P.C. Standley, probably knew that sailors survived on rock tripe during the ill-fated Franklin expedition to the Arctic, but apparently the species caused severe illness.[61] Under desperate conditions, most men would have preferred meals of other wild foods, but vitamin deficiency was a possible problem for those who relied on fish or wild game for an extended time. *Emergency Food in Arctic*

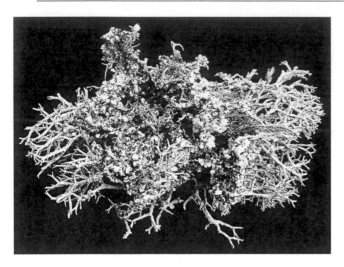

Survival manuals described lichens as a reliable food source in arctic habitats, organisms that lost airmen and sailors should not be afraid to consume. Edible species included reindeer moss, which was widespread and commonly used by local people (Verisimilus, Wikimedia Commons).

Canada recommended foraging for the wild mustards known as scurvy-grass (*Cochlearia* spp.) as a source of vitamin C in emergency arctic diets.[62] In fact, the 1st Combat Intelligence Platoon, a unit of the Alaska Scouts known as Castner's Cutthroats, relied on wild berries and other edible plants to survive; they fermented their dried fruit ration into an alcoholic drink which they named raisin jack, also the name of their boat.

Training films reinforced the strategies described in various manuals. Movie images with wry narration may have been a more engaging way to provide life or death information to young men. *Castaway* (Bureau of Aeronautics, 1944) described survival on a Pacific island following advice from *A Castaway's Baedecker to the South Seas*. A downed pilot finds and eats pigweed as an emergency food; he makes a sharpened stick for husking coconuts and survives on meals of coconuts, taro, and bananas. *Land and Live in the Jungle* (Army Air Forces, 1944) illustrated the survival strategies practiced by a flight crew lost in dense tropical vegetation. They consult the *Jungle Desert Arctic Emergencies* manual and follow its suggestions, from finding food and water to building beds and rafts from bamboo stems and vines.

In the War Department training film *Land and Live in the Arctic* (Army Air Forces, 1944) a downed airman survives in deep snow by building a shelter from conifer saplings and improvising shoes and socks from parachute cloth and canvas. The film suggests building snow shoes from willow branches and mentions that the inner bark of willows is edible, but ignores edible lichens. A rescue plane responds to SOS outlined in the snow with conifer branches. Another War Department film, *Land and Live in the Desert* (Army Air Forces, 1944), illustrates survival in a remote desert lacking vegetation, but the downed fliers camp under their parachutes and use oil, fuel, and rubber to make smoky signal fires. The Australian training film *Living off the Land* (Australian Army, Special Forces Jungle Food Course, 1944) begins bleakly; a search party discovers the body of a starved soldier, after the narrator reminded viewers that "food is all about you." Images and narration reveal how to collect drinking water from trees and vines and food from coconuts, tropical yams, cassava, ginger, sugar cane, and various fruits and nuts that grow wild in northern Queensland and nearby islands.

After the war, there was military interest in assessing survival strategies. The Arctic, Desert, Tropic Information Center (ADTIC), based at Maxwell Air Force Base in Alabama, coordinated the effort, and Richard Howard, a botanist who directed the Army Air Force jungle survival school in Florida, reviewed stories of survivors of land and sea emergencies for the important lessons that could be learned. Foremost, ingenuity and patience worked synergistically with the will to survive, supported by information recalled from films and read in manuals. According to personal accounts, men lost on Pacific islands improvised clothing and shoes from plant materials, including palm and banana leaves, woven grass, and the fibers surrounding the young leaves of coconut palms. Hollow bamboo stems and coconut shells were used to collect rain, and men experimented to find the vines that released the most water. Survivors tended to eat familiar foods such as bananas, mangoes, papayas, and coconuts (including the edible young seedlings), but desperate conditions resulted in experimentation with the unfamiliar ferns, roots, and fruits described in survival manuals. Grasses, including sugar cane and rice seedlings and other grains, were another option. Some safely prepared taro and cassava, both potentially toxic if directions in survival manuals were ignored. Food was surreptitiously harvested from gardens cultivated by Japanese occupiers. Local people shared garden crops, which included familiar vegetables such as tomatoes, squash, peas, beans, peanuts, and melons, many of which also escaped and naturalized on Pacific islands. Legumes were among the most nutritious foods that could be collected and eaten.[63]

Desert conditions lacked the diversity of plant materials, but a similar analysis of survival strategies revealed inventive plant uses. A pilot who crashed in a remote Arizona desert collected the pith of barrel cacti as a water source. Shrubs and grass hummocks served as supports for parachutes rigged as tenting, and green grass stalks were chewed as a water source and emergency food. Other wild foods collected by desert survivors included aloe berries (*Aloe* spp.), wild melons (particularly the seeds), pods of leguminous acacia trees (*Acacia* spp.), and dates (the fruit of the widely naturalized date palm, *Phoenix dactylifera*). Spines protect many desert species from herbivores, but they also cause injuries. The spines of various acacias and thistles (probably *Eryngium* spp.) caused dermatitis and small wounds, and the retrorse spines of cacti were a worse problem because they were difficult to remove and often caused infections.[64]

Deprivation, Starvation and Epigenetics

Dietary deprivation was a wartime reality for those imprisoned by Axis countries or living in occupied regions. Diaries and memoirs recorded the near starvation experienced by many, including prisoners of the Japanese who were fed vitamin-deficient diets of rice and little else. Interned civilians, many of them British colonials, held along the Kwai River in Burma (now Myanmar) and Siam (now Thailand) foraged for edible plants and cultivated gardens using whatever seeds and tools they could obtain. They experimented with fermenting rice using yeast, a source of B vitamins; an interned botanist discovered parasitic yeast on the inflorescences of palms and cultured it in rice to make a primitive vitamin supplement. Prisoners improvised communion services on a bamboo altar with substitutes for bread and wine made from rice. To quell malaria and scrub typhus (see Chapter 7), prisoners dug drainage ditches and cut grass that harbored rats. Cleanliness depended on water buckets crafted from robust stalks of bamboo, and imprisoned botanists advised on wild medicinal plants, including cures for dysentery and sources of narcotics to replace surgical anesthesia. Surgical instruments were sterilized with alcohol from fermented rice; tea leaves were used as sterile compresses for wounds and burns, and the covering seemed to prevent the spread of infections. Morale was also important. Christmas puddings were mixed up from rice, bananas, limes, and sugar obtained from palms, and a wreath made of jungle foliage helped to mark the holiday. Burned rice steeped in water served as a coffee substitute. Musical instruments were crafted from bamboo and wooden tea boxes and played in makeshift sets fashioned from rice sacks painted with plant pigments. Even prosthetic limbs were crafted available materials; prisoners foraged for kapok (seed hairs collected from the woody capsules of *Ceiba pentandra*, see Chapter 8) to line the baskets woven to hold the stumps of amputated legs.[65]

In the Philippines, the typical daily ration for internees was a cup of rice, but it was the unmilled *palai* type that had intact husks. Prisoners developed various strategies to pound or grind the grains into an edible meal, and they augmented their diet by foraging coconuts, bananas, yams, sweet potato leaves, and a succulent weed known as Philippine spinach (*Talinum fruticosum*). On Mindinao, prisoners were allowed to build huts using bamboo frames and woven palm leaves; roofing was made from the tough-leaved grass (*Imperata cylindrica*) associated with scrub typhus infections (see Chapter 7). They cultivated a vegetable garden, but their captors seized control of harvested crops and allocated prisoners a daily ration. Some also grew patola vines (*Luffa acutangula*), edible gourds that are relatives of *L. cylindrica*, the loofah sponges used as filters in shipboard engines (see Chapter 8). Starving prisoners resorted to palm leaves and entire banana plants, including the leaves and tough stems.[66] As described in survival manuals, coconuts in particular had many uses as a source of food and raw materials. Prisoners carved the shells as a pastime, and a coconut helped the crew of PT 109 avoid capture and imprisonment by the Japanese. After the loss of his wooden patrol torpedo boat (see Chapter 9) to fire, Lt. John Kennedy and surviving crew members were marooned on Naru Island in the Solomon archipelago; he scratched a succinct rescue message on the outer shell of a green coconut, which two local men delivered to the Allied base on Rendova Island.

Prison camp doctors in Hong Kong advised steeping pine needles in water as a source of vitamin C.[67] However, a diet of white rice still lacked thiamine (vitamin B1, see Chapter 3), which is provided by botanical foods such as leafy greens and whole grains. Severe thiamine deficiency from a rice diet caused beri-beri, resulting in lethargy, depression, and debilitating physical symptoms. Despite these hardships, women held at the Changi prison camp in eastern Singapore secretly embroidered cotton quilts with flowers, meaningful images, and messages to relatives. Red Cross workers shared the quilts with imprisoned men, who recognized the stitchery done by their wives and sisters.[68]

To avoid capture by the Japanese after the Allied defense of Burma collapsed in May 1942, General Joseph Stilwell led 103 men and women out of Burma and into India, and all managed to survive. Traveling on foot over 140 miles in twenty days (at the rate of 105 steps per minute, a brisk pace that became known as the Stilwell stride), the men and women foraged in the jungle for wild fruit, leafy greens, and other vegetables. They relied on local people for meals of potatoes, bananas, and coconut. According to a surgeon's memoirs, "We are all vegetable hungry," not surprising with field rations that were limited to tea, porridge, rice, and tinned beef. When they reached the Uru River, the party used rafts made of bamboo lashed with rattan to reach the Chindwin River. The Burmese nurses (staff of a hospital unit that joined the retreat) used local plants to thatch shelters aboard the rafts, which protected all of them from rainstorms and bright sun. At times they walked in stream beds to avoid impenetrable vegetation. Malaria and sores were commonplace; by the time that they arrived in Assam, several needed hospitalization, but all lived.[69]

Tropical botanist A.J. Kostermans recalled months of forced labor on the military road that the Japanese built from Thailand to Burma. Japanese guards allowed the prisoners to forage for jungle plants, including the edible leaves of sweet potato and *Amaranthus* spp. and the astringent bark of *Baccaurea* which had various medicinal uses. Using a milk tin as a still, they distilled clove oil for dentistry from tropical Asian basil (*Ocimum sanctum*) with high levels of eugenol. They also collected and ate various aroids, but it was essential to drink quantities of water to avoid oxalate accumulation and kidney stones. After the war, Kostermans collected 2,000 botanical specimens from the region, a project funded by the Arnold Arboretum and made possible by labor provided by former Japanese soldiers.[70]

By 1940, Jewish people in eastern Europe were forced into ghettoes. The Warsaw ghetto of 1.3 square miles was the largest of these segregated zones, with a population of more than 450,000 residents at the high point of its occupation. Crowded conditions and dietary deprivation were also elements of official policy; German occupiers limited daily rations to about three hundred calories, and bread flour was routinely adulterated with sawdust. Diet consisted of meals made in communal soup kitchens from rationed and cultivated potatoes, cabbages, and turnips. Early spring was a time of particular need, after winter supplies were used and before new crops had grown; even scraps of potato peels and outer cabbage leaves were consumed for their nutrients. During winter, the lack of heat increased caloric consumption, and ghetto residents scavenged for coal and wood, often burning woodwork and furniture. Poor sanitation resulted in the transmission of infectious diseases, including typhus and tuberculosis, exacerbated by poor nutrition and vitamin deficiencies. Paper shortages meant that little could be printed or recorded, and the absence of trees, lawns, public gardens, and parks contributed to depressing ghetto conditions.[71]

The Yiddish song "Undzer Friling!" composed by Mordecai Gebertig in May 1942 used botanical imagery to summarize bleakness inside the Krakow ghetto[72]:

Springtime in the trees, in the fields, in the forest,
But here, in the ghetto, it's autumnal and cold,
But here, in the ghetto, it's cheerless and bleak,
Like the house of a mourner—in grief

Springtime! Outside, the fields have been planted,
Here, around us, they've sowed only despair,
Here, around us, guarded walls rise,
Watched like a prison, through the darkest night.

Springtime, already! Soon it will be May,
But here, the air's filled with gunpowder and lead.
The hangman has plowed with his bloody sword
One giant graveyard—the earth.

Some ghetto residents escaped to join resistance groups of men and women in eastern Europe and the Soviet Union who worked to sabotage Nazi plans. Activities were conducted at night under the cover of dense forests, but partisans survived by constructing bunkers known as *zemlianka*, log buildings assembled in excavated pits and then covered with soil. Only a door and window were visible above ground, and the structures were cold, damp, unventilated, and flood-prone. Hygiene was impossible to maintain amidst mud, mosquitoes, and lice, and partisans suffered from scurvy, boils, and fungal infections. Lacking drugs and supplies, they used pine needles or clover infused in water as emergency sources of vitamin C and burned birch bark to make a black sap used to treat skin afflictions.[73] German troops fighting the partisans found the eastern forests daunting in size and scope. Leaf litter from deciduous trees decomposed slowly, forming a malodorous sodden forest floor beneath impenetrable growth and amidst insect-infested marshes.[74]

Most ghetto residents were deported to labor and concentration camps, where the nutritional deprivations of internment continued. Rations varied, depending on the work that prisoners performed; for instance, at Buchenwald in western Germany weekly rations in 1940 for a prisoner doing average labor officially included twelve or thirteen pounds of potatoes and other vegetables, five pounds of bread, and less than a pound of meat and cheese, quantities that decreased as the war continued. By 1945, prisoners at Buchenwald officially subsisted on a weekly ration of about four pounds of potatoes, a couple of pounds of bread, and a half pound of horse meat.[75] However, it is doubtful that this amount of food was ever actually dispersed. Most meals consisted of bread (sometimes containing undigestible straw) and thin soup made from paltry botanical ingredients, including potatoes, turnips, grasses, and nettles. Although nettles have a relatively high protein content (up to 25 percent of dry weight), the soup was so diluted that it provided few nutrients. Even nettle stems had a use; tough bast fibers (see Chapter 8) were woven into the striped cloth used for prison uniforms.[76]

At Theresienstadt in German-occupied Czechoslovakia, vegetable fields were cultivated by prisoners, but the crops were harvested for Nazi officers. Fresh vegetables were essential to maintaining health, so a barter economy arose in which inmates with access to fruits and vegetables traded for other goods. In fact, malnutrition was widespread despite a prison diet that included starchy dumplings, and there were more than 33,000 deaths at the camp, many resulting from dietary deficiencies and related diseases. To the outside world, Theresienstadt was presented as a model for Jewish resettlement, with decorative details such as flower boxes and gardens that were installed prior to visits of Red Cross officials.[77]

German military and civilian populations had priority over internees, which resulted in experimentation with alternatives to standard prison foods. In the Ukrainian concentration camp at Vapniarka, prisoners received bread rations made from the ground seeds of *Lathyrus sativus*, a widely naturalized wild pea that was traditionally used as fodder. Long known as an emergency food in time of famine, *Lathyrus sativus* causes leg paralysis and other neurodegenerative symptoms if the protein-rich seeds are consumed as a major part of diet for even a few months. The condition known as lathyrism results from the amino acid ODAP (oxalyldiaminopropionic acid), which affects motor neurons. More than 100 of the prisoners who ate bread made with the pea flour lost the ability to walk, a permanent condition first diagnosed by Dr. Arthur Kessler, a physician interned at Vapniarka. Ultimately he devoted much of his professional career to identifying the cause of lathyrism, to the extent of cultivating different varieties of the wild peas to determine chemical levels of the neurotoxin ODAP.[78]

Another abusive dietary experiment took place at the Mauthausen concentration camp in Austria, where prisoners were fed *Östliche Kostform* (eastern nutrition), a paste made from cellulose from plant cell walls, some of it obtained from the fibers in old cotton and linen clothing and rags. The substance was fed to hundreds of prisoners; in one six month trial of the paste as a subsistence food, over two-thirds of the experimental subjects died, no doubt the result of malnutrition because humans lack the enzymes needed to digest cellulose. However, German courts convened after the war determined that the cause of death was not necessarily malnutrition because camp conditions may have been contributing factors to poor health and survival.[79]

Prisoners in German POW camps survived under spartan conditions. Typical prison diets were limited to *ersatz* bread (often made of potato starch stretched with sawdust); *ersatz* coffee made from roasted acorns (see Chapter 5); soups and stews of root vegetables, cabbage, barley, and little meat. Red Cross packages from the U.S., England, Canada, and other Allied countries provided additional calories and nutrients that helped prisoners to survive. The parcels included botanical foods such as tea, chocolate, sugar, cocoa, coffee, biscuits, raisins and other dried fruit, margarine, fruit preserves, canned vegetables and fruit, condiments, and vitamin C tablets. These basic supplies were sometimes saved and repurposed for alternate needs and uses. Packets of Red Cross black pepper were routinely used to keep German guard dogs at bay, and captured Royal Air Force pilots compounded Red Cross chocolate, margarine, oatmeal, and vitamin supplements into energy-rich bars for those who escaped successfully from Stalag Luft III in Poland.[80] Beginning in late 1943, Nazi officials allowed the Red Cross to send food, medical supplies, and clothing to concentration camps including Dachau, Auschwitz, and Theresienstadt, but Third Reich policy demanded a specific prisoner's name and location for each package. Over a million Red Cross parcels were shipped to concentration camps, but many were derailed into the hands of prison commanders and guards.

Prior to D-Day, Axis prisoners were transported to rear areas, and many were sent to camps in the U.S. and Canada, but the situation changed dramatically in 1945 as the war in Europe ended. Despite the Geneva accords of 1929 and the field manual *Rules of Land Warfare* (1940) that mandated the humane treatment of POWs, some Axis prisoners endured poor conditions at the end of the war. Most German troops had surrendered or lost their personal equipment; lack of tentage meant that soldiers spent days and nights in open, muddy fields or temporary enclosures, while camps were organized and constructed. Canned rations were available but not plentiful, and prisoners ate with sticks; dysentery followed, and soil in the temporary encampments mixed with feces. Some men built fires in holes dug for shelter, but there were cases of death from carbon monoxide poisoning. Nutritional deficiencies appeared including pellagra and beri-beri, perhaps attributable to the high levels of unenriched flour used in POW rations. Vitamin capsules were distributed to the youngest prisoners and to those with signs of malnutrition; by the end of the war, the German army included boys who were members of the *Hitler Jugend* (see Chapters 6 and 9), youth who were considered most vulnerable to vitamin deficiencies. By the spring of 1945, there were seventeen of these temporary sites which held over a million *Wehrmacht* troops, men and boys who were awaiting medical care and de-nazification.[81]

Part of the Nazi desire for *Lebensraum* and the *Generalplan Ost* (General Plan for the East, see Chapter 6) involved *Der Hungerplan*, intentional food shortages in German-occupied territories. Historians have described *Der Hungerplan* as an engineered famine, caused by the seizure of food for Wehrmacht troops and for export to Germany, beginning with the invasion of the Soviet Union in 1941. *Der Hungerplan* caused the starvation deaths of over four million Soviet citizens, including prisoners of war and ghetto populations, when the loss of Ukrainian grain effectively reduced the daily bread ration to a few hundred calories. Survival depended exclusively on botanical foods; bread flour was stretched by adding oats, sawdust, and the leftover hulls from processing linseed oil. Rye bread baked from these ingredients was described as dense, with a clay-like interior, but bartered loaves were at the center of a life-sustaining economy. War workers and combat soldiers received a larger bread ration, while women and children made do with half the amount. Alcohol provided some calories in adult diets, but children were malnourished with the daily ration.[82]

By the winter of 1942–43, most farmers were in the military, so wheat supplies and bread rations dwindled further. Shop windows were boarded up, and the few remaining food displays were printed on cardboard. A common emergency food was thin soup made with millet (*Panicum miliaceum* and other small grass cultivars, traditionally used in porridge) and thickened with dry bread. Rural families ate and sold potatoes that they grew on small plots in collective farms, while city dwellers grew vegetables on available allotments. A black market flourished in which farmers traded potatoes for jewelry and clothing. Many foraged for emergency foods, including birch tree buds, pine needles, nettles, tree bark, grass, clover, and wallpaper paste, which was made from rye flour because of its high gluten content. In addition, acorns (the fruit of oaks, *Quercus* spp.) and beechnuts (the fruit of European beech trees, *Fagus sylvatica*) were widely collected across eastern Europe as emergency foods which could be stored for months. Both are in the family Fagaceae and have mast levels (collective nut production) that vary annually. Typically there is high mast production every two to seven years, followed by years of low yields. Both acorns and beechnuts can have high tannin levels (see Chapters 4 and 7), making them bitter and astringent; removing the germ (embryo) and soaking in water helped to make the nuts palatable.[83]

Beechnuts were widely collected across eastern Europe as an emergency food which could be stored for months. Tannins can impart a bitter, astringent taste, but removing the germ (embryo) and soaking the seeds in water helped to make them palatable (Frank Vincentz, Wikimedia Commons).

However, a botanical diet that provided some vitamins and high cellulose content could not sustain appetites and metabolism. Humans lack the enzymes needed to digest cellulose, so edible plants without stored starch or fats contributed few dietary calories. Edible leaves and buds filled stomachs, but provided little digestible tissue; bark provided some carbohydrates (sugars present in the inner layer of food-conducting phloem cells), but these were also minimal. Cold temperatures increased caloric demand, and coal shortages forced city dwellers to cut wood in nearby forests. Health declined, resulting in decreased productivity, fewer births, and heightened susceptibility to diseases that included tuberculosis, typhus, and typhoid fever. Family pets disappeared, and there were occasional reports of cannibalism.

In Holland, the cold months of 1944–45 became known as the *Hongerwinter* (hunger winter), which occurred when Germany blocked food shipments to the western Netherlands, where half of the population lived in Amsterdam, Rotterdam, and the Hague. Over half of all crops were already being forcibly exported to Germany or used by occupying German forces, so this was a further reduction in civilian food, beginning in the fall of 1944 as a two-month food embargo. The action retaliated for the Dutch railway strike in aid of the Allied attempt to liberate the Netherlands. However, unseasonably cold weather caused canals to freeze, blocking food shipments even when supplies were available. Low temperatures also increased the need for calories and heat, and wooden furniture and buildings were dismantled for fuel. By February, dwindling supplies provided a meager starvation diet for 4.5 million civilians, consisting of an approximate per person weekly ration of a pound of poor quality bread, some sugar beets, and perhaps a few potatoes. The ration supplied less than 30 percent of the pre-embargo caloric intake.[84]

As food supplies became scarce, families lived by their wits. Nazi occupiers forbid the transport of food, but there were some areas where civilians could move through German lines. Men feared deportation to Germany for forced labor if they ventured away from home, so women and girls pedaled on bicycles miles into the countryside in search of farms with surplus potatoes or wheat. They also foraged for sorrel, nettles, and other emergency foods; there were occasional reports of mushroom poisoning and gastrointestinal trouble caused by beechnuts, presumably due to high tannin concentrations. Wartime conditions had curtailed trade in horticultural bulbs, and thus desperate people turned to flower farms for food. In monocot families such as the Liliaceae, bulbs and corms evolved as asexual structures adapted to support the next season of growth and flowering. As modified stems that store starch and sugar, these cooked down into an edible puree that could be thickened with flour. While not usually considered a human food, cultivated tulips saved lives by providing dietary calories during the *Hongerwinter* when both bread and potatoes were in short supply.[85]

Help arrived following months of severe shortages that caused an estimated 20,000 starvation deaths. By spring, flour donations from Sweden helped to ease the bread shortage, and in Operation Manna, the Royal Air Force delivered flour, margarine, yeast, tea, chocolate, and other staple foods. A silk shortage precluded the use of parachutes, so hundreds of food parcels were packed into bomb bays and dropped from low altitudes, a rescue mission that involved 4,500 aircraft and over three million pounds of food.[86]

The *Hongerwinter* of 1944–45 had lasting effects on survivors. The incidence of tuberculosis increased; wooden huts sent from Sweden served as sanitariums for housing patients. Birth weights were low among infants born to starving mothers, and infant mortality increased. As adults, those who were starved while *in utero* developed a higher incidence of coronary heart disease, hypertension, glucose intolerance, and other conditions. Most remarkably, however, there were persistent health effects among grandchildren of women who were pregnant during the *Hongerwinter*, a phenomenon now known as epigenetics in which environment determines the expression of inherited genes. Several studies of cohorts of grandchildren have revealed an unexpectedly high incidence of neurological disorders, mental diseases (including schizophrenia), autoimmune diseases, respiratory conditions, and generally poor adult health. The mechanism of such epigenetic effects involves the ability of cells to regulate gene expression (i.e., turn genes on and off), probably by attaching $-CH_3$ (methyl) groups to DNA sequences, typically where the bases cytosine and guanine are adjacent. The addition of methyl groups (a process known as methylation) controls how tightly DNA coils, effectively turning certain genes and gene sequences on or off. There are other epigenetic markers as well, which combine to determine DNA (i.e., gene) activity. In short, malnutrition and other events early in life can be passed to future generations through the epigenetic control of genes. In the case of *Hongerwinter* survivors, a simple botanical diet of potatoes, root vegetables, and legumes would have provided sufficient nutrients and calories to preserve the health of unborn generations.[87]

In the U.S. there was little medical information about the effects of severe malnutrition and starvation. There was concern about feeding Europeans after the war and the best foods for reclaiming the health of millions of malnourished civilians. During 1945, an experiment at the University of Minnesota sought to quantify starvation, investigations organized by Ancel Keyes, the physiologist who also worked on developing the K rations carried by U.S. paratroopers. Controlled experiments examined the effect of severe dietary deprivation on young men, conscientious objectors who volunteered for the year-long experiment in which both physiological and psychological data were collected. After a few months of normal diet and baseline data, volunteers consumed a semi-starvation diet (half of normal caloric intake) for six months. Two meals daily of root vegetables, potatoes, and bread approximated the rations available in many European countries during the war years. A rehabilitation diet restored the men to normal body weight, closely monitored to obtain information useful for treating malnourished Europeans after the war. The outcomes were documented in a two-volume work, *The Biology of Human Starvation*, published by the University of Minnesota Press in 1950.[88]

However, months before the complete results of the Minnesota experiment were known, the single greatest need for nutritional rehabilitation arose. During the first six months of 1945, Allied forces liberated Auschwitz, Bergen-Belsen, Dachau, Ravensbrück, Theresienstadt, and other camps. Skeletal prisoners needed food, but there were anecdotal reports that victims of starvation could die from overeating. The phenomenon is now known as refeeding syndrome, in which neurological and cardiac symptoms result from electrolyte and fluid imbalances, vitamin deficiencies, and metabolic changes following prolonged starvation. Refeeding syndrome was first documented in prisoners held in the Far East during World War II, and counter-intuitively, its management begins with a low calorie diet.[89]

U.S. troops who liberated concentration camps had seemingly intuitive knowledge that feeding must begin slowly. Following the liberation of Dachau, inmates were housed in surplus U.S. Army tents outside of the concentration camp walls, and officers in General Patton's Seventh Army required that local villagers provide food, which they did. Amidst squalor and disease, prisoners had been subsisting on a ration of about six hundred calories daily. Most could not eat solid food, so soups were prepared from local potatoes, cabbage, carrots, turnips, and meat. The broth and vegetables were sufficiently nutritious to spur digestion among survivors but to circumvent refeeding syndrome. Some former prisoners did break into SS food supplies, but soon discovered that solid meals and Army chocolate were undigestible. Vitamin supplements helped to restore normal metabolism, and German army rations were distributed once former prisoners were able to eat normally.[90]

Subsistence Gardens

Captivity led to deprivation and boredom, which in equal measures led to gardening. Japanese-Americans interned at inland camps (see Chapter 6) cultivated fruits and vegetables to augment the diet of government food, and some also landscaped desert tracts in an effort to bring beauty to bleak surroundings. Before the war, many were farmers or horticultural landscapers; relocation began in the spring of 1942, and many carried edible and ornamental plants along to their new inland locales. Women cultivated vegetable plots outside of their temporary housing, small gardens (typically 10' × 50') that fit between blocks of barracks and provided traditional Japanese vegetables for their families. To improve the bleak landscape, landscapers and horticulturalists developed ornamental plantings, such as those outside of the mess halls at the Manzanar internment camp. Working in the California desert environment, residents moved tons of rock and soil, built ponds and waterfalls, and transplanted native cacti and Joshua trees (*Yucca brevifolia*). Some native plants such as sagebrush (*Artemisia* spp.) were trimmed and cultivated as decorative *bonsai*.[91]

In Europe, the Royal Horticultural Society worked with the Red Cross to send garden seeds to Allied soldiers imprisoned in Italy and Germany. Prison meals improved with the addition of tomatoes, lettuce, carrots, beets, cucumbers, and English marrows, the same cultivated squashes used to camouflage Anderson shelters in England (see Chapter 2). Seed packets also included flowers such as poppies and cornflowers, which prisoners cultivated to improve morale and to decorate graves in the prison cemetery. Some prisoners provided expert instruction for others, who had a chance to learn a new skill while waiting for the war to end. By 1943, the Royal Horticultural Society provided a means for interested prisoners to take their rigorous practical and written examinations in gardening.[92] For prisoners of the Japanese and Germans, gardening was a survival strategy because the vitamins from fresh vegetables helped to save lives. At least one prisoner of the Japanese devised a simple method of hydroponics, and in another case, sufficient vegetables were cultivated in a small greenhouse to forestall starvation among Allied officers held in Poland.[93]

Ghetto walls intentionally excluded public parklands and open spaces from which Jews were banned, and overcrowding was typical of ghetto life. For ghetto residents in eastern Europe, vegetable gardens supplemented meager rations; in Warsaw and Lodz, organizers bargained for land and obtained seeds and tools. Community groups and orphanages organized the efforts. Working in vacant lots and bomb sites, gardeners moved rubble and tilled hardpan soil with few tools, and they irrigated gardens with water carried in buckets. Vacant lots were converted into productive plots, but as occurred at Lodz in early 1941, ghetto boundaries could be moved at any time to exclude possible garden sites. At a time when subsistence gardens were essential to forestall starvation, memoirs recorded the impression of vegetable plots in every available piece of land. Potatoes, cabbages, turnips, carrots, onions, legumes, and kitchen and medicinal herbs were grown wherever possible, including courtyards, cemeteries, balconies, and even shop windows. Onions were planted in pots and window boxes; the bulbs flavored vegetable meals and also had antimicrobial properties (see Chapter 7). By the end of 1940, there were over 950 gardens cultivated in the Lodz ghetto, most of them small family plots in which intensive cultivation produced six cabbages per square meter. Nazi officials prohibited educational programs, but trade school horticulture classes often escaped notice; agricultural training was an ongoing process as the population changed as a result of deportations. Lectures covered the basics of soil preparation, seed germination, and weeding, while a two-year training course in agriculture provided hope and practical education for young ghetto residents, many of whom planned to emigrate after the war.

For ghetto residents in eastern Europe, vegetable gardens supplemented meager rations. Potatoes, cabbages, turnips, carrots, onions, legumes, and kitchen and medicinal herbs were grown wherever possible, including courtyards, cemeteries, balconies, and even shop windows. By the end of 1940, there were over 950 gardens cultivated in the Lodz ghetto, most of them small family plots in which intensive cultivation produced six cabbages per square meter (Ghetto Fighters' House Museum, Israel, Photo Archive).

However, there were no effective pesticides, and monoculture of a few essential crops heightened the risk of insect attack with devastating results. During the August heat wave of 1942, caterpillars completely skeletonized the cabbages that gardeners in the Lodz ghetto had planned to store for winter months.[94]

Regeneration

Bombing destroyed landscapes, but at the same time cleared land and created new habitats that plants colonized. In London, bomb craters were quickly covered by lush vegetation as the seeds of weedy species germinated in rubble. A sudden influx of wild-flower populations provided color in bleak areas such as docks and warehouses of the east end of the city; many interpreted this change in the urban landscape as a sign of postwar life. An article in *Life* noted, "Strangest of all is the appearance of 95 kinds of supposedly rare weeds, whose origin has become a heated English controversy. Some think they come from very old buried 'hard seeds'; others that they simply blew in."[95]

A postwar movie theater travelogue *Travel Talks—Looking at London* (Metro-Goldwyn-Mayer, 1946) reported on the widespread occurrence of fire flowers, a purple-flowering species that blanketed London bomb sites in numbers not seen since the Great Fire of 1666. Widely known in the countryside as rose-bay willow herb (*Chamaenerion angustifolium*, syn. *Epilobium angustifolium*), the species was among the first to colonize burned habitats. Willow herb requires sun and tolerates a range of soil types and pH, but its wartime growth was enhanced by the potash (potassium salts) produced by the wood fires caused by incendiary bombs. The young leaves were edible (see Chapter 4) and collected for salads, and the flowers attracted pollinating bees; a postwar analysis of local honey revealed a high incidence of nectar from willow herb. Most important, however, was seed production because single plant yielded 80,000 seeds, each with a tuft of seventy hairs adapted to wind dispersal.[96] During the summer of 1944, a note in the *New York Herald Tribune* observed, "London, paradoxically, is the gayest where she has been the most blitzed. The wounds made this summer by flying bombs are, of course, still raw and bare, but cellars and courts shattered into rubble by the German raids of 1940–41 have been taken over by an army of weeds which have turned them into wild gardens, sometimes as gay as any tilled by human hands. There is the brilliant rose-purple plant that Londoners call rose-bay willow herb. Americans call it fireweed because it blazes wherever a forest fire has raged. It will not grow in the shade, but there is little shade as yet in the London ruins."[97] Areas around Saint Paul's Cathedral and entire blocks in the Borough of Lambeth were blanketed in willow

Rose-bay willow herb was among the first plants to colonize bomb sites in London. The weedy species requires sun but tolerates a range of soil types and pH; its wartime growth was enhanced by the potash produced by incendiary bomb fires. A single plant yielded 80,000 seeds adapted to wind dispersal; populations were perennial and self-perpetuating.

herb. Populations were perennial and self-perpetuating, and for years during and after the war, huge numbers of willow herb seeds drifted over the city, germinating amidst rubble in soil scoured by bombs and fire.

Following the Blitz raids of 1940–41, there were documented changes in the urban flora of England as rubble became a common habitat. Another familiar flower was the garden saxifrage known as London pride (*Saxifraga* x *urbium*, a hybrid of *S. umbrosa* from Spain and *S. spathularis* from Ireland). The succulent plants readily colonized the xeric, sometimes shaded habitats of bomb sites, where they came to symbolize fortitude and resilience. In the lyrics of the popular song "London Pride" (1941), Noel Coward described the hybrid accurately as "Growing in the crevices by some London railing," while "Every Blitz your resistance toughening." The plants may have exhibited some hybrid vigor that allowed them to grow well in disturbed sites. Like many rubble plants, London pride produced hundreds of seeds, although they were not carried by wind.

Urban destruction provided unexpected opportunities for field botany. The London

Natural History Society sponsored surveys of the flora and fauna of bomb sites through the late 1940s. These included a five-year field study of the re-vegetation of a bomb crater on Bookham Common in Surrey, work that began in 1942 and entailed monthly observations. Bombed and burned sites revealed several wind-dispersed species, including ragwort (*Jacobaea vulgaris*, syn. *Senecio jacobaea*) and coltsfoot (*Tussilago farfara*). Both were known to Dioscorides and other ancient herbalists as medicinal plants, but were later recognized for their toxicity, even to other plants; ragwort and coltsfoot both establish territory by releasing toxins into the soil, an adaptation known as allelopathy. The Oxford ragwort (*Senecio squalidus*) also established itself in London, perhaps not surprising because the species originally evolved in the burned-over volcanic soils of Sicily. Many bomb sites also became entangled in nightshades (*Solanum dulcamara* and *S. nigrum*) and brambles (*Rubus* spp.) spread by birds that ate the fruit. A botanical survey revealed a total of 95 vascular plants that readily colonized bomb sites, including several familiar garden weeds such as dandelions and clover. Several of the colonizing plants coincidentally had medicinal uses, including coltsfoot, nightshade, chamomile, yarrow, and plantain, weedy species widely grown since ancient times as part of herbal tradition. Cellar holes provided wet microclimates inhabited by purple loosestrife (*Lythrum salicaria*), once valued as an astringent herb.[98]

Some plants that thrived in London bomb sites were entirely alien to Europe, including Canadian fleabane (*Erigeron canadensis*) and the Peruvian weed known as gallant soldier (*Galinsoga parviflora*), which had escaped years before from cultivation at the Royal Botanic Gardens (Kew). On some sites, tree of heaven (*Ailanthus altissima*), an allelopathic species introduced from China, quickly established and naturalized. Its seedlings grew several feet annually, providing shade while simultaneously releasing allelochemicals that prevented seeds of other species from germinating. Only one ornamental garden plant self-sowed among the weedy flora; the Asian shrub known as butterfly bush (*Buddleja davidii*) thrived in the dry, alkaline soil created by the rubble of old limestone-containing masonry. In short, disturbed sites were quickly blanketed by diverse, aggressive plants, including some non-native species, and the overall effect in the city was one of greenery, welcomed after years of blackouts and bombing.[99]

Bombing also resulted in changes to the German landscape, followed by regeneration of urban flora. After the war, Allied forces ordered local women (*Trümmerfrauen*) to work on sorting and moving rubble; using hand tools alone, teams worked together to salvage reusable wooden beams and other building materials. Remaining debris was used to fill bomb craters or mounded into *Trümmerberge* (rubble mountains), manmade hills that characterized the postwar terrain of Berlin, Cologne, Dresden, Munich, Nuremberg, and other bombed cities.

Weedy plants quickly colonized these new sites, which tended to be drier and warmer than natural habitats. Typical rubble vegetation included coltsfoot and mugwort (*Artemisia vulgaris*), both widely grown medicinal species that tolerate disturbed sites and variable climate and soil. In the course of postwar movement and migration, troops and refugees may have carried non-native seeds into Germany; postwar conditions also favored plants with efficient dispersal mechanisms, including several introduced weedy species. For instance, slender saltwort (*Salsola collina*, native to eastern Europe and Asia) functions as a tumbleweed that sheds seeds widely, and Jerusalem oak goosefoot (*Chenopodium botrys*, native to the Mediterranean region), is covered with viscid hairs which cling to boots and other surfaces. Both plants naturalized quickly across bombed areas, as did a wind-dispersed North American goldenrod (*Solidago giganteana*) that could easily have been introduced with American matériel.[100]

All of these are ruderal species, capable of germinating and surviving in disturbed habitats. Such plants typically produce large numbers of seeds and grow quickly in nutrient-poor soil without depending on symbiotic mycorrhizal fungi (see Chapter 9). Thus the initial influx of non-native ruderal weeds added humus to the thin soil of disturbed sites, and woody seedlings soon appeared in bombed areas. As in England, the Chinese tree of heaven (*Ailanthus altissima*) colonized the postwar ruins of German cities. Ecological succession on the dry alkaline soils of bomb sites resulted in woodlands of black locust (*Robinia pseudoacacia*), a species native to the southeastern U.S. but introduced to Europe by the 17th century. The seedlings tolerate disturbance and variable conditions, excluding wet or compacted soils; thus black locust thrived in the alkaline soil of rubble sites, where the soil was loosened by bomb blasts and excavation and enriched with calcium from limestone-containing masonry. Once established, the trees sprouted root suckers and quickly colonized former building sites with genetic clones; reproduction also occurred sexually by flowering and seed production. As legumes, the roots of black locust seedlings developed nodules that contained nitrogen-fixing *Rhizobium* bacteria (see Chapters 4 and 6) and so grew rapidly even in nitrogen-poor soils.

In the heavily bombed cities of Hamburg and Dresden, fast-growing poplars were planted for camouflage, and wood was needed for fuel. After the war, damaged and destroyed woody plants were difficult to replace. Tree nurseries were converted into vegetable farms to remedy postwar food shortages, so self-sown tree seedlings replaced the pre-war urban forest. Youth groups were organized to search the rubble for tree seedlings to transplant. The postwar changes in native vegetation led German botanists to focus on *Pflanzensoziologie* (phytosociology), an early ecological discipline that the Nazi regime had promoted as a means to understand populations and interactions among native German plants. Ironically, the postwar German landscape amounted to a vast experiment in field botany, in which damaged and diminished populations of native German plants competed for survival against non-native invasive species.[101]

Wartime conditions and Allied bombing also impacted the Japanese landscape. Trees were felled for fuel and coffins, and incendiary bombs ignited urban firestorms that burned or scarred living trees (see Chapter 7). Some species such as ginkgo (*Ginkgo biloba*) and camphor (*Cinnamomum camphora*) were fire resistant and grew new shoots following firestorm conditions. Nevertheless, the loss of woody plants was widespread; for instance, only about a third of all trees in Tokyo survived the war, although many of them grew in the protected grounds of shrines and temples.

The explosive force from the atomic bombs detonated over Hiroshima and Nagasaki broke tree trunks and sent entire trees into the air. Firestorms consumed vast amounts of wood in the hours following the blasts, and any remaining vegetation was exposed to high heat and radiation. The expectation seemed to be that all plant life within a kilometer of the hypocenter of the blast would be killed, but in Hiroshima, there were anecdotal reports of survivors sheltering in dense bamboo groves that charred but did not burn. Vast numbers of weeds appeared within a few weeks; apparently, "The bomb had not only left the underground organs of plants intact; it had stimulated them. Everywhere were bluets and Spanish bayonets, goosefoot, morning glories and day lilies, the hairy-fruited bean, purslane and clotbur and sesame and panic grass and feverfew."[102] Sickle senna (*Senna obtusifolia*, syn. *Cassia tora*) sprouted profusely in cracks and amidst masonry rubble; the weedy legume tolerated disturbance, and its seeds dispersed widely across Hiroshima. Within two months, there were reports of woody regeneration at distances 700 meters from the hypocenter. Buds opened on charred tree trunks to reveal new growth, and the cultivated cycads known as sago palm (*Cycas revoluta*) developed new leaves from their apical growth point.[103]

Trees that survived the atomic blast over Hiroshima were typically broad-leaved species, flowering plants rather than conifers. Known in Japan as *hibaku*, these included 150 trees located at 52 sites within a 2 kilometer radius of the hypocenter. Damage to the trees varied; some lost branches and charred only on the side facing the blast, while some woody trunks burned to the ground. Lone trees often resisted fire more readily than those that grew in clusters or woodlands that burned intensely. The most resistant species included ginkgo, camphor trees, figs, willows, azaleas, bamboos, eucalyptus, chinaberry (*Melia azedarach* var. *japonica*), oleander (*Nerium indicum*), and Japanese aralia (*Fatsia japonica*); black locust, known for colonizing bomb rubble in German cities, also survived in post-blast Hiroshima. The surviving tree closest to the blast hypocenter (300 m) was a willow (*Salix babylonica*), which grew new shoots from its roots. Regeneration was not necessarily immediate; the roots of a holly (*Ilex rotunda*) near the Rai Sanyo Shiseki Museum apparently survived but did not produce new shoots until 1949. In some cases, the subterranean bulbs of herbaceous species such as lilies (*Crinum* spp.) also survived the blast, as did the fast-growing Asian kudzu vines which re-grew from their starchy roots. Hiroshima survivors relied on kudzu roots as a food untainted by radiation.[104]

Radiation was the unknown factor in botanical survival. Trees near the hypocenter

Trees that survived the atomic blast over Hiroshima were typically broad-leaved species rather than conifers. Known in Japan as *hibaku*, these included 150 trees within a 2 kilometer radius of the hypocenter. Some lost branches and charred only on the side facing the blast, while some trunks burned to the ground and sprouted after the war. Lone trees often resisted fire more readily than those that grew in clusters or woodlands that burned intensely (Truman Library).

were exposed to the highest levels of gamma rays, ionizing radiation that can cause genetic mutations. Radiation decreased with distance from the blast, from 3,500 rad at locations a half kilometer from the hypocenter to 49 rad at sites 1.5 km away, followed by unmeasured levels of radioactive dust and rain that fell on all organisms that survived the initial blast. Some trees close to the hypocenter no doubt sustained genetic mutations, and studies have suggested that chromosome size influences the likelihood of DNA to mutate from ionizing radiation. Conifers such as pine and hemlock have comparatively large chromosomes, and the DNA in these chromosomes is more likely to mutate if irradiated. In contrast, broad-leaved trees have small chromosomes that are less prone to mutation[105] Of course, distance was not the only factor in exposure to radiation. Masonry buildings and walls protected some trees from radiation and heat, and roots remained sheltered in the soil and unexposed to the ionizing effects of gamma rays. The ability of many trees to regenerate new shoots at soil level reveals that many *hibaku* trees survived and regenerated from root stock alone following the atomic blasts at the end of World War II.

12

Botanical Gardens, Herbaria and Plant Science in Wartime

Botanical gardens remained open during the war years although staffing dwindled as both men and women entered military service and related war work and industries. Shortages of basic supplies vexed garden activities and maintenance, as noted in the 1943 annual report of the Arnold Arboretum, "The Arboretum has had its share of 'war troubles,' but the staff is trying to carry on as well as it can under the circumstances. The curtailment in gasolene and labor and inability to obtain new mechanical equipment and repair parts for old machines are the chief causes for conditions noted by the public. We are trying to maintain the grounds and the collections in good condition with the equipment and help available."[1] Nevertheless living plants were added to the collections, exchanges made with other institutions, and rare varieties shared with nurseries for propagation and sale.

Practical Knowledge

Staff shared botanical expertise wherever possible, and basic plant science yielded useful advice in areas such as the selection and maintenance of camouflage vegetation (see Chapter 11). The Office of Strategic Services (OSS) used collections of botanical photographs, maps, and field notes to glean useful information. Geographic details about Pacific island coastlines were essential to military cartography, and practical knowledge of Pacific plants was a critical need during the war with Japan. With this in mind, E.D. Merrill, wartime director of the Arnold Arboretum and a specialist in Philippine flora, authored *Plant Life of the Pacific World*; the text compiled information useful for U.S. troops and was republished in a Fighting Forces edition in 1945.[2] Decades of studying Philippine vegetation had also laid the groundwork for Merrill's *Emergency Food Plants of the Islands of the Pacific* (Technical Manual 10–420), a War Department survival manual written "to aid the individual who becomes separated from his unit" (see Chapter 11). Lily May Perry, an authority on Pacific botany, was Merrill's unacknowledged collaborator on the project; beginning in 1939, she translated from Dutch several manuscripts including those by H.J. Lam on the vegetation and people of Papua New Guinea, published originally as *Fragmenta Papuana* (1927–1929). During the Pacific war, Perry's translations were useful in both quinine research and military intelligence in Papua New Guinea and the Solomon Islands.[3]

On the home front, botanists searched arboreta and public gardens for edible plants and made lists of species suitable for foraging in the event of food shortages. Walnuts, blueberries, chicory, and dandelions were among the edible flora recommended by botanists at the Arnold Arboretum, but some suggested species such as pokeweed (*Phytolacca americana*) and sassafras (*Sassafras albidum*) are now considered too toxic to consume.[4] Horticulturalists supplied wartime information on pruning and insecticides (including arsenic compounds, which were still in use) to assure the best possible fruit crops despite shortages of some chemicals.[5] In addition to promoting victory gardens with lectures and classes, horticulturalists at the Brooklyn Botanic Garden supplied ornamental plants to landscape Army camps and cut flowers for the hospital at the Brooklyn Naval Yard.[6]

Botanical expertise extended to the study of algae and included research on agar at the Beaufort Marine Laboratory (see Chapter 7). In Germany, researchers at the Kaiser Wilhelm Institute for Biology examined the phosphorescent marine alga (*Noctiluca miliaris*), of interest for its potential implications in submarine detection.[7]

Maintaining living collections in wartime required propagation of plants already in cultivation both here and abroad. Bulbs were not exported from German-occupied Holland, so horticulturalists propagated narcissus and tulips both sexually from seeds and asexually from offsets and bulb scales. Public parks in England continued bulb displays during the war years. Vita Sackville-West noted a humorous occasion in which garden soil was used to fill sandbags, which were then banked against the walls and windows of a local hospital; the following spring, daffodil flowers burst through the coarse bags, making a colorful barricade.[8] Seedstock of ornamental plants was often difficult to obtain. Holland had exported many seeds until German occupation interfered, so the seeds of annuals and perennials were saved and grown for flower beds and borders. Staff planted victory gardens for public viewing and developed charts of planting times for various fruits and vegetables.[9] At the Royal Botanic Gardens (Kew), several acres of lawns were plowed under and planted in five varieties of potatoes; gardeners cultivated demonstration allotments patterned on Ministry of Agriculture "Dig for Victory" specifications and provided insights and answers for new vegetable gardeners.[10] A British Pathé newsreel "Stepping Out" (1943) featured scenes of the Royal Botanic Gardens, but avoided vegetable allotments and filmed only traditional Kew scenes: the landscape garden, lawns with naturalized crocus, rhododendron hedges, the lake, and pagoda. However, visitors to Kew saw the wartime changes that replaced picturesque views with vegetable plots. At Wisley, the garden of the Royal Horticultural Society, flowers trials were halted and replaced with vegetable allotments, and potato plants sprawled among experimental rhododendron plantings. Wisley gardeners conducted germination experiments on U.S. vegetable seeds provided as part of the Lend-Lease agreement (see Chapter 4).

Food plants were not the sole practical concern. Kew botanists studied nettle fibers and dyes, tung oil, rubber substitutes, drug plants, and vitamin-rich foods such as rosehips. The Ministry of Supply obtained seeds of latex-producing Russian dandelions (see Chapter 10), and the director of Kew distributed them for growth trials at twenty different locales. At the same time, botanists at Kew investigated British dandelions for latex production. They also collected data on the vitamin C content of all native British roses (about 20 species), cultivars, and hybrids, with surprising results; northern roses yielded more vitamin C than those found in the south, useful information in collecting rosehips for syrup (see Chapter 7). During wartime, gardeners at Kew included women trained

A 1943 Pathé newsreel featured wartime scenes of the Royal Botanic Gardens; two years earlier German bombs fell around the iconic Pagoda, but the structure survived. Its height proved useful for military engineers who used the ten-story structure to test the flight behavior of new bomb designs by dropping models 163 feet to the ground (Pathé).

in horticulture, and they took over many of the responsibilities of the formerly all-male staff. Faced with medicinal plant shortages, they cultivated foxglove, belladonna, and autumn crocus and collected clippings of bay laurel shrubs (*Laurus nobilis*) for wartime pharmaceutical use (see Chapters 7 and 8).[11]

Collections

Herbarium collections were a particular concern in light of air raids because most plant material for taxonomic study is pressed, dried, and paper-mounted, a flammable combination in the event of bombing. Evacuation seemed like the best option to preserve irreplaceable collections including the herbarium of Carolus Linnaeus, the 18th century Swedish botanist who developed binomial nomenclature. Linnaean Society headquarters in London housed his herbarium and natural history collections, but the likelihood of air raids mandated safe storage in the countryside. Among the plant specimens were the nomenclatural type specimens for the numerous plant species that he named. These are usually herbarium sheets, the physical record of scientific names, so their safekeeping is paramount to taxonomic botany. With funds from the Carnegie Corporation of America,

160,000 photographs were made on microfilm of the most important items in the collection, including type specimens, manuscripts, and books with marginal notations by Linnaeus. Copies of the microfilm were sent to the Arnold Arboretum and Smithsonian Institution, with the unstated intent that the photographs would replace the original nomenclatural types in the event of bombing or invasion. In April 1939, the herbarium and natural history specimens moved to Woburn Abbey in Bedfordshire and subsequently to Hertfordshire for the duration of the war.[12]

The herbarium of the Royal Botanic Gardens (Kew) also included numerous type specimens and other irreplaceable items, so a massive evacuation scheme relocated about a third of the collections and books to wartime locations in Oxford and Gloucestershire. Type specimens were placed in folders marked with bright red margins, a wartime innovation designed to facilitate quick removal. Evacuation involved moving hundreds of herbarium cases and organizing them to follow the taxonomic scheme of Bentham and Hooker still used at Kew; in Oxford, the New Bodleian building accommodated 600 cases in its reinforced concrete basement. Staffing dwindled as Kew botanists entered the military, but several accompanied the evacuated herbarium collections to their new sites where they carried on with administrative and research work. Relocated botanists took advantage of the relatively rural locations for fieldwork on violets, orchids, valerian, beech trees, and other native plants.[13] Botanists remaining at Kew carried on with research there, including the Index Kewensis, an ongoing compendium of all new plant names dating from the beginning of binomial nomenclature in 1753. Staff also identified unknown botanical specimens and substances captured from enemy countries, including medicinal plants and various *ersatz* coffee and tea substitutes.[14]

The fear of air raids was not unfounded. Over the course of the war, thirty high energy bombs and thousands of incendiary devices fell on the Royal Botanic Gardens, an area of 260 acres. Bombs broke glass in the Temperate House, Palm House, and herbarium building but did little irreparable damage. In 1941, German bombs fell around the iconic Pagoda, but the structure survived. Its height proved useful for military engineers who used the ten-story structure to test the flight behavior of new bomb designs; holes were drilled in each floor so that models could be dropped 163 feet to the ground. A special group of guards patrolled Kew grounds, and black-out conditions were required after dark; white paint used to mark roadside trees persisted for years after the war. Cold-sensitive plants were a particular concern after some living collections died in damaged greenhouses, but the curved glass of the historic Palm House posed a structural problem to replace. Kew botanists experimented with a glass substitute for greenhouses and windows; pliable sheets of sodium alginate purified from kelp (*Laminaria* spp.) were prepared to use as translucent substitutes for panes in the event of a glass shortage.[15]

Staff at U.S. botanical gardens worked to document and save collections here and abroad. Between 1929 and 1939, Francis MacBride, a botanist and curator from the Field Museum in Chicago, photographed type specimens at herbaria in Berlin and other major European cities. He made a valuable record of 40,000 photographs, including 15,800 images of type specimens in the Berlin herbarium, although the German *Reichsmarschall* Hermann Göring insisted that Berlin would not be bombed (see below). A survey conducted by the Botanical Society of America and American Society of Plant Taxonomists revealed that collections of type specimens at Cornell, Purdue, the U.S. National Herbarium, and seventeen herbaria were stored in buildings that could easily burn in the event of bombing. Staff were encouraged to separate type specimens, so that they could be

quickly removed in the event of air raids or invasion.[16] Coastal sites seemed most vulnerable to bombing, so herbaria in several cities took steps to remove collections to rural
and inland areas for safekeeping. Wartime locations for specimens were unpublicized.
The Los Angeles Museum stored type specimens in an inland vault, and the New York
Botanical Garden and other herbaria shipped valuable collections to rural campuses and
other institutions for safekeeping. In Morgantown, West Virginia, a plaque on the Clark
Hall of Chemistry recalls this era: "Through the hospitality of the Board of Governors,
President and faculty of the West Virginia University irreplaceable books and herbarium
specimens belonging to the New York Botanical Garden were graciously given shelter in
this building during the war years of 1942, 1943 and 1944."

Not all institutions were able to move collections away from urban areas, nor were
specimens safe from theft and looting. *Science News-Letter* reported extensive bombing
of the Komarov Institute in Leningrad; the greenhouses shattered, but the library and
herbarium collections survived German air raids.[17] In the Ukraine, known for its agricultural landscape, Nazi troops seized plant and insect collections from the Academy of
Sciences and shipped them to Germany. Presumably these specimens were plundered as
a source of information that might fuel the *Drang nach Osten* (drive eastward) into Slavic
countries (see Chapter 6).

Some herbaria worldwide were robbed of their collections, severely damaged, or
entirely destroyed. After years of Japanese occupation, the Philippine herbarium in Manila
was rebuilt with help from E.D. Merrill, an expert in Philippine flora, who coordinated
major herbaria to donate duplicate specimens and books.[18] In Paris, the herbarium at the
Musée d'Histoire Naturelle was left untouched, but the situation in Berlin was quite different. The herbarium of the botanic garden in Berlin (*Botanischer Garten und Botanisches
Museum Berlin-Dahlem*, located about seven miles outside of Berlin) contained over four
million specimens, including unique collections and numerous nomenclatural types.
Nazi leaders believed that the evacuation of specimens and books was bad for morale,
so the only collections moved to vaults for safekeeping were the 20,000 specimens comprising the Willdenow herbarium. Carl Ludwig Willdenow (1765–1812) was a botanist
and pharmacist who specialized in medicinal plants and plant geography, two significant
interests of the Nazi regime, and his herbarium included specimens collected by Alexander von Humboldt in South America. Within the herbarium building, some collections
were shifted into cellars and corridors for protection, but many type specimens were
overlooked. The spirit collection of fruit and flower specimens preserved in flammable
formaldehyde and alcohol were also stored in cellar areas, where they actually survived
intact.[19]

In early March 1943, Allied bombing of Berlin resulted in fires that destroyed most
of the herbarium building and the entire botanical library. Thousands of type specimens
burned, a loss with far-reaching taxonomic implications even now as plant groups are
studied and revised and new monographs are written. Specimens on loan from other
herbaria were also lost, including over four thousand herbarium sheets that German
botanists had borrowed from U.S. institutions for taxonomic study. The situation had
concerned U.S. botanists afraid of losing irreplaceable herbarium accessions on loan
abroad; E.D. Merrill compiled data from U.S. herbaria and determined that there were
over thirty thousand specimens on loan in Europe, including institutions in vulnerable
cities such as Hamburg, Munich, Vienna, Leningrad, and London. Despite concerns,
scholarship trumped hostilities, and few specimens if any were recalled.[20]

Occupation

After the war, there were complications stemming from occupation. In Berlin, the botanical garden was in the U.S. sector, while salvaged specimens had been taken to locations in the Russian sector and could not easily be moved. Collections were returned to the herbarium by 1948, but it took years to sort out the damaged herbarium specimens and to determine what survived the war, while building repairs were slowed by a shortage of wood needed to replace burned shelves and cabinets. A postwar report in *Kew Bulletin* provided comprehensive details of the surviving collections, a matter of particular interest to taxonomic botanists worldwide.[21]

Japanese expansion and occupation affected botanical gardens in the Pacific region. When troops took control in early 1942, two British botanists, R.E. Holttum and E.J.H. Corner, were in charge of the botanic garden in Singapore. Fortunately Hirohito, the Japanese emperor, was a marine biologist; he respected the plant sciences and insisted that research work continue at the botanical garden, but seconded local staff members to forced labor on the highway linking Burma to Bangkok. New administrators were appointed from a Japanese university, which allowed the captive British botanists to pursue fulltime research under tolerable but isolated conditions. Holttum undertook detailed studies of the orchids, ferns, and gingers of the Malayan region, work that laid the groundwork for postwar publications that included *Orchids of Malaya* (1953), *Gardening in the Lowlands of Malaya* (1953), *Plant Life in Malaya* (1954), and major contributions to the pteridophyte sections of *Flora Malesiana* (1959–82). Corner investigated the structure of local seeds and fruit and later published *The Seeds of Dicotyledons* (1976), a two volume work that included original illustrations. In addition, his tropical seed studies established the underpinnings of Corner's durian-based explanation of flowering plant origins, a somewhat farfetched evolutionary scenario explained in *The Durian Theory* (1949). He postulated that the spiny fruits and aril-enclosed seeds of the genus *Durio* are highly primitive, a hypothesis negated by more current research.

Some botanists were imprisoned but managed to continue with research. H.E. Desch did much of the work for the second volume of his comprehensive *Manual of Malayan Timbers* (Malayan Forest Records, 1954) while held for three years at the Changi prison in Singapore and other POW camps. Gerardus Johannes deJoncheere directed an Indonesian shipping company but was able to extend his interest in ferns while imprisoned in Java. A specialist in tropical staghorn ferns (*Platycerium* spp.), he became a pteridologist and curator at the herbarium in Utrecht. While serving with the Royal Air Force, J.L. Audus perfected botanical drawings of grasses and sedges, work that he was able to continue while imprisoned in Java. These survived the war, and some were later used as illustrations in *A Revised Flora of Malaya*.[22]

The botanical garden in Buitenzorg (now Bogor) was seized following the Japanese invasion in 1942, and Japanese staff replaced Dutch colonial botanists, many of whom were held as prisoners of war. Some were able to continue research in fossils, ferns, epiphytes, rice cultivation, latex-producing plants, and other botanical topics that may have been of interest to the Japanese. Although isolated by occupation conditions, with Japanese cooperation colonial botanists continued to publish *Annals of the Botanic Gardens Buitenzorg* and to stop the Japanese military from cutting specimen trees for lumber. Theft and neglect nevertheless compromised the garden, and living collections including the giant parasitic *Rafflesia* vanished.[23]

Field Botany

War provided coincidental opportunities for botanical exploration. During the construction of the ALCAN (Alaska-Canada Military) Highway in the early 1940s, two collecting expeditions scouted the wilderness during the summers of 1943 and 1944 for new lichens, mosses, and vascular plants. The highway was a strategic portal that linked the lower 48 states to Alaska, and it crossed unexplored territory across mountains and though forests, prairies, and alpine meadows. Construction of the ALCAN Highway provided access to habitats where botanists had never collected, wartime exploration supported by both governments. The Canadian Department of Mines and Resources provided field equipment, and the U.S. Army supplied transportation and access to Army depots for supplies. Hugh Raup (later appointed director of the Harvard Forest) and a team of other botanists collected 25,000 herbarium specimens from sites in British Columbia, across the Yukon Territory, and into Alaska.[24]

Botanists at the University of Michigan and Smithsonian collaborated on a program designed to interest servicemen in plant life and to encourage field work in the theaters of war. Described to colleagues as "a program of botanical collecting and study for servicemen," its stated goal was to encourage troops to cultivate an interest in natural history, plants in particular, as well as acquiring new specimens for U.S. herbaria and museums.[25]

During construction of the ALCAN Highway, botanical expeditions scouted the wilderness for new lichens, mosses, and vascular plants. The highway was a strategic portal that linked the lower 48 states to Alaska, and it crossed unexplored territory across mountains and though forests, prairies, and alpine meadows. A team of botanists collected 25,000 herbarium specimens from sites in British Columbia, across the Yukon Territory, and into Alaska (U.S. National Archives).

Organizers noted that Germany had practiced field botany this way for years, by enlisting the efforts of travelers, consuls, missionaries, and others who worked abroad to collect specimens; the U.S. in wartime could do the same. Their plan for training amateurs involved coaching and even flattery, "If he is a beginner, we shall give him close guidance by correspondence. More experienced men will need only occasional aid and advice.... Few will fail to be intrigued by the opportunity of becoming the best authority in the world on some bit of isolated land." Garrisoned military could also benefit from participation; field work provided distraction from boredom and miserable conditions. *A Field Collector's Manual in Natural History*, a Smithsonian publication for servicemen, noted, "In many areas remote from battle zones there will be stations where routine duties will become monotonous. Here natural history studies will provide welcome and valuable recreation for those interested, and may add to human knowledge. The United States National Museum, a branch of the Smithsonian Institution, throughout its existence has received large and valuable additions to its collections from service men in many regions and stands ready always to identify and provide information on plants and animals of all kinds."[26]

Known unofficially as Company D (named ironically for a special forces unit training at the University of Michigan), the collectors were issued *A Field Collector's Manual in Natural History*, which provided details on making a plant press from wooden slats, making complete field notes on growth habit and habitats, and drying plants quickly to prevent fungal attack.[27] In addition to dried and pressed specimens for herbarium collections, wood collections provided samples of potentially useful timber. Instructions were clearly slanted toward work in tropical habitats, and reprints of *The Pacific World* were distributed to spark an interest in natural history, plant life in particular.[28] At the University of Michigan, staff prepared a pamphlet series titled "Instructions to Naturalists in the Armed Forces" on specialized collecting methods for algae, fungi and lichens, mosses and liverworts, wood fungi, and plant fossils.

Botanists suggested possible participants in the field botany program. The program was widely publicized in scientific journals, and Professor Harley Bartlett at the University of Michigan and E.D. Merrill at the Arnold Arboretum enlisted former students. Eventually 41 servicemen and women participated, with 70 percent of the collections made in the Pacific region. Most were amateurs; only about a third had training in biological sciences, although a few had studied forestry or had photographed, sketched, or painted local plants before the war. Hundreds of letters were exchanged between servicemen and botanists who guided plant collections from afar. In return, herbaria benefited from wartime collections, which were shipped to the Smithsonian for dispersal; in 1945 alone, over 6,000 specimens were received. Some plants arrived moldy or damaged, but many arrived ready for mounting and accession. In 1945, the annual Director's Report of the Chicago Natural History Museum acknowledged 25 servicemen who provided new specimens for their collection. Support continued from botanical gardens and museums; botanists compiled literature that might prove useful to both professionals and amateurs botanizing in areas as remote as the Aleutians and vegetated Pacific atolls, and some military collectors such as Lt. G.B. van Schaack (see below) even mimeographed their own field notes.[29]

Of course, servicemen often had no idea of the identity of the plants that they collected. Herbarium staff determined the species and labeled each collection with pertinent information; E.D. Merrill took pride in identifying specimens received by the Arnold

Arboretum and writing to the collector within a day of receiving a shipment, which helped to maintain enthusiasm and interest. There were a few cases of military officers who viewed collecting as unmanly and forbid the shipment of specimens, but in most cases, botanical field work was tolerated if not entirely encouraged. Sometimes, collecting was done in the course of military duties. A collector found a new lupine species while hunting for Japanese troops on Kiska Island in the Aleutians, and a marine captain used a captured Japanese military manual to press grass specimens in Palau following the battle of Peleliu. Some medical units also collected local flora and fauna, including the Navy Medical Research Unit No. 2 stationed on Guam and the Typhus Commission in Burma (see Chapter 7), field work essential to understanding the etiology of malaria and scrub typhus.[30]

The Army and Navy intervened to waive the usual restrictions on imported plant material. However, occasionally the U.S. postal service refused to accept packages of pressed plants, to the frustration of collectors, some of whom continued to study botany as civilians. In 1945, Lt. Warren Wagner, a fern authority, commented on his collecting activities in Guam and in the Admiralty Islands, "I have learned a lot about Pacific vegetation and have secured some fine specimens of Pacific rarities. My pteridophyte collection … now totals over 700 collections. I am trying to get together a fern flora of Guam. …There are now 55 species known from there, of which 8 have never before been recorded. The results of our collections in the Admiralties are even more striking, the known number of species now being 165, whereas, so far as we can discover, only 39 had been reported earlier. We expect in the near future to publish papers on the pteridophytes of this group also, based on our 'extra-curricular' studies while in the service."[31]

Mosses and liverworts were of particular interest because the bryophyte flora was poorly known in many regions. Of course, mosses and liverworts are small, easy to collect, and convenient to dry, and thus the field of bryology benefited from wartime collections in areas as diverse as Greenland, Alaska, Bora-Bora, the Philippines, and Japan. A Red Cross worker and a medical doctor stationed on Attu Island in Alaska collected over two thousand mosses and other plant specimens.[32] Collections made by servicemen in the Pacific region included new species and provided information on ranges; as noted in *The Bryologist*, "World War II was not entirely without fruit for the various fields of the natural sciences. It presented an opportunity for extended travel, although not always to the satisfaction of the individual, and exposed new regions previously unknown to the average American. Perhaps the least known area thus uncovered was the Pacific and its many islands."[33]

Even the occupation years were seen as an opportunity to develop interests in natural history and continue botanical field work. Additional copies of *The Pacific World* were distributed to troops remaining in Japan and other areas after the war. Those who wanted formal botanical training could refer to *A Textbook of General Botany* (U.S. War Department Education Manual EM445), a paperback college-level text that covered plant morphology, anatomy, and genetics, with illustrations drawn from notable sources.[34]

Two of the most remarkable botanical discoveries of the 20th century date from the war years, however in both cases with no military connection to the field work involved. Collecting on Viti Levu in the Fiji Islands, botanist Otto Degener found a unique flowering tree, a species first collected in 1934 by A.C. Smith on the neighboring island of Vanua Levu. Smith's collection bore only fruit, but the flowers found by Degener in 1942 revealed a botanical surprise. They were the most primitive flowers recognized at the time, with leaf-like stamens and a single folded pistil. Smith, then a botanist at the Arnold Arboretum, named the new tree *Degeneria vitiensis* in honor of Degener. Widely known as a living fossil, *Degeneria* was placed in its own family (Degeneriaceae) as a genus that retains traits from one of the early lines of flowering plant evolution.[35] It was widely described in botanical literature as a primitive angiosperm. Despite its status as a remarkable botanical discovery, *Degeneria* is actually relatively common and well known to local people; its timber may have been harvested from Fijian rainforests for military uses.

Dawn redwood trees had long been known only as common Cenozoic fossils, but in 1941 living trees were discovered in Sichuan Province of central China. Postwar expeditions collected seeds that were sent to arboreta, colleges, and universities worldwide for planting and cultivation (Georgialh, Wikimedia Commons).

China yielded another unique living fossil during the war years. Trees of the genus *Metasequoia*, named by a Japanese paleobotanist in 1941, had long been known only from Cenozoic fossils found widely across the northern hemisphere. However, in 1941 foresters discovered a population of unknown conifers growing in a remote valley in the Sichuan Province of central China. After the war, botanists confirmed that these were indeed the same tree and that *Metasequoia* was still extant. The genus is related to the giant and coastal redwoods of North America (family Cupressaceae), but the specific epithet of the living species *Metasequoia glyptostroboides* reflects its resemblance to *Glyptostrobus*, the Chinese swamp cypress. Expeditions to the remote extant populations of *Metasequoia* included a 1948 collecting trip organized by staff at the Arnold Arboretum; seeds of the newly discovered dawn redwood were sent to arboreta, colleges, and universities worldwide for planting and cultivation.[36]

Germany and Native Plants

The Nazi zeal for Aryan genetics extended to botany, and native plants were regarded as genetically superior to plants that evolved outside of Germany. Nazi scientists pursued the study of plant geography (*Pflanzensoziologie*), presumably because it might illuminate the genetics and evolution of local vegetation, but complicit botanists even envisioned a correlation between vegetation and human evolution. Compared to forests, tundra vegetation was considered poorly developed, a subpar habitat that according to Nazi-era pseudoscience caused the evolution of primitive people.[37]

The practical implications of native plant preference were far-reaching. Official policy downplayed imported cultivars and advocated for plants native to the land, but need overruled history in the case of certain non-native medicinal and edible plants. Several widely used medicinal herbs originated in Asia or the Mediterranean region, but Nazi policy supported their cultivation and use in the practice of herbal medicine (see Chapter 7). Potatoes, essential to the German diet and also to the V2 rocket program (see Chapter 6), originated in South America. Sweet cherries (*Prunus avium*), a favorite fruit, evolved in Asia Minor, but were widely cultivated in Germany. Soybeans originated in Asia, but they were renamed *Nazi-bohne* (Nazi beans) and promoted as a healthy food; the goal was to "Germanize" the crop through selection and breeding of cultivars adapted to the German climate (see Chapter 6). Russian dandelions, a potential latex source, were another candidate for German adoption, all in the name of autarky (see Chapter 10).

Third Reich policy incorporated native plants into landscape design. The *Zentralstelle fur Vegetationskartierung des Deutsches Reiches* (central office for landscape mapping) was established in 1939 to recommend groupings of desirable natural plant species and to extirpate non-native vegetation. A campaign was mounted against *Impatiens parviflora*, a non-native Eurasian touch-me-not that German botanists believed was encroaching on native forest wildflowers. However, the definition of non-native plants was not based on actual ancestry; policy seemed to suggest that a plant species could become "German" through years of planting, cultivation, or association with German people.[38] Following this convenient re-interpretation, many non-native food crops and herbs were likely considered "native" by Nazi officials and their scientists.

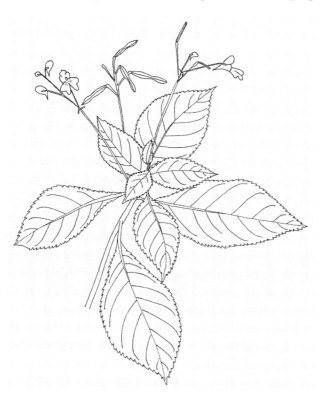

Third Reich policy incorporated native plants into landscape design, and a campaign was mounted against *Impatiens parviflora*, a non-native Eurasian touch-me-not thought to encroach on native forest wildflowers. However, the definition of non-native plants was not based on actual ancestry; Nazi policy suggested that a plant species could become "German" through years of planting, cultivation, or association with German people.

Alwin Seifert, a landscape architect who rejected the use of cultivated, imported plants in German gardens, was appointed state attorney for the landscape (*Reichslandschaftsanwalt*). He was tasked with the practical aspects of integrating Nazi *Blut und Boden* philosophy into German landscapes and in territories planned for *Lebensraum* as part of the *Generalplan Ost*, part of forging the ideological link between Aryan families and the land. Seifert followed the organic farming practices espoused by Rudolf Steiner (see Chapter 6), viewed good soil as essential to the German *Volk*, and used the American Dust Bowl to warn against desertification and the loss of fertile land.[39] The staff of Heinrich Himmler, *Reichsführer* of the SS, developed regulations that mandated naturalistic landscapes of German vegetation in Poland and other eastern areas planned for German resettlement. Aryan *Volk* could only be truly settled amidst plants native to Germany, thus reinforcing the bond of *Blut und Boden* (blood and soil). There were also practical matters to consider; for instance, naturalistic hedgerows required north to south orientation to interfere with future tank attacks. However, aside from a few model villages, these landscape plans for eastern territories were never realized.

In the U.S., similar ideas were voiced by Jens Jensen, a Danish-American landscape architect who rejected exotic cultivars, especially those from Asia and South America. Most of the colorful flowering plants grown as annuals by Victorian gardeners were exotic perennials, so Jensen in effect argued for the end of bright beds and borders. As a designer of public parklands and private estates, most notably the homes of Edsel Ford, Jensen operated with a Nordic perspective. During the 1930s he wrote for the German periodical *Gardenkunst* (garden art) on the desirability of native plants and Germanic landscapes that accompanied Hitler's notions of racial purity. Some have suggested that Jensen's affinity for native vegetation stemmed from racist views, citing in particular his contempt for "Latin spirit" and its effects on horticulture and landscape.[40] Others regarded him as a principled advocate of American landscapes, although he did advocate a native plant message in common with Nazi policy. Either way, Jensen was clearly suspicious of immigration, both human and botanical, and its influence on culture and landscape.

Landscape design during the Third Reich evolved from the nature garden, the 18th and 19th century counterpart of the British landscape garden. During the 1920s and 1930s, German landscape architects such as Willy Lange planted naturalistic habitats in which native plants were arranged in "social groupings" that resembled tidy woodlands, following the tenets of Nazi *Pflanzensoziologie*. Lange argued for informal design that mimicked Nordic forest ecology, and he rejected formality, topiaries, and non-native plants in his designs. In *Deutsche Gartenkunst* (*The German Art of Gardens*, 1938), Hans Hasler envisioned Nordic people amidst native plants cultivated to look utterly natural. In Nazi thinking, Aryan culture was influenced by the nature of the surrounding plant life, so decadent exotics were therefore replaced with orderly, cultivated woodlands of native trees, shrubs, and wildflowers.

German artists were pushed in the same direction. Modern paintings were reviled as degenerate art (*Entartete Kunst*), while realistic depictions of Germanic nature and plant life were revered. A 1937 government pamphlet used a botanical metaphor to explain the supposed effect of Jewish artists and modern art on German culture, "Dadaism, Futurism, Cubism, and all others isms are the poisonous flower of a Jewish parasitical plant grown on German soil.... Examples of these will be the strongest proof for the necessity of a radical solution of the Jewish question."[41] Realistic depictions of pastoral scenes and rural life interlaced with Nordic themes affirmed the goals of the Third Reich; images of agriculture and successful harvests forged and reinforced *Blut und Boden* connections between German *Volk* and the land (see Chapters 6 and 9). Almost half of the works displayed in state-sponsored art exhibitions were verdant landscapes with realistic vegetation painted in a traditional style.[42] In short, nature and native plants symbolized the Germanic landscape and *Lebensraum*, and the Third Reich demanded realism in their depiction. Modern works were shunned as part of the official state policy administered by Joseph Goebbels, the *Reichminister für Volksaufklärung und Propaganda* (Reich Minister for Public Enlightenment and Propaganda).

Ironically, the Nordic landscape message did not reach Camp Siegfried, a pro–Nazi youth camp in Yaphank, New York, operated during the 1930s by the German American Bund. Campers learned to salute, march, hunt, and shoot; there was also training in eugenics and Nazi doctrine, and reproduction was encouraged to produce Aryan offspring. The camp was landscaped with lawns and trimmed hedges; recently released photographs from the New York City Department of Records show a large flower bed in the shape of a swastika, several feet in diameter, outlined in boxwood and bedding plants, which were probably exotic species typically used in flower gardens. The camp was shuttered when the U.S. declared war on Germany. Some of the land became a residential area administered by the German American Settlement League, and until recently prospective buyers had to provide proof of German ancestry to purchase a house.

In contrast, the German writer, poet, and gardener Rudolf Borchardt argued for horticultural diversity, welcoming exotic cultivars into gardens and landscapes. He extolled botanical introductions that accompanied worldwide exploration and encouraged gardeners to grow unfamiliar, interesting species from seed. In *The Passionate Gardener* (written in 1938, but published posthumously in 1951), he criticized the exclusion of plants based on ancestry and questioned whether gardens should imitate nature or reflect horticultural transformation of landscapes; he preferred the latter and extolled the diversity of British gardens. Borchardt was soon recognized as an enemy of the Nazi regime and taken from Germany to Austria, where he died in 1945.

Hitler's *Berghof* (mountain farm) was situated at Obersalzberg in the Bavarian Alps, a spectacular natural site and settlement that Nazi officials took over during the 1930s. The property was essential to the image of alpine nature and traditional German life that Hitler wanted to project, and the architecture of the fortified chalet reflected the style of local farmhouses. Articles in *The New York Times Magazine* and *Homes and Gardens* detailed the setting and décor, which was the work of designer Gerdy Troost.[43]

The *Berghof* complex was situated amidst native alpine vegetation, visible through a massive window in the great hall and described in *Homes and Gardens* as "the fairest view in all of Europe." Receipts reveal the purchase of cultivated flowers, vines, and shrubs for window boxes and landscaping, and a kitchen garden supplied fresh produce for the kitchen. Jade green dominated the interior decoration, which included woodwork made from aromatic Swiss pine (*Pinus cembra*) and eighteenth century furnishings and wainscoting carved from oak and walnut.

Curtains were made from linen and other natural fibers at a time when shortages required civilians to make do with poor quality rayon manufactured from wood by-products (see Chapter 8). Hitler instructed the bureau in charge of allocating raw materials that all requests from Gerdy Troost were to be honored. In keeping with the rural motif of the *Berghof*, curtains in guest quarters and small rooms were decorated with botanical and *volkisch* patterns.[44] As an art student, Hitler used water colors to paint realistic studies of flowers including roses and dianthus and landscapes of trees and natural vegetation, some of which were displayed at the *Berghof*.

Majolica pots held Hitler's collection of cacti (family Cactaceae), succulents that are native only to the New World. As botanical curiosities apparently they were exempted from Hitler's stance on non-native plants, although his interest in cacti may have stemmed from peyote (*Lophophora williamsii*), source of the hallucinogenic alkaloid mescaline.

Hitler may have ingested peyote on occasion, and there were experiments with mescaline conducted on prisoners at the Dachau concentration camp. Curt Knebel, a plant breeder known for hybridizing cacti, introduced *Epiphyllum* 'Reichskanzler Adolf Hitler' (later shortened to 'Adolf Hitler') in 1935. Known for its large lilac-red flowers, the cultivar was renamed after the war to commemorate a California breeder and is now known among fanciers as *Epiphyllum* 'Sherman E. Beahm'.

There were opportunities for civilians to enjoy the countryside, part of the grander plan to connect German people to the land. The *Kraft durch Freude* program (see Chapter 10) offered subsidized excursions for German workers to the Harz mountains and other sites of natural beauty, and the *Hitler Jugend* (Hitler Youth) and the *Bund Deutscher Mädel* (League of German Girls) promoted the Aryan ideal of life on the land. During the summer of 1937, *Hitler Jugend* even bicycled through the English countryside, visits that were followed by systematic debriefing to garner information about natural features, terrain, and roads, as well as local political views. It is now believed that these bicycle tours were actually spying missions in preparation for an invasion.

Native vegetation played a significant role in this aspect of *Blut und Boden*, and perhaps the most iconic plant was edelweiss (*Leontopodium nivale*), an alpine wildflower adapted to montane habitats above 6000' elevation with limestone soils. The species is a composite (family Compositae or Asteraceae) with clustered flowers covered with white trichomes, a dense layer of plant hairs that evolved as an adaptation against direct sunlight and winds. Edelweiss became a German military symbol, in particular of the *Waffen-SS Gebirgsjäger* (mountain rangers), who wore edelweiss pins on their caps and sleeves, and the *Kampfgeschwader 51* (51st Bomber Wing), who flew planes with the emblem painted on the fuselage. Ironically the flower was also adopted as a badge by the *Edelweisspiraten* (edelweiss pirates) and *Edelweissbanden* (edelweiss bands), youth groups who sought to subvert the rigid structure of the *Hitler Jugend* and mock the authoritarianism of Nazi leaders. During the war, members assisted deserters, set fire to fuel supplies, supported the Allies, and waged undeclared war on the *Hitler Jugend*, but they also hiked and camped in the German countryside like the *Hitler Jugend*. Ultimately some *Edelweisspiraten* were imprisoned locally or in concentration camps, and six members were executed in 1944 as part of Gestapo action against anti–Nazi groups in Cologne.[45] A similar fate befell Munich students and professors who adopted the white rose to symbolize resistance; they published anti-Nazi leaflets until the Gestapo discovered and dismantled the alliance in 1943, sending members for execution or imprisonment.

Edelweiss also figured in music during the Third Reich. In 1934, the Wagnerian tenor Harry Steier recorded *"Adolf Hitlers Lieblingsblume ist das schlichte Edelweiss"* (Adolf Hitler's favorite flower is the simple edelweiss), composed to please the Nazi regime. German *Soldatenlieder* (soldier songs) included *"Es War ein Edelweiss"* (it was an edelweiss), which Herms Niel composed for the German Army in 1941. However, it was the cornflower (*Centaurea cyanus*) that Nazis wore to recognize each other when the party was banned in Austria during 1934–8. The bright blue composite had been the favorite flower of Kaiser Wilhelm and symbolized pan-German nationalism during the nineteenth century, also becoming the symbol of *Volksdeutsche* (racial Germans) living abroad.

Editions of *Du und Deine Harmonika Soldatenlieder* (Soldier Songs for You and Your Harmonika) provided lyrics and music for several other marching songs with sentimental references to plants and nature, including *"Drei Lilien"* (three lilies), *"Der Voglein im Wald"* (the small bird in the forest), *"Im Wald, im grünen Walde"* (in the forest, in the green forest), *"Schwarzbraun ist die Hazelnuss"* (black-brown is the hazelnut), *"Schon bluh'n die Heckenrosen"* (the wild roses flower beautifully), and *"Liebes Madel—Als in deinem kleinem Blumengarten"* (dear girl, as in your little flower garden).[46] Greeting cards designed by the *Reichspropagandaleitung* (central propaganda office) were sent to the families of fallen German soldiers. One example bore the message *"Den Müttern und Frauen unserer Gefallenen zum Muttertag 1944"* (For the Wives and Mothers of our Fallen on Mother's Day 1944) and included quotations from Hitler and Goebbels and the testimony of a German mother; it was illustrated with forget-me-nots and violets, botanical symbols of remembrance and love.[47]

Homefront Horticulture

Victory gardens in Allied countries provided essential food, and in areas where land was limited, wartime allotments replaced flowers and lawns. Magazines provided a forum to debate land use for food or flowers; an article in *House and Garden* asked, "The question of flowers arises. What part do they have in a war-time garden? A very important part indeed, for they nourish the spirit just as surely as vegetables serve the body."[48] Magazines recommended low maintenance perennials which did not tax the gardener who was also involved with victory gardening and war work.[49] Although vegetables replaced flowers on the covers of seed catalogues, common annuals and perennials were still sold and sown in beds and borders.

Ornamental gardens helped to sustain civilian morale, especially when travel was curtailed and lives revolved around home and war work. Some envisioned wartime beds of red, white, and blue flowers. Even before the attack on Pearl Harbor, an article in *Betters Homes and Gardens* advised readers, "We've mapped out spring planting maneuvers ... plan on reds, whites, and blues this year. If you haven't space for a tri-color border, put a patriotic edging to your paths ... remember this is one of the few countries in the world where people will plant flowers this spring."[50] Plant breeders also assumed a patriotic stance. Nursery catalogues featured two rose cultivars named for General Douglas MacArthur, a coral-colored hybrid tea variety and a climbing rose.

At the beginning of the war with Germany, English gardeners destroyed ornamental plantings and replaced them with vegetable plots. Lawns were the first to be tilled, followed by ornamental borders. Memoirs recorded gardeners' remorse. Many of the flowers and shrubs had been tended for generations, only to be replaced by cabbages and carrots as part of the Grow More Food and Dig for Victory campaigns (see Chapter 3). As part of an effort to preserve historic gardens, the Institute of Landscape Architects ran advertisements in the *Gardeners' Chronicle* offering their services to larger households in determining which areas should (and should not) be replaced with vegetable plots. On a smaller scale, many suburban gardens included rockeries made of local stone, clinkers, and concrete debris, the result of a 1930s fad for rock gardens and alpine plants. Garden writers recommended leaving these in place because moving the tonnage would have required considerable labor; alpine plants (no doubt including edelweiss) thus remained undisturbed for the duration of the war.

Flowers remained essential to British wartime morale. Dried arrangements of *Helichrysum* species (composites with petals that retain pigment colors when dried) and other "everlasting" cultivars were popular, and wartime publications also recommended forcing bulbs, assembling dish gardens, and planting window boxes.[51] Despite government insistence to prioritize vegetables over ornamentals, *Gardening Made Easy*, published mid-war, devoted an entire chapter to flower gardens.[52] Roses were popular during the war years, and seeds of annuals and perennials were still available, although the land that nurseries and growers could devote to non-food plants was limited. Supplies were sufficient that Sutton's Seeds marketed packets to U.S. customers as "Remembrances from 'Over There'" with the reminder, "In many an English garden U.S. soldiers find peace in the midst of war. You can grow the flowers they have smelled and admired—from seeds produced in England."[53] Flowers were never rationed, but florists' supplies were limited for the duration due to problems with both growing and shipping. Trains were occupied by military personnel and munitions, and the trains that brought flowers to London from growers in the Isles of Scilly and the West Country were cancelled in late 1942. When Churchill heard about flower shortages that resulted, he insisted for the sake of civilian morale that train service be restored to carry flower shipments to urban areas.[54]

Back in the U.S., an article in the *Journal of the Arnold Arboretum* described a young soldier's thoughts about British horticulture, "…what impressed me more than anything else was the English people's love for their flower-gardens … every house has its garden—the larger estate, the gardens often of renown—the smaller homes, gardens to fit the space, no matter how small it may be." He went on to discuss rhododendron displays, cottage gardens, and colorful plantings in ancient towns and villages. Sadly he also described the neglect and destruction of the grounds of country estates taken over by the military.[55] Large country estates suffered the effects of war most dramatically; great houses were typically situated amidst park-like grounds and tended gardens, often with surrounding farms maintained by resident tenant farmers. British military used great houses and their grounds for billeting and maneuvers; the private land was requisitioned for aerodromes, radio and telephone installations, munitions dumps, temporary buildings, and practice areas for bombs and landmines. Military trucks navigated shortcuts through groves of ancient landscape trees, and follies were vandalized. Rare plantings were replaced by vegetable plots, and untended gardens quickly overgrew with brambles and nettles for lack of care. However, not all wartime use of country estates was entirely destructive. Because of their rural locations, nearly two thousand such properties were requisitioned as homes for evacuated children, who found gardens and rural landscapes an entirely new experience in comparison to conditions in the 22 English cities that endured German bombing.

Rebirth

In England, World War II began with the German invasion of Poland in September 1939 and ended with the Japanese surrender in September 1945. Civilian life was drastically altered by six years of rationing, stringencies, evacuation, bombing, destruction, and deaths. With an end to the war in sight, there was concern for sustaining the British way of life, which required rebuilding both infrastructure and culture. *Britain in Pictures*, a series of slim volumes published during the war years, documented life in pre-war England. Edited by William James Turner, literary editor of the *Spectator*, the series emphasized rural life, with volumes devoted to agriculture, botany, farming practice, horticulture, herbs and vegetables, rural living, and garden design and history. The series provided descriptive records that cut across class lines, with occasional references to temporary stringencies and contingencies; the goal was to record British social history, as a blue-print for its reinvention and as a boost to national morale. A generation of children knew little of pre-war life, but *Britain in Pictures* volumes provided a detailed, albeit idealized, record of the rural landscape, practices, and natural history.

Botany remained an important discipline with connections to both worldwide exploration and local natural history, including recent ecological studies of newly vegetated bomb sites.[56] Concern mounted for native flora, although the British view on welcoming naturalized species and horticultural varieties from around the world stood in direct contrast to the German ideal of cultivating exclusively native plants. In fact, most species in the English countryside also grow in continental Europe, but the draining of wetlands and habitat destruction diminished populations of about 300 wildflowers, 13 percent of the native British flora. During the war years, medicinal plants also became increasingly rare; several species were collected aggressively (see Chapter 7), and military activity and vehicles damaged hedgerows and woodlands.[57] *English Gardens* envisioned a postwar rebirth of cottage gardens planted with traditional herbs and vegetables, noting that more than 80 percent of those surveyed during wartime Mass Observation polls envisioned "a small convenient house 'with a garden.'"[58] *British Herbs and Vegetables* recalled the recent revival of herb gardening and the importance of both traditional crops and wild foods during the war years.[59] *English Farming*, one of the first volumes in the series, noted in particular the precarious wartime food situation and the need to raise as many crops as possible in England, as well as the benefits of an agrarian economy that included "the interest that comes of dealing with living things and spending one's days in the open air, watching the growing crops … that furnish food for the nation."[60] While the language was idealistic, British self-sufficiency was indeed the most essential message for postwar restoration and rebuilding.

Chapter Notes

Chapter 1

1. *Guide for Planning the Local Victory Garden Program*, U.S. Office of Civil Defense, Washington, D.C., 1942, p. 3.
2. U.S. Department of Agriculture, "Victory Gardens: Miscellaneous Publication No. 483" (Washington, D.C., USDA, 1942).
3. L.A. Hawkins, *Have a Victory Garden* (Chicago, International Harvester Company, 1943), p. 2.
4. F. Thone, "Vegetables for Victory," *Science News-Letter*, March 28, 1942, pp. 198–199, 203.
5. F. Thone, "Victory Gardens," *Science News-Letter*, March 20, 1943, pp. 186–188.
6. D.M. Crooks, "Plants for Special Uses," *Economic Botany* 2, No. 1, 1948, p. 63.
7. F. Thone, "Victory Gardens," *Science News-Letter*, March 20, 1943, pp. 186–188.
8. U.S. Department of Agriculture, "Victory Gardens: Miscellaneous Publication No. 483" (Washington, D.C., USDA, 1942); U.S. Department of Agriculture, *Book IV. The Victory Garden Campaign* (Washington, D.C., USDA, 1943).
9. L.A. Hawkins, *Have a Victory Garden* (Chicago, International Harvester Company, 1943), pp. 15–20.
10. F. Thone, "Victory Gardens," *Science News-Letter*, March 20, 1943, p. 188.
11. T.H. Everett, "The Victory Gardens of 1942 and '43," *Journal of the New York Botanical Garden*, March 1943, p. 53.
12. *Ibid.*, p. 67.
13. W.H. Wisely, "Sewage Sludge for Victory Gardens?," *Sewage Works Journal*, July 1943, pp. 710–711.
14. U.S. Department of Agriculture, *Victory Garden Leader's Handbook* (Washington, D.C., USDA, 1943), p. 8.
15. C. Oderkirk, "Rodent Pests of Your Victory Garden," *The American Biology Teacher*, March 1944, pp. 128, 137.
16. U.S. Department of Agriculture, *Victory Garden Leader's Handbook* (Washington, D.C., USDA), p. 6.
17. M. Gregg [ed.], *The American Women's Voluntary Services Cook Book* (San Francisco, AWVS, 1942), p. 89.
18. "Preserve Garden Seeds," *Science News-Letter*, September 4, 1943, p. 150.
19. F. Thone, "Nature Ramblings: Hybrid Corn's Conquests," *Science News-Letter*, April 26, 1941, p. 271.
20. L.A. Hawkins, pp. 10–11.
21. M.G. Kains, *Food Gardens for Defense* (New York, Grosset and Dunlap, 1942).
22. "Gardens for U.S. at War," *Life*, March 30, 1942, pp. 81–84.
23. "Victory Gardens," *Life*, May 3, 1943, pp. 28–29.
24. "Vegetables Grow on Fifth Avenue," *American Cookery*, August-September 1942, p. 70.
25. "How Many Gardens?" *House and Garden*, June 1943, p. 15.
26. Boston Victory Gardens folders, Massachusetts Horticultural Society archives.
27. *Ibid.*
28. *Ibid.*
29. H. Watson, "Farming and Gardening at Mount Holyoke College During World War I and World War II" [unpublished paper based on research in the Mount Holyoke College archives], 2012.
30. E. Gabler, "School Gardens for Victory," *The Clearing House*, April 1942, pp. 469–472.
31. C.C. Culver, "Growing Plants for Victory Gardens," *The American Biology Teacher*, April 1942, pp. 217–218.
32. M.C. Lichtenwalter, "The Victory Garden and Biology," *The American Biology Teacher*, April 1942, pp. 206–8.
33. E. Gabler, pp. 469–472.
34. U.S. Department of Agriculture, *Victory Garden Leader's Handbook*, p. 2.
35. M. Leaf, *My Book to Help America* (Racine, Whitman, 1942), pp. 7–8.
36. Victory Garden Committee, War Services, *Victory Gardens: Handbook of the Victory Garden Committee* (Commonwealth of Pennsylvania, Pennsylvania State Council of Defense, 1944), p. 64.
37. M.A Russel, *Highland Park's School Victory Gardens*, 6 No. 8 (Highland Park, MI: The University of California Press on behalf of the National Association of Biology Teachers, May 1944), 171–174.
38. L. Elzey, "An Elementary School Garden Project," *The American Biology Teacher*, February 1944, pp. 115–118.
39. F.G. Heuchling, "Children's Gardens in Chicago," *The American Biology Teacher*, February 1944, pp. 103–107.
40. H.W. Hochbaum, "Victory Gardens in 1944—How Teachers May Help," *The American Biology Teacher*, February 1944, p. 101.
41. Boston Victory Gardens folders, Massachusetts Horticultural Society archives.
42. *Ibid.*
43. "Our Kids in Trouble," *Life*, December 20, 1943, pp. 96–108.

44. "Down to Earth Boys' Work," *The Rotarian*, May 1943, p. 21.

45. "Wartime 4-H Support—World War II," National 4-H History Preservation Program, https://4-hhistory preservation.com.

46. J. West, "Your Victory Garden," *Boys' Life*, May 1942, p. 3.

47. "Repairing Garden Implements," *Boys' Life*, May 1943, p. 2; "Merit Badge to Victory," *Boys' Life*, April 1945, p. 29.

48. B.J. Chute, "Weed 'Em and Reap," *Boys' Life*, May 1945, p. 14.

49. "The Facts About 1945 Victory Gardens," Massachusetts Horticultural Society archives.

50. Quoted in D. McCullough, *Truman* (New York, Simon and Schuster, 1992), p. 564.

51. "Notes on This and That," *Kiplinger's Personal Finance*, March 1948, p. 2.

52. "Garden for Fun and Health," *Science News-Letter*, March 15, 1952, pp. 170–171.

Chapter 2

1. U. Buchan, *A Green and Pleasant Land* (London, Windmill Books, 2013), p. 37.

2. L.B. and A.C. Horth, *101 Things to Do in Wartime* (London, B.T. Batsford, 1940), p. 82.

3. "Allotment and Garden Guide" (Ministry of Agriculture, December 1945), p. 6.

4. "In the Ruins—London Makes Use of the Scars Left by the Nazi Blitz of 1940," *Life*, September 27, 1943, pp. 41–44.

5. M. Grieve, *A Modern Herbal, Vol. 1* (Darien, CT, Hafner Publishing, 1970, reprint of the 1931 ed.), pp. 467–73.

6. "Home Gardener—Save the Rubbish," *Cairns Post*, April 17, 1942, p. 3.

7. "Garden Army Scheme," *Sydney Morning Herald*, March 12, 1943, p. 3.

8. *The Vegetable Garden Displayed* (Wisley, Royal Horticultural Society, 1941).

9. S.B. Whitehead, *Manures for the War-Time Garden* (London, W.H. & L. Collingridge Ltd., 1942).

10. L.B. and A.C. Horth, pp. 82–3.

11. "Home Gardener—Save the Rubbish," p. 3.

12. "Bomb Raids Will Find London Prepared," *Scientific American* 161, March 1939, pp. 138–9.

13. L.B. and A.C. Horth, pp. 80–1.

14. J.B.S. Haldane, *A.R.P—Air Raid Precautions* (London, Victor Gollancz, Ltd., 1938).

15. M. Patten, *We'll Eat Again in Victory Cookbook* (London, Chancellor Press, 2002, reprint of the 1985 ed.), pp. 65, 96.

16. J. Turowski, "The Schreber Garden," *Cabinet* 6, Spring 2002, cabinetmagazine.org.

17. W. Taub, "Report on the German People," *Collier's*, October 16, 1943, p. 17.

Chapter 3

1. E. Davis, "America Builds Food Defense," *Science News-Letter*, September 14, 1940, pp. 170–172.

2. M. Mead, "The Factor of Food Habits," *Annals of the American Academy of Political and Social Science* 225, 1943, p. 137.

3. "Bad Tempers, Inefficiency, Traced to Lack of Vitamin B1," *Science News-Letter*, August 9, 1941, p. 84.

4. U.S. Department of Agriculture, "Victory Gardens: Miscellaneous Publication No. 483" (Washington, D.C., USDA, 1942), p. 1.

5. R. Wilder, "Hitler's Secret Weapon Is Depriving People of Vitamin," *Science News-Letter*, April 12, 1941, pp. 237–238.

6. L.A. Hawkins, *Have a Victory Garden* (Chicago, International Harvester Company, 1943), pp. 75–7.

7. S.S. Arnon, R. Schecter, *et al.* "Botulinum Toxin as a Biological Weapon," *Journal of the American Medical Association* 285, February 28, 2001, pp. 1059–1070.

8. *Home Canners Textbook* (Cambridge, MA, Boston Woven Hose and Rubber Company, 1943).

9. "Home Canning," *Journal of Home Economics*, January 1944, p. 16.

10. *Canning at Home in 44—Cornell Bulletin for Homemakers 583, Supplement 1,* July 1944, p. 1.

11. "You're in the Army Too," *Good Housekeeping*, June 1942, pp. 110–111.

12. E.H. Scott, "Community Canning Centers," *Journal of Home Economics*, March 1944, pp. 141–142.

13. *Canning at Home in 44—Cornell Bulletin for Homemakers 583, Supplement 1,* p. 1.

14. H.W. Kendall and L. Chapman, "Your Home-Canned Food—Eat It, Don't Save It!, *Good Housekeeping*, February 1943, P. 81.

15. L.B. and A.C. Horth, *101 Things to Do in Wartime* (London, B.T. Batsford, 1940), P. 68.

16. L.B. and A.C. Horth, P. 70.

17. "'Square Meals' Literally," *Science News-Letter*, March 20, 1943, p. 180.

18. W.W. Wilcox, *The Farmer in the Second World War* (Ames. Iowa State College Press, 1947), p. 296.

19. "Eleanor Early Reports on Dehydrated Foods," *American Cookery*, November 1942, p. 140.

20. "How It Began," *American Cookery*, November 1942, p. 155.

Chapter 4

1. "Vermont Harvests Its Maple Syrup in Wartime," *Life*, April 27, 1942, pp. 47–50.

2. "Medicine: Dentists' Nightmare," *Time*, October 12, 1942, www.content.time.com.

3. "Sugar Rationing Called a 'Godsend' to National Health," *Science News-Letter*, March 14, 1942, p. 164.

4. "Patterns," *Time*, June 1942, www.content.time.com.

5. "Exit the Can Opener," *Time*, March 8, 1943, www.content.time.com.

6. "Wartime Living: 18,000,000 Gardens," *Time*, February 8, 1943, www.content. time.com.

7. R.N. Proctor, *The Nazi War on Cancer* (Princeton, New Jersey, Princeton University Press, 1999), p. 154.

8. *Ibid.*, pp. 165–169.

9. A. Bentley, *Eating for Victory: Food Rationing and the Politics of Domesticity* (Champaign, University of Illinois Press, 1998), p. 36.

10. C. A. Anderson, "Food Rationing and Morale," *American Sociological Review* 8 no. 1, 1943, p. 32.

11. W.D. Cocking, "Know Your Points," *The High School Journal*, January–February 1943, pp. 5–9.

12. "Happy New Year! and Happy Rationing!," *Journal of Home Economics,* January 1943, pp. 40–43.

13. F. Thone, "Rationing," *Science News-Letter*, July 3, 1943, pp. 12–13.

14. *The National Wartime Nutrition Guide* (Washington, D.C., War Food Administration, 1943).

15. "World War Two and the Vitamin Sea: Navy Propaganda Posters of the Florida Citrus Commission," Naval Historical Foundation, 2014, www.navalhistory.org.

16. E. Roosevelt, *It's Up to the Women* (New York, Stokes, 1933), pp. 64–65.

17. L. Shapiro, "The First Kitchen," *The New Yorker*, November 22, 2010, www.newyorker.com.

18. M. Gregg [ed.], *The American Women's Voluntary Services Cook Book* (San Francisco, AWVS, 1942), p. 89.

19. *"Meat Point Pointers—Wartime Meat Recipe Book"* (Chicago, National Live Stock and Meat Board, n.d.).

20. *"Victory Meat Extenders"* (Chicago, National Livestock and Meat Board, 1941).

21. *"Meat Point Pointers—Wartime Meat Recipe Book".*

22. "Tested Recipes of the Month," *American Cookery*, November 1942, p. 133.

23. A. Winn-Smith, *Thrifty Cooking for Wartime* (New York, Macmillan, 1942), p. 72.

24. S.B. Anthony, *Out of the Kitchen—Into the War* (Stephen Day, New York, 1943), p. 33.

25. *"Bright Spots for Wartime Meals—66 Ration-Wise Recipes"* (Minneapolis, General Foods Corporation, 1944).

26. H. Young, "Vegetables and Vitamins—How to Get the Latter Out of the Former," *American Cookery*, May 1942, pp. 418–419.

27. Dr. C. Sherwin, "A Q. and A. on Meals," *Good Housekeeping*, March 1942, p. 81.

28. "Do They Eat Around the Vegetables?," *Good Housekeeping*, April 1943, p. 83.

29. C.E.H. Daniel, "Food Waste Control," *The Journal of Higher Education*. 16 No. 11, 1945, pp. 24–28.

30. E. Borgwardt, *A New Deal for the World* (Cambridge, Harvard University, 2005), p. 47.

31. T.S. Harding, "The Science of Food Management in War and Peace," *Social Forces*, vol. 21, 1943, pp. 413–417.

32. "From the Victory Garden," *American Cookery*, June-July 1942, pp. 20–21.

33. "Betty Crocker Home Defense Supper Menu" (Minneapolis, General Mills, n.d.).

34. *"Health-For-Victory Meal Planning Guide"* (Mansfield, OH, Home Economics Institute, Westinghouse Electric and Manufacturing Co., May 1943).

35. "Eat Well to Work Well," *Cornell Bulletin for Homemakers—War Emergency Bulletin* 524, June 1942.

36. W.D. Salmon, "Soybeans for Human Food," *Journal of Home Economics* 35 No. 4, 1943, pp. 201–202.

37. J. K. Hale, "Soybeans in the Diet," *Journal of Home Economics* 35 No. 4, 1943, pp. 203–206.

38. C. Miller, "Bread and Whole Grain Cereals," *Cornell Bulletin for Homemakers—War Emergency Bulletin* 576, March 1943.

39. "Wartime Luncheons for Women's Clubs," *American Cookery*, November 1942, p. 141.

40. *Health-For-Victory Meal Planning Guide.*

41. *Report of the State Food Commission, New York Times*, June 11, 1943, p. 8.

42. C.M. McCay and J.B. McCay, *The Cornell Bread Book* (New York, Dover, 1980).

43. A. Winn-Smith, Preface.

44. "This Is the Month for Sweet Potatoes," *Good Housekeeping*, November 1943, pp. 90–91.

45. C. Scripture, "Can She Bake a Pumpkin Pie?," *Good Housekeeping*, November 1942, p. 152.

46. *Betty Crocker Cook Book of All-Purpose Baking* (Minneapolis, General Mills, 1942).

47. A. Winn-Smith, p. 18.

48. J.H. Martin and M.T. Jenkins, "New Uses for Waxy-Cereal Starches," in *Yearbook of Agriculture, 1950–51* (Washington, D.C., U.S. Government Printing Office, 1951), pp. 159–162.

49. P. Allen, "Mrs. Higgins and the Pot Herbs," *American Cookery*, April 1942, p. 384; "Queries and Answers," *American Cookery*, April 1942, p. 370.

50. A. Winn-Smith, p. 70.

51. P. Allen, p. 384.

52. "A.R.P. Home Storage of Food Supplies" (The Canned Foods Advisory Bureau, 1938).

53. M.F.K. Fisher, *How to Cook a Wolf* in *The Art of Eating* (New York, Macmillan, 1990), p. 339.

54. L.B. and A.C. Horth, *101 Things to Do in Wartime* (London, B.T. Batsford, 1940), p. 99.

55. S. Falasca-Zamponi, *Fascist Spectacle: The Aesthetics of Power in Mussolini's Italy* (Berkley, University of California Press, 2000), p. 105.

56. M. Patten, p. 95.

57. "Foreign News," *Time*, October 20, 1941, www.content.time.com.

58. V.D. Wickizer, *Coffee, Tea, and Cocoa: An Economic and Political Analysis* (Stanford, Stanford University Press, 1951), pp. 212–226.

59. L.B. and H.C. Horth, p. 88.

60. F. Blackwood, *Mrs. England Goes on Living* (New York, Creative Age Press, 1943), p. 107.

61. A.B. Hartley, *Unexploded Bomb—A History of Bomb Disposal* (New York, W.W. Norton, 1958), pp. 234–235.

62. G. Landemare, *Churchill's Kitchen* (London, Imperial War Museum, 2015).

63. M.F.K. Fisher, pp. 245–6.

64. R.J. Hammond, *Food and Agriculture in Britain, 1939–45* (Stanford, Stanford University Press, 1954), p. 179.

65. M. Patten, pp. 64, 76, 80.

66. U. Buchan, *A Green and Pleasant Land* (London, Windmill Books, 2013), p. 253.

67. M. Patten, p. 34.

68. "Britain Tightens Its Belt on Carrot and Potato Diet," *Life*, May 12, 1941, pp. 43–46.

69. M. Patten, p. 46.

70. M.F.K. Fisher, p. 286.

71. E.S. Rohde, *Hay Box Cookery* (London, Routledge, 1939).

72. "Your Anderson Shelter This Winter" (Ministry of Home Security, 1940).

73. F. Blackwood, p. 128.

74. J.E.B. Wright, "Feeding East London Children in Wartime," *Social Service Review* 20 No. 2, 1946, pp. 207–11.

75. J.B.S. Haldane, p. 189.

76. L.B. and H.C. Horth, pp. 111–112.

77. M. Patten, p. 11.

78. M.F.K. Fisher, p. 205.

79. "Hedgerow Harvest" (Ministry of Food, 1943).

80. Vicomte de Mauduit, *They Can't Ration These* (London, Michael Joseph, 1940).

81. G.M. Taylor, *British Herbs and Vegetables* (London, Collins, 1947), pp. 37–41.

82. E.P. Prentice, "Food in England," *Agricultural History* 24 No. 2, 1950, pp. 65–70.

83. E.P. Prentice, p. 70.

84. "Hitler's Mountain Home," *Homes and Gardens,* November 1938, p. 193.

85. T. Junge, *Hitler's Last Secretary: A Firsthand Account of Life with Hitler* (New York, Arcade, 2002); J. von Lang, *The Secretary—Martin Bormann: The Man Who Manipulated Hitler* (New York, Random House), pp. 97–98.

86. O.D. Tolischus, "Where Hitler Dreams and Plans," *The New York Times Magazine,* May 30, 1937, Section 8, p. 16.

87. G. Sullivan, "Hitler's Former Maid Remembers the Good Life at Der Fuhrer's Mountain Retreat," *Washington Post* (April 29, 2014), www.washingtonpost.com.

88. "Germany: Asparagus Sucker," *Time,* July 15, 1935, www.content.time.com.

89. "Hitler's Asparagus Eating Sends Six to Concentration Camp," *Chicago Daily Tribune* July 17, 1935, p. 1.

90. R.N. Proctor, *The Nazi War on Cancer.*

91. H. Ettlinger, *The Axis on the Air* (New York, The Bobbs-Merrill Company, 1943), p. 271.

92. J. Lund, "The Wages of Collaboration: The German Food Crisis 1939–1945 and the Supplies from Denmark," *Scandinavian Journal of History* 38 No. 4, 2013. P. 480.

93. translation from G. Bischof, F. Plasser, and B. Stelzl-Marx [eds.], *New Perspectives on Austrians and World War II* (New York, Routledge, 2015), pp. 147–148.

94. H.K. Smith, *Last Train from Berlin* (London, Cresset Press, 1942), pp. 91–92.

95. G. Bischof *et al.*, pp. 149).

96. "International: Who Eats?," *Time,* January 22, 1940, www.content.time.com.

97. A. Speer, *Infiltration: How Heinrich Himmler Schemed to Build a SS Industrial Empire,* New York, Macmillan, 1981), pp. 147–8.

98. E. Schmidt, "Food and Feed Yeast in Germany" (Food and Agriculture Organization of the United Nations, n.d.), www.fao.org.

99. C.L. Walker, "Secrets by the Thousands," *Harper's Magazine,* October 1946, p. 329, www.harpers.org.

100. G. Trienekens, 2000. "The Food Supply in the Netherlands During the Second World War," in D.F. Smith and J. Phillips [eds.], *Food, Science, Policy and Regulation in the Twentieth Century* (New York, Routledge, 2000), pp. 117–149.

101. "France: Hunger Cramps," *Time,* March 3, 1941, www.content.time.com.

102. "Japan: Last Days," *Time,* August 20, 1945, www.content.time.com.

103. J. Dusselier, "Does Food Make Place? Food Protests in Japanese American Concentration Camps," *Food and Foodways: Explorations in the History and Culture of Human Nourishment* 10 No. 3, 2002, pp. 137–165.

104. C.K. Tseng, "Seaweed Resources of North America," *Economic Botany* 1 No. 1, January–March 1947, pp. 69–97.

Chapter 5

1. I. Nehrling, "How America's Soldier Is Fed," *American Cookery,* March 1942, p. 342.

2. "Carrot Diet for Flyers May Be in Offing," *Science News Letter,* March 6, 1943, p. 153.

3. *National Archives, "Powers of Persuasion" Online Exhibit,* www.archives.gov/exhibits/powers-of-persuasion.

4. J.D. Tuthill, *He's in the Navy Now* (New York, McBride, 1941), pp. 90–93.

5. Green Giant advertisement, *Good Housekeeping,* May 1943, p. 167.

6. *Army Food and Messing: The Complete Manual of Mess Management,* 3rd ed. (Harrisburg, Military Service Publishing, 1943), pp. 428–29).

7. "The Army Has Mechanized Potato Peeler," *American Cookery,* November 1942, p. 153.

8. E.A. Croddy and J.J. Wirtz, [eds.] *Weapons of Mass Destruction: An Encyclopedia of Worldwide Policy, Technology, and History; Volume I: Chemical and Biological Weapons* (Santa Barbara, ABC-CLIO, 2004), p. 177.

9. *Army Food and Messing,* Chapter 5.

10. M. Davis, "Our Army's Menu-Maker," *American Cookery,* August-September 1942, p. 78.

11. Letters of Chaplain Maosao Yamada, Library of Congress.

12. *Army Food and Messing,* pp. 127, 172; "Vitamin-Enriched Flour Goes into Production," *Science News-Letter,* February 8, 1941, pp. 83–84.

13. *Methods for Laboratory Technicians—War Department Technical Manual No. 8–227* (Washington, D.C., War Department, 1941).

14. A.P. Stauffer, *The Quartermaster Corps: Operations in the War Against Japan* (Washington, D.C., U.S. Army, Center of Military History, 1956), p. 231.

15. W.F. Ross and C.F. Romanus, *Quartermaster Corps: Operations in the War Against Germany* (Washington, D.C., U.S. Army, Center of Military History, 1965), p. 143.

16. A.P. Stauffer, p. 231.

17. *Army Food and Messing,* pp. 73, 79.

18. A.P. Stauffer, pp. 160–177.

19. S.E. Anders, "Quartermaster Supply in the Pacific During World War II," *Quartermaster Professional Bulletin,* Spring 1999, www.qmfound.com.

20. A.P. Stauffer, pp. 160–177.

21. *Army Food and Messing,* pp. 395–6.

22. E. Risch, *Quartermaster Corps: Organization, Supply, and Services. Volume 1.* (Washington, D.C., U.S. Army, Center of Military History, 1953), p. 180.

23. W.M. Hammond, *Normandy: The U.S. Army Campaigns of World War II* (Washington, D.C., U.S. Army, Center of Military History, n.d.), p. 14; Staff of General MacArthur, *Reports of General MacArthur—MacArthur in Japan: The Occupation: Military Phase,* Vol. 1, Supplement (Washington, D.C., Department of the Army, 1966, 1994 facsimile), p. 49.

24. *Army Food and Messing,* p. 276.

25. M.L. Drazin, "Nutrition and National Defense," *Military Surgeon* 88, 1941, p. 39.

26. E. Risch, *Quartermaster Corps: Organization, Supply, and Services. Volume 1.* (Washington, D.C., U.S. Army, Center of Military History, 1953), p. 201.

27. W.F. Ross and C.F. Romanus, p. 132.

28. *Ibid.*, p. 142.

29. M. Pendergast, "Viewpoints: A Brief History of Coca-Colonization," *New York Times,* August 18, 1993, www.nytimes.com.

30. R.N. Proctor, *The Nazi War on Cancer* (Princeton, New Jersey, Princeton University Press, 1999), p. 154.

31. "Medicine: Feeding the Reichswehr," *Time,* July 28, 1941, www.content.time.com.

32. G. Sonnedecker, "Soybean Boom," *Science News Letter,* December 5, 1942, pp. 362–363.

33. *Factors Affecting the Nutritive Values of Foods—Miscellaneous Publication 664* (Washington, D.C., U.S. Department of Agriculture, 1948), p. 14.

34. B. Shishkin, "The Work of Soviet Botanists," *Science New Series* 97 No. 2530, 1943, pp. 354–355.

35. M. Gerson, "Feeding the German Army," *New York State Journal of Medicine* 41 No. 13, 1941, pp. 1471–1476.

36. C.L. Walker, "Secrets by the Thousands," *Harper's Magazine,* October 1946, p. 329, www.harpers.org.

37. J. Thompson, "Butter from Coal," *Chicago Sunday Tribune,* August 11, 1946, p. 2.

38. *Reports of General MacArthur—The Campaigns of MacArthur in the Pacific, Vol. I* (Washington, D.C., Department of the Army), 1994, p. 235; R.R. Smith, *The Approach to the Philippines* (Washington, D.C., U.S. Army, Center of Military History, 1996), p. 417.

39. F.K. Danquah, "Japanese Food Farming Policies in Wartime Southeast Asia: The Philippine Example, 1942–1944," *Agricultural History* 64 No. 3, 1990, pp. 64–66.

Chapter 6

1. The Great Plains during World War II—Agriculture, Center for Great Plains Studies, http://plainshumanities.unl.edu.

2. B. Gold, *Wartime Economic Planning in Agriculture* (New York, Columbia University Press, 1949), pp. 263–4.

3. W.W. Wilcox, *The Farmer in the Second World War* (Ames, Iowa State College Press, 1947), p. 293.

4. "Growth of Seeds Promoted by Adhesive Envelopes," *Science News-Letter,* April 10, 1943, p. 234.

5. "Rice Growing in Florida Promises a Major Crop," *Science News-Letter,* June 13, 1942, p. 372).

6. A.P. Stauffer, *The Quartermaster Corps: Operations in the War Against Japan* (Washington, D.C., U.S. Army, Center of Military History, 1956), pp. 129–133.

7. R.G. Bowman, "Army Farms and Agricultural Development in the Southwest Pacific," *Geographical Review* 36 No. 3, 1946, pp. 420–446.

8. R. Howard files, correspondence and notes from K. Mair, Pusey Library, Harvard University.

9. S. Milner, *The War in the Pacific: Victory in Papua* (Washington, D.C., U.S. Army, Center of Military History, 1989), p. 116, Footnote 39.

10. C.F. Greeves-Carpenter, "Plants by Liquid Culture," *Scientific American,* January 1939, pp. 5–7; N.W. Stuart, "About Hydroponics," in *Science in Farming—Yearbook of Agriculture, 1943–1947* (Washington, D.C., U.S. Government Printing Office, 1947), pp. 289–292).

11. F. Thone, "Nature Ramblings," *Science News-Letter,* August 19, 1933, p. 127.

12. L. Steele, "The Hybrid Corn Industry in the U.S.," in D.B. Walden [ed.], *Maize Breeding and Genetics* (New York, Wiley Interscience, 1978, p. 32).

13. L. Burbank, *The Training of the Human Plant* (New York, Century Co., 1909), pp. 58–59; K.C. Barrons, "Modern Plant Wizardry," *Scientific American,* July 1938, pp. 14–17; E.R. Sears, "Genetics and Farming" in *Science in Farming—Yearbook of Agriculture 1943–1947,* pp. 245–255 handbook.

14. W.W. Wilcox, p. 301.

15. "Bedlam: Food," *Time,* June 28, 1943, www.content.time.com.

16. W.W. Wilcox, p. 299.

17. *Soldier's Guide to the Japanese Army—Special Series No. 27* (Washington, D.C., Military Intelligence Service, 1944), p. 79.

18. W.W. Wilcox, p. 298; P.R. Henson, "Soybeans for the South," in *Science in Farming—Yearbook of Agriculture 1943–1947,* pp. 338–343.

19. "Production: Navy Bean Soup," *Time,* December 6, 1943, www.content.time.com.

20. W.W. Wilcox, pp. 57, 62.

21. R.D. Brigham, 1993. "Castor: Return of an Old Crop," in J. Janick and J.E. Simon [eds.], *New Crops* (New York, Wiley, 1993), pp. 380–383.

22. B. Gold, *Wartime Economic Planning in Agriculture* (New York, Columbia University Press, 1949), pp. 253–4.

23. "Hybrid Alfalfa Is Good for Livestock and Soil," *Science News-Letter,* June 6, 1942, p. 356.

24. "New Ration for Cows," *Science News-Letter,* September 4, 1943, p. 150.

25. F. Thone, "Cultivating by Fire," *Science News-Letter,* February 13, 1943, pp. 106–8.

26. Oil Sprays Kill Weeds in Carrot Gardens, *Science News-Letter,* April 4, 1945, p. 232.

27. W.W. Wilcox, p. 57).

28. "Harvesting Machine for Pyrethrum Flowers," *Science News-Letter,* April 12, 1941, p. 239.

29. E.C. Higbee, "Lonchocarpus: A Fish-Poison Insecticide," *Economic Botany* 1 No. 4, 1947, pp. 427–436.

30. J.A. Lockwood, 2009, *Six-Legged Soldiers: Using Insects as Weapons of War* (New York, Oxford University Press), pp. 128–138.

31. *Ibid.,* p. 134.

32. *Ibid.,* p. 134.

33. P. Rogers, S. Whitby, and M. Dando, "Biological Warfare Against Crops," *Scientific American,* June 1999, p. 73.

34. "Food: Crisis Coming," *Time,* November 2, 1942, www.content.time.com.

35. J. Brucato, "War Hits the Farmlands," *San Francisco News,* March 9, 1942, cited in www.sfmuseum.net.

36. "Life Visits the Harvesters of America," *Life,* September 27, 1943, pp. 119–129.

37. M.C. Wilson, "A Feminine Land Army: Plans in the Making Would Put City Women on Farms to Help Feed Forces," *New York Times,* February 28, 1943.

38. J.B. Litoff and D.C. Smith, "To the Rescue of the Crops: The Women's Land Army During World War II," *Prologue* 25, No. 4, Winter 1993, www.archives.gov.

39. A.P. Krammer, "When the Afrika Korps Came to Texas," the *Southwestern Historical Quarterly* 80 No. 30, 1977, P. 268.

40. J.M. Ward, "Nazis Hoe Cotton: Plants, POWs, and the Future of Farm Labor in the Deep South," *Agricultural History* 81 No. 4, 2007, p. 482.

41. *Ibid.,* pp. 482–483.

42. G. Bullett, *Achievement in Feeding Britain* (London, Pilot Press, 1944), p. 12.

43. J. Martin, "The Structural Transformation of British Agriculture: The Resurgence of Progressive, High-Input Arable Farming," in B. Short, C. Watkins, and J. Martin [eds.]. *The Front Line of Freedom: British Farming in the Second World War,* British Agricultural History Society, 2006, pp. 14–35.

44. "British Farmers Plough Their Fields by Night in Race Against Spring," *Life,* April 29, 1940, p. 33.

45. "War Agricultural Committee," *Nature* September 9, 1939, p. 473.

46. "Food Situation of the United Kingdom," Cabinet Memorandum, October 2, 1939, pp. 1–2, www.filestore. nationalarchives.gov.uk.

47. P. Brassley, "Wartime Productivity and Innovation, 1939–45," in B. Short, C. Watkins, and J. Martin, [eds.], *The Front Line of Freedom: British Farming in the Second World War*, British Agricultural History Society, 2006, p. 44.

48. *Ibid.*

49. E.J. Russell, *English Farming* (London, Collins, 1941), p. 16.

50. M. Riley, Silage for Self-Sufficiency? The Wartime Promotion of Silage and Its Use in the Peak District in B. Short, C. Watkins, and J. Martin [eds.], *The Front Line of Freedom: British Farming in the Second World War*, British Agricultural History Society, 2006, pp. 78–88.

51. W.E. Shewell-Cooper, *Land Girl Manual* (London, English Universities Press, 1940).

52. "Now We Are Three," *The Land Girl* April 1943, p. 1.

53. V. Sackville-West, *The Women's Land Army* (London, Michael Joseph, 1944), p. 112.

54. R.J. Moore-Collyer, "Kids in the Corn: School Harvest Camps and Farm Labour Supply in England, 1940–50," *The Agricultural History Review* 52 No. 2, 2004, p. 199.

55. B. Mayall and V. Morrow, *You Can Help Your Country: English Children's Work During the Second World War* (London, Institute of Education, University of London, 2011), pp. 145–157; R.J. Moore-Colyer, pp. 183–206.

56. W. Foot, The Impact of the Military on the Agricultural Landscape of England and Wales in the Second World War," *The Front Line of Freedom: British Farming in the Second World War* in B. Short, C. Watkins, and J. Martin, [eds.], *The Front Line of Freedom: British Farming in the Second World War*, British Agricultural History Society, 2006, pp. 132–142.

57. Quoted in E.J. Russell, *English Farming* (London, Collins, 1941), p. 10.

58. G. Gerhard, "Breeding Pigs and People for the Third Reich: Richard Walther Darré's Agrarian Ideology," in F. Bruggemeier, M. Cioc, and T. Zeller, *How Green Were the Nazis? Nature, Environment, and Nation in the Third Reich* (Athens, Ohio, Ohio University Press, 2005), pp. 129–146; C.R. Lovin, "Agricultural Reorganization in the Third Reich: The Reich Food Corporation," *Agricultural History* 43 No. 4, pp. 447–462.

59. *Ibid.*

60. N. Cameron and R.H. Stevens (transl.), *Hitler's Table Talk, 1941–1944: His Private Conversations* (New York, Enigma Books), p. 529.

61. MIRS London Branch, *The Hitler-Jugend* (Allied Expeditionary Force G-2 Counter Intelligence Sub-Division, n.d.), p. 16.

62. U. Deichmann, *Biologists Under Hitler* (Cambridge, Harvard University Press, 1996), pp. 134–136.

63. T. Wieland, "Autarky and Lebensraum. the Political Agenda of Academic Plant Breeding in Nazi Germany," *Journal of History of Science and Technology* 3, Fall 2009, p. 14.

64. G. Sonnedecker, "Soybean Boom," *Science News-Letter*, December 5, 1942, pp. 362–363.

65. A. Lang, 1987, "Elisabeth Schiemann: Life and Career of a Woman Scientist in Berlin," *Englera* 7, Pp. 17–28.

66. W. Gratzer, the *Undergrowth of Science: Delusion,*

Self-Deception, and Human Frailty (Oxford, Oxford University Press, 2000), p. 237.

67. S. Heim, *Plant Breeding and Agrarian Research in the Kaiser-Wilhelm Institutes 1933–1945* (Berlin, Springer Science, 2008), p. 170.

68. B. Gausemeier, "Political Networking and Scientific Modernization: Botanical Research at the KWI for Biology and Its Place in National Socialist Science Policy," in S. Heim, C. Sachse, and M. Walker [eds.], The Kaiser Wilhelm Society under National Socialism (New York, Cambridge University Press, 2009), pp. 242–243.

69. K. Macrakis, *Surviving the Swastika* (New York, Oxford University Press, 1993), p. 122.

70. B. Gausemeier, pp. 237–238.

71. "Nazi Raw Material Handicaps," *Illustrated London News*, August 3, 1940.

72. F. Strauss, "The Food Problem in the German War Economy," *The Quarterly Journal of Economics* 55 No. 3, 1941, p. 374.

73. C.L. Sulzberger, "Oswiecim Killings Placed at 4, 000, 000," *New York Times*, May 8, 1945.

74. M. Lamer, *The World Fertilizer Economy* (Stanford, CA, Stanford University Press, 1957), pp. 539–542.

75. *Ibid.*, p. 539.

76. *Ibid.*, pp. 539–542.

77 B.F. Johnston, M. Hosoda, and Y. Kusumi, *Japanese Food Management in World War II* (Stanford, CA, Stanford University Press, 1953), pp. 39–41, 86.

78. Staff of General MacArthur, *Reports of General MacArthur—MacArthur in Japan: The Occupation: Military Phase*, Vol. 1, Supplement (Washington, D.C., Department of the Army, 1966, 1994 facsimile), pp. 215, 217.

79. B.F. Johnston, M. Hosoda, and Y. Kusumi, pp. 118–119.

80. *Ibid.*, pp. 118–119, 122–126.

81. D.C. Earhart, *Certain Victory: Images of World War II in the Japanese Media* (Armonk, New York, M.E. Sharpe, 2008), p. 445.

82. *Ibid.*, pp. 451–452.

Chapter 7

1. E.F. Woodward, "Botanical Drugs: A Brief Review of the Industry with Comments on Recent Developments," *Economic Botany* 1 No. 4, p. 410.

2. *Military Sanitation, War Department Field Manual FM21-10* (Washington, D.C., War Department, 1945), p. 166.

3. H.S. Gentry, A.J. Verbiscar, and T.F. Banigan, "Red Squill (*Urginea maritima*, Liliaceae)," *Economic Botany* 41 No. 2, pp. 267–282, 1987.

4. H.W. Youngken, "The Medicinal Plant Garden of the Massachusetts College of Pharmacy," *Arnoldia* 2 No. 7, pp. 37–40.

5. D.B. Worthen, *Pharmacy in World War II* (New York The Haworth Press), p. 94.

6. D.M. Crooks, "Plants for Special Uses," *Economic Botany* 2, No. 1, 1948, pp. 61–63.

7. E.F. Woodward, p. 413.

8. *Medical Field Manual—Medical Service of Field Units FM 8-10* (Washington, D.C., War Department, 1942), pp. 253–254.

9. G.A. Cosmas and A.E. Cowdrey, *The Medical Department: Medical Service in the European Theater of Operations* (Washington, D.C., U.S. Army, Center of Military History, 1992), p. 363; *The Basic Field Man-*

Notes. Chapter 7

ual—*First Aid for Soldiers FM-21-11* (Washington, D.C., War Department, 1943), pp. 107–108.

10. J. Lewy, "The Drug Policy of the Third Reich," *Social History of Alcohol and Drugs* 22 No. 2, 2008), pp. 148–149.

11. H.N. Harkins, "Treatment of Shock from War Injuries," *Journal of the Michigan Medical Society* 41, April 1942, pp. 287–293; D.B. Kendrick, *Blood Program in World War II*, Medical Department, U.S. Army in World War II, http://history.amedd.army.mil, pp. 378–379.

12. *Ibid.*, p. 380.

13. B. Krauss, *Keneti: South Seas Adventures of Kenneth Emory* (Honolulu, University of Hawaii Press, 1988), p. 295.

14. D. Campbell-Falck, T. Thomas, T.M. Falck, N. Tutuo, and K. Clem, "The Intravenous Use of Coconut Water," *American Journal of Emergency Medicine* 18 No. 1, 2000, pp. 108–111.

15. G. Majori, "Short History of Malaria and Its Eradication in Italy with Short Notes on the Fight Against the Infection in the Mediterranean Basin," *Mediterranean Journal of Hematology and Infectious Diseases* 4 No. 1, 2012, www.mjhid.org.

16. L.D. Heaton, *Preventive Medicine in World War II. Vol. VI Communicable Diseases: Malaria*. Medical Department, U.S. Army in World War II, http://history.amedd.army.mil, p. 1).

17. M. Davis, "Malaria," *Good Housekeeping*, August 1943, p. 22.

18. L.D. Heaton, *Preventive Medicine in World War II. Vol. VI Communicable Diseases*, Medical Department, U.S. Army in World War II, http://history.amedd.army.mil, pp. 1–8; *Military Sanitation, War Department Field Manual FM21-10* (Washington, D.C., War Department, 1945), pp. 120–123.

19. L.D. Heaton, p. 129.

20. A.P. Stauffer, *The Quartermaster Corps: Operations in the War Against Japan* (Washington, D.C., U.S. Army, Center of Military History, 1956), p. 298.

21. D.H. Killeffer, "Insects Can Be Controlled," *Scientific American*, July 1944, pp. 13–15.

22. I. Stewart, *Organizing Scientific Research for War* (Boston, Little Brown, 1948), p. 126.

23. R. Fosberg *Columbian Cinchona Manual* (Bogota, Colombia, Foreign Economic Administration, 1943).

24. I. Stewart, pp. 114–115.

25. W. Kaempffert, "Synthetic Quinine, of High Medical Importance, Achieved at Last by Two American Chemists," *New York Times*, May 5, 1944, p. 18.

26. C.B. Philip, "Tsutsugamushi Disease (Scrub Typhus) in World War II," *The Journal of Parasitology* 34 No. 3, 1948, pp. 168–191.

27. *Military Sanitation, War Department Field Manual FM21-10*, p. 156.

28. *Jungle Warfare—War Department Field Manual FM 72-20* (Washington, D.C., War Department), 1944, p. 17.

29. E. Risch, *Quartermaster Corps: Organization, Supply, and Services. Volume 1.* (Washington, D.C., U.S. Army, Center of Military History, 1953), pp. 98–100.

30. B. Shishkin, "The Work of Soviet Botanists," *Science New Series* 97 No. 2530, 1943, pp. 354–5.

31. "Onion Paste Reduces Infection and Helps Heal Wounds," *Popular Mechanics,* June 1944, p. 32; B. Tokin, "Effect of Phyoneides Upon Protozoa," *American Review of Soviet Medicine* 1 No. 3, 1944, pp. 237–9.

32. C.J. Cavallito and J.H. Bailey, "Allicin, the Antibacterial Principle of *Allium sativum*. I. Isolation, Physical Properties and Antibacterial Action," *Journal of the American Chemical Society* 66 No. 11, 1944, pp. 1950–51.

33. C.F. Carson, K.A. Hammer, and T.V. Riley, "*Melaleuca alternifolia* (Tea Tree) Oil: A Review of Antimicrobial and Other Medicinal Properties," *Clinical Microbiology Reviews* 19 No. 1, 2006, pp. 50–62.

34. C.A. McAvoy, "First Aid for Burns," *Scientific American*, September 1940, pp. 126–127.

35. "Treatment of Burns," *Lancet* 2, November 16, 1940, pp. 621, 627; "Burns of the Hands and Face," *Lancet* 2, November 23, 1940, p. 655).

36. B. Cannon, "Plastic and Reconstructive Surgery at the MGH," *The Massachusetts General Hospital Surgical Society Newsletter,* Summer 2003, pp. 16–17.

37. I. Stewart, pp. 105–106.

38. *Methods for Laboratory Technicians—War Department Technical Manual No. 8-227* (Washington, D.C., War Department, 1941), p. 163.

39. K.B. Raper, "Penicillin," in *Science in Farming—Yearbook of Agriculture, 1943–1947* (Washington, D.C., U.S. Government Printing Office, 1947), pp. 699–710.

40. E. Gallardo, "Sensitivity of Bacteria from Infected Wounds to Penicillin, *War Medicine*" 7, February 1945, pp. 100–103.

41. D. Doyle, "Adolf Hitler's Medical Care," *Journal of the Royal College of Physicians of Edinburgh* 35, 2005, p. 78.

42. "Immersion Foot Prevented," *Science News-Letter*, March 20, 1943, p. 179.

43. J.A. Doull, *Preventive Medicine in World War II. Vol. IV Communicable Diseases*, Medical Department, Chapter 4. Leprosy, U.S. Army in World War II, http://history.amedd.army.mil, pp. 34–36.

44. L.M. Miller, "Chlorophyll for Healing," *Science News-Letter*, March 15, 1941, pp. 170–171.

45. S. Mowbray, "The Antibacterial Activity of Chlorophyll," *British Medical Journal,* February 2, 1957, pp. 268–269.

46. H. Keen, "Orphan Agar," *Scientific American*, August 1943, pp. 73–75.

47. *Methods for Laboratory Technicians—War Department Technical Manual No. 8-227* (Washington, D.C., War Department, 1941), pp. 154–168.

48. H. Keen, pp. 73–75.

49. H. Humm, "Seaweeds at Beaufort, NC, as a Source of Agar," *Science* 96, 1942, pp. 230–231.

50. H.J. Humm, "Agar: A Pre-War Japanese Monopoly," *Economic Botany* 1 No. 3, 1947, pp. 317–329.

51. "Drug Supplies in Wartime," *Nature* January 25, 1941, p. 112.

52. National Federation of Women's Institutes, *Town Children Through Country Eyes: A Survey on Evacuation* (Dorking, Surrey, NFWI, 1940).

53. B. Keen and J. Armstrong, *Herb Gathering* (London, Brome and Schimmer, 1941).

54. H.G. Bruenn, "Clinical Notes on the Illness and Death of President Franklin D. Roosevelt," *Annals of Internal Medicine* 72 No. 4, 1970, pp. 579–591.

55. Ministry of Supply, *Herb Collector' Bulletin No. 1*, 1942.

56. Ministry of Supply, *Herb Collectors' Bulletin No. 4*, 1942.

57. Ministry of Supply, *Herb Collectors' Bulletin No. 3*, 1942.

58. B. Shishkin, pp. 354–5.

59. M. Grieve, *A Modern Herbal, Vol. 2* (Darien, CT, Hafner Publishing, 1970, reprint of the 1931 ed.), pp. 824–9.

60. "Plants Used in Medicine Growing in N.Z. Help to Meet War Shortage," *The Dominion*, April 2, 1942.

61. R.J. Evans, 2005, The *Third Reich in* Power (New York, Penguin Books, 2005), p. 444.

62. *Ibid.*, pp. 317–319.

63. *Ibid.*, p. 319.

64. *Ibid.*, p. 439.

65. R. Proctor, *The Nazi War on Cancer*, pp. 157, 159.

66. "Gelernt Ist Gelernt: Mit Bildbericht Aus Der Reichsbräute- Und Heimmütterschule Husbäke in Oldenburg," *NS Frauen Warte* 8 No. 2, Maiheft 1940.

67. R. Proctor, *Racial Hygiene: Medicine Under the Nazis* (Cambridge, Harvard University Press, 1988), p. 249.

68. U. Deichmann, *Biologists Under Hitler* (Cambridge, Harvard University Press, 1996), pp. 137–138.

69. R. Sigel, "The Cultivation of Medicinal Herbs in the Concentration Camp—The Plantation as Dachau," in W. Benz, and B. Distel [eds.], *History of Nazi Concentration Camps—Studies, Reports, Documents Vol. 2, Dachau Review 2*, Dachau, *1990*, pp. 81–83).

70. U. Deichmann, p. 253.

71. R. Sigel, "The Cultivation of Medicinal Herbs in the Concentration Camp—The Plantation as Dachau," in W. Benz, and B. Distel [eds.], *History of Nazi Concentration Camps—Studies, Reports, Documents Vol. 2, Dachau Review 2*, 1990, p. 85.

72. *Ibid.*, pp. 78, 86.

73. D. Doyle, "Adolf Hitler's Medical Care," *Journal of the Royal College of Physicians of Edinburgh* 35, 2005, pp. 81–82.

74. K. Rendell collection, Museum of World War II, Natick, Massachusetts.

Chapter 8

1. W.W. Wilcox, *The Farmer in the Second World War* (Ames. Iowa State College Press, 1947), pp. 216–218; E.E. Berkley and H.D. Barker, "What Makes Cotton Good?," in *Science in Farming—Yearbook of Agriculture, 1943–1947* (Washington, D.C., U.S. Government Printing Office, 1947), pp. 289–292).

2. M.E. Condon-Rall and A.E. Cowdrey, *The Medical Department: Medical Service in the War Against Japan* (Washington, D.C., U.S. Army, Center of Military History, 1998), pp. 133–134.

3. V. Torrey, "What Makes the Rocket Go," *Popular Science*, August 1945, p. 68.

4. "Better Cotton, Tobacco, New Berry Resulting from Drug," *Science News-Letter*, August 12, 1939, pp. 99–100; M.G. Morrow, "Nature Paints Cotton," *Science News-Letter*, July 8, 1944, pp. 26–27.

5. E. Risch, *Quartermaster Corps: Organization, Supply, and Services. Volume 1.* (Washington, D.C., U.S. Army, Center of Military History, 1953), pp. 67, 72, 97–101, 117, 167.

6. *Cornell Bulletin for Homemakers: War Emergency Bulletin* 506, May 1942.

7. C.L. Walker, "Secrets by the Thousands," *Harper's Magazine,* October 1946, www.harpers.org.

8. "Fiber from Redwood Bark Is Wool Substitute," *Popular Mechanics*, May 1942, p. 49.

9. J.L. Forsythe, "World Cotton Technology During World War II," *Agricultural History* 54 No. 1, Agricultural History Symposium: Science and Technology in Agriculture, January 1980, pp. 208–222.

10. E. Risch, p. 68; H.T. Edwards, "The Introduction of Abacá [Manila Hemp] into the Western Hemisphere," *Annual Report of the Board of Regents of the Smithsonian Institution* (Washington, D.C., U.S. Government Printing Office, 1945), pp. 327–349.

11. E. Marcovitz and H.J. Myers, "The Marijuana Addict in the Army," *War Medicine* 6: December 1944, 382–391.

12. W.W. Wilcox, pp. 39–40.

13. J.H. Garland, "Hemp: A Minor American Fiber Crop," *Economic Geography* 22 No. 2, 1946, pp. 126–132.

14. A.L. Ash, "Hemp: Production and Utilization," *Economic Botany* 2 No. 2, 1948, pp. 158–169.

15. D.W. Fishler, "Fiber Flax in Oregon," *Economic Botany* 3 No. 4, 1949, pp. 395–406.

16. W.W. Wilcox, pp. 39–40.

17. R. Howard, "The Role of Botanists During World War II in the Pacific Theatre," *The Botanical Review* 60 No. 2, 1994, pp. 197–257.

18. J. Lewis, Changing Direction: British Military Planning for Post-war Strategic Defence, 1942–47 (London, Routledge, 2002), p. 212.

19. G. Luxbacher, "Raw and Advanced Materials for an Autarktic Germany," in S. Heim, C. Sachse, and M. Walker [eds.], The Kaiser Wilhelm Society under National Socialism (New York, Cambridge University Press, 2009), pp. 200–226).

20. "Nettle-Growing for Textile Manufacture," *Journal of the Royal Society of Arts*, January 24, 1919, pp. 146–147.

21. R. Milne and L. Hastings, "Home-Spun Solutions," *Kew*, Spring 1998, pp. 10–11.

22. B. Berkman, "Milkweed: A War Strategic Material and a Potential Industrial Crop for Sub-Marginal Lands in the U.S.," *Economic Botany* 3 No. 3, 1949, pp. 223–239.

23. "Milkweed at the Front," *The Herbarist* 74, 2008, pp. 91–93.

24. *Ibid.*

25. "Cat-Tail Parachutes Tested for Wartime Use," *Popular Science,* October 1943, p. 65.

26. E. Risch, *The Quartermaster Corps: Organization, Supply, and Services—Volume I,* U.S. Army, Washington, 1995, pp. 70–71.

27. "How to Darn Holes and Tears," Board of Trade Chart Leaflet No. 5, n.d.

28. "Getting Ready for Baby," Make Do and Mend Leaflet No. 1, Board of Trade, n.d.

29. *Tents and Tent Pitching—War Department Field Manual FM-2015* (Washington, D.C., Department of the Army, 1945), p. 55.

30. *Ibid.*, p. 54.

31. S.M. Spencer, "Chemical Guardians of Fabrics," *Scientific American*, October 1944, pp. 163–165.

32. W.G. Hutchinson, "The Deterioration of Matériel in the Tropics," *The Scientific Monthly* 6 No. 3, 1946, pp. 165–177.

33. Quoted in L.R. Thiesmeyer and J.E. Burchard, *Combat Scientists* (Boston, Little, Brown and Company, 1947), p. 160.

34. "Fungus-Proof Fabric Is Promising Development," *Science News-Letter*, September 8, 1945, p. 152.

35. A.P. Stauffer, *The Quartermaster Corps: Operations in the War Against Japan* (Washington, D.C., U.S. Army, Center of Military History, 1956), pp. 205–205.

36. L. Malkin, *Krueger's Men: The Secret Nazi Counterfeit Plot and the Prisoners of Block 19* (New York, Little Brown, 2006).

Chapter 9

1. W.W. Wilcox, *The Farmer in the Second World War* (Ames. Iowa State College Press, 1947), pp. 113–114; B.H. Paul, "Better Timbers from Farms," in *Science in Farming—Yearbook of Agriculture, 1943–1947* (Washington, D.C., U.S. Government Printing Office, 1947), pp. 455–460).

2. "Discretion of Defense Uses of Natural Resources Advised," *Science News-Letter*, March 1, 1941, p. 141; W.W. Wilcox, pp. 113–114).

3. G.H. Collingwood, "Science in the Forest," *Scientific American*, December 1942, pp. 270–273.

4. T.W. Patton, "Forestry and Politics: Franklin D. Roosevelt as Governor of New York," *New York History* 75 No. 4, 1994, pp. 397–418.

5. D. Brinkley, *Rightful Heritage: Franklin D. Roosevelt and the Land of America* (New York, Harper Collins, 2016), p. 257.

6. *Ibid.*, pp. 258–9.

7. M.B. Hopkins, "Wood Grown to Order," *Scientific American*, March 1938, p. 141.

8. A. Tabak, *Fort Devens, from Boys to Men* (Charleston, SC, CreateSpace, 2012), pp. 156–157.

9. E.D. Merrill and L.M. Perry, Plantae Papuanae Archiboldianae, XVI, *Journal of the Arnold Arboretum* 26 No. 3, 1945, pp. 229–266.

10. J.H. Kraemer, *Native Woods for Construction Purposes in the Western Pacific Region* (Washington, D.C., U.S. Government Printing Office, 1944), p. 109.

11. J.H. Kraemer, *Native Woods for Construction Purposes in the South China Sea Region* (Washington, D.C., U.S. Government Printing Office, 1945).

12. A.H. Oxholm, "How French Forests Kept the American Army Warm," *Journal of Forestry* 44, 1946, pp. 326–329.

13. E. Vickers, "'The Forgotten Army of the Woods': The Women's Timber Corps During the Second World War," *The Agricultural History Review* 59, 2011, pp. 101–112.

14. *A Handbook of Home-Grown Timbers—War Emergency Edition* (London, Her Majesty's Stationery Office, 1941).

15. *Handbook on German Military Forces—War Department Technical Manual TM-E 30-451* (Washington, D.C., U.S. Government Printing Office, 1945), Chapter VIII.

16. *Fifth Army at the Winter Line* (Washington, D.C., U.S. Army, Center of Military History, 1990), p. 88.

17. *Anzio Beachhead* (Washington, D.C., U.S. Army, Center of Military History 1990), p. 18.

18. R. Howard files, correspondence and notes from Knut Faegri, Pusey Library, Harvard University.

19. *The War Against Japan—Pictorial Record* (Washington, D.C., U.S. Army, Center of Military History 2001), p. 157.

20. K.C. Dod, *The Corps of Engineers: The War Against Japan* (Washington, D.C., U.S. Army, Center of Military History 1987), p. 198.

21. *Papuan Campaign: The Buna-Sanananda Operation* (Washington, D.C., U.S. Army, Center of Military History, 1990), pp. 14–16.

22. M.E. Condon-Rall and A.E. Cowdrey, *The Medical Department: Medical Service in the War Against Japan* (Washington, D.C., U.S. Army, Center of Military History 1998), pp. 28, 30, 33, 63, 141, 300.

23. K.C. Dod, pp. 93–94.

24. M.H. Cannon, *Leyte: Return to the Philippines* (Washington, D.C., U.S. Army, Center of Military History, 1993), p. 133.

25. L. Morton, *Fall of the Philippines* (Washington, D.C., U.S. Army, Center of Military History, 1993), p. 322.

26. C.F. Romanus, *China-Burma-India Theater: Time Runs Out in CBI* (Washington, D.C., U.S. Army, Center of Military History, 1999), pp. 187–88.

27. D.W. Hogan, *U.S. Army Special Operations in World War II*, Center of Military History, U.S. Army, Washington, DC, 1992, p. 109).

28. *St-Lo 7 July-19 July 1944* (Washington, D.C. Historical Division, War Department, U.S. Army, 1984), p. 62.

29. M. Blumenson, *Breakout and Pursuit* (Washington, D.C., U.S. Army, Center of Military History, 1993), pp. 11, 42, 150, 156, 159, 162, 177.

30. *St-Lo 7 July-19 July 1944*, p. 4.

31. M. Blumenson, pp. 205–7; A. Beck, A. Bortz, C. Lynch, L. Mayo, and R. Weld, *The Corps of Engineers: The War Against Germany* (Washington, D.C., U.S. Army, Center of Military History, 1985), p. 367.

32. W. Walton, "The Battle of the Hürtgen Forest," *Life*, January 1, 1945, pp. 33–36.

33. A.H. Lloyd, "Timber Supplies for the Allied Expeditionary Force, 1944–45," *Empire Forestry Journal* 24 No. 2, 1945, pp. 141–149.

34. "The War Effort," *Journal of the Arnold Arboretum*, 25, 1944, pp. 490–491.

35. K. Ingram, "Botanists at War," *Australasian Systematic Botany Society Newsletter* 75, June 1993, pp. 6–9.

36. *Bandaging and Splinting—War Department Field Manual FM 8-50* (Washington, D.C., U.S. Government Printing Office, 1944), p. 62; *Basic Field Manual—First Aid for Soldiers FM 21-11* (Washington, D.C., U.S. Government Printing Office, 1943), pp. 66–67.

37. T.D. Perry, "Rolling Off a Log," *Scientific American*, March 1942, pp. 125–128.

38. *Germanischer Lloyd Rules for Surveying and Testing of Plywood for Aircraft* (Berlin, Germanischer Lloyd SE, 1953).

39. "Building the Colditz Glider," NOVA, www.pbs.org, 2001.

40. G.R. Thompson, *The Signal Corps: The Outcome*, (Washington, D.C., U.S. Army, Center of Military History, 1991), pp. 190–191.

41. T. Cutler [ed.], *The U.S. Naval Institute on the U.S. Naval Reserve* (Annapolis, Naval Institute Press, 2015), p. 70.

42. Jim Anderson and Dirk A.D. Smith, "A Tale of Two Semi-Submersible Submarines," *Studies in Intelligence* 58 No. 4, 2014, pp. 19–28.

43. L. Schmeller, *Ice Railway Bridge Over the Dnieper [Foreign Military Studies]*, Washington, D.C, U.S. Army, 1953).

44. C.E. Randall, "Science Enters the Woods," *Scientific American*, August 1943, pp. 64–65.

45. B. Mayall and V. Morrow, *You Can Help Your Country: English Children's Work During the Second World War* (London, Institute of Education, University of London, 2011), p. 106.

46. *Graves Registration—War Department Field Manual FM 10-63* (Washington, D.C., U.S. Government Printing Office, 1945), pp. 39–41.

47. A.P. Stauffer, *The Quartermaster Corps: Operations in the War Against Japan* (Washington, D.C., U.S. Army, Center of Military History, 1956), pp. 182–183.

48. L.B. and A.C. Horth, *101 Things to Do in Wartime*

(London, B.T. Batsford, 1940), p. 100–103; "Your Home as an Air Raid Shelter," (Ministry of Home Security, 1940); Ministry of Information, *The British Home-Front Pocket-Book, 1940–42* (London, Conway, 2010, pp. 110, 114; D.C. Earhart, *Certain Victory: Images of World War II in the Japanese Media* (Armonk, New York, M.E. Sharpe, 2008), pp. 115–116.

49. J.Y. Cole [ed.], "Books in Action: The Armed Services Editions, Library of Congress, Washington," http://catdir.loc.gov, 1984.

50. C.L. Walker, "Secrets by the Thousands," *Harper's Magazine*, October 1946, p. 329, www.harpers.org.

51. W.M. Tuttle, *Daddy's Gone to War* (New York, Oxford University Press, 1993), p. 10.

52. R.C. Mikesh, *Japan's World War II Balloon Bomb Attacks on North America* (Washington, D.C., Smithsonian Institution Press, 1973), pp. 25, 27.

53. *Ibid.*, p. 8.

54. *Ibid.*, pp. 13, 15, 23.

55. R. Howard files, correspondence and notes, Pusey Library, Harvard University; R. Howard, "The Role of Botanists During World War II in the Pacific Theatre," *The Botanical Review* 60 No. 2, 1994, p 230.

56. H.T. Cook and T.F. Cook, *Japan at War: An Oral History* (New York, New Press, 1992), pp. 187–192.

57. R.C. Mikesh, pp. 13, 69–77.

58. E. Risch, *Quartermaster Corps: Organization, Supply, and Services. Volume 1.* (Washington, D.C., U.S. Army, Center of Military History, 1953), pp. 73, 103, 157–159.

59. J. Coster-Mullen, *Atom Bombs: The Top Secret Inside Story of Little Boy and Fat Man* (J. Coster-Mullen, 2010), p. 41.

60. W.G. Hutchinson, "The Deterioration of Matériel in the Tropics," *The Scientific Monthly* 6 No. 3, 1946, pp. 170–171.

61. "Cork Faces Trouble," *Scientific American*, February 1942, p. 67; "'Cow Apple' Roots May Be Source of Substitute," *Scientific American*, June 1943, p. 254; E.C. Lathrop, "The Celotex and Cane-Sugar Industries," *Industrial and Engineering Chemistry*, 22 No. 5, 1930, pp. 449–460.

62. C.M. Hackett, "Coal Tar Began It," *Scientific American*, September 1940, pp. 117–119.

63. R. Grant, "Seven Trillion Dollar Treasure," *Popular Mechanics*, January 1945, pp. 50–53.

64. E. Vickers, pp. 101–112.

65. C.G. Deuber, "Effects on Trees of an Illuminating Gas in the Soil," *Plant Physiology* 11 No. 2, 1936, pp. 401–412.

66. G. Egloff, "Ersatz Motor Fuels," *Scientific American*, July 1939, pp. 5–7.

67. L. Brophy, W. Miles, and R. Cochrane, *The Chemical Warfare Service: From Laboratory to Field* (Washington, D.C., U.S. Army, Center of Military History, 1988), pp. 79–81.

68. A. Beck *et al.*, p. 102.

69. J. Lucas, *War on the Eastern Front, 1941–1945: The German Soldier in Russia* (New York, Stein and Day, 1980), p. 86.

70. F. Uekoetetter, *The Green and the Brown: A History of Conservation in Nazi Germany* (New York, Cambridge University Press, 2006), pp. 70–71, 74.

71. K. Neumann, *Shifting Memories: The Nazi Past in the New Germany* (Ann Arbor, University of Michigan Press, 2000), p. 179.

72. E. Hiemer, *Der Giftpilz* (Nürnberg, Julius Streicher/Stürmer Verlag, 1938).

73. Ministry of Information, p. 83.

74. L.B. and H.C. Horth, pp. 76- 78, 84–87.

75. N. Catford, *Improvised Toys for Nurseries and Refugee Camps* (Bickley, Kent, University of London Press, 1944).

76. L.B. and H.C. Horth, p. 97.

77. B. den Hond, "Tree Rings Tell a Tale of Wartime Privations." *Eos* No. 99, April 11, 2018, www.eos.org; J. Trevino, "Norwegian Trees Still Bear Evidence of a World War II Battleship." *Smithsonian*, April 12, 2018, www.smithsonian.com.

78. S. Perkins, "Seeing Past the Dirt," *Science News*, July 30, 2005, pp. 72–74.

Chapter 10

1. J. Lucas, *War on the Eastern Front, 1941–1945: The German Soldier in Russia* (New York, Stein and Day, 1980), p. 16.

2. A. Speer, *Infiltration: How Heinrich Himmler Schemed to Build a SS Industrial Empire* (New York, Macmillan, 1981), pp. 147–8.

3. U.S. Naval Technical Mission to Japan, *Japanese Fuels and Lubricants—Article 1. Fuel and Lubricant Technology. Index No. X-38 (N)-1*, 1946, p. 11.

4. Speer, p. 148.

5. "Oil from Florida Trees," *Popular Mechanics*, August 1929, pp. 291–295.

6. W.T. Gillis, "Poison-Ivy and Its Kin," *Arnoldia*, March 1975, p. 95.

7. *Gopher Peavey* (St. Paul, University of Minnesota, Forestry School, 1942), p. 23.

8. A.L. Murray," Save Your Tires," *Scientific American*, April 1943, p. 170.

9. H.J. Fuller, "War-Time Rubber Exploitation in Tropical America," *Economic Botany* 5 No. 4, 1951, pp. 311–337.

10. "Guayule and Kok-Saghyz Sources Now Striding Ahead," *Scientific American*, April 1942, pp. 172–3.

11. James Bonner, correspondence and notes, R. Howard files, Pusey Library, Harvard University.

12. "Rubber from Milkweed," *Popular Mechanics*, March 1942, p. 88.

13. *Report of the Science Services* (Canada, Dominion Department of Agriculture, March 31, 1945), p. 19.

14. "Rubber Facts That Don't Stretch," *Scientific American*, June 1942, pp. 276–7.

15. H.J. Fuller, pp. 311–337.

16. T. Wieland, "Autarky and Lebensraum. the Political Agenda of Academic Plant Breeding in Nazi Germany," *Journal of History of Science and Technology* 3, Fall 2009, pp. 26–9.

17. S. Heim, "Kok-Sagyz—A Vital War Resource," in S. Heim, C. Sachse, and M. Walker [eds.], *The Kaiser Wilhelm Society Under National Socialism* (New York, Cambridge University Press, 2009), pp. 173–199.

18. E.P. Hoyt, *U-Boats: A Pictorial History* (New York, McGraw-Hill Book Company, 1987), pp. 164, 248, 250, 257.

19. "German Shrub May Yield Gutta-Percha," *Science News-Letter*, September 6, 1941, p. 149.

20. "Decoy Army Fooled Nazi Masterminds," *Popular Science*, February 1946, p. 126.

21. A.P. Stauffer, *The Quartermaster Corps: Operations in the War Against Japan* (Washington, D.C., U.S. Army, Center of Military History, 1956), pp. 292–297.

22. D.C. Earhart, *Certain Victory: Images of World*

War II in the Japanese Media (Armonk, NY, M.E. Sharpe, 2008), p. 287.

23. G.A. Cosmas and A.E. Cowdrey, *Medical Service in the European Theater of Operations* (Washington, D.C., U.S. Army, Center of Military History, 1992), pp. 143–144.

24. *Military Sanitation, War Department Field Manual FM21-10* (Washington, D.C., War Department, 1945), p. 24.

25. *Logistics in World War II—Final Report of the Army Service Forces* (Washington, D.C., U.S. Army, Center of Military History, 1993), p. 107.

26. L.B. and A.C. Horth, *101 Things to Do in Wartime* (London, B.T. Batsford, 1940) pp. 108–109.

27. B.E. Kleber and D. Birdsell, *The Chemical Warfare Service: Chemicals in Combat* (Washington, D.C., U.S. Army, Center of Military History, 1990), pp. 165, 175.

28. "Assault Combat Mask," *Popular Science*, March 1944, p. 74.

29. B.E. Kleber and D. Birdsell, pp. 70, 185, 259.

30. *Ibid.*, pp. 221, 232, 233.

31. L. Brophy, W. Miles, and R. Cochrane, *The Chemical Warfare Service: From Laboratory to Field* (Washington, D.C., U.S. Army, Center of Military History, 1988), pp. 85–86.

32. U. Lee, *The Employment of Negro Troops* (Washington, D.C., U.S. Army, Center of Military History), 2001, p. 592; R.G. Ruppenthal, *Logistical Support of the Armies, Volume 1* (Washington, D.C., U.S. Army, Center of Military History, 1995), p. 398.

33. G.R. Thompson and D.R. Harris, *The Signal Corps: The Outcome [Mid-1943 Through 1945]* (Washington, D.C., U.S. Army, Center of Military History, 1991), pp. 169–170.

34. Enid Marx Obituary, *The Independent*, May 18, 1998, www.independent.co.uk.

35. S.J. French, "Synthetic Elastomers," *Scientific American*, July 1942, pp. 10–13.

Chapter 11

1. *Jungle Warfare—War Department Field Manual FM 72-20* (Washington, D.C., War Department, 1944, p. 1.

2. M.E. Condon-Rall and A.E. Cowdrey, *The Medical Department: Medical Service in the War Against Japan* (Washington, D.C., U.S. Army, Center of Military History, 1998), p. 25.

3. *Jungle Warfare—War Department Field Manual FM 72-20*, p. 7.

4. "Body of WWII Airman Found Dangling from Tree," *The Telegraph*, August 28, 2008, www.telegraph.co.uk.

5. S. Milner, *Merrill's Marauders, February–May 1944* (Washington, D.C., U.S. Army, Center of Military History, 1990), p. 20.

6. C.F. Romanus and R. Sunderland, *Stilwell's Command Problems* (Washington, D.C., U.S. Army, Center of Military History, 1987), p. 170.

7. M.E. Condon-Rall and A.E. Cowdrey, pp. 33, 104, 119, 141.

8. "The Study of Art in War Time," *College Art Journal* 2 No. 1, 1942, pp. 13–19; M. Wheeler [ed.], *Britain at War*, Museum of Modern Art, New York, 1941; First Service Command Tactical School, Sturbridge, MA, Advanced Course [notes], Harvard Forest Archives; Camouflage Envelope HF 1942-10, Interstaff Correspondence, Photographs, Notes, Reports, Harvard Forest Archives.

9. "The Infra-Red Problem," *Camouflage Bulletin #9*, August 1, 1942; R. Howard, "The Role of Botanists During World War II in the Pacific Theatre," *The Botanical Review* 60 No. 2, 1994, p. 214.

10. "Plant Materials Commercially Available in the U.S.," *Camouflage Memorandum 120*, Camouflage Section, Fort Belvoir, VA, The Engineer Board, August 1, 1942 [rev.].

11. L.M. Hutchings, B. Epstein, and F.M. Bullock, "High School Biology Goes to War," *The American Biology Teacher* 6 No. 1, 1943, pp. 5–8.

12. "The Museum and the War," *The Bulletin of the Museum of Modern Art* 10 No. 1, 1942, pp. 3–19.

13. D. Wyman, "Available Rapid Growing Vines for the U.S.," *Arnoldia* 4 No. 9, 1944, p. 45.

14. *Ibid.*, p. 48.

15. D.H. Alderman, "Channing Cope and the Making of a Miracle Vine," *Geographical Review* 94 No. 2, 2004, pp. 157–177.

16. *Camouflage of Field Artillery—War Department Field Manual FM 5-20D* (War Department, Corps of Engineers, Washington, D.C., 1944.

17. K.C. Dod, *The Corps of Engineers: The War Against Japan*, Washington, D.C., U.S. Army, Center of Military History, 1987), pp. 291, 346, 361.

18. *Camouflage of Individuals and Infantry Weapons—War Department Field Manual FM 5-20A* (War Department, Washington, D.C., 1944), p. 7.

19. J.E. Johnson, *Wing Leader* (New York, Random Century, 1956), p. 137.

20. *Camouflage of Bivouacs, Command Posts, Supply Points, and Medical Installations, War Department Field Manual FM 5-20C* (War Department, Corps of Engineers, Washington, D.C., 1944).

21. *Camouflage, Basic Principles—War Department Field Manual FM 5-20 C* (War Department, Corps of Engineers, Washington, D.C., 1944), p. 34.

22. Camouflage Envelope HF 1942-10, Interstaff Correspondence, Photographs, Notes, Reports, Harvard Forest Archives.

23. K.A. Grossenbacher, S.H. Spurr, and J. Vlamis, "Lasting Properties of Cut Foliage," *Journal of the Arnold Arboretum* 26 No. 2, 1945, p. 214.

24. "Using Cut Foliage for Camouflage" (Cambridge, Harvard Camouflage Committee, August 1943), p. 3.

25. *Ibid.*, p. 14.

26. *Ibid.*, p. 13.

27. "Using Cut Foliage for Camouflage. Supplement on Tropical Pacific Islands" (Cambridge, Harvard Camouflage Committee, November 1943), pp. 5, 7, 10, 11, 18.

28. *Ibid.*, pp. 16, 18.

29. Camouflage Envelope HF 1942-10, Interstaff Correspondence, Photographs, Notes, Reports, Harvard Forest Archives.

30. "HMAS *Abraham Crijnssen*," Royal Australian Navy, www.navy.gov.au/node.

31. A.P. Stauffer, *The Quartermaster Corps: Operations in the War Against Japan* (Washington, D.C., U.S. Army, Center of Military History, 1956), pp. 291, 292.

32. M.E. Condon-Rall and A.E. Cowdrey, p. 134.

33. D. Wyman, "Available Rapid Growing Vines for the U.S.," p. 45.

34. S. Milner, *Victory in Papua* (Washington, D.C., U.S. Army, Center of Military History, 1989), pp. 92, 134, 323.

35. *Camouflage of Individuals and Infantry Weapons—War Department Field Manual FM 5-20A* (War Department, Corps of Engineers, Washington, D.C., 1944), pp. 12–15, 32, 37–39, 50, 51.

36. K.C. Dod, p. 614.

37. *Camouflage of Vehicles—War Department Field Manual FM 5-20B* (War Department, Corps of Engineers, Washington, D.C., 1944), pp. 36, 37, 44.

38. A.B. Godshall, "Edible, Poisonous, and Medicinal Fruits of Central America" (Panama Canal, 1942).

39. U.S. Army Air Forces, *Jungle and Desert Emergencies* (Washington, D.C., U.S.A.A.F., 1943); U.S. Army Air Forces, *Jungle Desert Arctic Emergencies* (Washington, D.C., U.S.A.A.F., 1943).

40. U.S. Army Air Forces, *Jungle Desert Arctic Emergencies*, pp. 25, 37.

41. E.D. Merrill, *Emergency Food Plants and Poisonous Plants of the Pacific—Technical Manual 10-420* (War Department, Washington, D.C., 1943).

42. E.D. Merrill, "Emergency Food Manuals, "*Arnoldia* 4 No. 7, 1944, pp. 29–36, 30.

43. E.D. Merrill, *Emergency Food Plants and Poisonous Plants of the Pacific—Technical Manual 10-420*, p. 11.

44. *Ibid.*, pp. 16–17.

45. *Jungle Warfare—War Department Field Manual FM 72-20*, pp. 112, 114.

46. *Ibid.*, pp. 108–112.

47. General Staff, L.H.Q. Australia, *Friendly Fruits and Vegetables* (Melbourne, Allied Forces, Southwest Pacific Area, 1943).

48. L. Cranwell, *Food Is Where You Find It—A Guide to Emergency Foods of the Western Pacific* (Auckland, NZ, Auckland Institute and Museum, 1943).

49. S. Milner, the *War in the Pacific: Victory in Papua* (Washington, D.C., U.S. Army, Center of Military History, 1989), p. 151.

50. K.P. Emory, a *Castaway's Baedecker to the South Seas* (Pearl Harbor, HI, Objective Data Section, Intelligence Center, Pacific Ocean Area, 1942).

51. K.P. Emory, *South Sea Lore* (Honolulu, Bernice B. Bishop Museum Special Publication 36 1943).

52. K.P. Emory, "Every Man His Own Robinson Crusoe: A Novel Program to Teach Our South Seas Fighters How to Fare for Themselves in Time of Need by Use of Ingenious Native Methods," *Natural History Magazine*, June 1943, pp. 8–15.

53. B.E. Dahlgren and P.C. Standley, *Edible and Poisonous Plants of the Caribbean Region* (Washington, D.C., U.S. Government Printing Office, U.S. Navy, Bureau of Medicine and Surgery, 1944).

54. *Ibid.*, p. 71.

55. E.M. Satulsky and C.A. Wirts, "Dermatitis Venenata Caused by the Manzanillo Tree: Further Observations and Report of Sixty Cases," *Archives of Dermatology and Syphilis*, 47, June 1943, p. 797.

56. B.E. Dahlgren and P.C. Standley, p. 59.

57. Ethnographic Board and Staff of the Smithsonian Institution, *Survival on Land and Sea* (Washington, D.C., U.S. Navy, Office of Naval Intelligence, 1943).

58. *Ibid.*, pp. 149–164.

59. G.A. Llano, "Economic Uses of Lichens," *Economic Botany* 2 No. 1, 1948. p. 25.

60. P.C. Standley, *Edible Plants of the Arctic Region* (Navy Bureau of Medicine and Surgery, 1943).

61. G.A. Llano, pp. 24–25.

62. A.E. Porsild, *Emergency Food in Arctic Canada* (Ottawa, National Museum of Canada, Special Contribution No. 45-1, 1945).

63. R.A. Howard, *999 Survived: An Analysis of Survival Experiences in the Southwest Pacific—ADTIC Publication No. T-100* (Maxwell Air Force Base, AL, Arctic, Desert, Tropic Information Center, 1950), pp. 15–18, 21–29.

64. R.A. Howard, *Sun, Sand, and Survival: An Analysis of Survival Experiences in the Desert—ADTIC Publication No. D-102* (Maxwell Air Force Base, AL, Arctic, Desert, Tropic Information Center, 1953), pp. 16, 17, 23, 27.

65. E. Gordon, *Through the Valley of the Kwai* (New York, Harper Collins, 1962), pp. 146–7, 157–169, 180–186; C.O. Kelly, *The Flamboya Tree* (New York, Random House, 2002), p. 55; R. Howard, "The Role of Botanists During World War II in the Pacific Theatre," *The Botanical Review* 60 No. 2, 1994, p. 240.

66. L. Nova and I. Lourie [eds.], *Interrupted Lives: Four Women's Stories of Internment During World War II in the Philippines* (Nevada City, CA, Artemis Books, 1995), pp. 4, 5, 19, 20, 23, 24, 41, 92.

67. G. Priestwood, *Through Japanese Barbed Wire* (New York, D. Appleton-Century Company, 1943), p. 73.

68. "The Changi Quilt: Secrets and Survival," British Red Cross, http://www.redcross.org.uk; The Secrets of the Changi Girl Guide Quilt, *The Telegraph*, June 1, 2010, www.telegraph. co.uk.

69. G.S. Seagrave, *Burma Surgeon* (New York, W.W. Norton, 1943), pp. 250, 247, 249–252; "Flight from Burma: Stillwell Leads Way Through Jungle to India," *Life*, August 10, 1942, pp. 26–27.

70. R. Howard files, correspondence and notes from A.J. Kostermans, Pusey Library, Harvard University.

71. "Diary of Stanislaw Rozycki," in J. Noakes and G. Pridham, [eds.], *Nazism 1919–1945 Vol. 3: Foreign Policy, War and Racial Extermination—A Documentary Reader* (Exeter, University of Exeter Press, 1988), pp. 460–462; L. Dobroszycki [ed.], *The Chronicle of the Lodz Ghetto, 1941–1944* (New Haven, Yale University Press, 1984), pp. 356–7.

72. "Undzer Friling!", *Holocaust Encyclopedia*, U.S. Holocaust Museum, www.ushmm.org.

73. A. Levine, *Fugitives of the Forest* (Guilford, CT, Lyons Press, 2009), pp. 244–251.

74. J. Lucas, *War on the Eastern Front, 1941–1945: The German Soldier in Russia* (New York, Stein and Day, 1980), pp. 73–4.

75. D.A. Hackett [ed.], *The Buchenwald Report* (Boulder, CO, Westview Press, 1995), pp. 146–147.

76. J.N. Siedlecki, K. Olszewski, and T. Borowski, *We Were in Auschwitz* (New York, Welcome Rain Publishers, 1946).

77. E. Krasa, personal comm., January 2013.

78. D. Kessler, "Dr. Arthur Kessler 1903–2000," *Lathyrus Lathyrism Newsletter* 3, 2003, pp. 2–4, https://www.researchgate.net.

79. R.J. Evans, The *Third Reich at War* (New York, Penguin Press, 2009), p. 606; A. Jacobson, *Operation Paperclip* (New York, Little, Brown, and Company, 2014), p. 303.

80. E. Williams, *The Wooden Horse* (Hammonsworth, England, Penguin Books, 1984), pp. 21, 29, 65, 110, 111, 40, 103, 214; O. Philpot, *Stolen Journey* (New York, E.P. Dutton, 1952), pp. 313–314.

81. G.A. Cosmas and A.E. Cowdrey, *The Medical Department: Medical Service in the European Theater of Operations* (Washington, D.C., U.S. Army, Center of Military History), pp. 561–568.

82. A.V. Bremzen, *Mastering the Art of Soviet Cook-*

ing (New York, Broadway Books, 2013), pp. 106–109; E. Snow, *People on Our Side* (New York, Random House, 1944), pp. 157, 162–163; J. Barber and M. Harrison, *The Soviet Home Front, 1942-1945: A Social and Economic History of the USSR in World War II* (New York, Longman, 1991), pp. 79–93.

83. A.V. Bremzen, pp. 106–109; E. Snow, *People on Our Side* (New York, Random House, 1944), pp. 157, 162–163; J. Barber and M. Harrison, *The Soviet Home Front, 1942-1945: A Social and Economic History of the USSR in World War II* (New York, Longman, 1991), pp. 79–93.

84. M.J.L. Dols and D.J.A.M. van Arcken, "Food Supply and Nutrition in the Netherlands During and Immediately After World War II," *The Milbank Memorial Fund Quarterly* 24 No. 4, 1946, pp. 319–358.

85. C. Banning and H.A. Lohr, "Occupied Holland," *British Medical Journal* 1 No. 4502, 1947, pp. 537–542.

86. M.J.L. Dols and D.J.A.M. van Arcken, pp. 319–358.

87. C. Banning and H.A. Lohr, pp. 539–542; K. Boekelheide, B. Blumberg, R.E. Chapin, I. Cote, J.H. Graziano, A. Janesick, R. Lane, K. Lillycrop, L. Myatt, J.C. States, K.A. Thayer, M.P. Waalkes and J.M. Rogers, "Predicting Later-Life Outcomes of Early-Life Exposures," *Environmental Health Perspectives* 120 No. 10, 2012, pp. 1353–1361; M.J.L. Dols and D.J.A.M. van Arcken pp. 319–358.

88. T. Tucker, *The Great Starvation Experiment: Ancel Keys and the Men Who Starved for Science.* (New York, Free Press, 2006).

89. S.D. Hearing, "*Refeeding Syndrome,*" *British Medical Journal* 328, April 17, 2004, Pp. 908–909.

90. Professor Walter Pauk, *Notes and Interview*, July 26, 1994; G.A. Cosmas and A.E. Cowdrey, pp. 572–578.

91. K. Helphand, *Defiant Gardens: Making Gardens in Wartime* (San Antonio, Trinity University Press, 2006), pp. 155–200; "Gardens in Camp," *Densho Encyclopedia*, www.encyclopedia.densho.org; L. Gordon and G.Y. Okihiro [eds.], *Impounded—Dorothea Lang and the Censored Images of Japanese American Internment* (New York, W.W. Norton, 2006), pp. 160, 169, 175, 181, 192, 193.

92. T. Way and M. Brown, *Digging for Victory* (Sevenoaks, Kent, Sabrestorm Publishing, 2010), pp. 32–33.

93. R. Howard files, Pusey Library, Harvard University, correspondence and notes, from Andy Thomson and John Creech.

94. L. Dobroszycki [ed.], *The Chronicle of the Lodz Ghetto, 1941-1944* (New Haven, Yale University Press, 1984), pp. 21, 72, 243–44; K. Helphand, pp. 60–105.

95. "In the Ruins—London Makes Use of the Scars Left by the Nazi Blitz of 1940," *Life*, September 27, 1943, pp. 41–44.

96. G. Grigson, *Wild Flowers in Britain* (London, Collins, 1944), p. 45.

97. L. Gannett, *New York Herald Tribune*, July 25, 1944.

98. C.P. Castell, "The Survey of Bookham Common," *London Naturalist* 34, 1954.

99. E.J. Salisbury, "The Flora of Bombed Areas," *Nature* 151, 1943, pp. 462–466.

100. H. Sukopp, "Flora and Vegetation Reflecting the Urban History of Berlin," *Die Erde* 134, 2003, pp. 295–316.

101. J. Lachmund, "Exploring the City of Rubble: Botanical Fieldwork in Bombed Cities in Germany After World War II," *Osiris* (2nd Series) 18, 2003, pp. 234–254; J. Stilgenbauer and J.R. McBride, "Reconstruction of Urban Forests in Hamburg and Dresden After World War II," *Landscape Journal* 29 No. 2, 2010, pp. 144–160.

102. J. Hersey, "Hiroshima," *The New Yorker*, August 31, 1946, www.newyorker.com.

103. *Ibid.*; M. Laird, "Regeneration of Trees in Hiroshima," *New Zealand Science Review*, December 1946, pp. 53–4.

104. P. Del Tredici, "Hibaku Trees of Hiroshima," *Arnoldia* 53 No. 3, 1993, pp. 25–9; Database of Hibaku Jumoku, Atomic-Bombed Trees of Hiroshima, Green Legacy Hiroshima, www.unitar.org; S. Cheng and J.R. McBride, "Restoration of the Urban Forests of Tokyo and Hiroshima Following World War II," *Urban Forestry and Urban Greening* 5 No. 4, 2006, pp. 155–168.

105. F.W. Whicker and L. Fraley, "Effects of Ionizing Radiation on Terrestrial Plant Communities," *Advances in Radiation Biology* 4, 1974, pp. 317–366.

Chapter 12

1. "The Arnold Arboretum During the Fiscal Year Ended June 30, 1943," *Journal of the Arnold Arboretum* 24 No. 4, 1943, pp. 488–497.

2. E.D. Merrill, *Plant Life of the Pacific [Fighting Forces Series]* (Washington, D.C., The Infantry Journal, 1945).

3. E.D. Merrill, *Emergency Food Plants and Poisonous Plants of the Pacific—Technical Manual 10-420* (War Department, Washington, D.C., 1943); R.A. Howard, "Lily May Perry [1895–1992]," *Taxon* 41 No. 4, 1992, pp. 792–796.

4. E.J. Palmer," Food Plants in the Arnold Arboretum," *Arnoldia* 4 No. 1, 1944, pp. 1–7.

5. D. Wyman, "Short Guide to Care of the Garden in Wartime," *Arnoldia* 4 No. 2–3, March 24, 1944, pp. 9–16.

6. "The Brooklyn Botanic Garden," *Science, New Series* 97 No. 2524, 1943, p. 437.

7. B. Gausemeier, "Political Networking and Scientific Modernization: Botanical Research at the KWI for Biology and Its Place in National Socialist Science Policy," in S. Heim, C. Sachse, and M. Walker [eds.], *The Kaiser Wilhelm Society under National Socialism* (New York, Cambridge University Press, 2009), p. 248.

8. V. Sackville-West, *Country Notes in Wartime* (Garden City, NY, Doubleday, Doran, and Company, 1939), p. 59.

9. D. Wyman, "Planting Vegetables," *Arnoldia* 3 No. 1, March 26, 1943, pp. 1–7.

10. P. Cornwell, "The Kew Demonstration Plot," *Journal of the Kew Guild* 6 No. 49, 1942, pp. 174–175.

11. "Kew in War Time," *Journal of the Kew Guild*, 6 No. 48, 1941, pp. 31–34; G. Evans, "Economic Botany at Kew in War Time," *Journal of the Kew Guild*, 6 No. 49, 1942, pp. 143–147.

12. J.R. Norman, "A Photographic Record of the Linnaean Collections," *Proceedings of the Linnean Society of London* 154, 1942, pp. 50–57; "The Arnold Arboretum During the Fiscal Year Ended June 30, 1943," pp. 488–497.

13. "Letters from the Evacuated Staffs," *Journal of the Kew Guild* 6 No. 48, 1941, pp. 39–44.

14. "Review of the Work of the Royal Botanic Gardens, Kew, During 1940," *Bulletin of Miscellaneous Information*, No. 1, 1941, pp. 1- 8.

15. "The Museums," *Journal of the Kew Guild* 6 No. 48, 1941, pp. 36–38.

16. F.R. Fosberg, "Segregation of Type Specimens," *Science, New Series* 107 No. 2789, 1942, pp. 515–516.

17. "In Science Fields," *Science News-Letter*, April 14, 1945, p. 233.

18. I. Hay, "E.D. Merrill, from Maine to Manila," *Arnoldia* 54 No. 1, 1998, pp. 11–19.

19. "The Herbarium: The History of the Collections of the Botanical Museum Berlin-Dahlem. Part 3," Botanical Museum Berlin, www.bgbm.org.

20. E.D. Merrill, "Destruction of the Berlin Herbarium," *Science, New Series* 98 No. 2553, 1943, pp. 490–491.

21. E.B. Babcock, "The Berlin Botanic Garden," *Science, New Series* 107 No. 2789, 1948, p. 622; H. Sleumer, "The Botanic Gardens and Museum at Berlin-Dahlem," *Kew Bulletin* 4 No. 2, 1949, pp. 172–175.

22. H.R. Gilliland, *A Revised Flora of Malaya, Volume III* (Singapore, Botanic Gardens, Government Printing Office, 1971).

23. R. Howard files, correspondence and notes from M.J. van Steenis, Pusey Library, Harvard University.

24. H.M. Raup, "Expeditions to the Alaska Military Highway 1943–44," *Arnoldia* 4 No. 12, 1944, pp. 65–72.

25. H.H. Bartlett and E.H. Walker, "A Program of Botanical Collecting and Study for Servicemen," *Chronica Botanica* IX, 1945, pp. 135–137.

26. *A Field Collector's Manual in Natural History— Publication 3766* (Washington, D.C., Smithsonian Institution, 1944), pp. 2–3.

27. *Ibid.*, pp. 72–78.

28. F. Osborn [ed.], *The Pacific World* (New York, W.W. Norton, 1944).

29. E.H. Walker, "Natural History in the Armed Forces. A Resume of Some Recent Literature, Mostly Botanical, of Interest to Servicemen," *The Scientific Monthly* 61 No. 4, 1945, pp. 307–12.

30. E.H. Walker, "Biological Collecting During World War II, the *Scientific Monthly* 63 No. 5, 1946, pp. 333–340.

31. *Ibid.*, P. 339.

32. A.M. Harvill, "Notes on the Moss Flora of Alaska. I. the Mosses of Attu Island Collected by Margaret Bell Howard and George B. Van Schaack," *The Bryologist* 50, 1947, p. 169.

33. E.B. Bartram, "Okinawa Mosses," *The Bryologist* 50, 1947, pp. 158–9.

34. R. Holman and W. Robbins, *A Textbook of General Botany* (U.S. War Department Education Manual EM445) (Madison, WI, U.S. Armed Forces Institute, 1944).

35. I.W. Bailey and A.C. Smith, "Degeneriaceae: A New Family of Flowering Plants from Fiji," *Journal of the Arnold Arboretum* 23 No. 2, 1942, pp. 356–365.

36. E.D. Merrill, "*Metasequoia*, Another 'Living Fossil'" *Arnoldia* 8 No. 1, 1948, pp. 13–16; H.H. Hu, "How Metasequoia, the 'Living Fossil,' Was Discovered in China," *Arnoldia* 58 No. 4, pp. 4–7.

37. G. Groening and J. Wolschke-Bulmahn, "Some Notes on the Mania for Native Plants in Germany," *Landscape Journal* 11 No. 2, 1992, pp. 116–126.

38. *Ibid.*

39. T. Zeller, "Molding the Landscape of Nazi Environmentalism: Alwin Seifert and the Third Reich," in F. Bruggemeier, M. Cioc, and T. Zeller, *How Green Were the Nazis? Nature, Environment, and Nation in the Third Reich* (Athens, OH, Ohio University Press, 2005), pp. 147–170.

40. S.J. Gould, "An Evolutionary Perspective on Strengths, Fallacies, and Confusions in the Concept of Native Plants," *Arnoldia* 58 No. 1, 1998, pp. 3–10.

41. P. Adam, *Art of the Third Reich* (New York, Harry N. Abrams, 1992), p. 12.

42. *Ibid.*, p. 97.

43. O.D. Tolischus, "Where Hitler Dreams and Plans," *The New York Times Magazine*, May 30, 1937, Section 8, p. 1; "Hitler's Mountain Home," *Homes and Gardens*, November 1938, pp. 193–5; D. Stratigakos, *Hitler at Home* (New Haven, Yale University Press, 2015).

44. D. Stratigakos, pp. 87, 123.

45. R.J. Evans, The *Third Reich at War* (New York, Penguin Press, 2009), p. 207; MIRS London Branch *The Hitler Jugend* (Allied Expeditionary Force G-2 Counter Intelligence Sub-Division, n.d.), p. 30).

46. *Du Und Deine Harmonika Soldatenlieder* (Trossingen, Max Hohner, 1936).

47. German Propaganda Archive, Calvin College, http://www.bytwerk.com.

48. E. Keays, "Roses—Some Kinds That Require Almost No Care," *House and Garden*, June 1943, p. 63.

49. "Iris, Peonies, and Poppies, How to Plant and Care For, and Select the Best Varieties," *House and Garden*, July 1943, p. 53.

50. L. Richardson, "Grow Your Colors," *Better Homes and Gardens*, March 1942, p. 28.

51. L.B. and A.C. Horth, *101 Things for the Housewife to Do* (London, B.T. Batsford, 1939), pp. 54–61.

52. A. Miall and B. Miall, *Gardening Made Easy* (London, John Gifford, 1943).

53. "Sutton's Seeds—Britain's Best" advertisement, *Better Homes and Gardens*, January 1943, p. 69.

54. R. MacKay, *Half the Battle—Civilian Morale in Britain During the Second World War* (Manchester, Manchester University Press, 2002), pp. 215–216.

55. C.E. Kobuski, "British Gardens in War Time as Seen by an American Soldier," *Journal of the Arnold Arboretum* 5 No. 12, 1945), pp. 77–88.

56. J. Gilmour, *British Botanists* (London, Collins, 1944), p. 47.

57. G. Grigson, *Wild Flowers in Britain* (London, Collins, 1944), pp. 42–44, 47.

58. H. Roberts, *English Gardens* (London, Collins, 1944), p. 48.

59. G.M. Taylor, *British Herbs and Vegetables* (London, Collins, 1947), pp. 40–46.

60. E.J. Russell, *English Farming* (London, Collins, 1941), pp. 45–48.

Bibliography

Adam, P. *Art of the Third Reich*. New York, Harry N. Abrams, 1992.

Alderman, D.H. "Channing Cope and the Making of a Miracle Vine." *Geographical Review* 94 No. 2, 2004, pp. 157–177.

Allen, P. "Mrs. Higgins and the Pot Herbs." *American Cookery*, April 1942, pp. 384–385, 396.

"Allotment and Garden Guide." Ministry of Agriculture, December 1945.

Anders, S.E. "Quartermaster Supply in the Pacific During World War II." *Quartermaster Professional Bulletin*, Spring 1999, www.qmfound.com.

Anderson, C.A. "Food Rationing and Morale." *American Sociological Review* 8 no. 1, 1943.

Anderson, Jim, and Smith, Dirk A.D. "A Tale of Two Semi-Submersible Submarines." *Studies in Intelligence* 58 No. 4, 2014, pp. 19–28.

Anthony, S.B. *Out of the Kitchen—Into the War*. Stephen Day, New York, 1943.

Anzio Beachhead. Washington, D.C., U.S. Army, Center of Military History 1990.

Army Food and Messing: The Complete Manual of Mess Management, 3rd ed., Harrisburg, Military Service Publishing, 1943.

"The Army Has Mechanized Potato Peeler." *American Cookery*, November 1942, p. 153.

"The Arnold Arboretum During the Fiscal Year Ended June 30, 1943." *Journal of the Arnold Arboretum* 24 No. 4, 1943, pp. 488–497.

Arnon, S.S., Schecter, R., *et al.* "Botulinum Toxin as a Biological Weapon." *Journal of the American Medical Association* 285, February 28, 2001, pp. 1059–1070.

"A.R.P. Home Storage of Food Supplies." The Canned Foods Advisory Bureau, 1938.

Ash, A.L. "Hemp: Production and Utilization." *Economic Botany* 2 No. 2, 1948, pp. 158–169.

"Assault Combat Mask." *Popular Science*, March 1944, p. 74.

Babcock, E.B. "The Berlin Botanic Garden." *Science, New Series* 107 No. 2789, 1948, p. 622.

_____. "Bad Tempers, Inefficiency, Traced to Lack of Vitamin B1." *Science News-Letter*, August 9, 1941, p. 84.

Bailey, I.W., and Smith, A.C. "Degeneriaceae: A New Family of Flowering Plants from Fiji," *Journal of the Arnold Arboretum* 23 No. 2, 1942, pp. 356–650.

Bandaging and Splinting—War Department Field Manual FM 8-50., Washington, D.C., U.S. Government Printing Office, 1944.

Banning, C., and Lohr, H.A. "Occupied Holland." *British Medical Journal* 1 No. 4502, 1947, pp. 539–542.

Barber, J., and Harrison, M. *The Soviet Home Front, 1942–1945: A Social and Economic History of the USSR in World War II*. New York, Longman, 1991.

Barrons, K.C. "Modern Plant Wizardry." *Scientific American*, July 1938, pp. 14–17.

Bartlett, H.H., and Walker, E.H. "A Program of Botanical Collecting and Study for Servicemen." *Chronica Botanica* IX, 1945, pp. 135–137.

Bartram, E.H. "Okinawa Mosses." *The Bryologist* 50, 1947, pp. 158–9.

Basic Field Manual—First Aid for Soldiers FM 21-11. Washington, D.C., U.S. Government Printing Office, 1943.

The Basic Field Manual—First Aid for Soldiers FM-21-11. Washington, D.C., War Department, U.S. Government Printing Office, 1943.

Beck, A., Bortz, A., Lynch, C., Mayo, L., and Weld, R. *The Corps of Engineers: The War Against Germany*. Washington, D.C., U.S. Army, Center of Military History, 1985.

"Bedlam: Food," *Time*, June 28, 1943, www.content.time.com.

Bentley, A. *Eating for Victory: Food Rationing and the Politics of Domesticity*. Champaign, University of Illinois Press, 1998.

Berkley, E.E., and Barker, H.D. "What Makes Cotton Good?" in *Science in Farming—Yearbook of Agriculture, 1943–1947*, Washington, D.C., U.S. Government Printing Office, 1947, pp. 289–292.

Berkman, B. "Milkweed: A War Strategic Material and a Potential Industrial Crop for Sub-Marginal Lands in the U.S." *Economic Botany* 3 No. 3, 1949, pp. 223–239.

"Better Cotton, Tobacco, New Berry Resulting from Drug," *Science News-Letter*, August 12, 1939, pp. 99–100.

Betty Crocker Cook Book of All-Purpose Baking. Minneapolis, General Mills, 1942.

"Betty Crocker Home Defense Supper Menu." Minneapolis, General Mills, n.d.

Bischof, G., Plasser, F., and Stelzl-Marx, B. [eds.], *New Perspectives on Austrians and World War II*. New York, Routledge, 2015.

Blackwood, F. *Mrs. England Goes on Living*. New York, Creative Age Press, 1943.

Blumenson, M. *Breakout and Pursuit*. Washington, D.C., U.S. Army, Center of Military History, 1993.

Body of WWII Airman Found Dangling from Tree." *The Telegraph,* August 28, 2008, www.telegraph.co.uk.

Boekelheide, K., Blumberg, B., Chapin, R.E., Cote, I., Graziano, J.H., Janesick, A., Lane, R., Lillycrop, K., Myatt, L., States, J.C., Thayer, K.A., Waalkes M.P., and Rogers, J.M. "Predicting Later-Life Outcomes of Early-Life Exposures." *Environmental Health Perspectives* 120 No. 10, 2012.

"Bomb Raids Will Find London Prepared," *Scientific American* 161, March 1939, pp. 138–9.

Borgwardt, E. *A New Deal for the World.* Cambridge, Harvard University, 2005.

Bowman, R.G. "Army Farms and Agricultural Development in the Southwest Pacific." *Geographical Review* 36 No. 3, 1946, pp. 420–446.

Brassley, P. "Wartime Productivity and Innovation, 1939–45," in Short, B., Watkins, C., and Martin, J. [eds.], *The Front Line of Freedom: British Farming in the Second World War,* British Agricultural History Society, 2006, pp. 36–54.

Bremzen, A.V. *Mastering the Art of Soviet Cooking.* New York, Broadway Books, 2013.

Brigham, R.D. 1993. "Castor: Return of an Old Crop," in Janick, J., and Simon, J.E. [eds.], *New Crops* (New York, Wiley, 1993), pp. 380–383.

"Bright Spots for Wartime Meals—66 Ration-Wise Recipes." Minneapolis, General Foods Corporation, 1944.

Brinkley, D. *Rightful Heritage: Franklin D. Roosevelt and the Land of America.* New York, HarperCollins, 2016.

"Britain Tightens Its Belt on Carrot and Potato Diet." *Life,* May 12, 1941, pp. 43–46.

"British Farmers Plough Their Fields by Night in Race Against Spring." *Life,* April 29, 1940, p. 33.

"The Brooklyn Botanic Garden." *Science, New Series* 97 No. 2524, 1943, p. 437.

Brophy, L. Miles, W., and Cochrane, R. *The Chemical Warfare Service: From Laboratory to Field.* Washington, D.C., U.S. Army, Center of Military History, 1988.

Brucato, J. "War Hits the Farmlands." *San Francisco News,* March 9, 1942, cited in www.sfmuseum.net.

Bruenn, H.G. "Clinical Notes on the Illness and Death of President Franklin D. Roosevelt." *Annals of Internal Medicine,* 72 No. 4, 1970, pp. 579–591.

Buchan, U. *A Green and Pleasant Land.* London, Windmill Books, 2013.

"Building the Colditz Glider." NOVA, 2001, www.pbs.org.

Bullett, G. *Achievement in Feeding Britain.* London, Pilot Press, 1944.

Burbank, L. *The Training of the Human Plant.* New York, Century Co., 1909.

Burns of the Hands and Face." *Lancet* 2, November 23, 1940, p. 655.

Cameron, N., and Stevens, R.H. [transl.]. *Hitler's Table Talk, 1941–1944: His Private Conversations.* New York, Enigma Books, 2000.

Camouflage, Basic Principles—War Department Field Manual FM 5-20 C. Washington, D.C., War Department, Corps of Engineers, 1944.

Camouflage of Bivouacs, Command Posts, Supply Points, and Medical Installations—War Department Field Manual FM 5-20C. Washington, D.C., War Department, Corps of Engineers, 1944.

Camouflage of Field Artillery—War Department Field Manual FM 5-20D. Washington, D.C., War Department, Corps of Engineers, 1944.

Camouflage of Individuals and Infantry Weapons—War

Department Field Manual FM 5-20A. Washington, D.C., War Department, Corps of Engineers.

Camouflage of Vehicles—War Department Field Manual FM 5-20B. Washington, D.C., War Department, Corps of Engineers, 1944.

Campbell-Falck, D., Thomas, T., Falck, T.M., Tutuo, N., and Clem K. "The Intravenous Use of Coconut Water." *American Journal of Emergency Medicine* 18 No. 1, 2000, pp. 108–111.

Canning at Home in 44—Cornell Bulletin for Homemakers 583, Supplement 1, July 1944.

Cannon, B. "Plastic and Reconstructive Surgery at the MGH." *The Massachusetts General Hospital Surgical Society Newsletter,* Summer 2003, pp. 16–17.

Cannon, M.H. *Leyte: Return to the Philippines.* Washington, D.C., U.S. Army, Center of Military History, 1993.

"Carrot Diet for Flyers May Be in Offing." *Science News-Letter,* March 6, 1943, p. 153.

Carson, C.F., Hammer, K.A., and Riley, T.V. "*Melaleuca alternifolia* (Tea Tree) Oil: A Review of Antimicrobial and Other Medicinal Properties." *Clinical Microbiology Reviews* 19 No. 1, 2006, pp. 50–62.

Castell, C.P. "The Survey of Bookham Common." *London Naturalist* 34, 1954.

"Cat-Tail Parachutes Tested for Wartime Use." *Popular Science,* October 1943, p. 65.

Catford, N. *Improvised Toys for Nurseries and Refugee Camps.* Bickley, Kent, University of London Press, 1944.

Cavallito, C.J., and Bailey, J.H. "Allicin, the Antibacterial Principle of *Allium sativum.* I. Isolation, Physical Properties and Antibacterial Action." *Journal of the American Chemical Society* 66 No. 11, 1944, pp. 1950–51.

"The Changi Quilt: Secrets and Survival." British Red Cross, http://www.redcross.org.uk.

Cheng, S., and McBride, J.R. "Restoration of the Urban Forests of Tokyo and Hiroshima Following World War II." *Urban Forestry and Urban Greening* 5 No. 4, 2006, pp. 155–168.

Chute, B.J. "Weed 'Em and Reap." *Boys' Life,* May 1945, p. 14.

Cocking, W.D. "Know Your Points." *The High School Journal,* January–February 1943, pp. 5–9.

Cole, J.Y. [ed.]. "Books in Action: The Armed Services Editions, Library of Congress, Washington." http://catdir.loc.gov, 1984.

A Collector's Manual in Natural History—Publication 3766, Washington, D.C., Smithsonian Institution, 1944.

Collingwood, G.H. "Science in the Forest." *Scientific American,* December 1942, pp. 270–273.

Condon-Rall, M.E., and Cowdrey, A.E. *The Medical Department: Medical Service in the War Against Japan.* Washington, D.C., U.S. Army, Center of Military History, 1998.

Cook, H.T., and Cook, T.F. *Japan at War: An Oral History.* New York, New Press, 1992.

"Cork Faces Trouble." *Scientific American,* February 1942, p. 67.

Cornell Bulletin for Homemakers: War Emergency Bulletin 506, May 1942.

Cornwell, P. "The Kew Demonstration Plot." *Journal of the Kew Guild* 6 No. 49, 1942, pp. 174–175.

Cosmas, G.A., and Cowdrey, A.E. *The Medical Department: Medical Service in the European Theater of Operations.* Washington, D.C., U.S. Army, Center of Military History, 1992.

Coster-Mullen, J. *Atom Bombs: The Top Secret Inside Story of Little Boy and Fat Man,* J. Coster-Mullen, 2010.

"'Cow Apple' Roots May Be Source of Substitute." *Scientific American,* June 1943, p. 254.

Cranwell, L. *Food Is Where You Find It—A Guide to Emergency Foods of the Western Pacific.* Auckland, NZ, Auckland Institute and Museum, 1943.

Crooks, D.M. "Plants for Special Uses." *Economic Botany* 2, No. 1, 1948, pp. 58–72.

Croddy E.A., and Wirtz, J.J. [eds.]. *Weapons of Mass Destruction: An Encyclopedia of Worldwide Policy, Technology, and History; Volume I: Chemical and Biological Weapons.* Santa Barbara, ABC-CLIO, 2004.

Culver, C.C. "Growing Plants for Victory Gardens." *The American Biology Teacher,* April 1942, pp. 217–218.

Cutler, T. [ed.]. *The U.S. Naval Institute on the U.S. Naval Reserve.* Annapolis, Naval Institute Press, 2015.

Dahlgren, B.E., and Standley, P.C. *Edible and Poisonous Plants of the Caribbean Region.* Washington, D.C., U.S. Government Printing Office, U.S. Navy, Bureau of Medicine and Surgery, 1944.

Daniel, C.E.H. "Food Waste Control." *The Journal of Higher Education* 16 No. 11, 1945.

Danquah, F.K. "Japanese Food Farming Policies in Wartime Southeast Asia: The Philippine Example, 1942–1944." *Agricultural History* 64 No. 3, 1990, pp. 64–66.

Database of Hibaku Jumoku, Atomic-bombed Trees of Hiroshima, Green Legacy Hiroshima, www.unitar.org.

Davis, B.L. *Flags and Standards of the Third Reich,* London, Macdonald and Jane's, 1975.

Davis, E. "America Builds Food Defense." *Science News-Letter,* September 14, 1940, pp. 170–172.

Davis, M. "Malaria." *Good Housekeeping,* August 1943, pp. 22, 153–154.

_____ "Our Army's Menu-Maker." *American Cookery,* August–September 1942, p. 78.

Decoy Army Fooled Nazi Masterminds." *Popular Science,* February 1946, p. 126.

Deichmann, U. *Biologists Under Hitler.* Cambridge, Harvard University Press, 1996.

Del Tredici, P. "Hibaku Trees of Hiroshima." *Arnoldia* 53 No. 3, 1993, pp. 25–9.

De Mauduit, Vicomte. *They Can't Ration These.* London, Michael Joseph, 1940.

den Hond, B. "Tree Rings Tell a Tale of Wartime Privations." *Eos* No. 99, April 11, 2018, www.eos.org.

Deuber, C.G. "Effects on Trees of an Illuminating Gas in the Soil." *Plant Physiology* 11 No. 2, 1936, pp. 401–412.

"Diary of Stanislaw Rozycki" in Noakes, J., and Pridham, G. [eds.]. *Nazism 1919–1945 Vol. 3: Foreign Policy, War and Racial Extermination—A Documentary Reader.* Exeter, University of Exeter Press, 1988.

Dickison, W.C. *Integrative Plant Anatomy,* San Diego, Harcourt/Academic Press, 2000.

"Discretion of Defense Uses of Natural Resources Advised." *Science News-Letter,* March 1, 1941, p. 141.

"Do They Eat Around the Vegetables?" *Good Housekeeping,* April 1943.

Dobroszycki, L. [ed.], *The Chronicle of the Lodz Ghetto, 1941–1944.* New Haven, Yale University Press, 1984.

Dod, K.C. *The Corps of Engineers: The War Against Japan.* Washington, D.C., U.S. Army, Center of Military History, 1987.

Dols, M.L.J., and van Arcken, D.J.A.M. "Food Supply and Nutrition in the Netherlands During and Imme-

diately After World War II." *The Milbank Memorial Fund Quarterly* 24 No. 4, 1946, pp. 319–358.

Doull, J.A. *Preventive Medicine in World War II.* Vol. IV *Communicable Diseases,* Medical Department, Chapter 4. Leprosy, U.S. Army in World War II, http://history.amedd.army.mil, pp. 25–36.

"'Down to Earth Boys' Work." *The Rotarian,* May 1943, p. 21.

Doyle, D. "Adolf Hitler's Medical Care." *Journal of the Royal College of Physicians of Edinburgh* 35, 2005, pp. 75–82.

Drazin, M.L. "Nutrition and National Defense." *Military Surgeon* 88, 1941, p. 39.

Drug Supplies in Wartime." *Nature* January 25, 1941, p. 112.

Du Und Deine Harmonika Soldatenlieder. Trossingen, Max Hohner, 1936.

Dusselier, J. "Does Food Make Place? Food Protests in Japanese American Concentration Camps." *Food and Foodways: Explorations in the History and Culture of Human Nourishment* 10 No. 3, 2002, pp. 137–165.

Earhart, D.C. *Certain Victory: Images of World War II in the Japanese Media.* Armonk, NY, M.E. Sharpe, 2008.

"Eat Well to Work Well," *Cornell Bulletin for Homemakers—War Emergency Bulletin.* 524, June 1942.

Edwards, H.T. "The Introduction of Abacá [Manila Hemp] into the Western Hemisphere." *Annual Report of the Board of Regents of the Smithsonian Institution,* Washington, D.C., U.S. Government Printing Office, 1945, pp. 327–349.

Egloff, G. "Ersatz Motor Fuels." *Scientific American,* July 1939, pp. 5–7.

"Eleanor Early Reports on Dehydrated Foods." *American Cookery,* November 1942, pp. 140, 149.

Elzey, L. "An Elementary School Garden Project." *The American Biology Teacher,* February 1944, pp. 115–118.

Emory, K.P. *South Sea Lore.* Honolulu, Bernice B. Bishop Museum Special Publication 36 1943.

_____. *A Castaway's Baedecker to the South Seas.* Pearl Harbor, Objective Data Section, Intelligence Center, Pacific Ocean Area, 1942.

_____. "Every Man His Own Robinson Crusoe: A Novel Program to Teach Our South Seas Fighters How to Fare for Themselves in Time of Need by Use of Ingenious Native Methods," *Natural History Magazine,* June 1943, pp. 8–15.

Enid Marx: Obituary. *The Independent,* May 18, 1998, www.independent.co.uk.

Ethnographic Board and Staff of the Smithsonian Institution, *Survival on Land and Sea.* Washington, D.C., U.S. Navy, Office of Naval Intelligence, 1943.

Ettlinger, H. *The Axis on the Air.* New York, The Bobbs-Merrill Company, 1943.

Evans, G. "Economic Botany at Kew in War Time." *Journal of the Kew Guild,* 6 No. 49, 1942, pp. 143–147.

Evans, R.J. *The Third Reich in Power.* New York, Penguin Books, 2005.

_____. *The Third Reich at War.* New York, Penguin Press, 2009.

Everett, T.H. "The Victory Gardens of 1942 and '43," *Journal of the New York Botanical Garden,* March 1943.

Evert, R.F., and Eichhorn, S.E. *Esau's Plant Anatomy,* 3rd. ed., Hoboken, New Jersey, Wiley Interscience, 2006.

"Exit the Can Opener." *Time,* March 8, 1943, www.content.time.com.

Factors Affecting the Nutritive Values of Foods—Miscel-

laneous Publication 664. Washington, D.C., U.S. Department of Agriculture, 1948.

Falasca-Zamponi, S. *Fascist Spectacle: The Aesthetics of Power in Mussolini's Italy*. Berkley, University of California Press, 2000.

"Fiber from Redwood Bark Is Wool Substitute." *Popular Mechanics*, May 1942, p. 49.

Fifth Army at the Winter Line. Washington, D.C., U.S. Army, Center of Military History, 1990.

Fisher, M.F.K. *How to Cook a Wolf* in *The Art of Eating*. New York, Macmillan, 1990.

Fishler, D.W. "Fiber Flax in Oregon." *Economic Botany* 3 No. 4, 1949, pp. 395–406.

"Flight from Burma: Stillwell Leads Way Through Jungle to India." *Life*, August 10, 1942, pp. 26–27.

"Food: Crisis Coming." *Time*, November 2, 1942, www.content.time.com.

"Food Situation of the United Kingdom." Cabinet Memorandum, October 2, 1939, pp. 1–2, www.filestore.nationalarchives.gov.uk.

Foot, W. "The Impact of the Military on the Agricultural Landscape of England and Wales in the Second World War," in Short, B., Watkins, C., and Martin, J. [eds.], *The Front Line of Freedom: British Farming in the Second World War*, British Agricultural History Society, 2006, pp. 132–142.

"Foreign News." *Time*, October 20, 1941, www.content.time.com.

Forsythe, J.L. "World Cotton Technology During World War II." *Agricultural History* 54 No. 1, Agricultural History Symposium: Science and Technology in Agriculture, January 1980, pp. 208–222.

Fosberg, F.R. "Segregation of Type Specimens." *Science, New Series* 107 No. 2789, 1942, pp. 515–516.

Fosberg, R. *Columbian Cinchona Manual*. Bogota, Colombia, Foreign Economic Administration, 1943.

"France: Hunger Cramps." *Time*, March 3, 1941, www.content.time.com.

French, S.J. "Synthetic Elastomers." *Scientific American*, July 1942, pp. 10–13.

"From the Victory Garden." *American Cookery*, June–July 1942, pp. 20–21.

Fuller, H.J. "War-Time Rubber Exploitation in Tropical America." *Economic Botany* 5 No. 4, 1951, pp. 311–337.

"Fungus-Proof Fabric Is Promising Development." *Science News-Letter*, September 8, 1945, p. 152.

Gabler, E. "School Gardens for Victory." *The Clearing House*, April 1942, pp. 469–472.

Gallardo, E. "Sensitivity of Bacteria from Infected Wounds to Penicillin, *War Medicine*" 7, February 1945, pp. 100–103.

Gannett, L. *New York Herald Tribune*, July 25, 1944.

"Garden Army Scheme." *Sydney Morning Herald*, March 12, 1943, p. 3.

"Garden for Fun and Health." *Science News-Letter*, March 15, 1952, pp. 170–171.

Gardens for U.S. at War." *Life*, March 30, 1942, pp. 81–84.

"Gardens in Camp," *Densho Encyclopedia*, www.encyclopedia.densho.org.

Garland, J.H. "Hemp: A Minor American Fiber Crop," *Economic Geography* 22 No. 2, 1946, pp. 126–132.

Gausemeier, B. "Political Networking and Scientific Modernization: Botanical Research at the KWI for Biology and Its Place in National Socialist Science Policy," in Heim, S., Sachse, C., and Walker, M. [eds.]. *The Kaiser Wilhelm Society Under National Socialism*. New York, Cambridge University Press, 2009, pp. 227–282.

"Gelernt Ist Gelernt: Mit Bildbericht Aus Der Reichs-braute- Und Heimmütterschule Husbäke in Oldenburg," *NS Frauen Warte* 8 No. 2, Maiheft 1940.

General Staff, L.H.Q. Australia, *Friendly Fruits and Vegetables*. Melbourne, Allied Forces, Southwest Pacific Area, 1943.

Gentry, H.S., Verbiscar, A.J., and Banigan, T.F. "Red Squill (*Urginea maritima*, Liliaceae)." *Economic Botany* 41 No. 2, 1987, pp. 267–282.

Gerhard, G. "Breeding Pigs and People for the Third Reich: Richard Walther Darré's Agrarian Ideaology," in Bruggemeier, F., Cioc, M., and Zeller, T. *How Green Were the Nazis? Nature, Environment, and Nation in the Third Reich*, Athens, OH, Ohio University Press, 2005, pp. 129–146.

"German Shrub May Yield Gutta-Percha." *Science News-Letter*, September 6, 1941, p. 149.

Germanischer Lloyd Rules for Surveying and Testing of Plywood for Aircraft. Berlin, Germanischer Lloyd SE, 1953.

"Germany: Asparagus Sucker." *Time*, July 15, 1935, www.content.time.com.

Gerson, M. "Feeding the German Army." *New York State Journal of Medicine* 41 No. 13, 1941, pp. 1471–1476.

"Getting Ready for Baby." Make Do and Mend Leaflet No. 1, Board of Trade, n.d.

Gilliland, H.R. *A Revised Flora of Malaya, Volume III*. Singapore, Botanic Gardens, Government Printing Office, 1971).

Gillis, W.T. "Poison-Ivy and Its Kin." *Arnoldia*, March 1975, pp. 93–121.

Gilmour, J. *British Botanists*. London, Collins, 1944.

Godshall, A.B. "Edible, Poisonous, and Medicinal Fruits of Central America." Panama Canal, 1942.

Gold, B. *Wartime Economic Planning in Agriculture*. New York, Columbia University Press, 1949.

Gopher Peavey. St. Paul, University of Minnesota, Forestry School, 1942.

Gordon, E. *Through the Valley of the Kwai*. New York, HarperCollins, 1962.

Gordon, L., and Okihiro, G.Y. [eds.]. *Impounded—Dorothea Lang and the Censored Images of Japanese American Internment*. New York, W.W. Norton, 2006.

Gould, S.J. "An Evolutionary Perspective on Strengths, Fallacies, and Confusions in the Concept of Native Plants." *Arnoldia* 58 No. 1, 1998, pp. 3–10.

Grant, R. "Seven Trillion Dollar Treasure." *Popular Mechanics*, January 1945, pp. 50–53.

Gratzer, W. *The Undergrowth of Science: Delusion, Self-Deception, and Human Frailty*. Oxford, Oxford University Press, 2000.

Graves Registration—War Department Field Manual FM 10-63. Washington, D.C., U.S. Government Printing Office, 1945.

"The Great Plains During World War II—Agriculture." Center for Great Plains Studies, http://plainshumanities.unl.edu.

Greeves-Carpenter, C.F. "Plants by Liquid Culture." *Scientific American*, January 1939, pp. 5–7.

Gregg, M. [ed.]. *The American Women's Voluntary Services Cook Book*. San Francisco, AWVS, 1942.

Grieve, M. *A Modern Herbal, Vol. 1*. Darien, CT, Hafner Publishing, 1970 [reprint of the 1931 ed.].

Grigson, G. *Wild Flowers in Britain*. London, Collins, 1944.

Groening, G., and J. Wolschke-Bulmahn, J. "Some Notes on the Mania for Native Plants in Germany." *Landscape Journal* 11 No. 2, 1992, pp. 116–126.

Grossenbacher, K.A., Spurr, S.H., and Vlamis, J. "Lasting Properties of Cut Foliage." *Journal of the Arnold Arboretum* 26 No. 2, 1945, pp. 214–228.

"Growth of Seeds Promoted by Adhesive Envelopes." *Science News-Letter,* April 10, 1943, p. 234.

"Guayule and Kok-Saghyz Sources Now Striding Ahead." *Scientific American,* April 1942, pp. 172–3.

Guide for Planning the Local Victory Garden Program, U.S. Office of Civil Defense, Washington, D.C., 1942.

Hackett, C.M. "Coal Tar Began It." *Scientific American,* September 1940, pp. 117–119.

Hackett, D.A. [ed.], *The Buchenwald Report.* Boulder, CO, Westview Press, 1995.

Haldane, J.B.S. *A.R.P—Air Raid Precautions.* London, Victor Gollancz, Ltd., 1938.

Hale, J.K. "Soybeans in the Diet." *Journal of Home Economics* 35 No. 4, 1943, pp. 203–206.

Hammond, R.J. *Food and Agriculture in Britain, 1939–45.* Stanford, CA, Stanford University Press, 1954.

Hammond, W.M. *Normandy: The U.S. Army Campaigns of World War II.* Washington, D.C., U.S. Army, Center of Military History, n.d.

A Handbook of Home-Grown Timbers—War Emergency Edition. London, Her Majesty's Stationery Office, 1941.

Handbook on German Military Forces—War Department Technical Manual TM-E 30-451. Washington, D.C., U.S. Government Printing Office, 1945.

"Happy New Year! and Happy Rationing!" *Journal of Home Economics,* January 1943, pp. 40–43.

Harding, T.S. "The Science of Food Management in War and Peace." *Social Forces* 21, 1943, pp. 413–417.

Harkins, H.N. "Treatment of Shock from War Injuries." *Journal of the Michigan Medical Society* 41, April 1942, pp. 287–293.

Hartley, A.B. *Unexploded Bomb—A History of Bomb Disposal.* New York, W.W. Norton, 1958.

"Harvesting Machine for Pyrethrum Flowers," *Science News-Letter,* April 12, 1941, p. 239.

Harvill, A.M. "Notes on the Moss Flora of Alaska. I. the Mosses of Attu Island Collected by Margaret Bell Howard and George B. Van Schaack." *The Bryologist* 50, 1947, pp. 169–177.

Hawkins, L.A. *Have a Victory Garden.* Chicago, International Harvester Company, 1943.

Hay, I. "E.D. Merrill, from Maine to Manila." *Arnoldia* 54 No. 1, 1998, pp. 11–19.

"Health-For-Victory Meal Planning Guide." Mansfield, OH, Home Economics Institute, Westinghouse Electric and Manufacturing Co., May 1943.

Hearing, S.D. "Refeeding Syndrome." *British Medical Journal* 328, April 17, 2004, pp. 908–909.

Heaton, L.D. *Preventive Medicine in World War II. Vol. VI Communicable Diseases: Malaria.* Medical Department, U.S. Army in World War II, http://history.amedd.army.mil, pp. 1–580.

"Hedgerow Harvest." Ministry of Food, 1943.

Heim, S. *Plant Breeding and Agarian Research in the Kaiser-Wilhelm Institutes 1933–1945.* Berlin, Springer Science, 2008.

Heim, S. "Kok-sagyz—A Vital War Resource" in Heim, S., Sachse, C., and Walker, M. [eds.]. *The Kaiser Wilhelm Society Under National Socialism.* New York, Cambridge University Press, 2009, pp. 173–199.

Helphand, K. *Defiant Gardens: Making Gardens in Wartime.* San Antonio, Trinity University Press, 2006.

Henson, P.R. "Soybeans for the South" in *Science in Farming—Yearbook of Agriculture 1943-1947,* Washington, D.C., U.S. Government Printing Office, 1947, pp. 338–343.

"The Herbarium: The History of the Collections of the Botanical Museum Berlin-Dahlem. Part 3." Botanical Museum Berlin, www.bgbm.org.

Hersey, J. "Hiroshima," *The New Yorker,* August 31, 1946, www.newyorker.com

Heuchling, F.G. "Children's Gardens in Chicago." *The American Biology Teacher,* February 1944, pp. 103–107.

Hiemer, E. *Der Giftpilz.* Nürnberg, Julius Streicher/Stürmer Verlag, 1938.

Higbee, E.C. "Lonchocarpus: A Fish-Poison Insecticide." *Economic Botany* 1 No. 4, 1947, pp. 427–436.

Hill, A.F. *Economic Botany: A Textbook of Useful Plants and Plant Products,* New York, McGraw-Hill, 1952.

"Hitler's Asparagus Eating Sends Six to Concentration Camp." *Chicago Daily Tribune,* July 17, 1935, p. 1.

"Hitler's Mountain Home." *Homes and Gardens,* November 1938, pp. 193–5.

"HMAS *Abraham Crijnssen.*" Royal Australian Navy, www.navy.gov.au/node.

Hochbaum, H.W. "Victory Gardens in 1944—How Teachers May Help." *The American Biology Teacher,* February 1944, pp. 101–103.

Hogan, D.W. *U.S. Army Special Operations in World War II,* Center of Military History, U.S. Army, Washington, D.C., 1992.

Holman, R., and Robbins, W. *A Textbook of General Botany—U.S. War Department Education Manual EM445.* Madison, WI, U.S. Armed Forces Institute, 1944.

Home Canners Textbook. Cambridge, MA, Boston Woven Hose and Rubber Company, 1943.

"Home Canning." *Journal of Home Economics,* January 1944, p. 16.

"Home Gardener—Save the Rubbish." *Cairns Post,* April 17, 1942, p. 3.

Hopkins, M.P. "Wood Grown to Order." *Scientific American,* March 1938, p. 141.

Horth, L.B., and A.C. *101 Things for the Housewife to Do.* London, B.T. Batsford, 1939.

_____. *101 Things to Do in Wartime.* London, B.T. Batsford, 1940.

"How It Began." *American Cookery,* November 1942, p. 155.

"How Many Gardens?" *House and Garden,* June 1943, p. 15.

"How to Darn Holes and Tears." Board of Trade Chart Leaflet No. 5, n.d.

Howard, R.A. "Lily May Perry [1895–1992]." *Taxon* 41 No. 4, 1992, pp. 792–796.

_____. *999 Survived: An Analysis of Survival Experiences in the Southwest Pacific—ADTIC Publication No. T-100.* Maxwell Air Force Base, AL, Arctic, Desert, Tropic Information Center, 1950.

_____. "The Role of Botanists During World War II in the Pacific Theatre." *The Botanical Review* 60 No. 2, 1994, pp. 197–257.

_____. *Sun, Sand, and Survival: An Analysis of Survival Experiences in the Desert—ADTIC Publication No. D-102.* Maxwell Air Force Base, AL, Arctic, Desert, Tropic Information Center, 1953.

Hoyt, E.P. *U-Boats: A Pictorial History.* New York, McGraw-Hill Book Company, 1987.

Hu, H.H. "How Sequoia, the 'Living Fossil,' Was Discovered in China," *Arnoldia* 58 No. 4, 1998, pp. 4–7.

Humm, H.J. "Agar: A Pre-War Japanese Monopoly." *Economic Botany* 1 No. 3, 1947, pp. 317–329.

_____. "Seaweeds at Beaufort, NC as a Source of Agar." *Science* 96, 1942, pp. 230–231.

Hutchings, L.M., Epstein, B., and Bullock, F.M. "High

School Biology Goes to War." *The American Biology Teacher* 6 No. 1, 1943, pp. 5–8.

Hutchinson, W.G. "The Deterioration of Matériel in the Tropics." *The Scientific Monthly* 6 No. 3, 1946, pp. 165–177.

"Hybrid Alfalfa Is Good for Livestock and Soil." *Science News-Letter,* June 6, 1942, p. 356.

"Immersion Foot Prevented." *Science News-Letter,* March 20, 1943, p. 179.

"In Science Fields." *Science News-Letter.* April 14, 1945, p. 233.

"In the Ruins—London Makes Use of the Scars Left by the Nazi Blitz of 1940." *Life,* September 27, 1943, pp. 41–44.

"The Infra-Red Problem." *Camouflage Bulletin #9,* August 1, 1942.

Ingram, K. "Botanists at War." *Australasian Systematic Botany Society Newsletter* 75, June 1993, pp. 6–9.

"International: Who Eats?" *Time,* January 22, 1940, www.content.time.com.

"Iris, Peonies, and Poppies, How to Plant and Care For, and Select the Best Varieties." *House and Garden,* July 1943, p. 53.

Jacobson, A. *Operation Paperclip.* New York, Little, Brown, and Company, 2014.

"Japan: Last Days." *Time,* August 20, 1945, www.content.time.com.

Johnson, J.E. *Wing Leader.* New York, Random Century, 1956.

Johnston, B.F., Hosoda, M., and Kusumi, Y. *Japanese Food Management in World War II.* Stanford, CA, Stanford University Press, 1953.

Junge, T. *Hitler's Last Secretary: A Firsthand Account of Life with Hitler.* New York, Arcade, 2002.

Jungle Warfare—War Department Field Manual FM 72-20. Washington, D.C., War Department, 1944.

Kaempffert, W. "Synthetic Quinine, of High Medical Importance, Achieved at Last by Two American Chemists." *New York Times,* May 5, 1944, p. 18.

Kains, M.G. *Food Gardens for Defense.* New York, Grosset and Dunlap, 1942.

Keays, E. "Roses—Some Kinds That Require Almost No Care." *House and Garden,* June 1943, p. 63.

Keen, B., and Armstrong, J. *Herb Gathering,* London, Brome and Schimmer, 1941.

Keen, K. "Orphan Agar." *Scientific American,* August 1943, pp. 73–75.

Kelly, C.O. *The Flamboya Tree.* New York, Random House, 2002.

Kendall, H.W., and Chapman, L. "Your Home-Canned Food—Eat It, Don't Save It!" *Good Housekeeping,* February 1943, pp. 81–83.

Kendrick, D.B. *Blood Program in World War II,* Medical Department, U.S. Army in World War II, http://history.amedd.army.mil, pp. 1–810.

Kessler, D. "Dr. Arthur Kessler 1903–2000." *Lathyrus Lathyrism Newsletter* 3, 2003, pp. 2–4, https://www.researchgate.net.

"Kew in War Time." *Journal of the Kew Guild,* 6 No. 48, 1941, pp. 31–34.

Killeffer, D.H. "Insects Can Be Controlled," *Scientific American,* July 1944, pp. 13–15.

Kleber, B.E., and Birdsell, D. *The Chemical Warfare Service: Chemicals in Combat.* Washington, D.C., U.S. Army, Center of Military History, 1990.

Kobuski, C.E. "British Gardens in War Time as Seen by an American Soldier." *Journal of the Arnold Arboretum* 5 No. 12, 1945, pp. 77–88.

Kraemer, J.H. *Native Woods for Construction Purposes in the South China Sea Region.* Washington, D.C., U.S. Government Printing Office, 1945.

_____. *Native Woods for Construction Purposes in the Western Pacific Region.* Washington, D.C., U.S. Government Printing Office, 1944.

Krammer, A.P. "When the Afrika Korps Came to Texas." *The Southwestern Historical Quarterly* 80 No. 30, 1977, pp. 247–282.

Krauss, B. *Keneti: South Seas Adventures of Kenneth Emory.* Honolulu, University of Hawaii Press, 1988.

Lachmund, J. "Exploring the City of Rubble: Botanical Fieldwork in Bombed Cities in Germany After World War II." *Osiris* (2nd Series) 18, 2003, pp. 234–254.

Laird, M. "Regeneration of Trees in Hiroshima." *New Zealand Science Review,* December 1946, pp. 53–4.

Lamer, M. *The World Fertilizer Economy.* Stanford, CA, Stanford University Press, 1957.

Landemare, G. *Churchill's Kitchen.* London, Imperial War Museum, 2015.

Lang, A. "Elisabeth Schiemann: Life and Career of a Woman Scientist in Berlin." *Englera* 7, 1987, pp. 17–28.

Lathrop, E.C. "The Celotex and Cane-Sugar Industries." *Industrial and Engineering Chemistry,* 22 No. 5, 1930, pp. 449–460.

Leaf, M. *My Book to Help America.* Racine, Whitman, 1942.

Lee, U. *The Employment of Negro Troops.* Washington, D.C., U.S. Army, Center of Military History, 2001.

"Letters from the Evacuated Staffs." *Journal of the Kew Guild* 6 No. 48, 1941, pp. 39–44.

Levine, A. *Fugitives of the Forest.* Guilford, CT, Lyons Press, 2009.

Lewis, J. *Changing Direction: British Military Planning for Post-War Strategic Defence, 1942–47.* London, Routledge, 2002.

Lewis, W.H., and Elvin-Lewis, M.P.F. *Medical Botany: Plants Affecting Human Health,* 2nd ed. Hoboken, New Jersey, Wiley Interscience, 2003.

Lewy, J. "The Drug Policy of the Third Reich." *Social History of Alcohol and Drugs* 22 No. 2, 2008), pp. 144–167.

Lichtenwalter, M.C. "The Victory Garden and Biology." *The American Biology Teacher,* April 1942, pp. 206–8.

"Life Visits the Harvesters of America." *Life,* September 27, 1943, pp. 119–129.

Litoff, J.B., and Smith, D.C. "To the Rescue of the Crops: The Women's Land Army During World War II." *Prologue* 25, No. 4, Winter 1993, www.archives.gov.

Llano, G.A. "Economic Uses of Lichens," *Economic Botany* 2 No. 1, 1948. pp. 15–45.

Lloyd, A.H. "Timber Supplies for the Allied Expeditionary Force, 1944–45." *Empire Forestry Journal* 24 No. 2, 1945, pp. 141–149.

Lockwood, J.A. *Six-Legged Soldiers: Using Insects as Weapons of War.* New York, Oxford University Press, 2009.

Logistics in World War II—Final Report of the Army Service Forces. Washington, D.C., U.S. Army, Center of Military History, 1993.

Lovin, C.R. "Agricultural Reorganization in the Third Reich: The Reich Food Corporation." *Agricultural History* 43 No. 4, pp. 447–462.

Lucas, J. *War on the Eastern Front, 1941–1945: The German Soldier in Russia.* New York, Stein and Day, 1980.

Lund, J. "The Wages of Collaboration: The German Food Crisis 1939–1945 and the Supplies from Denmark." *Scandinavian Journal of History* 38 No. 4, 2013, pp. 480–501.

Luxbacher, G. "Raw and Advanced Materials for an Autarktic Germany," in Heim, S., Sachse, C., and Walker, M. [eds.]. *The Kaiser Wilhelm Society Under National Socialism.* New York, Cambridge University Press, 2009, pp. 200–226.

MacKay, R. *Half the Battle—Civilian Morale in Britain During the Second World War.* Manchester, Manchester University Press, 2002.

Macrakis, K. *Surviving the Swastika.* New York, Oxford University Press, 1993.

Majori, G. "Short History of Malaria and Its Eradication in Italy with Short Notes on the Fight Against the Infection in the Mediterranean Basin." *Mediterranean Journal of Hematology and Infectious Diseases* 4 No. 1, 2012, www.mjhid.org.

Malkin, L. *Krueger's Men: The Secret Nazi Counterfeit Plot and the Prisoners of Block 19.* New York, Little Brown, 2006.

Marcovitz, E., and Myers, H.J. "The Marijuana Addict in the Army." *War Medicine* 6: December 1944, 382–391.

Martin, J. "The Structural Transformation of British Agriculture: The Resurgence of Progressive, High-Input Arable Farming," in Short, B., Watkins, C., and Martin, J. [eds.],*The Front Line of Freedom: British Farming in the Second World War,* British Agricultural History Society, 2006, pp. 14–35.

Martin, J.H., and Jenkins, M.T. "New Uses for Waxy-Cereal Starches" in *Yearbook of Agriculture, 1950–51.* Washington, D.C., U.S. Government Printing Office, 1951, pp. 159–162.

Mayall, B., and Morrow, V. *You Can Help Your Country: English Children's Work During the Second World War.* London, Institute of Education, University of London, 2011.

McAvoy, C.A. "First Aid for Burns." *Scientific American,* September 1940, pp. 126–127.

McCay. C.M., and McCay, J.B. *The Cornell Bread Book.* New York, Dover, 1980.

McCullough, D. *Truman.* New York, Simon & Schuster, 1992.

Mead, M. "The Factor of Food Habits." *Annals of the American Academy of Political and Social Science* 225, 1943, pp. 136–141.

Meat Point Pointers—Wartime Meat Recipe Book." Chicago, National Live Stock and Meat Board, n.d.

Medical Field Manual—Medical Service of Field Units FM 8-10. Washington, D.C., War Department, 1942.

"Medicine: Dentists' Nightmare." *Time,* October 12, 1942, www.content.time.com.

"Medicine: Feeding the Reichswehr." *Time,* July 28, 1941, www.content.time.com.

"Merit Badge to Victory," *Boys' Life,* April 1945, p. 29.

Merrill, E.D. "Destruction of the Berlin Herbarium." *Science, New Series* 98 No. 2553, 1943, pp. 490–491.

———. "Emergency Food Manuals, "*Arnoldia* 4 No. 7, 1944, Pp. 29–36, 30.

———. *Emergency Food Plants and Poisonous Plants of the Pacific—Technical Manual 10-420.* Washington, D.C., War Department, 1943.

———. "*Metasequoia,* Another 'Living Fossil'" *Arnoldia* 8 No. 1, 1948, pp. 1–8.

———. *Plant Life of the Pacific [Fighting Forces Series].* Washington, D.C., The Infantry Journal, 1945.

Merrill, E.D., and Perry, L.M. "Plantae Papuanae Archiboldianae, XVI," *Journal of the Arnold Arboretum* 26 No. 3, 1945, pp. 229–266.

Methods for Laboratory Technicians—War Department Technical Manual No. 8-227. Washington, D.C., War Department, 1941.

Miall, A. and Miall, B. *Gardening Made Easy.* London, John Gifford, 1943.

Mikesh, R.C. *Japan's World War II Balloon Bomb Attacks on North America.* Washington, D.C., Smithsonian Institution Press, 1973.

Military Sanitation, War Department Field Manual FM21-10. Washington, D.C., War Department, 1945.

"Milkweed at the Front," *The Herbarist* 74, 2008, pp. 91–93.

Miller, C. "Bread and Whole Grain Cereals," *Cornell Bulletin for Homemakers—War Emergency Bulletin* 576, March 1943.

Miller, L.M. "Chlorophyll for Healing." *Science News-Letter,* March 15, 1941, pp. 170–171.

Milne, R., and Hastings, L. "Home-Spun Solutions." *Kew,* Spring 1998, pp. 10–11.

Milner, S. *Merrill's Marauders, February-May 1944.* Washington, D.C., U.S. Army, Center of Military History, 1990.

———. *Victory in Papua.* Washington, D.C., U.S. Army, Center of Military History, 1989.

———. *The War in the Pacific: Victory in Papua.* Washington, D.C., U.S. Army, Center of Military History, 1989.

Ministry of Information. *The British Home-Front Pocket-Book, 1940–42.* London, Conway, 2010.

Ministry of Supply. *Herb Collectors' Bulletin No. 1,* 1942.

———. *Herb Collectors' Bulletin No. 3,* 1942.

———. *Herb Collectors' Bulletin No. 4,* 1942.

MIRS London Branch, *The Hitler Jugend.* Allied Expeditionary Force G-2 Counter Intelligence Sub-Division, n.d.

Moore-Collyer, R.J. "Kids in the Corn: School Harvest Camps and Farm Labour Supply in England, 1940–50." *The Agricultural History Review* 52 No. 2, 2004, pp. 183–206.

Morrow, M.G. "Nature Paints Cotton." *Science News-Letter,* July 8, 1944, pp. 26–27.

Morton, L. *Fall of the Philippines.* Washington, D.C., U.S. Army, Center of Military History, 1993.

Mowbray, S. "The Antibacterial Activity of Chlorophyll," *British Medical Journal,* February 2, 1957, pp. 268–269.

Murray, A.L." Save Your Tires." *Scientific American,* April 1943, pp. 170–171.

"The Museum and the War." *The Bulletin of the Museum of Modern Art* 10 No. 1, 1942, pp. 3–19.

"The Museums." *Journal of the Kew Guild* 6 No. 48, 1941, pp. 36–38.

National Archives, *"Powers of Persuasion" Online Exhibit,* www.archives.gov/exhibits/ powers-of-persuasion.

National Federation of Women's Institutes, *Town Children Through Country Eyes: A Survey on Evacuation,* Dorking, Surrey, NFWI, 1940.

The National Wartime Nutrition Guide. Washington, D.C., War Food Administration, 1943.

"Nazi Raw Material Handicaps." *Illustrated London News,* August 3, 1940.

Nehrling, I. "How America's Soldier Is Fed." *American Cookery,* March 1942, p. 342.

Nettle-Growing for Textile Manufacture." Journal of the Royal Society of Arts, January 24, 1919, pp. 146–147.

Neumann, K. *Shifting Memories: The Nazi Past in the New Germany.* Ann Arbor, University of Michigan Press, 2000.

"New Ration for Cows." *Science News-Letter,* September 4, 1943, p. 150. New York: Macmillan, 1981.

Norman, J.R, "A Photographic Record of the Linnaean Collections." *Proceedings of the Linnean Society of London* 154, 1942, pp. 50–57.

"Notes on This and That." *Kiplinger's Personal Finance,* March 1948, p. 2.

Nova, L., and Lourie, I. [eds.]. *Interrupted Lives: Four Women's Stories of Internment During World War II in the Philippines.* Nevada City, CA, Artemis Books, 1995.

"Now We Are Three." *The Land Girl,* April 1943, p. 1.

Oderkirk, C. "Rodent Pests of Your Victory Garden," *The American Biology Teacher,* March 1944, pp. 128, 137–138.

"Oil from Florida Trees." *Popular Mechanics,* August 1929, pp. 291–295.

"Oil Sprays Kill Weeds in Carrot Gardens." *Science News-Letter,* April 4, 1945, p. 232.

"Onion Paste Reduces Infection and Helps Heal Wounds." *Popular Mechanics,* June 1944, p. 32.

Osborn, F. [ed.], *The Pacific World.* New York, W.W. Norton, 1944.

"Our Kids in Trouble." *Life,* December 20, 1943, pp. 96–108.

Oxholm, A.H. "How French Forests Kept the American Army Warm." *Journal of Forestry* 44, 1946, pp. 326–329.

Palmer, E.J. "Food Plants in the Arnold Arboretum." *Arnoldia* 4 No. 1, 1944, pp. 1–7.

Papuan Campaign: The Buna-Sanananda Operation. Washington, D.C., U.S. Army, Center of Military History, 1990.

Patten, M. *We'll Eat Again in Victory Cookbook.* London, Chancellor Press, 2002 [reprint of the 1985 ed.].

"Patterns." *Time,* June 1942, www.content.time.com.

Patton, T.W. "Forestry and Politics: Franklin D. Roosevelt as Governor of New York." *New York History* 75 No. 4, 1994, pp. 397–418.

Paul, B.H. "Better Timbers from Farms" in *Science in Farming—Yearbook of Agriculture, 1943–1947,* Washington, D.C., U.S. Government Printing Office, 1947, pp. 455–460.

Pendergast, M. "Viewpoints: A Brief History of Coca-Colonization." *New York Times,* August 18, 1993, www.nytimes.com.

Perkins, S. "Seeing Past the Dirt." *Science News,* July 30, 2005, pp. 72–74.

Perry, T.D. "Rolling Off a Log," *Scientific American,* March 1942, pp. 125–128.

Philip, C.B. "Tsutsugamushi Disease (Scrub Typhus) in World War II." *The Journal of Parasitology* 34 No. 3, 1948, pp. 168–191.

Philpot, O. *Stolen Journey.* New York, E.P. Dutton, 1952.

"Plant Materials Commercially Available in the U.S." Camouflage Memorandum 120, Camouflage Section, Fort Belvoir, VA The Engineer Board, August 1, 1942 [rev.].

"Plants Used in Medicine Growing in N.Z. Help to Meet War Shortage." *The Dominion,* April 2, 1942.

Porsild, A.E. *Emergency Food in Arctic Canada.* Ottawa, National Museum of Canada, Special Contribution No. 45–1, 1945.

Prentice, E.P. "Food in England," *Agricultural History* 24 No. 2, 1950, pp. 65–70.

"Preserve Garden Seeds." *Science News-Letter,* September 4, 1943, p. 150.

Priestwood, G. *Through Japanese Barbed Wire.* New York, D. Appleton-Century Company, 1943.

Proctor, R. *Racial Hygiene: Medicine Under the Nazis,* Cambridge, Harvard University Press, 1988.

Proctor, R.N. *The Nazi War on Cancer.* Princeton, New Jersey, Princeton University Press, 1999.

"Production: Navy Bean Soup." *Time,* December 6, 1943, www.content.time.com.

"Queries and Answers." *American Cookery,* April 1942, p. 370.

Randall, C.E. "Science Enters the Woods." *Scientific American,* August 1943, pp. 64–65.

Raper, K.B. "Penicillin" in *Science in Farming—Yearbook of Agriculture, 1943–1947,* Washington, D.C., U.S. Government Printing Office, 1947, pp. 699–710.

Raup, H.M. "Expeditions to the Alaska Military Highway 1943–44." *Arnoldia* 4 No. 12, 1944, pp. 65–72.

"Repairing Garden Implements," *Boys' Life,* May 1943, p. 2.

Report of the Science Services. Canada, Dominion Department of Agriculture, March 31, 1945.

"Report of the State Food Commission," *New York Times,* June 11, 1943, p. 8.

Reports of General MacArthur—The Campaigns of MacArthur in the Pacific, Vol. I. Washington, D.C., Department of the Army, 1994.

"Review of the Work of the Royal Botanic Gardens, Kew, During 1940." *Bulletin of Miscellaneous Information,* No. 1, 1941, pp. 1-8.

"Rice Growing in Florida Promises a Major Crop." *Science News-Letter,* June 13, 1942, p. 372.

Richardson, L. "Grow Your Colors." *Better Homes and Gardens,* March 1942, p. 28.

Riley, M. "Silage for Self-Sufficiency? The Wartime Promotion of Silage and Its Use in the Peak District," in Short, B., Watkins, C., and Martin, J. [eds.],*The Front Line of Freedom: British Farming in the Second World War,* British Agricultural History Society, 2006, pp. 78–88.

Risch, E. *Quartermaster Corps: Organization, Supply, and Services. Volume 1.* Washington, D.C., U.S. Army, Center of Military History, 1953.

Roberts, H. *English Gardens.* London, Collins, 1944.

Rogers, P., Whitby, S., and Dando, M. "Biological Warfare Against Crops." *Scientific American,* June 1999, pp. 70–75.

Rohde, E.S. *Hay Box Cookery.* London, Routledge, 1939.

Romanus, C.F. *China-Burma-India Theater: Time Runs Out in CBI.* Washington, D.C., U.S. Army, Center of Military History, 1999.

Romanus, C.F., and Sunderland, R. *Stilwell's Command Problems.* Washington, D.C., U.S. Army, Center of Military History, 1987.

Roosevelt, E. *It's Up to the Women.* New York, Stokes, 1933.

Ross, W.F., and Romanus, C.F. *Quartermaster Corps: Operations in the War Against Germany.* Washington, D.C., U.S. Army, Center of Military History, 1965.

"Rubber Facts That Don't Stretch." *Scientific American,* June 1942, pp. 276–277.

"Rubber from Milkweed." *Popular Mechanics,* March 1942, pp. 88–89, 163.

Ruppenthal, R.G. *Logistical Support of the Armies, Vol. 1.* Washington, D.C., U.S. Army, Center of Military History, 1995.

Russel, M.A., "Highland Park's School Victory Gardens." 6 No. 8, Highland Park, MI: The University of California Press on behalf of the National Association of Biology Teachers, May 1944.

Russell, E.J. *English Farming.* London, Collins, 1941.

Sackville-West, V. *Country Notes in Wartime*. Garden City, NY, Doubleday, Doran, and Company, 1939.

_____. *The Women's Land Army*. London, Michael Joseph, 1944.

St-Lo 7 July-19 July 1944. Washington, D.C. Historical Division, War Department, U.S. Army, 1984.

Salisbury, E.J. "The Flora of Bombed Areas." *Nature* 151, 1943, pp. 462–466.

Salmon, W.D. "Soybeans for Human Food." *Journal of Home Economics* 35 No. 4, 1943, pp. 201–202.

Satulsky, E.M., and Wirts, C.A. "Dermatitis Venenata Caused by the Manzanillo Tree: Further Observations and Report of Sixty Cases." *Archives of Dermatology and Syphilis*, 47, June 1943.

Schmeller, L. *Ice Railway Bridge Over the Dnieper [Foreign Military Studies]*. Washington, D.C, U.S. Army, 1953.

Schmidt, E. "Food and Feed Yeast in Germany." Food and Agriculture Organization of the United Nations, n.d., www.fao.org.

Scott, E.H. "Community Canning Centers." *Journal of Home Economics*, March 1944, pp. 141–142.

Scripture, C. "Can She Bake a Pumpkin Pie?" *Good Housekeeping*, November 1942, p. 152.

Seagrave, G.S. *Burma Surgeon*. New York, W.W. Norton, 1943.

Sears, E.R. "Genetics and Farming" in *Science in Farming—Yearbook of Agriculture 1943-1947*, Washington, D.C., U.S. Government Printing Office, 1947, pp. 245–255 handbook.

"The Secrets of the Changi Girl Guide Quilt." *The Telegraph*, June 1, 2010, www.telegraph.co.uk.

Shapiro, L. "The First Kitchen," *The New Yorker*, November 22, 2010, www.newyorker.com.

Sherwin, C. "A Q. and A. on Meals." *Good Housekeeping*, March 1942.

Shewell-Cooper, W.E. *Land Girl Manual*. London, English Universities Press, 1940.

Shishkin, B. "The Work of Soviet Botanists." *Science* New Series 97 No. 2530, 1943, pp. 354–355.

Siedlecki, J.N., Olszewski, K., and Borowski, T. *We Were in Auschwitz*. New York, Welcome Rain Publishers, 1946.

Sigel, R. "The Cultivation of Medicinal Herbs in the Concentration Camp—The Plantation as Dachau" in Benz, W., and Distel, B. [eds.], *History of Nazi Concentration Camps—Studies, Reports, Documents Vol. 2, Dachau Review 2*, Dachau, 1990, pp. 78–86.

Simpson, B.S., and Ogorzaly, M. *Economic Botany: Plants in Our World*, 3rd ed. New York, McGraw-Hill, 2000.

Sleumer, H. "The Botanic Gardens and Museum at Berlin-Dahlem." *Kew Bulletin* 4 No. 2, 1949, pp. 172–175.

Smith, D.F., and Phillips, J. [eds.], *Food, Science, Policy and Regulation in the Twentieth Century*. New York, Routledge, 2000.

Smith, H.K. *Last Train from Berlin*. London, Cresset Press, 1942.

Smith, R.R. *The Approach to the Philippines*. Washington, D.C., U.S. Army, Center of Military History, 1996.

Snow, E. *People on Our Side*. New York, Random House, 1944.

Soldier's Guide to the Japanese Army—Special Series No. 27. Washington, D.C., Military Intelligence Service, 1944.

Sonnedecker, G. "Soybean Boom." *Science News-Letter*, December 5, 1942, pp. 362–363.

Speer, A. *Infiltration: How Heinrich Himmler Schemed to Build a SS Industrial Empire*. New York, Macmillan, 1981.

Spencer, S.M. "Chemical Guardians of Fabrics." *Scientific American*, October 1944, pp. 163–165.

"Square Meals' Literally," *Science News-Letter*, March 20, 1943, p. 180.

Standley, P.C., *Edible Plants of the Arctic Region*. Navy Bureau of Medicine and Surgery, 1943.

Staff of General MacArthur, *Reports of General MacArthur—MacArthur in Japan: The Occupation: Military Phase, Vol. 1*. Supplement. Washington, D.C., Department of the Army, 1966 [1994 facsimile].

Stamper, Anne, "Countrywomen in War Time, Women's Institutes 1938-1945." The Second National Conference on the History of Voluntary Action, Roehampton Institute, University of Surrey, September 9–11, 2003.

Stauffer, A.P. *The Quartermaster Corps: Operations in the War Against Japan*. Washington, D.C., U.S. Army, Center of Military History, 1956.

Steele, L. "The Hybrid Corn Industry in the U.S." in Walden, D.B. [ed.], *Maize Breeding and Genetics*. New York, Wiley Interscience, 1978, pp. 29–39.

Stewart, I. *Organizing Scientific Research for War*. Boston, Little Brown, 1948.

Stilgenbauer, J., and McBride, J.R. "Reconstruction of Urban Forests in Hamburg and Dresden After World War II." *Landscape Journal* 29 No. 2, 2010, pp. 144–160.

Stratigakos, D. *Hitler at Home*. New Haven, Yale University Press, 2015.

Strauss, F. "The Food Problem in the German War Economy." *The Quarterly Journal of Economics* 55 No. 3, 1941, pp. 364–412.

Stuart, N.W. "About Hydroponics" in *Science in Farming—Yearbook of Agriculture, 1943-1947*, Washington, D.C., U.S. Government Printing Office, 1947, pp. 289–292.

"The Study of Art in War Time." *College Art Journal* 2 No. 1, 1942, pp. 13–19.

Sugar Rationing Called a 'Godsend' to National Health." *Science News-Letter*, March 14, 1942, p. 164.

Sukopp, H. "Flora and Vegetation Reflecting the Urban History of Berlin." *Die Erde* 134, 2003, pp. 295–316.

Sullivan, G. "Hitler's Former Maid Remembers the Good Life at Der Fuhrer's Mountain Retreat." *Washington Post*, April 29, 2014, www.washingtonpost.com.

Sulzberger, C.L. "Oswiecim Killings Placed at 4,000,000." *New York Times*, May 8, 1945.

Sumner, J. *American Household Botany: A History of Useful Plants 1620-1900*. Portland, OR, Timber Press, 2004.

_____. *The Natural History of Medicinal Plants*. Portland, OR, Timber Press, 2000.

Tabak, A. *Fort Devens, from Boys to Men*. Charleston, SC, CreateSpace, 2012.

Taub, W. "Report on the German People." *Collier's*, October 16, 1943, p. 17.

Taylor, G.M. *British Herbs and Vegetables*. London, Collins, 1947.

Tents and Tent Pitching—War Department Field Manual FM-2015. Washington, D.C., Department of the Army, 1945.

"Tested Recipes of the Month." *American Cookery*, November 1942, p. 133.

Thiesmeyer, L.R., and J.E. Burchard, J.E. *Combat Scientists*, Boston, Little, Brown and Company, 1947.

"This Is the Month for Sweet Potatoes." *Good House-keeping,* November 1943, pp. 90–91.

Thompson, G.R. *The Signal Corps: The Outcome.* Washington, D.C., U.S. Army, Center of Military History, 1991.

Thompson, G.R., and Harris, D.R. *The Signal Corps: The Outcome [Mid-1943 Through 1945].* Washington, D.C., U.S. Army, Center of Military History, 1991.

Thompson, J. "Butter from Coal." *Chicago Sunday Tribune,* August 11, 1946, p. 2.

Thone, F. "Cultivating by Fire." *Science News-Letter,* February 13, 1943, pp. 106–8.

_____. "Nature Ramblings: Hybrid Corn's Conquests." *Science News-Letter,* April 26, 1941, p. 271.

_____. "Nature Ramblings." *Science News-Letter,* August 19, 1933, p. 127.

_____. "Rationing." *Science News-Letter,* July 3, 1943, pp. 12–13.

_____. "Vegetables for Victory." *Science News-Letter.* March 28, 1942, pp. 198–199, 203.

_____. "Victory Gardens." *Science News-Letter.* March 20, 1943, pp. 186–188.

Tokin, B. "Effect of Phyoneides Upon Protozoa." *American Review of Soviet Medicine* 1 No. 3, 1944, pp. 237–9.

Tolischus, O.D. *They Wanted War.* New York, Reynal and Hitchcock, 1940.

_____. "Where Hitler Dreams and Plans." *The New York Times Magazine,* May 30, 1937, Section 8, pp. 1–2. 16.

Torrey, V. "What Makes the Rocket Go." *Popular Science,* August 1945, pp. 68–71, 214, 218.

"Treatment of Burns." *Lancet* 2, November 16, 1940, pp. 621, 627.

Trevino, J. "Norwegian Trees Still Bear Evidence of a World War II Battleship." *Smithsonian,* April 12, 2018, www.smithsonian.com.

Trienekens, G. 2000. "The Food Supply in the Netherlands During the Second World War" in D.F. Smith and J. Phillips [eds.], *Food, Science, Policy and Regulation in the Twentieth Century,* New York, Routledge, 2000, pp. 117–149.

Tseng, C.K. "Seaweed Resources of North America." *Economic Botany* 1 No. 1, January–March 1947, pp. 69–97.

Tucker, T. *the Great Starvation Experiment: Ancel Keys and the Men Who Starved for Science. New York, Free Press, 2006.*

Turowski, J. "The Schreber Garden." *Cabinet* 6, Spring 2002, cabinetmagazine.org.

Tuthill, J.D. *He's in the Navy Now.* New York, McBride, 1941.

Tuttle, W.M. *Daddy's Gone to War.* New York, Oxford University Press, 1993.

Uekoetetter, F. *The Green and the Brown: A History of Conservation in Nazi Germany.* New York, Cambridge University Press, 2006.

U.S. Army Air Forces. *Jungle and Desert Emergencies.* Washington, D.C., U.S.A.A.F., 1943.

_____. *Jungle Desert Arctic Emergencies.* Washington, D.C., U.S.A.A.F., 1943.

U.S. Department of Agriculture. *Book IV. the Victory Garden Campaign.* Washington, D.C., USDA, 1943.

_____. *Victory Garden Leader's Handbook.* Washington, D.C., USDA, 1943.

U.S. Department of Agriculture. "Victory Gardens: Miscellaneous Publication No. 483." Washington, D.C., USDA, 1942.

U.S. Naval Technical Mission to Japan, *Japanese Fuels and Lubricants—Article 1. Fuel and Lubricant Technology. Index No. X-38 (N)-1,* 1946.

"Using Cut Foliage for Camouflage." Cambridge, Harvard Camouflage Committee, August 1943.

"Using Cut Foliage for Camouflage. Supplement on Tropical Pacific Islands." Cambridge. Harvard Camouflage Committee, November 1943.

The Vegetable Garden Displayed. Wisley, Royal Horticultural Society, 1941.

"Vegetables Grow on Fifth Avenue." *American Cookery,* August–September 1942, p. 70.

"Vermont Harvests Its Maple Syrup in Wartime." *Life,* April 27, 1942, pp. 47–50.

Vickers, E. "'The Forgotten Army of the Woods': The Women's Timber Corps During the Second World War." *The Agricultural History Review* 59, 2011, pp. 101–112.

"Victory Garden Committee," War Services, *Victory Gardens: Handbook of the Victory Garden Committee.* Pennsylvania State Council of Defense, 1944.

"Victory Gardens." *Life,* May 3, 1943, pp. 28–29.

"Victory Meat Extenders." Chicago, National Livestock and Meat Board, 1941.

"Vitamin-Enriched Flour Goes into Production." *Science News-Letter,* February 8, 1941, pp. 83–84.

von Lang, J. *The Secretary—Martin Bormann: The Man Who Manipulated Hitler.* New York, Random House, 1979.

Walker, C.L. "Secrets by the Thousands." *Harper's Magazine,* October 1946, www.harpers.org.

Walker, E.H. "Biological Collecting During World War II." *The Scientific Monthly* 63 No. 5, 1946, pp. 333–340.

_____. "Natural History in the Armed Forces. A Resume of Some Recent Literature, Mostly Botanical, of Interest to Servicemen," *The Scientific Monthly* 61 No. 4, 1945, pp. 307–12.

Walton, W. "The Battle of the Hürtgen Forest." *Life,* January 1, 1945, pp. 33–36.

The War Against Japan—Pictorial Record. Washington, D.C., U.S. Army, Center of Military History 2001.

"War Agricultural Committee." *Nature,* September 9, 1939, p. 473.

"The War Effort." *Journal of the Arnold Arboretum* 25, 1944, pp. 490–491.

Ward, J.M. "Nazis Hoe Cotton: Plants, POWs, and the Future of Farm Labor in the Deep South." *Agricultural History* 81 No. 4, 2007, pp. 471–492.

"Wartime Living: 18,000,000 Gardens." *Time,* February 8, 1943, www.content.time.com.

"Wartime Luncheons for Women's Clubs." *American Cookery,* November 1942, pp. 141, 152.

Watson, H. "Farming and Gardening at Mount Holyoke College During World War I and World War II" [Unpublished paper based on research in the Mount Holyoke College archives], 2012.

Way, T., and Brown, M., *Digging for Victory.* Sevenoaks, Kent, Sabrestorm Publishing, 2010.

West, J. "Your Victory Garden." *Boys' Life,* May 1942, p. 3.

Wheeler, M. [ed.]. *Britain at War.* New York, Museum of Modern Art, 1941.

Whicker, F.W., and Fraley, L. "Effects of Ionizing Radiation on Terrestrial Plant Communities." *Advances in Radiation Biology* 4, 1974, pp. 317–366.

Whitehead, S.B. *Manures for the War-Time Garden.* London, W.H. & L. Collingridge Ltd., 1942.

Wickizer, V.D. *Coffee, Tea, and Cocoa: An Economic and Political Analysis.* Stanford, CA, Stanford University Press, 1951.

Wieland, T. "Autarky and Lebensraum. the Political Agenda of Academic Plant Breeding in Nazi Germany." *Journal of History of Science and Technology* 3, Fall 2009, pp. 14–34.

Wilcox, W.W. *The Farmer in the Second World War.* Ames, Iowa State College Press, 1947.

Wilder, R. "Hitler's Secret Weapon Is Depriving People of Vitamin," *Science News-Letter,* April 12, 1941, pp. 237–238.

Williams, E. *The Wooden Horse.* Hammonsworth, England, Penguin Books, 1984.

Wilson, M.C. "A Feminine Land Army: Plans in the Making Would Put City Women on Farms to Help Feed Forces." *New York Times,* February 28, 1943.

Winn-Smith, A. *Thrifty Cooking for Wartime.* New York, Macmillan, 1942.

Wisely, W.H. "Sewage Sludge for Victory Gardens?" *Sewage Works Journal,* July 1943, pp. 710–711.

Woodward, E.F. "Botanical Drugs: A Brief Review of the Industry with Comments on Recent Developments." *Economic Botany* 1 No. 4, pp. 402–414.

World War Two and the Vitamin Sea: Navy Propaganda Posters of the Florida Citrus Commission," 2014, Naval Historical Foundation, www.navalhistory.org.

Worthen, D.B. *Pharmacy in World War II.* New York, The Haworth Press, 2004.

Wright, J.E.B. "Feeding East London Children in Wartime." *Social Service Review* 20 No. 2, 1946.

Wyman, D. "Available Rapid Growing Vines for the U.S." *Arnoldia* 4 No. 9, 1944, pp. 45–64.

_____. "Planting Vegetables." *Arnoldia* 3 No. 1, March 26, 1943, pp. 1–7.

_____. "Short Guide to Care of the Garden in Wartime," *Arnoldia* 4 No. 2–3, March 24, 1944, pp. 9–16.

Young, H. "Vegetables and Vitamins—How to Get the Latter Out of the Former." *American Cookery,* May 1942, p. 419.

Youngken, H.W. "The Medicinal Plant Garden of the Massachusetts College of Pharmacy." *Arnoldia* 2 No. 7, pp. 37–40.

"Your Anderson Shelter This Winter." Ministry of Home Security, 1940.

"Your Home as an Air Raid Shelter." Ministry of Home Security, 1940.

"You're in the Army Too." *Good Housekeeping,* June 1942, pp. 110–111.

Zeller, T. "Molding the Landscape of Nazi Environmentalism: Alwin Seifert and the Third Reich," in Bruggemeier, F., Cioc, M., and Zeller, T. *How Green Were the Nazis? Nature, Environment, and Nation in the Third Reich,* Athens, OH, Ohio University Press, 2005, pp. 147–170.

Index

Numbers in **bold italics** indicate pages with illustrations

351